The Concise
St. Martin's
Guide to Writing

SEVENTH EDITION

The Concise
St. Martin's
Guide to Writing

Rise B. Axelrod
University of California, Riverside

Charles R. Cooper
University of California, San Diego

Bedford / St. Martin's
Boston ◆ New York

For Bedford/St. Martin's

Vice President, Editorial, Macmillan Higher Education Humanities: Edwin Hill
Editorial Director for English and Music: Karen S. Henry
Publisher for Composition and Business and Technical Writing: Leasa Burton
Executive Editor: Molly Parke
Executive Development Manager: Jane Carter
Associate Editor: Leah Rang
Senior Production Editor: Pamela Lawson
Senior Production Supervisor: Dennis Conroy
Marketing Manager: Emily Rowin
Director of Rights and Permissions: Hilary Newman
Senior Art Director: Anna Palchik
Text Design: Jerilyn Bockorick
Cover Design: Marine Miller
Composition: Cenveo Publisher Services
Printing and Binding: RR Donnelley and Sons

Manufactured in the United States of America.

9 8 7 6 5
f e d c b

For information, write: Bedford/St. Martin's, 75 Arlington Street,
Boston, MA 02116 (617-399-4000)

ISBN 978-1-4576-6955-2

Acknowledgments

Preface

When we first wrote *The Concise St. Martin's Guide to Writing*, our goal was to provide students with the clear guidance and practical strategies they needed to harness their potential as writers—an achievement that will be key to their success in college, at work, and in the wider world. We also wanted to provide instructors with the hands-on tools they needed to help their students write with a clear understanding of their rhetorical situation. Our goals have remained the same, and so *The Concise St. Martin's Guide* retains the core features that over the years have drawn so many instructors and programs to the *Concise Guide*. But now it also includes many new features that we believe will keep the *Concise Guide* the most practical hands-on text for teachers and students.

Core Features of the *Concise Guide*

The Concise St. Martin's Guide retains its emphasis on active learning—learning by doing—by providing practical guides to writing, promoting genre awareness to aid the transfer of writing skills from one genre or context to another, and integrating reading and writing through hands-on activities of critical thinking, reading, and analysis.

Practical Guides to Writing

Each chapter in Part One offers practical, flexible guides that help students draft and revise essays in a variety of analytical and argumentative genres. Commonsensical and easy to follow, these writing guides teach students to

- assess the rhetorical situation, focusing on their purpose and audience, with special attention to the genre and medium in which they are writing;
- ask probing analytical questions;
- practice finding answers through various kinds of research, including memory search, field research, and traditional source-based research.

These flexible guides to writing begin with a **Starting Points** chart to offer students multiple ways of finding the help they need when they need it. Each also includes a **Critical Reading Guide** to help students assess their own writing and the writing of their classmates and a **Troubleshooting Guide** to help students find ways to improve their drafts. All these guides are organized and color-coded to emphasize the genre's basic features. In short, the Guides to Writing help students make their writing thoughtful, clear, organized, and compelling—in a word, effective for the rhetorical situation.

A CRITICAL READING GUIDE

A Focused, Well-Defined Problem

Has the writer framed the problem effectively?

Summarize: Tell the writer what you understand the problem to be.

Praise: Give an example where the problem and its significance come across effectively such as where an example dramatizes the problem or statistics establish its significance.

Critique: Tell the writer where readers might need more information about the problem's causes and consequences, or where more might be done to establish its seriousness.

A Well-Argued Solution

Has the writer argued effectively for the solution?

Summarize: Tell the writer what you understand the proposed solution to be.

Praise: Give an example in the essay where support for the solution is presented especially effectively—for example, note particularly strong reasons, writing strategies that engage readers, or design or visual elements that make the solution clear and accessible.

Critique: Tell the writer where the argument for the solution could be strengthened—for example, where steps for implementation could be laid out more clearly, where the practicality of the solution could be established more convincingly, or where additional support for reasons should be added.

Genre Awareness

Each chapter in Part One introduces a genre of writing. By working through several genres, students learn how writers employ the basic features and strategies of a genre to achieve their purpose with their readers. The Arguing a Position essay, for example, teaches students to examine critically their views on a controversial issue, as well as those of their prospective readers, with an eye toward developing an argument that not only is well reasoned and well supported but also responds constructively to readers' likely questions and concerns. Studying multiple genres—as well as multiple examples of each genre—helps students gain genre awareness that helps them understand how we actually communicate with one another in a variety of contexts and situations. Genre awareness makes us better communicators, better readers and writers, in whatever medium we are using.

Systematic Integration of Critical Reading and Reflective Writing

Students are asked to read and analyze essays in the genre they are learning to write. The activities following the professional reading selections prompt students to read actively by asking them to reflect on the essay and relate it to their own experience, and to read like a writer, paying attention to the strategies the writer uses to convey his or her ideas and communicate effectively with readers.

What's New

Although the seventh edition of the *The Concise St. Martin's Guide to Writing* builds on the success of previous editions, many of the strategies the *Concise Guide* employs have changed in order to connect more effectively with a new generation of teachers and students. Even in the years since the publication of the previous edition, there have been increasingly burdensome demands on the time, attention, and energy of teachers and students and tremendous growth in access to and reliance upon the Internet. So the guiding principle for this edition has been to maximize **active learning** by enhancing the book's **visual rhetoric,** giving students more opportunities for **hands-on learning,** and providing students and instructors with **more readings** and more interactive activities than ever before: more showing, more doing, more options, more learning.

 ## More Readings

In addition to new professional and student writing selections (and resources to access even *more* student essays), the new LaunchPad Solo for *The Concise St. Martin's Guide to Writing* features e-readings that come alive online with video, Web sites, comics, and more. The e-readings offer multimodal content and interactive activities in the online workspace students prefer, making it possible for us to include more diverse reading selections and writing instruction in the *Concise Guide* than ever before:

- **More student essays** are available in both print and LaunchPad Solo. Each is accompanied by a headnote identifying the student writer and describing the assignment that the essay was written to fulfill. Additional student essays are also available in *Sticks and Stones,* a collection of student essays from across the country that is available free to adopters.

- **Multimodal readings** take advantage of what the Web can do to give instructors more choices than ever before. Each reading is accompanied by a headnote describing the writer and the venue in which the selection originally appeared, and each is followed by Analyze & Write and Reflect activities that ask students to think and write about how the selection employs a basic feature of the genre.

- **For additional information** about LaunchPad Solo, see page xix and a list of the contents in the back of your book.

- **New professional readings** give instructors more opportunity to engage students with interesting topics and strong models of writing (see Desmond-Harris on the next page). Each reading is accompanied by a headnote describing the writer and the venue in which the selection originally appeared, and each is followed by Analyze & Write activities and a Consider Possible Topics feature that ask students to think and write about the basic features of the genre.

Jenée Desmond-Harris | *Tupac and My Non-thug Life*

Courtesy of Jenée Desmond-Harris

JENÉE DESMOND-HARRIS is a staff writer at the *Root*, an online magazine dedicated to African American news and culture. She writes about the intersection of race, politics, and culture in a variety of formats, including personal essays. She has also contributed to *Time* magazine, MSNBC's *Powerwall*, and *xoJane* on topics ranging from her relationship with her grandmother, to the political significance of Michelle Obama's hair, to the stereotypes that hinder giving to black-teen mentoring programs. She has provided television commentary on CNN, MSNBC, and Current TV. Desmond-Harris is a graduate of Howard University and Harvard Law School. The following selection was published in the *Root* in 2011. It chronicles Desmond-Harris's reaction to the murder of gangsta rap icon Tupac Shakur in a Las Vegas drive-by shooting in 1996. She mentions Tupac's mother, Afeni, as well as the "East Coast–West Coast war"—the rivalry between Tupac and the Notorious B.I.G. (Biggie), who was suspected of being involved in Tupac's murder. As you read, consider the photograph that appeared in the *Root* article and that is reproduced here:

- What does it capture about the fifteen-year-old Desmond-Harris?
- What does its inclusion say about Desmond-Harris's perspective on her adolescent self and the event she recollects?

1 I learned about Tupac's death when I got home from cheerleading practice that Friday afternoon in September 1996. I was a sophomore in high school in Mill Valley, Calif. I remember trotting up my apartment building's stairs, physically tired but buzzing with the frenetic energy and possibilities for change that accompany fall and a new school year. I'd been cautiously allowing myself to think during the walk home about a topic that felt frighteningly taboo (at least in my world, where discussion of race was avoided as delicately as obesity or mental illness): what it meant to be biracial and on the school's mostly white cheerleading team instead of the mostly black dance team. I remember acknowledging, to the sound of an 8-count that still pounded in my head as I walked through the door, that I didn't really have a choice: I could memorize a series of stiff and precise motions but couldn't actually dance.

2   My private musings on identity and belonging—not original in the least, but novel to me—were interrupted when my mom heard me slam the front door and drop my bags: "*Your friend died!*" she called out from another room. Confused silence. "*You know, that rapper you and Thea love so much!*"

Mourning a Death in Vegas

3 The news was turned on, with coverage of the deadly Vegas shooting. Phone calls were made. Ultimately my best friend, Thea, and I were left to our own 15-year-old devices to mourn that weekend. Her mother and stepfather were out of town. Their expansive, million-dollar home was perched on a hillside less than an hour from Tupac's former stomping grounds in Oakland and Marin City. Of course, her home was also worlds away from both places.

4   We couldn't "pour out" much alcohol undetected for a libation, so we limited

Active Learning

Leaner chapters make it easier for instructors to get and keep students reading and to focus their attention on what matters most. This edition of *The Concise St. Martin's Guide to Writing* is tighter and more focused than ever.

A new design helps guide students through the chapters, with **headings** that show students where they are, where they've been, and where they're going in the chapter and that **help students identify the activities** and **understand the purpose they serve in active learning**.

Gladwell   *What College Rankings Really Tell Us* ▶ **GUIDE TO READING**
                                                      GUIDE TO WRITING
                                                      THINKING CRITICALLY

winning football team, with a particular religious orientation, with opportunities for undergraduates to do scientific research?

- How would comparing the criteria you used with the criteria your classmates used help you better understand the ideology—values and beliefs—behind your choices?

[ANALYZE] Use the basic features.

A WELL-PRESENTED SUBJECT: INTRODUCING A COMPLICATED SUBJECT

Every year, *U.S. News* publishes a special edition that ranks colleges and universities across the nation. In his essay, Gladwell does not simply evaluate one year's ratings; he evaluates the ranking system itself. But he begins by focusing on the ranking system of another magazine, *Car and Driver*.

[ANALYZE & WRITE]

Write a paragraph or two analyzing and evaluating how Gladwell introduces *U.S. News*'s ranking system:

1. Reread paragraph 1. Why do you think Gladwell begins his evaluation of *U.S. News*'s college ranking system by discussing the system used by another magazine to rank cars? How is Gladwell's evaluation of *Car and Driver*'s ranking system preparing the reader for his evaluation of *U.S. News*'s ranking system?

2. Now reread paragraph 2. What cues does Gladwell provide to help readers follow his transition from the ranking system of *Car and Driver* to that of *U.S. News*?

3. What does Gladwell mean when he describes *U.S. News*'s ranking system as striving to be both comprehensive and heterogeneous?

A **mini table of contents** and a **Starting Points** chart at the opening of each Guide to Writing section in Part One help students find the information they need. **Starting Points, Critical Reading,** and **Troubleshooting** guides use speech bubbles to prompt students to reflect on, interrogate, and revise their writing on their own.

GUIDE TO WRITING

The Writing Assignment	171
Writing a Draft: Invention, Research, Planning, and Composing	172
Evaluating the Draft: Getting a Critical Reading	182
Improving the Draft: Revising, Formatting, Editing, and Proofreading	184

The Writing Assignment

Write an essay arguing a controversial position: Start by learning more about the issue and the debate surrounding it, and then take a position. Present the issue so readers recognize that it merits their attention, and develop a well-supported argument that will confirm, challenge, or change your readers' views.

This Guide to Writing is designed to help you compose your own position argument and apply what you have learned from reading other position arguments. This Starting Points chart will help you find answers to questions you might have about composing a position argument. Use the chart to find the guidance you need, when you need it.

STARTING POINTS: ARGUING A POSITION

How do I come up with an issue to write about?

- Consider possible topics. (pp. 162–63, 170)
- Choose a controversial issue on which to take a position. (p. 173)
- Test Your Choice (p. 174)

A Focused, Well-Presented Issue

How can I effectively frame the issue for my readers?

- Assess the genre's basic features: A focused, well-presented issue. (pp. 147–49)
- A Focused, Well-Presented Issue: Framing an Argument for a Diverse Group of Readers (pp. 160–61)
- A Focused, Well-Presented Issue: Reframing through Contrast (p. 168)
- Frame the issue for your readers. (pp. 174–75)
- A Troubleshooting Guide: A Focused, Well-Presented Issue (p. 184)

A Well-Supported Position

How do I come up with a plausible position?

- Assess the genre's basic features: A well-supported position. (pp. 149–50)
- Formulate a working thesis stating your position. (p. 176)
- Develop the reasons supporting your position. (pp. 176–77)
- Research your position. (p. 177)
- Use sources to reinforce your credibility. (pp. 177–78)

(continued)

171

Color-coded highlighting and annotations *show* students the techniques writers use to communicate effectively with their readers.

In addition to asserting the thesis, writers sometimes preview the reasons in the same order they will bring them up later in the essay, as in this example of a *forecasting statement by* Jessica Statsky:

Transition	. . . too often played to adult standards, which are developmentally inappro-
Reason 1	priate for children and can be both physically and psychologically harmful.
	Furthermore, because they . . . , they are actually counterproductive for
Reason 2	developing either future players or fans. Finally, because they . . . *provide*
Reason 3	*occasions for some parents and coaches to place their own fantasies and needs*
	ahead of children's welfare. (par. 2)

Integrated sentence strategies foreground the sentence patterns writers use to communicate effectively with their readers. Examples from the reading selections demonstrate the flexibility of the pattern.

A FOCUSED, WELL-PRESENTED ISSUE: REFRAMING THROUGH CONTRAST

Writers sometimes have to remind their readers why an issue is controversial. Beginning with the title, Solove works to undermine the widely held assumption that the erosion of privacy should not be a concern. He does this primarily by contrasting two different ways of thinking about threats to privacy, which he calls Orwellian and Kafkaesque, based on the novels *1984,* by George Orwell, and *The Trial,* by Franz Kafka. To present this contrast, Solove uses sentence patterns like these:

▶ Not _____ , but _____ .

▶ _____ focus on _____ , which is characterized by _____ , and they don't even notice _____ , which is characterized by _____ .

Here are a couple of examples from Solove's position argument:

The problems are not just Orwellian but Kafkaesque. (par. 10)

Legal and policy solutions focus too much on the problems under the Orwellian metaphor—those of surveillance—and aren't adequately addressing the Kafkaesque problems—those of information processing. (par. 9)

In the Guide to Writing, **sentence strategies are integrated into the Ways In activities** to invite students to use them for their own rhetorical purpose and to make them their own as they revise.

∷ Frame the issue for your readers.

Once you have made a preliminary choice of an issue, consider how you can frame (or reframe) it so that readers who support opposing positions will listen to your argument. To do this, consider how the issue has been debated in the past and what your readers are likely to think. Use the following questions and sentence strategies to help you put your ideas in writing.

WAYS IN

HOW CAN I EXPLORE THE ISSUE?

What groups or notable individuals have shaped the debate on this issue? What positions have they taken?

▶ It may surprise you that _____ is a controversial issue. Although many people take _____ for granted, [individuals/groups] oppose it on the grounds that _____ .

▶ Whereas supporters of _____ have argued that _____, opponents such as [list individuals/groups] contend that _____ .

WHAT DO MY READERS THINK?

What values and concerns do I and my readers share regarding the issue?

▶ Concern about _____ leads many of us to oppose _____ . We worry that _____ will happen if _____ .

▶ _____ is a basic human right that needs to be protected. But what does it mean in everyday practice when _____ ?

What fundamental differences in worldview or experience might keep me and my readers from agreeing?

Council of Writing Program Administrators (WPA) Outcomes Statement

The Concise St. Martin's Guide to Writing, Seventh Edition, helps students build proficiency in the four categories of learning that writing programs across the country use to assess their students' work: rhetorical knowledge; critical thinking, reading, and writing; writing processes; and knowledge of conventions. The chart on the following pages shows in detail how the *Concise Guide* helps students develop these proficiencies.

Note: This chart aligns with the latest WPA Outcomes Statement, ratified in July 2014.

WPA OUTCOMES	RELEVANT FEATURES OF *THE CONCISE ST. MARTIN'S GUIDE*
Rhetorical Knowledge	
Learn and use key rhetorical concepts through analyzing and composing a variety of texts	Chapter 1, "Thinking about Writing," prepares students to communicate in various rhetorical situations. From there, students **read, analyze,** and **compose a variety of texts** in Part 1, "Writing Assignments" (Chs. 2–7). In each of these chapters, a Guide to Reading asks students to analyze texts (including professional articles, student essays, and multimodal e-readings), in terms of **purpose, audience,** and **genre features.** Each Guide to Writing (in Chs. 2–7) supports student composers with detailed help for responding to different rhetorical situations: remembering events, writing profiles, explaining concepts, arguing a position, proposing a solution, and justifying an evaluation.
	See also Part 2, "Strategies for Critical Thinking, Reading, and Writing" (Chs. 8–13). In particular, Chapter 12, Analyzing Visuals, guides students in evaluating visual texts including advertisements and photographs.
Gain experience reading and composing in several genres to understand how genre conventions shape and are shaped by readers' and writers' practices and purposes	See above. In addition, a rich collection of **multimodal e-readings** give students practice in reading various **genres** in various **rhetorical contexts.** Chapter-opening features (in Pt. 1, Chs. 2–7)—In College Courses, In the Community, and In the Workplace—show students how genres work in different settings.
	The **readings** in Part 1, which represent a range of texts and genres, are annotated and framed with comments and questions that **focus students on key aspects of genres** and help spark ideas for their own compositions.
	The **composing practice** in Part 1 is built around six genre assignments. Students are asked to create texts in which they remember an event; profile a person, activity, or place; explain a concept; argue a position; propose a solution; and justify an evaluation. These chapters emphasize the connection between **reading and composing in a particular genre:** Each begins with a group of readings with apparatus that introduces students to basic features and conventions of the genre; then a Guide to Writing leads them through the process of applying these features to an essay of their own.
Develop facility in responding to a variety of situations and contexts, calling for purposeful shifts in voice, tone, level of formality, design, medium, and/or structure	In Part 1, students **practice responding** to a variety of rhetorical situations and contexts, as noted above. These chapters also point out what makes a text structurally sound, while the Guides to Writing help students systematically develop their own processes and structures. Sentence Strategies sections in these chapters help composers deal with issues of **voice, tone, and formality.**
	In Part 2, Chapter 14, "Designing Documents," takes students through the **rhetorical choices** involved in the **design** of any text.
Understand and use a variety of technologies to address a range of audiences	One of the book's assumptions is that most students compose in digital spaces for varied audiences and use different media for doing so. This is woven throughout, especially in Chapters 2 through 7. Further, online tutorials include **how-tos for using technology:** e.g., digital writing for specific **audiences** and purposes, creating presentations, integrating photos, and appealing to a prospective employer. E-readings include samples of Web, video, and other multimodal models.
Match the capacities of different environments (e.g., print and electronic) to varying rhetorical situations	Multimodal e-readings, addressing a variety of rhetorical situations, represent digital-first texts and also show how **genres can be adapted** to a visual or online format. (See the table of contents.)

(continued)

WPA OUTCOMES	RELEVANT FEATURES OF *THE CONCISE ST. MARTIN'S GUIDE*
Rhetorical Knowledge (continued)	
	Chapter 14, "Designing Documents," provides guidance on how to make effective **rhetorical choices** with electronic documents, from academic formatting and font sizes to adding visuals and screen shots.
Critical Thinking, Reading, and Composing	
Use composing and reading for inquiry, learning, thinking, and communicating in various rhetorical contexts	See the Processes section above, Part 1 (Chs. 2–7), and also Part 2, **"Strategies for Critical Thinking, Reading, and Writing"** (Chs. 8–13). Chapter 8, "Strategies for **Invention** and **Inquiry**," and Chapter 9, "Strategies for Reading Critically," prompt students to engage actively in reading and writing actively.
	Analyze and Write activities in Part 1 (Chs. 2–7) ask students to evaluate each professional reading and develop their ideas in paragraphs. Make Connections, a recurring section in the apparatus following the professional readings in Part 1 (Chs. 2–7), encourages students to put what they've read in the context of the world they live in. These preliminary reflections come into play in the Guides to Writing, in which students are asked to draw on their experiences in college, community, and career in order to begin writing.
	Thinking Critically sections, which conclude Chapters 2 through 7, ask students to reconsider what they have learned, often in a social/political context.
Read a diverse range of texts, attending especially to relationships between assertion and evidence, to patterns of organization, to interplay between verbal and nonverbal elements, and how these features function for different audiences and situations	See the Rhetorical Knowledge section above, especially the first two sections that discuss **texts, genres,** and **rhetorical situations.** Each Guide to Reading highlights Basic Features of each genre and always directs attention to supporting details and evidence as well as a clear, logical organization. Further, each chapter in Part 1 includes a multimodal selection in the online e-readings which demonstrates how purpose and medium interact.
	The Concise Guide is also available as an **e-book;** adopters of print or digital versions also have access to **online tutorials** and activities in **LearningCurve,** an adaptive game-like quizzing tool.
Locate and evaluate primary and secondary research materials, including journal articles, essays, books, databases, and informal Internet sources	Chapters 16 and 17 offer extensive coverage of **finding, evaluating, and using** print and electronic resources with guidance for responsibly using the Internet, e-mail, and online communities for research. Chapter 16 addresses **primary** and secondary **research.**
Use strategies—such as interpretation, synthesis, response, critique, and design/redesign—to compose texts that integrate the writer's ideas with those from appropriate sources	Chapter 11, "Analyzing and Synthesizing Arguments," focuses specifically on evaluating ideas and finding common ground among sources in order to support an argument. Chapter 18, "Using Sources to Support Your Ideas," offers detailed **strategies** for **integrating research into a composition.** Specifically, there is advice on how to integrate and introduce quotations, how to cite paraphrases and summaries so as to distinguish them from the writer's own ideas, and how to avoid plagiarism. Sentence strategies and research coverage in several Part 1 chapters offer additional support.
	In Chapters 6 through 8, which cover argument, there is also extensive discussion of the need to **anticipate opposing positions** and readers' objections to the writer's thesis. These chapters are complemented by argument strategies for making assertions, offering support, avoiding logical fallacies, and using sentence strategies in Chapter 13, "Arguing."

WPA OUTCOMES	RELEVANT FEATURES OF *THE CONCISE ST. MARTIN'S GUIDE*
Processes	
Develop a writing project through multiple drafts	The need for the critical reading and **revision of drafts** is emphasized in Chapter 1. In Chapters 2 through 7, Guides to Writing prompt students to compose and revise. They are offered specific steps for inventing, researching, planning, and composing—and for evaluating and improving their work over the course of **multiple drafts.**
Develop flexible strategies for reading, drafting, reviewing, collaboration, revising, rewriting, rereading, and editing	The Guides to Writing in Chapters 2 through 7 offer extensive, genre-specific advice on **rethinking and revising** at multiple stages. Ways In activities, Starting Points charts, and Troubleshooting charts in Part 1 chapters encourage students to discover, review, and revise their own process(es) of writing. Activities urge students to start from their strengths, and Starting Points and Troubleshooting charts offer specific, targeted advice for students with different challenges.
	These chapters also offer genre-specific coverage of invention and research, getting a critical reading of a draft (peer review), revising, editing, and proofreading. See also, section below: "Experience the **collaborative** and social aspects of writing processes."
	A dedicated Chapter 8, "Strategies for Invention and Inquiry," offers numerous helpful suggestions for idea generation.
Use composing processes and tools as a means to discover and reconsider ideas	Central to Chapters 2 through 7 is the idea of using **composing to discover ideas.** Students are offered specific steps for inventing, researching, planning, and composing—and for evaluating and improving their work over the course of multiple drafts.
	Specifically, the Guides to Writing in Chapters 2 through 7 break writing assignments down into doable focused thinking and writing activities that engage students in the **recursive process of invention** and research to find, analyze, question, and synthesize information and ideas.
	See also, Chapter 8, "Strategies for Invention and Inquiry" and Chapter 15, "Planning a Research Project."
Experience the collaborative and social aspects of writing processes	This goal is implicit in several **collaborative activities:** Practicing the Genre activities at the beginning of the chapter, Make Connections activities after the readings, and, in the Guides to Writing, Test Your Choice activities in the Critical Reading Guide.
Learn to give and act on productive feedback to works in progress	The Evaluating the Draft, Critical Reading Guide, Improving the Draft, and Troubleshooting Guide sections in the Guides to Writing in each Part 1 chapter all offer students **specific advice on constructively criticizing**—and praising—their own work and the work of their classmates, then reflecting and acting upon the comments they've received.
Adapt composing processes for a variety of technologies and modalities	As noted in the Rhetorical Knowledge section above, one of the book's assumptions is that most students compose in digital spaces for varied audiences and use different media for doing so. This is woven throughout, especially in Chapters 2 through 7. Further, integrated digital tutorials include online **how-tos for using technology:** e.g., digital writing, creating presentations, integrating photos, and appealing to a prospective employer. E-readings include samples of Web, video, and other multimodal models.
Reflect on the development of composing practices and how those practices influence their work	See the section above: "Use composing processes and tools as a means to discover and reconsider ideas."

(continued)

WPA OUTCOMES	RELEVANT FEATURES OF *THE CONCISE ST. MARTIN'S GUIDE*
Processes (continued)	
	In addition, a Thinking Critically section concludes each Part 1 (Chs. 2–7) chapter and asks students to reflect on what they've learned about the genre and about their own composing experiences.
Knowledge of Conventions	
Develop knowledge of linguistic structures, including grammar, punctuation, and spelling, through practice in composing and revising	Genre-specific **editing** and **proofreading** appears in the Editing and Proofreading sections in each chapter in Part 1. Additional practice activities of sentence-level skills are featured in the **LearningCurve quizzing,** available in the online media.
Understand why genre conventions for structure, paragraphing, tone, and mechanics vary	Chapters 2 through 7 present several basic **features of a specific genre,** which are introduced up front and then consistently reinforced throughout the chapter. **Genre-specific issues of structure,** paragraphing, tone, and mechanics are also addressed in the Sentence Strategies and Editing and Proofreading sections of each Guide to Reading.
Gain experience negotiating variations in genre conventions	Students **read, analyze,** and **compose a variety of texts** in Part 1, "Writing Assignments" (Chs. 2–7). In each of these chapters, a Guide to Reading asks students to analyze texts (including ads, student essays, and multimodal e-readings), in terms of **purpose, audience,** and **Basic Features** (or genre conventions). Each Guide to Writing (in Chs. 2–7) supports student composers with detailed help for responding to different rhetorical situations: remembering events, writing profiles, explaining concepts, arguing a position, proposing a solution, and justifying an evaluation.
Learn common formats and/or design features for different kinds of texts	Document design is covered in a dedicated Chapter 14. Examples of specific formats for a range of texts appear on pages 457–65 (research paper) and pages 301–03 (table, diagram, graph, chart, map, and other figures).
Explore the concepts of intellectual property (such as fair use and copyright) that motivate documentation conventions	The book's research coverage (mainly Chs. 18–20) teaches specific strategies of evaluating and integrating source material—and **citing the work of others.** A dedicated section, "Acknowledging Sources and Avoiding Plagiarism," appears on pages 428–29.
	Chapter 9, "Strategies for Reading Critically," covers various strategies useful in working with sources, including annotating, summarizing, and synthesizing. Chapter 18, **"Using Sources to Support Your Ideas,"** offers detailed coverage of finding, evaluating, using, and acknowledging primary and secondary sources, while Chapter 15, "Planning a Research Project," instructs students on creating an annotated bibliography.
Practice applying citation conventions systematically in their own work	Chapter 18 offers detailed advice on how to integrate and introduce quotations, how to cite paraphrases and summaries so as to distinguish them from the writer's own ideas, and how to avoid plagiarism. Chapters 19 and 20 offer coverage of **MLA and APA documentation** in addition to an annotated sample student research paper. Chapter 12, "Analyzing Visuals," also offers a complete student paper with MLA documentation. In addition, research sections in each Guide to Writing in the Part 1 chapters help students with the details of using and appropriately documenting sources by providing genre-specific examples of what (and what not) to do.

Acknowledgments

We owe an enormous debt to all the rhetoricians and composition specialists whose theory, research, and pedagogy have informed *The Concise St. Martin's Guide to Writing.* We would be adding many pages to an already long book if we were to name everyone to whom we are indebted; suffice it to say that we have been eclectic in our borrowing.

We must also acknowledge immeasurable lessons learned from all the writers, professional and student alike, whose work we analyzed and whose writing we used in this and earlier editions.

So many instructors and students have contributed ideas and criticism over the years. The members of the advisory board for the tenth edition of *The St. Martin's Guide to Writing,* a group of dedicated composition instructors from across the country, have provided us with extensive insights and suggestions and have given us the benefit of their advice on new readings and other new features. For their many contributions, we would like to thank Lisa Bickmore, Salt Lake Community College; Mary Brantley, Holmes Community College–Ridgeland; Jo Ann Buck, Guilford Technical Community College; Wallace Cleaves, University of California, Riverside; Leona Fisher, Chaffey College; Gwen Graham, Holmes Community College–Grenada; Lesa Hildebrand, Triton College; Stephanie Kay, University of California, Riverside; Donna Nelson-Beene, Bowling Green State University; Gail Odette, Baton Rouge Community College; Gray Scott, Texas Woman's University; and David Taylor, St. Louis Community College.

Many other instructors have also helped us improve the book. For responding to detailed questionnaires about the *Concise Guide,* Sixth Edition, we thank Diane Baker, Castleton State College; Nolan Belk, Wilkes Community College; Crystal Bickford, Southern New Hampshire University; Toni Borge, Bunker Hill Community College; Danielle Bienvenue Bray, University of Georgia at Athens; Barbara Campbell, Butler University; Sherry Cisler, Arizona State University; Christine Peters Cucciarre, University of Delaware; Catherine De Leon, North Shore Community College; Daniel de Roulet, Irvine Valley College; Merry Dennehy, Monterey Peninsula College; Helen Doss, Wilbur Wright College; Marie Eckstrom, Rio Hondo College; Leona Fisher, Chaffey College; Laura Franey, Millsaps College; Howard Hendrix, California State University, Fresno; Laurel Hendrix, California State University, Fresno; Richard Hishmeh, Palomar College; Ferdinand Hunter, GateWay Community College; Elizabeth Jones, Georgia Gwinnett College; Katherine Kapitan, Buena Vista University; Odeana Kramer, Prince George's Community College; Carrie Krantz, Washtenaw Community College; Tamara Kuzmenkov, Tacoma Community College; Carmen Lind, Morton College; Timothy Mercer, University of Arizona; Susan Miller-Cochran, North Carolina State University; Patricia Murphy, State University of New York Institute of Technology; Douglas Okey, Spoon River College; Gordon Petry, Bradley University; Timothy Rogers, University of Massachusetts, Lowell; Derri Scarlett, Bismarck State College; Gray Scott, Texas Women's University; Elizabeth Shelley, Aquinas College; Pearl Shields, Auburn University; Celeste Sonnier, Morton College; Joseph Teller, College of the Sequoias; Marilynn Turner, Asnuntuck Community College; Kristi Walker, Tacoma Community College; and Mike Wilcomb, Northern Essex Community College.

For the tenth edition of *The St. Martin's Guide,* from which the *Concise Guide* is derived, we also gratefully acknowledge the special contributions of Gray Scott, who made recommendations of reading selections, helped draft some of the reading apparatus, and was generally available as a sounding board and a font of good advice; Natasha Cooper, Syracuse University, who provided expert advice on the revised coverage of research; Christine Garbett, Bowling Green State University, who wrote all comprehension quizzes for the reading selections that appear on the Web site and in the instructor's manual; Beth Castrodale, who helped find e-readings and wrote the apparatus to accompany them; and Leona Fisher, who revised and updated the instructor's manual. Finally, we are especially grateful to the student authors for allowing us to use their work in *Sticks and Stones* and the *Concise Guide.*

We want to thank many people at Bedford/St. Martin's, especially the *Concise Guide* editor Leah Rang, who made this edition possible; Executive Development Manager Jane Carter, without whom this book would not have been written; Pamela Lawson, who worked miracles keeping all the details straight and keeping us on schedule; and Kimberly Hampton, Rebecca Merrill, and Katie Schultz, without whom we would have no online media.

Diana Puglisi George made many valuable contributions to this revision with her careful copyediting, as did Steve Patterson and Deanna Hegle with their meticulous proofreading, and Jake Kawatski, with his indexing of the text. Sue Brown, Shuli Traub, Elise Kaiser, and Dennis Conroy kept the whole process running smoothly.

Thanks also to the immensely talented design team—book designer Jerilyn Bockorick as well as Bedford/St. Martin's art directors Lucy Krikorian and Anna Palchik—for making the seventh edition the most beautiful and most functional yet. Our gratitude also goes to Linda Winters, Margaret Gorenstein, Martha Friedman, and Connie Gardner for their hard work clearing permissions.

We also want to thank Karen Henry, Editorial Director for English and Music and Leasa Burton, Publisher for Composition and Business and Technical Writing—who both offered valued advice at many critical stages in the process. Thanks as well to Denise Wydra for her skillful guidance of Bedford/St. Martin's, and Marketing Manager Emily Rowin and Executive Editor Molly Parke—along with the extraordinarily talented and hardworking sales staff—for their tireless efforts on behalf of the *Concise Guide.*

Rise dedicates this book to two young women whose writing she very much looks forward to reading: Sophie and Amalia Axelrod-Delcampo.

Get the most out of your course with *The Concise St. Martin's Guide to Writing*

Bedford/St. Martin's offers resources and format choices that help you and your students get even more out of your book and course. To learn more about or to order any of the following products, contact your Macmillan sales representative, go to **macmillanhighered.com /getsupport** or visit the Web site at **macmillanhighered.com/conciseguide.**

LaunchPad Solo for *The Concise St. Martin's Guide to Writing:* Where Students Learn

LaunchPad Solo provides engaging content and new ways to get the most out of your course. Get **unique, book-specific materials** combined with **writing tutorials and game-like quizzing** in a customizable course space; then assign and mix our resources with yours. A complete list of the LaunchPad Solo materials can be found on the last page of the book.

- **Multimodal Selections**   Six multimodal selections — one for each Part One writing genre chapter — include a unique comic, animated graphic, podcast interview, and more. Just like the readings in the printed text, each multimedia selection is preceded by a headnote and accompanied by activities that ask students to analyze and reflect on each writer's technique and use of the genre's basic features.

- **Pre-built units** — including readings, videos, quizzes, discussion groups, and more — are **easy to adapt and assign** by adding your own materials and mixing them with our high-quality multimedia content and ready-made assessment options, such as **LearningCurve** adaptive quizzing.

- A **streamlined interface** helps students focus on what's due. Use LaunchPad Solo on its own or integrate it with your school's learning management system so that your class is always on the same page.

To get the most out of your course, order LaunchPad Solo for *The Concise St. Martin's Guide to Writing* packaged with the print book **at no additional charge.** (LaunchPad Solo for *The Concise St. Martin's Guide to Writing* can also be purchased on its own.) An activation code is required. To order LaunchPad for *The Concise St. Martin's Guide to Writing* with the print book, use **ISBN 978-1-319-00686-0.**

Choose from Alternative Formats of *The Concise St. Martin's Guide to Writing*

Bedford/St. Martin's offers a range of affordable e-books, including portable, download-able versions of *The Concise St. Martin's Guide to Writing,* Seventh Edition, in popular formats — allowing students to choose the one that works best for them. For details, visit **macmillanhighered.com/conciseguide/formats**.

Select Value Packages

Add value to your text by packaging one of the following resources with *The Concise St. Martin's Guide to Writing.* To learn more about package options for any of these products, contact your Bedford/St. Martin's sales representative or visit **macmillanhighered.com /conciseguide/catalog**.

LearningCurve for Readers and Writers, Bedford/St. Martin's adaptive quizzing program, quickly learns what students already know and helps them practice what they don't yet understand. Game-like quizzing motivates students to engage with their course, and reporting tools help teachers discern their students' needs. *LearningCurve for Readers and Writers* can be packaged with the *Concise Guide* at a significant discount. An activation code is required.

Portfolio Keeping, **Third Edition, by Nedra Reynolds and Elizabeth Davis,** provides all the information students need to use the portfolio method successfully in a writing course. *Portfolio Teaching,* a companion guide for instructors, provides the practical information instructors and writing program administrators need to use the portfolio method successfully in a writing course.

Sticks and Stones and Other Student Essays, **Eighth Edition,** is a collection of more than forty essays written by students across the nation using *The St. Martin's Guide to Writing.* Each essay is accompanied by a headnote that spotlights some of the ways the writer uses the genre successfully, invites students to notice other achievements, and supplies context where necessary. To order *Sticks and Stones,* use ISBN 978-1-4576-1262-6.

Make Learning Fun with *ReWriting 3*

macmillanhighered.com/rewriting
New open online resources with videos and interactive elements engage students in new ways of writing. You'll find tutorials about using common digital writing tools, an interactive peer review game, *Extreme Paragraph Makeover,* and more — all for free and for fun. Visit **macmillanhighered.com/rewriting**.

Instructor Resources

macmillanhighered.com/conciseguide
You have a lot to do in your course. Bedford/St. Martin's wants to make it easy for you to find the support you need — and to get it quickly.

The Instructor's Resource Manual for the Concise St. Martin's Guide to Writing is available as a PDF that can be downloaded from the Bedford/St. Martin's online catalog at the URL above. In addition to chapter overviews, the instructor's manual includes sample course plans and syllabi, teaching tips, and classroom activities.

Teaching Central offers the entire list of Bedford/St. Martin's print and online professional resources in one place. You'll find landmark reference works, sourcebooks on pedagogical issues, award-winning collections, and practical advice for the classroom — all free for instructors — at **macmillanhighered.com/teachingcentral**.

Bits collects creative ideas for teaching a range of composition topics in an easily searchable blog format at **bedfordbits.com.** A community of teachers — leading scholars, authors, and editors — discuss revision, research, grammar and style, technology, peer review, and much more. Take, use, adapt, and pass the ideas around. Then, come back to the site to comment or share your own suggestion.

Contents

Preface   v

1 | Introduction: Thinking about Writing   1

Why Write?   1

Write to communicate effectively in different rhetorical situations.   2
■ Write to think.   2   ■ Write to learn.   3   ■ Write to succeed.   3
■ Write to know yourself and connect to other people.   3

How *The Concise St. Martin's Guide to Writing* Helps You Learn to Write   4

Learn to write by using the Guides to Reading.   4   ■ Learn to write by using the Guides to Writing.   4

THINKING CRITICALLY   5

REFLECTION: A Literacy Narrative   5

PART 1   Writing Activities

2 | Remembering an Event   8

PRACTICING THE GENRE: Telling a Story   10

GUIDE TO READING   11

Analyzing Remembered Event Essays   11

Determine the writer's purpose and audience.   11   ■ Assess the genre's basic features.   11

Readings   13

Jean Brandt, *Calling Home*   13

 e-readings > Shannon Lewis, *We Were Here* (STUDENT ESSAY)

Annie Dillard, *An American Childhood*   17

Jenée Desmond-Harris, *Tupac and My Non-thug Life*   23

e-readings > Kelsey C. Roy, *The Daily Grind* (COMIC)

GUIDE TO WRITING   29

The Writing Assignment   29

STARTING POINTS: Remembering an Event   29

Writing a Draft: Invention, Research, Planning, and Composing   30

Choose an event to write about.   31

TEST YOUR CHOICE   32

Shape your story.   32

WAYS IN: Bringing Your Story into Focus   32

Organize your story to enhance the drama.   33

TEST YOUR CHOICE   34

Choose your tense and plan time cues.   35   ▪ Use dialogue to tell your story.   35   ▪ Develop and refine your descriptions.   36

WAYS IN: Describing People and Places   37

Incorporate descriptive details throughout your story.   38

WAYS IN: Working Descriptions into Action Sequences   38

Consider ways to convey your event's autobiographical significance.   39

WAYS IN: Conveying the Event's Autobiographical Significance   39

Write the opening sentences.   41   ▪ Draft your story.   41

Evaluating the Draft: Getting a Critical Reading   41

A CRITICAL READING GUIDE   42

Improving the Draft: Revising, Formatting, Editing, and Proofreading   43

Revise your draft.   43

A TROUBLESHOOTING GUIDE   43

Edit and proofread your draft.   45

LearningCurve > Subject-Verb Agreement

THINKING CRITICALLY   48

Reflecting on What You Have Learned   48

Reflecting on the Genre 48

e **Tutorials** > Digital Writing > Audio Editing in Audacity

3 | Writing Profiles 50

PRACTICING THE GENRE: Conducting an Interview 52

GUIDE TO READING 53

Analyzing Profiles 53

Determine the writer's purpose and audience. 53 ▪ Assess the genre's basic features. 53

Readings 55

Brian Cable, *The Last Stop* 55

e **e-readings** > Brianne O'Leary, *Fatty's Custom Tattooz and Body Piercing* (STUDENT ESSAY)

Amanda Coyne, *The Long Good-Bye: Mother's Day in Federal Prison* 61

Gabriel Thompson, *A Gringo in the Lettuce Fields* 68

e **e-readings** > Sarah Kate Kramer/WNYC, *Niche Market: Fountain Pen Hospital* (ARTICLE AND SLIDESHOW)

GUIDE TO WRITING 75

The Writing Assignment 75

STARTING POINTS: Writing a Profile 75

Writing a Draft: Invention, Research, Planning, and Composing 76

Choose a subject to profile. 77

TEST YOUR CHOICE 77

Conduct your field research. 78

WAYS IN: Managing Your Time 78

WAYS IN: Setting Up and Conducting Interviews and Observations 79

Integrate quotations from your interviews. 82 ▪ Create an outline that will organize your profile effectively for your readers. 83 ▪ Determine your role in the profile. 84

WAYS IN: Determining Your Role   84

Develop your perspective on the subject.   85

WAYS IN: Developing Your Perspective   86

Write the opening sentences.   88 ▪ Draft your profile.   88

Evaluating the Draft: Getting a Critical Reading   88

A CRITICAL READING GUIDE   89

Improving the Draft: Revising, Formatting, Editing, and Proofreading   90

Revise your draft.   90

A TROUBLESHOOTING GUIDE   91

Edit and proofread your draft.   93

ⓔ LearningCurve > Fragments

A Common Problem for Multilingual Writers: Determining Adjective Order   95

THINKING CRITICALLY   96

Reflecting on What You Have Learned   96

Reflecting on the Genre   96

ⓔ Tutorials > Digital Writing > Job Search/Personal Branding

4 | Explaining a Concept   98

PRACTICING THE GENRE: Explaining an Academic Concept   100

GUIDE TO READING   101

Analyzing Concept Explanations   101

Determine the writer's purpose and audience.   101 ▪ Assess the genre's basic features.   101

Readings

Patricia Lyu, *Attachment: Someone to Watch over You*   104

ⓔ e-readings > Ammar Rana, *Jihad: The Struggle in the Way of God* (STUDENT ESSAY)

Anastasia Toufexis, *Love: The Right Chemistry*   111

Susan Cain, *Shyness: Evolutionary Tactic?*   117

ⓔ e-readings > National Geographic Online, *Mapping Memory* (INTERACTIVE GRAPHIC)

ⓔ LaunchPad Solo for *The Concise St. Martin's Guide to Writing*

GUIDE TO WRITING 125

The Writing Assignment 125

STARTING POINTS: Explaining a Concept 125

Writing a Draft: Invention, Research, Planning, and Composing 127

Choose a concept to write about. 127

TEST YOUR CHOICE 128

Conduct initial research on the concept. 128

WAYS IN: Determining What You Know and What You Need to Learn 128

Focus your explanation of the concept. 129

WAYS IN: Making the Concept Interesting to You and Your Readers 129

TEST YOUR CHOICE 130

Conduct further research on your focused concept. 130 ▪ Draft your working thesis. 130 ▪ Organize your concept explanation effectively for your readers. 131 ▪ Consider the explanatory strategies you should use. 131

WAYS IN: Using Writing Strategies to Explain the Focused Concept 132

Use summaries, paraphrases, and quotations from sources to support your points. 133 ▪ Use visuals or multimedia illustrations to enhance your explanation. 133 ▪ Use appositives to integrate sources. 133 ▪ Use descriptive verbs in signal phrases to introduce information from sources. 134 ▪ Write the opening sentences. 135 ▪ Draft your explanation. 135

Evaluating the Draft: Getting a Critical Reading 136

A CRITICAL READING GUIDE 136

Improving the Draft: Revising, Formatting, Editing, and Proofreading 137

Revise your draft. 137

A TROUBLESHOOTING GUIDE 138

Edit and proofread your draft. 140

THINKING CRITICALLY 142

Reflecting on What You Have Learned 142

Reflecting on the Genre 142

5 | Arguing a Position   144

PRACTICING THE GENRE: Debating a Position   146

GUIDE TO READING   147

Analyzing Position Arguments   147

Determine the writer's purpose and audience.   147 ▪ Assess the genre's basic features.   147

Readings   152

Jessica Statsky, *Children Need to Play, Not Compete*   152

🄔 **e-readings** > Michael Niechayev, *It's Time to Ban Head First Tackles and Blocks* (STUDENT ESSAY)

Amitai Etzioni, *Working at McDonald's*   157

Daniel J. Solove, *Why Privacy Matters Even If You Have "Nothing to Hide"*   163

🄔 **e-readings** > U.S. Department of Transportation/The Ad Council, *The "It's Only Another Beer" Black and Tan* (ADVERTISEMENT)

GUIDE TO WRITING   171

The Writing Assignment   171

STARTING POINTS: Arguing a Position   171

Writing a Draft: Invention, Research, Planning, and Composing   172

Choose a controversial issue on which to take a position.   173

TEST YOUR CHOICE   174

Frame the issue for your readers.   174

WAYS IN: Exploring and Framing the Issue and What Your Readers Think   174

TEST YOUR CHOICE   175

Formulate a working thesis stating your position.   176

WAYS IN: Devising an Arguable Thesis   176

Develop the reasons supporting your position.   176

WAYS IN: Devising Reasons to Support Your Position   176

Research your position.   177 ▪ Use sources to reinforce your credibility.   177 ▪ Identify and respond to your readers' likely reasons and objections.   178

WAYS IN: Identifying and Responding to Readers' Concerns   179

Create an outline that will organize your argument effectively for your readers.   180   ▪   Write the opening sentences.   181   ▪   Draft your position argument.   182

Evaluating the Draft: Getting a Critical Reading   182

A CRITICAL READING GUIDE   182

Improving the Draft: Revising, Formatting, Editing, and Proofreading   184

Revise your draft.   184

A TROUBLESHOOTING GUIDE   184

Edit and proofread your draft.   185

🄴 LearningCurve > Appropriate Language

> Commas

> Run-ons and Comma Splices

THINKING CRITICALLY   188

Reflecting on What You Have Learned   188

Reflecting on the Genre   188

6 │ Proposing a Solution   190

PRACTICING THE GENRE: Arguing That a Solution Is Feasible   192

GUIDE TO READING   193

Analyzing Proposals   193

Determine the writer's purpose and audience.   193   ▪   Assess the genre's basic features.   193

Readings   197

Patrick O'Malley, *More Testing, More Learning*   197

🄴 e-readings > Molly Coleman, *Missing the Fun* (STUDENT ESSAY)

David Bornstein, *Fighting Bullying with Babies*   204

Karen Kornbluh, *Win-Win Flexibility*   210

🄴 e-readings > Phoebe Sweet and Zach Wise, *The Problem with Lawns: The Transforming Landscape of Las Vegas* (VIDEO)

GUIDE TO WRITING 218

The Writing Assignment 218

STARTING POINTS: Proposing a Solution 218

Writing a Draft: Invention, Research, Planning, and Composing 219

Choose a problem for which you can propose a solution. 220

TEST YOUR CHOICE 220

Frame the problem for your readers. 221

WAYS IN: Identifying the Problem and Figuring Out Why Readers Will Care 221

TEST YOUR CHOICE 223

Use statistics to establish the problem's existence and seriousness. 223 ▪ Assess how the problem has been framed, and reframe it for your readers. 224

WAYS IN: Framing and Reframing the Problem 224

Develop a possible solution. 225

WAYS IN: Solving the Problem 225

Explain your solution. 226

WAYS IN: Explaining the Solution and Showing Its Feasibility 226

Research your proposal. 226 ▪ Develop a response to objections and alternative solutions. 227

WAYS IN: Drafting a Refutation or Concession 227

Create an outline that will organize your proposal effectively for your readers. 228 ▪ Write the opening sentences. 229 ▪ Draft your proposal. 229

Evaluating the Draft: Getting a Critical Reading 229

A CRITICAL READING GUIDE 230

Improving the Draft: Revising, Formatting, Editing, and Proofreading 231

Revise your draft. 231

A TROUBLESHOOTING GUIDE 231

Edit and proofread your draft. 232

🄴 LearningCurve > Active and Passive Voice

THINKING CRITICALLY   234

   Reflecting on What You Have Learned   234

   Reflecting on the Genre   234

7 | Justifying an Evaluation   236

PRACTICING THE GENRE: Choosing Appropriate Criteria
and Examples   238

GUIDE TO READING   239

   Analyzing Evaluations   239

   Determine the writer's purpose and audience.   239   ▪ Assess the
genre's basic features.   239

   Readings   243

   William Akana, Scott Pilgrim vs. the World: *A Hell of a Ride*   243

   e e-readings > Brittany Lemus, Requiem for a Dream: *Fantasy versus
Reality* (STUDENT ESSAY)

   Malcolm Gladwell, *What College Rankings Really Tell Us*   249

   Christine Rosen, *The Myth of Multitasking*   255

   e e-readings > Yelp, *Kuma's Corner* (WEB PAGE)

GUIDE TO WRITING   263

   The Writing Assignment   263

     STARTING POINTS: Justifying an Evaluation   263

   **Writing a Draft: Invention, Research, Planning,
and Composing**   264

   Choose a subject to evaluate.   264

     TEST YOUR CHOICE   265

   Assess your subject and consider how to present it to
your readers.   266

     WAYS IN: Determining What You and Your Readers Think   266

   Formulate a working thesis stating your overall judgment.   267

     WAYS IN: Asserting a Tentative Overall Judgment   267

Develop the reasons and evidence supporting your judgment.   268

WAYS IN: Devising Reasons and Evidence to Support
Your Judgment   268

Research your evaluation.   269 ▪ Respond to a likely objection or
alternative judgment.   269

WAYS IN: Responding Effectively to Readers   270

Organize your draft to appeal to your readers.   271 ▪ Write the
opening sentences.   272 ▪ Draft your evaluation.   272

Evaluating the Draft: Getting a Critical Reading   272

A CRITICAL READING GUIDE   273

**Improving the Draft: Revising, Formatting, Editing,
and Proofreading**   274

Revise your draft.   274

A TROUBLESHOOTING GUIDE   274

Edit and proofread your draft.   277

THINKING CRITICALLY   279

Reflecting on What You Have Learned   279

Reflecting on the Genre   279

PART 2   Strategies for Critical Thinking, Reading, and Writing

8 | Strategies for Invention and Inquiry   282

Mapping   282

Create a cluster diagram.   282 ▪ Make a list.   283 ▪ Create an
outline.   284

Writing   287

Use cubing.   288 ▪ Construct a dialogue.   288 ▪ Use the five elements
of dramatizing.   289 ▪ Freewrite for a set amount of time.   290
▪ Keep a journal.   291 ▪ Use looping.   291 ▪ Ask questions.   292

9 | Strategies for Reading Critically   294

Annotating   295

Martin Luther King Jr., *An Annotated Sample from "Letter from Birmingham Jail"*   295

🄴 LearningCurve > Critical Reading

Taking Inventory   302

Outlining   302

Paraphrasing   304

Summarizing   306

Synthesizing   307

Contextualizing   308

Exploring the Significance of Figurative Language   309

Looking for Patterns of Opposition   310

Reflecting on Challenges to Your Beliefs and Values   312

Evaluating the Logic of an Argument   312

Test for appropriateness.   313 ▪ Test for believability.   313 ▪ Test for consistency and completeness.   314

Recognizing Emotional Manipulation   315

Judging the Writer's Credibility   315

Test for knowledge.   315 ▪ Test for common ground.   316 ▪ Test for fairness.   316

10 | Cueing the Reader   317

Orienting Statements   317

Use thesis statements to announce the main idea.   317 ▪ Use forecasting statements to preview topics.   318

🄴 LearningCurve > Topics and Main Ideas

Paragraphing 319

Paragraph indents signal related ideas. 319 ▪ Topic sentences announce the paragraph's focus. 320

[e] **LearningCurve** > Topic Sentences and Supporting Details

Cohesive Devices 323

Pronouns connect phrases or sentences. 323 ▪ Word repetition aids cohesion. 324 ▪ Synonyms connect ideas. 325 ▪ Sentence structure repetition emphasizes connections. 325 ▪ Collocation creates networks of meaning. 325

Transitions 326

Transitions emphasize logical relationships. 327 ▪ Transitions can indicate a sequence in time. 328 ▪ Transitions can indicate relationships in space. 328

Headings and Subheadings 329

Headings indicate sections and levels. 330 ▪ Headings are not common in all genres. 330 ▪ At least two headings are needed at each level. 330

11 | Analyzing and Synthesizing Arguments 332

Analyzing Arguments 332

Applying the criteria for analyzing arguments. 332 ▪ Annotating a text and creating a chart. 334

[e] **Tutorials** > Critical Reading > Active Reading Strategies

Coming up with a focus for your analysis. 334

Sentence Strategies for Analysis 336

A Sample Analysis 336

Mirko Bagaric and Julie Clarke, *A Case for Torture* 336

Melissa Mae's annotaions. 338 ▪ Melissa Mae's analysis. 339

From Analysis to Synthesis 344

A Sample Synthesis 344

Melissa Mae's process. 344

12 | Analyzing Visuals 352

Criteria for Analyzing Visuals 355
e Tutorials > Critical Reading > Reading Visuals: Purpose
                                 > Reading Visuals: Audience

A Sample Analysis 356

13 | Arguing 366

Asserting a Thesis 366
Make arguable assertions. 367 ▪ Use clear and precise
wording. 367 ▪ Qualify the thesis appropriately. 368

Giving Reasons and Support 369
Use representative examples for support. 369 ▪ Use up-to-date,
relevant, and accurate statistics. 370 ▪ Cite reputable authorities
on relevant topics. 371 ▪ Use vivid, relevant anecdotes. 372
▪ Use relevant textual evidence. 374

Responding to Objections and Alternatives 375
Acknowledge readers' concerns. 375 ▪ Concede readers'
concerns. 376 ▪ Refute readers' objections. 377

Recognizing Logical Fallacies 378

Sentence Strategies for Argument 379

14 | Designing Documents 383

The Impact of Document Design 383

Considering Context, Audience, and Purpose 384

Elements of Document Design 385
e Tutorials > Digital Writing > Word Processing
Choose readable fonts. 385 ▪ Use headings to organize your
writing. 387 ▪ Use lists to highlight steps or key points. 387
▪ Use colors with care. 388 ▪ Use white space to make text
readable. 389

Adding Visuals 390

Choose and design visuals with their final use in mind. 390

🄴 **Tutorials** > Digital Writing > Presentations

> Photo Editing Basics with GIMP

Number, title, and label visuals. 390 ▪ Cite visual sources. 393 ▪ Integrate the visual into the text. 393 ▪ Use common sense when creating visuals on a computer. 394

PART 3 Strategies for research

15 | Planning a Research Project 396

Analyzing Your Rhetorical Situation and Setting a Schedule 397

Choosing a Topic and Getting an Overview 399

Narrowing Your Topic and Drafting Research Questions 400

Establishing a Research Log 400

Creating a Working Bibliography 401

Annotating Your Working Bibliography 402

Taking Notes on Your Sources 403

16 | Finding Sources and Conducting Field Research 404

Searching Library Catalogs and Databases 404

Use appropriate search terms. 404 ▪ Narrow (or expand) your results. 405 ▪ Find books (and other sources) through your library's catalog. 405 ▪ Find articles in periodicals using your library's databases. 407 ▪ Find government documents and statistical information. 408 ▪ Find Web sites and interactive sources. 409

🄴 **Tutorials** > Digital Writing > Online Research Tools

Conducting Field Research   412

Conduct observational studies.   412

PRACTICING THE GENRE: Collaborating on an Observational Study   413

Conduct interviews.   414

PRACTICING THE GENRE: Interviewing a Classmate   416

Conduct surveys.   416

17 | Evaluating Sources   420

Choosing Relevant Sources   420

Choosing Reliable Sources   421

Who wrote it?   422 ▪ When was it published?   422 ▪ Is the source scholarly, popular, or for a trade group?   423 ▪ Who published it?   423 ▪ How is the source written?   426 ▪ What does the source say?   426

18 | Using Sources to Support Your Ideas   427

Synthesizing Sources   427

Acknowledging Sources and Avoiding Plagiarism   428

What does and does not need to be acknowledged?   428

ⓔ **Tutorials** > Documentation and Working with Sources > Do I Need to Cite That?

Avoid plagiarism by acknowledging sources and quoting, paraphrasing, and summarizing carefully.   428

Using Information from Sources to Support Your Claims   429

Decide whether to quote, paraphrase, or summarize.   430

ⓔ **LearningCurve** > Working with Sources (MLA)

> Working with Sources (APA)

Copy quotations exactly, or use italics, ellipses, and brackets to indicate changes.   431 ▪ Use in-text or block quotations.   434 ▪ Use punctuation to integrate quotations into your writing.   435 ▪ Paraphrase sources carefully.   435 ▪ Summaries should present the source's main ideas in a balanced and readable way.   437

19 | Citing and Documenting Sources in MLA Style 438

e Tutorials > Documentation and Working with Sources
> How to Cite an Article in MLA style
> How to Cite a Book in MLA Style
> How to Cite a Database in MLA Style
> How to Cite a Web Site in MLA Style

Citing Sources in the Text 439

DIRECTORY TO IN-TEXT-CITATION MODELS 439

Creating a List of Works Cited 442

DIRECTORY TO WORKS-CITED-LIST MODELS 442

Student Research Project in MLA Style 456

20 | Citing and Documenting Sources in APA Style 466

e Tutorials > Documentation and Working with Sources
> How to Cite a Database in APA Style
> How to Cite a Web Site in APA Style

Citing Sources in the Text 466

DIRECTLY TO IN-TEXT-CITATION MODELS 466

Creating a List of References 468

DIRECTORY TO REFERENCE-LIST MODELS 468

A Sample References List 474

Acknowledgments A-1

Index I-1

Edit and Proofread Your Draft I-19

The Concise
St. Martin's
Guide to Writing

1

Introduction: Thinking about Writing

More people are writing today than ever before, and many are switching comfortably from one genre or medium to another—from tweeting to blogging to creating multi-media Web pages. Learning to be effective as a writer is a continuous process as you find yourself in new writing situations using new technologies and trying to anticipate the concerns of different audiences. "The illiterate of the 21st century will not be those who cannot read and write," futurist Alvin Toffler predicted, "but those who cannot learn, unlearn, and relearn."

Learning anything—especially learning to communicate in new ways—benefits from what we call reflection, thinking critically about *how* as well as *what* you are learning. Extensive research confirms what writers have known for a long time: that reflection makes learning easier and faster. In fact, recent studies show that writing even a few sentences about your thoughts and feelings before a high-stress paper or exam helps students reduce stress and boost performance. That is why in this chapter and throughout this book, we ask you to think about your experience as a writer, and we recommend using writing to explore and develop your ideas. The activities that conclude this chapter invite you to compose a **literacy narrative,** a multifaceted exploration of yourself as a writer.

To get started thinking about writing, we will look at some of the important contri-butions writing makes. Then, we'll preview how *The Concise St. Martin's Guide to Writing* can help you become a better, more confident, and more versatile writer.

Why Write?

"Why write?" is an important basic question, especially today, when many people assume technology has eliminated the need to learn to write well. Obviously, writing enables you to communicate, but it also helps you think and learn, enhances your chances of success, contributes to your personal development, and strengthens your relationships.

1

Write to communicate effectively in different rhetorical situations.

Writing is a powerful means of communicating with diverse audiences in different genres and media. We use the term **rhetorical situation** to emphasize the fact that writing is social and purposeful. The rhetorical situation includes four interrelated factors:

Why?	Your *purpose* for writing
Who?	The *audience* you are addressing
What?	The *genre* or type of text you are writing
How?	The *medium* in which your text will be read

Writing with an awareness of the rhetorical situation means writing not only to express yourself but also to reach out to your readers (audience) by engaging their interest and responding to their concerns. You write to influence how your readers think and feel about a subject and, depending on the genre, perhaps also to inspire them to action.

Writing with genre awareness affects your composing decisions—what you write about (subject choice), the claims you make (thesis), how you support those claims (reasons and evidence), and how you organize it all. **Genres** are simply ways of categorizing texts—for example, we can distinguish between fiction and nonfiction; subdivide fiction into romance, mystery, and science fiction genres; or break down mystery even further into hard-boiled detective, police procedural, true crime, and classic whodunit genres. Each genre has a set of conventions or **basic features** readers expect texts in that genre to use. Although individual texts within the same genre vary a great deal—for example, no two *proposals*, even those arguing for the same solution, will be identical—they nonetheless follow a general pattern that provides a certain amount of predictability. Without such predictability, communication would be difficult, if not impossible. But these conventional patterns should not be thought of as recipes. Conventions are broad frameworks within which writers are free to be creative. Most writers, in fact, find that working within a framework makes creativity possible. Depending on the formality of the rhetorical situation and the audience's openness to innovation, writers may also play with genre conventions, remixing features of different genres to form new mash-ups, as you will see in the integrated media selections for each Part One chapter.

Like genre, the medium in which you are working also affects many of your design and content choices. For example, written texts can use color, type fonts, charts, diagrams, and still images to heighten the visual impact of the text, delivering information vividly and persuasively. If you are composing Web pages or apps, you have many more options to make your text truly multimedia—for example, by adding hyperlinks, animation, audio, video, and interactivity to your written text.

Write to think.

The very act of writing—crafting and combining sentences—helps you think creatively and logically. You create new ideas by putting words together to make meaningful sentences and by linking sentences with *logical transitions,* like *however* or *because,* to form a coherent chain of meaning. Many writers equate thinking with writing: "How can I tell what I think," the novelist E. M. Forster famously wrote,

> "How can I tell what I think," the novelist E. M. Forster famously wrote, "till I see what I say?"

"till I see what I say?" Other writers have echoed the same idea. Columnist Anna Quindlen, for example, put it this way: "As a writer, I would find out most clearly what I thought, and what I only thought I thought, when I saw it written down." Finally, here's the way physicist James Van Allen explained the connection between writing and thinking: "The mere process of writing is one of the most powerful tools we have for clarifying our own thinking."

Write to learn.

As a student, you are probably keenly aware of the many ways writing can help you do well in courses throughout the curriculum. The physical act of writing—from simply making notes as you read, to listing main points, to summarizing—is a potent memory aid. Writing down your rudimentary ideas and posing questions can lead to deeper understanding. *Analyzing* and *synthesizing* ideas and information from different sources can extend your learning. Most important, thinking about what you are learning and how—what are called *methodologies* in many disciplines—can open up new directions for further learning.

Write to succeed.

Writing contributes to success in school and at work. We've already suggested some of the ways writing can both help you think analytically and logically and aid your learning and remembering. In school, you need to use writing to demonstrate your learning. You will be asked to write essays *explaining* and *applying concepts* and to construct academic *arguments* using sources and other kinds of evidence. Your skill at doing these things will most likely affect your grades. Writing also helps in practical ways as you apply for internships, admission to professional school, and a job. At work, you may need to write for a variety of rhetorical situations—for example, to *evaluate* staff you supervise, to collaborate with colleagues *proposing* a new project, to e-mail suggestions for resolving conflicts or ideas about new initiatives, or to prepare year-end reports *justifying* expenditures and priorities. Just as your achievement in school is influenced by your ability to write well, so, too, may your professional success depend on your ability to write effectively to different audiences in varied genres and media.

Write to know yourself and connect to other people.

Writing can help you grow as an individual and also help you maintain and build relationships with friends and colleagues. Journal writing has long been used as a means of self-discovery. Many people blog for the same reason. Becoming an author confers *authority,* giving you confidence to assert your ideas and opinions. Whether you're tweeting to let friends know what's happening, posting comments on a Web site, taking part in a class discussion, or participating in political debate and decision making, writing enables you to offer your own point of view and invites others to share theirs in return.

How *The Concise St. Martin's Guide to Writing* Helps You Learn to Write

There are many myths about writing and writers. Perhaps the most enduring myth is that people who are good at writing do not have to learn to write—they just naturally know how. Writing may be easier and more rewarding for some people, but no one is born knowing how to write. Writing must be learned. To learn to write, as Stephen King explained, "you must do two things above all others: read a lot and write a lot." That is precisely how the *Concise Guide* works—by providing both a Guide to Reading and a Guide to Writing for each genre you will be writing.

> To learn to write, as Stephen King explained, "you must do two things above all others: read a lot and write a lot."

Learn to write by using the Guides to Reading.

These guides teach you to analyze how texts work in particular rhetorical situations. By analyzing several texts in the genre you will be writing in, you can see how writers employ the genre's basic features differently to achieve their purpose with their audience. In other words, you will see in action the many strategies writers can use to achieve their goals.

Learn to write by using the Guides to Writing.

These guides help you apply to your own writing what you are learning from reading and analyzing examples of the genre. They provide a scaffold to support your writing as you develop a repertoire of strategies for using the genre's basic features to achieve your purpose with your audience.

Each Guide to Writing begins with a Starting Points chart that will enable you to find answers to your composing questions. You can follow your own course, dipping into the Guide for help when you need it, or you can follow the sequence of exploratory activities, from Writing a Draft through Evaluating the Draft to Improving the Draft. Although many people assume that good writers begin with their first sentence and go right through to their last sentence, professional writers know that writing is a process of discovery. Most writers begin with preliminary planning and exploratory writing that at some point turns into a rough draft. Then, as the draft takes shape, they may reconsider the organization, do additional research to fill in gaps, rewrite passages that need clarification, or continue drafting. Essayist Dave Barry describes his typical writing process this way: "It's a matter of piling a little piece here and a little piece there, fitting them together, going on to the next part, then going back and gradually shaping the whole piece into something."

A challenge for most writers comes when they have a draft but don't know how to improve it. It is sometimes hard for them to see what a draft actually says as opposed to what they want to convey. Instructors often set aside class time for a draft workshop or ask students to do an online peer critique.

> Essayist Dave Barry describes his typical writing process this way: "It's a matter of piling a little piece here and a little piece there, fitting them together, going on to the next part, then going back and gradually shaping the whole piece into something."

Each chapter's Guide to Writing includes a Critical Reading Guide for this purpose. You may find that reading someone else's draft can be especially helpful to you as a writer because it's often easier to recognize problems and see how to fix them in someone else's draft than it is to see similar problems in your own writing. The Critical Reading Guide is also keyed to a Troubleshooting Guide that will help you find ways to revise and improve your draft. The Guide to Writing also includes advice on proofreading and editing that you can use to check for sentence-level errors.

THINKING CRITICALLY

In addition to modeling good writing and providing guides for reading and writing, *The Concise St. Martin's Guide to Writing* helps you think critically about your writing. Each writing assignment chapter in Part One of the *Concise Guide* includes many opportunities for you to think critically and reflect on your understanding of the rhetorical situation in which you are writing. In addition, a section titled Thinking Critically concludes each chapter, giving you an opportunity to look back and reflect on how you used your writing process creatively and how you expanded your understanding of the genre. The following activity gives you the opportunity to reflect on your own experience with reading and writing, your own literacy narrative. Why not start now to become a better writer by thinking critically about your own experience?

REFLECTION

A Literacy Narrative

Write several pages telling about your experience with writing. Consider the following suggestions:

- Recall an early experience of writing: What did you write? Did anyone read it? What kind of feedback did you get? How did you feel about yourself?
- Think of a turning point when your attitude toward writing changed or crystallized. What happened? What changed?

- Recall a person — a teacher, a classmate, a family member, a published writer, or someone else — who influenced your writing, for good or ill. How was your writing affected?

- Cast yourself as the main character of a story about writing. How would you describe yourself — as a talented writer, as someone who struggles to write well, or somewhere in between? Consider your trajectory, or *narrative arc*: Over the years, would you say you have showed steady improvement? Ups and downs? More downs than ups? A decline?

- Think about literacy more broadly and write about how you acquired academic literacy (perhaps focusing on how you learned to think, talk, and write as a scientist or a historian), workplace literacy (perhaps focusing on how you learned to communicate effectively with customers or managers), sports literacy (perhaps as a player, coach, or fan), music literacy (perhaps as a performer or composer), community literacy (perhaps focusing on how you learned to communicate with people of different ages or with people who speak different languages or dialects), or any other kind of literacy you have mastered.

PART 1

Writing
Activities

2 Remembering an Event   8

3 Writing Profiles   50

4 Explaining a Concept   98

5 Arguing a Position   144

6 Proposing a Solution   190

7 Justifying an Evaluation   236

2
Remembering an Event

Writing about the memorable events and people in our lives can be exhilarating. This kind of writing can lead us to think deeply about why certain experiences are meaningful and continue to touch us. It can help us understand the cultural influences that helped shape who we are and what we value. It can also give us an opportunity to represent ourselves and connect with others. In college courses, we can use our experience to better understand what we are studying; in the community, we can use personal stories for inspiration; and in the workplace, we can use experience to catalyze needed change.

© Yellow Dog Productions/Getty Images

IN COLLEGE COURSES

For a linguistics course, a student writes an essay analyzing a recent conversation with her brother in light of a book she read for the class: Deborah Tannen's *Gender and Discourse*, in which Tannen argues that when discussing problems, women tend to focus on the problem and their feelings about it, while men typically cut short talk about feelings and focus on possible solutions. The student begins her essay by reconstructing the conversation with her brother, quoting some dialogue from her diary and paraphrasing other parts from memory. Then she analyzes the conversation. Using Tannen's ideas, she discovers that what bothered her about the conversation was less its content than her brother's way of communicating.

IN THE COMMUNITY

As part of a local history series in a newspaper serving a small western ranching community, an amateur historian helps an elderly rancher write about the winter of 1938, when a six-foot snowfall isolated the rancher's family for nearly a month. The rancher talks about how he, his wife, and the couple's infant survived, including an account of how he snowshoed eight miles to get word to relatives. The details the rancher includes, like the suspenseful description of his exhausting trek, make the event vivid and dramatic for the newspaper's readers.

IN THE WORKPLACE

A respected longtime regional manager gives the keynote speech at the highway department's statewide meeting on workplace safety. He opens his speech with a dramatic recounting of a confrontation he had with a disgruntled employee who complained bitterly about his work schedule and threatened the safety of the manager and his family. Setting the scene (a lonely office after hours) to help audience members enter into his experience, he describes the taste of fear in his mouth and his relief when a contractor entered the office. The manager follows the anecdote with data showing the frequency of such workplace incidents nationwide and concludes by calling for new departmental guidelines on how to defuse such confrontations effectively.

In this chapter, we ask you to write about a remembered event that will engage readers and that has significance for you. From reading and analyzing the selections in the Guide to Reading that follows, you will learn how to make your own story interesting, even exciting, to read. The Guide to Writing later in the chapter will support you as you compose your remembered event essay, showing you ways to use the basic features of the genre to tell your story vividly and dramatically, entertaining readers but also giving them insight into the event's significance—its meaning and importance—in your life.

| PRACTICING THE GENRE |

Telling a Story

The success of remembered event writing depends on how well the story is told. Some memorable events are inherently dramatic, but most are not. The challenge is to make the story entertaining and meaningful for readers. The most effective autobiographical stories make readers care about the storyteller and curious to know what happened. To practice creating an engaging story based on a memorable event in your life, get together with two or three other students and follow these guidelines:

Part 1. Choose a memorable event that you feel comfortable describing to this group. (Make sure you can tell your story in just a few minutes.) Take five minutes to sketch out a plan: Think about what makes the event memorable (for example, a conflict with someone else or within yourself, the strong or mixed feelings it evokes, the cultural attitudes it reflects). What will be the turning point, or climax, of the story, and how will you build up to it? Then take turns telling your stories.

Part 2. After telling your stories, discuss what you learned about the genre:

- **What did you learn about the genre from others' stories?** To think about purpose and audience in the genre of autobiography, tell each other what struck you most on hearing each other's stories. For example, identify something in the story that was moving, suspenseful, edgy, or funny. What in the story, if anything, helped you identify or sympathize with the storyteller? What do you think the point or significance of the story is — in other words, what makes the event so memorable?

- **What did you learn about the genre from constructing your own autobiographical story?** With the others in your group, compare your thoughts on what was easiest and hardest about telling the story: for example, choosing an event, portraying the conflict and making the story dramatic, selecting what to put in and leave out, or letting the story speak for itself without explaining.

Analyzing Remembered Event Essays

As you read the selections in this chapter, you will see how different authors craft stories about an important event in their lives. Analyzing how these writers tell a dramatic, well-focused story, use vivid, specific description to enliven their writing, and choose the details and words that enable them to convey their perspective on the event will help you see how you can employ these same techniques when writing your own autobiographical story.

Determine the writer's purpose and audience.

Many people write about important events in their lives to archive their memories and to learn something about themselves. Keep in mind, however, that unless you are writing in your diary, remembered event writing is a public genre meant to be read by others. So it is important to think about self-presentation as well as self-discovery.

Memorable events are by definition full of potential meaning, and insightful readers often see larger themes or deeper implications—what we call **significance**—beyond those the writer consciously intends to communicate or even acknowledges. This richness of meaning makes autobiographical writing fascinating to read and to write. When reading the selections about remembered events that follow, ask yourself the following questions about the writer's purpose and audience:

- What seems to be the writer's main *purpose*—for example, to understand what happened and why, perhaps to confront unconscious and possibly uncomplimentary motives; to relive an intense experience, perhaps to work through complex and ambivalent feelings; to win over readers, perhaps to justify or rationalize choices made, actions taken, or words used; to reflect on cultural attitudes at the time the event occurred, perhaps in contrast to current ways of thinking?

- What does the author assume about the *audience*—for example, that readers will have had similar experiences and therefore appreciate what the writer went through and not judge the writer too harshly; that they will see the writer as innocent, well meaning, a victim, or something else; that readers will laugh with and not at the writer, seeing the writer's failings as amusing foibles and not serious shortcomings; that readers will reflect on the cultural context in which the event occurred and how it influenced the writer?

Assess the genre's basic features.

Basic Features
A Well-Told Story
Vivid Description
Significance

As you read remembered event essays in this chapter, you will see how different authors incorporate the basic features of the genre. The examples that follow are taken from the reading selections that appear later in this Guide to Reading.

A WELL-TOLD STORY

Read first to enjoy the story. The best autobiographical stories are first and foremost a pleasure to read.

FIGURE 2.1 Dramatic Arc
The shape of the arc varies. Not all stories devote the same amount of space to each element, and some may omit an element or include more than one.

- **Exposition/Inciting Incident:** Background information, scene setting, or an introduction to the characters or an initial conflict or problem that sets off the action, arousing curiosity and suspense
- **Rising Action:** The developing crisis, possibly leading to other conflicts and complications
- **Climax:** The emotional high point, a turning point marking a change for good or ill
- **Falling Action:** Resolution of tension and unraveling of conflicts; may include a final surprise
- **Resolution/Reflection:** Conflicts come to an end but may not be fully resolved, and writer reflects on the event's meaning and importance—its significance

Examine the story to see if it is well told. Does it let readers into the narrator's point of view, enabling us to empathize with the writer? Does it arouse curiosity and suspense by structuring the narrative around conflict? Does it lead to a change or discovery of some kind? These elements can be visualized in the form of a **dramatic arc** (see Figure 2.1), which you can analyze to see how a narrative creates and resolves dramatic tension.

Look also to see how *dialogue* is used to portray people, help readers understand their point of view, and heighten the drama. There are three ways to present dialogue: by quoting, paraphrasing, or summarizing. **Quoting** dramatizes the dialogue through a combination of actual spoken words and descriptive *speaker tags* that surround them:

> Speaker tag "You stupid kids," he began perfunctorily. (Dillard, par. 18)

Paraphrasing reports the content of what was said but doesn't quote the actual words or use quotation marks:

> I asked her if she thought I should buy the button. She said it was cute and if I wanted it to go ahead and buy it. (Brandt, par. 2)

Summarizing gives the gist without the detail:

> I was read my rights and questioned. (Brandt, par. 19)

VIVID DESCRIPTION OF PEOPLE AND PLACES

Look for descriptions of people and places to see how the describing strategies of *naming, detailing,* and *comparing* are used to portray vividly what people look like and how they dress, gesture, and talk, as well as to convey graphic sensory images showing what the narrator saw, heard, smelled, touched, and tasted. For example, take a look at Desmond-Harris's description of people and Dillard's description of a place:

Naming My hair has recently been straightened with my first (and last) relaxer and
Detailing a Gold 'N Hot flatiron on too high a setting. Hers is slicked back with the
Comparing mixture of Herbal Essences and Blue Magic that we formulated in a bath-
room laboratory. (Desmond-Harris, par. 6)

The cars' tires laid behind them on the snowy street a complex trail of
beige chunks like crenellated castle walls. I had stepped on some earlier;
they squeaked. (Dillard, par. 5)

AUTOBIOGRAPHICAL SIGNIFICANCE

Read finally to understand the story's autobiographical significance. This is the point the
writer is trying to make—the purpose for writing to a particular audience. Notice how
writers convey mixed or ambivalent feelings, how they acknowledge still-unresolved
conflict, how they avoid making the story seem clichéd or sentimental.

To convey the richness of meaning that makes the event worth writing about, writers tell as well as show

- by *remembering feelings and thoughts* from the time the event took place:

    The thought of going to jail terrified me. . . . I felt alone and scared." (Brandt, par. 17)

    It was an immense discovery, pounding into my hot head with every sliding, joyous
    step, that this ordinary adult evidently knew what I thought only children . . . knew.
    (Dillard, par. 13)

- by reflecting on the past from the *present perspective*:

    I mourned Tupac's death then, and continue to mourn him now, because his music
    represents the years when I was both forced and privileged to confront what it meant to
    be black. (Desmond-Harris, par. 9)

- by choosing details and words that create a *dominant impression*: Brandt, for example,
  describes her rapidly changing feelings: naïve optimism, fear, humiliation, excitement, shame, worry, relief. This cinematic technique of quick cuts from one feeling or
  thought to another conveys the volatility of her emotions.

Readings

Jean Brandt | *Calling Home*

As a first-year college student, Jean Brandt wrote about a memorable event that occurred
when she was thirteen. Reflecting on how she felt at the time, Brandt writes, "I was afraid,
embarrassed, worried, mad." In disclosing her tumultuous and contradictory remembered
feelings, Brandt makes her story dramatic and resonant. Even if readers have not had a similar experience, they are likely to empathize with Brandt and grasp the significance of this
event in her life.

As you read, do the following:

- Look for places where Brandt lets us know how she felt at the time the event occurred.
- Identify the parts of the dramatic arc that she emphasizes or complicates, that she downplays or eliminates.
- Consider the questions in the margin. Your instructor may ask you to post answers to these questions to a class blog or discussion board or bring them to class.

Basic Features
A Well-Told Story
Vivid Description
Significance

1   As we all piled into the car, I knew it was going to be a fabulous day. My grandmother was visiting for the holidays; and she and I, along with my older brother and sister, Louis and Susan, were setting off for a day of last-minute Christmas shopping. On the way to the mall, we sang Christmas carols, chattered, and laughed. With Christmas only two days away, we were caught up with holiday spirit. I felt light-headed and full of joy. I loved shopping — especially at Christmas.

How well do these descriptive details help you visualize the scene?

2   The shopping center was swarming with frantic last-minute shoppers like ourselves. We went first to the General Store, my favorite. It carried mostly knickknacks and other useless items which nobody needs but buys anyway. I was thirteen years old at the time, and things like buttons and calendars and posters would catch my fancy. This day was no different. The object of my desire was a 75-cent Snoopy button. Snoopy was the latest. If you owned anything with the Peanuts on it, you were "in." But since I was supposed to be shopping for gifts for other people and not myself, I couldn't decide what to do. I went in search of my sister for her opinion. I pushed my way through throngs of people to the back of the store where I found Susan. I asked her if she thought I should buy the button. She said it was cute and if I wanted it to go ahead and buy it.

What is your first impression of Brandt?

3   When I got back to the Snoopy section, I took one look at the lines at the cashiers and knew I didn't want to wait thirty minutes to buy an item worth less than one dollar. I walked back to the basket where I found the button and was about to drop it when suddenly, instead, I took a quick glance around, assured myself no one could see, and slipped the button into the pocket of my sweatshirt.

How do these action verbs (highlighted) and dialogue contribute to the drama?

4   I hesitated for a moment, but once the item was in my pocket, there was no turning back. I had never before stolen anything; but what was done was done. A few seconds later, my sister appeared and asked, "So, did you decide to buy the button?"

5   "No, I guess not." I hoped my voice didn't quaver. As we headed for the entrance, my heart began to race. I just had to get out of that store. Only a few more yards to go and I'd be safe. As we crossed the threshold, I heaved a sigh of relief. I was home free. I thought about how sly I had been and I felt proud of my accomplishment.

6   An unexpected tap on my shoulder startled me. I whirled around to find a middle-aged man, dressed in street clothes, flashing some type of badge and politely asking me to empty my pockets. Where did this man come from? How did he know? I was so sure that no one had seen me! On the verge of panicking, I told myself that all I had to do was give this man his button back, say I was sorry, and go on my way. After all, it was only a 75-cent item.

7   Next thing I knew, he was talking about calling the police and having me arrested and thrown in jail, as if he had just nabbed a professional thief instead of a terrified kid. I couldn't believe what he was saying.

8   "Jean, what's going on?"

9   The sound of my sister's voice eased the pressure a bit. She always managed to get me out of trouble. She would come through this time too.

10   "Excuse me. Are you a relative of this young girl?"

11   "Yes, I'm her sister. What's the problem?"

12   "Well, I just caught her shoplifting and I'm afraid I'll have to call the police."

13   "What did she take?"

14   "This button."

15   "A button? You are having a thirteen-year-old arrested for stealing a button?"

16   "I'm sorry, but she broke the law."

17   The man led us through the store and into an office, where we waited for the police officers to arrive. Susan had found my grandmother and brother, who, still shocked, didn't say a word. The thought of going to jail terrified me, not because of jail itself, but because of the encounter with my parents afterward. Not more than ten minutes later, two officers arrived and placed me under arrest. They said that I was to be taken to the station alone. Then, they handcuffed me and led me out of the store. I felt alone and scared. I had counted on my sister being with me, but now I had to muster up the courage to face this ordeal all by myself.

How does your understanding of Brandt deepen or change through what she reveals about her feelings and thoughts?

18   As the officers led me through the mall, I sensed a hundred pairs of eyes staring at me. My face flushed and I broke out in a sweat. Now everyone knew I was a criminal. In their eyes I was a juvenile delinquent, and thank God the cops were getting me off the streets. The worst part was thinking my grandmother might be having the same thoughts. The humiliation at that moment was overwhelming. I felt like Hester Prynne being put on public display for everyone to ridicule.

19   That short walk through the mall seemed to take hours. But once we reached the squad car, time raced by. I was read my rights and questioned. We were at the police station within minutes. Everything happened so fast I didn't have a chance to feel remorse for my crime. Instead, I viewed what was happening to me as if it were a movie. Being searched, although embarrassing, somehow seemed to be exciting. All the movies and television programs I had seen were actually coming to life. This is what it was really like. But why were criminals always portrayed as frightened and regretful? I was having fun. I thought I had nothing to fear — until I was allowed my one phone call. I was trembling as I dialed home. I didn't know what I was going to say to my parents, especially my mother.

20   "Hi, Dad, this is Jean."

21   "We've been waiting for you to call."

22   "Did Susie tell you what happened?"

How does this dialogue add to the drama?

23   "Yeah, but we haven't told your mother. I think you should tell her what you did and where you are."

24   "You mean she doesn't even know where I am?"

25   "No, I want you to explain it to her."

26   There was a pause as he called my mother to the phone. For the first time that night, I was close to tears. I wished I had never stolen that stupid pin. I wanted to give the phone to one of the officers because I was too ashamed to tell my mother the truth, but I had no choice.

27   "Jean, where are you?"

28   "I'm, umm, in jail."

29   "Why? What for?"

30   "Shoplifting."

31   "Oh no, Jean. Why? Why did you do it?"

32   "I don't know. No reason. I just did it."

33   "I don't understand. What did you take? Why did you do it? You had plenty of money with you."

34   "I know but I just did it. I can't explain why. Mom, I'm sorry."

35   "I'm afraid sorry isn't enough. I'm horribly disappointed in you."

36   Long after we got off the phone, while I sat in an empty jail cell, waiting for my parents to pick me up, I could still distinctly hear the disappointment and hurt in my mother's voice. I cried. The tears weren't for me but for her and the pain I had put her through. I felt like a terrible human being. I would rather have stayed in jail than confront my mom right then. I dreaded each passing minute that brought our encounter closer. When the officer came to release me, I hesitated, actually not wanting to leave. We went to the front desk, where I had to sign a form to retrieve my belongings. I saw my parents a few yards away and my heart raced. A large knot formed in my stomach. I fought back the tears.

What is the effect of interweaving storytelling and describing with re-membering thoughts and feelings in this paragraph?

37   Not a word was spoken as we walked to the car. Slowly, I sank into the back seat anticipating the scolding. Expecting harsh tones, I was relieved to hear almost the opposite from my father.

What do you learn from Brandt's account of her father's reaction?

38   "I'm not going to punish you and I'll tell you why. Although I think what you did was wrong, I think what the police did was more wrong. There's no excuse for locking a thirteen-year-old behind bars. That doesn't mean I condone what you did, but I think you've been punished enough already."

How well does this final paragraph help you understand the event's significance?

39   As I looked from my father's eyes to my mother's, I knew this ordeal was over. Although it would never be forgotten, the incident was not mentioned again.

For an additional student reading, go to **macmillanhighered.com/conciseguide.**
E-readings > Shannon Lewis, *We Were Here*

Annie Dillard | *An American Childhood*

Phyllis Rose

ANNIE DILLARD, professor emeritus at Wesleyan University, won the Pulitzer Prize for nonfiction writing in 1975 with her first book, *Pilgrim at Tinker Creek* (1974). Since then, she has written eleven other books in a variety of genres. They include *Teaching a Stone to Talk* (1988), *The Writing Life* (1990), *The Living* (1993), *Mornings Like This* (1996), and *The Maytrees* (2007). Dillard also wrote an autobiography of her early years, *An American Childhood* (1987), from which the following selection comes.

As you read, consider Dillard's opening paragraphs:

- Why do you think Dillard chose to introduce the event with this reflection when she could have begun with paragraph 3?
- How do the opening paragraphs prepare readers to understand the event's significance?

1 Some boys taught me to play football. This was fine sport. You thought up a new strategy for every play and whispered it to the others. You went out for a pass, fooling everyone. Best, you got to throw yourself mightily at someone's running legs. Either you brought him down or you hit the ground flat out on your chin, with your arms empty before you. It was all or nothing. If you hesitated in fear, you would miss and get hurt: you would take a hard fall while the kid got away, or you would get kicked in the face while the kid got away. But if you flung yourself wholeheartedly at the back of his knees—if you gathered and joined body and soul and pointed them diving fearlessly—then you likely wouldn't get hurt, and you'd stop the ball. Your fate, and your team's score, depended on your concentration and courage. Nothing girls did could compare with it.

2 Boys welcomed me at baseball, too, for I had, through enthusiastic practice, what was weirdly known as a boy's arm. In winter, in the snow, there was neither baseball nor football, so the boys and I threw snowballs at passing cars. I got in trouble throwing snowballs, and have seldom been happier since.

3 On one weekday morning after Christmas, six inches of new snow had just fallen. We were standing up to our boot tops in snow on a front yard on trafficked Reynolds Street, waiting for cars. The cars traveled Reynolds Street slowly and evenly; they were targets all but wrapped in red ribbons, cream puffs. We couldn't miss.

4 I was seven; the boys were eight, nine, and ten. The oldest two Fahey boys were there—Mikey and Peter—polite blond boys who lived near me on Lloyd Street, and who already had four brothers and sisters. My parents approved Mikey and Peter Fahey. Chickie McBride was there, a tough kid, and Billy Paul and Mackie Kean too, from across Reynolds, where the boys grew up dark and furious, grew up skinny, knowing, and skilled. We had all drifted from our houses that morning looking for action, and had found it here on Reynolds Street.

5 It was cloudy but cold. The cars' tires laid behind them on the snowy street a complex trail of beige chunks like crenellated castle walls. I had stepped on some earlier; they squeaked. We could not have wished for more traffic. When a car came, we all popped it one. In the intervals between cars we reverted to the natural solitude of children.

6 I started making an iceball—a perfect iceball, from perfectly white snow, perfectly spherical, and squeezed perfectly translucent so no snow remained all the way through. (The Fahey boys and I considered it unfair actually to throw an iceball at somebody, but it had been known to happen.)

7 I had just embarked on the iceball project when we heard tire chains come clanking from afar. A black Buick was moving toward us down the street. We all spread out, banged together some regular snowballs, took aim, and, when the Buick drew nigh, fired.

8 A soft snowball hit the driver's windshield right before the driver's face. It made a smashed star with a hump in the middle.

9 Often, of course, we hit our target, but this time, the only time in all of life, the car pulled over and stopped. Its wide black door opened; a man got out of it, running. He didn't even close the car door.

10   He ran after us, and we ran away from him, up the snowy Reynolds sidewalk. At the corner, I looked back; incredibly, he was still after us. He was in city clothes: a suit and tie, street shoes. Any normal adult would have quit, having sprung us into flight and made his point. This man was gaining on us. He was a thin man, all action. All of a sudden, we were running for our lives.

11   Wordless, we split up. We were on our turf; we could lose ourselves in the neighborhood backyards, everyone for himself. I paused and considered. Everyone had vanished except Mikey Fahey, who was just rounding the corner of a yellow brick house. Poor Mikey, I trailed him. The driver of the Buick sensibly picked the two of us to follow. The man apparently had all day.

12   He chased Mikey and me around the yellow house and up a backyard path we knew by heart: under a low tree, up a bank, through a hedge, down some snowy steps, and across the grocery store's delivery driveway. We smashed through a gap in another hedge, entered a scruffy backyard and ran around its back porch and tight between houses to Edgerton Avenue; we ran across Edgerton to an alley and up our own sliding woodpile to the Halls' front yard; he kept coming. We ran up Lloyd Street and wound through mazy backyards toward the steep hilltop at Willard and Lang.

13   He chased us silently, block after block. He chased us silently over picket fences, through thorny hedges, between houses, around garbage cans, and across streets. Every time I glanced back, choking for breath, I expected he would have quit. He must have been as breathless as we were. His jacket strained over his body. It was an immense discovery, pounding into my hot head with every sliding, joyous step, that this ordinary adult evidently knew what I thought only children who trained at football knew: that you have to fling yourself at

what you're doing, you have to point yourself, forget yourself, aim, dive.

14   Mikey and I had nowhere to go, in our own neighborhood or out of it, but away from this man who was chasing us. He impelled us forward; we compelled him to follow our route. The air was cold; every breath tore my throat. We kept running, block after block; we kept improvising, backyard after backyard, running a frantic course and choosing it simultaneously, failing always to find small places or hard places to slow him down, and discovering always, exhilarated, dismayed, that only bare speed could save us—for he would never give up, this man—and we were losing speed.

15   He chased us through the backyard labyrinths of ten blocks before he caught us by our jackets. He caught us and we all stopped.

16   We three stood staggering, half blinded, coughing, in an obscure hilltop backyard: a man in his twenties, a boy, a girl. He had released our jackets, our pursuer, our captor, our hero: he knew we weren't going anywhere. We all played by the rules. Mikey and I unzipped our jackets. I pulled off my sopping mittens. Our tracks multiplied in the backyard's new snow. We had been breaking new snow all morning. We didn't look at each other. I was cherishing my excitement. The man's lower pants legs were wet; his cuffs were full of snow, and there was a prow of snow beneath them on his shoes and socks. Some trees bordered the little flat backyard, some messy winter trees. There was no one around: a clearing in a grove, and we the only players.

17   It was a long time before he could speak. I had some difficulty at first recalling why we were there. My lips felt swollen; I couldn't see out of the sides of my eyes; I kept coughing.

18   "You stupid kids," he began perfunctorily.

19   We listened perfunctorily indeed, if we listened at all, for the chewing out was redundant, a mere formality, and beside the point. The point was that he had chased us passionately without giving up, and so he had caught us. Now he came down to earth. I wanted the glory to last forever.

20   But how could the glory have lasted forever? We could have run through every backyard in North America until we got to Panama. But when he trapped us at the lip of the Panama Canal, what precisely could he have done to prolong the drama of the chase and cap its glory? I brooded about this for the next few years. He could only have fried Mikey Fahey and me in boiling oil, say, or dismembered us piecemeal, or staked us to anthills. None of which I really wanted, and none of which any adult was likely to do, even in the spirit of fun. He could only chew us out there in the Panamanian jungle, after months or years of exalting pursuit. He could only begin, "You stupid kids," and continue in his ordinary Pittsburgh accent with his normal righteous anger and the usual common sense.

21   If in that snowy backyard the driver of the black Buick had cut off our heads, Mikey's and mine, I would have died happy, for nothing has required so much of me since as being chased all over Pittsburgh in the middle of winter—running terrified, exhausted—by this sainted, skinny, furious redheaded man who wished to have a word with us. I don't know how he found his way back to his car.

[REFLECT] **Make connections: Acting fearlessly.**

At the beginning of the essay, Dillard tells about being taught by the neighborhood boys the joy of playing football, particularly the "all or nothing" of diving "fearlessly" (par. 1). Recall an occasion when you had an opportunity to dive fearlessly into an activity that posed some challenge or risk or required special effort. For example, you may have been challenged, like Dillard, by your teammates at a football game or by a group of volunteers helping during a natural disaster. Or you may have felt pressured by friends to do something that went against your better judgment, was illegal, or was dangerous. Your instructor may ask you to post your thoughts to a class discussion board or to discuss them with other students in class. Use these questions to get started:

- What made you embrace the challenge or resist it? What do you think your choice tells about you at the time of the event?
- Dillard uses the value term *courage* to describe the fearless behavior she learned playing football. What value term would you use to describe your experience? For example, were you being *selfless* or *self-serving; responsible* or *irresponsible; a follower, a leader,* or *a self-reliant individual*?

[ANALYZE] **Use the basic features.**

A WELL-TOLD STORY: CONSTRUCTING AN ACTION SEQUENCE

Throughout the excerpt from *An American Childhood*, Dillard combines *action verbs* and *prepositional phrases* to create compelling *action sequences*. Consider this example:

Action verb	He chased Mikey and me around the yellow house and up a backyard path
Prepositional phrases	we knew by heart: under a low tree, up a bank, through a hedge, down some snowy steps, and across the grocery store's delivery driveway. (par. 12)

ANALYZE & WRITE

Write a paragraph analyzing Dillard's action sequences:

1. Skim paragraphs 11–13, circling the action verbs and underlining the prepositional phrases.

2. Think about how this series of prepositional phrases contributes to the effectiveness of the scene.

VIVID DESCRIPTION OF PEOPLE AND PLACES: USING NAMES AND DETAILS

Describing—naming objects and detailing their colors, shape, size, textures, and other qualities—is an important strategy in remembered event writing. Writers use this strategy to create vivid images of the scene in which the story takes place. They also use describing to give readers thumbnail portraits of people.

ANALYZE & WRITE

Write a paragraph analyzing Dillard's use of naming and detailing:

1. Reread paragraph 4, noting the names of her friends and underlining the details she gives to describe each boy. How do these details help you imagine what each boy was like?

2. Look closely at Dillard's description of an iceball to see how she uses these describing strategies:

Naming	I started making an iceball —a perfect iceball, from perfectly white snow,
Detailing	perfectly spherical, and squeezed perfectly translucent so no snow remained all the way through. (par. 6)

What attributes of the iceball does Dillard point out? Why do you think she repeats the words *perfect* and *perfectly*? Notice also that in the next sentence, she tells us that it was against the rules to throw an iceball at someone. So why do you imagine she tries to make such a "perfect" iceball?

AUTOBIOGRAPHICAL SIGNIFICANCE: SHOWING AND TELLING

Writers use both *showing* and *telling* to convey significance. **Showing**, through the careful choice of words and details, creates an overall or dominant impression. **Telling** presents the narrator's remembered feelings and thoughts together with her present perspective on what happened and why it is significant.

To alert readers that they are telling, not showing, writers may announce their experience by using a verb like *felt* or a noun like *thought*:

Verb	▶ I felt _____. (Example: "I felt alone and scared" [Brandt, par. 17])
Noun	▶ The thought of _____. (Example: "The thought of going to jail terrified me" [Brandt, par. 17])

A more direct strategy is to choose words that tell readers which emotion or thought was experienced:

▶ The [terror/exhilaration/excitement] was _____. (Example: "The humiliation at that moment was overwhelming" [Brandt, par. 18])

Writers may also use **stream of consciousness,** which captures remembered thoughts and feelings by relating what went through the narrator's mind at the time. The following example re-creates the mash-up of feelings and thoughts, seemingly uncensored, that went through Jean Brandt's mind as she was being stopped for shoplifting:

> Where did this man come from? How did he know? I was so sure that no one had seen me! . . . I told myself that all I had to do was give this man his button back, say I was sorry, and go on my way. After all, it was only a 75-cent item. (par. 6)

Much of the telling in autobiographical stories includes what the writer remembers thinking and feeling at the time the incident occurred. But writers also occasionally insert comments telling what they think and feel now, from the **present perspective,** as they look back and reflect on the event's significance.

ANALYZE & WRITE

Write a paragraph or two analyzing Dillard's use of showing and telling to create autobiographical significance:

1 Skim paragraphs 7, 10, 13, 16, 18, and 20–21, highlighting the details Dillard uses to describe the man, how he dresses, the car he drives, and especially the way he talks when he catches her and her friend. What is the dominant impression you get of the man from these details, and what do they suggest about why he chases the kids?

2 Review paragraphs 13–21, adding notes where Dillard tells us what she thought and felt at the time. Notice also how Dillard conveys her present perspective—for example, by using adult vocabulary such as "perfunctorily," "redundant," and "mere formality" (par. 19). Highlight any other details that help convey Dillard's adult authorial voice. What does Dillard's telling add to the dominant impression, and how does it help you better understand the event's significance?

[RESPOND] ## Consider possible topics: Remembering unexpected adult actions and reactions.

Like Dillard, you could write about a time when an adult did something entirely unexpected during your childhood; an action that seemed dangerous or threatening to you; or something humorous, kind, or generous. Consider unpredictable actions of adults in your immediate or extended family, adults you had come to know outside your family, and strangers. As you consider these possible topics, think about your purpose and audience: What would you want your instructor and classmates to learn about you from reading about this event?

Jenée Desmond-Harris | *Tupac and My Non-thug Life*

Courtesy of Jenée Desmond-Harris

JENÉE DESMOND-HARRIS is a staff writer at the *Root*, an online magazine dedicated to African American news and culture. She writes about the intersection of race, politics, and culture in a variety of formats, including personal essays. She has also contributed to *Time* magazine, MSNBC's *Powerwall*, and *xoJane* on topics ranging from her relationship with her grandmother, to the political significance of Michelle Obama's hair, to the stereotypes that hinder giving to black-teen mentoring programs. She has provided television commentary on CNN, MSNBC, and Current TV. Desmond-Harris is a graduate of Howard University and Harvard Law School. The following selection was published in the *Root* in 2011. It chronicles Desmond-Harris's reaction to the murder of gangsta rap icon Tupac Shakur in a Las Vegas drive-by shooting in 1996. She mentions Tupac's mother, Afeni, as well as the "East Coast–West Coast war"—the rivalry between Tupac and the Notorious B.I.G. (Biggie), who was suspected of being involved in Tupac's murder. As you read, consider the photograph that appeared in the *Root* article and that is reproduced here:

- What does it capture about the fifteen-year-old Desmond-Harris?

- What does its inclusion say about Desmond-Harris's perspective on her adolescent self and the event she recollects?

1   I learned about Tupac's death when I got home from cheerleading practice that Friday afternoon in September 1996. I was a sophomore in high school in Mill Valley, Calif. I remember trotting up my apartment building's stairs, physically tired but buzzing with the frenetic energy and possibilities for change that accompany fall and a new school year. I'd been cautiously allowing myself to think during the walk home about a topic that felt frighteningly taboo (at least in my world, where discussion of race was avoided as delicately as obesity or mental illness): what it meant to be biracial and on the school's mostly white cheerleading team instead of the mostly black dance team. I remember acknowledging, to the sound of an 8-count that still pounded in my head as I walked through the door, that I didn't really have a choice: I could memorize a series of stiff and precise motions but couldn't actually dance.

2   My private musings on identity and belonging—not original in the least, but novel to me—were interrupted when my mom heard me slam the front door and drop my bags: *"Your friend died!"* she called out from another room. Confused silence. *"You know, that rapper you and Thea love so much!"*

Mourning a Death in Vegas

3   The news was turned on, with coverage of the deadly Vegas shooting. Phone calls were made. Ultimately my best friend, Thea, and I were left to our own 15-year-old devices to mourn that weekend. Her mother and stepfather were out of town. Their expansive, million-dollar home was perched on a hillside less than an hour from Tupac's former stomping grounds in Oakland and Marin City. Of course, her home was also worlds away from both places.

4   We couldn't "pour out" much alcohol undetected for a libation, so we limited

ourselves to doing somber shots of liqueur from a well-stocked cabinet. One each. Tipsy, in a high-ceilinged kitchen surrounded by hardwood floors and Zen flower arrangements, we baked cookies for his mother. We packed them up to ship to Afeni with a handmade card. ("Did we really do that?" I asked Thea this week. I wanted to ensure that this story, which people who know me now find hilarious, hadn't morphed into some sort of personal urban legend over the past 15 years. "Yes," she said. "We put them in a lovely tin.")

5   On a sound system that echoed through speakers perched discreetly throughout the airy house, we played "Life Goes On" on a loop and sobbed. We analyzed lyrics for premonitions of the tragedy. We, of course, cursed Biggie. Who knew that the East Coast–West Coast war had two earnest soldiers in flannel pajamas, lying on a king-size bed decorated with pink toe shoes that dangled from one of its posts? There, we studied our pictures of Tupac and re-created his tattoos on each other's body with a Sharpie. I got "Thug Life" on my stomach. I gave Thea "Exodus 1811" inside a giant cross. Both are flanked by "West Side."

6   A snapshot taken that Monday on our high school's front lawn (seen here) shows the two of us lying side by side, shirts lifted to display the tributes in black marker. Despite our best efforts, it's the innocent, bubbly lettering of notes passed in class and of poster boards made for social studies presentations. My hair has recently been straightened with my first (and last) relaxer and a Gold 'N Hot flatiron on too high a setting. Hers is slicked back with the mixture of Herbal Essences and Blue Magic that we formulated in a bathroom laboratory.

7   My rainbow-striped tee and her white wifebeater capture a transition between our skater-inspired Salvation Army shopping phase and the next one, during which we'd wear the same jeans slung from our hip bones, revealing peeks of flat stomach, but transforming ourselves from Alternative Nation to MTV Jams imitators. We would get bubble coats in primary colors that Christmas and start using silver eyeliner, trying—and failing—to look something like Aaliyah.[1]

Mixed Identities: Tupac and Me

8   Did we take ourselves seriously? Did we feel a real stake in the life of this "hardcore" gangsta rapper, and a real loss in his death? We did, even though we were two mixed-race girls raised by our white moms in a privileged community where we could easily rattle off the names of the small handful of other kids in town who also had one black parent: Sienna. Rashea. Brandon. Aaron. Sudan. Akio. Lauren. Alicia. Even though the most subversive thing we did was make prank calls. Even though we hadn't yet met our first boyfriends, and Shock G's proclamations about putting satin on people's panties sent us into

The author (left) with her friend Thea
Courtesy of Jenée Desmond-Harris

---

[1] A hit rhythm-and-blues and hip-hop recording artist. Aaliyah Dana Haughton died in a plane crash at age twenty-two. [Editor's note]

absolute giggling fits. And even though we'd been so delicately cared for, nurtured and protected from any of life's hard edges—with special efforts made to shield us from those involving race—that we sometimes felt ready to explode with boredom. Or maybe because of all that.

9   I mourned Tupac's death then, and continue to mourn him now, because his music represents the years when I was both forced and privileged to confront what it meant to be black. That time, like his music, was about exploring the contradictory textures of this identity: The ambience and indulgence of the fun side, as in "California Love" and "Picture Me Rollin'." But also the burdensome anxiety and outright anger—"Brenda's Got a Baby," "Changes" and "Hit 'Em Up."

10   For Thea and me, his songs were the musical score to our transition to high school, where there emerged a vague, lunchtime geography to race: White kids perched on a sloping green lawn and the benches above it. Below, black kids sat on a wall outside the gym. The bottom of the hill beckoned. Thea, more outgoing, with more admirers among the boys, stepped down boldly, and I followed timidly. Our formal invitations came in the form of unsolicited hall passes to go to Black Student Union meetings during free periods. We were assigned to recite Maya Angelou's "Phenomenal Woman" at the Black History Month assembly.

11   Tupac was the literal sound track when our school's basketball team would come charging onto the court, and our ragtag group of cheerleaders kicked furiously to "Toss It Up" in a humid gymnasium. Those were the games when we might breathlessly join the dance team after our cheer during time-outs if they did the single "African step" we'd mastered for BSU performances.

Everything Black—and Cool

12   . . . Blackness became something cool, something to which we had brand-new access. We flaunted it, buying Kwanzaa candles and insisting on celebrating privately (really, just lighting the candles and excluding our friends) at a sleepover. We memorized "I Get Around"[2] and took turns singing verses to each other as we drove through Marin County suburbs in Thea's green Toyota station wagon. Because he was with us through all of this, we were in love with Tupac and wanted to embody him. On Halloween, Thea donned a bald cap and a do-rag, penciled in her already-full eyebrows and was a dead ringer.

13   Tupac's music, while full of social commentary (and now even on the Vatican's playlist), probably wasn't made to be a treatise on racial identity. Surely it wasn't created to accompany two girls (*little* girls, really) as they embarked on a coming-of-age journey. But it was there for us when we desperately needed it.

---

[2] Tupac Shakur's first top-twenty single, released in 1993 on *Strictly 4 My N.I.G.G.A.Z.*, Shakur's second studio album. [Editor's note]

[REFLECT] ## Make connections: Remembering idols.

We often find ourselves profoundly affected by what happens to people we've never met. You may remember where you were and how you reacted to the death of Michael Jackson or Whitney Houston, for example. In "Tupac and My Non-thug Life," Desmond-Harris captures the emotional connection between a teen and her slain idol, showing us not only how Tupac's death affected her then but what she thinks of her teenage self's obsession now that she is older.

Recall a time when the emotional impact of an event that happened to someone else (or to other people) was powerful enough to affect your behavior, decisions, or actions for the day or longer. Consider the reasons for your reactions. Your instructor may ask you to post your thoughts to a class discussion board or blog, or to discuss them with other students in class. Use these questions to get started:

- Why did you identify so closely with the person (or people) you heard about?
- What does your reaction say about who you were and what you valued?
- Would you react the same way today? What would be different and why?

⎡ANALYZE⎤ Use the basic features.

A WELL-TOLD STORY: USING DIALOGUE

Dialogue is a narrating strategy that helps writers dramatize a story. Quoting with descriptive speaker tags—

Speaker tag   ▶ He said, "_____."   ▶ She asked, "_____?"

—is an especially effective way of making readers feel as though they were there, overhearing what was said and how it was said. But all of the dialogue strategies—quoting, paraphrasing, and summarizing—can help readers identify with or understand a writer's point of view and give us an impression of the speakers. Desmond-Harris includes only a few lines of dialogue in "Tupac and My Non-thug Life," but those she does include demonstrate how effective this sentence strategy can be.

| ANALYZE & WRITE |

Write a paragraph analyzing how Desmond-Harris uses dialogue:

1 Skim the story, highlighting the dialogue and underlining the speaker tags. Also note where Desmond-Harris summarizes or paraphrases a conversation.

2 Consider each bit of dialogue, paraphrase, or summary to see what role it plays. Does it tell you something about the speaker or her relationship with another person? Does it convey feelings or attitudes? Does it advance the narrative or something else?

To learn more about quoting with speaker tags, paraphrasing, and summarizing in autobiographical stories, see pp. 35–36.

VIVID DESCRIPTION OF PEOPLE AND PLACES: USING VISUALS AND BRAND NAMES

Desmond-Harris provides lots of concrete details to enliven her narrative. She also uses a photo and refers to brand names to convey to readers an exact sense of what the girls were like. Notice that she recounts the Sharpie tattooing and then actually shows us a photo of the girls displaying their tattoos. But Desmond-Harris does not let the photo speak for itself; instead, she describes the picture, pointing out features, such as their hairstyles and outfits, that mark their identity. Consider the references to particular styles and brand names (such as "our skater-inspired Salvation Army shopping phase") that tag the various roles they were trying on at that time of their lives (par. 7).

ANALYZE & WRITE
───

Write a paragraph or two analyzing Desmond-Harris's use of a photograph and brand names to enhance her descriptions:

1. Skim paragraphs 5–7, highlighting the specific details in the photo that Desmond-Harris points out as well as the brand names (usually capitalized) and the modifiers that make them more specific (as in *skater-inspired*).

2. Look closely at the photograph itself, and consider its purpose: Why do you think Desmond-Harris included it? What does the photograph contribute or show us that the text alone does not convey?

3. Consider the effect that the photo and the brand names have on you as a reader (or might have on readers of about Desmond-Harris's age). How do they help readers envision these girls? What is the dominant impression you get of the young Desmond-Harris from these descriptive details? Where, if anywhere, in this passage do you detect the adult author's self-irony?

For more on analyzing visuals, see Chapter 12.

AUTOBIOGRAPHICAL SIGNIFICANCE: HANDLING COMPLEX EMOTIONS

Remembered events that have lasting significance nearly always involve mixed or ambivalent feelings. Therefore, readers expect and appreciate some degree of complexity. Multiple layers of meaning make autobiographical stories more, not less, interesting. Significance that seems simplistic or predictable makes stories less successful.

ANALYZE & WRITE
───

Write a paragraph or two analyzing Desmond-Harris's handling of the complex personal and cultural significance of her remembered event:

1. Skim the last two sections (pars. 8–13), noting passages where Desmond-Harris tells readers her remembered feelings and thoughts at the time and her present perspective as an adult reflecting on the experience. Consider Desmond-Harris's dual perspective—that of the fifteen-year-old experiencing the event and the thirty-year-old writing about it. How does she use this dual perspective to convey complexity?

2. Look closely at paragraph 8, and highlight the following sentence strategies:
   - Rhetorical questions (questions writers answer themselves)
   - Repeated words and phrases
   - Stylistic sentence fragments (incomplete sentences used for special effect)

   What effect do these sentence strategies have on readers? How do they help convey the significance of the event?

Note that in academic writing, stylistic fragments may be frowned on; one of the instructor's purposes in assigning a writing project is to teach students to use formal academic writing conventions, and it may not be clear from the context whether the student is using a fragment purposely for rhetorical effect or whether the student does not know how to identify and correct sentence fragments.

[RESPOND] **Consider possible topics: Recognizing a public event as a turning point.**

Like Desmond-Harris, you could write about how a public event, like a celebrity death or marriage, an act of heroism or charity, or even the passage of a law helped (or forced) you to confront an aspect of your identity. Consider the complexities of your reaction—the significance the event had for you at the time and the significance the event has for you now. You might make a list of physical traits, as well as beliefs about or aspects of your sense of identity that changed as a result of the event.

macmillanhighered.com/conciseguide
What does remembering an event look like as a comic?
E-readings > Kelsey C. Roy, *The Daily Grind*

GUIDE TO WRITING

The Writing Assignment	29
Writing a Draft: Invention, Research, Planning, and Composing	30
Evaluating the Draft: Getting a Critical Reading	41
Improving the Draft: Revising, Formatting, Editing, and Proofreading	43

The Writing Assignment

Write an essay about an event in your life that will engage readers and that will, at the same time, help them understand the significance of the event. Tell your story dramatically and vividly.

This Guide to Writing is designed to help you compose your own remembered event essay and apply what you have learned from reading other essays in the same genre. The following Starting Points chart will help you find answers to many of the questions you might have about composing a remembered event essay. Use the chart to find the guidance you need, when you need it.

STARTING POINTS: REMEMBERING AN EVENT

A Well-Told Story

How can I come up with an event to write about?

- Consider possible topics. (pp. 22, 28)
- Choose an event to write about. (p. 31)
- Test Your Choice (p. 32)

How can I interest my audience and hold its attention?

- Shape your story. (pp. 32–33)
- Organize your story to enhance the drama. (pp. 33–34)
- Test Your Choice (p. 34)
- Write the opening sentences. (p. 41)

How can I make the story of my event dramatic?

- Assess the genre's basic features: A well-told story. (pp. 11–12)
- A Well-Told Story: Constructing an Action Sequence (pp. 20–21)
- A Well-Told Story: Using Dialogue (p. 26)
- Shape your story. (pp. 32–33)
- Organize your story to enhance the drama. (pp. 33–34)
- Use dialogue to tell your story. (pp. 35–36)

How should I organize my story?

- Assess the genre's basic features: A well-told story. (pp. 11–12)
- Organize your story to enhance the drama. (pp. 33–34)
- Choose your tense and plan time cues. (p. 35)

(continued)

Vivid Description of People and Places

How can I describe the place where the event took place vividly and specifically?

- Assess the genre's basic features: Vivid description of people and places. (pp. 11–13)
- Develop and refine your descriptions. (pp. 36–38)
- Incorporate descriptive details throughout your story. (pp. 38–39)

How can I make the people in my story come alive?

- Assess the genre's basic features: A well-told story. (pp. 11–12)
- Vivid Description of People and Places: Using Names and Details (pp. 9–21)
- A Well-Told Story: Using Dialogue (p. 26)
- Develop and refine your descriptions. (pp. 36–38)
- Incorporate descriptive details throughout your story. (pp. 38–39)

Autobiographical Significance

How can I help readers grasp the significance of my remembered event?

- Assess the genre's basic features: Autobiographical significance. (p. 13)
- Autobiographical Significance: Showing and Telling (pp. 21–22)
- Consider ways to convey your event's autobiographical significance. (pp. 39–40)

How can I create a dominant impression?

- Assess the genre's basic features: Autobiographical significance. (p. 13)
- Autobiographical Significance: Showing and Telling (pp. 21–27)
- Consider ways to convey your event's autobiographical significance. (pp. 39–40)

Writing a Draft: Invention, Research, Planning, and Composing

The activities in this section will help you choose an event to write about and develop it into a well-told, vivid, significant story. Your writing in response to many of these activities can be used in a rough draft that you will be able to improve after receiving feedback from your classmates and instructor. Do the activities in any order that makes sense to you (and your instructor), and return to them as needed as you revise.

:: Choose an event to write about.

To make a compelling story, the event you choose to write about should

- take place over a short period of time (preferably just a few hours);
- center on a conflict (an internal struggle or an external confrontation with another person or idea);
- disclose something significant about your life;
- reveal complex or ambivalent feelings (rather than superficial and sentimental ones).

Make a list of events that fit the bill. If you're like most people, you may have trouble coming up with events to write about. To get your creative juices flowing, try the following:

- Review the Consider Possible Topics sections on pp. 22 or 28, or reread any notes you made in response to those suggestions.
- Consult Web sites where people post stories about their lives, such as the Story Preservation Initiative, the Sixties Project, or StoryCorps. Try also typing *storytelling memory project, survivor stories,* or a similar word string into the search box of your browser.

If you need more ideas, the following may give you a jumping-off point:

- A difficult situation (for example, when you had to make a tough choice and face the consequences, or when you let someone down or someone you admired let you down)
- An occasion when things did not turn out as expected (for example, when you expected to be criticized but were praised or ignored instead, or when you were convinced you would succeed but failed)
- An incident that changed you or that revealed an aspect of your personality (such as initiative, insecurity, ambition, jealousy, or heroism)
- An incident in which a conflict or a serious misunderstanding with someone made you feel unjustly treated or caused you to mistreat someone else
- An experience that made you reexamine a basic value or belief (such as a time when you were expected to do something that went against your values or had to make a decision about which you were deeply conflicted)
- An encounter with another person that led you to consider seriously someone else's point of view, that changed the way you viewed yourself, or that altered your ideas about how you fit into a group or community
- An event that revealed to you other people's surprising assumptions about you (as a student, friend, colleague, or worker)

After you have made a tentative choice, ask yourself the following questions:

- Will I be able to reconstruct enough of the story and describe the place and people in vivid detail to make my story dramatic and create a dominant impression?
- Do I feel drawn toward understanding what this event meant to me then and what it means to me now? (You may not yet know what the significance of the event is, but you should feel compelled to explore it.)
- Do I feel comfortable writing about this event for my instructor and classmates? This isn't a diary entry, after all. You are going to share your writing with others and should be comfortable doing so.

If you lose confidence in your choice, return to your list and choose another event.

Shape your story.

Once you have selected an event, consider how you might structure your story to make it compelling. To do this, first create a *quick sketch* or *outline* of what happened during the event. Sketch out the moments in simple, chronological order. You can fill in details and revise later.

Once you have a quick sketch of the event, use the following questions and advice to help you put your ideas in writing. (Some writers may prefer to work out the dramatic structure of the story before developing the key moments. If that is true of you, move on to the next section, "Organize your story to enhance the drama," and come back to this section later on.)

WAYS IN

WHAT DOES MY STORY NEED?

Compare your story sketch with the dramatic arc in Figure 2.1 (p. 12):

Sketch out the backstory, or exposition, your readers will need to understand what happened.

- In (year), while I was (_____ ing) in (location), _____.

- John knew all about _____ because he was a/an _____, an expert on _____.

- In past years, I had previously _____.

HOW CAN I INTEREST READERS?

Analyze your audience:

Consider who will be reading your story and what aspect of the story they will find most interesting. Often, it's the conflict, but it could be the setting or the activity you were taking part in.

Pick a moment in your story that you think might hook readers, such as a bit of dialogue or an inciting incident, and try writing about that moment.

Practice writing the "inciting incident," the conflict that triggers the story. To dramatize it, try using narrative actions and dialogue, including speaker tags and quotation marks.

> A black Buick was moving toward us down the street. We all spread out, banged together some regular snowballs, took aim, and, when the Buick drew nigh, fired. (Dillard, par. 7)

Prep. phrase

Action verbs

Dramatize the moment of surprise, confrontation, crisis, or discovery that may become the climax of your story, using narrative action and dialogue to bring the action to life.

> He chased us through the backyard labyrinths of ten blocks before he caught us by our jackets. He caught us and we all stopped. . . . "You stupid kids," he began perfunctorily. (Dillard, pars. 15, 18)

Augment your memory by asking people who were there what they remember; look through family photographs, yearbooks, e-mails, or videos, and write briefly about what you found:

> A snapshot taken that Monday on our high school's front lawn (seen here) shows the two of us lying side by side, shirts lifted to display the tributes in black marker. (Desmond-Harris, par. 6)

My private musings on identity and belonging—not original in the least, but novel to me—were interrupted when my mom heard me slam the front door and drop my bags: *"Your friend died!"* she called out from another room. Confused silence. *"You know, that rapper you and Thea love so much!"* (Desmond-Harris, par. 2)

As an alternative, practice opening with exposition, as Dillard does.

> Some boys taught me to play football. (Dillard, par. 1)

Experiment with ways to end your story so that the ending reminds readers of the beginning—repetition with a difference.

> As we all piled into the car, I knew it was going to be a fabulous day. (Brandt, par. 1)

> As I looked from my father's eyes to my mother's, I knew this ordeal was over. (Brandt, par. 39)

▪ Organize your story to enhance the drama.

Once you have sketched out your event and (perhaps) done some writing to help you focus on key moments, you may be ready to revisit the structure of your story. Think about how you can structure it to make it more exciting or moving for your readers. Following are organizational plans based on the dramatic arc in Figure 2.1 (p. 12) that you can use or modify to fit your needs.

If your readers are likely to understand the setting and activities described in the story, you might think about opening directly with the conflict's inciting incident:

I. **Inciting Incident:** Hook readers' attention by showing immediately how the conflict or problem started.

II. **Exposition:** Then rewind a bit to tell us what you had been doing when the event happened, and how you ended up in that situation.

III. **Rising Action:** Return to the main action, showing how the crisis developed or worsened.

IV. **Climax:** Describe the most critical moment of the event.

V. **Falling Action:** Narrate what happened after the climax.

VI. **Resolution/Reflection:** Tell how the event ended, and reflect on its autobiographical significance. What impact has this event had on you?

If the situation you were in when the conflict or problem developed is one that might be interesting to readers or might require some explanation, you might open with exposition:

I. **Exposition:** Tell us what you were doing when the event happened, and how you got there.

II. **Inciting Incident:** Show us how the conflict or problem started.

III. **Rising Action:** Show how the crisis developed or worsened.

IV. **Climax:** Describe the most critical moment of the event.

V. **Falling Action:** Narrate what happened after the climax.

VI. **Resolution/Reflection:** Tell us how the event ended, and reflect on its autobiographical significance. What impact has this event had on you?

If you have drafted parts of your story already (based on the "Ways In" section on pp. 32–33 or other writing you have done), try putting it all together now, so you can see what details your story still needs. You can always change the organization and move the scenes around as you continue drafting and revising.

| TEST YOUR CHOICE |

Get together with two or three other students to try out your story. Your classmates' reactions will help you determine whether you are telling it in an interesting or exciting way.

Storytellers.   Take turns telling your stories briefly. Try to pique your listeners' curiosity and build suspense, and watch your audience to see if your story is having the desired reaction.

Listeners.   Briefly tell each storyteller what you found most intriguing about the story. For example, consider these questions:

- Were you eager to know how the story would turn out?
- What was the inciting incident? Did it seem sufficient to motivate the climax?
- Was there a clear conflict that seemed important enough to write about?

⸬ Choose your tense and plan time cues.

To prevent readers from becoming confused about the sequence of actions in time, writers use a combination of verb tenses and transitional words and phrases related to time. Although writing about your remembered event in the present tense can give your narrative a sense of immediacy, *writing about the event itself in the past tense will make it easier to manage your other tenses.* For example, you may need to talk about what happened before the event took place or how you feel about the event now, as Desmond-Harris does here:

Past tense for event
Present tense for
current reflection

I mourned Tupac's death then, and continue to mourn him now, because his music represents the years when I was both forced and privileged to confront what it meant to be black. (par. 9)

Managing the tenses for these breaks from the timeline can be tough if you aren't already writing most of the story in the past tense. Try rewriting the preceding sentence with the event described in the present tense: "I mourn Tupac's death, and . . ." Can you see how to do it? Most writers write about past events in the past tense because it makes these moves much easier.

Cite calendar *or* clock time *to establish when the event took place and help readers follow the action over time.* Writers often situate the event in terms of the date or time. Brandt, for example, establishes in the opening paragraph that the event occurred when she went to the mall for "a day of last-minute Christmas shopping." Dillard also identifies when the event took place and how old she was at the time: "On one weekday morning after Christmas. . . . I was seven." (pars. 3, 4).

Use transitions of time, such as *after, before, in the meantime,* and *simultaneously, to help readers follow a sequence of actions.* In the following example, *when* signals that one action followed another:

Transition of time
First action
Second action

When I got back to the Snoopy section, I took one look at the lines. (Brandt, par. 3)

In the following example, *as* indicates that the first action occurred at the same time as the second action.

As the officers led me through the mall, I sensed a hundred pairs of eyes staring at me. (Brandt, par. 18)

⸬ Use dialogue to tell your story.

Although writers may not remember exactly what was said, they often reconstruct dialogue through quotation, paraphrase, or summary. Quotation emphasizes a conversation, while paraphrase or summary enables you to move past less important conversations quickly.

For more on transitions of time, see also p. 328 in Chapter 10.

When you quote, enclose the words, phrases, or sentences within quotation marks. Each time a new speaker is quoted, start a new paragraph:

Security guard   "Excuse me. Are you a relative of this young girl?"

Brandt's sister   "Yes, I'm her sister. What's the problem?"

Security guard   "Well, I just caught her shoplifting and I'm afraid I'll have to call the police." (Brandt, pars. 10–12)

In the example above, Brandt is careful to let readers know who is speaking by having the security guard ask Jean's sister if she's a relative, and by having her sister identify herself as such. In addition, writers can indicate who is speaking in the paragraphs that precede the dialogue:

References to *mother* prepare us for mother's line   There was a pause as he called my mother to the phone. For the first time that night, I was close to tears. I wished I had never stolen that stupid pin. I wanted to give the phone to one of the officers because I was too ashamed to tell my mother the truth, but I had no choice.

Reference to *Jean* prepares us for Jean's reply   "Jean, where are you?"

I'm tells us it is Jean's turn again   "I'm, umm, in jail." (Brandt, pars. 26–28)

You can also use **speaker tags** to identify the speaker:

"You stupid kids," he began perfunctorily. (Dillard, par. 18)

("Did we really do that?" I asked Thea this week. . . . "Yes," she said. "We put them in a lovely tin.") (Desmond-Harris, par. 4)

To learn more about using speaker tags, see pp. 12 and 26 in this chapter and pp. 82–83 in Chapter 3.

Use paraphrase to repeat the substance of what was said in your own words:

Next thing I knew, he was talking about calling the police and having me arrested and thrown in jail. (Brandt, par. 7)

Use summary to convey the gist of the discussion without the details of what was said:

We listened perfunctorily indeed, if we listened at all, for the chewing out was redundant, a mere formality, and beside the point. (Dillard, par. 19)

:: Develop and refine your descriptions.

To be effective, a remembered event should include specific details about the people and places involved. Describe people in detail—what they looked like and how they dressed, talked, and gestured. Describe the setting—what you saw, heard, smelled, touched, and tasted. Once you've described the people and places involved, try incorporating them into the action. The following activities will help you get started.

WAYS IN

HOW CAN I MAKE MY DESCRIPTIONS OF PEOPLE AND PLACES MORE VIVID?

- Consult *memorabilia,* like scrapbooks or souvenirs (ticket stubs, T-shirts), for details you may have forgotten.

- Look at *photographs* from your own albums, visit the Facebook pages of key people, or consult Google Earth views to sharpen your descriptions. Consider scanning, uploading, or attaching images of the memorabilia to your essay.

- Come up with a list of *names* or *nouns* to describe the most important people and locations in the story.

People	Places
Consider the job(s) they have, the roles they play, their facial features or accents, articles of clothing they wore, or items they carried.	Consider the type of location (clothing store, funeral parlor), the architectural features it had, or what it was near.
Brandt's security guard: man, street clothes, badge.	*Brandt's store:* General Store, knick-knacks, buttons, calendars, posters, lines at the cashiers, basket, threshold, office.
Dillard's pursuer: man, driver, city clothes, suit and tie, street shoes, jacket; *after the pursuit:* cuffs full of snow, prow of snow on shoes and socks, Pittsburgh accent.	*Dillard's neighborhood:* Reynolds Street, cars' tires, trail of chunks, sidewalk, house, path, tree, hedge, bank, grocery store driveway, porch, gap in hedge, alley, woodpile, backyards, hilltop.

- Come up with a list of *narrative actions* that remind you of the ways people acted, moved, and talked or that capture what was happening in the setting.

People	Places
Brandt's security guard: tapped shoulder, flashed badge.	*Brandt's shopping center:* was swarming with frantic last-minute shoppers.
Desmond-Harris and her friend: baked, played, sobbed, analyzed, cursed Biggie, studied.	*Desmond-Harris's high school:* perched on a sloping green lawn, sat on a wall, come charging onto the court, kicked furiously to "Toss It Up."

- Use detailing to flesh out descriptions.

People	Places
Brandt's security guard: unexpected tap, middle-aged man, some type of badge, politely asking.	*Brandt's store:* other useless items, 75-cent Snoopy button.
Dillard's pursuer: thin man, red-headed, chased silently, pants legs were wet.	*Desmond-Harris's friend's house:* well-stocked liquor cabinet, high-ceilinged kitchen, speakers perched discreetly.

(continued)

- Use similes or metaphors to compare people or places with other people or things.

People

Desmond-Harris and her friend Thea: were two earnest soldiers in the East Coast–West Coast war.

Brandt: felt like Hester Prynne being put on display for everyone to ridicule.

Places

Dillard's neighborhood: a complex trail of beige chunks like crenellated castle walls; mazy backyards.

Remember that you can rearrange the components of your description in any way that makes sense to you.

Incorporate descriptive details throughout your story.

Look over the details you've generated, your organizational plan, and any sections you've already drafted, and weave the descriptive details into your action sequences. Because readers often skip lengthy descriptions, spreading the details out over the whole story may work best.

WAYS IN

HOW CAN I WORK DESCRIPTIONS INTO MY ACTION SEQUENCES?

1. Begin with a simple sentence—an independent clause consisting of a subject (noun or pronoun) and a verb, for example:

   Amalia and Sophie ran.

2. **To describe people,** add descriptive naming and detailing as well as narrative actions to show what the people said and did, as in this example:

Narrative actions	Yelling "Grandma!" at the top of their lungs, the curly-headed
Independent clause	five-year-old twins, Amalia and Sophie, ran to their laughing
Descriptive naming and detailing	curly-headed grandmother, who was getting out of a silver hybrid sedan.

   Here's an example from Jean Brandt's essay (par. 6):

Independent clause	I whirled around to find a middle-aged man, dressed in street
Descriptive naming and detailing	clothes, flashing some type of badge and politely asking me to
Narrative actions	empty my pockets.

3. **To describe the place,** add descriptive naming, detailing, and comparing along with narrative actions, including prepositional phrases to show where each

object is located in the scene, as in this example (with only the new information marked):

Narrative actions	Yelling "Grandma!" at the top of their lungs, Amalia and Sophie ran to their laughing grandmother, a tall, thin woman getting out of a silver hybrid sedan she had just parked at the yellow loading-only zone in front of the old-fashioned yellow-clapboard elementary school.
Descriptive naming and detailing	

Here's an example from Annie Dillard's essay (par. 12):

Descriptive naming and detailing	He chased Mikey and me around the yellow house and up a back-yard path we knew by heart: under a low tree, up a bank, through a hedge, down some snowy steps, and across the grocery store's delivery driveway.
Narrative actions	

▓ Consider ways to convey your event's autobiographical significance.

The following activities should help you move from the notes you already have to some strategies for showing and telling readers why your event matters to you. Often, your word choices—what you focus on and how you describe it, especially the comparisons you draw—can tell readers a lot about your feelings. It might also help to move back and forth between your memory of the experience and how you see it now, examining changes in your attitude toward the event and your younger self.

WAYS IN →

HOW CAN I CONVEY THE AUTOBIOGRAPHICAL SIGNIFICANCE OF MY STORY?

Revisit your purpose and audience

Who are your readers, and what do you want them to think, feel, or believe about you or the event? The following sentence strategy can help you come up with an answer:

▶ Aside from my classmates and instructor, the people I imagine being most interested in what I'm saying would fit this description: _____. I think they will be most surprised by _____. I hope that when they are done reading they will think of me as _____ and be more aware that _____.

Think about your main point

What do you want your readers to understand or believe after reading your story?

▶ When readers finish my story, they will better appreciate how [society and culture/an individual person/the human condition] _____.

Explore the significance of your story's conflict

How does the event reflect what you were going through, and how can you drama-tize what occurred? Following are some sentence strategies you may use to start

(continued)

generating ideas, though you may want to revise or restructure them before including them in your paper.

▸ During this event, I found myself locked in conflict with _____. (Elaborate.)

▸ Although I struggled with [a factor outside myself], I also was at war with myself while it happened: I kept wondering, should I _____ or should I _____? (Elaborate.)

Consider the dominant impression you want to convey

Write for a few minutes about the kind of impression (of the setting, of the characters) you are hoping to create. What mood (scary, lighthearted, gloomy) do you want to convey? If you were filming the event, what would the lighting be like? What sound track would you use?

Now reread the writing you have already done. Identify any details that might undermine or contradict the dominant impression. Can you strengthen the dominant impression you want to convey by deleting or replacing any words that carry the wrong connotation (or associations)? Or are these contradictions actually part of the dominant impression and complex significance you want to convey? If so, consider how you could emphasize or deepen the complexity and ambivalence you felt at the time or feel now as you reflect on the event.

Explore how you felt at the time

Write for a few minutes, exploring how you felt and what you thought at the time the event occurred (for example, angry, subdued, in control, vulnerable, proud, embarrassed, or a combination of feelings). The following sentence strategies may help you put your feelings into words:

▸ As the event started [or during or right after the event], I felt _____ and _____. I hoped others would think of me as _____.

▸ I showed or expressed these feelings by _____.

Explore your present perspective

Write for a few minutes, exploring what you think about the event now. What can you say or show that will let readers know what you think and feel as you look back? The following sentence strategies may help you put your feelings into words:

▸ My feelings since the event [have/have not] changed in the following ways: _____.

▸ At the time, I had been going through _____, which may have affected my experience by _____.

▸ Looking back at the event, I realize I was probably trying to _____, though I didn't appreciate that at the time.

Write the opening sentences.

Review what you have already written to see if you have something that would work to launch your story. If not, experiment with ways to begin, and review the readings to see how they begin. Here are some additional ideas:

- A graphic description of a place or person
- A startling action that you or someone else took
- A telling bit of dialogue
- Your present reflections on your past self or on the context of the event

Don't agonize over the first sentences, because you may think of better approaches after you've written a rough draft.

Draft your story.

By this point, you have done a lot of writing

- to develop a plan for a well-told story;
- to come up with vivid details to help your readers imagine what happened;
- to think of strategies for showing or telling the autobiographical significance of your event;
- to try out a way to launch your story.

Now stitch that material together to create a draft. The next two parts of this Guide to Writing will help you evaluate and improve your draft.

Evaluating the Draft: Getting a Critical Reading

Your instructor may arrange a peer review session in class or online where you can exchange drafts with your classmates and give each other a thoughtful critical reading, pointing out what works well and suggesting ways to improve the draft. A good critical reading does three things:

1. It lets the writer know how clear, vivid, and meaningful the story seems to readers.
2. It praises what works best.
3. It indicates where the draft could be improved and makes suggestions on how to improve it.

A CRITICAL READING GUIDE

A Well-Told Story

How effectively does the writer tell the story?

Summarize: Circle or highlight the inciting incident and the climax of the story.

Praise: Give an example in the story where the storytelling is especially effective — for example, a place where the story seems to flow smoothly and maintain the reader's interest, or where narrative action is compelling or exciting.

Critique: Tell the writer where the storytelling could be improved — for example, where the suspense slackens, the story lacks tension or conflict, or the chronology is confusing.

Vivid Description of People and Places

Do the descriptions help you imagine what happened?

Summarize: Choose a passage of description and analyze how and how well it uses the describing strategies of naming, detailing, and comparing.

Praise: Identify a description that is particularly vivid — for example, a graphic sensory description or an apt comparison that makes a person or place come alive.

Critique: Tell the writer where the description could be improved — for example, where objects in the scene are not named or described with enough specific detail (colors, sounds, smells, textures), or where the description is sparse. Note any description that contradicts the dominant impression; it may suggest how the significance can be made more complex and interesting.

Autobiographical Significance

Is it clear why the event was important to the author?

Summarize: Briefly describe the story's dominant impression, and tell the writer why you think the event was significant.

Praise: Give an example where the significance comes across effectively — for example, where remembered feelings are expressed poignantly, where the present perspective seems insightful, or where the description creates a strong dominant impression that clarifies the significance.

Critique: Tell the writer where the significance could be strengthened — for example, if the conflict is too easily resolved, if a moral seems tacked on at the end, or if more interesting meanings could be drawn out of the experience.

Before concluding your peer review, be sure to address any of the writer's concerns that have not been discussed already.

Improving the Draft: Revising, Formatting, Editing, and Proofreading

Start improving your draft by reflecting on what you have written thus far:

- Review critical reading comments from your classmates, instructor, or writing center tutor. What are your readers getting at?
- Take another look at your notes and ideas. What else should you consider?
- Review your draft. What else can you do to make your story compelling?

Revise your draft.

If your readers are having difficulty with your draft, try some of the strategies listed in the Troubleshooting Guide below. They can help you fine-tune your presentation of the genre's basic features.

A TROUBLESHOOTING GUIDE

A Well-Told Story

My readers tell me that the story starts too slowly.

- Shorten the exposition, spread it out more within the story, or move it to a later part of the story.
- Move a bit of dialogue or narrative action up front.
- Start with something surprising but critical to the story.
- Begin with a flashback or flashforward.

My readers find the chronology confusing.

- Add or change time transitions.
- Look for inadvertent tense shifts and fix them.

My readers feel that the suspense slackens or that the story lacks drama.

- Add remembered feelings and thoughts to heighten anticipation.
- Add dialogue and narrative action to emphasize critical moments in the story.
- Cut or shorten background exposition and unnecessary description.
- Build rising action in stages, with multiple high points.

(continued)

A Well-Told Story

My readers find the conflict vague or unconnected to the autobiographical significance.

- Think about the conflict's multiple and possibly contradictory meanings.
- Add remembered feelings or thoughts to suggest multiple meanings, and cut those that don't clarify the significance.
- Add your present perspective to make the significance clearer and bring out the implications.
- Add dialogue or narrative action to clarify the conflict.

Vivid Description of People and Places

My readers feel that the people in the story don't come alive.

- Add details about distinctive physical features or mannerisms.
- Add speaker tags that characterize people and show their feelings.
- Read your dialogue aloud, and revise to make the language more natural and appropriate to the person.

My readers have trouble visualizing the places I describe.

- Name objects in the scene.
- Add sensory details (colors, sounds, smells, textures).
- Use a comparison — metaphor or simile — to evoke a particular mood or attitude.
- Add a visual — a photograph or other memorabilia.

My readers feel that some descriptions weaken the dominant impression.

- Omit unnecessary details.
- Add adjectives, similes, or metaphors to strengthen the dominant impression.
- Rethink the impression you want your writing to convey and the significance it suggests.

Autobiographical Significance

My readers do not identify or sympathize with me.

- Add background details or explain the context.
- Reveal the cultural influences acting on you or emphasize the historical period in which the event occurred.
- Show readers how you have changed or were affected by the experience.

> My readers don't understand the significance of the story.

Autobiographical Significance

- Use irony or humor to contrast your present perspective with your past behavior, feelings, or attitudes.
- Show that the event ended but that the conflict was not resolved.
- Use dialogue to show how your relationship with people in your story changed.
- Indicate how the event continues to influence your thoughts or actions.

> My readers think the significance seems too pat or simplistic.

- Develop contradictions or show ambivalence to enrich the implications.
- Use humor to comment ironically on your past behavior or current contradictory feelings.
- Stress the social or cultural dimensions of the event.
- Revise Hollywood-movie clichés, simple resolutions, or tagged-on morals.

Edit and proofread your draft.

Three problems commonly appear in essays about remembered events: misused words and expressions, incorrectly punctuated or formatted dialogue, and misused past-perfect verbs. The following guidelines will help you check your essay for these common errors.

Using the Right Word or Expression

The Problem   Many familiar sayings and expressions are frequently heard but not often seen in writing, so writers often mistake the expression. Consider the following sentences:

> Chock it up to my upbringing, but having several children play butt naked around my feet certainly curved my appetite for parenthood.

> The deer was still jerking in its death throws, but for all intensive purposes it was dead.

Within those two sentences are five commonly mangled expressions. To the ear, they may sound right, but in each case the author has heard the expression incorrectly and written down the wrong words.

Note: the expressions should be: chalk it up, buck naked, curbed my appetite, death throes, for all intents and purposes.

The Correction   You can find and debug these kinds of errors by following these steps:

1. Highlight or circle common expressions of two or more words in your writing project (especially those you've heard before but haven't seen in writing).
2. Check each expression in a dictionary or in a list of frequently misused words.

3. Consider revising the expression: If you have heard the expression so often that it "sounds right," it may be a cliché. A fresh expression will be more powerful.

The Problem   Early drafts often include vague or overly general word choices and flabby sentences. Cutting words that add little, making verbs active, and replacing weak word choices with stronger ones can greatly increase the power of a remembered event essay.

The Correction   The following three steps can help you tighten your language and make it more powerful.

1. Circle empty intensifiers, such as *just, very, certain,* and *really.* Now reread each sentence, omitting the circled word. If the sentence still makes sense without the word, delete it.

2. Circle all forms of the verb *to be* (such as *am, is, are, was,* and *were*). Now reread each sentence that includes a circled word, and ask yourself, "Could I revise the sentence or combine it with another sentence to create an active construction?" Examples:

   barking
   ▶ The dog was barking. He took off after Jasper, as he raced toward Third Avenue.
   ^

   Sarah double-knotted the rope
   ▶ The rope was tied around the oak in the front yard.
   ^

3. Review your descriptions, highlighting or underlining adjectives, adverbs, and prepositional phrases. Now reread them, imagining a more specific noun or verb that could convey the same idea in fewer words.

   A Humvee sped
   ▶ A large, black truck moved quickly across the parking lot.
   ^

Incorporating Dialogue

The Problem   Remembered event essays often include dialogue, but writers sometimes have trouble using the conventions of dialogue correctly. One common problem occurs with punctuation marks:

- In American English, the opening quotation mark hugs the first word of the quotation. Commas belong inside the closing quotation mark, but end punctuation can go inside or outside the closing quotation mark, depending on whether the end punctuation belongs to the quotation or the end of the sentence.

- Speaker tags reflect what the speaker was thinking, feeling, or doing.

- A new paragraph is typically used to indicate a change in speaker.

The Correction   Revise the punctuation, add speaker tags, or start a new paragraph as needed:

   ?
   ▶ "Jean, what's going on," my sister asked?
   ^

▶ "Jean, what's going on?" my sister ~~questioned~~. *asked*

▶ A few seconds later, my sister appeared and asked, "So, did you decide to buy the

button?" "No, I guess not." *¶*

Using the Past Perfect

The Problem   Remembered event essays often mention events that occurred before the main action. To convey this sequence of events, writers use the past-perfect tense rather than the simple past tense:

Past Perfect	Simple Past
had traveled	traveled
had been	was
had begun	began

Failing to use the past perfect when it is needed can make your meaning unclear. (What happened when, exactly?)

The Correction   Check places where you recount events to verify that you are using the past perfect to indicate actions that had already been completed at the time of another past action (she *had finished* her work when we saw her).

▶ I had three people in the car, something my father told me not to do that very morning. *had*

▶ Coach Kernow told me I ran faster than ever before. *had run*

Note for Multilingual Writers   It is important to remember that the past perfect is formed with *had* followed by a past participle. Past participles usually end in *-ed, -d, -en, -n,* or *-t*—*worked, hoped, eaten, taken, bent*—although some are irregular (such as *begun* or *chosen*).

▶ Before Tania went to Moscow last year, she had not really speak Russian. *spoken*

THINKING CRITICALLY

To think critically means to use all of the knowledge you have acquired from the information in this chapter, your own writing, the writing of other students, and class discussions to reflect deeply on your work for this assignment and the genre (or type) of writing you have produced. The benefit of thinking critically is proven and important: Thinking critically about what you have learned will help you remember it longer, ensuring that you will be able to put it to good use well beyond this writing course.

Reflecting on What You Have Learned

In this chapter, you have learned a great deal about this genre from reading several autobiographical stories and writing one of your own. To consolidate your learning, reflect not only on what you learned but also on how you learned it.

ANALYZE & WRITE

Write a blog post, a letter to your instructor or a classmate, or an e-mail message to a student who will take this course next term, using the writing prompt that seems most productive for you:

- Explain how what you wanted your readers to learn about you from reading your story influenced one of your decisions as a writer, such as how you used the dramatic arc to shape your story around a conflict, how you used dialogue to intensify the drama and convey the significance, or how you integrated your remembered thoughts and feelings into your storytelling.

- Discuss what you learned about yourself as a writer in the process of writing this essay. For example, what part of the process did you find most challenging, or did you try anything new, like getting a critical reading of your draft or outlining your draft in order to revise it? If so, how well did it work?

- If you were to give advice to a fellow student who was about to write a remembered event essay, what would you say?

- Which of the readings (in this chapter or elsewhere) influenced your choice of an event to write about or how you told the story? Explain the influence, citing specific examples comparing the two.

- If you got good advice from a critical reader, explain exactly how the person helped you — perhaps by questioning the conflict in a way that enabled you to develop your story's significance, or by pointing out passages that needed clearer time markers to better orient readers.

Reflecting on the Genre

We've said throughout this chapter that writing a remembered event essay leads to self-discovery, but what do we mean by the "self"? Should we think of the self as our "true" essence or as the different roles we play in different situations? If we accept the idea of an essential self, writing about significant events in our lives can help us in the search to discover who we truly are. Given this idea of the self, we might see Jean Brandt, for example, as searching to understand whether she is the kind of person who breaks the law and only cares when she is caught and has to face her parents' disapproval. If, on the other hand, we accept the idea that the various roles we play are ways we construct the self in different situations, then writing about a remembered event allows us to examine a side of our personality and the influences that shaped it. This view of the self assumes that we present different self-images to different people in different situations. Given this idea, we might see Brandt as presenting her sassy teenage side to the police but keeping her vulnerability hidden from them and perhaps also from her family, with some painful loss of intimacy.

ANALYZE & WRITE

Write a page or two explaining how the genre prompts you to think about self-discovery. In your discussion, you might consider one or more of the following:

1 **Consider how your remembered event essay might be an exercise in self-discovery.** Planning and writing your essay, did you see yourself as discovering your true self or examining how you reacted in a particular situation? Do you think your essay reveals your single, essential, true self, or does it show only an aspect of the person you understand yourself to be?

2 **Write a page or so explaining your ideas about self-discovery and truth in remembered event essays.** Connect your ideas to your own essay and to the readings in this chapter.

---

 macmillanhighered.com/conciseguide
How can you incorporate oral storytelling into a remembered event project?
Tutorials > **Digital Writing** > Audio Editing in Audacity

3
Writing Profiles

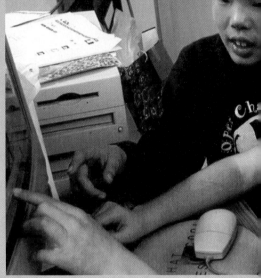

© Bill Aron/PhotoEdit

Profiles are analytical, informative, and thought-provoking portraits of a person or place, or of an activity that brings people together. They may be cultural ethnographies, ranging from a day-in-the-life to extended immersion studies of communities or people at work and at play. They are intensively researched, centering on the field research techniques of colorful observations and edifying interviews. As a result, profiles are always entertaining to read, sometimes amusing, and often compelling. Whether written in a college course, for the broader community, or about the workplace, at their best profiles bring their subjects to life, taking us behind the scenes.

IN COLLEGE COURSES

A college student who plans to become a teacher visits a middle school class to study how a group of sixth graders collaborate on a project. During multiple visits, she makes notes of her observations and her interviews with the students and their teacher. To keep the focus on the children's activities, she reports as a spectator, weaving her insights about their collaborative process into a detailed narrative of a typical half-hour session. As she writes, the central idea emerges that the success of their collaboration depends on the children's frequent talk—both planning what to do next and reflecting on what they have already accomplished. After completing her ethnographic profile, she posts it on the class bulletin board for her classmates and others interested in collaborative learning.

© H. Lorren Au Jr./The Orange County Register/
ZUMAPRESS.com/Alamy

Radius Images/Alamy

IN THE COMMUNITY

A newspaper reporter is assigned to write a profile of a mural project recently commissioned by the city of Los Angeles, so he visits the studio of the local artist in charge of the project. They discuss the specifics of the mural project and the artist's views of other civic art projects, and the artist invites the reporter to spend the following day at the site. The next day, the artist puts the reporter to work alongside two volunteers. The reporter intends to use his firsthand experience, interviews with volunteers, and photos of the project to describe the painting from a participant-observer's point of view. Later, writing copy for the Sunday paper, the reporter organizes the profile around the artist's goals for the project, the experience of volunteers, and the mural's importance as civic art.

IN THE WORKPLACE

For a company newsletter, a public-relations officer profiles the corporation's new chief executive officer (CEO). He follows the CEO from meeting to meeting, taking photographs and observing her interactions with colleagues. Between meetings, he interviews her about her management philosophy and her five-year plan for the corporation. Immediately after the interviews, he makes notes and writes down questions to ask as follow-up. A day later, the CEO invites the writer to visit her at home. He watches her help her daughter with homework, chats with her husband, and takes more photographs. The writer decides to illustrate the profile with images of the CEO at her desk working and with her daughter. As he reports on some of the challenges the CEO anticipates for the corporation, he tries to convey the confidence she shows both at work and at home.

In this chapter, we ask you to write a profile. Whether you choose something you know well or something you want to learn about, focus on it as if for the first time, and choose details that will not only make it come alive for your readers but also show them why your subject is intriguing and important. As you write your profile, consider how you can most effectively convey your insights to your readers. Consider, too, whether using visuals or multimedia would help your readers more fully grasp your subject.

| PRACTICING THE GENRE |

Conducting an Interview

Part 1.   Get together in a small group to practice interviewing, a crucial skill in profile writing. Have one group member take the role of the interviewee and the rest of the group taking turns as interviewers. (Choose as the interviewee a group member who is knowledgeable about a subject, such as a sport, a type of music or video game, an academic subject, or a kind of work.) Interviewers should take a couple of minutes to prepare questions and then spend five minutes taking turns asking questions. Listen to what is being said, and respond with follow-up questions as needed. All interviewers should take notes on what is being said (quoting or summarizing) plus any details about the way it is said (Is it sarcastic, excited, uncertain?) that could give readers a sense of the interviewee's attitude.

Part 2.   Discuss what you learned about profiles and about conducting an interview:

- **What did you learn about profiles?** For a profile to be effective, it must depict the subject vividly and be thought provoking. Assume that other members of your class do not know much about the subject, and take turns identifying one thing the interviewee said — for example, an illuminating fact, an amusing anecdote, or a surprising judgment — that would engage readers' interest. What other questions would readers want answered?

- **What did you learn about conducting an interview?** Compare your thoughts with those of the others in your group on what was easiest and hardest—for example, preparing questions, listening and following up, taking notes, or considering what to include in your profile.

Analyzing Profiles

As you read the selections in this chapter, you will see how different authors create a compelling profile. Analyzing how they describe and report on what they observed, how they organize the profile, the role they take, and the dominant impression they create will help you see how you can employ these same techniques to convey your perspective on the subject to your readers.

Determine the writer's purpose and audience.

Although crafting a profile helps writers understand their subjects, most write profiles to impart their own special insight. When reading the following profiles, ask yourself questions like these about the writer's purpose and audience:

- What seems to be the writer's main *purpose*—for example, to inform readers about some aspect of everyday life (the places and activities around us that we rarely get to know intimately); to give readers a behind-the-scenes look at an intriguing or unusual activity; to surprise readers by presenting unusual subjects or familiar ones in new ways; to offer a new way to look at and think about the cultural significance of the subject; or to bridge the distance between outsiders' preconceptions and the lived experience of people as they try to communicate, construct their identities, and define their values?

- What does the author assume about the *audience*—for example, that audience members know nothing or very little about the subject; that they will be interested and possibly amused by a particular aspect of the subject; or that they will be intrigued by the perspective the writer takes or fascinated by certain quotes or descriptive details?

Assess the genre's basic features.

> **■■ Basic Features**
> ■■
> Detailed Information
> A Clear, Logical
> Organization
> Writer's Role
> Perspective on the
> Subject

Use the following to help you analyze and evaluate how profile writers employ the genre's basic features. The examples are drawn from the reading selections in this chapter.

DETAILED INFORMATION ABOUT THE SUBJECT

Read first to learn about the subject. Much of the pleasure of reading a profile comes from the way the writer interweaves bits of information into a tapestry of lively narrative, arresting quotations, and vivid descriptions.

Examine the describing strategies of *naming, detailing,* and *comparing* to see how they create a vivid image, as in Brian Cable's description of coffins on display:

Naming	We passed into a bright, fluorescent-lit "**display room**." Inside were thirty
Detailing	**coffins**. . . . Like new cars on the showroom floor. . . (Cable, par. 18)
Comparing	

Although most information in a profile comes from observation (and is therefore described), information may also come from interviews and background research. To present information from sources, profile writers rely on three basic strategies—**quotation**, paraphrase, and summary:

QUOTATION	"We're in *Ripley's Believe It or Not,* along with another funeral home whose owners' names are Baggit and Sackit," Howard told me, without cracking a smile. (Cable, par. 14)
PARAPHRASE	Goodbody Mortuary, upon notification of someone's death, will remove the remains from the hospital or home. They then prepare the body for viewing, whereupon features distorted by illness or accident are restored to their natural condition. (Cable, par. 6)
SUMMARY	I came across several articles describing the causes of a farmworker shortage. The stories cited an aging workforce, immigration crackdowns, and long delays at the border that discourage workers with green cards. (Thompson, par. 5)

Profile writers nearly always research the subject thoroughly. Convention dictates that selections published in popular publications like magazines, blogs, and general-interest books not cite their sources. Not so for academic or scholarly essays: Unless the information is widely known by educated adults, most instructors require you to cite your sources and provide a list of references or works cited.

See Chapters 19 and 20 to learn about the conventions for citing and documenting sources.

A CLEAR, LOGICAL ORGANIZATION

Profiles can be organized narratively, as a guided tour of a place or as a story, or they can be organized as an array of topics. In narratives, look for time markers, such as narrative actions, which combine actors (nouns and pronouns) with action verbs; prepositional phrases, which locate objects in space or actions in time; verb tenses, which show how actions relate in time; calendar and clock time; and transitions of time and space.

NARRATIVE ACTIONS	I climbed the stone steps to the entrance. (Cable, par. 4)
PREPOSITIONAL PHRASES	Services are held in one of three chapels at the mortuary, and afterward the casket is placed in a "visitation room." (Cable, par. 6) On my first day . . . (Thompson, par. 6)
VERB TENSES	I bend over, noticing that most of the crew has turned to watch. (Thompson, par. 8)
CALENDER AND CLOCK TIME	It's now 3:00. (Coyne, par. 19) The Goodbody family started the business way back in 1915. Today, they do over five hundred services a year. (Cable, par. 13)
TRANSITIONS OF TIME	But after we hand the children over to their mothers . . . (Coyne, par. 3) Next, he . . . he then . . . (Thompson, par. 7)

TRANSITIONS OF SPACE	. . . through the glass doors and out the exit. (Coyne, par. 26)
	Ahead of us . . . (Cable, par. 15)

In topical sections, look for *logical transitions* such as these that announce a

CONTRADICTION	. . . but it's widely assumed . . . (Thompson, par. 5)
	On the contrary, his bitterness . . . (Coyne, par. 13)
CAUSE	Because of their difference in skin color, there would be . . . (Coyne, par. 11)
CONCLUSION	So I am to be very careful and precise . . . (Thompson, par. 12)
SPECULATION	Perhaps such an air of comfort makes it easier for the family to give up their loved one. (Cable, par. 24)

Whereas a narrative tour or story may be more engaging, a topical organization may deliver information more efficiently. As you read the profiles in this chapter, consider the writer's decision on how to organize the information. What was gained and lost, if anything?

To learn more about cueing the reader, see Chapter 10.

THE WRITER'S ROLE

Look also at the role that the writer assumes in relation to his or her subject:

- As a **spectator** or **detached observer,** the writer's position is like that of the reader — an outsider looking in on the people and their activities (such as the college student in the first scenario, p. 50, and Brian Cable in his profile below).

- As a **participant observer,** the writer participates in the activity being profiled and acquires insider knowledge (such as Gabriel Thompson in his profile, pp. 68–71).

Sometimes writers use both the spectator and the participant role, as Amanda Coyne does in her profile on pp. 61–65.

A PERSPECTIVE ON THE SUBJECT

All of the basic features listed previously — detailed information, the way the information is organized, and the writer's role — develop the writer's **perspective on the subject,** the main idea or cultural significance that the writer wants readers to take away from reading the profile. Profiles create a dominant impression through their description and narration. But they also analyze and interpret the subject, conveying their perspective explicitly through commentary as well as implicitly through tone (such as irony).

Readings

Brian Cable | *The Last Stop*

THIS PROFILE of a neighborhood mortuary was originally written when Brian Cable was a first-year college student. "Death," as he explains in the opening sentence, "is a subject largely ignored by the living," so it is not surprising that he notices people averting their eyes as they walk past the mortuary on a busy commercial street. Cable, however, walks in and takes readers on a guided tour of the premises. As he presents information he learned from observing how the mortuary works—from the reception room up front to the embalming room in back— and from interviewing the people who work there, Cable invites us to reflect on our own feelings and cultural attitudes about death. As you read, do the following:

- Notice how Cable uses humor to defuse the inherent seriousness of his subject.
- Consider the questions in the margin. Your instructor may ask you to post your answers to a class blog or discussion board or to bring them to class.

Basic Features
Detailed Information
A Clear, Logical Organization
Writer's Role
Perspective on the Subject

Let us endeavor so to live that when we come to die even the undertaker will be sorry.

— Mark Twain, *Pudd'nhead Wilson*

1   Death is a subject largely ignored by the living. We don't discuss it much, not as children (when Grandpa dies, he is said to be "going away"), not as adults, not even as senior citizens. Throughout our lives, death remains intensely private. The death of a loved one can be very painful, partly because of the sense of loss, but also because someone else's mortality reminds us all too vividly of our own.

2   More than a few people avert their eyes as they walk past the dusty-pink building that houses the Goodbody Mortuary. It looks a bit like a church — tall, with gothic arches and stained glass — and somewhat like an apartment complex — low, with many windows stamped out of red brick.

Cable tells us what he expected. How does the opening — including the title and epigraph (introductory quote) — influence what you expect from his profile?

3   It wasn't at all what I had expected. I thought it would be more like Forest Lawn, serene with lush green lawns and meticulously groomed gardens, a place set apart from the hustle of day-to-day life. Here instead was an odd pink structure set in the middle of a business district. On top of the Goodbody Mortuary sign was a large electric clock. What the hell, I thought. Mortuaries are concerned with time, too.

What organizational plan for the profile emerges in pars. 4 and 5?

4   I was apprehensive as I climbed the stone steps to the entrance. I feared rejection or, worse, an invitation to come and stay. The door was massive, yet it swung open easily on well-oiled hinges. "Come in," said the sign. "We're always open." Inside was a cool and quiet reception room. Curtains were drawn against the outside glare, cutting the light down to a soft glow.

5   I found the funeral director in the main lobby, adjacent to the reception room. Like most people, I had preconceptions about what an undertaker looked like. Mr. Deaver fulfilled my expectations entirely. Tall and thin, he even had beady eyes and a bony face. A low, slanted forehead gave way to a beaked nose. His skin, scrubbed of all color, contrasted sharply with his jet black hair. He was wearing a starched white shirt, gray pants, and black shoes. Indeed, he looked like death on two legs.

What does the detailed description of Deaver in pars. 5 and 6 contribute to Cable's profile of the mortuary?

6   He proved an amiable sort, however, and was easy to talk to. As funeral director, Mr. Deaver ("Call me Howard") was responsible for a wide range of services. Goodbody Mortuary, upon notification of someone's death, will remove the remains from the hospital or home. They then prepare the body for viewing, whereupon features distorted by illness or accident are restored to their natural condition. The body is embalmed and then placed in a casket selected by the family of the deceased. Services are held in one of three chapels at the mortuary, and afterward the casket is placed in a "visitation room," where family and friends can pay their last respects. Goodbody also makes arrangements for the purchase of a burial site and transports the body there for burial.

What role has Cable adopted in writing the profile? When does it become clear?

Why do you think Cable summarizes the information in par. 6 instead of quoting Howard?

7   All this information Howard related in a well-practiced, professional manner. It was obvious he was used to explaining the specifics of his profession. We sat alone in the lobby. His desk was bone clean, no pencils or paper, nothing—just a telephone. He did all his paperwork at home; as it turned out, he and his wife lived right upstairs. The phone rang. As he listened, he bit his lips and squeezed his Adam's apple somewhat nervously.

8   "I think we'll be able to get him in by Friday. No, no, the family wants him cremated."

9   His tone was that of a broker conferring on the Dow Jones. Directly behind him was a sign announcing "Visa and Master Charge Welcome Here." It was tacked to the wall, right next to a crucifix.

What does this observation reveal about Cable's perspective?

10   "Some people have the idea that we are bereavement specialists, that we can handle emotional problems which follow a death: Only a trained therapist can do that. We provide services for the dead, not counseling for the living."

Why do you think Cable quotes Howard in par. 10 instead of paraphrasing or summarizing?

11   Physical comfort was the one thing they did provide for the living. The lobby was modestly but comfortably furnished. There were several couches, in colors ranging from earth brown to pastel blue, and a coffee table in front of each one. On one table lay some magazines and a vase of flowers. Another supported an aquarium. Paintings of pastoral scenes hung on every wall. The lobby looked more or less like that of an old hotel. Nothing seemed to match, but it had a homey, lived-in look.

What does this observation contribute to the dominant impression?

12   "The last time the Goodbodies decorated was in '59, I believe. It still makes people feel welcome."

13   And so "Goodbody" was not a name made up to attract customers but the owner's family name. The Goodbody family started the business way back in 1915. Today, they do over five hundred services a year.

14   "We're in *Ripley's Believe It or Not*, along with another funeral home whose owners' names are Baggit and Sackit," Howard told me, without cracking a smile.

How does Cable make the transition from topic to topic in pars. 15–18?

15   I followed him through an arched doorway into a chapel that smelled musty and old. The only illumination came from sunlight filtered through a stained glass ceiling. Ahead of us lay a casket. I could see that it contained a man dressed in a black suit. Wooden benches ran on either side of an aisle that led to the body. I got no closer. From the red roses across the dead man's chest, it was apparent that services had already been held.

16   "It was a large service," remarked Howard. "Look at that casket — a beautiful work of craftsmanship."

17   I guess it was. Death may be the great leveler, but one's coffin quickly reestablishes one's status.

18   We passed into a bright, fluorescent-lit "display room." Inside were thirty coffins, lids open, patiently awaiting inspection. Like new cars on the showroom floor, they gleamed with high-gloss finishes.

What does the comparison to a new-car showroom in pars. 18–21 reveal about Cable's perspective?

19   "We have models for every price range."

20   Indeed, there was a wide variety. They came in all colors and various materials. Some were little more than cloth-covered cardboard boxes, others were made of wood, and a few were made of steel, copper, or bronze. Howard told me prices started at $500 and averaged about $1,800. He motioned toward the center of the room: "The top of the line."

21   This was a solid bronze casket, its seams electronically welded to resist corrosion. Moisture-proof and air-tight, it could be hermetically sealed off from all outside elements. Its handles were plated with 14-karat gold. The Promethean casket made by the Batesville Casket Company is the choice of celebrities and the very wealthy. The price: a cool $25,000.

REUTERS/Mario Anzuoni/Landov

Fig. 1   "The top of the line." The Promethean casket that Michael Jackson was buried in.

22   A proper funeral remains a measure of respect for the deceased. But it is expensive. In the United States, the amount spent annually on funerals is around $12 billion (Grassley). Among ceremonial expenditures, funerals are second only to weddings. As a result, practices are changing. Howard has been in this business for forty years. He remembers a time when everyone was buried. Nowadays, with burials costing more than $7,000 a shot (Grassley), people often opt instead for cremation — as Howard put it, "a cheap, quick, and easy means of disposal." In some areas of the country, according to Howard, the cremation rate is now over 60 percent. Observing this trend, one might wonder whether burials are becoming obsolete. Do burials serve an important role in society?

Where does the information in pars. 22–23 come from? How can you tell?

Why do you think Cable uses a rhetorical question here?

23   For Tim, Goodbody's licensed mortician, the answer is very definitely yes. Burials will remain in common practice, according to the slender embalmer with the disarming smile, because they allow family and friends to view the deceased. Painful as it may be, such an experience brings home the finality of death. "Something deep within us demands a confrontation with death," Tim explained. "A last look assures us that the person we loved is, indeed, gone forever."

24

Whose perspective does this statement reflect? How do you know?

Apparently, we also need to be assured that the body will be laid to rest in comfort and peace. The average casket, with its innerspring mattress and pleated satin lining, is surprisingly roomy and luxurious. Perhaps such an air of comfort makes it easier for the family to give up their loved one. In addition, the burial site fixes the deceased in the survivors' memory, like a new address. Cremation provides none of these comforts.

25

Is Tim's definition of mortuary science helpful? Why or why not?

Tim started out as a clerk in a funeral home but then studied to become a mortician. "It was a profession I could live with," he told me with a sly grin. Mortuary science might be described as a cross between pre-med and cosmetology, with courses in anatomy and embalming as well as in restorative art.

26

Which information in par. 26 comes from observation and which comes from interviewing Tim? How do you know?

Tim let me see the preparation, or embalming, room, a white-walled chamber about the size of an operating room. Against the wall was a large sink with elbow taps and a draining board. In the center of the room stood a table with equipment for preparing the arterial embalming fluid, which consists primarily of formaldehyde, a preservative, and phenol, a disinfectant. This mixture sanitizes and also gives better color to the skin. Facial features can then be "set" to achieve a restful expression. Missing eyes, ears, and even noses can be replaced.

27

I asked Tim if his job ever depressed him. He bridled at the question: "No, it doesn't depress me at all. I do what I can for people and take satisfaction in enabling relatives to see their loved ones as they were in life." He said that he felt people were becoming more aware of the public service his profession provides. Grade-school classes now visit funeral homes as often as they do police stations and museums. The mortician is no longer regarded as a minister of death.

28

How effective is this ending?

Before leaving, I wanted to see a body up close. I thought I could be indifferent after all I had seen and heard, but I wasn't sure. Cautiously, I reached out and touched the skin. It felt cold and firm, not unlike clay. As I walked out, I felt glad to have satisfied my curiosity about dead bodies, but all too happy to let someone else handle them.

Works Cited

Grassley, Chuck. "Opening Statement of Chairman Grassley." U.S. Senate Special Committee on Aging. 21 Sept. 2000. Web. 6 Jan. 2012.

Twain, Mark. *Pudd'nhead Wilson*. New York: Pocket Books, 2004: 45. Print.

Amanda Coyne | *The Long Good-Bye: Mother's Day in Federal Prison*

Courtesy of Amanda Coyne

AMANDA COYNE earned a master of fine arts degree in creative writing at the University of Iowa, where she was the recipient of an Iowa Arts Fellowship. She is the cofounder and writer of the *Alaska Dispatch,* an award-winning online news site. Her work has appeared in such publications as *Harper's,* the *New York Times Magazine, Bust, Newsweek,* and the *Guardian.* Most recently, she is the coauthor with her husband of a book about oil and politics in Alaska entitled *Crude Awakening: Money, Mavericks, and Mayhem in Alaska* (2011).

"The Long Good-Bye," her first piece of published writing, originally appeared in *Harper's.* This selection takes a more ethnographic turn than the other profiles in this chapter in that Coyne uses direct observation and interview to study the behavior of a particular community. In this profile, Coyne examines women who have been incarcerated and separated from their children to see how the mothers and children negotiate their difficult relationships. As you read, think about what you learn about the stresses on these parent-child relationships:

- What stresses seem to affect the family relationships described in this profile?
- What do you think is the author's attitude toward these stresses? How can you tell what she thinks and feels?

1 You can spot the convict-moms here in the visiting room by the way they hold and touch their children and by the single flower that is perched in front of them — a rose, a tulip, a daffodil. Many of these mothers have untied the bow that attaches the flower to its silver-and-red cellophane wrapper and are using one of the many empty soda cans at hand as a vase. They sit proudly before their flower-in-a-Coke-can, amid Hershey bar wrappers, half-eaten Ding Dongs, and empty paper coffee cups. Occasionally, a mother will pick up her present and bring it to her nose when one of the bearers of the single flower — her child — asks if she likes it. And the mother will respond the way that mothers always have and always will respond when presented with a gift on this day. "Oh, I just love it. It's perfect. I'll put it in the middle of my Bible." Or, "I'll put it on my desk, right next to your school picture." And always: "It's the best one here."

2 But most of what is being smelled today is the children themselves. While the other adults are plunking coins into the vending machines, the mothers take deep whiffs from the backs of their children's necks, or kiss and smell the backs of their knees, or take off their shoes and tickle their feet and then pull them close to their noses. They hold them tight and take in their own second scent — the scent assuring them that these are still their children and that they still belong to them.

3 The visitors are allowed to bring in pockets full of coins, and today that Mother's Day flower, and I know from previous visits to my older sister here at the Federal Prison Camp for women in Pekin, Illinois, that there is always an aberrant urge to gather immediately around the vending machines. The sandwiches are stale, the coffee weak, the candy bars the ones we always pass up in a convenience store. But

after we hand the children over to their mothers, we gravitate toward those machines. Like milling in the kitchen at a party. We all do it, and nobody knows why. Polite conversation ensues around the microwave while the popcorn is popping and the processed-chicken sandwiches are being heated. We ask one another where we are from, how long a drive we had. An occasional whistle through the teeth, a shake of the head. "My, my, long way from home, huh?" "Staying at the Super 8 right up the road. Not a bad place." "Stayed at the Econo Lodge last time. Wasn't a good place at all." Never asking the questions we really want to ask: "What's she in for?" "How much time's she got left?" You never ask in the waiting room of a doctor's office either. Eventually, all of us—fathers, mothers, sisters, brothers, a few boyfriends, and very few husbands— return to the queen of the day, sitting at a fold-out table loaded with snacks, prepared for five or so hours of attempted normal conversation.

4   Most of the inmates are elaborately dressed, many in prison-crafted dresses and sweaters in bright blues and pinks. They wear meticulously applied makeup in corresponding hues, and their hair is replete with loops and curls—hair that only women with the time have the time for. Some of the better seamstresses have crocheted vests and purses to match their outfits. Although the world outside would never accuse these women of making haute-couture fashion statements, the fathers and the sons and the boyfriends and the very few husbands think they look beautiful, and they tell them so repeatedly. And I can imagine the hours spent preparing for this visit—hours of needles and hooks clicking over brightly colored yards of yarn. The hours of discussing, dissecting, and bragging about these visitors— especially the men. Hours spent in the other world behind the door where we're not allowed, sharing lipsticks

and mascaras, and unraveling the occasional hair-tangled hot roller, and the brushing out and lifting and teasing . . . and the giggles that abruptly change into tears without warning—things that define any female-only world. Even, or especially, if that world is a female federal prison camp.

5   While my sister Jennifer is with her son in the playroom, an inmate's mother comes over to introduce herself to my younger sister, Charity, my brother, John, and me. She tells us about visiting her daughter in a higher-security prison before she was transferred here. The woman looks old and tired, and her shoulders sag under the weight of her recently acquired bitterness.

6   "Pit of fire," she says, shaking her head. "Like a pit of fire straight from hell. Never seen anything like it. Like something out of an old movie about prisons." Her voice is getting louder and she looks at each of us with pleading eyes. "My *daughter* was there. Don't even get me started on that place. Women die there."

7   John and Charity and I silently exchange glances.

8   "My daughter would come to the visiting room with a black eye and I'd think, 'All she did was sit in the car while her boyfriend ran into the house.' She didn't even touch the stuff. Never even handled it."

9   She continues to stare at us, each in turn. "Ten years. That boyfriend talked and he got three years. She didn't know anything. Had nothing to tell them. They gave her ten years. They called it conspiracy. Conspiracy? Aren't there real criminals out there?" She asks this with hands outstretched, waiting for an answer that none of us can give her.

10   The woman's daughter, the conspirator, is chasing her son through the maze of chairs and tables and through the other children. She's a twenty-four-year-old blonde, whom I'll call Stephanie, with Dorothy Hamill hair and matching dimples.

She looks like any girl you might see in any shopping mall in middle America. She catches her chocolate-brown son and tickles him, and they laugh and trip and fall together onto the floor and laugh harder.

11   Had it not been for that wait in the car, this scene would be taking place at home, in a duplex Stephanie would rent while trying to finish her two-year degree in dental hygiene or respiratory therapy at the local community college. The duplex would be spotless, with a blown-up picture of her and her son over the couch and ceramic unicorns and horses occupying the shelves of the entertainment center. She would make sure that her son went to school every day with stylishly floppy pants, scrubbed teeth, and a good breakfast in his belly. Because of their difference in skin color, there would be occasional tension—caused by the strange looks from strangers, teachers, other mothers, and the bullies on the playground, who would chant after they knocked him down, "Your Momma's white, your Momma's white." But if she were home, their weekends and evenings would be spent together transcending those looks and healing those bruises. Now, however, their time is spent eating visiting-room junk food and his school days are spent fighting the boys in the playground who chant, "Your Momma's in prison, your Momma's in prison."

12   He will be ten when his mother is released, the same age my nephew will be when his mother is let out. But Jennifer, my sister, was able to spend the first five years of Toby's life with him. Stephanie had Ellie after she was incarcerated. They let her hold him for eighteen hours, then sent her back to prison. She has done the "tour," and her son is a well-traveled six-year-old. He has spent weekends visiting his mother in prisons in Kentucky, Texas, Connecticut (the Pit of Fire), and now at last here, the camp—minimum security, Pekin, Illinois.

13   Ellie looks older than his age. But his shoulders do not droop like his grandmother's. On the contrary, his bitterness lifts them and his chin higher than a child's should be, and the childlike, wide-eyed curiosity has been replaced by defiance. You can see his emerging hostility as he and his mother play together. She tells him to pick up the toy that he threw, say, or to put the deck of cards away. His face turns sullen, but she persists. She takes him by the shoulders and looks him in the eye, and he uses one of his hands to swat at her. She grabs the hand and he swats with the other. Eventually, she pulls him toward her and smells the top of his head, and she picks up the cards or the toy herself. After all, it is Mother's Day and she sees him so rarely. But her acquiescence makes him angrier, and he stalks out of the playroom with his shoulders thrown back.

14   Toby, my brother and sister and I assure one another, will not have these resentments. He is better taken care of than most. He is living with relatives in Wisconsin. Good, solid, middle-class, churchgoing relatives. And when he visits us, his aunts and his uncle, we take him out for adventures where we walk down the alley of a city and pretend that we are being chased by the "bad guys." We buy him fast food, and his uncle, John, keeps him up well past his bedtime enthralling him with stories of the monkeys he met in India. A perfect mix, we try to convince one another. Until we take him to see his mother and on the drive back he asks the question that most confuses him, and no doubt all the other children who spend much of their lives in prison visiting rooms: "Is my Mommy a bad guy?" It is the question that most seriously disorders his five-year-old need to clearly separate right from wrong. And because our own need is perhaps just as great, it is the question that haunts us as well.

15   Now, however, the answer is relatively simple. In a few years, it won't be. In a few years we will have to explain mandatory minimums, and the war on drugs, and the murky conspiracy laws, and the enormous amount of money and time that federal agents pump into imprisoning low-level drug dealers and those who happen to be their friends and their lovers. In a few years he might have the reasoning skills to ask why so many armed robbers and rapists and child-molesters and, indeed, murderers are punished less severely than his mother. When he is older, we will somehow have to explain to him the difference between federal crimes, which don't allow for parole, and state crimes, which do. We will have to explain that his mother was taken from him for five years not because she was a drug dealer but because she made four phone calls for someone she loved.

16   But we also know it is vitally important that we explain all this without betraying our bitterness. We understand the danger of abstract anger, of being disillusioned with your country, and, most of all, we do not want him to inherit that legacy. We would still like him to be raised as we were, with the idea that we live in the best country in the world with the best legal system in the world—a legal system carefully designed to be immune to political mood swings and public hysteria; a system that promises to fit the punishment to the crime. We want him to be a good citizen. We want him to have absolute faith that he lives in a fair country, a country that watches over and protects its most vulnerable citizens: its women and children.

17   So for now we simply say, "Toby, your mother isn't bad, she just did a bad thing. Like when you put rocks in the lawn mower's gas tank. You weren't bad then, you just did a bad thing."

18   Once, after being given this weak explanation, he said, "I wish I could have done something really bad, like my Mommy. So I could go to prison too and be with her."

19   It's now 3:00. Visiting ends at 3:30. The kids are getting cranky, and the adults are both exhausted and wired from too many hours of conversation, too much coffee and candy. The fathers, mothers, sisters, brothers, and the few boyfriends, and the very few husbands are beginning to show signs of gathering the trash. The mothers of the infants are giving their heads one last whiff before tucking them and their paraphernalia into their respective carrying cases. The visitors meander toward the door, leaving the older children with their mothers for one last word. But the mothers never say what they want to say to their children. They say things like, "Do well in school," "Be nice to your sister," "Be good for Aunt Berry, or Grandma." They don't say, "I'm sorry I'm sorry I'm sorry. I love you more than anything else in the world and I think about you every minute and I worry about you with a pain that shoots straight to my heart, a pain so great I think I will just burst when I think of you alone, without me. I'm sorry."

20   We are standing in front of the double glass doors that lead to the outside world. My older sister holds her son, rocking him gently. They are both crying. We give her a look and she puts him down. Charity and I grasp each of his small hands, and the four of us walk through the doors. As we're walking out, my brother sings one of his banana songs to Toby.

21   "Take me out to the — " and Toby yells out, "Banana store!"

22   "Buy me some — "

23   "Bananas!!"

24   "I don't care if I ever come back. For it's root, root, root for the — "

25   "Monkey team!"

26   I turn back and see a line of women standing behind the glass wall. Some of them are crying, but many simply stare with dazed eyes. Stephanie is holding both of her son's hands in hers and speaking urgently to him. He is struggling, and his head is twisting violently back and forth. He frees one of his hands from her grasp,

balls up his fist, and punches her in the face. Then he walks with purpose through the glass doors and out the exit. I look back at her. She is still in a crouched position. She stares, unblinking, through those doors. Her hands have left her face and are hanging on either side of her. I look away, but before I do, I see drops of blood drip from her nose, down her chin, and onto the shiny marble floor.

⌈ REFLECT ⌉ Make connections: Unfair punishment.

Coyne reflects near the end of the essay that she wishes her nephew Toby would "have absolute faith that he lives in a fair country" (par. 16). Yet she expects that, like Stephanie's son, Ellie, Toby will become bitter and angry when he understands that "his mother was taken from him for five years not because she was a drug dealer but because she made four phone calls for someone she loved" (par. 15).

Think about an occasion when you were punished harshly—for breaking a school rule, perhaps, or neglecting to fulfill an expectation of your parents. Although you willingly admit having done it, you may still feel that the punishment was unjustified. Consider what you did and why you think the punishment was unfair. Your instructor may ask you to post your thoughts on a class discussion board or to discuss them with other students in class. Use these questions to get started:

- Why do you think the punishment was unfair? For example, were the rules or expectations that you broke unclear or unreasonable? Were they applied to everyone or applied selectively or at the whim of those in power?

- Coyne uses the value term *unfair* to describe what's wrong with the punishment her sister and some of the other women received. Why do you think Coyne believes her sister's punishment is unfair? Why does Stephanie's mother think Stephanie's punishment was unfair? Do you agree or disagree?

⌈ ANALYZE ⌉ Use the basic features.

DETAILED INFORMATION ABOUT THE SUBJECT: USING ANECDOTES

Including **anecdotes**—brief narratives about one-time events—can be a powerful way to convey detailed information about a subject. Coyne, for example, exposes the effects of separation on mothers and children through powerful anecdotes portraying what happened between Stephanie and her son, Ellie, during their visit.

ANALYZE & WRITE

Write a few paragraphs analyzing Coyne's use of anecdotes to present information:

1. Reread paragraphs 13 and 26, underlining the words that Coyne uses to present Ellie's actions and putting brackets around the words Coyne uses to present his mother's reactions.

2. What do you learn from these anecdotes about the effects on Stephanie and Ellie of enforced separation?

A CLEAR, LOGICAL ORGANIZATION: NARRATING A DAY IN THE LIFE

Coyne uses narrative as a kind of exoskeleton, a shell within which to hold the information and ideas she wants to present to her readers. The occasion is specific: visiting hours at the Federal Prison on Mother's Day. The opening paragraphs situate the profile in time and space, and the concluding paragraphs—signaled with the time marker "It's now 3:00. Visiting ends at 3:30" (par. 19)—recount what happened at the end of the visit. Within this narrative framework, however, Coyne does not follow a strict chronological order. Some events occur at the same time as other events. For example, paragraphs 1 to 3 present actions that occur at the same time: while mothers are getting reacquainted with their children (pars. 1 and 2), the family members are using the vending machines and chatting with one another (par. 3).

ANALYZE & WRITE

Write a couple of paragraphs analyzing Coyne's use of narrative organization:

1. Reread the essay, noting in the margin when the events are happening in relation to the events in earlier paragraphs and highlighting any time markers, such as prepositional phrases locating actions in time, clock time, or verb tenses (past, present, future, and so on).

2. Coyne could have organized her essay topically, by presenting a series of insights and impressions from the many visits she has made instead of focusing on one Mother's Day. How does her choice help you understand the situation of the women and their families?

THE WRITER'S ROLE: ALTERNATING PARTICIPANT AND SPECTATOR ROLES

Instead of choosing between the roles of participant-observer or spectator, writers may also alternate between these two roles, as Coyne does in "The Long Good-Bye." Notice how Coyne uses pronouns (first-, second-, and third-person) to let readers know which role she is taking.

The **spectator,** or **eyewitness,** role shows what is unfolding before the writer's eyes.

2nd-person pronoun   You can spot the convict-moms here in the visiting room by the way they hold

3rd-person pronouns   and touch their children. (par. 1)

The participant-observer role puts Coyne and the other adult visitors into the scene.

1st-person pronouns   I know from previous visits to my older sister. (par. 3)

ANALYZE & WRITE

Write a couple of paragraphs analyzing how Coyne uses these two roles:

1. Analyze the rest of paragraphs 1 and 3, highlighting the first-, second-, and third-person pronouns.

2. Look closely at the way the pronouns are used. Note, for example, that writers seldom use the second-person pronoun *you*; why do you think Coyne uses it here? Who is Coyne referring to with the first-person plural pronoun *we*?

3 Consider the effect that alternating between spectator and participant roles has on the reader. How would your experience as a reader be different if Coyne had stuck with one role or the other? Also think about how alternating the roles helps convey her perspective — for example, how the pronouns align the speaker with certain people and distance her from others (*us* versus *them*).

A PERSPECTIVE ON THE SUBJECT: USING CONTRAST AND JUXTAPOSITION

Profiles may offer a clear perspective on a subject, but unlike an argument for a position or a justification of an evaluation, which tell readers directly what the writer thinks and why, profiles may be more effective when they provide information and ideas that allow readers to draw their own conclusions. One strategy is to use transitions that point out different elements and identify the contrast between them.

Some of them are crying, but many simply stare with dazed eyes. (Coyne, par. 26)

A related strategy is to juxtapose (place next to one another) contrasting elements without explaining the relationship between them:

Some of them are crying. Many simply stare with dazed eyes.

To learn more about transitions indicating a contrasting or opposing view, see p. 327 in Chapter 10.

| ANALYZE & WRITE |

Write a couple of paragraphs analyzing how Coyne uses transitions indicating contrast and juxtaposition to convey her perspective:

1 Skim Coyne's profile, highlighting the transitional words and phrases that indicate contrast. Analyze at least one of the contrasts you've found. What is being contrasted? How does the transition help you understand?

2 Note in the margin which paragraphs focus on Coyne's sister Jennifer and her son, Toby, and which focus on Stephanie and her son, Ellie. What differences between the two families does Coyne emphasize? Contrasts tend to be worth pointing out when there are also important similarities. What similarities do you think Coyne wants readers to think about?

3 Consider how Coyne's use of contrast and juxtaposition—between people, between the world of the prison and the world outside, and between what is and what could have been—helps convey her perspective on the plight of women like her sister and children like her nephew.

[RESPOND] Consider possible topics: Profiling one instance of a recurring event.

Like Coyne, you can also profile an activity occurring over a short period of time, in a relatively small space, involving only a few people. Consider, for example, profiling a team practicing, a musical group rehearsing, or researchers working together in a lab. Try to make more than one observational visit to see the group in action, and arrange to talk with people on every visit, perhaps capturing a few digital images you could use to help you prepare the profile and possibly also to illustrate it.

Gabriel Thompson | *A Gringo in the Lettuce Fields*

GABRIEL THOMPSON has worked as a community organizer and written extensively about the lives of undocumented immigrants in the United States. He has published numerous articles in periodicals such as *New York* magazine, the *New York Times,* and the *Nation.* His books include *There's No José Here: Following the Hidden Lives of Mexican Immigrants* (2006), *Calling All Radicals: How Grassroots Organizers Can Help Save Our Democracy* (2007), and *Working in the Shadows: A Year of Doing the Jobs (Most) Americans Won't Do* (2010), from which the following selection is taken. The photograph showing lettuce cutters at work (p. 69) is from Thompson's blog, *Working in the Shadows.*

"A Gringo in the Lettuce Fields" falls into the category of immersion journalism, a cultural ethnography that uses undercover participant observation over an extended period of time to get an insider's view of a particular community. As you read, consider the ethical implications of this kind of profile:

- What does Thompson's outsider status enable him to understand—or prevent him from understanding—about the community?

- How does Thompson avoid—or fail to avoid—stereotyping or exploiting the group being profiled?

- Toward the end, Thompson tells us that one of the workers "guesses" that he "joined the crew . . . to write about it" (par. 17). Not all participant-observers go undercover; why do you think Thompson chose to do so? What concerns would you have if you were the writer or if you were a member of the group being profiled?

1   I wake up staring into the bluest blue I've ever seen. I must have fallen into a deep sleep because I need several seconds to realize that I'm looking at the Arizona sky, that the pillow beneath my head is a large clump of dirt, and that a near-stranger named Manuel is standing over me, smiling. I pull myself to a sitting position. To my left, in the distance, a Border Patrol helicopter is hovering. To my right is Mexico, separated by only a few fields of lettuce. "*Buenos días,*" Manuel says.

2   I stand up gingerly. It's only my third day in the fields, but already my 30-year-old body is failing me. I feel like someone has dropped a log on my back. And then piled that log onto a truck with many other logs, and driven that truck over my thighs. "Let's

go," I say, trying to sound energetic as I fall in line behind Manuel, stumbling across rows of lettuce and thinking about "the five-day rule." The five-day rule, according to Manuel, is simple: Survive the first five days and you'll be fine. He's been a farmworker for almost two decades, so he should know. I'm on day three of five—the goal is within sight. Of course, another way to look at my situation is that I'm on day three of what I promised myself would be a two-month immersion in the work life of the people who do a job that most Americans won't do. But thinking about the next seven weeks doesn't benefit anyone. *Day three of five.*

3   "Manuel! Gabriel! Let's go! *¡Vámonos!*" yells Pedro, our foreman. Our short break is over. Two dozen crew members standing

near the lettuce machine are already putting on gloves and sharpening knives. Manuel and I hustle toward the machine, grab our own knives from a box of chlorinated water, and set up in neighboring rows, just as the machine starts moving slowly down another endless field.

4   Since the early 1980s, Yuma, Ariz., has been the "winter lettuce capital" of America. Each winter, when the weather turns cold in Salinas, California—the heart of the nation's lettuce industry—temperatures in sunny Yuma are still in the 70s and 80s. At the height of Yuma's growing season, the fields surrounding the city produce virtually all of the iceberg lettuce and 90 percent of the leafy green vegetables consumed in the United States and Canada.

5   America's lettuce industry actually needs people like me. Before applying for fieldwork at the local Dole headquarters, I came across several articles describing the causes of a farmworker shortage. The stories cited an aging workforce, immigration crackdowns, and long delays at the border that discourage workers with green cards who would otherwise commute to the fields from their Mexican homes.[1] Wages have been rising somewhat in response to the demand for laborers (one prominent member of the local growers association tells me average pay is now between $10 and $12 an hour), but it's widely assumed that most U.S. citizens wouldn't do the work at any price. Arizona's own Senator John McCain created a stir in 2006 when he issued a challenge to a group of union members in Washington, D.C. "I'll offer anybody here $50 an hour if you'll go pick lettuce in Yuma this season, and pick for the whole season," he said. Amid jeers, he didn't back down, telling the audience, "You can't do it, my friends."

6   On my first day I discover that even putting on a lettuce cutter's uniform is challenging (no fieldworkers, I learn, "pick" lettuce). First, I'm handed a pair of black galoshes to go over my shoes. Next comes the *gancho,* an S-shaped hook that slips over my belt to hold packets of plastic bags. A white glove goes on my right hand, a gray glove, supposedly designed to offer protection from cuts, goes on my left. Over the cloth gloves I pull on a pair of latex gloves. I put on a black hairnet, my baseball cap, and a pair of protective sunglasses. Adding to my belt a long leather sheath, I'm good to go. I feel ridiculous.

inga spence/Alamy

7   The crew is already working in the field when Pedro walks me out to them and introduces me to Manuel. Manuel is holding an 18-inch knife in his hand. "Manuel has been cutting for many years, so watch him to see how it's done," Pedro says. Then he walks away. Manuel resumes cutting, following a machine that rolls along just ahead of the crew. Every several seconds Manuel bends down, grabs a head of iceberg lettuce with his left hand, and makes a quick cut with the knife in his right hand, separating the lettuce from its roots. Next, he lifts the lettuce to his stomach and

---

[1] A green card is an immigration document that allows noncitizens to work legally in the United States, whether they live here or commute across the border. Undocumented workers (or illegal immigrants, depending on your position) lack green cards. [Editor's note]

makes a second cut, trimming the trunk. He shakes the lettuce, letting the outer leaves fall to the ground. With the blade still in his hand, he then brings the lettuce toward the *gancho* at his waist, and with a flick of the wrist the head is bagged and dropped onto one of the machine's extensions. Manuel does this over and over again, explaining each movement. "It's not so hard," he says. Five minutes later, Pedro reappears and tells me to grab a knife. Manuel points to a head of lettuce. "Try this one," he says.

8   I bend over, noticing that most of the crew has turned to watch. I take my knife and make a tentative sawing motion where I assume the trunk to be, though I'm really just guessing. Grabbing the head with my left hand, I straighten up, doing my best to imitate Manuel. Only my lettuce head doesn't move; it's still securely connected to the soil. Pedro steps in. "When you make the first cut, it is like you are stabbing the lettuce." He makes a quick jabbing action. "You want to aim for the center of the lettuce, where the trunk is," he says.

9   Ten minutes later, after a couple of other discouraging moments, I've cut maybe 20 heads of lettuce and am already feeling pretty accomplished. I'm not perfect: If I don't stoop far enough, my stab—instead of landing an inch above the ground—goes right through the head of lettuce, ruining it entirely. The greatest difficulty, though, is in the trimming. I had no idea that a head of lettuce was so humongous. In order to get it into a shape that can be bagged, I trim and trim and trim, but it's taking me upward of a minute to do what Manuel does in several seconds.

10   Pedro offers me a suggestion. "Act like the lettuce is a bomb," he says. "Imagine you've only got five seconds to get rid of it."

11   Surprisingly, that thought seems to work, and I'm able to greatly increase my speed. For a minute or two I feel euphoric. "Look at me!" I want to shout at Pedro; I'm in the zone. But the woman who is packing the lettuce into boxes soon swivels around to face me. "Look, this lettuce is no good." She's right: I've cut the trunk too high, breaking off dozens of good leaves, which will quickly turn brown because they're attached to nothing. With her left hand she holds the bag up, and with her right she smashes it violently, making a loud pop. She turns the bag over and the massacred lettuce falls to the ground. She does the same for the three other bags I've placed on the extension. "It's okay," Manuel tells me. "You shouldn't try to go too fast when you're beginning." Pedro seconds him. "That's right. Make sure the cuts are precise and that you don't rush."

12   So I am to be very careful and precise, while also treating the lettuce like a bomb that must be tossed aside after five seconds.

13   That first week on the job was one thing. By midway into week two, it isn't clear to me what more I can do to keep up with the rest of the crew. I know the techniques by this time and am moving as fast as my body will permit. Yet I need to somehow *double* my current output to hold my own. I'm able to cut only one row at a time while Manuel is cutting two. Our fastest cutter, Julio, meanwhile can handle three. But how someone could cut two rows for an hour—much less an entire day—is beyond me. "Oh, you will get it," Pedro tells me one day. "You will most definitely get it." Maybe he's trying to be hopeful or inspiring, but it comes across as a threat.

14   That feeling aside, what strikes me about our 31-member crew is how quickly they have welcomed me as one of their own. I encountered some suspicion at first, but it didn't last. Simply showing up on the second day seemed to be proof enough that I was there to work. When I faltered in the field and fell behind, hands would come across from adjacent rows to grab a head or two of my lettuce so I could catch up. People whose names I didn't yet know

would ask me how I was holding up, reminding me that it would get easier as time went by. If I took a seat alone during a break, someone would call me into their group and offer a homemade taco or two.

15   Two months in, I make the mistake of calling in sick one Thursday. The day before, I put my left hand too low on a head of lettuce. When I punched my blade through the stem, the knife struck my middle finger. Thanks to the gloves, my skin wasn't even broken, but the finger instantly turned purple. I took two painkillers to get through the afternoon, but when I wake the next morning it is still throbbing. With one call to an answering machine that morning, and another the next day, I create my own four-day weekend.

16   The surprise is that when I return on Monday, feeling recuperated, I wind up having the hardest day of my brief career in lettuce. Within hours, my hands feel weaker than ever. By quitting time—some 10 hours after our day started—I feel like I'm going to vomit from exhaustion. A theory forms in my mind. Early in the season—say, after the first week—a farmworker's body gets thoroughly broken down. Back, legs, and arms grow sore, hands and feet swell up. A tolerance for the pain is developed, though, and two-day weekends provide just enough time for the body to recover from the trauma. My four-day break had been too long; my body actually began to recuperate, and it wanted more time to continue. Instead, it was thrown right back into the mix and

rebelled. Only on my second day back did my body recover that middle ground. "I don't think the soreness goes away," I say to Manuel and two other co-workers one day. "You just forget what it's like not to be sore." Manuel, who's 37, considers this. "That's true, that's true," he says. "It always takes a few weeks at the end of the year to get back to normal, to recover."

17   An older co-worker, Mateo, is the one who eventually guesses that I have joined the crew because I want to write about it. "That is good," he says over coffee at his home one Sunday. "Americans should know the hard work that Mexicans do in this country."

18   Mateo is an unusual case. There aren't many other farmworkers who are still in the fields when they reach their 50s. It's simply not possible to do this work for decades and not suffer a permanently hunched back, or crooked fingers, or hands so swollen that they look as if someone has attached a valve to a finger and pumped vigorously. The punishing nature of the work helps explain why farmworkers don't live very long; the National Migrant Resources Program puts their life expectancy at 49 years.

19   "Are you cutting two rows yet?" Mateo asks me. "Yes, more or less," I say. "I thought I'd be better by now." Mateo shakes his head. "It takes a long time to learn how to really cut lettuce. It's not something that you learn after only one season. Three, maybe four seasons—then you start understanding how to really work with lettuce."

[REFLECT] Make connections: Switching perspectives.

Thompson joins a community of lettuce cutters to write about their work from the inside. Have you ever experienced an unfamiliar activity or culture? Perhaps you visited relatives in another country, joined a friend's family for an event, or tried out an unfamiliar sport or hobby with a group of experts. Consider what you learned about the culture, the participants, and yourself. Your instructor may ask you to post your thoughts about the experience on a class discussion board or to discuss them with other students in class. Use these questions to get started:

- How fully were you able to immerse yourself in the community? What, if anything, held you back? How did the group members treat you—for example, welcome you warmly, keep you at arm's length, or make you earn their respect?

- How valuable are such immersion experiences to the individual observing, to the group being observed, and to readers in general? What ethical challenges do you see with this kind of participant observation, especially if the writer is undercover, hiding his true purpose, as Thompson was?

- Suppose Thompson wanted to join a community of which you are a member in order to write about it—such as a religious group, sports team, fraternity, or sorority. What elements of Thompson's profile, if any, would cause you to trust or distrust his reporting?

[ANALYZE] Use the basic features.

DETAILED INFORMATION ABOUT THE SUBJECT: USING QUOTATION, PARAPHRASE, AND SUMMARY

Profile writers—like all writers—depend on the three basic strategies for presenting source material: quoting, paraphrasing, and summarizing. Each strategy has advantages and disadvantages. It's obvious why Cable chose this quotation: "We're in *Ripley's Believe It or Not,* along with another funeral home whose owners' names are Baggit and Sackit" (par. 14). But decisions about what to quote and what to paraphrase or summarize are not always that easy.

ANALYZE & WRITE

Write a few paragraphs analyzing Thompson's decisions about how to present information from different sources:

1. Skim the essay to find at least one example of a quotation and one paraphrase or summary of information gleaned from an interview or from background research.

2. Why do you think Thompson chooses to quote certain things and paraphrase or summarize other things? What could be a good rule of thumb for you to apply when deciding whether to quote, paraphrase, or summarize? (Note that when writing for an academic audience in a paper for a class or in a scholarly publication, all source material—whether it is quoted, paraphrased, or summarized — should be cited.)

To learn more about quotation, paraphrase, and summary, see Chapter 18, pp. 430–37.

A CLEAR, LOGICAL ORGANIZATION: NARRATING AN EXTENDED PERIOD

Some profile writers do field research, observing and interviewing over an extended period of time. As an immersive journalist, Thompson spent more than two months as a member of one crew. To give readers a sense of the chronology of events, he uses time markers (such as calendar and clock time, transitions like *next,* and prepositional phrases such as *on my first day*). These cues are especially useful because Thompson's narrative does not always follow a straightforward chronology.

ANALYZE & WRITE

Write a few paragraphs analyzing Thompson's use of time markers and process narration:

1 Skim the profile, highlighting the time markers. Why do you imagine Thompson decided not to follow a linear chronology? How well does he use time markers to keep readers from becoming confused?

2 Why do you think Thompson devotes so much space (pars. 6–12) to narrating the process of cutting lettuce? What does this detailed depiction provide to readers?

For more on time markers, see pp. 54–55.

THE WRITER'S ROLE: PARTICIPATING IN A GROUP

Thompson acts as both a participant and an observer: He does not watch lettuce cutters from the sidelines but works among them for two months. His informal interviews take place during work or on breaks (even at the homes of his coworkers). Nevertheless, there is a significant difference between a two-month experiment and a personal account written by a lettuce cutter like Mateo after a lifetime on the job. A profile writer may participate but is always an outsider looking in.

ANALYZE & WRITE

Write a paragraph or two analyzing Thompson's use of the participant-observer role:

1 Skim the text, highlighting each time Thompson

- reminds readers of his status as an outsider (for example, when he refers to a coworker as a "near-stranger" [par. 1]);

- tells readers about something he thinks will be unfamiliar to them (for example, when he explains that people do not "'pick' lettuce" [par. 6]);

- calls attention to his own incompetence or failings (for example, when he describes his first attempt to cut lettuce [par. 8]).

2 Why do you think Thompson tells us about his errors and reminds us that he is an outsider? What effect are these moves likely to have on his audience?

3 How do the writers whose profiles appear in this chapter use their outsider status to connect with readers? What are the advantages, if any, of adopting the participant-observer role (as Thompson does) instead of the spectator role (as Cable does)?

A PERSPECTIVE ON THE SUBJECT: PROFILING A CONTROVERSIAL SUBJECT

Two of the profiles in this chapter touch on a controversial subject about which people have strong opinions. Cable addresses the commercialization of death, and Coyne, the unfairness of the legal system. While profiles do not engage such debates head on, the way essays arguing a position do, they do offer a perspective on an issue. In doing so, they provide readers with certain kinds of information that they might not get from more explicit arguments.

| ANALYZE & WRITE |

Write a few paragraphs analyzing Thompson's perspective:

1 Start by identifying the subject of the profile. Point to a couple of specific passages in the text that tell you what the subject is.

2 Identify Thompson's perspective on the subject. Consider the title of the profile ("A Gringo in the Lettuce Fields") and the title of the book from which it is excerpted, *Working in the Shadows: A Year of Doing the Jobs (Most) Americans Won't Do*. What do these titles tell you about Thompson's perspective?

3 What do you think Thompson wants readers to take away from the profile? How does the political debate raging in this country about undocumented (or illegal) immigration affect how you understand the subject and perspective of this profile?

[RESPOND] **Consider possible topics: Immersing yourself.**

Thompson's experience suggests two possible avenues for research: You could embed yourself in a group, participating alongside group members, and then write about that experience. For example, you might join a club on campus or try an unusual sport. Alternatively, you could observe life in an unfamiliar group, watching how a meeting or event unfolds, interviewing members to learn about their practices, and conducting additional research to learn about the group.

macmillanhighered.com/conciseguide
How can a slideshow enhance a profile?
E-readings > Sarah Kate Kramer/WNYC, *Niche Market:* Fountain Pen Hospital

The Writing Assignment | 75

Writing a Draft: Invention, Research, Planning, and Composing | 76

Evaluating the Draft: Getting a Critical Reading | 88

Improving the Draft: Revising, Formatting Editing, and Proofreading | 90

The Writing Assignment

Write a profile on an intriguing person, a group of people, a place, or an activity in your community. Observe your subject closely, and then present what you have learned in a way that both informs and engages readers.

This Guide to Writing is designed to help you compose your own profile essay and apply what you have learned from reading other profiles. This Starting Points chart will help you find answers to questions you might have about composing a profile. Use the chart to help you find the guidance you need, when you need it.

STARTING POINTS: WRITING A PROFILE

How do I come up with an appropriate subject to profile?

- Consider possible topics. (pp. 67, 74)
- Choose a subject to profile. (p. 77)
- Test Your Choice (pp. 77–78)
- Conduct your field research. (pp. 78–82)

Detailed Information about the Subject

How can I gather information on my subject?

- Conduct your field research. (pp. 78–82)
- Chapter 16, "Finding Sources and Conducting Field Research"

How can I make my subject come to life?

- Assess the genre's basic features: Detailed information about the subject. (pp. 53–54)
- Detailed Information about the Subject: Using Anecdotes (p. 65)
- Detailed Information about the Subject: Using Quotation, Paraphrase, and Summary (p. 72)
- Integrate quotations from your interviews. (pp. 82–83)
- A Troubleshooting Guide: Detailed Information about the Subject (p. 91)

(continued)

A Clear, Logical Organization

How should I organize my profile?

- Assess the genre's basic features: A clear, logical organization. (pp. 54–55)
- A Clear, Logical Organization: Narrating a Day in the Life (p. 66)
- A Clear, Logical Organization: Narrating an Extended Period (p. 72)
- Create an outline that will organize your profile effectively for your readers. (pp. 83–84)
- A Troubleshooting Guide: A Clear, Logical Organization (p. 92)

The Writer's Role

What role should I adopt in researching and presenting my subject?

- Assess the genre's basic features: The writer's role. (p. 55)
- The Writer's Role: Alternating Participant and Spectator Roles (pp. 66–67)
- The Writer's Role: Participating in a Group (p. 73)
- Determine your role in the profile. (pp. 84–85)
- A Troubleshooting Guide: The Writer's Role (p. 93)

A Perspective on the Subject

How do I develop and express a clear perspective on the subject?

- Determine the writer's purpose and audience. (p. 53)
- Assess the genre's basic features: A perspective on the subject. (p. 55)
- A Perspective on the Subject: Using Contrast and Juxtaposition (p. 67)
- A Perspective on the Subject: Profiling a Controversial Subject (p. 73)
- Develop your perspective on the subject. (pp. 85–87)
- A Troubleshooting Guide: A Perspective on the Subject (p. 93)

Writing a Draft: Invention, Research, Planning, and Composing

The activities in this section will help you choose a subject to profile and develop your perspective on the subject. Do the activities in any order that makes sense to you (and your instructor), and return to them as needed as you revise.

Although some of the activities will take only a few minutes each to complete, the essential field research — making detailed observations and conducting interviews — will

take a good deal of time to plan and carry out. Your writing in response to many of these activities can be used in a rough draft, which you will be able to improve after receiving feedback from your classmates and instructor.

⸬ Choose a subject to profile.

To create an informative and engaging profile, your subject — whether it's a person, a group of people, a place, or an activity — should be

- a subject that sparks your interest or curiosity;
- a subject your readers will find interesting and informative;
- a subject you can gain access to and observe in detail in the time allowed;
- a subject about which (or with whom) you can conduct in-depth interviews.

Note: Whenever you write a profile, consider carefully the ethics involved in such research: You will want to be careful to treat participants fairly and with respect in the way you both approach and depict them. Discuss the ethical implications of your research with your instructor, and think carefully about the goals of your research and the effect it will have on others. You may also need to obtain permission from your school's ethics review board.

Make a list of appropriate subjects. Review the "Consider possible topics" on pp. 67 and 74, and consult your school's Web site to find intriguing places, activities, or people on campus. The following ideas may suggest additional possibilities to consider:

- A place where people come together because they are of the same age, gender, sexual orientation, or ethnic group (for example, a foreign language–speaking dorm or fraternity or sorority), or a place where people of different ages, genders, sexual orientations, or ethnic groups have formed a community (for example, a Sunday morning pickup basketball game in the park, LGBT club, or barbershop)
- A place where people are trained for a certain kind of work (for example, a police academy, cosmetology program, truck driving school, or boxing ring)
- A group of people working together for a particular purpose (for example, students and their teacher preparing for the academic decathlon competition, employees working together to produce something, law students and their professor working to help prisoners on death row, or scientists collaborating on a research project)

<hr/>

TEST YOUR CHOICE

After you have made a tentative choice, ask yourself the following questions:

1. Do I feel curious about the subject?
2. Am I confident that I will be able to make the subject interesting for my readers?
3. Do I believe that I can research this subject sufficiently in the time I have?

Then get together with two or three other students:

Presenters.   Take turns identifying your subjects. Explain your interest in the subject, and speculate about why you think it will interest readers.

Listeners.   Briefly tell each presenter what you already know about his or her subject, if anything, and what might make it interesting to readers.

⸬ Conduct your field research.

To write an effective profile, you must conduct field research—interviews and observations— to collect detailed, firsthand information about your subject. The following activities will help you plan and carry out your field research.

Many writers begin with observations to get the lay of the land and identify people to interview, but you can start with interviews. You may even be able to make observations and conduct interviews during the same visit. Regardless of how you start your field research, come prepared: Dress appropriately, and bring preliminary questions and equipment for taking notes (be sure to ask permission before recording or filming).

To learn more about making observations and conducting interviews, see Chapter 16, pp. 412–15.

WAYS IN

HOW CAN I MANAGE MY TIME?

One of the best strategies for scheduling your time so that everything gets done by your deadline is *backward planning*.

1. Buy or make a calendar (in print or online).

2. Write the date the project is due and any other interim due dates (such as the date that your first draft is due) on the calendar. (Some writers like to give them- selves a personal due date — the day before the official due date — so they have some wiggle room.)

3. Move backward through the calendar, writing in due dates for other parts of the project:

   ▪ Interview and observation write-ups completed (organize your scribbled and abbreviated notes into logical categories, add reflections or additional thoughts, and type your notes in complete sentences)

   ▪ All field research completed

   ▪ Follow-up observations or interviews completed

   ▪ Initial interviews and observations conducted (leave at least a week for this process)

   ▪ Interviews and observations scheduled (leave at least several days for this process)

A Sample Schedule

October						
Sunday	Monday	Tuesday	Wednesday	Thursday	Friday	Saturday
	1 Arrange ——— interviews & observa- tions	2	3	4 ——————▶	5 Research interview subject, locations	6
7	8 Conduct ——— interviews & observa- tions	9	10	11	12 ——▶	13
14	15	16 Write-ups completed	17	18	19 First draft due	20 Conduct any extra research
21	22 Call/E-mail with follow- up questions	23 Revise draft —	24	25	26 ▶ Revised draft due	27
28	29	30	31			

WAYS IN

HOW DO I SET UP AND PREPARE FOR INTERVIEWS AND OBSERVATIONS?

1. Make a list of people you would like to interview or places you would like to observe. Include a number of possibilities in case your first choice doesn't work out.

2. Write out your intentions and goals, so you can explain them clearly to others.

3. Call or e-mail for an appointment with your interview subject, or make arrangements to visit the site. Explain who you are and what you are doing. Student research projects are often embraced, but be prepared for your request to be rejected.

(continued)

Note: Be sure to arrange your interview or site visit as soon as possible. The most common error students report making on this assignment is waiting too long to make that first call. Be aware, too, that the people and places you contact may not respond immediately (or at all); be sure to follow up if you have not gotten an answer to your request within a few days.

4. Make notes about what you expect to learn before you write interview questions, interview your subject, or visit your site. Writing a paragraph or two responding to the following questions might help:

Interview	Observation
▪ How would I define or describe the subject?	▪ How would I define or describe my subject?
▪ What is the subject's purpose or function?	▪ What typically takes place at this location?
▪ Who or what seems to be associated with it?	▪ Who will I likely observe?
▪ Why do I assume it will be interesting to me and to my readers?	▪ Why will my readers be interested in this location or the people who frequent it?
▪ What do I hope to learn about it?	▪ How will my presence affect those I am observing?
	▪ What do I expect to learn about my subject?

5. Write some interview questions in advance, or ask yourself some questions to help you determine how best to conduct the observation.

Interview	Observation
Ask for stories:	Should I observe from different vantage points or from the same location?
▶ Tell me how you got into _____ .	Should I visit the location at different times of day or days of the week, or would it be better to visit at the same time every day?
▶ Tell me about something that surprised, pleased, frustrated you _____ .	
Give subjects a chance to correct misconceptions, including your own:	Should I focus on specific people, or should I identify roles and focus on people as they adopt those roles?
▶ What myths about _____ would you most like to bust?	
Ask for their thoughts about the subject's past and future:	
▶ How has _____ changed over the years, and where do you think it's going?	

6. Conduct some preliminary research on your subject or related subjects if possible, and revise your questions or plans accordingly.

HOW DO I CONDUCT INTERVIEWS?

Take notes

- Clearly distinguish *quotations* from paraphrases/summaries by inserting quotation marks where needed.

- Make an audio recording of what people say, if allowed, but also take notes. If you're worried about keeping pace with a pen, politely ask interviewees to speak slowly, repeat themselves, or confirm your quotations. (Interviewees often fear being misquoted and will usually appreciate your being careful.)

- In addition to writing down what your subject says, describe the interviewee's tone, gestures, and mannerisms.

- To generate *anecdotes,* ask how the interviewee first got involved; if there was a key event worth noting; what most concerns the interviewee; what has been the biggest influence, for good or ill.

- To elicit *process narratives,* ask how something works; what happens if it breaks; whether it was always done the same way; how it has changed; how it could be improved.

- To *classify, compare,* or *contrast,* ask what kind of thing it is; how it's like and unlike others of its kind; how it compares to what it was like in the past.

- To help you with your perspective, ask why the subject is important, how it contributes to the community, or how it could be improved. Ask who would disagree with these perspectives.

- Finally, ask for the interviewee's preferences for handling follow-up questions you might have later.

HOW DO I CONDUCT OBSERVATIONS?

Take notes

- Note your surroundings, using all of your senses: sight, hearing, smell, taste, touch.

- Describe the place from multiple vantage points, noting furnishings, decor, and so on, and sketch the layout.

- Describe people's appearance, dress, gestures, and actions.

- Make a record of interesting overheard conversation.

- Note your reactions and ideas, especially in relation to your preconceptions. What surprises you?

- If you can get permission, look closely over the shoulders of people who are centrally involved.

Consider your perspective

- If you are new to the subject and would like to have a participant-observer role, ask permission to take part in a small way for a limited time.

- If you are an insider, find a new angle so that you learn something new. (For example, if you're on the football team, focus on the cheerleaders or the people who maintain the field.)

Collect artifacts, or take videos or photos

- Collect any brochures or other written material you might be able to use, either to prepare for interviews or to include in your essay.

- Consider taking photographs or videos, if allowed. Try a pan shot scanning the scene from side to side or a tracking shot indicating what you see as you enter or tour the place.

(continued)

Reflect on the interview

Review your notes for five minutes after the interview. Focus on first impressions. Mark promising material, such as

- anything that calls into question your or your readers' likely preconceptions;
- sensory details that could paint a vivid portrait of the place, people, and activity;
- quotable phrases that could help you capture the tone or mood of the subject;
- questions you still need answered.

Reflect on your observations

Take five minutes right after your visit to think about what you observed, and write a few sentences about your impressions of the subject:

- ▶ The most interesting aspect of the subject is _____ because _____ .

- ▶ Although my visit confirmed that _____ , I was surprised to learn that _____ .

- ▶ My dominant impression of the subject is _____ .

Write up your interview

Write a few paragraphs, deciding what to quote, summarize, paraphrase, or omit. Describe the person's tone of voice, gestures, and appearance, as well as details you noticed about the place. You may use some of this material later in your draft. If your interviewee said you could follow up to check facts, e-mail or call with requests for clarification or questions.

Write up your observations

Write a few paragraphs reporting on your visit. This write-up may produce language you can use in your draft. It will also help you think about how to describe your subject, what dominant impression you want to create, and the perspective your profile should take.

Consider another interview

You might also arrange to talk to another person who has different kinds of information to share.

Consider a follow-up observation

Consider a follow-up visit, possibly combined with an interview. Examine other aspects of the place or activity, and try to answer questions you still have. Does the impression you had on the first visit still hold?

⁘ Integrate quotations from your interviews.

Good profiles quote sources so readers can hear what people have to say in their own voices. As you write, choose quotations from your notes to reveal the style and character of the people you interviewed, and integrate these quotations smoothly into your sentences.

When you quote someone directly (rather than paraphrasing or summarizing), you'll need to identify the speaker. The principal way to do so is with a speaker tag. You may rely on an all-purpose verb (such as *says*) or a more descriptive verb (such as *yells out*) to help readers imagine speakers' attitudes and personal styles:

"Try this one," he says. (Thompson, par. 7)

"Take me out to the—" and Toby yells out, "Banana store!" (Coyne, par. 21)

You may also add a word or phrase to a speaker tag to describe the speaker or to reveal more about how, where, when, or why the speaker speaks:

"We're in *Ripley's Believe It or Not,* along with another funeral home whose owners' names are Baggit and Sackit," Howard told me, without cracking a smile. (Cable, par. 14)

Once, after being given this weak explanation, he said, "I wish I could have done something really bad, like my Mommy. So I could go to prison too and be with her." (Coyne, par. 18)

In addition to being carefully introduced, quotations must be precisely punctuated. Fortunately, there are only two general rules:

1. Enclose all quotations in quotation marks. These always come in pairs: one at the beginning, and one at the end of the quotation.

2. Separate the quotation from its speaker tag with appropriate punctuation, usually a comma. But if you have more than one sentence (as in the last example above), be careful to punctuate the separate sentences properly.

Create an outline that will organize your profile effectively for your readers.

Outlining what you have can help you organize the profile effectively for your audience. Compare the following possible outlines to see how you might organize your essay, depending on whether you prefer a narrative or a topical plan. Even if you wish to blend features of both outlines, seeing how each basic plan works can help you combine them.

For more on clustering and outlining, see Chapter 8, pp. 282–87.

If you plan to arrange your material *narratively as a tour,* plot the key events on a timeline. (Brian Cable's profile of the Goodbody Mortuary is a good example of narrative organization.) The following suggests one way to organize a narrative profile of a place:

I. **Begin by describing the place from the outside.**

II. **Present background information.**

III. **Describe what you see as you enter.**

If you plan to arrange your material *topically,* use *clustering* or *outlining* to help you divide and group related information. Here is a suggested outline for a topical profile about a person:

I. **Begin with a vivid image of the person in action.**

II. **Present the first topic.** (A topic could be a characteristic of the person or one aspect of his or her work.) Use dialogue, description, narration, process description,

(continued)

IV. **Introduce the people and activities.**

V. **Tour the place, describing what you see as you move from one part to the next.**

VI. **Fill in information wherever you can, and comment about the place or the people.**

VII. **Conclude with reflections on what you have learned about the place.**

evaluation, or interpretation to illustrate this topic.

III. **Present the second topic.** Use dialogue, description, narration, process description, evaluation, or interpretation to`illustrate this topic.

IV. **Present the third topic** (and continue as above until you have presented all topics).

V. **Conclude with a bit of action or dialogue.**

The tentative plan you choose should reflect the possibilities in your material as well as your purpose and your understanding of your audience. As you begin drafting, you will almost certainly discover new ways of organizing parts of your material.

:: Determine your role in the profile.

Based on your work so far, decide whether you want to adopt a participant-observer role, a spectator role, or some blend of the two. All three options can be engaging and help readers identify with you. The following questions can help you choose, and the sentence strategies will give you some tools for expressing these roles in your paper.

WAYS IN

WHAT ARE THE ADVANTAGES AND DRAWBACKS OF A PARTICIPANT-OBSERVER ROLE?

Advantages

The participant-observer role is a good way to profile physical activities that readers won't know unless you describe them in detail.

▶ As I tried to _____ like the _____, I was surprised to find that _____.

▶ I picked up the _____. It felt like _____ to the touch, and [smelled/tasted/sounded] like _____.

▶ After _____ [hours/minutes/days] of _____, I felt like _____.

WHAT ARE THE ADVANTAGES AND DRAWBACKS OF A SPECTATOR ROLE?

Advantages

The spectator role is a good way to profile places or people. By focusing attention on the subject rather than yourself, you improve the clarity of the picture.

▶ On the other side of _____, a _____ [appeared/came into view/did something].

▶ [Person] talked as he _____-ed. "_____," he said. "_____."

▶ _____ing [at/down/along/with/on] _____, [person] remarked that _____.

If you try to do what the people you're observing do, readers can imagine going through the same experience.

The participant-observer role enables you to explore the effect your actions might have had on the scene.

▶ I interrupted _____ as [he/she] _____ to ask why _____ .

▶ I can't be sure whether that interruption led to _____, but I think _____ .

Disadvantages

The participant-observer role can become distracting if it's overdone—the profile starts to feel like it's about you, rather than the subject. This is particularly true when you are profiling a person or place.

▶ The _____ is [impressive/strange/easy to miss], with [its/his/her] _____, _____, and _____ .

If you describe a place readers may never have been, they can see it through your eyes as you learn about it and look over the shoulders of the people there.

The spectator role enables you to build an aura of objectivity—you're just reporting what you saw and heard.

▶ _____ makes [person] angry. [She/he] says it's because: "_____."

Disadvantages

The spectator role can feel detached, particularly if you are profiling a physical or difficult activity.

WHAT ARE THE ADVANTAGES AND DRAWBACKS TO ALTERNATING BETWEEN PARTICIPANT AND SPECTATOR ROLES?

Advantages

You gain the best of both worlds: By switching back and forth, as Cable and Coyne do, you make activities come alive while portraying places and people without much interference from you.

▶ [Above/around/before] me, [activity happened]. I tried to _____ [an object or activity], and found it _____ . "_____," [person] said, watching, "_____."

Disadvantages

It can be challenging to juggle both roles. When it's not handled well, the result can be confusing to readers.

:: Develop your perspective on the subject.

The following activities will help you deepen your analysis and think of ways to help your readers gain a better understanding of your subject's cultural significance. Complete them in any order that seems helpful to you, and try using the sentence strategies to come up with ideas.

WAYS IN

HOW CAN I DEVELOP A PERSPECTIVE FOR MY PROFILE?

Explore your perspective

Write for five minutes exploring your perspective on the subject — what about the subject seems important and meaningful?

> If you are focusing on a place, ask yourself what you find interesting about its culture: What rituals or habits are practiced there? Who visits it? What is its function in the community?

▶ Without [name of place], [life/business/academics] would be different in [name of community or larger place], according to [interview subject]: [type of people] would/would no longer _____ because _____ .

> If you are focusing on an activity, consider how it has changed over time, for good or ill; how outsiders are initiated into the activity; who benefits from it; and what its value is for the community.

▶ Although [activity] might seem _____, it's important to _____ because _____, says [interviewee]. _____, in particular, benefit from it in the following ways: _____ .

▶ [Activity] today is [somewhat/very] different from [activity] [in the past/long ago/just a few years ago]: Instead of _____, a change brought on by _____, those interested in participating are in for _____ .

> If you are focusing on a person or group, ask yourself what sense of identity they have; what customs and ways of communicating they have; what their values and attitudes are; what they think about social hierarchies or gender differences; and how they see their role in the community.

▶ Despite common assumptions that _____, [subject] thinks of [himself/herself] as _____, an identity that comes across [in/through] _____ .

▶ [She/he] cares less about _____ than about _____, to the point of _____ .

Define your purpose for your readers

Write for five minutes exploring what you want your readers to learn about the subject. Use these sentence strategies to help you clarify your thinking:

▶ In addition to my teacher and classmates, I envision my ideal readers as _____ .

▶ They probably know _____ about my subject and have these opinions: _____ .

▶ They would be most surprised to learn _____ and most interested in the following facets of the subject: _____ .

▶ I can help change their opinions of the subject by _____ and get them to think about the subject's social and cultural significance by _____ .

▶ What I've learned about the subject implies _____ about our shared values and concerns, and I can help readers understand this by _____ .

Consider your main point

Review what you have written, and add a couple of sentences summarizing the main idea you want readers to take away from your profile. Readers don't expect a profile to have an explicit thesis statement, as they do an argumentative essay, but the descriptive details and other information need to work together to convey the main idea.

Clarify the dominant impression

Although you need to create a dominant impression, readers appreciate profiles that reveal the richness and complexity of a subject. Even as Cable shows that the Goodbody Mortuary is guided by commercialism, he also gets readers to think about cultural attitudes toward death, perhaps exemplified in his own complex feelings. To create a dominant impression, try reviewing your notes and write-ups, highlighting in one color the descriptive language that supports the dominant impression you want your essay to create. Then highlight in a second color any descriptions that seem to create a different impression. Finally, write for a few minutes exploring how these different impressions relate to one another. Consider whether they reveal complexity in the subject or ambivalence in your perspective that could be developed further in your essay. You might start with one of the following sentence strategies and elaborate from there.

▶ Although [subject] clearly seemed _____ , I couldn't [shake the feeling that/ignore/stop thinking about] _____ .

▶ Although [subject] [tries to/pretends to/has made progress toward] _____ , [overall/for the most part/primarily] [he/she/it] _____ .

Present the information

Review the notes from your interviews and observations, noting which information you should include in your draft and how you might present it. Consider including the following:

- Definitions of key terms
- Comparisons or contrasts that make information clearer or more memorable
- Lists or categories that organize information
- Ways to show processes or causes and effects vividly
- Quotes that reveal the character of the speaker as well as something about the subject

Write the opening sentences.

You could try out one or two different ways of beginning your essay — possibly from the list that follows — but don't agonize over the first sentences because you are likely to discover the best way to begin only as you draft your essay. Review your invention writing to see if you have already written something that would work to launch your essay. To engage your readers' interest from the start, consider the following opening strategies:

- A surprising statement
- A remarkable thought or occasion that triggers your observational visit (like Cable)
- A vivid description (like Coyne and Thompson)
- An arresting quotation
- A fascinating bit of information
- An amusing anecdote

Draft your profile.

By this point, you have done a lot of research and writing

- to develop something interesting to say about a subject;
- to devise a plan for presenting that information;
- to identify a role for yourself in the essay;
- to explore your perspective on the subject.

Now stitch that material together to create a draft. As you do so, you will notice that some of the sentences you have written based on the sentence strategies in this chapter feel awkward or forced. Revise them, keeping the content but putting the ideas into words and sentence structures that feel natural to you. The next two parts of this Guide to Writing will help you evaluate and improve your draft.

Evaluating the Draft: Getting a Critical Reading

Your instructor may arrange a peer review session in class or online, where you can exchange drafts with your classmates and give one another a thoughtful critical reading, pointing out what works well and suggesting ways to improve the draft. A good critical reading does three things:

1. It lets the writer know how well the reader understands the point of the essay.
2. It praises what works best.
3. It indicates where the draft could be improved and makes suggestions on how to improve it.

A CRITICAL READING GUIDE

Detailed Information about the Subject

Does the writer portray the subject in enough well-chosen detail to show us why it's interesting?

Summarize: Tell the writer one thing you learned about the subject from reading the essay.

Praise: Point out one passage where the description seems especially vivid, a quotation stands out, or another writing strategy works particularly well to present information.

Critique: Point out one passage where description could be added or where the description could be made more vivid, where a quotation that falls flat should be paraphrased or summarized, or where another writing strategy could be used.

A Clear, Logical Organization

Is the profile easy to follow?

Summarize: Identify the kind of organization — narrative, topical, or a blend of the two — that the writer uses.

Praise: Comment on the cues the writer gives that make the profile easy to follow. For example, point to a place where one topic leads logically to the next or where transitions help you follow the tour or narrative. Also, indicate what in the opening paragraphs grabs your attention or why you think the ending works well.

Critique: Point to information that seems out of place or instances where the chronology is confusing. If you think the opening or ending could be improved, suggest an alternative passage in the essay that could work as an opening or an ending.

The Writer's Role

Is the author's role, whether spectator, participant observer, or both, clear?

Summarize: Identify the role the writer adopts.

Praise: Point to a passage where the spectator or participant-observer role enables you to identify with the writer, enhancing the essay's immediacy or interest.

Critique: Point out any problems with the role — for example, if the participant-observer role becomes distracting, or if the spectator role seems too distant.

(continued)

> **Does the author have a clear point of view on the subject?**

A Perspective on the Subject

Summarize: State briefly what you believe to be the writer's perspective on the subject and the dominant impression you get from the essay.

Praise: Give an example where you have a strong sense of the writer's perspective through a comment, description, quotation, or bit of information.

Critique: Tell the writer if the essay does not have a clear perspective or convey a dominant impression. To help him or her find one, explain what interests you about the subject and what you think is important. If you see contradictions in the draft that could be developed to make the profile more complex and illuminating, briefly explain.

Before concluding your review, be sure to address any of the writer's concerns that have not already been addressed.

Improving the Draft: Revising, Formatting, Editing, and Proofreading

Start improving your draft by reflecting on what you have written thus far:

- Review critical reading comments from your classmates, instructor, or writing center tutor. What are your readers getting at?
- Take another look at the notes from your interviews, observations, and earlier writing activities. What else should you consider?
- Review your draft. What else can you do to make your profile compelling?

Revise your draft.

If your readers are having difficulty with your draft, try some of the strategies listed in the Troubleshooting Guide that follows. It can help you fine-tune your presentation of the genre's basic features.

A TROUBLESHOOTING GUIDE

My readers tell me the people do not come alive.

- Describe a physical feature, a mannerism, or an emotional reaction that will help readers imagine or identify with the person.
- Include speaker tags that characterize how people talk.
- Paraphrase long, dry quotations that convey basic information.
- Use short quotations that reveal character or the way someone speaks.
- Make comparisons.
- Use anecdotes or action sequences to show the person in action.

My readers say the place is hard to visualize.

- Name objects in the scene.
- Add sensory detail — sight, sound, smell, taste, touch, temperature.
- Make comparisons.
- Consider adding a visual — a photograph or sketch, for example.

Detailed Information about the Subject

My readers say there is too much information — it is not clear what is important.

- Prioritize based on the perspective and dominant impression you want to convey, cutting information that complicates or does not reinforce that perspective.
- Break up long blocks of informational text with quotations, narration of events, or examples.
- Vary the writing strategies used to present the information: Switch from raw factual reporting to comparisons, examples, or process descriptions.
- Consider which parts of the profile would be more engaging if presented through dialogue or summarized more succinctly.

My readers say visuals could be added or improved.

- Use a photo, a map, a drawing, a cartoon, or any other visual that might make the place or people easier to imagine or the information more understandable.
- Consider adding textual references to any images in your essay or positioning images more effectively.

(continued)

A Clear, Logical Organization

My readers say the narrative plan drags or rambles.

- Try adding drama through dialogue or action sequences.
- Summarize or paraphrase any dialogue that seems dry or uninteresting.
- Give the narrative shape: Establish a conflict, build tension toward a climax, and resolve it.
- Make sure the narrative unfolds or develops and has a clear direction.

My readers say my topically arranged essay seems disorganized or out of balance.

- Rearrange topics into new patterns, choosing the structure that makes the most sense for your subject. (Describe a place from outside to inside or from biggest to smallest; describe a process from start to finish or from cause to effect).
- Add clearer, more explicit transitions or topic sentences.
- Move, remove, or condense information to restore balance.

My readers say the opening fails to engage their attention.

- Consider alternatives: Think of a question, an engaging image, or dialogue you could open with.
- Go back to your notes for other ideas.
- Recall how the writers in this chapter open their profiles: Cable stands on the street in front of the mortuary; Thompson awakens in the lettuce fields, his break over.

My readers say that transitions are missing or are confusing.

- Look for connections between ideas, and try to use those connections to help readers move from point to point.
- Add appropriate transitional words or phrases.

My readers say the ending seems weak.

- Consider ending earlier or moving a striking insight to the end. (Often first drafts hit a great ending point and then keep going. Deleting the last few sentences often improves papers.)
- Consider ending by reminding readers of something from the beginning.
- Recall how the writers in this chapter end their profiles: Cable touches the cold flesh of a cadaver; Coyne watches a mother bleed after being punched by her son.

My readers say the visual features are not effective.

- Consider adding textual references to any images in your essay or positioning images more effectively.
- Think of other design features — drawings, lists, tables, graphs, cartoons, headings — that might make the place and people easier to imagine or the information more understandable.

The Writer's Role

> My readers say the spectator role is too distant.

- Consider placing yourself in the scene as you describe it.
- Add your thoughts and reactions to one of the interviews.

> My readers say my approach to participation is distracting.

- Bring other people forward by adding material about them.
- Reduce the material about yourself.

A Perspective on the Subject

> My readers say the perspective or dominant impression is unclear.

- Try stating your perspective by adding your thoughts or someone else's.
- Make sure the descriptive and narrative details reinforce the dominant impression you want to convey.
- If your perspective is complex, you may need to discuss more directly the contradictions or complications you see in the subject.

> My readers don't find my perspective interesting.

- An "uninteresting" perspective is sometimes an unclear one. Check with your readers to see whether they understood it. If they didn't, follow the tips above.
- Readers sometimes say a perspective is "uninteresting" if it's too simple or obvious. Go back through your notes, looking for contradictions, other perspectives, surprises, or anything else that might help you complicate the perspective you are presenting.

Edit and proofread your draft.

Several errors often occur in profiles, including problems with the punctuation of quotations and the integration of *participial phrases*. The following guidelines will help you check your essay for these common errors.

Checking the Punctuation of Quotations

Because most profiles are based in part on interviews, you have probably quoted one or more people in your essay. When you proofread your writing, check to make sure you have observed the strict conventions for punctuating quotations:

What to Check For

- All quotations should have quotation marks at the beginning and the end.

  ▶ "What exactly is civil litigation?ˮI asked.

- Commas and periods go *inside* quotation marks.

  ▶ "I'm here to see Anna Post," I replied nervously.

  ▶ Tony explained, "Fraternity boys just wouldn't feel comfortable at the Chez Moi Café."

- Question marks and exclamation points go *inside* closing quotation marks if they are part of the quotation, *outside* if they are not.

  ▶ After a pause, the patient asked, "Where do I sign?"

  ▶ Willie insisted, "You can *too* learn to play Super Mario!"

  ▶ When was the last time someone you just ticketed said to you, "Thank you, Officer, for doing a great job"?

- Use commas with speaker tags (*he said, she asked*) that accompany direct quotations.

  ▶ "This sound system costs only four thousand dollars," Jorge said.

  ▶ I asked, "So where were these clothes from originally?"

Integrating Participial Phrases

The Problem   Consider the following sentence:

▶ Snoring blissfully, <u>Bob</u> reclined in his chair.

You know that "Snoring blissfully" applies to Bob, because in English, modifying phrases or clauses like *snoring blissfully* are understood to apply to the nouns they precede or follow. That's why, when you read

▶ Exhausted after 28 hours of studying, <u>Regina</u> sighed loudly.

you know that Regina studied for twenty-eight hours. So what does the following sentence, taken from a 2003 government press release, mean?

▶ Suspected to have been started by an arsonist, <u>the fire investigation team</u> . . . continues its search for the person(s) responsible.

—that the fire investigation team was started by an arsonist? That may not be what the author of this sentence meant, but that's what the sentence says. This kind of error—called a *dangling modifier* — can confuse readers (or make them chuckle).

The Correction   When editing or proofreading your writing, look for modifying clauses or phrases. In each case, ask yourself whether the person or thing performing the action in the modifier is named immediately before or after the modifier. If it isn't, you have several options for fixing the error:

Change the subject of the sentence.

▶ Suspected to have been started by an arsonist, <u>the fire</u> burned nearly 60,000 acres before being brought under control.

Change the modifier.

▶ Suspecting that an arsonist started the fire, the fire investigation team . . . continues its search for the person(s) responsible.

Move the modifying phrase or clause.

▶ The fire investigation team continues its investigation into the fire, suspected to have been started by an arsonist.

macmillanhighered.com/conciseguide
LearningCurve > Fragments

A Common Problem for Multilingual Writers: Determining Adjective Order

The Problem   In trying to present the subject of your profile vividly and in detail, you have probably included many descriptive adjectives. When you include more than one adjective in front of a noun, you may have difficulty sequencing them. For example, do you write *a large old ceramic pot* or *an old large ceramic pot*?

The Correction   The following list shows the order in which adjectives are ordinarily arranged in front of a noun:

1. *Amount* (a/an, the, six)
2. *Evaluation* (good, beautiful, ugly, serious)
3. *Size* (large, small, tremendous)
4. *Shape, length* (round, long, short)
5. *Age* (young, new, old)
6. *Color* (red, black, green)
7. *Origin* (Asian, Brazilian, German)
8. *Material* (wood, cotton, gold)
9. Noun used as an adjective (computer [as in *computer program*], cake [as in *cake pan*])

   1   3   6
Seventeen small green buds appeared on my birch sapling.

         1 2 5   6   9
He tossed his daughter a nice new yellow tennis ball.

  1   4   7   8
The slender German-made gold watch cost a great deal of money.

THINKING CRITICALLY

To think critically means to use all of the knowledge you have acquired from the information in this chapter, your own writing, the writing and responses of other students, and class discussions to reflect deeply on your work for this assignment and the genre (or type) of writing you have produced. The benefit of thinking critically is proven and important: Thinking critically about what you have learned will help you remember it longer, ensuring that you will be able to put it to good use well beyond this writing course.

Reflecting on What You Have Learned

In this chapter, you have learned a great deal about this genre by reading several profiles and writing one of your own. To consolidate your learning, reflect not only on what you learned but on how you learned it.

| ANALYZE & WRITE |

Write a blog post, a letter to your instructor or a classmate, or an e-mail message to a student who will take this course next term, using the writing prompt that seems most productive for you:

- Explain how your purpose and audience — what you wanted your readers to learn about your subject from reading your profile — influenced *one* of your decisions as a writer, such as what kinds of descriptive detail you included, what method of organization you used, or the role you adopted in writing about your subject.

- Discuss what you learned about yourself as a writer in the process of writing this profile. For example, what part of the process did you find most challenging? Did you try anything new, like getting a critical reading of your draft or outlining your draft in order to revise it? If so, how well did it work?

- If you were to give advice to a fellow student who was about to write a profile, what would you say?

- Which of the readings in this chapter influenced your essay? Explain the influence, citing specific examples from your profile and the reading.

- If you got good advice from a critical reader, explain exactly how the person helped you — perhaps by questioning your perspective in a way that enabled you to refocus your profile's dominant impression, or by pointing out passages that needed more information or clearer chronology to better orient readers.

Reflecting on the Genre

Profiles broaden our view of the world by entertaining and informing us with portraits of people, places, or activities. But even effective profiles sometimes offer a limited view of their subjects. For example, the impulse to entertain readers may lead a profile writer to focus exclusively on the dramatic, colorful, or humorous aspects of a person, place, or activity, ignoring the equally important humdrum, routine, or otherwise less appealing aspects. Imagine a profile that focuses on the dramatic moments in an emergency-room doctor's shift but ignores the routine cases and the slow periods when nothing much is happening. Such a profile would provide a limited and distorted picture of an emergency-room doctor's work. In addition, by focusing on the dramatic or glamorous aspects of a subject, profile writers tend to ignore economic or social consequences and to slight supporting players. Profiling the highly praised chef in a trendy new restaurant, a writer might not ask who the kitchen workers and waitstaff are, how the chef treats them, or how much they are paid.

ANALYZE & WRITE

Write a page or two explaining how the genre prompts you to think about the subject of a profile. In your discussion, you might consider one or more of the following:

1 **Consider whether any of the profiles you have read glamorize or sensationalize their subjects.** Do they ignore less colorful but centrally important people or everyday activities? Is this a problem with your own profile?

2 **Write a page or so explaining what the omissions signify.** What do they suggest about the readers' desires to be entertained and the profile writer's reluctance to present the subject in a more complete way?

 macmillanhighered.com/conciseguide
How might you profile yourself for prospective employers?
Tutorials > Digital Writing > Job Search/Personal Branding

4
Explaining a Concept

Concepts are central to the understanding of virtually every subject — in the community, at work, and especially in college. Much of your reading and writing as a student involves learning the concepts that are the building blocks of academic subjects. Concepts include principles or ideals (such as *equal justice* or *the American dream*), theories (such as *relativity* or *evolution*), ideas (such as *commodification* or *states' rights*), conditions (such as *state of flow* or *paranoia*), phenomena (such as *quarks* or *inflation*), and processes (such as *high-intensity interval training* or *socialization*). To communicate effectively and efficiently about a particular subject — whether you are writing to insiders or to novices — you need to be able to use and explain concepts clearly and compellingly.

IN COLLEGE COURSES

For a cultural studies course, a student responds to a writing assignment to analyze the politics of sexuality in advertising. She decides to use the concept of framing she had learned in her first-year composition course the previous term. After reviewing her old class notes, she researches *cultural framing theory* in relation to sexual politics. She finds several sources and cites them to explain the concept. Then, she uses cultural framing to analyze a couple of advertisements she downloaded from the Web. Finally, she posts to her class Web site the final paper, along with the advertisements she analyzed.

© Visage/Stockbyte/Getty Images

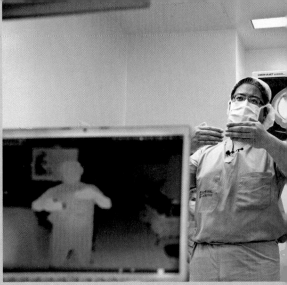

© Doug Nicholson/Media Source

IN THE COMMUNITY

A manager at a marketing research firm gives a presentation on *surveying,* an important research method, to fifth-grade science students. She begins by having students fill out a brief survey on their television-watching habits, and then asks them to speculate on what they expect their answers to show and how this data might be used by advertisers and programmers. Then, with the students' help, she selects the variables that seem significant: the respondents' gender, the number of hours spent watching television, and the types of shows watched. She distributes graphs detailing her analysis and asks the students to see whether the results match their assumptions. She concludes by passing out a quiz to find out how much the students have learned about surveys.

IN THE WORKPLACE

At a seminar for small business owners with minimal knowledge of programming, a technology consultant gives a multimedia presentation on what has been called the *Kinect effect.* He begins by explaining what Kinect is and how it works, showing two clips from the film *Minority Report* to illustrate Kinect's gesture-driven 3-D imaging (multitouch computer interface) and personalized advertising (retina-scanning talking billboards). Then he demonstrates some of its many potential medical uses—for example, enabling surgeons to use gesture to examine a patient's MRI scans during surgery or providing navigational assistance for the visually impaired.

In this chapter, we ask you to explain a concept that is unfamiliar to your readers. Whether you tackle a concept you've studied in college or choose one from your work or your favorite sport, you need to answer your readers' inevitable "So what?" Why should they want to understand the concept? Analyzing the selections in the Guide to Reading that follows will help you learn how to make your concept explanation interesting as well as informative. The Guide to Writing later in the chapter will show you ways to use the basic features of the genre, including how to use visuals and multimedia, to make an unfamiliar concept appealing and understandable to your readers.

PRACTICING THE GENRE

Explaining an Academic Concept

Part 1.   Get together in a small group to practice explaining a concept. First, think of a concept you recently learned in one of your courses. Next, take a few minutes to plan how you will explain it to group members who may not know anything about the subject. Consider whether it would be helpful to identify the course and the context in which you learned it, to give your listeners a dictionary definition, to tell them what kind of concept it is, to compare it to something they may already know, to give them an example, or to explain why the concept is important or useful. Then, take two or three minutes each to explain your concept.

Part 2.   Discuss what you learned about explaining concepts:

- **What did you learn from others' explanations?** To think about purpose and audience in explaining a concept, tell one another whether you felt the "So what?" question was adequately answered: What, if anything, piqued your interest or made you feel that the concept might be worth learning about? If you were to try to explain the concept to someone else, what would you be able to say?

- **What did you learn by constructing your own explanation?** Compare your thoughts with others in your group about what was easiest and hardest about explaining a concept—for example, choosing a concept you understood well enough to explain to others; making it interesting, important, or useful; or deciding what to say about it in the time you had.

Analyzing Concept Explanations

As you read the selections in this chapter, you will see how different authors explain concepts. Analyzing how these writers focus their explanations, organize their writing, use examples and other writing strategies, and integrate sources will help you see how you can employ these techniques to make your own explanation of a concept clear and compelling for your readers.

Determine the writer's purpose and audience.

How well a writer explains a concept can demonstrate how well the writer understands the concept. That is why this kind of writing is so frequently assigned in college courses. But it is also a popular genre outside of the classroom, where writers typically know more about the subject than their readers do. It is especially important to anticipate readers' "So what?" question and excite their curiosity. When reading the concept explanations that follow, ask questions like these about the writer's purpose and audience:

- What seems to be the writer's main *purpose* in explaining this concept—for example, to inform readers about an important idea or theory, to show how a concept has promoted original thinking and research in an area of study, to better understand the concept by explaining it to others, or to demonstrate knowledge of the concept and the ability to apply it?

- What does the writer assume about the *audience*—for example, that readers will be unfamiliar with the concept and need an introduction that will capture their interest, that readers will know something about the concept but want to learn more about it, or that the primary reader will be an instructor who knows more about the concept than the writer does and who is evaluating the writer's knowledge?

Assess the genre's basic features.

■■ Basic Features
A Focused Explanation
A Clear, Logical Organization
Appropriate Explanatory Strategies
Smooth Integration of Sources

Use the following to help you analyze and evaluate how writers of concept explanations employ the genre's basic features. The examples are drawn from the reading selections in this chapter.

A FOCUSED EXPLANATION

Read first to identify the concept. Then ask yourself, "What is the focus or main point?" This point is the *thesis* of a concept explanation, comparable to what we call autobiographical significance in remembered event essays and perspective in profiles. The point answers the "So what?" question: Why are you telling me about this concept? Why is it interesting or important?

Focusing requires that there be thoughtful selection of what to include and what to leave out. For college writing and some other contexts, the focus may be dictated by a specific question or prompt. For example, Patricia Lyu's instructor asked students to do two things: explain a concept they had learned about in a course, and apply that concept to a passage in *The Things They Carried,* a book the class was reading. In the textbook for her Introduction to Psychology course, Lyu had recently read about infant attachment and the research that had been done to establish the concept in the field of developmental psychology. She saw immediately how the concept could be applied to *The Things They Carried,* in particular to explain Dobbins's "peculiar" attachment to "his girlfriend's pantyhose" (Lyu, par. 10).

A CLEAR, LOGICAL ORGANIZATION

Effective concept explanations have to be clearly and logically organized. As you read the essays in this chapter, notice how each writer develops a plan that does the following:

- States the thesis or main point early on

Concept	Let's put love under a microscope. . . . When rigorous people with Ph.D.s after their names do that, what they see is not some silly
Main point	senseless thing. No, their probe reveals that love rests firmly on the foundations of evolution, biology, and chemistry. (Toufexis, pars. 1–2)

- Divides the information into clearly distinguishable topics and forecasts them

Rhetorical questions often announce the topics	How does that bond develop and how does it affect romantic relationships later in life? John Bowlby and Mary Ainsworth's theory of attachment answers both of these questions. (Lyu, par. 1)

- Guides readers by providing cues or road signs

Logical transitions often used in topic sentences	Thus, Harlow's research validated attachment theory . . .
	As an adult, however, . . .
Topic sentence may summarize topic of preceding paragraph and introduce topic of current paragraph	Moreover, . . . (Lyu, pars. 8, 11, 12)
	If, in nature's design, romantic love is not eternal, neither is it exclusive. (Toufexis, par. 8)

APPROPRIATE EXPLANATORY STRATEGIES

Writers explaining a concept typically use a variety of writing strategies, such as *definition, classification, comparison-contrast, example, illustration,* and *cause-effect:*

DEFINITION Defining characteristic Term to be defined	Each person carries in his or her mind a unique subliminal guide to the ideal partner, a "love map," ". . . (Toufexis, par. 17)

CLASSIFICATION Cue signaling classification	From this research, Ainsworth identified three basic types of attachment that children form with their primary caregiver: *secure, anxious* (or *anxious-resistant*), and *avoidant*. (Lyu, par. 4)
COMPARISON-CONTRAST Juxtaposition Cues	Shyness and introversion are not the same thing. Shy people fear negative judgment; introverts simply prefer quiet, minimally stimulating environments. (Cain, par. 9) In contrast, . . . (Cain, par. 19)
EXAMPLE Cues Examples	We find them in recent history, in figures like Charles Darwin, Marcel Proust and Albert Einstein, and, in contemporary times, think of Google's Larry Page, or Harry Potter's creator, J. K. Rowling. (Cain, par. 11) Anxiety . . . can serve an important social purpose; for example, . . . (Cain, par. 22) Despite . . . side effects—nausea, loss of sex drive, seizures—drugs like Zoloft . . . (Cain, par. 3)
ILLUSTRATION (WITH VISUAL) Reference to a visual in the text	The infant monkeys were separated from their biological mothers and raised by a surrogate mother made of wood and covered with terry cloth or made from uncovered heavy wire (see fig. 2). (Lyu, par. 7)
CAUSE-EFFECT Cues	A meeting of eyes, a touch of hands or a whiff of scent sets off a flood. . . . The results are familiar: flushed skin, sweaty palms, heavy breathing. (Toufexis, par. 9)

SMOOTH INTEGRATION OF SOURCES

Although writers often draw on their own experiences and observations in explaining a concept, they almost always conduct research into their subject. As you read, think about how the writer establishes her or his authority by smoothly integrating information from sources into the explanation. Does the writer quote, paraphrase, or summarize the source material? How does the writer establish the source's expertise and credibility?

QUOTE Signal phrase plus background Parenthetical citation (qtd. in = quoted in)	The association between infant attachment and adult relationships was first investigated in Cindy Hazan and Phillip Shaver's appropriately titled breakthrough study, "Romantic Love Conceptualized as an Attachment Process." Since then, attachment theory "has become one of the major frameworks for the study of romantic relationships" (Fraley and Shaver 132). This expansion of the concept of attachment should be no surprise given that Bowlby himself described the formation of attachment as "falling in love" (qtd. in Cassidy 5). (Lyu, par. 11)
PARAPHRASE	It is the difference between passionate and compassionate love, observes Walsh, a psychobiologist at Boise State University in Idaho. (Toufexis, par. 14)

SUMMARY   Studies dating back to the 1960s by the psychologists Jerome Kagan
           and Ellen Siegelman found that cautious, solitary children playing matching
           games spent more time considering all the alternatives than impulsive children
           did. . . . (Cain, par. 19)

How writers treat sources depends on the writing situation. Certain formal situations, such as college assignments or scholarly publications, require writers to cite sources in the text and document them in a bibliography (called a list of **works cited** in many humanities disciplines and a list of **references** in the sciences and social sciences). Students and scholars are expected to cite their sources formally because readers judge their work in part by what the writers have read and how they have used their reading, and also so that those interested can locate the sources and read more about the topic for themselves. (See student Patricia Lyu's essay, pp. 105–10, for an example of academic citation.) For more informal writing—magazine and newspaper articles, for example— readers do not expect references or publication information to appear in the article, but they do expect sources to be identified and their expertise established in some way. (See the articles by Toufexis and Cain, on pp. 111–14, and 117–21, respectively, for examples of informal citation.)

Readings

Patricia Lyu | *Attachment: Someone to Watch over You*

ORIGINALLY, Patricia Lyu wrote this essay explaining the concept of infant attachment for her composition course. You will see that following her instructor's recommendation, Lyu chose a concept she had learned about in another course, Introduction to Psychology, and she quotes from that course's textbook. She also uses a number of other sources, including articles and books, some of which she accessed through the library's Web site and others that she found in print in the library. As you read, consider the following questions as well as those in the margin:

- How effectively does Lyu integrate source material into her own sentences?
- What strategies does she use to cite her sources? Why do you think citing sources this way is expected in most college papers?

> "Babies are such nice ways to start people."
>
> —Don Herrold

Basic Features

A Focused Explanation

A Clear, Logical Organization

Appropriate Explanatory Strategies

Smooth Integration of Sources

1   Fortunately, most people agree with humorist Don Herrold, because infants depend for their well-being, indeed for their very survival, on the goodwill of others. Developmental psychologists have wondered about the bond that needs to form between newborns and caregivers in order for infants to survive and thrive. How does that bond develop and how does it affect romantic relationships later in life? John Bowlby and Mary Ainsworth's theory of attachment answers both of these questions.

2   Bowlby theorized that humans have evolved in ways that made infants and caretakers "biologically predisposed" to send and receive signals ("attachment behaviors" such as crying, smiling, and cooing) that bring the child into close contact with the caretaker, which assures the child's safety, feeding, and likelihood of surviving to reproductive age (Cassidy 4–5). According to psychology professor R. Chris Fraley's "A Brief Overview of Adult Attachment Theory and Research," children develop what Bowlby called an "attachment behavioral system." This system ensures that the attachment object (usually a parent or primary caregiver) will be physically present and attentive to the child's needs. But attachment does not end in childhood. As Bowlby famously stated, it continues to play an important role throughout life, from "the cradle to the grave" (qtd. in Fraley 3). Attachment begins in need and is intensified by fear. As we will see, Tim O'Brien's character Henry Dobbins in *The Things They Carried* provides a fascinating example of how the trauma of war affects adult attachment behavior and may even help explain religious faith.

3   Bowlby's understanding of attachment came from observations after World War II of children separated from parents or other primary caregivers. He saw that "separation anxiety" — being physically apart from the caregiver or perceiving the "threat" of separation — "activates the attachment system" (Kobak and Madsen 30). In his "Overview,"

What strategies does Lyu use in the epigraph and opening paragraphs to introduce the concept to readers? How well do they work to engage readers and give them a map to follow the analysis?

Fraley describes the way the attachment system works and also illustrates it with the flowchart shown in fig. 1:

> the attachment system essentially "asks" the following fundamental question: "Is the attachment figure nearby, accessible, and attentive?" If the child perceives the answer to this question to be "yes," he or she feels loved, secure, and confident, and, behaviorally, is likely to explore his or her environment, play with others, and be sociable. If, however, the child perceives the answer to this question to be "no," the child experiences anxiety and, behaviorally, is likely to exhibit attachment behaviors ranging from simple visual searching on the low extreme to active following and vocal signaling on the other (1–2).

How effectively does Lyu integrate information from sources to support her explanation?

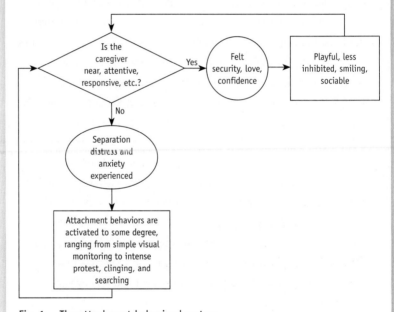

Fig. 1. The attachment behavioral system
Fraley, R. Chris and Phillip R. Shaver. "Adult Romantic Attachment: Theoretical Developments, Emerging Controversies, and Unanswered Questions." *Review of General Psychology*, 2000, 4(2): 132–154. American Psychological Association, publisher. Adapted with permission.

How well do the figures that appear here and elsewhere in the paper help explain the concept of attachment?

4   Developmental psychologist Mary Ainsworth "contributed the concept of the attachment figure as a secure base from which an infant can explore the world" (Bretherton 759). She also designed a series of experiments using "the strange situation" in which researchers watched twelve- to twenty-month-old children through a one-way mirror as they played in an

unfamiliar laboratory playroom, first while their attachment figure was with them and then as the caregiver stepped out of the room for a few moments. From this research, Ainsworth identified three basic types of attachment that children form with their primary caregiver: *secure, anxious* (or *anxious-resistant*), and *avoidant* (Fraley 4).

How does Lyu use Ainsworth's categories to organize this section of her paper?

5   The secure child cries when the caregiver leaves, but goes to the caregiver and calms down when he or she returns. According to Ainsworth, these children feel secure because their primary caregiver has been reliably responsive to their needs over the course of their short lives.

6   Ainsworth classifies the other two styles of attachment as insecure compared to the first attachment style. Anxious children may be clingy, get very upset when the caregiver leaves, and seem afraid of the stranger. They do not calm down when the caregiver returns, crying inconsolably and seeming very mad at the caregiver. Avoidant children ignore the caregiver when he or she returns. They seem emotionally distant and may even move away from him or her to play with toys.

7   Attachment theory was revolutionary: "Before widespread acceptance of Bowlby's theory, psychologists viewed attachment as a secondary drive, derived from primary drives like hunger" ("Attachment" 1). Harry Harlow's primate research lent support to attachment theory, showing that infant monkeys bond to whatever is soft and cuddly. A psychologist at the Primate Laboratory at the University of Wisconsin, Harlow conducted a series of famous and rather disturbing experiments with infant monkeys. The infant monkeys were separated from their biological mothers and raised by a surrogate mother made of wood and covered with terry cloth or made from uncovered heavy wire (see fig. 2). Kimble, Garmezy, and Zigler, in their introductory psychology textbook, describe Harlow's research this way:

How effectively does Lyu transition to and demonstrate the relevance of Harlow's research to the concept of attachment?

> In one experiment, both types of surrogates were present in the cage, but only one was equipped with a nipple from which the infant could nurse. Some infants received nourishment from the wire mother, and others were fed from the cloth mother. Even when the wire mother was the source of nourishment, the infant monkey spent a greater amount of time clinging to the cloth surrogate. (21)

Fig. 2.   Harlow's infant monkey cuddling the cloth surrogate and turning its back on the wire surrogate with the bottle.
Photo by Nina Leen/Time Life Pictures/Getty Images

8   Thus, Harlow's research validated attachment theory by showing that the infant monkeys attached themselves to the more cuddly terry cloth "surrogate" even if it did not have a bottle and therefore could not feed them. Harlow demonstrated that attachment, the need for closeness and comfort, is as strong as the need for food.

9   In other experiments, he also showed that fear is a strong motivator of attachment, leading the infant monkeys to seek consolation from the surrogate. In these experiments, Harlow put a strange object in the cage. If the surrogate was absent or if only the wire surrogate was present, the baby monkey would be afraid, often crying, sucking its thumb, and hiding in the corner. But if the terry cloth surrogate was present, the monkey would run to it, cling for a while, and then, apparently reassured, venture out again to explore the cage and confront the intruder. The conclusion drawn from this research is that the attachment figure provides security, especially in times of fear.

How does Lyu signal the reader that she is shifting from a discussion of infant attachment to a discussion of attachment in adult relationships?

10   The original research on attachment, plus Harlow's monkey experiments, underlines the idea that "the attachment and fear systems are inter-twined" (Cassidy 8). During a time of war, fear obviously is intensified, especially for soldiers in harm's way. Therefore, we can see how applying the

concept of attachment to *The Things They Carried* can be illuminating. It is especially helpful in understanding Henry Dobbins's peculiar habit of wearing "his girlfriend's pantyhose around his neck before heading out on ambush" (O'Brien 117). Fear triggers Dobbins's attachment behavior. Like Harlow's monkey, he seeks comfort from his attachment figure.

11   As an adult, however, Dobbins's attachment figure is the object of his romantic love, his girlfriend. The association between infant attachment and adult relationships was first investigated in Cindy Hazan and Phillip Shaver's appropriately titled breakthrough study, "Romantic Love Conceptualized as an Attachment Process." Since then, attachment theory "has become one of the major frameworks for the study of romantic relationships" (Fraley and Shaver 132). This expansion of the concept of attachment should be no surprise given that Bowlby himself described the formation of attachment as "falling in love" (qtd. in Cassidy 5).

12   Moreover, O'Brien's description of Dobbins's behavior shows that for adults under extreme duress, the attachment process includes the use of substitutes. For Dobbins, in the absence of his girlfriend, her stockings serve as a substitute attachment object, Dobbins's security blanket: "He sometimes slept with the stockings up against his face, the way an infant sleeps with a flannel blanket, secure and peaceful. More than anything, though, the stockings were a talisman for him. They kept him safe" (117–18).

How effectively does this quotation support Lyu's claim about Dobbins?

13   O'Brien makes the further point that the power of the security object comes from Dobbins's unwavering faith in it: "he believed firmly and absolutely in the protective power of the stockings. They were like body armor" (118). Even after his girlfriend abandons him, Dobbins's faith is not shaken because the object itself had taken her place in his attachment system. Dobbins clearly has a very secure attachment style.

14   Through Dobbins's example, we can see that O'Brien appears to be making a connection between having absolute confidence in one's attachment figure and having strong religious beliefs. By calling the stockings Dobbins's "talisman" and emphasizing their magical powers, O'Brien makes the connection explicit. Dobbins's faith, in fact, is so strong that it seems to be contagious. The other soldiers somehow "came to appreciate the mystery of it" (118). Ultimately, we as readers also become invested in

What does Lyu achieve in this conclusion? How does it work for you?

this belief system because, as O'Brien tells us: "Dobbins was invulnerable. Never wounded. Never a scratch" (118). The example of Henry Dobbins suggests that attachment is not only the evolutionary mechanism by which helpless infants survive, but it may also be a precursor to religious belief, the faith that someone is watching over you.

Works Cited

What makes Lyu's sources seem authoritative (or not)?

"Attachment." *Gale Encyclopedia of Psychology*. *Encyclopedia.com*, 2001. Web. 5 Mar. 2012.

Bretherton, Inge. "The Origins of Attachment Theory: John Bowlby and Mary Ainsworth." *Developmental Psychology* 28 (1992): 759–75. Print.

Cassidy, Jude. "The Nature of the Child's Ties." *Handbook of Attachment: Theory, Research, and Clinical Applications*. Ed. Jude Cassidy and Phillip R. Shaver. 2nd ed. New York: Guilford, 2008. 3–22. Print.

Fraley, R. Chris. "A Brief Overview of Adult Attachment Theory and Research." *Dept. of Psychology*. University of Illinois, 2010. Web. 5 Mar. 2012.

What can you learn about creating a list of works cited from this example?

Fraley, R. Chris, and Phillip R. Shaver. "Adult Romantic Attachment: Theoretical Developments, Emerging Controversies, and Unanswered Questions." *Review of General Psychology* 4.2 (2000): 132–54. *PsycArticles*. Web. 6 Mar. 2012.

Hazan, Cindy, and Phillip Shaver. "Romantic Love Conceptualized as an Attachment Process." *Journal of Personality and Social Psychology* 52.3 (1987): 511–24. *PsycArticles*. Web. 4 Mar. 2012.

Kimble, Gregory, Norman Garmezy, and Edward Zigler. *Principles of General Psychology*, 5th ed. New York: Wiley, 1980. Print.

Kobak, Roger, and Stephanie Madsen. "Disruptions in Attachment Bonds." *Handbook of Attachment: Theory, Research, and Clinical Applications*. Ed. Jude Cassidy and Phillip R. Shaver. 2nd ed. New York: Guilford, 2008. 23–47. Print.

O'Brien, Tim. *The Things They Carried*. Boston: Houghton, 1990. Print.

Passman, Richard H. "Security Objects." *Gale Encyclopedia of Psychology*. *Encyclopedia.com*, 2001. 5 Mar. 2012.

For an additional student reading, go to **macmillanhighered.com/conciseguide**. **E-readings** > Ammar Rana, *Jihad: The Struggle in the Way of God*

Anastasia Toufexis | *Love: The Right Chemistry*

ANASTASIA TOUFEXIS has been an associate editor of *Time*, senior editor of *Discover*, and editor in chief of *Psychology Today*. She has written on subjects as diverse as medicine, health and fitness, law, the environment, education, science, and national and world news. Toufexis has won a number of awards for her writing, including a Knight-Wallace Fellowship at the University of Michigan and an Ocean Science Journalism Fellowship at Woods Hole Oceanographic Institution. She has also lectured on science writing at Columbia University, the University of North Carolina, and the School of Visual Arts in New York. As you read, consider these questions:

- How would you describe the tone Toufexis adopts in this essay, at least in the beginning? How effective do you think this tone was for her original *Time* magazine readers? How appropriate would it be for a college paper?

- Given her purpose and audience, how helpful is the visual in helping readers understand her rather technical explanation?

Love is a romantic designation for a most ordinary biological—or, shall we say, chemical?—process. A lot of nonsense is talked and written about it.

> —Greta Garbo to Melvyn
> Douglas in *Ninotchka*

1   O.K., let's cut out all this nonsense about romantic love. Let's bring some scientific precision to the party. Let's put love under a microscope.

2   When rigorous people with Ph.D.s after their names do that, what they see is not some silly, senseless thing. No, their probe reveals that love rests firmly on the foundations of evolution, biology and chemistry. What seems on the surface to be irrational, intoxicated behavior is in fact part of nature's master strategy—a vital force that has helped humans survive, thrive and multiply through thousands of years. Says Michael Mills, a psychology professor at Loyola Marymount University in Los Angeles: "Love is our ancestors whispering in our ears."

3   It was on the plains of Africa about 4 million years ago, in the early days of the human species, that the notion of romantic love probably first began to blossom or at least that the first cascades of neurochemicals began flowing from the brain to the bloodstream to produce goofy grins and sweaty palms as men and women gazed deeply into each other's eyes. When mankind graduated from scuttling around on all fours to walking on two legs, this change made the whole person visible to fellow human beings for the first time. Sexual organs were in full display, as were other characteristics, from the color of eyes to the span of shoulders. As never before, each individual had a unique allure.

4   When the sparks flew, new ways of making love enabled sex to become a romantic encounter, not just a reproductive act. Although mounting mates from the rear was, and still is, the method favored among most animals, humans began to enjoy face-to-face couplings; both looks and personal attraction became a much greater part of the equation.

5   Romance served the evolutionary purpose of pulling males and females into long-term partnership, which was essential to child rearing. On open grasslands, one parent would have a hard—and

dangerous—time handling a child while foraging for food. "If a woman was carrying the equivalent of a 20-lb. bowling ball in one arm and a pile of sticks in the other, it was ecologically critical to pair up with a mate to rear the young," explains anthropologist Helen Fisher, author of *Anatomy of Love.*

6   While Western culture holds fast to the idea that true love flames forever (the movie *Bram Stoker's Dracula* has the Count carrying the torch beyond the grave), nature apparently meant passions to sputter out in something like four years. Primitive pairs stayed together just "long enough to rear one child through infancy," says Fisher. Then each would find a new partner and start all over again.

7   What Fisher calls the "four-year itch" shows up unmistakably in today's divorce statistics. In most of the 62 cultures she has studied, divorce rates peak around the fourth year of marriage. Additional youngsters help keep pairs together longer. If, say, a couple have another child three years after the first, as often occurs, then their union can be expected to last about four more years. That makes them ripe for the more familiar phenomenon portrayed in the Marilyn Monroe classic *The Seven-Year Itch.*

8   If, in nature's design, romantic love is not eternal, neither is it exclusive. Less than 5% of mammals form rigorously faithful pairs. From the earliest days, contends Fisher, the human pattern has been "monogamy with clandestine adultery." Occasional flings upped the chances that new combinations of genes would be passed on to the next generation. Men who sought new partners had more children. Contrary to common assumptions, women were just as likely to stray. "As long as prehistoric females were secretive about their extramarital affairs," argues Fisher, "they could garner extra resources, life insurance, better genes and more varied DNA for their biological futures. . . ."

9   Lovers often claim that they feel as if they are being swept away. They're not mistaken; they are literally flooded by chemicals, research suggests. A meeting of eyes, a touch of hands or a whiff of scent sets off a flood that starts in the brain and races along the nerves and through the blood. The results are familiar: flushed skin, sweaty palms, heavy breathing. If love looks suspiciously like stress, the reason is simple: the chemical pathways are identical.

10   Above all, there is the sheer euphoria of falling in love—a not-so-surprising reaction, considering that many of the substances swamping the newly smitten are chemical cousins of amphetamines. They include dopamine, norepinephrine and especially phenylethylamine (PEA). Cole Porter knew what he was talking about when he wrote, "I get a kick out of you." "Love is a natural high," observes Anthony Walsh, author of *The Science of Love: Understanding Love and Its Effects on Mind and Body.* "PEA gives you that silly smile that you flash at strangers. When we meet someone who is attractive to us, the whistle blows at the PEA factory."

11   But phenylethylamine highs don't last forever, a fact that lends support to arguments that passionate romantic love is short-lived. As with any amphetamine, the body builds up a tolerance to PEA; thus it takes more and more of the substance to produce love's special kick. After two to three years, the body simply can't crank up the needed amount of PEA. And chewing on chocolate doesn't help, despite popular belief. The candy is high in PEA, but it fails to boost the body's supply.

12   Fizzling chemicals spell the end of delirious passion; for many people that marks the end of the liaison as well. It is particularly true for those whom Dr. Michael Liebowitz of the New York State Psychiatric

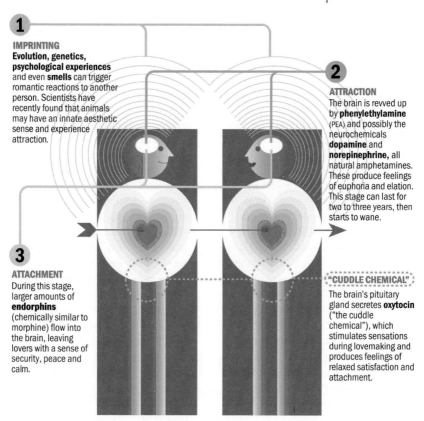

1

IMPRINTING
Evolution, genetics,
psychological experiences
and even **smells** can trigger
romantic reactions to another
person. Scientists have
recently found that animals
may have an innate aesthetic
sense and experience
attraction.

2

ATTRACTION
The brain is revved up
by **phenylethylamine**
(PEA) and possibly the
neurochemicals
dopamine and
norepinephrine, all
natural amphetamines.
These produce feelings
of euphoria and elation.
This stage can last for
two to three years, then
starts to wane.

3

ATTACHMENT
During this stage,
larger amounts of
endorphins
(chemically similar to
morphine) flow into
the brain, leaving
lovers with a sense of
security, peace and
calm.

"CUDDLE CHEMICAL"

The brain's pituitary
gland secretes **oxytocin**
("the cuddle
chemical"), which
stimulates sensations
during lovemaking and
produces feelings of
relaxed satisfaction and
attachment.

Diagram by Nigel Holmes for TIME Magazine

Institute terms "attraction junkies." They crave the intoxication of falling in love so much that they move frantically from affair to affair just as soon as the first rush of infatuation fades.

13   Still, many romances clearly endure beyond the first years. What accounts for that? Another set of chemicals, of course. The continued presence of a partner gradually steps up production in the brain of endorphins. Unlike the fizzy amphetamines, these are soothing substances. Natural painkillers, they give lovers a sense of security, peace and calm. "That is one reason why it feels so horrible when we're abandoned or a lover dies," notes Fisher. "We don't have our daily hit of narcotics."

14   Researchers see a contrast between the heated infatuation induced by PEA, along with other amphetamine-like chemicals, and the more intimate attachment fostered and prolonged by endorphins. "Early love is when you love the way the other person makes you feel," explains psychiatrist Mark Goulston of the University of California, Los Angeles. "Mature love is when you love the person as he or she is." It is the difference between passionate and compassionate love, observes Walsh, a psychobiologist at Boise State University in Idaho. "It's Bon Jovi vs. Beethoven."

15   Oxytocin is another chemical that has recently been implicated in love. Produced by the brain, it sensitizes nerves and stimulates muscle contraction. In women it helps uterine contractions during childbirth as well as production of breast milk, and seems to inspire mothers to nuzzle their

infants. Scientists speculate that oxytocin might encourage similar cuddling between adult women and men. The versatile chemical may also enhance orgasms. In one study of men, oxytocin increased to three to five times its normal level during climax, and it may soar even higher in women.

16   Chemicals may help explain (at least to scientists) the feelings of passion and compassion, but why do people tend to fall in love with one partner rather than a myriad of others? Once again, it's partly a function of evolution and biology. "Men are looking for maximal fertility in a mate," says Loyola Marymount's Mills. "That is in large part why females in the prime child-bearing ages of 17 to 28 are so desirable." Men can size up youth and vitality in a glance, and studies indeed show that men fall in love quite rapidly. Women tumble more slowly, to a large degree because their requirements are more complex; they need more time to check the guy out. "Age is not vital," notes Mills, "but the ability to provide security, father children, share resources and hold a high status in society are all key factors."

17   Still, that does not explain why the way Mary walks and laughs makes Bill dizzy with desire while Marcia's gait and giggle leave him cold. "Nature has wired us for one special person," suggests Walsh, romantically. He rejects the idea that a woman or a man can be in love with two people at the same time. Each person carries in his or her mind a unique subliminal guide to the ideal partner, a "love map," to borrow a term coined by sexologist John Money of Johns Hopkins University.

18   Drawn from the people and experiences of childhood, the map is a record of whatever we found enticing and exciting—or disturbing and disgusting. Small feet, curly hair. The way our mothers patted our head or how our fathers told a joke. A fireman's uniform, a doctor's stethoscope. All the information gathered while growing up is imprinted in the brain's circuitry by adolescence. Partners never meet each and every requirement, but a sufficient number of matches can light up the wires and signal, "It's love." Not every partner will be like the last one, since lovers may have different combinations of the characteristics favored by the map.

19   O.K., that's the scientific point of view. Satisfied? Probably not. To most people—with or without Ph.D.s—love will always be more than the sum of its natural parts. It's a commingling of body and soul, reality and imagination, poetry and phenylethylamine. In our deepest hearts, most of us harbor the hope that love will never fully yield up its secrets, that it will always elude our grasp.

[REFLECT] Make connections: How love works.

The chemistry of love is easily summarized: Amphetamines fuel romance; endorphins and oxytocin sustain lasting relationships. As Toufexis makes clear, however, these chemical reactions do not explain why people are attracted to each other in the first place. Rather, she claims that an attraction occurs because each of us carries a "unique subliminal guide," or "love map" (par. 17), that leads us unerringly to a partner. Make a short list of the qualities in a partner that would appear on your "love map," and then consider Toufexis's explanation. Your instructor may ask you to post your thoughts on a class discussion board or to discuss them with other students in class. Use these questions to get started:

- What role do factors such as family, friends, community, the media, and advertising play in constructing your love map?

- Why do you think Toufexis ignores the topic of sexual orientation?

- According to Toufexis, men typically look for "maximal fertility," whereas women look for security, resources, status, and a willingness to father children (par. 16). Does this explanation seem convincing to you? Why or why not?

[ANALYZE]   Use the basic features.

A FOCUSED EXPLANATION: EXCLUDING OTHER TOPICS

In writing about a concept as broad as love, Toufexis has to find a way to narrow her focus. Writers choose a focus in part by considering the **rhetorical situation**—the purpose, audience, and genre—in which they are writing. Student Patricia Lyu is limited by the fact that she is writing in response to her instructor's assignment. As a science writer for *Time* magazine, Toufexis probably also had an assignment to report on current scientific research. The question is, though, how does she make the science interesting to her readers?

ANALYZE & WRITE

Write a paragraph analyzing how Toufexis focuses her explanation:

1. What is the focus or main point of Toufexis's essay? How do you think she answers readers' potential "So what?" question?

2. How do the title, epigraph, and opening paragraphs help you identify this focus or main point?

3. How do you think Toufexis's purpose, audience, and genre (an article for a popular newsmagazine) affected the focus she was assigned or chose?

A CLEAR, LOGICAL ORGANIZATION: CUEING THE READER

Experienced writers know that readers often have trouble making their way through new and difficult material. To avoid having them give up in frustration, writers strive to construct a reader-friendly organization: They include a thesis statement that asserts the focus or main point—the answer to the "So what?" question. In addition writers sometimes include a *forecasting statement,* which alerts readers to the main topics to be discussed, and include *transitional words and phrases* to guide readers from topic to topic.

ANALYZE & WRITE

Write a paragraph or two analyzing the strategies Toufexis uses to organize her essay for readers:

1. Skim the essay, and note in the margin where she announces her concept and forecasts the topics she uses to organize her explanation. Then highlight the passage where she discusses each topic. How well does her forecast work to make her essay readable?

2. Study how Toufexis connects the topic of "love maps" (pars. 17–18) to the topics she discussed earlier in the essay. Identify any sentences that connect the two parts of the article, and assess how well they work.

APPROPRIATE EXPLANATORY STRATEGIES: USING VISUALS

Patricia Lyu, like Toufexis, uses a flowchart to show the stages of a process she is describing in her essay. In Lyu's case, the visual comes from one of her sources. In contrast, Toufexis's visual was most likely created after her article was written, by the magazine's art editor, Nigel Holmes. Notice also that whereas Lyu, following a convention of academic writing, refers in the text of her essay to her visuals, labels them "Fig. 1" and "Fig. 2," and includes captions, Toufexis does not refer to the visual in her text, and the visual does not have a caption.

ANALYZE & WRITE

Write a paragraph or two analyzing Toufexis's use of the visual:

1 Analyze the visual included in Toufexis's *Time* magazine article. Consider it apart from the rest of the article. What can you learn from the visual itself? What makes it easy or hard to read?

2 Skim Toufexis's essay to mark where she discusses each of the stages in the process described in the flowchart. Considering her original audience, how well does the flowchart work as a map to help readers navigate through the somewhat technical content of her explanation? Would it have been helpful had Toufexis referred to and labeled the visual?

SMOOTH INTEGRATION OF SOURCES: ESTABLISHING CREDIBILITY

To establish their authority on the subject, writers need to convince readers that the information they are using is authoritative. They can do this in a number of ways, but giving the professional credentials of their sources is a conventional strategy.

ANALYZE & WRITE

Write a paragraph or two analyzing how Toufexis establishes the credentials of her sources:

1 Skim the essay, underlining the name of each source she mentions. Then go back through the essay to highlight each source's credentials. When Toufexis provides credentials, what kinds of information does she include?

2 Consider the effectiveness of Toufexis's strategies for letting readers know the qualifications of her sources. Given her original audience (*Time* magazine readers), how well do you think she establishes her sources' credentials? If she were writing for an academic audience (for example, for your class), what would she have to add?

[RESPOND] Consider possible topics: Examining other aspects of love.

Like Toufexis, you could write an essay about love or romance, but you could choose a different focus—for example, the history of romantic love (how did the concept of romantic love develop in the West, and when did it become the basis of marriage?), love's cultural characteristics (how is love regarded by different American ethnic groups or in world cultures?), its excesses or extremes (what is sex addiction?), or the phases of falling in and out of love (what is infatuation?). You could also consider writing about other concepts involving personal relationships, such as jealousy, codependency, stereotyping, or homophobia.

Susan Cain | *Shyness: Evolutionary Tactic?*

SUSAN CAIN is the author of the book *Quiet: The Power of Introverts in a World That Can't Stop Talking* (2012). She also writes a popular blog about introversion and has contributed to the magazine *Psychology Today* on this topic. The selection that appears here was originally published in the *New York Times*. Note that Cain did not include references (as is customary when writing in popular periodicals like newspapers and magazines). As you read, consider these questions:

- Notice the title of this reading and the title of Cain's book. What do these titles lead you to expect? How accurate is your prediction?

- Given that this selection was first published in a newspaper, consider how effective the opening paragraph is as a hook to catch readers' attention.

1   A beautiful woman lowers her eyes demurely beneath a hat. In an earlier era, her gaze might have signaled a mysterious allure. But this is a 2003 advertisement for Zoloft, a selective serotonin reuptake inhibitor (SSRI) approved by the FDA to treat social anxiety disorder. "Is she just shy? Or is it Social Anxiety Disorder?" reads the caption, suggesting that the young woman is not alluring at all. She is sick.

2   But is she?

3   It is possible that the lovely young woman has a life-wrecking form of social anxiety. There are people too afraid of disapproval to venture out for a job interview, a date or even a meal in public. Despite the risk of serious side effects—nausea, loss of sex drive, seizures—drugs like Zoloft can be a godsend for this group.

4   But the ad's insinuation aside, it's also possible the young woman is "just shy," or introverted—traits our society disfavors. One way we manifest this bias is by encouraging perfectly healthy shy people to see themselves as ill.

5   This does us all a grave disservice, because shyness and introversion—or more precisely, the careful, sensitive temperament from which both often spring—are not just normal. They are valuable. And they may be essential to the survival of our species.

6   Theoretically, shyness and social anxiety disorder are easily distinguishable. But a blurry line divides the two. Imagine that the woman in the ad enjoys a steady paycheck, a strong marriage and a small circle of close friends—a good life by most measures—except that she avoids a needed promotion because she's nervous about leading meetings. She often criticizes herself for feeling too shy to speak up.

7   What do you think now? Is she ill, or does she simply need public-speaking training?

8   Before 1980, this would have seemed a strange question. Social anxiety disorder did not officially exist until it appeared in that year's Diagnostic and Statistical Manual, the DSM-III, the psychiatrist's bible of mental disorders, under the name "social phobia." It was not widely known until the 1990s, when pharmaceutical companies received FDA approval to treat

social anxiety with SSRI's and poured tens of millions of dollars into advertising its existence. The current version of the Diagnostic and Statistical Manual, the DSM-IV, acknowledges that stage fright (and shyness in social situations) is common and not necessarily a sign of illness. But it also says that diagnosis is warranted when anxiety "interferes significantly" with work performance or if the sufferer shows "marked distress" about it. According to this definition, the answer to our question is clear: the young woman in the ad is indeed sick.

9   The DSM inevitably reflects cultural attitudes; it used to identify homosexuality as a disease, too. Though the DSM did not set out to pathologize shyness, it risks doing so, and has twice come close to identifying introversion as a disorder, too. (Shyness and introversion are not the same thing. Shy people fear negative judgment; introverts simply prefer quiet, minimally stimulating environments.)

10   But shyness and introversion share an undervalued status in a world that prizes extroversion. Children's classroom desks are now often arranged in pods, because group participation supposedly leads to better learning; in one school I visited, a sign announcing "Rules for Group Work" included, "You can't ask a teacher for help unless everyone in your group has the same question." Many adults work for organizations that now assign work in teams, in offices without walls, for supervisors who value "people skills" above all. As a society, we prefer action to contemplation, risk-taking to heed-taking, certainty to doubt. Studies show that we rank fast and frequent talkers as more competent, likable and even smarter than slow ones. As the psychologists William Hart and Dolores Albarracin point out, phrases like "get active," "get moving," "do something" and similar calls to action surface repeatedly in recent books.

11   Yet shy and introverted people have been part of our species for a very long time, often in leadership positions. We find them in the Bible ("Who am I, that I should go unto Pharaoh?" asked Moses, whom the Book of Numbers describes as "very meek, above all the men which were upon the face of the earth.") We find them in recent history, in figures like Charles Darwin, Marcel Proust and Albert Einstein, and, in contemporary times: think of Google's Larry Page, or Harry Potter's creator, J. K. Rowling.

12   In the science journalist Winifred Gallagher's words: "The glory of the disposition that stops to consider stimuli rather than rushing to engage with them is its long association with intellectual and artistic achievement. Neither $E = mc^2$ nor *Paradise Lost* was dashed off by a party animal."

13   We even find "introverts" in the animal kingdom, where 15 percent to 20 percent of many species are watchful, slow-to-warm-up types who stick to the sidelines (sometimes called "sitters") while the other 80 percent are "rovers" who sally forth without paying much attention to their surroundings. Sitters and rovers favor different survival strategies, which could be summed up as the sitter's "Look before you leap" versus the rover's inclination to "Just do it!" Each strategy reaps different rewards.

14   In an illustrative experiment, David Sloan Wilson, a Binghamton evolutionary biologist, dropped metal traps into a pond of pumpkinseed sunfish. The "rover" fish couldn't help but investigate—and were immediately caught. But the "sitter" fish stayed back, making it impossible for Professor Wilson to capture them. Had Professor Wilson's traps posed a real threat, only the sitters would have survived. But had the sitters taken Zoloft and become more like bold rovers, the entire family of pumpkinseed sunfish would have been wiped out. "Anxiety" about the trap saved the fishes' lives.

15   Next, Professor Wilson used fishing nets to catch both types of fish; when he carried them back to his lab, he noted that the rovers quickly acclimated to their new environment and started eating a full five days earlier than their sitter brethren. In this situation, the rovers were the likely survivors. "There is no single best . . . [animal] personality," Professor Wilson concludes in his book, *Evolution for Everyone,* "but rather a diversity of personalities maintained by natural selection."

16   The same might be said of humans, 15 percent to 20 percent of whom are also born with sitter-like temperaments that predispose them to shyness and introversion. (The overall incidence of shyness and introversion is higher—40 percent of the population for shyness, according to the psychology professor Jonathan Cheek, and 50 percent for introversion. Conversely, some born sitters never become shy or introverted at all.)

17   Once you know about sitters and rovers, you see them everywhere, especially among young children. Drop in on your local Mommy and Me music class: there are the sitters, intently watching the action from their mothers' laps, while the rovers march around the room banging their drums and shaking their maracas.

18   Relaxed and exploratory, the rovers have fun, make friends and will take risks, both rewarding and dangerous ones, as they grow. According to Daniel Nettle, a Newcastle University evolutionary psychologist, extroverts are more likely than introverts to be hospitalized as a result of an injury, have affairs (men) and change relationships (women). One study of bus drivers even found that accidents are more likely to occur when extroverts are at the wheel.

19   In contrast, sitter children are careful and astute, and tend to learn by observing instead of by acting. They notice scary things more than other children do, but they also notice more things in general.

Studies dating all the way back to the 1960s by the psychologists Jerome Kagan and Ellen Siegelman found that cautious, solitary children playing matching games spent more time considering all the alternatives than impulsive children did, actually using more eye movements to make decisions. Recent studies by a group of scientists at Stony Brook University and at Chinese universities using functional MRI technology echoed this research, finding that adults with sitter-like temperaments looked longer at pairs of photos with subtle differences and showed more activity in brain regions that make associations between the photos and other stored information in the brain.

20   Once they reach school age, many sitter children use such traits to great effect. Introverts, who tend to digest information thoroughly, stay on task, and work accurately, earn disproportionate numbers of National Merit Scholarship finalist positions and Phi Beta Kappa keys, according to the Center for Applications of Psychological Type, a research arm for the Myers-Briggs personality type indicator—even though their IQ scores are no higher than those of extroverts. Another study, by the psychologists Eric Rolfhus and Philip Ackerman, tested 141 college students' knowledge of 20 different subjects, from art to astronomy to statistics, and found that the introverts knew more than the extroverts about 19 subjects— presumably, the researchers concluded, because the more time people spend socializing, the less time they have for learning.

21   The psychologist Gregory Feist found that many of the most creative people in a range of fields are introverts who are comfortable working in solitary conditions in which they can focus attention inward. Steve Wozniak, the engineer who founded Apple with Steve Jobs, is a prime example: Mr. Wozniak describes his creative process as

an exercise in solitude. "Most inventors and engineers I've met are like me," he writes in "iWoz," his autobiography. "They're shy and they live in their heads. They're almost like artists. In fact, the very best of them are artists. And artists work best alone. . . . Not on a committee. Not on a team."

22   Sitters' temperaments also confer more subtle advantages. Anxiety, it seems, can serve an important social purpose; for example, it plays a key role in the development of some children's consciences. When caregivers rebuke them for acting up, they become anxious, and since anxiety is unpleasant, they tend to develop pro-social behaviors. Shy children are often easier to socialize and more conscientious, according to the developmental psychologist Grazyna Kochanska. By six they're less likely than their peers to cheat or break rules, even when they think they can't be caught, according to one study. By seven they're more likely to be described by their parents as having high levels of moral traits such as empathy.

23   When I shared this information with the mother of a "sitter" daughter, her reaction was mixed. "That is all very nice," she said, "but how will it help her in the tough real world?" But sensitivity, if it is not excessive and is properly nurtured, can be a catalyst for empathy and even leadership. Eleanor Roosevelt, for example, was a courageous leader who was very likely a sitter. Painfully shy and serious as a child, she grew up to be a woman who could not look away from other people's suffering—and who urged her husband, the constitutionally buoyant F.D.R., to do the same; the man who had nothing to fear but fear itself relied, paradoxically, on a woman deeply acquainted with it.

24   Another advantage sitters bring to leadership is a willingness to listen to and implement other people's ideas. A groundbreaking study led by the Wharton management professor Adam Grant, to be published this month in *The Academy of Management Journal*,[1] found that introverts outperform extroverts when leading teams of proactive workers—the kinds of employees who take initiative and are disposed to dream up better ways of doing things. Professor Grant notes that business self-help guides often suggest that introverted leaders practice their communication skills and smile more. But, he told me, it may be extrovert leaders who need to change, to listen more and say less.

25   What would the world look like if all our sitters chose to medicate themselves? The day may come when we have pills that "cure" shyness and turn introverts into social butterflies—without the side effects and other drawbacks of today's medications. (A recent study suggests that today's SSRI's not only relieve social anxiety but also induce extroverted behavior.) The day may come—and might be here already—when people are as comfortable changing their psyches as the color of their hair. If we continue to confuse shyness with sickness, we may find ourselves in a world of all rovers and no sitters, of all yang and no yin.

26   As a sitter who enjoys an engaged, productive life, and a professional speaking career, but still experiences the occasional knock-kneed moment, I can understand why caring physicians prescribe available medicine and encourage effective non-pharmaceutical treatments such as cognitive-behavioral therapy.

27   But even non-medical treatments emphasize what is wrong with the people who use them. They don't focus on what is right. Perhaps we need to rethink our approach to social anxiety: to address the pain, but to respect the temperament that

---

[1]The article, "Leading with Meaning: Beneficiary Contact, Prosocial Impact, and the Performance Effects of Transformational Leadership" was published in the April 2012 edition, Volume 55.2. [Editor's note]

underlies it. The act of treating shyness as an illness obscures the value of that temperament. Ridding people of social unease need not involve pathologizing their fundamental nature, but rather urging them to use its gifts.

28   It's time for the young woman in the Zoloft ad to rediscover her allure.

[REFLECT] Make connections: What's wrong with being shy?

Cain asserts that "shyness and introversion share an undervalued status in a world that prizes extroversion. . . . As a society, we prefer action to contemplation, risk-taking to heed-taking, certainty to doubt" (par. 10). To explore these categories of introversion and extroversion and to test Cain's assertion about society's valuing one personality type over the other, think of someone you would describe as introverted and someone else who seems to be extroverted. (Include yourself, if you like.) What in particular leads you to classify these individuals as introverts or extroverts? Consider whether personality type has any effect on how other people react to them or whether they are more or less successful in school or in social or work contexts. Your instructor may ask you to post your thoughts on a class discussion board or to discuss them with other students in class. Use these questions to get you started:

- What do you think are the defining characteristics of these two personality types?
- Which, if any, of these characteristics seem to be overvalued or devalued? By whom and in what contexts? Why?
- Cain raises a question about the way psychiatrists and the pharmaceutical industry may be pathologizing shyness or introversion—in other words, "encouraging perfectly healthy shy people to see themselves as ill" (par. 4). What do you think about this issue?

[ANALYZE] Use the basic features.

A FOCUSED EXPLANATION: PRESENTING ESTABLISHED INFORMATION AND YOUR OWN IDEAS

Writing for her instructor and classmates in an English class, Patricia Lyu can assume that the psychological concept she is explaining is unfamiliar to her audience, and because it is a topic in her Introduction to Psychology textbook, she can be confident that it is widely accepted and a basic building block of the field. However, when she applies the concept to a book her readers know well and uses the concept to interpret Henry Dobbins's "peculiar habit" in *The Things They Carried* (par. 10), Lyu's purpose becomes more complicated. She is not only reporting established information about a concept but also presenting her own ideas. Her readers are not likely to question the concept, as long as she provides authoritative sources to back it up, but they may very well question her application of the concept. Therefore, Lyu needs to provide evidence, quoting from *The Things They Carried* to convince readers that her use of the concept makes sense and that it helps to explain Dobbins's behavior. Concept explanations nearly always entail this kind of shift from reporting established information to presenting the writer's own ideas about the concept and offering supportive evidence.

Write a paragraph or two analyzing how Cain reports information and also presents her own ideas:

1. Reread paragraph 5, in which Cain states her thesis. How does the phrase between dashes in the first sentence ("or more precisely, the careful, sensitive temperament from which both often spring") help to unify the different phenomena she describes in this article?

2. Consider the second and third sentences in paragraph 5. How do these sentences help convey Cain's purpose?

3. Skim the rest of the article, looking for places where Cain restates the ideas she conveys in sentences 2 and 3 of paragraph 5. Highlight the words and phrases that restate this theme.

4. Consider how effective Cain's tactics are: After reading the article, do you know what shyness is? Are you persuaded that it is underrated? Why or why not?

A CLEAR, LOGICAL ORGANIZATION: CREATING CLOSURE

Patricia Lyu refers to British psychologist John Bowlby near the beginning and the end of her paper. In paragraph 2, she introduces the concept of attachment as a survival strategy, and then in paragraph 10, she notes Bowlby's assessment of attachment as "intertwined" with fear. With these two references to Bowlby, Lyu creates a sense of closure, a sense that readers have come full circle. Cain also uses this strategy.

Write a paragraph or two analyzing how Cain creates a sense of closure in her article:

1. Skim paragraphs 1–8 and 25–28 to remind yourself of how Cain begins and ends the reading selection. What image does she start with? What image does she end with? How does she make sense of this image for her readers? What context does she put it in?

2. Notice the pronouns she uses: *she, we, us, they, I*. How does the shift—from talking about the shy, the introverted, the "sitters," in the third person (*she/he/they*) to talking about them in the first person (*I/we*)—change the context in which the Zoloft ad is presented? How does this shift in the pronouns Cain uses add or detract from the sense of closure?

APPROPRIATE EXPLANATORY STRATEGIES: USING COMPARISON-CONTRAST

Writers explaining concepts often use comparison and contrast. Research has shown that seeing how unfamiliar concepts are similar to or different from concepts we already know facilitates the learning of new concepts. Even when both concepts are unfamiliar, comparing foregrounds commonalities, while contrasting makes visible inconsistencies we might not otherwise notice.

Writers employ many strategies to signal comparisons and contrasts, including words that emphasize similarity or difference, and repeating sentence patterns to highlight the differences:

COMPARISONS	Like Harlow's monkey, he seeks comfort from his attachment figure.
Like: word emphasizing similarity	(Lyu, par. 10)
CONTRASTS	"Early love is when you love the way the other person makes you
Repeated sentence pattern highlights the contrast	feel." . . . "Mature love is when you love the person as he or she is." It is the difference between passionate and compassionate love. . . . "It's Bon Jovi vs. Beethoven." (Toufexis, par. 14)

ANALYZE & WRITE

Write a paragraph or two analyzing Cain's strategies for showing contrast:

1. Find and highlight two or three of the sentence patterns Cain uses for cueing contrast in paragraphs 3–4, 9, 10, 13, 18, and 19.

2. Analyze what is being contrasted and how each contrast works.

3. Why do you think Cain uses contrast so often in this essay?

SMOOTH INTEGRATION OF SOURCES: USING EVIDENCE FROM A SOURCE TO SUPPORT A CLAIM

Cain's article first appeared in the *New York Times*. So, like Toufexis, whose article was originally published in a popular periodical, Cain names her sources and mentions their credentials but does not cite them as you must do when writing a paper for a class. While Cain does not cite her sources formally, as academic writing requires, she does integrate her sources effectively by

- Making a claim of her own

- Showing how the evidence she provides supports her claim

- Naming her source author(s) in a signal phrase (name plus an appropriate verb) and mentioning his, her, or their credentials

- Providing appropriate, relevant supporting evidence

Look at how Cain achieves these goals:

Cain's idea	*As a society, we prefer action to contemplation, risk-taking to heed-*
Research findings supporting Cain's idea	*taking, certainty to doubt.* Studies show that we rank fast and frequent talkers as more competent, likable and even smarter
Author credentials and signal phrase	than slow ones. As the psychologists William Hart and Dolores Albarracin point out, phrases like "get active," "get moving,"
Links Cain's idea and research findings	"do something" and similar calls to action surface repeatedly in recent books. (par. 10)

ANALYZE & WRITE

Write a paragraph analyzing how Cain integrates source material elsewhere in her article:

1. Examine paragraphs 18–19 or 20–21 to see how Cain uses a pattern similar to the one described above.

2 Find and mark the elements: Cain's idea; the name(s) and credentials of the source or sources; what the source found; text linking the source's findings to the original idea or extending the idea in some way.

3 When writers use information from sources, why do you think they often begin by stating their own idea (even if they got the idea from a source)? What do you think would be the effect on readers if the opening sentence of paragraph 18 or 20 began with the source instead of with Cain's topic sentence?

[RESPOND] Consider possible topics: Correcting a misunderstood concept.

Cain writes in this article about a concept she thinks has been misunderstood or misused. Consider other concepts that you think need clarification. For example, you might consider concepts such as *attention-deficit hyperactivity disorder (ADHD)*, *autism spectrum*, or *transgender*. Alternatively, you might consider contested political concepts such as *liberal, conservative, corporate personhood, American exceptionalism,* or *regime change*.

macmillanhighered.com/conciseguide
How can a graphic illustrate and explain a concept?
E-readings > National Geographic Online, *Mapping Memory*

GUIDE TO WRITING

The Writing Assignment | **125**

Writing a Draft: Invention, Research, Planning, and Composing | **127**

Evaluating the Draft: Getting a Critical Reading | **136**

Improving the Draft: Revising, Formatting, Editing, and Proofreading | **137**

The Writing Assignment

Write an essay explaining an important and interesting concept, one you already know well or are just learning about. Consider what your readers are likely to know and think about the concept, what you might want them to learn about it, and whether you can research it sufficiently in the time you have.

This Guide to Writing is designed to help you compose your own concept explanation and apply what you have learned from reading other concept explanations. This Starting Points chart will help you find answers to questions you might have about explaining a concept. Use it to find the guidance you need, when you need it.

STARTING POINTS: EXPLAINING A CONCEPT

How do I come up with a concept to write about?

- Consider Possible Topics (pp. 116–17 and 124)
- Choose a concept to write about. (p. 127)
- Test Your Choice (p. 128)

How can I decide on a focus for my concept?

- Assess the genre's basic features: A focused explanation. (pp. 101–102)
- Conduct initial research on the concept. (p. 128)
- Focus your explanation of the concept. (p. 129)
- Test Your Choice (p. 130)
- Conduct further research on your focused concept. (p. 130)

A Focused Explanation

How can I make my concept interesting to my readers?

- A Focused Explanation: Presenting Established Information and Your Own Ideas (p. 121)
- Focus your explanation of the concept. (p. 129)
- Test Your Choice (p. 130)
- Draft your working thesis. (pp. 130–31)
- Write the opening sentences. (p. 135)
- A Troubleshooting Guide: A Focused Explanation (p. 138)

(continued)

A Clear, Logical Organization

How should I organize my explanation so that it's logical and easy to read?

- Assess the genre's basic features: A clear, logical organization. (p. 102)
- A Clear, Logical Organization: Creating Closure (p. 122)
- Organize your concept explanation effectively for your readers. (p. 131)
- A Troubleshooting Guide: A Clear, Logical Organization (pp. 138–39)

What kinds of cues should I provide?

- Assess the genre's basic features: A clear, logical organization. (p. 1)
- A Clear, Logical Organization: Cueing the Reader (p. 115)
- Draft your working thesis. (pp. 130–31)

Appropriate Explanatory Strategies

What's the best way to explain my concept? What writing strategies should I use?

- Assess the genre's basic features: Appropriate explanatory strategies. (pp. 102–103)
- Appropriate Explanatory Strategies: Using Visuals (p. 116)
- Appropriate Explanatory Strategies: Using Comparison-Contrast (pp. 122–23)
- Consider the explanatory strategies you should use. (pp. 131–32)
- Use summaries, paraphrases, and quotations from sources to support your points. (p. 133)
- Use visuals or multimedia illustrations to enhance your explanation. (p. 133)
- A Troubleshooting Guide: Appropriate Explanatory Strategies (pp. 139–40)

Smooth Integration of Sources

How should I integrate sources so that they support my argument?

- Assess the genre's basic features: Smooth integration of sources. (pp. 103–104)
- Use appositives to integrate sources. (pp. 133–34)
- Use descriptive verbs in signal phrases to introduce information from sources. (p. 134)
- A Troubleshooting Guide: Smooth Integration of Sources (p. 140)

Writing a Draft: Invention, Research, Planning, and Composing

The activities in this section will help you choose a concept and develop an explanation that will appeal to your readers, using appropriate explanatory strategies as well as photographs, tables, charts, and other illustrations. Do the activities in any order that makes sense to you (and your instructor), and return to them as needed as you revise. They are easy to complete and should take only a few minutes each. Spreading them out over several days will stimulate your creativity, enabling you to find a concept and strategies for explaining it that work for you and your readers. Remember to keep good notes: You'll need them when you draft and revise.

▪▪ Choose a concept to write about.

Come up with a list of possible concepts you might write about. For the best results, your concept should be one that

- you understand well or feel eager to learn more about;
- you think is important and will interest your readers;
- you can research sufficiently in the allotted time;
- you can explain clearly in the length prescribed by your instructor.

To get your juices flowing, review the Consider Possible Topics activities on pages 116 and 124 or reread notes you made in response to those suggestions. The following list suggests some good concepts:

College Courses

- **Literature and cultural studies:** irony, semiotics, dystopia, canon, postmodernism, realism, genre, connotation
- **Psychology and sociology:** assimilation/accommodation, social cognition, emotional intelligence, the Stroop effect, trauma, theory of mind, deviance, ethnocentrism, social stratification, acculturation, cultural relativism, patriarchy
- **Biology, nursing, and the physical sciences:** morphogenesis, electron transport, phagocytosis, homozygosity, diffusion, mass, energy, gravity, entropy, communicable diseases, epidemiology, toxicology, holistic medicine, pathogen

Community

- **Identity and community:** multiculturalism, racism, social contract, community policing, social Darwinism, identity politics, public space
- **Environment:** fracking, toxic waste, endangered species, sustainability

Workplace and Business Management

- **Work:** private and public sector, minimum wage, affirmative action, glass ceiling, downsizing, collective bargaining, robotics
- **Management and finance:** risk management, leveraged buyout, deregulation, branding, economy of scale, monopoly capitalism, socially conscious investing

To decide whether to proceed with this concept, ask yourself the following questions:

- Can I answer my readers' inevitable "So what?" question and make the concept seem interesting and worth knowing about?
- Am I interested in the concept and can I focus my explanation?
- Do I know enough about the concept now, or can I research it in the time I have?

Conduct initial research on the concept.

You will need to research your concept in three stages:

1. Gain an overview of the concept.
2. Identify an aspect of the concept to focus on.
3. Conduct enough research to learn about this aspect of the concept.

The following activities will help you begin putting your ideas into words that you may be able to use as you draft.

WAYS IN

WHAT DO I ALREADY KNOW?

Describe what you already know about the concept, reviewing textbooks and lecture notes as needed.

Why have you chosen the concept and why do you find it interesting?

- ▶ My concept is important/useful for the study of _____ because _____.

Explain the concept briefly, using as a starting point the sentence strategies below.

- ▶ My concept can be divided into _____ categories: _____, _____, _____.

- ▶ Examples of my concept include _____, _____, and _____.

- ▶ My concept is a _____ [member of a larger category] that is/does/has _____ [defining characteristics].

- ▶ My concept is [similar to/different from] _____ in these ways: _____.

WHAT DO I NEED TO LEARN?

Conduct a search on your concept using a reference database such as the Gale Virtual Reference Library or Web of Science. After reading several articles, list the following:

- *Names* of experts on your subject
- Terms, phrases, or synonyms that you might use as *search terms* later
- *Interesting aspects* of the concept that you might want to focus on

Conduct a search for relevant books on your topic, and then click on each library record to find additional subject terms.

Enter the word *overview* or *definition* with the name of your concept into a search engine, and skim the top ten search results to get a general sense of your topic. Bookmark useful links, or save a copy (.*edu*, .*gov*, or .*org* sites are more likely to be reliable than .*com* sites).

⠿ Focus your explanation of the concept.

You cannot realistically explain every aspect of your concept thoroughly in a short writing project. Instead, focus on an aspect of the concept that interests you and will interest your readers. The following activities will help you choose a tentative focus, which you will likely refine as you do further research and writing.

WAYS IN

WHAT MAKES THE CONCEPT INTERESTING TO ME AND MY READERS?

- List two or three aspects of your concept that interest you, and then answer these questions:
  - Why does it interest you?
  - How is it relevant to your life, family, community, work, or studies?
  - What do you already know about this aspect of the concept? What would you like to learn about it?
- Ask yourself questions about your concept:
  - What is it similar to?
  - How is it different from related concepts?
  - What parts or features distinguish it from other concepts?
  - What are its cultural or historical contexts?
- Write for five minutes about your concept, focusing on what you already know.
- Analyze your audience by brainstorming answers to the following questions:
  - Who are your readers, and what is the context in which they will be reading your explanation? What aspects of the concept do you think they would want to know about?
  - How would you answer your readers' "So what?" question? Think of at least one aspect of the concept that is relevant to their life, family, community, work, or studies.
  - What are your readers likely to know about the concept, about related concepts, or about the subject in general? How can you build on what they already know?
  - If you suspect your readers are likely to have faulty assumptions, misunderstandings, or outdated ideas about the concept (or about the subject in general), how can you clarify the concept for them?
- After completing the activities above, choose an aspect of your concept on which to focus, and write a sentence explaining why it interests you and why it will interest your audience.

If you find that you don't have enough to write about, return to the previous section (pp. 127–28) to conduct additional research, broaden your concept by adding cultural or historical contexts, or check sources or class readings to look for broader concepts of which your concept is a part.

Get together with two or three other students to test your choice:

Presenters   Briefly describe your intended audience, identify the aspect of the concept that you will focus on, and explain what you find interesting or relevant about it and what you think your readers will find interesting or relevant. (If your listeners do not find your focus appropriate or interesting, consider returning to your list of possible concepts and repeating the activities above.)

Listeners   Briefly tell the presenter whether the focus sounds appropriate and interesting for the intended audience. Share what you think readers are likely to know about the concept and what information might be especially interesting to them.

⁜ Conduct further research on your focused concept.

Your instructor may expect you to do in-depth research or may limit the number and type of sources you can use. Readers will want to be sure that your sources are reliable and perhaps read your sources for themselves.

To learn more about finding and developing sources, see Chapter 16, and for evaluating your sources, see Chapter 17.

⁜ Draft your working thesis.

An essay explaining a concept is made up of three basic parts:

- An attempt to engage readers' interest
- A thesis statement, announcing the concept and its focus, and forecasting the main topics
- Information about the concept, organized by topic

You may want to draft a working thesis statement and other parts of your explanation before deciding on an opening that will engage readers' attention. If, however, you prefer to sketch out an opening first, turn to the section "Write the opening sentences" (p. 135), and return to this section later.

The thesis statement in a concept explanation announces the concept to be explained and identifies the aspect of the concept that the writer will focus on. It may also forecast the topics to be explored. Here's an example of a thesis statement from "Love: The Right Chemistry" (pp. 111–14):

Concept	O.K., let's cut out all this nonsense about <u>romantic love</u>. Let's bring some
Focus	scientific precision to the party. Let's put love under a microscope.
	When rigorous people with Ph.D.s after their names do that, what
Forecast topics	they see is not some silly, senseless thing. No, their probe reveals that love rests firmly on the foundations of evolution, biology and chemistry.
	(Toufexis, pars. 1–2)

To draft your thesis statement, consider using some of your writing from the Ways In activities in the section "Focus your explanation of the concept" (pp. 129–30). Alternatively, simply state directly the concept you will explain and the approach you will take. You may also want to forecast the topics you will cover.

Organize your concept explanation effectively for your readers.

Once you have drafted a working thesis, you may want to devise a tentative outline drawing on your invention and research notes. An effective outline for a concept explanation should be divided into separate topics that are conceptually parallel. Patricia Lyu, for example, forecasts her topics in two *rhetorical questions:* "How does that bond develop and how does it affect romantic relationships later in life?" (par. 1) From this sentence, readers know what she will focus on. Toufexis focuses on the scientific foundations of love, and so she divides the topics she will cover into evolution, biology, and chemistry. Once you have decided on your topics, present them in a logical order (for example, from most familiar to least familiar).

Below is a simple *scratch outline* for an essay explaining a concept, which you may use as a starting point:

> I. **Introduction:** Attempts to gain readers' interest in the concept, but may not name the concept immediately.
>
> II. **Thesis:** This part is usually a single sentence that identifies the concept. But it may be several sentences, including a brief definition, an example, or another strategy to clarify the focus. It may also include a forecast listing the topics that will be addressed later.
>
> III. **Topic 1:** For each topic, note the explanatory strategies you will use, the source materials you will include, and any visuals you already have or need to find.
>
> IV. **Topic 2:**
>
> V. **Topic 3 (etc.):**
>
> VI. **Conclusion:** Might summarize information, give advice about how to use or apply the information, or speculate about the future of the concept.

Use your outline to guide your drafting, but do not feel tied to it. You may figure out a better way to sequence your topics as you write.

Consider the explanatory strategies you should use.

To explain your concept, consider how you would define it, examples you can provide to help readers understand it, how it is similar to or different from other related concepts, how it happens or gets done, and what its causes or effects are. Keep in mind that your goal is not only to inform your readers but also to engage their interest. The following activities provide sentence strategies you may use to explore the best ways to explain your concept, and they may also get you started drafting your essay.

WAYS IN

WHAT WRITING STRATEGIES CAN I USE TO EXPLAIN MY FOCUSED CONCEPT?

What are the concept's defining characteristics? What broader class does it belong to, and how does it differ from other members of its class? (*definition*)

▶ [Concept] is a _____ in which _____ [list defining characteristics].

What examples or anecdotes can make the concept less abstract and more understandable? (*example*)

▶ [Experts/scientists/etc.] first became aware of [concept] in [year], when _____ (citation).

▶ Interest in [concept] has been [rising/declining/steady] [because of/in spite of] [recent examples/a shortage of recent examples] like _____, _____, and _____.

How is this concept like or unlike related concepts with which your readers may be more familiar? (*comparison and contrast*)

▶ Many people think the term [concept] means _____, but it might be more accurate to say it means _____.

▶ [Concept] is similar in some ways to [similar concept]: [list areas of similarity]. However, unlike [similar concept], it [list areas of difference].

▶ [Concept], a kind of [grown-up, children's, bigger, smaller, local, international, or other adjective] version of [similar concept], [is/does/has] _____.

How can an explanation of this concept be divided into parts to make it easier for readers to understand? (*classification*)

▶ Experts like [name of expert] say there are [number] [categories, types, subtypes, versions] of [concept], ranging from _____ to _____ (citation).

How does this concept happen, or how does one go about doing it? (*process narration*)

▶ To perform [concept or task related to concept], a [person, performer, participant, etc.] starts by _____. Then [he/she/it] must [verb], [verb], and [verb]. [Insert or remove sections as necessary.] The process ends when [he/she/it] [verb].

What are this concept's known causes or effects? (*cause and effect*)

▶ [Concept or concept-related result] happens because _____.

▶ Before [concept or concept-related result] can [happen/take place/occur], [identify a condition that has to be met first]. However, [that condition] isn't enough by itself: [second condition] must also [happen/take place/be established].

▶ Experts disagree over the causes of [concept]. Some, like [name 1], believe _____ (citation). Others, like [name 2], contend that _____ (citation).

Use summaries, paraphrases, and quotations from sources to support your points.

Summaries, paraphrases, and quotations from sources are frequently used to explain concepts or reinforce an explanation. Chapter 18 (in Part 3, "Strategies for Research"), explains how to write an effective summary or paraphrase and to decide when to summarize, paraphrase, or quote from a source. But keep the following in mind:

- Use *summary* to give the gist of a research report or other information.
- Use *paraphrase* to provide specific details or examples when the language of the source is not especially memorable.
- Use *quotation* to emphasize source material that is particularly vivid or clear, to convey an expert's voice, or to discuss the source's choice of words.

In academic writing projects, you will need to cite the sources of all summaries, paraphrases, and quotations.

Also remember that your readers will want you to explain how the ideas from the sources you cite reinforce the points you are making. So make sure you comment on sources, making the relationship between your own ideas and the supporting information from sources absolutely clear. (For help with integrating information from sources, see p. 134.)

Use visuals or multimedia illustrations to enhance your explanation.

Concept explanations do not require illustrations, but they can be an effective tool. The medium in which your concept explanation appears will determine the types of illustrations you can use. For example, papers can include visual images such as photographs and flowcharts. Web pages can include music, film clips, and animated graphs. Oral presentations can use the Web or presentation slides (such as PowerPoint).

When deciding whether to include illustrations, consider whether you can create your own graphics (for example, using spreadsheet software to create bar graphs or pie charts) or whether you will need to borrow materials that others have created (for example, downloading materials from the Internet, taking screenshots from Web sites or DVDs, or scanning visuals from books or magazines). Borrowed material must be cited, including the sources of data you use to create graphs and tables. If your writing is going to be published on a Web site that is not password protected, you also need to obtain permission from the source.

Use appositives to integrate sources.

When you write your essay, you'll have to tell readers about the credentials of experts you quote, paraphrase, and summarize. Instead of providing this information in separate sentences, you can use an *appositive* to embed this information smoothly and clearly into a single sentence.

An **appositive** is a noun or pronoun that, along with modifiers, gives more information about another noun or pronoun. Here is an example from one of the reading selections earlier in the chapter:

Noun
Appositive

"Love is a natural high," observes Anthony Walsh, author of *The Science of Love: Understanding Love and Its Effects on Mind and Body*. (Toufexis, par. 10)

By placing the credentials right after the expert's name, sentences with appositives can provide readers with the information they need, exactly where they need it.

Appositives can also be used for many different purposes, as these examples suggest:

TO DEFINE A KEY TERM   Each person carries in his or her mind a unique subliminal guide to the ideal partner, a "love map." (Toufexis, par. 17)

TO IDENTIFY PEOPLE AND THINGS   Says Michael Mills, a psychology professor at Loyola Marymount University in Los Angeles: "Love is our ancestors whispering in our ears." (Toufexis, par. 2)

TO GIVE EXAMPLES   Despite the risk of serious side effects—nausea, loss of sex drive, seizures—drugs like Zoloft can be a godsend for this group. (Cain, par. 3)

Notice that the last example uses dashes instead of commas to set off the appositive from the rest of the sentence. Although commas are more common, dashes are often used if the writer wants to give the appositive more emphasis or if the appositive itself contains commas, as in the last example above.

Use descriptive verbs in signal phrases to introduce information from sources.

When introducing quotations, paraphrases, or summaries, writers often use a **signal phrase**—the source author's name plus an appropriate verb—to alert readers to the fact that they are borrowing someone else's words or ideas. Often the verb is neutral, as with the following two examples (the verbs are italicized):

Signal phrase

"That is one reason why it feels so horrible when we're abandoned or a lover dies," *notes* Fisher. (Toufexis, par. 13)

Mr. Wozniak *describes* his creative process as an exercise in solitude. "Most inventors and engineers I've met are like me," he *writes* in "iWoz," his autobiography (Cain, par. 21)

Sometimes, however, the verb may be more descriptive—even evaluative:

"As long as prehistoric females were secretive about their extramarital affairs," *argues* Fisher, "they could garner extra resources, life insurance, better genes and more varied DNA for their biological futures. . . ." (Toufexis, par. 8)

The verb *argues* emphasizes the fact that what is being reported is an interpretation that others may disagree with. As you refer to sources in your concept explanation, choose carefully among a wide variety of precise verbs to introduce your sources. Here are some possibilities: *suggests, reveals, questions, finds, notices, observes, underscores*.

In academic writing, merely mentioning the author's name in a signal phrase is not sufficient. In most cases, you must also include in-text citations that provide the page number from which the borrowed material is taken and include full bibliographic information in a list of works cited or references, so readers can trace the source for themselves. Writers may also include the source author's name in a signal phrase. But often the information provided in parentheses following the borrowed passage is sufficient, particularly if the source author has already been identified or if the source's identity is not relevant (as when citing facts):

The original research on attachment, plus Harlow's monkey experiments, underlines the idea that "the attachment and fear systems are inter-

Parenthetical citation

twined" (Cassidy 8). During a time of war, fear obviously is intensified, especially for soldiers in harm's way. Therefore, we can see how applying the concept of attachment to *The Things They Carried* can be illuminating. It is especially helpful in understanding Henry Dobbins's peculiar habit of wearing "his girlfriend's pantyhose around his neck before heading out on ambush" (O'Brien 117). Fear triggers Dobbins's attachment behavior. Like Harlow's monkey, he seeks comfort from his attachment figure. (Lyu, par. 10)

For more about integrating sources into your sentences and constructing signal phrases, see Chapter 18.

Write the opening sentences.

Review your invention writing to see if you have already written something that would work to launch your essay, or try out one or two ways of beginning your essay—possibly from the list that follows:

- A surprising or provocative quotation (like Toufexis and Lyu)
- An anecdote illustrating the concept
- A concrete example (like Cain)
- A paradox or surprising aspect of the concept
- A comparison or contrast that relates the concept to something readers know

Your goal should be to engage your readers' interest from the start, but do not agonize over the first sentences, because you are likely to discover the best way to begin only after you have written a rough draft.

Draft your explanation.

By this point, you have done a lot of research and writing to

- focus your explanation and develop a working thesis statement;
- try out writing strategies that can help you explain your concept;
- create an outline for presenting that information;
- come up with ways to smoothly integrate your sources;
- consider opening sentences.

Now stitch that material together to create a draft. As you do so, you will notice that some of the sentences you have written based on the sentence strategies in this chapter feel awkward or forced. If so, revise them, retaining the content but experimenting with new ways to present them. The next two parts of this Guide to Writing will help you evaluate and improve your draft.

Evaluating the Draft: Getting a Critical Reading

Your instructor may arrange a peer review session in class or online, where you can exchange drafts with your classmates and give one another a thoughtful critical reading, pointing out what works well and suggesting ways to improve the draft. A good critical reading does three things:

1. It lets the writer know how well the reader understands the point of the essay.

2. It praises what works best.

3. It indicates where the draft could be improved and makes suggestions on how to improve it.

Before concluding your review, be sure to address any of the writer's concerns that have not already been addressed.

A CRITICAL READING GUIDE

A Focused Explanation

Is the explanation focused?

Summarize: Tell the writer, in one sentence, what you understand the concept to mean and why it is important or useful.

Praise: Give an example of something in the draft that you think will especially interest the intended readers.

Critique: Tell the writer about any confusion or uncertainty you have about the concept's meaning, importance, or usefulness. Indicate if the focus could be clearer or more appropriate for the intended readers or if the explanation could have a more interesting focus.

A Clear, Logical Organization

Is the explanation easy to follow?

Summarize: Look at the way the essay is organized by making a scratch outline.

Praise: Give an example of where the essay succeeds in being readable — for instance, in its overall organization, forecast of topics, or use of transitions.

Critique: Identify places where readability could be improved — for example, the beginning made more appealing, a topic sentence made clearer, or transitions or headings added.

Appropriate Explanatory Strategies

Is the concept explained effectively?

Summarize: Note which explanatory strategies the writer uses, such as definition, comparison, example, cause-effect, or process analysis.

Praise: Point to an explanatory strategy that is especially effective, and highlight research that is particularly helpful in explaining the concept.

Critique: Point to any places where a definition is needed, where more (or better) examples might help, or where another explanatory strategy could be improved or added. Note where a visual (such as a flowchart or graph) would make the explanation clearer.

Smooth Integration of Sources

Are the sources incorporated into the essay effectively?

Summarize: Note each source mentioned in the text, and check to make sure it appears in the list of works cited, if there is one. Highlight signal phrases and in-text citations, and identify appositives used to provide experts' credentials.

Praise: Give an example of the effective use of sources — a particularly well-integrated quotation, paraphrase, or summary that supports and illustrates the point. Note any especially descriptive verbs used to introduce information.

Critique: Point out where experts' credentials are needed. Indicate quotations, paraphrases, or summaries that could be more smoothly integrated or more fully interpreted or explained. Suggest verbs in signal phrases that may be more appropriate.

Improving the Draft: Revising, Formatting, Editing, and Proofreading

Start improving your draft by reflecting on what you have written thus far:

- Review critical reading comments from your classmates, instructor, or writing center tutor. What are your readers getting at?

- Take another look at the notes from your earlier research and writing activities. What else should you consider?

- Review your draft. What else can you do to make your explanation effective?

Revise your draft.

If your readers are having difficulty with your draft, or if you think there is room for improvement, try some of the strategies listed in the Troubleshooting Guide that follows. It can help you fine-tune your presentation of the genre's basic features:

A TROUBLESHOOTING GUIDE

A Focused Explanation

I don't have enough to write about. (The focus is too narrow.)

- Broaden your concept by adding cultural or historical comparisons and contrasts.
- Look up your concept using reference sources to find additional subject terms for larger concepts that include it.
- Conduct a Web search using the name of your concept and *overview* or *definition*. Use the Advanced Search feature to focus on sites with a *.edu, .gov,* or *.org* domain.
- If your concept comes from another course you are taking, check your textbook or lecture notes for broader, related topics.

Readers don't find my focus interesting.

- Conduct additional research, focusing on finding information likely to be of value and interest to your readers.
- Consider how you can answer your readers' "So what?" question. Show them, perhaps, how they could use the concept; build on their interests or what they already know; or clarify their mistaken, faulty, or outdated assumptions or ideas.
- Consider using humor, anecdotes, or visuals to engage readers' interest.
- Ask yourself whether the focus is interesting to you. If it isn't, choose a different focus. If it is, ask yourself how you can communicate your enthusiasm to your readers —perhaps with anecdotes, examples, or illustrations.

A Clear, Logical Organization

The organization is not clear and logical.

- Reread your thesis statement to be sure that it clearly announces the concept and forecasts the topics in the order they appear in the essay.
- Outline your material to be sure that it is divided into separate topics that are conceptually parallel and presented in a logical order.
- Look for topic sentences in each paragraph. (If you find them difficult to locate, your reader will, too.) Clarify where necessary.

The beginning does not draw readers in.

- Review your opening paragraphs to be sure that you clearly introduce your concept and your focus.
- Try starting with an anecdote, an interesting quotation, a surprising aspect of the concept, a concrete example, or a similar lead-in.
- Consider stating explicitly what makes the concept worth thinking about and how it relates to your readers' interests.

A Clear, Logical Organization

The essay doesn't flow smoothly from one part to the next.

- Outline your essay, dividing it into major parts — introduction, main topics, and conclusion. Reread the end of each major part and the beginning of the next to make sure you have provided transitional cues (for example, the strategic repetition of words or phrases; use of synonyms; rhetorical questions). If there are none, add some.
- Consider adding headings to make the topical sections easier to identify.

The ending falls flat.

- Consider ending by speculating on what the future will bring — how the concept might be redefined, for example.
- Consider relating the ending to the beginning — for example, by recalling an example or a comparison.

Appropriate Explanatory Strategies

Readers don't understand my explanation.

- Consider whether you have used the most appropriate writing strategies for your topic — defining, classifying, comparing and contrasting, narrating, illustrating, describing, or explaining cause and effect.
- Recheck your definitions for clarity. Be sure that you have explicitly defined any key terms your readers might not know.
- Consider forecasting the topics you will cover explicitly.
- Add transitional cues (transitional words and phrases, strategic repetition, rhetorical questions, etc.).
- Add headings and bulleted or numbered lists to help readers follow the discussion.

Readers want more information about certain aspects of the concept.

- Expand or clarify definitions by adding examples or using appositives.
- Add examples or comparisons and contrasts to relate the concept to something readers already know.
- Conduct additional research on your topic, and cite it in your essay.

Readers want visuals to help them understand certain aspects of the concept.

- Check whether your sources use visuals (tables, graphs, drawings, photographs, and the like) that might be appropriate for your explanation. (If you are publishing your concept explanation online, consider video clips, audio files, and animated graphics as well.)
- Consider drafting your own charts, tables, or graphs, or adding your own photographs or illustrations.

(continued)

Appropriate Explanatory Strategies

> Summaries lack oomph; paraphrases are too complicated; quotations are too long or uninteresting.

- Revise the summaries to emphasize a single key idea.
- Restate the paraphrases more succinctly, omitting irrelevant details. Consider quoting important words.
- Use ellipses to tighten the quotations to emphasize the memorable words.

> Readers aren't sure how source information supports my explanation of the concept.

- Check to be sure that you have appropriately commented on all cited material, making its relation to your own ideas absolutely clear.
- Expand or clarify accounts of research that your readers find unconvincing on grounds apart from the credibility of the source.

Smooth Integration of Sources

> Quotes, summaries, and/or paraphrases don't flow smoothly with the rest of the essay.

- Reread all passages where you quote outside sources. Ask yourself whether you provide enough context for the quotation or establish clearly enough the credentials of the source author.
- Use signal phrases to place sources in context. Consider using descriptive verbs in signal phrases to give your readers more information about what your source is saying and why you are referring to it.
- Use appositives to integrate information about your sources smoothly and clearly.

> Readers are concerned that my list of sources is too limited.

- Do additional research to balance your list, taking particular care that you have an adequate number of scholarly sources.
- If you have difficulty finding appropriate material, ask your instructor or a reference librarian for help.

> My readers wonder whether my sources are credible.

- Clearly identify all sources, and fully state the credentials of all cited authorities, using appositives where appropriate.
- Eliminate sources that are clearly identified and well integrated but not considered relevant, credible, or otherwise appropriate.

Edit and proofread your draft.

Two kinds of errors occur often in concept explanations: mixed constructions and missing or unnecessary commas around adjective clauses. The following guidelines will help you check your essay for these common errors.

Avoiding Mixed Constructions

What Is a Mixed Construction?   A **mixed construction** in a sentence is a combination of structures that don't work together properly according to the rules of logic or English grammar. Mixed constructions often occur when a writer attributes information to a source, defines a term, or provides an explanation. In particular, watch out for definitions that include *is when* or *is where* and explanations that include *the reason . . . is because,* which are likely to be both illogical and ungrammatical.

The Problem   Sentences are logically or grammatically incoherent.

The Correction   Replace *when* or *where* with a noun that renames the subject or with an adjective that describes the subject.

▶ Depression is ~~where~~ people feel sad, guilty, or worthless, and lack energy or focus.
  a disorder in which

Delete either *the reason . . . is* or *because.*

▶ ~~The reasons~~ ponds become meadows is because plant life collects in the bottom.
  p

Check subjects and predicates to make sure they are logically and grammatically matched, and delete any redundant expressions.

▶ ~~According to Eleanor Smith,~~ she said that the best movie of the year was *Queen Margot.*

▶ According to Eleanor Smith, ~~she said that~~ the best movie of the year was *Queen Margot.*

Using Punctuation with Adjective Clauses

What Is an Adjective Clause?   An **adjective clause** includes both a subject and a verb, gives information about a noun or a pronoun, and often begins with *who, which,* or *that*:

▶ It is common for schizophrenics to have delusions *that they are being persecuted.*
  └────── adjective clause ──────┘
                          subj. verb

Because adjective clauses add information about the nouns they follow—defining, illustrating, or explaining—they can be useful in writing that explains a concept.

The Problem   Adjective clauses may or may not need to be set off with a comma or commas. To decide, determine whether the clause is essential to the meaning of the sentence. Essential clauses should *not* be set off with commas; nonessential clauses *must* be set off with commas.

The Correction   Mentally delete the clause. If taking out the clause does not change the basic meaning of the sentence or make it unclear, add a comma or commas.

▶ Postpartum neurosis‚ which can last for two weeks or longer‚ can adversely affect a mother's ability to care for her infant.

If the clause follows a proper noun, add a comma or commas.

▶ Nanotechnologists defer to K. Eric Drexler‚ who speculates imaginatively about the use of nonmachines.

If taking out the clause changes the basic meaning of the sentence or makes it unclear, do *not* add a comma or commas.

▶ Seasonal affective disorders are mood disturbances‚ that occur in fall/winter.

THINKING CRITICALLY

To think critically means to use all of the knowledge you have acquired from the information in this chapter, your own writing, the writing and responses of other students, and class discussions to reflect deeply on your work for this assignment and the genre (or type) of writing you have produced. The benefit of thinking critically is proven and important: Thinking critically about what you have learned will help you remember it longer, ensuring that you will be able to put it to good use well beyond this writing course.

Reflecting on What You Have Learned

In this chapter, you have learned a great deal about this genre from reading several explanations of a concept and writing a concept explanation of your own. To consolidate your learning, reflect not only on what you learned but also on how you learned it.

ANALYZE & WRITE

Write a blog post, a letter to your instructor or a classmate, or an e-mail message to a student who will take this course next term, using the writing prompt that seems most productive for you:

- Explain how your purpose and audience — what you wanted your readers to learn from reading your concept explanation — influenced *one* of your decisions as a writer, such as how you focused the concept, how you organized your explanation, how you used writing strategies to convey information, or how you integrated sources into your essay.

- If you were to give advice to a fellow student who was about to write a concept explanation, what would you say?

- Which of the readings in this chapter influenced your essay? Explain the influence, citing specific examples from your essay and the reading.

- If you got good advice from a critical reader, explain exactly how the person helped you — perhaps by questioning your definitions, your use of visuals, the way you began or ended your essay, or the kinds of sources you used.

- Discuss what you learned about yourself as a writer in the process of writing this essay. For example, what part of the process did you find most challenging? Did you try anything new like getting a critical reading of your draft or outlining your draft in order to revise it?

Reflecting on the Genre

Writers explaining concepts typically present knowledge as established and uncontested. They presume to be unbiased and objective, and they assume that readers will not doubt or challenge the truth or the value of the knowledge they present. This stance encourages readers to feel confident about the validity of the explanation. But should explanatory writing always be accepted at face value? Textbooks and reference materials, in particular, sometimes present a simplified or limited view of knowledge in an academic discipline. Because they must be highly selective, they necessarily leave out certain sources of information and types of knowledge.

Write a page or two considering how concept explanations may distort knowledge. In your discussion, you might consider one or more of the following:

1 **Consider the claim that concept explanations attempt to present their information as uncontested truths.** Identify a reading in this chapter that particularly seems to support this claim, and then think about how it does so. Do the same for a chapter or section in a textbook you are reading for another course.

2 **Write a page or two explaining your initial assumptions about the knowledge or information you presented about the concept in your essay.** When you were doing research on the concept, did you discover that some of the information was being challenged by experts? Or did the body of knowledge seem settled and established? Did you at any point think that your readers might question any of the information you were presenting? How did you decide what information might seem new or even surprising to readers? Did you feel comfortable in your roles as the selector and giver of knowledge?

5

Arguing
a Position

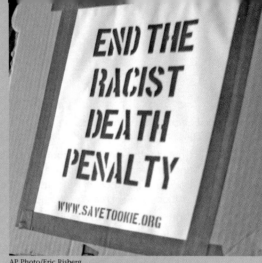

Because of the in-your-face kind of arguing in blogs and on talk shows, you may associate arguing to support your position on a controversial issue with quarreling. Although this kind of "argument" lets people vent strong feelings, it seldom leads them to consider seriously other points of view or to think critically about their own reasons or underlying values. A more thoughtful, deliberative kind of position argument, one that depends on a critical analysis of an issue, on giving logical reasons rather than raising voices, is more likely to convince others in the workplace, in the community, and especially in college courses to accept—or even to take seriously—a controversial position.

IN COLLEGE COURSES

For a law and society course, a student writes an essay analyzing racial discrepancies in sentencing, especially in death-penalty cases. She cites studies that have found, surprisingly, that the race of the murder victim, not the perpetrator, is the crucial factor: If the victim is white, the defendant is more likely to receive the death sentence. Based on her research, she argues that the main reason for this disparity is due not to the decision of the jury but to the decision of prosecutors who seek the death penalty more often when the murder victim is white. She concludes that although there is no evidence that sentencing decisions are racially discriminatory, outcomes often are, and this fact makes people think the justice system is unjust.

Radius images/Alamy   © Proehl Studios/Corbis

IN THE COMMUNITY

In an open letter, a group of parents asks the school board to institute a Peacemakers program at the local middle school. The group's impassioned letter begins with anecdotal reports of bullying at the school to underscore the need for action and to appeal to board members' compassion. It then describes the Peacemakers program and details the negotiation procedure children are taught. It acknowledges that the program will add to the school's budget, but it claims that the negotiation skills the children will learn will help them now and throughout their lives.

IN THE WORKPLACE

At a business conference, a consultant makes a presentation arguing that adopting sustainable business practices is good for business. He displays poll results showing that two-thirds of businesses see sustainability as a necessity to compete in the global marketplace—up more than 50 percent from the previous year—and that a third increased profits as a direct result of their sustainability efforts. Citing several examples, he shows how companies can develop a strategic sustainability plan by changing performance reviews or by offering compensation packages to reward employees who implement sustainability practices and achieve goals. He concludes by urging audience members to log on to his blog to read inspiring examples and to add their own.

In this chapter, we ask you to write about your position on a controversial issue for the purpose of convincing readers to adopt your point of view or at least to consider it seriously. Analyzing the selections in the Guide to Reading that follows, you will learn how writers engage their readers' attention and make a compelling argument. As you read, consider whether visuals would help readers more fully grasp the issue or accept the position.

| PRACTICING THE GENRE |

Debating a Position

To get a sense of what's involved in arguing a position, get together with two or three students to discuss an issue you have strong feelings about. Here are some guidelines to follow:

Part 1.   As a group, think of a college issue you all know and care about, or choose one from the following list:

- Should admission to college be based solely on high school grade point average?
- Should there be a community service requirement for graduation from college?
- Should college students be required to take courses outside of their major?
- Should the federal government subsidize everyone's college education?
- Should drinking alcohol on college campuses be permitted?
- Should college athletes be paid?

First, identify your purpose and audience: Is your goal to convince readers to change their minds, confirm their opinions, or move them to action? Who constitutes your audience — college administrators, parents, or fellow students — and what values or interests do you think they will find most important? What values or interests are most important to you?

Second, divide into two teams — those in favor and those opposed (at least, for this activity) — and take a few minutes to think of reasons why your audience should accept your position.

Third, take turns presenting your argument.

Part 2.   Reflect on what you learned, and discuss these questions in your group:

- How did clarifying your purpose and knowing whether you were addressing administrators, parents, or students affect which reasons you used and how you presented them?
- Why did you expect your audience to find these particular reasons convincing?

Your instructor may ask you to write about what you learned and present your conclusions to the rest of the class.

Analyzing Position Arguments

As you read the selections in this chapter, you will see how different authors argue a position. Analyzing how these writers present and support their position, respond to opposing views, and organize their writing will also help you see how you can employ these techniques to make your own position argument clear and compelling for your readers.

Determine the writer's purpose and audience.

Although arguing a position helps writers clarify their own reasons for taking that particular position, writers typically aim to influence others. When reading the position arguments that follow, ask yourself these questions about the writer's purpose and audience:

- What seems to be the writer's main *purpose* in arguing for a position—for example, to change readers' minds by convincing them to look at the issue in a new way, to confirm readers' opinions by providing them with authoritative arguments, to move readers to take action by stressing the urgency or seriousness of the issue, or to remind readers what is at stake and establish common ground on which people might be able to agree?

- What does the writer assume about the *audience*—for example, that audience members are already knowledgeable about the issue, that they will be only mildly interested and need to be inspired to care about the issue, or that they have strong convictions and are likely to have serious objections to the writer's position?

Assess the genre's basic features.

Basic Features
A Focused,
Well-Presented Issue
A Well-Supported Position
An Effective Response to
Opposing Views
A Clear, Logical
Organization

Use the following to help you analyze and evaluate how writers of position arguments use the genre's basic features. The strategies position writers typically use to make a convincing case are illustrated below with examples from the readings in this chapter as well as sentence strategies you can experiment with later, as you write your own position argument.

A FOCUSED, WELL-PRESENTED ISSUE

Read first to see how the issue is presented and to determine whether it is clearly focused and well presented, given the writer's purpose and original audience. To identify the issue, look at the title and the opening paragraphs. The title of Daniel J. Solove's position argument (pp. 163–67), for example, identifies both the topic and his position:

Topic   Why Privacy Matters Even If You Have "Nothing to Hide"
Position

For current, hotly debated issues, the title may be enough to identify the issue for readers, and writers may use their opening paragraphs merely to remind readers about what is at stake or what the position is that they oppose, using a simple sentence pattern like this:

▶ When [issue/event] happens, most people think _____ , but I think _____ .

147

For example, Solove uses this strategy in his position paper about privacy:

> When the government gathers or analyzes personal information, many people say . . . (par. 1)

His "but I think . . ." response to the common view takes up the bulk of the essay.

When writers know the issue will be unfamiliar to their audience, they need to establish its significance, as student Jessica Statsky does in her position essay:

> "Organized sports for young people have become an institution in North America," reports sports journalist Steve Silverman, attracting more than 44 million youngsters according to a recent survey by the National Council of Youth Sports ("History"). (par. 1)

To establish the significance of the issue, Statsky quotes a respected authority and also cites statistics.

To present their positions effectively, writers must focus on a specific aspect of their issue, one they can address fully in the space allowed. An issue like the death penalty, for example, is too complex to be tackled fully in a relatively brief space. So writers must focus on one aspect of the issue. A writer taking a position on the death penalty might address the more specific question of whether race influences prosecutors to seek the death penalty, as does the student in the In College Courses scenario on page 144.

Also consider how the writer frames the issue. **Framing an issue** is like cropping and resizing a photograph to focus the viewer's eye on one part of the picture (see Figure 5.1). Writers typically frame the issue in a way that sets the stage for their argument and promotes their point of view, usually by suggesting that particular values are at stake or by raising in readers' minds certain concerns. As you read, notice how each writer frames the issue, asking yourself questions like these:

- Who does the writer associate with each position, and how does the writer characterize their views? For example, does one side appear thoughtful, moderate, and knowledgeable, and the other side extreme, unreasonable, or self-interested? What does the writer suggest is really at stake, and for whom?

- How does the way the writer frames the issue affect your own thinking about it? If the issue was unfamiliar to you before reading the essay, what did the writer lead you

FIGURE 5.1 Framing an issue.
By cropping this photograph of a protest march to focus on the little boy, the photographer softens the message, framing it in terms of saving the planet for this child.

© Patrick Ward/Alamy

to think and feel about it? If you were already familiar with the issue, which of your preconceptions were reinforced and which were challenged by the writer's way of framing the issue?

A WELL-SUPPORTED POSITION

To argue effectively, writers need to *assert an arguable **position**—*that is, an opinion, not a fact that can be proved or disproved or a belief taken on faith—that can be supported with convincing *reasons* and trustworthy *evidence*. Read first to identify the position, usually declared in a *thesis statement* early in the essay. Then determine whether the position is clear and appropriately qualified (for example, using words like *may* and specifying conditions). Notice, for example, how Jessica Statsky states her thesis:

> Qualifying terms   When overzealous parents and coaches impose adult standards on children's sports, the result can be activities that are neither satisfying nor beneficial to children.
>
>   I am concerned about all organized sports activities for children between the ages of six and twelve. (pars. 1–2)

Then examine the main reasons and the evidence the writer provides, making sure that the reasons clearly support the writer's position and that the evidence (such as statistics, research studies, or authorities) is credible. (Writers of position arguments often *forecast* the reasons they will develop; to see how Statsky does this, see the section that follows on organization.) Look for sentence strategies like these that introduce supporting reasons:

> Position   ▶ What makes _____ [problematic/praiseworthy] is _____ .
>
> Reason   ▶ Because _____ , I [support/oppose] _____ .

> **EXAMPLE**   This statistic illustrates another reason I oppose competitive sports
>
> Position   for children: because they are so highly selective, very few children get
>
> Reason   to participate. (Statsky, par. 7)

The following examples demonstrate some approaches to introducing supporting evidence:

> Statistics   24 percent . . . worked . . . five to seven days. . . . There is just no way such
>
> Reason   amounts of work will not interfere with school work, especially homework. In an informal survey . . . , 58 percent of seniors acknowledged that their jobs interfere with their school work. (Etzioni, par. 13)

> Authority   Leonard Koppett in *Sports Illusion, Sports Reality* claims that . . . , sometimes
>
> Reason   resulting in lifelong injuries (294). (Statsky, par. 3)

Position arguments are most convincing when writers are able to appeal to readers on three levels:

- **Logos:** Appeal to readers' intellect, presenting them with logical reasoning and reliable evidence.
- **Ethos:** Appeal to readers' perception of the writer's credibility and fairness.
- **Pathos:** Appeal to readers' values and feelings.

To learn more about evaluating sources, see Chapter 9.

When reading a position argument (or writing your own), consider how well the writer has used these appeals. Ask yourself questions like these: Is the argument logical and reasonable (logos)? Does the writer appear credible and trustworthy (pathos)? Are the values and feelings sincere or manipulative (ethos)?

To learn more about constructing an argument, see Chapter 13.

AN EFFECTIVE RESPONSE TO OPPOSING VIEWS

An effective argument anticipates readers' objections and opposing arguments and refutes or concedes them. Writers **refute** (argue against) opposing views when they can show that the opposing view is weak or flawed. A typical refutation states the problem with the opposing view and then explains why the view is problematic, using sentence strategies like these:

- ▶ One problem with [opposing view] is that _____.

- ▶ Some claim [opposing view], but in reality _____.

Notice that writers often introduce the refutation with a *transition* that indicates *contrast*, such as *but, although, nevertheless,* or *however*:

> Transition
> Refutation
>
> Yet another problem with government gathering and use of personal data is distortion. Although personal information can reveal quite a lot about people's personalities and activities, it often fails to reflect the whole person. It can paint a distorted picture. (Solove, par. 14)

Writers may also **concede** (accept) valid objections, concerns, or reasons. A typical way of conceding is to use sentence strategies like these:

- ▶ I agree that _____.

- ▶ _____ is certainly an important factor.

Here is an example from Jessica Statsky's essay (pp. 152–57):

> Concession
>
> Some children *want* to play competitive sports; they are not being forced to play. These children are eager to learn skills, to enjoy the camaraderie of the team, and earn self-respect by trying hard to benefit their team. I acknowledge that some children may benefit from playing competitive sports. (par. 12)

Conceding a strong opposing view reassures readers that the writer shares their values and builds a bridge of common concerns.

Frequently, though, writers reach out to readers by making a concession but then go on to point out where they differ. We call this the **concession-refutation move**. Writers making the concession-refutation move often employ sentence patterns like these, which include transitions that indicate contrast, like *but, although, nevertheless,* or *however,* to indicate that an exception or refinement is coming.

- ▶ _____ may be true for _____, *but* not for _____.

- ▶ *Although* _____, I think _____.

- ▶ _____ insists that _____. *Nevertheless,* in spite of her good intentions, _____.

Analyzing Position Arguments   **GUIDE TO READING**
GUIDE TO WRITING
THINKING CRITICALLY   **151**

Here's an example:

| Concession | True, you still have to have the gumption to get yourself over to the ham- |
| Refutation | burger stand, but once you don the prescribed uniform, your task is spelled out in minute detail. (Etzioni, par.7) |

While reading position arguments, assess the effectiveness of the responses:

▨ Do the concessions seem significant or trivial, genuine or insincere? Do they add to or detract from the writer's credibility (ethos)?

▨ Do the refutations appeal to shared values (pathos) or question readers' priorities? Do they offer compelling reasons and credible evidence (logos) or simply make unsubstantiated assertions? Do they draw on authorities whose expertise is established (ethos) or merely refer vaguely to "some" or "many" people with whom they agree? Do they misrepresent the opposition (committing a *straw man fallacy*) or attack people personally (committing an *ad hominem fallacy*)?

To learn more about logical fallacies, see pp. 378–79 in Chapter 13.

A CLEAR, LOGICAL ORGANIZATION

When reading a position argument, first *look for a thesis statement that directly asserts the writer's position.* For example, Amitai Etzioni begins with an alarming sentence that states in a surprising way what he goes on to clarify in the next sentence:

McDonald's is bad for your kids. I do not mean the flat patties and the white-flour buns; I refer to the jobs teen-agers undertake, mass-producing these choice items. (par. 1)

In addition to asserting the thesis, writers sometimes preview the reasons in the same order they will bring them up later in the essay, as in this example of a *forecasting statement by* Jessica Statsky:

Transition	...too often played to adult standards, which are developmentally inappro-
Reason 1	priate for children and can be both physically and psychologically harmful. Furthermore, because they . . . , they are actually counterproductive for
Reason 2	developing either future players or fans. Finally, because they . . . *provide*
Reason 3	*occasions for some parents and coaches to place their own fantasies and needs ahead of children's welfare.* (par. 2)

Notice also where the writer uses *logical transitions:* to indicate supporting evidence (*because*), exceptions (*however*), concessions (*admittedly*), refutations (*on the other hand*), or conclusions (*therefore*) as well as to list reasons (*first, finally*). Transitions may be useful in a forecasting statement, as in the preceding example, or in the *topic sentence* of a paragraph or group of paragraphs, as in the following examples from Solove's position argument:

One such harm, for example, . . . Another potential problem with . . . is . . . A related problem involves. . . . Yet another problem. . . . (pars. 11–14)

Finally, check for logical fallacies—such as *oversimplifying, personal attack* (ad hominem), *slanting,* and *false analogy.*

To learn more about transition cues, see pp. 321–22 in Chapter 10.

Readings

Jessica Statsky | *Children Need to Play, Not Compete*

THIS ESSAY by Jessica Statsky about children's competitive sports was written for a college composition course. When you were a child, you may have had experience playing competitive sports, in or out of school, for example, in Peewee Football, Little League Baseball, American Youth Soccer, or some other organization. Or you may have had relatives or friends who were deeply involved in sports. As you read, consider the following:

- In your experience and observation, was winning unduly emphasized or was more value placed on having a good time, learning to get along with others, developing athletic skills, or something else altogether?
- The questions in the margin: Your instructor may ask you to post your answers to a class blog or discussion board or to bring them to class.

Basic Features

A Focused, Well-Presented Issue

A Well-Supported Position

An Effective Response to Opposing Views

A Clear, Logical Organization

How does Statsky present the issue in a way that prepares readers for her argument?

How does she qualify her position in par. 2?

What reasons does she forecast here, and in which paragraphs does she discuss each reason? Do her reasons appeal primarily to readers' intellect (logos), to their sense of fairness and what's credible (ethos), or to their feelings (pathos)?

1   "Organized sports for young people have become an institution in North America," reports sports journalist Steve Silverman, attracting more than 44 million youngsters according to a recent survey by the National Council of Youth Sports ("History"). Though many adults regard Little League Baseball and Peewee Football as a basic part of childhood, the games are not always joyous ones. When overzealous parents and coaches impose adult standards on children's sports, the result can be activities that are neither satisfying nor beneficial to children.

2   I am concerned about all organized sports activities for children between the ages of six and twelve. The damage I see results from noncontact as well as contact sports, from sports organized locally as well as those organized nationally. Highly organized competitive sports such as Peewee Football and Little League Baseball are too often played to adult standards, which are developmentally inappropriate for children and can be both physically and psychologically harmful. Furthermore, because they eliminate many children from organized sports before they are ready to compete, they are actually counterproductive for developing either future players or fans. Finally, because they emphasize competition and winning, they unfortunately provide occasions for some parents and coaches to place their own fantasies and needs ahead of children's welfare.

3   One readily understandable danger of overly competitive sports is that they entice children into physical actions that are bad for growing bodies.

"There is a growing epidemic of preventable youth sports injuries," according to the STOP Sports Injuries campaign. "Among athletes ages 5 to 14, 28 percent of football players, 25 percent of baseball players, 22 percent of soccer players, 15 percent of basketball players, and 12 percent of softball players were injured while playing their respective sports." Although the official Little League Web site acknowledges that children do risk injury playing baseball, it insists that "severe injuries . . . are infrequent," the risk "far less than the risk of riding a skateboard, a bicycle, or even the school bus" ("What about My Child?"). Nevertheless, Leonard Koppett in *Sports Illusion, Sports Reality* claims that a twelve-year-old trying to throw a curve ball, for example, may put abnormal strain on developing arm and shoulder muscles, sometimes resulting in lifelong injuries (294). Contact sports like football can be even more hazardous. Thomas Tutko, a psychology professor at San Jose State University and coauthor of the book *Winning Is Everything and Other American Myths*, writes:

> I am strongly opposed to young kids playing tackle football. It is not the right stage of development for them to be taught to crash into other kids. Kids under the age of fourteen are not by nature physical. Their main concern is self-preservation. They don't want to meet head on and slam into each other. But tackle football absolutely requires that they try to hit each other as hard as they can. And it is too traumatic for young kids. (qtd. in Tosches A1)

4   As Tutko indicates, even when children are not injured, fear of being hurt detracts from their enjoyment of the sport. The Little League Web site ranks fear of injury as the seventh of seven reasons children quit ("What about My Child?"). One mother of an eight-year-old Peewee Football player explained, "The kids get so scared. They get hit once and they don't want anything to do with football anymore. They'll sit on the bench and pretend their leg hurts..." (qtd. in Tosches A1). Some children are driven to even more desperate measures. For example, in one Peewee Football game, a reporter watched the following scene as a player took himself out of the game:

> "Coach, my tummy hurts. I can't play," he said. The coach told the player to get back onto the field. "There's nothing wrong with your stomach," he said. When the coach turned his head the seven-year-old stuck a finger down his throat and made himself

How does Statsky try to establish the cred-ibility of her sources in pars. 3–5 (ethos)?

Why do you think she uses block quotations instead of integrating these quotes into her own sentences?

vomit. When the coach turned back, the boy pointed to the ground and told him, "Yes there is, coach. See?" (Tosches A33)

5 Besides physical hazards and anxieties, competitive sports pose psychological dangers for children. Martin Rablovsky, a former sports editor for the *New York Times*, says that in all his years of watching young children play organized sports, he has noticed very few of them smiling. "I've seen children enjoying a spontaneous pre-practice scrimmage become somber and serious when the coach's whistle blows," Rablovsky says. "The spirit of play suddenly disappears, and sport becomes joblike" (qtd. in Coakley 94). The primary goal of a professional athlete — winning — is not appropriate for children. Their goals should be having fun, learning, and being with friends. Although winning does add to the fun, too many adults lose sight of what matters and make winning the most important goal. Several studies have shown that when children are asked whether they would rather be warming the bench on a winning team or playing regularly on a losing team, about 90 percent choose the latter (Smith, Smith, and Smoll 11).

How does Statsky try to refute this objection?

6 Winning and losing may be an inevitable part of adult life, but they should not be part of childhood. Too much competition too early in life can affect a child's development. Children are easily influenced, and when they sense that their competence and worth are based on their ability to live up to their parents' and coaches' high expectations — and on their ability to win — they can become discouraged and depressed. Little League advises parents to "keep winning in perspective" ("Your Role"), noting that the most common reasons children give for quitting, aside from change in interest, are lack of playing time, failure and fear of failure, disapproval by significant others, and psychological stress ("What about My Child?"). According to Dr. Glyn C. Roberts, a professor of kinesiology at the Institute of Child Behavior and Development at the University of Illinois, 80 to 90 percent of children who play competitive sports at a young age drop out by sixteen (Kutner).

How effective do you think Statsky's argument in par. 7 is? Why?

7 This statistic illustrates another reason I oppose competitive sports for children: because they are so highly selective, very few children get to participate. Far too soon, a few children are singled out for their athletic promise, while many others, who may be on the verge of developing the

necessary strength and ability, are screened out and discouraged from trying out again. Like adults, children fear failure, and so even those with good physical skills may stay away because they lack self-confidence. Consequently, teams lose many promising players who with some encouragement and experience might have become stars. The problem is that many parent-sponsored, out-of-school programs give more importance to having a winning team than to developing children's physical skills and self-esteem.

8   Indeed, it is no secret that too often scorekeeping, league standings, and the drive to win bring out the worst in adults who are more absorbed in living out their own fantasies than in enhancing the quality of the experience for children (Smith, Smith, and Smoll 9). Recent newspaper articles on children's sports contain plenty of horror stories. *Los Angeles Times* reporter Rich Tosches, for example, tells the story of a brawl among seventy-five parents following a Peewee Football game (A33). As a result of the brawl, which began when a parent from one team confronted a player from the other team, the teams are now thinking of hiring security guards for future games. Another example is provided by a *Los Angeles Times* editorial about a Little League manager who intimidated the opposing team by setting fire to one of their team's jerseys on the pitcher's mound before the game began. As the editorial writer commented, the manager showed his young team that "intimidation could substitute for playing well" ("The Bad News").

9   Although not all parents or coaches behave so inappropriately, the seriousness of the problem is illustrated by the fact that Adelphi University in Garden City, New York, offers a sports psychology workshop for Little League coaches, designed to balance their "animal instincts" with "educational theory" in hopes of reducing the "screaming and hollering," in the words of Harold Weisman, manager of sixteen Little Leagues in New York City (Schmitt). In a three-and-one-half-hour Sunday morning workshop, coaches learn how to make practices more fun, treat injuries, deal with irate parents, and be "more sensitive to their young players' fears, emotional frailties, and need for recognition." Little League is to be credited with recognizing the need for such workshops.

10   Some parents would no doubt argue that children cannot start too soon preparing to live in a competitive free-market economy. After all, secondary

In criticizing some parents' behavior in pars. 8–9, Statsky risks alienating her readers. How effective is this part of her argument?

How effective is Statsky's use of concession and refutation here?

schools and colleges require students to compete for grades, and college admission is extremely competitive. And it is perfectly obvious how important competitive skills are in finding a job. Yet the ability to cooperate is also important for success in life. Before children are psychologically ready for competition, maybe we should emphasize cooperation and individual performance in team sports rather than winning.

11   Many people are ready for such an emphasis. In 1988, one New York Little League official who had attended the Adelphi workshop tried to ban scoring from six- to eight-year-olds' games — but parents wouldn't support him (Schmitt). An innovative children's sports program in New York City, City Sports for Kids, emphasizes fitness, self-esteem, and sportsmanship. In this program's basketball games, every member on a team plays at least two of six eight-minute periods. The basket is seven feet from the floor, rather than ten feet, and a player can score a point just by hitting the rim (Bloch). I believe this kind of local program should replace overly competitive programs like Peewee Football and Little League Baseball. As one coach explains, significant improvements can result from a few simple rule changes, such as including every player in the batting order and giving every player, regardless of age or ability, the opportunity to play at least four innings a game (Frank).

How effectively does Statsky conclude her argument?

12   Some children *want* to play competitive sports; they are not being forced to play. These children are eager to learn skills, to enjoy the camaraderie of the team, and earn self-respect by trying hard to benefit their team. I acknowledge that some children may benefit from playing competitive sports. While some children do benefit from these programs, however, many more would benefit from programs that avoid the excesses and dangers of many competitive sports programs and instead emphasize fitness, cooperation, sportsmanship, and individual performance.

Are Statsky's sources adequate to support her position, in number and kind? Has she documented them clearly and accurately?

Works Cited

"The Bad News Pyromaniacs?" Editorial. *Los Angeles Times* 16 June 1990: B6. *LexisNexis*. Web. 16 May 2008.

Bloch, Gordon B. "Thrill of Victory Is Secondary to Fun." *New York Times* 2 Apr. 1990, late ed.: C12. *LexisNexis*. Web. 14 May 2008.

Coakley, Jay J. *Sport in Society: Issues and Controversies.* St. Louis: Mosby, 1982. Print.

Frank, L. "Contributions from Parents and Coaches." *CYB Message Board.*
AOL, 8 July 1997. Web. 14 May 2008.

Koppett, Leonard. *Sports Illusion, Sports Reality.* Boston: Houghton, 1981.
Print.

Kutner, Lawrence. "Athletics, through a Child's Eyes." *New York Times*
23 Mar. 1989, late ed.: C8. *LexisNexis.* Web. 15 May 2008.

Schmitt, Eric. "Psychologists Take Seat on Little League Bench." *New York
Times* 14 Mar. 1988, late ed.: B2. *LexisNexis.* Web. 14 May 2008.

Silverman, Steve. "The History of Youth Sports." Livestrong.com. Demand
Media, Inc., 26 May 2011. Web. 10 Dec. 2011.

Smith, Nathan, Ronald Smith, and Frank Smoll. *Kidsports: A Survival Guide
for Parents.* Reading: Addison, 1983. Print.

STOPSportsInjuries.org. American Orthopaedic Society for Sports Medicine,
n.d. Web. 10 Dec. 2011.

Tosches, Rich. "Peewee Football: Is It Time to Blow the Whistle?" *Los
Angeles Times* 3 Dec. 1988: A1+. *LexisNexis.* Web. 22 May 2008.

"What about My Child?" *Little League Online.* Little League Baseball,
Incorporated, 1999. Web. 30 May 2008.

"Your Role as a Little League Parent." *Little League Online.* Little League
Baseball, Incorporated, 1999. Web. 30 May 2008.

 For an additional student reading, go to **macmillanhighered.com/conciseguide.**
E-readings > Michael Niechayev, *It's Time to Ban Head First Tackles and Blocks*

Amitai Etzioni | *Working at McDonald's*

Jessica McConnell Burt/The George
Washington University

AMITAI ETZIONI is a sociologist who has taught at Columbia, Harvard,
and George Washington Universities, where he currently directs the
Institute for Communitarian Policy Studies. He has written numerous articles and more than two dozen books reflecting his commitment to peace
in a nuclear age—for example, *Winning without War* (1964); overcoming
excessive individualism through communitarianism—for example, *The
Spirit of Community: The Reinvention of American Society* (1983); limiting the
erosion of privacy in an age of technological surveillance—for example,

The Limits of Privacy (2004); and, most recently, rethinking foreign policy in an age of terrorism—for example, *Hot Spots: American Foreign Policy in a Post-Human-Rights World* (2012). The following reading was originally published on the opinion page of the *Miami Herald* newspaper. As you read, consider the following:

- What may Etzioni's teenage son Dari, who helped his father write the essay, have contributed?
- What have you learned from the various summer and school-year jobs you have held?

1   McDonald's is bad for your kids. I do not mean the flat patties and the white-flour buns; I refer to the jobs teen-agers undertake, mass-producing these choice items.

2   As many as two-thirds of America's high school juniors and seniors now hold down part-time paying jobs, according to studies. Many of these are in fast-food chains, of which McDonald's is the pioneer, trend-setter and symbol.

3   At first, such jobs may seem right out of the Founding Fathers' educational manual for how to bring up self-reliant, work-ethic-driven, productive youngsters. But in fact, these jobs undermine school attendance and involvement, impart few skills that will be useful in later life, and simultaneously skew the values of teen-agers — especially their ideas about the worth of a dollar.

4   It has been a longstanding American tradition that youngsters ought to get paying jobs. In folklore, few pursuits are more deeply revered than the newspaper route and the sidewalk lemonade stand. Here the youngsters are to learn how sweet are the fruits of labor and self-discipline (papers are delivered early in the morning, rain or shine), and the ways of trade (if you price your lemonade too high or too low . . .).

5   Roy Rogers, Baskin Robbins, Kentucky Fried Chicken, et al. may at first seem nothing but a vast extension of the lemonade stand. They provide very large numbers of teen jobs, provide regular employment, pay quite well compared to many other teen jobs and, in the modern equivalent of toiling over a hot stove, test one's stamina.

6   Closer examination, however, finds the McDonald's kind of job highly uneducational in several ways. Far from providing opportunities for entrepreneurship (the lemonade stand) or self-discipline, self-supervision and self-scheduling (the paper route), most teen jobs these days are highly structured — what social scientists call "highly routinized."

7   True, you still have to have the gumption to get yourself over to the hamburger stand, but once you don the prescribed uniform, your task is spelled out in minute detail. The franchise prescribes the shape of the coffee cups; the weight, size, shape and color of the patties; and the texture of the napkins (if any). Fresh coffee is to be made every eight minutes. And so on. There is no room for initiative, creativity, or even elementary rearrangements. These are breeding grounds for robots working for yesterday's assembly lines, not tomorrow's high-tech posts.

8   There are very few studies on the matter. One of the few is a 1984 study by Ivan Charper and Bryan Shore Fraser. The study relies mainly on what teen-agers write in response to questionnaires rather than actual observations of fast-food jobs. The authors argue that the employees develop many skills such as how to operate a food-preparation machine and a cash register. However, little attention is paid to how long it takes to acquire such a skill, or what its significance is.

9   What does it matter if you spend 20 minutes to learn to use a cash register, and then — "operate" it? What "skill" have you acquired? It is a long way from learning to work with a lathe or carpenter tools in the olden days or to program computers in the modern age.

10   A 1980 study by A. V. Harrell and P. W. Wirtz found that, among those students who worked at least 25 hours per week while in school, their unemployment rate four years later was half of that of seniors who did not work. This is an impressive statistic. It must be seen, though, together with the finding that many who begin as part-time employees in fast-food chains drop out of high school and are gobbled up in the world of low-skill jobs.

11   Some say that while these jobs are rather unsuited for college-bound, white, middle-class youngsters, they are "ideal" for lower-class, "non-academic," minority youngsters. Indeed, minorities are "over-represented" in these jobs (21 percent of fast-food employees). While it is true that these places provide income, work and even some training to such youngsters, they also tend to perpetuate their disadvantaged status. They provide no career ladders, few marketable skills, and undermine school attendance and involvement.

12   The hours are often long. Among those 14 to 17, a third of fast-food employees (including some school dropouts) labor more than 30 hours per week, according to the Charper-Fraser study. Only 20 percent work 15 hours or less. The rest: between 15 and 30 hours.

13   Often the stores close late, and after closing one must clean up and tally up. In affluent Montgomery County, Md., where child labor would not seem to be a widespread economic necessity, 24 percent of the seniors at one high school in 1985 worked as much as five to seven days a week; 27 percent, three to five. There is just no way such amounts of work will not interfere with school work, especially homework. In an informal survey published in the most recent yearbook of the high school, 58 percent of seniors acknowledged that their jobs interfere with their school work.

14   The Charper-Fraser study sees merit in learning teamwork and working under supervision. The authors have a point here.

However, it must be noted that such learning is not automatically educational or wholesome. For example, much of the supervision in fast-food places leans toward teaching one the wrong kinds of compliance: blind obedience, or shared alienation with the "boss."

15   Supervision is often both tight and woefully inappropriate. Today, fast-food chains and other such places of work (record shops, bowling alleys) keep costs down by having teens supervise teens with often no adult on the premises.

16   There is no father or mother figure with which to identify, to emulate, to provide a role model and guidance. The work-culture varies from one place to another: Sometimes it is a tightly run shop (must keep the cash registers ringing); sometimes a rather loose pot party interrupted by customers. However, only rarely is there a master to learn from, or much worth learning. Indeed, far from being places where solid adult work values are being transmitted, these are places where all too often delinquent teen values dominate. Typically, when my son Oren was dishing out ice cream for Baskin Robbins in upper Manhattan, his fellow teen-workers considered him a sucker for not helping himself to the till. Most youngsters felt they were entitled to $50 severance "pay" on their last day on the job.

17   The pay, oddly, is the part of the teen work-world that is most difficult to evaluate. The lemonade stand or paper route money was for your allowance. In the old days, apprentices learning a trade from a master contributed most, if not all, of their income to their parents' household. Today, the teen pay may be low by adult standards, but it is often, especially in the middle class, spent largely or wholly by the teens. That is, the youngsters live free at home ("after all, they are high school kids") and are left with very substantial sums of money.

18   Where this money goes is not quite clear. Some use it to support themselves, especially among the poor. More middle-class kids set some money aside to help pay for

college, or save it for a major purchase — often a car. But large amounts seem to flow to pay for an early introduction into the most trite aspects of American consumerism: flimsy punk clothes, trinkets and whatever else is the last fast-moving teen craze.

19   One may say that this is only fair and square; they are being good American consumers and spend their money on what turns them on. At least, a cynic might add, these funds do not go into illicit drugs and booze. On the other hand, an educator might bemoan that these young, yet unformed individuals, so early in life driven to buy objects of no intrinsic educational, cultural or social merit, learn so quickly the dubious merit of keeping up with the Joneses in ever-changing fads, promoted by mass merchandising.

20   Many teens find the instant reward of money, and the youth status symbols it buys, much more alluring than credits in calculus courses, European history or foreign languages. No wonder quite a few would rather skip school—and certainly homework — and instead work longer at a Burger King. Thus, most teen work these days is not providing early lessons in the work ethic; it fosters escape from school and responsibilities, quick gratification and a short cut to the consumeristic aspects of adult life.

21   Thus, parents should look at teen employment not as automatically educational. It is an activity — like sports — that can be turned into an educational opportunity. But it can also easily be abused. Youngsters must learn to balance the quest for income with the needs to keep growing and pursue other endeavors that do not pay off instantly—above all education.

22   Go back to school.

[REFLECT] Make connections: Useful job skills.

Etzioni argues that fast-food jobs do not qualify as meaningful work experience because they do not teach young people the skills and habits they will need for fulfilling careers: "entrepreneurship . . . or self-discipline, self-supervision and self-scheduling" (par. 6).

To judge Etzioni's argument against your own experience, consider what you have learned from your own summer and after-school jobs, either paid or volunteer. Your instructor may ask you to post your thoughts on a class discussion board or to discuss them with other students in class. Use these questions to get started:

- Which, if any, of the skills and habits Etzioni lists as important did you practice at your job or through the activities in which you participated?

- Why do you think these skills and habits are worth learning? If you think other skills and habits are as important or even more important, explain what they are and why you think so.

[ANALYZE] Use the basic features.

A FOCUSED, WELL-PRESENTED ISSUE: FRAMING AN ARGUMENT FOR A DIVERSE GROUP OF READERS

When Jessica Statsky wrote "Children Need to Play, Not Compete," she knew she would be addressing her classmates. But writers of position essays do not always have such a homogeneous audience. Often, they have to direct their argument to a diverse group of readers, many of whom do not share their concerns or values. From the first sentence, it is clear that Etzioni's primary audience is the parents of teenagers, but his concluding sentence is a direct address to the teenagers themselves: "Go back to school."

ANALYZE & WRITE

Write a paragraph or two analyzing and evaluating how Etzioni presents the issue to a diverse group of readers:

1. Reread paragraphs 1–7, highlighting the qualities—values and skills—associated with traditional jobs (the newspaper route and lemonade stand of yesteryear) and with today's McDonald's-type jobs, at least according to Etzioni. How does Etzioni use these values and skills to lead parents to reconsider their assumption that McDonald's-type jobs are good for their kids?

2. As we point out in the headnote, Etzioni's teenage son Dari helped him write the essay. Skim the essay looking for places where Etzioni appeals to teenagers themselves. Notice, for example, how he represents teenagers' experience and values. Explain how effective you think Etzioni's appeal would be to teenage readers and how effective you think it would be for you and your classmates.

A WELL-SUPPORTED POSITION: USING STATISTICS

Statistics—numerical data about a given population sample—are often used to support position arguments because readers tend to find statistical evidence especially convincing. Numbers can seem impressive—as, for example, when Jessica Statsky refers to the research finding that about 90 percent of children would choose to play regularly on a losing team rather than sit on the bench of a winning team (par. 5). Readers are likely to accept such a high percentage at face value because they would probably share the preference for playing over watching. However, without knowing the size of the sample (90 percent of 10 people, 100 people, or 10,000 people?), it is impossible to judge the significance of the statistic. Moreover, without knowing who the researchers are and how their research was funded and conducted, it is also difficult to judge the credibility of the statistic. That's why most critical readers want to know the source of statistics to see whether the research is **peer-reviewed**—that is, whether it has been evaluated by other researchers knowledgeable about the subject and able to judge the reliability of its findings.

ANALYZE & WRITE

Write a couple of paragraphs analyzing and evaluating Etzioni's use of statistics, and write a paragraph explaining how you could use statistics to enhance your credibility with readers:

1. Reread paragraphs 8–14, and highlight the statistics Etzioni uses. What is each statistic being used to illustrate or prove?

2. Identify what you would need to know about these research studies before you could accept their statistics as credible. Consider also what you would need to know about Etzioni himself before you could decide whether to rely on statistics he calls "impressive" (par. 10). How does your personal experience and observation influence your decision?

3. Based on this analysis, explain how you think you should present statistics that you want your readers to accept as trustworthy.

AN EFFECTIVE RESPONSE: PRESENTING AND REINTERPRETING EVIDENCE TO UNDERMINE OBJECTIONS

At key points throughout his essay, Etzioni acknowledges readers' likely objections and then responds to them. One strategy Etzioni uses is to cite research that appears to undermine his claim and then offer a new interpretation of that evidence. For example, he cites a study by Harrell and Wirtz (par. 10) that links work as a student with greater likelihood of employment later on. He then reinterprets the data from this study to show that the high likelihood of future employment could be an indication that workers in fast-food restaurants are more likely to drop out of school rather than an indication that workers are learning important employment skills. This strategy of presenting and reinterpreting evidence can be especially effective in academic writing, as Etzioni (a professor of sociology) well knows.

ANALYZE & WRITE

Write a couple of paragraphs analyzing and evaluating Etzioni's use of this strategy elsewhere in his essay:

1 Reread paragraphs 8–9, in which Etzioni responds to the claim that employees in McDonald's-type jobs develop many useful skills.

2 Reread paragraphs 14–16, in which Etzioni discusses the benefits and shortcomings of various kinds of on-the-job supervision.

3 Identify the claim that appears in the research Etzioni cites, point out how Etzioni reinterprets it, and explain whether you find his reinterpretation persuasive.

A CLEAR, LOGICAL ORGANIZATION: PROVIDING CUES FOR READERS

Writers of position arguments generally try to make their writing logical and easy to follow. Providing **cues,** or road signs—for example, by forecasting their reasons in a thesis statement early in the argument, using topic sentences to announce each reason as it is supported, and employing transitions (such as *furthermore, in addition,* and *finally*) to guide readers from one point to another—can be helpful, especially in newspaper articles, the readers of which do not want to spend a lot of time deciphering arguments.

ANALYZE & WRITE

Write a paragraph analyzing and evaluating the cueing strategies Etzioni uses to help his readers follow his argument:

1 Find and highlight his thesis statement, the cues forecasting his reasons, the transitions he provides, and any other cueing devices Etzioni uses.

2 Identify the paragraphs in which Etzioni develops each of his reasons.

3 Explain how Etzioni helps readers track his reasons and how effective his cues are.

[RESPOND] **Consider possible topics: Issues facing students.**

Etzioni focuses on a single kind of part-time work, takes a position on how worthwhile it is, and recommends against it. You could write a similar kind of essay. For example, you could take a position for or against students' participating in other kinds of part-time work or recreation during the high school or college academic year or over the summer—for example, playing on a sports team, volunteering, completing an internship, studying a musical instrument or a foreign language, or taking an elective class. If you work to support yourself and pay for college, you could focus on why the job either strengthens or weakens you as a person, given your life and career goals. Writing for other students, you would either recommend the job or activity to them or discourage them from pursuing it, giving reasons and support for your position.

Daniel J. Solove | *Why Privacy Matters Even If You Have "Nothing to Hide"*

© Dirk Anschütz

DANIEL J. SOLOVE is the John Marshall Harlan Research Professor of Law at the George Washington University Law School. In addition to writing numerous books and articles on issues of privacy and the Internet, Solove is the founder of a company that provides privacy and data security training to corporations and universities. Among his books are *The Future of Reputation: Gossip, Rumor, and Privacy on the Internet* (2007), which won Fordham University's McGannon Award for Social and Ethical Relevance in Communications Policy Research, and *Nothing to Hide: The False Tradeoff between Privacy and Security* (2011). An earlier and longer version of this essay in a law review journal included citations that had to be eliminated for publication in the *Chronicle of Higher Education* in 2011, but we have restored them so that you can see how Solove uses a variety of sources to support his position. As you read, consider the following:

- The sources cited in the opening paragraphs: How do they contribute to your understanding of why many people think privacy is not something they should be concerned about?

- Do you use Internet privacy settings, and should you be concerned about protecting your privacy on social networking and other Web sites?

1   When the government gathers or analyzes personal information, many people say they're not worried. "I've got nothing to hide," they declare. "Only if you're doing something wrong should you worry, and then you don't deserve to keep it private." The nothing-to-hide argument pervades discussions about privacy. The data-security expert Bruce Schneier calls it the "most common retort against privacy advocates." The legal scholar Geoffrey Stone refers to it as an "all-too-common refrain." In its most compelling form, it is an argument that the privacy interest is generally minimal, thus making the contest with security concerns a foreordained victory for security.

2   The nothing-to-hide argument is everywhere. In Britain, for example, the government has installed millions of public-surveillance cameras in cities and towns, which are watched by officials via

closed-circuit television. In a campaign slogan for the program, the government declares: "If you've got nothing to hide, you've got nothing to fear" (Rosen 36). Variations of nothing-to-hide arguments frequently appear in blogs, letters to the editor, television news interviews, and other forums. One blogger in the United States, in reference to profiling people for national-security purposes, declares: "I don't mind people wanting to find out things about me, I've got nothing to hide! Which is why I support [the government's] efforts to find terrorists by monitoring our phone calls!" (greatcarrieoakey).

3   On the surface, it seems easy to dismiss the nothing-to-hide argument. Everybody probably has something to hide from somebody. As Aleksandr Solzhenitsyn declared, "Everyone is guilty of something or has something to conceal. All one has to do is look hard enough to find what it is" (192). . . . One can usually think of something that even the most open person would want to hide. As a commenter to my blog post noted, "If you have nothing to hide, then that quite literally means you are willing to let me photograph you naked? And I get full rights to that photograph—so I can show it to your neighbors?" (Andrew) . . .

4   But such responses attack the nothing-to-hide argument only in its most extreme form, which isn't particularly strong. In a less extreme form, the nothing-to-hide argument refers not to all personal information but only to the type of data the government is likely to collect. Retorts to the nothing-to-hide argument about exposing people's naked bodies or their deepest secrets are relevant only if the government is likely to gather this kind of information. In many instances, hardly anyone will see the information, and it won't be disclosed to the public. Thus, some might argue, the privacy interest is minimal, and the security interest in preventing terrorism is much more important. In this less extreme form, the nothing-to-hide argument is a formidable one. However, it stems from certain faulty assumptions about privacy and its value. . . .

5   Most attempts to understand privacy do so by attempting to locate its essence—its core characteristics or the common denominator that links together the various things we classify under the rubric of "privacy." Privacy, however, is too complex a concept to be reduced to a singular essence. It is a plurality of different things that do not share any one element but nevertheless bear a resemblance to one another. For example, privacy can be invaded by the disclosure of your deepest secrets. It might also be invaded if you're watched by a peeping Tom, even if no secrets are ever revealed. With the disclosure of secrets, the harm is that your concealed information is spread to others. With the peeping Tom, the harm is that you're being watched. You'd probably find that creepy regardless of whether the peeper finds out anything sensitive or discloses any information to others. There are many other forms of invasion of privacy, such as blackmail and the improper use of your personal data. Your privacy can also be invaded if the government compiles an extensive dossier about you. Privacy, in other words, involves so many things that it is impossible to reduce them all to one simple idea. And we need not do so. . . .

6   To describe the problems created by the collection and use of personal data, many commentators use a metaphor based on George Orwell's *Nineteen Eighty-Four*. Orwell depicted a harrowing totalitarian society ruled by a government called Big Brother that watches its citizens obsessively and demands strict discipline. The Orwell metaphor, which focuses on the harms of surveillance (such as inhibition and social control), might be apt to describe government monitoring of citizens. But much of

the data gathered in computer databases, such as one's race, birth date, gender, address, or marital status, isn't particularly sensitive. Many people don't care about concealing the hotels they stay at, the cars they own, or the kind of beverages they drink. Frequently, though not always, people wouldn't be inhibited or embarrassed if others knew this information.

7   Another metaphor better captures the problems: Franz Kafka's *The Trial*. Kafka's novel centers around a man who is arrested but not informed why. He desperately tries to find out what triggered his arrest and what's in store for him. He finds out that a mysterious court system has a dossier on him and is investigating him, but he's unable to learn much more. *The Trial* depicts a bureaucracy with inscrutable purposes that uses people's information to make important decisions about them, yet denies the people the ability to participate in how their information is used.

8   The problems portrayed by the Kafkaesque metaphor are of a different sort than the problems caused by surveillance. They often do not result in inhibition. Instead they are problems of information processing—the storage, use, or analysis of data— rather than of information collection. They affect the power relationships between people and the institutions of the modern state. They not only frustrate the individual by creating a sense of helplessness and powerlessness, but also affect social structure by altering the kind of relationships people have with the institutions that make important decisions about their lives.

9   Legal and policy solutions focus too much on the problems under the Orwellian metaphor—those of surveillance—and aren't adequately addressing the Kafkaesque problems—those of information processing. The difficulty is that commentators are trying to conceive of the problems caused by databases in terms of surveillance when, in fact, those problems are different.

Commentators often attempt to refute the nothing-to-hide argument by pointing to things people want to hide. But the problem with the nothing-to-hide argument is the underlying assumption that privacy is about hiding bad things. By accepting this assumption, we concede far too much ground and invite an unproductive discussion about information that people would very likely want to hide. As the computer-security specialist Schneier aptly notes, the nothing-to-hide argument stems from a faulty "premise that privacy is about hiding a wrong." Surveillance, for example, can inhibit such lawful activities as free speech, free association, and other First Amendment rights essential for democracy.

10   The deeper problem with the nothing-to-hide argument is that it myopically views privacy as a form of secrecy. In contrast, understanding privacy as a plurality of related issues demonstrates that the disclosure of bad things is just one among many difficulties caused by government security measures. To return to my discussion of literary metaphors, the problems are not just Orwellian but Kafkaesque. Government information-gathering programs are problematic even if no information that people want to hide is uncovered. In *The Trial*, the problem is not inhibited behavior but rather a suffocating powerlessness and vulnerability created by the court system's use of personal data and its denial to the protagonist of any knowledge of or participation in the process. The harms are bureaucratic ones—indifference, error, abuse, frustration, and lack of transparency and accountability.

11   One such harm, for example, which I call aggregation, emerges from the fusion of small bits of seemingly innocuous data. When combined, the information becomes much more telling. By joining pieces of information we might not take pains to guard, the government can glean information about us that we might indeed wish to

conceal. For example, suppose you bought a book about cancer. This purchase isn't very revealing on its own, for it indicates just an interest in the disease. Suppose you bought a wig. The purchase of a wig, by itself, could be for a number of reasons. But combine those two pieces of information, and now the inference can be made that you have cancer and are undergoing chemotherapy. That might be a fact you wouldn't mind sharing, but you'd certainly want to have the choice.

12   Another potential problem with the government's harvest of personal data is one I call exclusion. Exclusion occurs when people are prevented from having knowledge about how information about them is being used, and when they are barred from accessing and correcting errors in that data. Many government national-security measures involve maintaining a huge database of information that individuals cannot access. Indeed, because they involve national security, the very existence of these programs is often kept secret. This kind of information processing, which blocks subjects' knowledge and involvement, is a kind of due-process problem. It is a structural problem, involving the way people are treated by government institutions and creating a power imbalance between people and the government. To what extent should government officials have such a significant power over citizens? This issue isn't about what information people want to hide but about the power and the structure of government.

13   A related problem involves secondary use. Secondary use is the exploitation of data obtained for one purpose for an unrelated purpose without the subject's consent. How long will personal data be stored? How will the information be used? What could it be used for in the future? The potential uses of any piece of personal information are vast. Without limits on or accountability for how that information is used, it is hard for people to assess the dangers of the data's being in the government's control.

14   Yet another problem with government gathering and use of personal data is distortion. Although personal information can reveal quite a lot about people's personalities and activities, it often fails to reflect the whole person. It can paint a distorted picture, especially since records are reductive—they often capture information in a standardized format with many details omitted. For example, suppose government officials learn that a person has bought a number of books on how to manufacture methamphetamine. That information makes them suspect that he's building a meth lab. What is missing from the records is the full story: The person is writing a novel about a character who makes meth. When he bought the books, he didn't consider how suspicious the purchase might appear to government officials, and his records didn't reveal the reason for the purchases. Should he have to worry about government scrutiny of all his purchases and actions? Should he have to be concerned that he'll wind up on a suspicious-persons list? Even if he isn't doing anything wrong, he may want to keep his records away from government officials who might make faulty inferences from them. He might not want to have to worry about how everything he does will be perceived by officials nervously monitoring for criminal activity. He might not want to have a computer flag him as suspicious because he has an unusual pattern of behavior. . . .

15   Privacy is rarely lost in one fell swoop. It is usually eroded over time, little bits dissolving almost imperceptibly until we finally begin to notice how much is gone. When the government starts monitoring the phone numbers people call, many may shrug their shoulders and say, "Ah, it's just numbers, that's all." Then the government might start monitoring some phone calls. "It's just a few phone calls, nothing more."

The government might install more video cameras in public places. "So what? Some more cameras watching in a few more places. No big deal." The increase in cameras might lead to a more elaborate network of video surveillance. Satellite surveillance might be added to help track people's movements. The government might start analyzing people's bank records. "It's just my deposits and some of the bills I pay—no problem." The government may then start combing through credit-card records, then expand to Internet-service providers' records, health records, employment records, and more. Each step may seem incremental, but after a while, the government will be watching and knowing everything about us.

16   "My life's an open book," people might say. "I've got nothing to hide." But now the government has large dossiers of everyone's activities, interests, reading habits, finances, and health. What if the government leaks the information to the public? What if the government mistakenly determines that based on your pattern of activities, you're likely to engage in a criminal act? What if it denies you the right to fly? What if the government thinks your financial transactions look odd—even if you've done nothing

wrong—and freezes your accounts? What if the government doesn't protect your information with adequate security, and an identity thief obtains it and uses it to defraud you? Even if you have nothing to hide, the government can cause you a lot of harm. . . .

Works Cited

Andrew. Weblog comment. *Concurring Opinions*. 16 Oct. 2006. Web. 24 May 2012.

greatcarrieoakey. "Reach For The Stars!" *Blogspot.com*. 14 May 2006. Web. 24 May 2012.

Rosen, Jeffrey. *The Naked Crowd: Reclaiming Security and Freedom in an Anxious Age*. New York: Random House, 2004. Print.

Schneier, Bruce. "The Eternal Value of Privacy." *Wired*. 18 May 2006. Web. 24 May 2012.

Solzhenitsyn, Aleksandr. *Cancer Ward*. Trans. Nicholas Bethell and David Burg. New York: Farrar, Straus and Giroux, 1969. Print.

Stone, Geoffrey R. "Freedom and Public Responsibility." *Chicago Tribune* 21 May 2006: 11. Print.

⎡REFLECT⎤ **Make connections: Privacy concerns on the Internet.**

Whereas Solove's position argument focuses on concerns about government collection and use of personal information, many people today are concerned as well about corporate collection and use of personal information. For example, students about to graduate from college have been surprised to discover that potential employers search blogs and social media Web sites to gather information about job candidates and to check their résumés. Corporations also use data mining to personalize advertising, sending diaper coupons, for example, to women in their thirties who have recently bought diaper bags or baby monitors online. (You may recall the talking billboards depicted in the film *Minority Report:* "John Anderton! You could use a Guinness right about now.")

Think about the implications of corporate data mining, and reflect on how this could affect your own sense of online privacy. Your instructor may ask you to post your thoughts on a class discussion board or to discuss them with other students in class. Use these questions to get started:

- How, if at all, do you manage the privacy preferences or settings on sites you use? Do you ever de-friend people or click the "do not track" tool when you have the opportunity to do so? Would you untag photos or delete comments on social networking sites like Facebook that you didn't want potential employers to see?

- Do you think you should be concerned or learn more about privacy problems, such as identity theft, cyberstalking, or personalized advertising?

- What are the advantages and disadvantages of corporate data mining? Have targeted advertisements been a boon to you, or are you distressed about a corporation's knowing so much about you?

[ANALYZE] Use the basic features.

A FOCUSED, WELL-PRESENTED ISSUE: REFRAMING THROUGH CONTRAST

Writers sometimes have to remind their readers why an issue is controversial. Beginning with the title, Solove works to undermine the widely held assumption that the erosion of privacy should not be a concern. He does this primarily by contrasting two different ways of thinking about threats to privacy, which he calls Orwellian and Kafkaesque, based on the novels *1984*, by George Orwell, and *The Trial*, by Franz Kafka. To present this contrast, Solove uses sentence patterns like these:

▶ Not _____, but _____.

▶ _____ focus on _____, which is characterized by _____, and they don't even notice _____, which is characterized by _____.

Here are a couple of examples from Solove's position argument:

> The problems are not just Orwellian but Kafkaesque. (par. 10)

> Legal and policy solutions focus too much on the problems under the Orwellian metaphor—those of surveillance—and aren't adequately addressing the Kafkaesque problems—those of information processing. (par. 9)

ANALYZE & WRITE

Write a few paragraphs analyzing and evaluating the effectiveness of Solove's use of contrast to reframe the issue for readers:

1. Notice how Solove uses sources in his first two paragraphs. Given his purpose to reframe a commonly held view of privacy, why do you think he begins this way?

2. Reread paragraphs 6–7 to see how Solove explains the two contrasting metaphors. Then skim paragraphs 8–10, highlighting any sentence patterns used to mark the contrast.

3. Has Solove's reframing of the discussion affected your understanding of privacy and your concerns about its loss? Why or why not?

A WELL-SUPPORTED POSITION: USING SOURCES

Writers of position arguments often quote, paraphrase, and summarize sources. Usually, they use sources to support their positions, as Jessica Statsky does in her argument about children's sports. Sometimes, however, they use sources to highlight opposing positions to which they will respond, as Solove does in this essay.

In the following example, Solove signals his opinion through the words he chooses to characterize the source:

> As the computer-security specialist Schneier aptly notes, the nothing-to-hide argument stems from a faulty "premise that privacy is about hiding a wrong." (par. 9)

Elsewhere, readers have to work a little harder to determine how Solove is using the source.

Solove also uses what we might call **hypothetical quotations**—sentences that quote not what someone actually said but what they *might* have said:

Signal phrase	Many people say they're not worried. "I've got nothing to hide," they
Hypothetical quotation	declare. "Only if you're doing something wrong should you worry, and then you don't deserve to keep it private." (par. 1)
	"My life's an open book," people might say. "I've got nothing to hide." (par. 16)

You can tell from a signal phrase like "people might say" or "many people say" that no actual person made the statement, but Solove does not always supply such cues.

ANALYZE & WRITE ─────────────────────────────────

Write a couple of paragraphs analyzing and evaluating Solove's use of quotations:

1. Find and mark the quotations, noting which actually quote someone and which are hypothetical.

2. Identify the quotations — real or hypothetical — that Solove agrees with and those that represent an opposing view.

3. Consider how effective Solove's quoting strategy was likely to have been, given his purpose and audience. (Remember that this article appeared in the *Chronicle of Higher Education*, a weekly newspaper for college faculty and administrators.) How effective did you find his quoting strategy?

To learn more about using patterns of opposition to read critically, see pp. 310–11 in Chapter 9.

AN EFFECTIVE RESPONSE: REFUTING BY DEMONSTRATING THE EFFECTS

As his title suggests, Solove refutes the claim that privacy does not matter "if you have 'nothing to hide.'" His primary way of refuting the nothing-to-hide argument is to argue that the collection and use of personal information (the cause) has negative effects, which he sometimes calls "problems" and sometimes calls "harms" (pars. 5 and 6).

ANALYZE & WRITE

Write a few paragraphs analyzing and evaluating Solove's use of cause and effect reasoning to refute the claim that privacy only matters if you have something to hide:

1 Reread paragraphs 6–14, noting where Solove discusses potential problems or harms that could result from the collection of personal data.

2 Choose one of these harms, and examine Solove's argument more closely. How does he support this part of the argument — for example, what are his reasons, his evidence, the values and beliefs he uses to appeal to his audience?

3 How effective are Solove's reasons and evidence for you? How effective might they have been for his original audience?

A CLEAR, LOGICAL ORGANIZATION: USING CUEING DEVICES

Solove uses a number of cueing devices to help readers keep track of his argument. Perhaps the most obvious and helpful cues are the topic sentences that begin each paragraph and the logical transitions ("One such harm . . . ," "Another potential problem . . . ," "A related problem . . . ," "Yet another problem . . ." [pars. 11–14]) that signal connections between and within paragraphs. In addition, Solove uses rhetorical questions, such as the series of "What if" questions in the final paragraph.

ANALYZE & WRITE

Write a few paragraphs analyzing and evaluating the effectiveness of Solove's use of cueing devices to help readers follow his argument:

1 Choose a couple of paragraphs that seem to you to use topic sentences and logical transitions effectively. Look closely at the way Solove uses these cueing devices, and determine what makes them so effective.

2 Highlight the rhetorical questions posed in paragraphs 12–14 and 16. Why do you imagine Solove uses so many of them, especially in the final paragraph? Given his purpose and audience, how effective do you think these rhetorical questions were likely to have been? How effective do you find them?

[RESPOND] **Consider possible topics: Issues concerning privacy.**

Solove focuses on one concern about the erosion of privacy. You could write a similar type of essay, taking a position on issues such as state laws requiring women to have ultrasounds before terminating a pregnancy; airport security requiring passengers either to go through a full-body scanner or to submit to a "pat-down" before boarding a flight; cell phones making it possible for individuals to be located and tracked without their consent or knowledge; or houses, offices, and even people on the street being depicted on Google Maps without their knowledge or consent.

 macmillanhighered.com/conciseguide
How can a visual make a strong argument?
E-readings > U.S. Department of Transportation/The Ad Council, *The "It's Only Another Beer" Black and Tan*

The Writing Assignment	171
Writing a Draft: Invention, Research, Planning, and Composing	172
Evaluating the Draft: Getting a Critical Reading	182
Improving the Draft: Revising, Formatting, Editing, and Proofreading	184

The Writing Assignment

Write an essay arguing a controversial position: Start by learning more about the issue and the debate surrounding it, and then take a position. Present the issue so readers recognize that it merits their attention, and develop a well-supported argument that will confirm, challenge, or change your readers' views.

This Guide to Writing is designed to help you compose your own position argument and apply what you have learned from reading other position arguments. This Starting Points chart will help you find answers to questions you might have about composing a position argument. Use the chart to find the guidance you need, when you need it.

STARTING POINTS: ARGUING A POSITION

How do I come up with an issue to write about?

- Consider possible topics. (pp. 162–63, 170)
- Choose a controversial issue on which to take a position. (p. 173)
- Test Your Choice (p. 174)

A Focused, Well-Presented Issue

How can I effectively frame the issue for my readers?

- Assess the genre's basic features: A focused, well-presented issue. (pp. 147–49)
- A Focused, Well-Presented Issue: Framing an Argument for a Diverse Group of Readers (pp. 160–61)
- A Focused, Well-Presented Issue: Reframing through Contrast (p. 168)
- Frame the issue for your readers. (pp. 174–75)
- A Troubleshooting Guide: A Focused, Well-Presented Issue (p. 184)

A Well-Supported Position

How do I come up with a plausible position?

- Assess the genre's basic features: A well-supported position. (pp. 149–50)
- Formulate a working thesis stating your position. (p. 176)
- Develop the reasons supporting your position. (pp. 176–77)
- Research your position. (p. 177)
- Use sources to reinforce your credibility. (pp. 177–78)

(continued)

A Well-Supported Position

How do I come up with reasons and evidence supporting my position?

- A Well-Supported Position: Using Statistics (p. 161)
- A Well-Supported Position: Using Sources (p. 169)
- Formulate a working thesis stating your position. (p. 176)
- Develop the reasons supporting your position. (pp. 176–77)
- Research your position. (p. 177)

An Effective Response to Opposing Views

How do I respond to possible objections to my position?

- Assess the genre's basic features: An effective response to opposing views. (pp. 150–51)
- Identify and respond to your readers' likely reasons and objections. (pp. 178–80)
- Write the opening sentences. (pp. 181–82)

How do I respond to possible alternative positions?

- Assess the genre's basic feature: An effective response to opposing views (pp. 150–51)
- An Effective Response: Presenting and Reinterpreting Evidence to Undermine Objections (p. 162)
- An Effective Response: Refuting by Demonstrating the Effects (p. 169)
- Research your position (p. 177)
- Identify and respond to your readers' likely reasons and objections. (pp. 178–80)

A Clear, Logical Organization

How can I help my readers follow my argument?

- Assess the genre's basic features: A clear, logical organization. (p. 151)
- A Clear, Logical Organization: Providing Cues for Readers (p. 162)
- A Clear, Logical Organization: Using Cueing Devices (p. 170)
- Create an outline that will organize your argument effectively for your readers. (pp. 180–81)
- A Troubleshooting Guide: A Clear, Logical Organization (p. 185)

Writing a Draft: Invention, Research, Planning, and Composing

The activities in this section will help you choose and research an issue as well as develop and organize an argument for your position. Do the activities in any order that makes sense to you (and your instructor), and return to them as needed as you revise. Your writing in response to many of these activities can be used in a rough draft that you will be able to improve after receiving feedback from your classmates and instructor.

Choose a controversial issue on which to take a position.

When choosing an issue, keep in mind that the issue must be

- controversial—an issue that people disagree about;
- arguable—a matter of opinion on which there is no absolute proof or authority;
- one that you can research, as necessary, in the time you have; and
- one that you care about.

Choosing an issue in which you have special interest or knowledge usually works best. For example, if you are thinking of addressing an issue of national concern, focus on a local or at least a specific aspect of it: For example, instead of addressing censorship in general, write about a recent lawmaker's effort to propose a law censoring the Internet, a city council attempt to block access to Internet sites at the public library, or a school board's ban on certain textbooks.

You may already have an issue in mind. If you do, skip to Test Your Choice (p. 172). If you do not, the topics that follow, in addition to those following the readings (pp. 162 and 170), may suggest an issue you can make your own:

Issues Related to School

- Should particular courses, community service, or an internship be a graduation requirement at your high school or college?
- Should students attending public colleges be required to pay higher tuition fees if they have been full-time students but have not graduated within four years?
- Should your large lecture or online courses have frequent (weekly or biweekly) exams instead of only a midterm and final?

Issues Related to Your Community

- Should children raised in this country whose parents entered illegally be given an opportunity to become citizens upon finishing college or serving in the military?
- Should the racial, ethnic, or gender makeup of the police force resemble the makeup of the community it serves?
- Should the football conference your school (or another school in the area) participates in be allowed to expand?

Issues Related to Work

- Should you look primarily for a job that is well paid or for a job that is personally fulfilling or socially responsible?
- Should public employees be allowed to unionize and to bargain collectively for improved working conditions, pay, or pensions?
- Should the state or federal government provide job training for those who are unemployed but able to work?

Ask yourself the following questions:

- Does the issue matter to me and to my readers? If the issue is not currently one of widespread concern, would I be able to argue convincingly at the beginning of my essay that it *ought* to be of concern?
- Do I know enough about the issue to take a position that I can support effectively, or can I learn what I need to know in the time I have?
- Have I begun to understand the issue well enough to frame or reframe it in a way that might open readers to my point of view?
- What can I realistically hope to achieve with my readers — convince them to adopt my point of view; get them to reconsider what's at stake; show them that arguments they trust are unfair, inaccurate, or logically flawed?

As you plan and draft your argument, you will probably want to consider these questions. If at any point you cannot answer them with a confident *yes*, you may want to consider modifying your position on the issue or choosing a different issue to write about. If you have serious doubts, discuss them with your instructor.

Frame the issue for your readers.

Once you have made a preliminary choice of an issue, consider how you can frame (or reframe) it so that readers who support opposing positions will listen to your argument. To do this, consider how the issue has been debated in the past and what your readers are likely to think. Use the following questions and sentence strategies to help you put your ideas in writing.

WAYS IN

HOW CAN I EXPLORE THE ISSUE?

What groups or notable individuals have shaped the debate on this issue? What positions have they taken?

- ▶ It may surprise you that _____ is a controversial issue. Although many people take _____ for granted, [individuals/groups] oppose it on the grounds that _____.
- ▶ Whereas supporters of _____ have argued that _____, opponents such as [list individuals/groups] contend that _____.

WHAT DO MY READERS THINK?

What values and concerns do I and my readers share regarding the issue?

- ▶ Concern about _____ leads many of us to oppose _____. We worry that _____ will happen if _____.
- ▶ _____ is a basic human right that needs to be protected. But what does it mean in everyday practice when _____?

What fundamental differences in world-view or experience might keep me and my readers from agreeing?

How has the issue, or people's opinions about the issue, changed? What makes the issue important now?

▶ [Recent research reports/incidents reported in the news] have changed some people's minds on this issue. Instead of assuming _____, many people now think _____ .

▶ The debate over whether _____ should _____ was initially concerned with _____, but now the main concern seems to be that _____ .

▶ Those who disagree about _____ often see it as a choice between _____ and _____. But both are important. We don't have to choose between them because _____ .

▶ While others may view it as a matter of _____, for me, the issue hinges on _____ .

▶ According to _____, what's at stake in this issue is _____. For me, however, what is most important is _____ .

HOW CAN I FRAME THE ISSUE EFFECTIVELY?

Once you have a good idea of how the issue has been debated and what your readers think, use these sentence strategies to frame the issue for your readers.

What is the issue, and why should my readers be concerned about it?

▶ I'm concerned about _____ because _____ .

EXAMPLE   I'm concerned about the high cost of tuition at state colleges like ours because students are having to borrow more money to pay for their education than they will be able to repay.

Why are popular approaches or attitudes inappropriate or inadequate?

▶ Although some argue _____, I think _____ because _____ .

EXAMPLE   Although some argue that college football players should be paid, I think the current system should be maintained because it is only the money earned from football that enables our school to fund other, less lucrative sports programs.

TEST YOUR CHOICE

Ask two or three other students to consider the way you have framed your issue.

Presenters.   Briefly explain the values and concerns you think are at stake. (The sentence strategies in the Ways In section can help you articulate your position and approach.)

Listeners.   Tell the presenter what response this way of framing the issue elicits from you and why. Use language that follows as a model for structuring your response, or use language of your own.

▶ I'm [also/not] concerned about the high cost of tuition because _____ .

▶ I [agree/disagree] that college football players should not be paid because _____ .

Formulate a working thesis stating your position.

You may already have a position on the issue; if so, try drafting a working thesis statement now. (Alternatively, if you prefer to conduct research or develop your argument before trying to formulate a thesis, skip this activity and return to it when you're ready.) As you develop your argument, rework this assertion to make it a compelling thesis statement by sharpening the language and perhaps forecasting your reasons. You may also need to qualify it, with words like *often, sometimes,* or *in part.*

WAYS IN

HOW CAN I DEVISE AN ARGUABLE THESIS?

A good strategy is to begin by describing the issue, possibly indicating where others stand on it or what's at stake, and then saying what you think. These sentence strategies may help you get started:

- ▶ On this issue, X and Y say _____. Although I understand and to some degree sympathize with their point of view, this is ultimately a question of _____. What's at stake is not _____ but _____. Therefore, we must _____.

- ▶ This issue is dividing our community. Some people argue _____ . Others contend _____. And still others believe _____. It is in all of our interests to _____, however, because _____.

- ▶ Conventional wisdom is that _____. But I take a different view: _____.

Develop the reasons supporting your position.

The following activities will help you find plausible reasons and evidence for your position. Begin by writing down what you already know. You can do some focused research later to fill in the details, or skip ahead to conduct research now.

For more idea-generating strategies, see Chapter 8.

WAYS IN

HOW CAN I COME UP WITH REASONS THAT SUPPORT MY POSITION?

One way to generate ideas is to write steadily for at least five minutes exploring your reasons. Ask yourself questions like these:

- How can I show readers that my reasons lead logically to my position?
- In addition to appealing to readers' intellect (logos), how can I convince my readers that I am trustworthy (ethos) or appeal to their feelings (pathos)?

At this point, don't worry about the exact language you will use in your final draft. Instead, just write the reasons you hold your position and the evidence (such as anecdotes, examples, statistics, expert testimony) that supports it. Keep your readers in mind—what would they find most convincing?

If you prefer to brainstorm a list of reasons, try this:

- Start by writing your position at the top of the page.
- List as many potential reasons as you can think of to support your position. (Don't judge at this point.)
- Make notes about the kinds of evidence you would need to show how each reason supports your position. You may be able to use this list and your notes as a starting point for further research and drafting.

▪▪ Research your position.

Do some research to find out how others have argued in support of your position:

- Try entering keywords or phrases related to the issue or your position in the search box of an all-purpose database, such as *Academic OneFile* (InfoTrac) or *Academic Search Complete* (EBSCOHost), to find relevant articles in magazines and journals, or use the database *Lexis/Nexis* to find articles in newspapers. For example, Jessica Statsky could have tried a combination of keywords, such as *children's sports,* or variations on her terms (*youth sports*) to find relevant articles. A similar search of your library's catalog could also be conducted to locate books and other resources on your topic.
- If you think your issue has been dealt with by a government agency, explore the state, local, or tribal sections of USA.gov—the U.S. government's official Web portal—or visit the Library of Congress page on state government information (www.loc.gov/rr/news/stategov/stategov.html) and follow the links.

Remember to bookmark promising sites and to record the URL and information you will need to cite and document any sources or visuals you use.

To learn more about searching a database or catalog, or about finding government documents, see Chapter 16, pp. 404–408.
To learn more about documenting sources, consult Chapter 19 (MLA) or Chapter 20 (APA).

▪▪ Use sources to reinforce your credibility.

How you represent your sources can quickly establish your credibility (ethos)—or the reverse. For example, by briefly describing the author's credentials the first time she *summarizes, paraphrases,* or *quotes* from a source, Jessica Statsky establishes the source's authority and demonstrates that she has selected sources appropriately:

Signal phrase and author's credentials	Martin Rablovsky, a former sports editor for the *New York Times,* says that in all his years of watching young children play organized sports, he
Source summary	has noticed very few of them smiling. "I've seen children enjoying a

Quotations can also reinforce the accuracy of your summary or paraphrase and establish your fairness to opposing points of view. In the following sentence, Jessica Statsky demonstrates her fairness by quoting from the Web site of the Little League, a well-known organization, and she establishes her credibility by demonstrating that even those who disagree with her recognize that injuries occur:

<table>
<tr><td>In-text citation
follows quotation</td><td>spontaneous pre-practice scrimmage become somber and serious when the coach's whistle blows," Rablovsky says . . . (qtd. in Coakley 94).</td></tr>
</table>

<table>
<tr><td>Statsky's introduction:
Summarizes source

In-text citation follows
quotation</td><td>Although the official Little League Web site acknowledges that children do risk injury playing baseball, it insists that "severe injuries . . . are infrequent," the risk "far less than the risk of riding a skate-board, a bicycle, or even the school bus" ("What about My Child?").</td></tr>
</table>

In both of these examples from "Children Need to Play, Not Compete" (pars. 5 and 3, respectively), Statsky introduces the source to her readers, explaining the relevance of the source material, including the author's credentials, for readers rather than leaving them to figure out its relevance for themselves.

Whenever you borrow information from sources, be sure to double-check that you are summarizing, paraphrasing, and quoting accurately and fairly. Compare Statsky's sentence with the source passage (that follows). (The portions she uses are highlighted.) Notice that she has inserted ellipsis (. . .) to indicate that she has left out words from her source's second sentence.

Source

Injuries seem to be inevitable in any rigorous activity, especially if players are new to the sport and unfamiliar with its demands. But because of the safety precautions taken in Little League, severe injuries such as bone fractures are infrequent. Most injuries are sprains and strains, abrasions and cuts and bruises. The risk of serious injury in Little League Baseball is far less than the risk of riding a skateboard, a bicycle, or even the school bus.

In both of the preceding examples, Statsky uses quotation marks to indicate that she is borrowing the words of a source and provides an in-text citation so that readers can locate the sources in her list of works cited. Doing both is essential to avoiding plagiarism; one or the other is not enough.

For more on integrating language from sources into your own sentences and avoiding plagiarism, see Chapter 18, pp. 428–29.

▪▪ Identify and respond to your readers' likely reasons and objections.

The following activity will help you anticipate reasons your readers may use to support their argument or objections they may have. You may want to return to this activity as you do additional research and learn more about the issue and the arguments people make. Use the research strategies on pp. 176–77 or consult Chapter 16, "Finding Sources and Conducting Field Research."

WAYS IN →

HOW CAN I FIGURE OUT WHAT MY READERS WILL BE CONCERNED ABOUT?

1. Start by listing the reasons you expect your readers to have for their position and the objections (including those based on logical fallacies) you expect them to raise to your argument. To think of readers' concerns, consider how you differ on values, beliefs, and priorities.

2. Analyze your list of readers' likely reasons and objections. Which can you refute, and how? Which may you need to concede?

For more logical fallacies, see pp. 378–79 in Chapter 13.

HOW CAN I RESPOND TO READERS' REASONS AND OBJECTIONS?

Now, choose a reason or objection, and try out a response:

1. Summarize it accurately and fairly. (Do not commit the "straw man" fallacy of knocking down something that no one really takes seriously.)

2. Decide whether you can refute it, need to concede it, or can refute part and concede part.

Try sentence strategies like these to refute, concede, or concede and refute reasons supporting readers' arguments or their objections to your argument:

To Refute

Reason or Objection Lacks Credible Support

▶ My opponents cite research to support their [reason/objection], but the credibility of that research is questionable because _____. In contrast, reliable research by _____ shows _____.

▶ This [reason/objection] seems plausible because it is consistent with our preconceptions. Nevertheless, evidence shows _____.

Readers' Values and Concerns Are Better Served by Your Position

▶ Some insist _____. Still, in spite of their good intentions, _____ would [take away a basic right/make things even worse].

▶ X and Y think this issue is about _____. But what is really at stake here is _____.

Reasoning Is Flawed

▶ Proponents object to my argument on the grounds that _____. However, they are confusing results with causes. What I am arguing is _____.

▶ Polls show that most people favor _____, but an opinion's popularity does not make it true or right.

▶ While most would agree that _____, it does not necessarily follow that _____.

(continued)

Times Have Changed

▶ One common complaint is _____. In recent years, however, _____.

To Concede

Accept an Objection Well Taken

▶ To be sure, _____ is true.

▶ Granted, _____ must be taken into consideration.

Qualify on Common Ground

▶ Some people argue that _____. I understand this reservation, and therefore, I think we should _____.

Refocus Your Argument

▶ A common concern about this issue is _____. That's why my argument focuses on [a different aspect of the issue].

To Concede and Refute

And Instead of Or

▶ I agree that _____ is important, and so is _____.

Yes, But

▶ I agree that _____ is important, but my opponents also need to consider _____.

On the One Hand . . . On the Other Hand

▶ On the one hand, I accept X's argument that _____, but on the other hand, I still think _____ is ultimately more important because _____.

Note: If a reason or an objection seems so damaging that you cannot refute it convincingly or concede it without undermining your own argument, discuss with your instructor how you could modify your position or whether you should choose a new issue to write about. If you do not know enough about readers' views to anticipate their reasons or likely objections to your argument, do more research.

Create an outline that will organize your argument effectively for your readers.

Whether you have rough notes or a complete draft, making an outline of what you have written can help you organize the essay effectively for your audience. Compare the possible outlines that follow to see how you might organize your essay depending on whether your readers primarily agree or disagree with you.

Readers Primarily Agree with You	**Readers Primarily Disagree with You**
Strengthen their convictions by organizing your argument around a series of reasons backed by supporting evidence or by refuting opposing arguments point by point:	Begin by emphasizing common ground, and make a concession to show that you have considered the opposing position carefully and with an open mind:
I. **Presentation of the issue**	I. **Presentation of the issue:** Reframe the issue in terms of common values
II. **Thesis statement:** A direct statement of your position	II. **Concession:** Acknowledge the wisdom of an aspect of the opposing position
III. **Your most plausible reasons and evidence**	III. **Thesis statement:** A direct statement of your position, qualified as necessary
IV. **Concession or refutation of opposing reasons or objections to your argument**	IV. **Your most plausible reasons and evidence**
V. **Conclusion:** Reaffirmation of your position	V. **Conclusion:** Reiteration of shared values

Whatever organizational strategy you adopt, do not hesitate to change your outline as necessary while drafting and revising. For instance, you might find it more effective to hold back on presenting your own position until you have discussed unacceptable alternatives. Or you might find a more powerful way to order the reasons for supporting your position. The purpose of an outline is to identify the basic components of your argument and to help you organize them effectively, not to lock you into a particular structure.

For more on outlining, see pp. 284–87 in Chapter 8.

Write the opening sentences.

Notice how the writers of the selections in this chapter have used their opening sentences to frame or reframe the issue for their readers while also grabbing their attention:

- Jessica Statsky provides statistics to help readers understand the importance of her topic:

  "Organized sports for young people have become an institution in North America," reports sports journalist Steve Silverman, attracting more than
  44 million youngsters according to a recent survey by the National Council of Youth Sports ("History"). (p. 152)

- Amitai Etzioni uses a surprising statement to capture readers' attention:

  McDonald's is bad for your kids. (p. 158)

- Daniel J. Solove uses a hypothetical quotation to indicate how people typically think about the issue:

  When the government gathers or analyzes personal information, many people say they're not worried. "I've got nothing to hide," they declare. (p. 163)

Additional strategies you could try include comparing your issue to a different issue about which your readers may agree or using a rhetorical question to arouse your readers' concerns about the issue. To engage your readers and set the stage for your position, try reworking your framing sentences (p. 175) and using them to open your essay, but do not agonize over the first sentences because you are likely to discover the best way to begin only after you have written a rough draft.

Draft your position argument.

By this point, you have done a lot of writing to

- Devise a focused, well-presented issue and take a position on it
- Frame your issue so that readers will be open to your argument
- Support your position with reasons and evidence your readers will find persuasive
- Refute or concede alternative viewpoints on the issue
- Organize your ideas to make them clear, logical, and effective for readers

Now stitch that material together to create a draft. The next two parts of this Guide to Writing will help you evaluate and improve that draft.

Evaluating the Draft: Getting a Critical Reading

Your instructor may arrange a peer review session in class or online, where you can exchange drafts with your classmates and give each other a thoughtful critical reading—pointing out what works well and suggesting ways to improve the draft. A good critical reading does three things:

1. It lets the writer know how the reader understands the point of the argument.

2. It praises what works best.

3. It indicates where the draft could be improved and makes suggestions how to improve it.

One strategy for evaluating a draft is to use the basic features of a position argument as a guide.

A CRITICAL READING GUIDE

How well does the writer present the issue?

**A Focused
Well-Presented
Issue**

Summarize: Tell the writer what you understand the issue to be. If you were already familiar with it and understand it differently, briefly explain.

Praise: Give an example from the essay where the issue and its significance come across effectively.

Critique: Tell the writer where more information about the issue is needed, where more might be done to establish its seriousness, or how the issue could be framed or reframed in a way that would better prepare readers for the argument.

A Well-Supported Position

How well does the writer argue in support of the position?

Summarize: Underline the thesis statement and the main reasons.

Praise: Give an example in the essay where the argument is especially effective; for example, indicate which reason is especially convincing or which supporting evidence is particularly compelling.

Critique: Tell the writer where the argument could be strengthened; for example, indicate how the thesis statement could be made clearer or more appropriately qualified, how the argument could be developed, or where additional support is needed.

An Effective Response to Opposing Views

How effectively has the writer responded to others' reasons and likely objections?

Summarize: Identify where the writer responds to a reason others use to support their argument or an objection they have to the writer's argument.

Praise: Give an example in the essay where a concession seems particularly well done or a refutation is convincing.

Critique: Tell the writer how a concession or refutation could be made more effective, identify a reason or objection the writer should respond to, or note where common ground could be found.

A Clear, Logical Organization

How clearly and logically has the writer organized the argument?

Summarize: Find the sentence(s) in which the writer states the thesis and forecasts supporting reasons, as well as transitions or repeated key words and phrases.

Praise: Give an example of how or where the essay succeeds in being especially easy to read, perhaps in its overall organization, clear presentation of the thesis, clear transitions, or effective opening or closing.

Critique: Tell the writer where the readability could be improved. Can you, for example, suggest better forecasting or clearer transitions? If the overall organization of the essay needs work, make suggestions for rearranging parts or strengthening connections.

Before concluding your peer review, be sure to address any of the writer's concerns that have not been discussed already.

Improving the Draft: Revising, Formatting, Editing, and Proofreading

Start improving your draft by reflecting on what you have written thus far:

- Review critical reading comments from your classmates, instructor, or writing center tutor: What problems are your readers identifying?
- Consider your invention writing: What else should you consider?
- Review your draft: What can you do to support your position more effectively?

Revise your draft.

If your readers are having difficulty with your draft, or if you think there is room for improvement, try some of the strategies listed in the Troubleshooting Guide that follows. It can help you fine-tune your presentation of the genre's basic features.

A TROUBLESHOOTING GUIDE

A Focused, Well-Presented Issue

My readers don't get the point.

- Quote experts or add information—statistics, examples, anecdotes, and so on—to help readers understand what's at stake.
- Consider adding visuals, graphs, tables, or charts to present the issue more clearly.

My readers have a different perspective on the issue than I do.

- Show the limitations of how the issue has traditionally been understood.
- Reframe the issue by showing how it relates to values, concerns, needs, and priorities you share with readers.
- Give concrete examples or anecdotes, facts, and details that could help readers see the issue as you see it.

A Well-Supported Position

My readers do not find my argument clear and/or persuasive.

- Revisit your thesis statement to make sure your position is stated clearly and directly.
- Reconsider your reasons, or explain how they support your position.
- Add supporting evidence—statistics, examples, authorities, and so on.
- Consider adding visuals, graphs, tables, or charts to support your argument.
- Strengthen the logical, ethical, and/or emotional appeals of your argument.
- Try outlining your argument; if your organization is weak or illogical, or if your transitional strategies are not working, try reorganizing the material, adding transitional words and phrases, or repeating key words strategically.

An Effective Response to Opposing Views

My readers question my response to opposing arguments or objections to my argument.

- If your refutation is weak, strengthen it with additional or more compelling reasons and evidence.
- If your concession weakens your argument, qualify your position with words like *sometimes* or *often*.
- Consider adding a refutation to your concession.

A Clear, Logical Organization

My readers are confused by my essay or find it difficult to read.

- Outline your essay. If necessary, move, add, or delete sections to strengthen coherence.
- Consider adding a forecasting statement with key terms that are repeated in topic sentences throughout the essay.
- Check for appropriate transitions between sentences, paragraphs, and major sections of your essay.
- Review your opening and closing paragraphs. Be sure that your thesis is clearly expressed and that you reaffirm your position in your closing.

Edit and proofread your draft.

Students frequently struggle to maintain a neutral tone when arguing a position they hold dearly. Our research also indicates that incorrect comma usage in sentences with *coordinating conjunctions* and punctuation errors in sentences that use *conjunctive adverbs* are common in position arguments. The following guidelines will help you check your essay for these common errors.

Editing for Tone

To demonstrate that you are treating alternative viewpoints fairly, use words with a positive or neutral connotation (emotional resonance) and avoid name-calling.

▶ Too often . . . the drive to win ~~turns~~ *encourages* parents ~~into monsters~~ ~~threatening~~ *to threaten* umpires.

As you edit your position argument, also watch out for language that is puffed up or pompous:

▶ A coach who had attended the Adelphi workshop tried to ~~operationalize~~ *put into practice* what he had

learned there, but the players' ~~progenitors~~ *parents* would not support him.

Using Commas before Coordinating Conjunctions

In essays that argue a position, writers often use coordinating conjunctions (*and, but, for, or, nor, so,* and *yet*) to join related **independent clauses**—groups of words that can stand alone as complete sentences—to create *compound sentences*. Consider this example from Jessica Statsky's essay:

Compound sentence: two independent clauses linked by a coordinating conjunction

coord. conj.

▶ Winning and losing may be an inevitable part of adult life, but they
— independent clause 1 —   comma
should not be part of childhood. (par. 6)
— independent clause 2 —

In this sentence, Statsky links two complete ideas of equal importance with the coordinating conjunction *but* to emphasize contrast.

The Problem   Two common errors occur in sentences like these:

1. A comma may be left out when two independent clauses are linked by a coordinating conjunction.
2. A comma may be inserted before the coordinating conjunction when one of the sentence parts is not an independent clause.

The Correction   Add a comma before coordinating conjunctions that join two independent clauses, as in the following example:

▶ The new immigration laws will bring in more skilled people but their presence will take jobs away from other Americans

Omit the comma when coordinating conjunctions join phrases that are not independent clauses:

▶ We need people with special talents, and diverse skills to make the United States a stronger nation.

 macmillanhighered.com/conciseguide
LearningCurve > Commas

Avoiding Comma Splices When Using Conjunctive Adverbs to Link Independent Clauses

Conjunctive adverbs (such as *consequently, furthermore, however, moreover, therefore,* and *thus*) indicate the logical relationships among ideas. For example, words like *thus* and *therefore* are used to alert readers that a conclusion is coming, and words like *furthermore* and *moreover* are used to alert readers to expect additional ideas on the same topic. When writers take a position, they often use conjunctive adverbs to link independent clauses.

Consider this example:

conj. adv.

▶ Children watching television recognize violence but not its intention; thus, they
— independent clause 1 —   semicolon   comma
become desensitized to violence.
— independent clause 2 —

In this sentence, the writer uses the word *thus* to indicate that he is drawing a conclusion.

The Problem   A *comma splice* is one error that often occurs when writers use a comma before a conjunctive adverb linking two independent clauses.

The Correction   Use a semicolon before and a comma after a conjunctive adverb when it links two independent clauses:

▶ The recent vote on increasing student fees produced a disappointing turnout, moreover

  the presence of campaign literature on ballot tables violated voting procedures.

Make sure that both parts of the sentence are independent clauses before inserting a semicolon, a conjunctive adverb, and a comma to link them. If one or both parts cannot stand alone, add a subject, a verb, or both as needed to avoid a *sentence fragment:*

▶ Children watching television recognize violence; however, not its intention.

Alternatively, you may replace the semicolon, conjunctive adverb, and comma with a coordinating conjunction:

but

▶ Children watching television recognize violence; however, not its intention.

macmillanhighered.com/conciseguide
LearningCurve > Run-ons and Comma Splices

A Common Problem for Multilingual Writers: Detecting Subtle Differences in Meaning

Because the distinctions in meaning among some common conjunctive adverbs are subtle, nonnative speakers often have difficulty using them accurately. For example, the difference between *however* and *nevertheless* is small; each is used to introduce a contrasting statement. But *nevertheless* emphasizes the contrast, whereas *however* softens it. Check usage of such terms in an English dictionary rather than a bilingual one. *The American Heritage Dictionary of the English Language* has special usage notes to help distinguish frequently confused words.

THINKING CRITICALLY

To think critically means to use all of the knowledge you have acquired from the information in this chapter, your own writing, the writing of other students, and class discussions to reflect deeply on your work for this assignment and the genre (or type) of writing you have produced. The benefit of thinking critically is proven and important: Thinking critically about what you have learned will help you remember it longer, ensuring that you will be able to put it to good use well beyond this writing course.

Reflecting on What You Have Learned

In this chapter, you have learned a great deal about arguing for a position from reading several position arguments and from writing one of your own. To consolidate your learning, reflect not only on what you learned but also on how you learned it.

ANALYZE & WRITE

Write a blog post to classmates, a letter to your instructor, or an e-mail message to a student who will take this course next term, using the writing prompt that seems most productive for you:

- Explain how your purpose and audience influenced one of your decisions as a writer, such as how you presented the issue, the strategies you used in arguing your position, or the ways in which you attempted to counter possible objections.

- Discuss what you learned about yourself as a writer in the process of writing this essay. For example, what part of the process did you find most challenging? Did you try anything new, like getting a critical reading of your draft or outlining your draft in order to revise it?

- Choose one of the readings in this chapter and explain how it influenced your essay. Be sure to cite specific examples from your essay and the reading.

- If you got good advice from a critical reader, explain exactly how the person helped you—perhaps by questioning the way you addressed your audience or the kinds of evidence you offered in support of your position.

Reflecting on the Genre

While you were writing your position argument, we encouraged you to frame your position in terms of values you share with your readers and to provide logical reasons and evidence in support of your position. However, some critics argue that privileging reasoned argument over other ways of arguing is merely a means to control dissent. Instead of expressing what may be legitimate outrage and inciting public concern through passionate language, dissenters are urged to be dispassionate and reasonable even though they are arguing with people whose views they find repugnant. In the end, trying to present a well-reasoned, well-supported argument may serve to maintain the status quo by silencing the more radical voices within the community. What do you think about this controversy?

Write a page or two explaining your ideas about whether the genre's requirement that writers give reasons and support suppresses dissent. Connect your ideas to your own position argument and to the readings in this chapter. In your discussion, you might consider one or more of the following questions:

1. **In your own experience of arguing a position on a controversial issue, did having to give reasons and support discourage you from choosing any particular issue or from expressing strong feelings?** Reflect on the issues you listed as possible subjects for your essay and how you made your choice. Did you reject any issues because you could not come up with reasons and support for your position? When you made your choice, did you think about whether you could be dispassionate and reasonable about it?

2. **Consider the readings in this chapter and the position arguments you read by other students in the class.** Do you think any of these writers felt limited by the need to give reasons and support for their position? Which of the essays you read, if any, seemed to you to express strong feelings about the issue? Which, if any, seemed dispassionate?

3. **Consider the kind of arguing you typically witness in the media — radio, television, newspapers, magazines, the Internet.** In the media, have giving reasons and support and anticipating readers' objections been replaced with a more contentious, in-your-face style of arguing? Think of media examples of these two different ways of arguing. What do these examples lead you to conclude about the contention that reasoned argument can stifle dissent?

6

Proposing a Solution

© Children's Television Workshop/Getty Images

A proposal urges readers to take action to solve a problem. To be convincing, proposals need to demonstrate that the problem must be solved and that the proposed solution is the best available option. In college, proposals may be written to solve campus problems, such as residence hall noise, or they may be more specialized, such as research proposals to seek funding to investigate how to preserve indigenous languages. Workplace proposals may be addressed to the company's management (such as the need for investment in new technology) or to another company seeking a contract to perform certain services. In the community, proposals seek to get things done, from a neighborhood proposal for a traffic signal at a dangerous intersection to a congressional recommendation to improve the health care system.

IN COLLEGE COURSES

For an early childhood education class, a student writes a proposal that Congress require broadcast networks to provide programming to help preschool children learn English. He establishes the need for such regulation by citing statistics showing that the children of non-English-speaking parents are less likely than the children of English speakers to attend preschool. To lend credibility to his proposal, he cites a researcher specializing in the impact of media on children's language acquisition and interviews via e-mail the programming coordinator for a national network. He counters possible objections of impracticality by citing two model programs, public television's *Sesame Street* and cable's *Mi Casita* (*My Little House*). He concludes by reminding his readers — not only his instructor but also his local Congressional representative — that those who use publicly owned airwaves are required by law to serve the public interest.

Claudia Wiens/Alamy

© Blend Images/Alamy

IN THE COMMUNITY

A social services administrator in a large city becomes concerned about a rise in the number of adolescents in jail. To help solve this problem, he proposes that his department intervene at the first sign of delinquent behavior in eight- to twelve-year-olds. He describes the consequences of jailing young criminals, focusing on the cost of incarceration and the high rate of recidivism (the return to criminal activity), and he provides statistics and case histories showing the positive effects of intervention for very young first offenders. He then discusses the major components of his program: finding mentors for struggling adolescents and placing social workers with troubled families. The administrator acknowledges the costs of the program but points to savings if incarceration rates are lowered.

IN THE WORKPLACE

A truck driver notices that her employer is unable to find enough short-haul drivers for deliveries. To solve this problem, she suggests in an e-mail message to her boss that the company initiate a training program to bring more women into the workforce. By interviewing other female truck drivers, she had learned that women tend to be turned off by the male-dominated truck-driving schools, so she proposes that qualified recruits be placed with experienced drivers serving as paid mentors. She recognizes that the program must not adversely affect the company's bottom line, so she suggests that the cost of the mentorship be offset by a rookie-driver tuition fee. She concludes by pointing out that the company would not only get the skilled drivers it needs at no cost but also create an incentive (additional income) for experienced drivers to remain with the company.

In this chapter, we ask you to identify a problem you care about and write a proposal to solve it. Analyzing the reading selections that follow will help you learn how to make a convincing case for the solution you propose. The Guide to Writing later in the chapter will show you ways to use the basic features of the genre to make your proposal inventive as well as practical.

PRACTICING THE GENRE

Arguing That a Solution Is Feasible

Proposals often succeed or fail on the strength of the argument that the proposed solution is feasible. To practice making a feasibility argument, get together with two or three other students and follow these guidelines:

Part 1.   Begin by identifying a problem you face as a student in one of your college courses (this course or a different one). Next, discuss the problem in your group, and choose one of the following solutions (or think of another solution). The instructor should:

- drop one of the assigned books;
- offer special study sessions;
- post study sheets on the readings.

Then discuss the following questions to determine how you could demonstrate to the instructor that your solution is feasible:

- Is it doable? List specific steps that the instructor would need to take.
- Is it worth doing? Identify what implementing the solution would cost the instructor (in terms of time, for example) compared to how much it would benefit the students (in terms of learning, for example).
- Would it work? To prove it would actually help solve the problem, you could show that it eliminates a cause of the problem or that it has worked elsewhere, for example.

Part 2.   As a group, discuss what you learned from this activity.

- Which part of the argument — identifying a problem, finding a solution, or arguing that the solution is doable, is worth doing, and would work — was easiest? Hardest?
- If the instructor objected that your proposed solution would be unfair to those students who are doing well in the course, how could you respond in a way that assures the instructor that it would be fair?
- Imagine that you were writing this proposal to a different audience — for example, a group of professors at a conference about undergraduate teaching or an administrator who controls the budget or schedule. How might you change your argument or the way you present it for a different audience?

Analyzing Proposals

As you read the selections in this chapter, you will see how different authors propose a solution. Analyzing how these writers define their problems, argue for their solutions, respond to opposing views, and organize their writing will help you see how you can use these techniques to make your own proposals clear and compelling for your readers.

Determine the writer's purpose and audience.

When reading the proposals in this chapter, ask yourself the following questions about the writer's purpose and audience:

- What seems to be the writer's main *purpose*—for example, to convince readers that the problem truly exists and needs immediate action; to persuade readers that the writer's proposed solution is better than alternative solutions; or to rekindle readers' interest in a long-standing problem?

- What does the writer assume about the *audience*—for example, that readers will be unaware of the problem; that they will recognize the existence of the problem but fail to take it seriously; that they will think the problem has already been solved; or that they will prefer an alternative solution?

Assess the genre's basic features.

> ### Basic Features
>
> A Focused, Well-Defined Problem
>
> A Well-Argued Solution
>
> An Effective Response to Objections and Alternative Solutions
>
> A Clear, Logical Organization

Use the following to help you analyze and evaluate how proposal writers use the genre's basic features. The writing strategies they typically use to convince readers to adopt the proposed solution are illustrated below with examples from the readings in this chapter as well as sentence strategies you can experiment with later, as you write your own proposal.

A FOCUSED, WELL-DEFINED PROBLEM

Read first to see how the writer defines or frames the problem. Framing a problem is a way of preparing readers for the proposed solution by focusing on the aspect of the problem the proposal tries to solve. In "More Testing, More Learning," for example, student Patrick O'Malley frames the problem in terms of the detrimental effects of high-stakes exams on students' learning. If O'Malley were writing to students instead of their teachers, he might have framed the problem in terms of students' poor study habits or procrastination. By framing the problem as he did, he indicates that teachers, rather than students, have the ability to solve the problem and tries to convince readers that it is real and serious. Consider, for example, how (and how well) the writer frames the problem

- by recounting *anecdotes* or constructing *scenarios* to show how the problem affects people

EXAMPLE   It's late at night. The final's tomorrow. (O'Malley, par. 1)

   by giving *examples* to make the problem less abstract

EXAMPLE   [Tyler Clementi was] a victim of cyber-bullying. (Bornstein, par. 1)

   by listing the negative *effects* of the problem

EXAMPLE   Cause   As a result of the unaffordable and low quality nature of child care
              Transition   in this country, a disturbing number of today's children are left
              Effect   home alone. (Kornbluh, par. 13)

   by describing the ongoing discussion of the problem and debate over solutions

EXAMPLE   The typical institutional response to bullying is to get tough. (Bornstein, par. 2)

Probably the most convincing strategy writers use to demonstrate the severity of the problem is to cite *research studies* and *statistics*. As you read, look for source material, and notice whether the writer emphasizes the credibility of the research by including the expert's name and credentials or by identifying the publication in which the study appeared at the beginning of the sentence in which the study is mentioned:

Placement   ▶ A study published in [name of journal or university press] shows that _____.
emphasizes
credibility of   **EXAMPLE**   A 2006 study reported in the journal *Psychological Science*
expert/   concluded that "taking repeated tests . . . leads to better . . .
publication   retention" . . . according to the study's coauthors, Henry L.
                                 Roediger and Jeffrey Karpicke (ScienceWatch.com, 2008).
                                 (O'Malley, par. 4)

        ▶ [Name], [title] at [institution], has found that _____.

            EXAMPLE   Ervin Staub, professor emeritus of psychology at the University of
                                 Massachusetts, has studied . . . and found that . . . ("Biographical
                                 Note"). (Bornstein, par. 9)

Alternatively, the writer may emphasize the source material by putting the information about the study up front and identifying the source later in the sentence or in the parenthetical citation, as in the following:

Placement   ▶ _____ percent of [group studied] [believe/work/struggle] _____.
emphasizes
study   **EXAMPLE**   Fifty-nine percent of these caregivers either work or have worked
                                 while providing care ("Caregiving"). (Kornbluh, par. 8)

        ▶ [Research findings] show that _____ (source).

            EXAMPLE   Moreover, many employees . . . lack the ability to take a day off to
                                 care for a family member (Lovell). (Kornbluh, par. 2)

Then assess whether the problem is focused enough to have been treated in the depth needed to achieve the writer's purpose with the original audience. To make their proposal manageable, writers concentrate on one aspect of a broad problem.

A WELL-ARGUED SOLUTION

To argue convincingly for a solution to a problem, writers need to *make clear exactly what is being proposed and offer supporting reasons and evidence* showing that the proposed solution

- will help solve the problem;
- can be implemented;
- is worth the expense, time, and effort to do so.

Read first to find the proposed solution, usually declared in a *thesis statement* early in the essay. Typically, the thesis describes the proposed solution briefly and indicates how it would solve the problem, as in this example:

Problem and its *disadvantages*	So, not only do high-stakes exams *discourage frequent study* and *undermine students' performance,* they also *do long-term damage to students' cognitive*
Thesis proposing solution and its benefits	*development.* If professors gave brief exams at frequent intervals, students would be spurred to learn more and worry less. They would study more regularly, perform better on tests, and enhance their cognitive functioning. (O'Malley, par. 2)

Then check to see how the writer presents the *supporting reasons* and *evidence,* and consider how compelling the argument will be to the writer's purpose and audience. The following sentence and examples suggest the kinds of reasons, evidence, and writing strategies proposal writers often employ to present their argument:

Cause/effect
- The proposed solution would reduce or eliminate a major cause of the problem and would (or could) have beneficial effects:

  ▶ As research shows, [the proposed solution] would [lead to/encourage] _____ and would [stop something harmful, change habits, reverse a decline].

EXAMPLE
But programs like the one I want to discuss today show the potential of augmenting our innate impulses to care for one another instead of just falling back on punishment as a deterrent. (Bornstein, par. 2)

Comparison
- A similar solution has worked elsewhere:

  ▶ Research shows that [program Y] has been effective in [solving/causing] _____.

EXAMPLE
It seems that it's not only possible to make people kinder, it's possible to do it systematically at scale—at least with school children. That's what one organization based in Toronto called Roots of Empathy has done. (Bornstein, par. 4)

Process analysis
- The necessary steps to put the solution into practice can be taken without excessive cost or inconvenience:

  ▶ [The solution] is easy to implement: first do _____ and then do _____.

EXAMPLE
Ideally, a professor would give an in-class test or quiz after each unit. . . . These exams should be given weekly or at least twice monthly. . . . Exams should take no more than 15 or 20 minutes. (O'Malley, par. 3)

Statistics   ■ Stakeholders could come together behind the proposal:

> ▶ Statistical surveys suggest that [the solution] will appeal to those who are concerned about _____ as well as those worried about _____ because [it would alleviate both groups' concerns/is in the best interests of everyone].

EXAMPLE   This should be a popular priority. A recent poll found that 77 percent of likely voters feel . . . Eighty-four percent of voters agree that . . . (Kornbluh, par. 15)

AN EFFECTIVE RESPONSE TO OBJECTIONS AND ALTERNATIVE SOLUTIONS

Writers proposing solutions need to *anticipate and respond to readers' likely objections and to the alternative solutions readers may prefer.* Writers typically respond in one or more of the following ways:

- ■ By **conceding** (accepting) a valid objection and modifying the argument to accommodate it
- ■ By **refuting** (arguing against) criticism—for example, by demonstrating that an objection is without merit or arguing that an alternative solution would be more costly or less likely to solve the problem than the proposed solution

A typical way of conceding is to use a sentence strategy like this:

> ▶ To accommodate [critic A's concern], instead of doing _____, you could do _____.

Before writing his proposal, student Patrick O'Malley interviewed professors so that he could respond to their objections. Notice how his concession is really a compromise designed to convince readers of his proposal's flexibility:

> If weekly exams still seem too time-consuming to some professors, their frequency could be reduced to every other week or their length to 5 or 10 minutes. In courses where multiple-choice exams are appropriate, several questions could be designed to take only a few minutes to answer. (O'Malley, par. 9)

A typical refutation summarizes the objection or alternative solution and then explains why the criticism is problematic. Proposal writers refute objections and alternative solutions more often than they concede. Following are common sentence strategies used to refute objections and alternative solutions:

> ▶ Some object that the proposed solution would [cost too much/cause too much disruption]. However, when you take into consideration the fact that [inaction would cost even more/cause more disruption than doing nothing], you have to conclude that _____.

> ▶ Although X and Y prefer [alternative approach], my solution would be [less expensive/ easier to implement] because _____.

Here are a few examples showing how the proposals in this chapter refute objections or alternative solutions. Notice that proposal writers often introduce the refutation with a *transition* that indicates contrast, such as *but, although, nevertheless,* or *however:*

Contrasts alternative and proposed solutions   Some believe that . . . From the student's perspective, however, this time is well spent. (O'Malley, par. 9)

> The typical institutional response to bullying is to get tough. . . . But programs like the one I want to discuss today show the potential of augmenting our innate impulses to care for one another instead of just falling back on punishment as a deterrent. (Bornstein, par. 2)

When reading a proposal, consider whether the writer presents others' views fairly and accurately and whether the writer's rebuttal is likely to be convincing to readers. Pay special attention to the writer's tone in responding to other views, noting any place the tone seems sarcastic or dismissive and considering whether such a tone would be effective given the writer's purpose and audience.

To learn more about constructing arguments, see Chapter 13.

A CLEAR, LOGICAL ORGANIZATION

Look for cues or signposts that help readers identify the parts of the proposal. Identify the topic and find the thesis, which in a proposal asserts the solution. Bornstein identifies the topic in his title— "Fighting Bullying with Babies"—and asserts his thesis in paragraph 4:

> It seems that it's not only possible to make people kinder, it's possible to do it systematically at scale—at least with school children.

Look also for topic sentences, particularly those that announce the parts of the proposal argument. Notice also any transitions and how they function. For example, all of the transitions in the following topic sentences (*another, moreover, still,* and *furthermore*) indicate items in a list. Other transitions you can expect in proposals signal causes or effects (*because, as a result*), exceptions (*but*), concessions (*although*), refutations (*however*), emphasis (*more important*), conclusions (*then, therefore*), and enumerations (*first, second*). Here are the beginnings of several topic sentences from O'Malley's essay:

The main reason professors should give frequent exams is that . . . (par. 4)

Transitions   Another, closely related argument in favor of multiple exams is that . . . (par. 6)

Moreover, professors object to frequent exams because . . . (par. 10)

Still another solution might be to . . . (par. 12)

Furthermore, professors could . . . (par. 13)

Finally, if headings or visuals (such as flowcharts, graphs, tables, photographs, or cartoons) are included, determine how they contribute. Notice whether visuals are referred to in the text and whether they have titles or captions.

Readings

Patrick O'Malley | *More Testing, More Learning*

FRUSTRATED BY what he calls "high-stakes exams," Patrick O'Malley wrote the following proposal while he was a first-year college student. To conduct research into opposing viewpoints, O'Malley interviewed two professors (his writing instructor and the writing program director), talked with several students, and read published research on testing. He cited his sources using APA style, as his instructor had requested.

As you read, consider the questions in the margin. Your instructor may ask you to post your answers or bring them to class. Also consider the following:

- How does O'Malley respond to likely objections?
- How does he respond to preferred alternative solutions?

Basic Features

A Focused, Well-Defined Problem

A Well-Argued Solution

An Effective Response to Objections and Alternative Solutions

A Clear, Logical Organization

What is the function of the opening paragraph?

How does framing the problem this way set up the solution?

How does O'Malley use the key terms introduced here throughout the essay?

What does par. 3 contribute to the argument?

---

1   It's late at night. The final's tomorrow. You got a C on the midterm, so this one will make or break you. Will it be like the midterm? Did you study enough? Did you study the right things? It's too late to drop the course. So what happens if you fail? No time to worry about that now — you've got a ton of notes to go over.

2   Although this last-minute anxiety about midterm and final exams is only too familiar to most college students, many professors may not realize how such major, infrequent, high-stakes exams work against the best interests of students both psychologically and cognitively. They cause unnecessary amounts of stress, placing too much importance on one or two days in the students' entire term, judging ability on a single or dual performance. Reporting on recent research at Cornell University Medical School, Sian Beilock, a psychology professor at the University of Chicago, points out that "stressing about doing well on an important exam can backfire, leading students to 'choke under pressure' or to score less well than they might otherwise score if the stakes weren't so high." Moreover, Cornell's research using fMRI brain scans shows that "the pressures of a big test can reach beyond the exam itself — stunting the cognitive systems that support the attention and memory skills every day" (Beilock 2010). So, not only do high-stakes exams discourage frequent study and undermine students' performance, they also do long-term damage to students' cognitive development. If professors gave brief exams at frequent intervals, students would be spurred to learn more and worry less. They would study more regularly, perform better on tests, and enhance their cognitive functioning.

3   Ideally, a professor would give an in-class test or quiz after each unit, chapter, or focus of study, depending on the type of class and course material. A physics class might require a test on concepts after every chapter covered, while a history class could necessitate quizzes covering certain

time periods or major events. These exams should be given weekly or at least twice monthly. Whenever possible, they should consist of two or three essay questions rather than many multiple-choice or short-answer questions. To preserve class time for lecture and discussion, exams should take no more than 15 or 20 minutes.

4   The main reason professors should give frequent exams is that when they do and when they provide feedback to students on how well they are doing, students learn more in the course and perform better on major exams, projects, and papers. It makes sense that in a challenging course containing a great deal of material, students will learn more of it and put it to better use if they have to apply or "practice" it frequently on exams, which also helps them find out how much they are learning and what they need to go over again. A 2006 study reported in the journal *Psychological Science* concluded that "taking repeated tests on material leads to better long-term retention than repeated studying," according to the study's coauthors, Henry L. Roediger and Jeffrey Karpicke (ScienceWatch.com, 2008). When asked what the impact of this breakthrough research would be, they responded: "We hope that this research may be picked up in educational circles as a way to improve educational practices, both for students in the classroom and as a study strategy outside of class." The new field of mind, brain, and education research advocates the use of "retrieval testing." For example, research by Karpicke and Blunt (2011) published in *Science* found that testing was more effective than other, more traditional methods of studying both for comprehension and for analysis. Why retrieval testing works is not known. UCLA psychologist Robert Bjork speculates that it may be effective because "when we use our memories by retrieving things, we change our access" to that information. "What we recall," therefore, "becomes more recallable in the future" (qtd. in Belluck, 2011).

(margin note) How does O'Malley introduce this reason? What kinds of support does he offer?

(margin note) How does O'Malley integrate and cite sources in pars. 4 and 5?

5   Many students already recognize the value of frequent testing, but their reason is that they need the professor's feedback. A Harvard study notes students' "strong preference for frequent evaluation in a course." Harvard students feel they learn least in courses that have "only a midterm and a final exam, with no other personal evaluation." Students believe they learn most in courses with "many opportunities to see how they are doing" (Light, 1990, p. 32). In a review of a number of studies of student learning, Frederiksen (1984) reports that students who take weekly quizzes achieve

higher scores on final exams than students who take only a midterm exam and that testing increases retention of material tested.

How does O'Malley support this reason? Why does he include it?

6   Another, closely related argument in favor of multiple exams is that they encourage students to improve their study habits. Greater frequency in test taking means greater frequency in studying for tests. Students prone to cramming will be required — or at least strongly motivated — to open their textbooks and notebooks more often, making them less likely to resort to long, kamikaze nights of studying for major exams. Since there is so much to be learned in the typical course, it makes sense that frequent, careful study and review are highly beneficial. But students need motivation to study regularly, and nothing works like an exam. If students had frequent exams in all their courses, they would have to schedule study time each week and would gradually develop a habit of frequent study. It might be

How does O'Malley introduce and respond to this possible objection?

argued that students are adults who have to learn how to manage their own lives, but learning history or physics is more complicated than learning to drive a car or balance a checkbook. Students need coaching and practice in learning. The right way to learn new material needs to become a habit, and I believe that frequent exams are key to developing good habits of study and learning. The Harvard study concludes that "tying regular evaluation to good course organization enables students to plan their work more than a few days in advance. If quizzes and homework are scheduled on specific days, students plan their work to capitalize on them" (Light, 1990, p. 33).

7   By encouraging regular study habits, frequent exams would also decrease anxiety by reducing the procrastination that produces anxiety. Students would benefit psychologically if they were not subjected to the emotional ups and downs caused by major exams, when after being virtually worry-free for weeks they are suddenly ready to check into the psychiatric ward. Researchers at the

How effectively does O'Malley use this source?

University of Vermont found a strong relationship among procrastination, anxiety, and achievement. Students who regularly put off studying for exams had continuing high anxiety and lower grades than students who procrastinated less. The researchers found that even "low" procrastinators did not study regularly and recommended that professors give frequent assignments and exams to reduce procrastination and increase achievement (Rothblum, Solomon, & Murakami, 1986, pp. 393–394).

8   Research supports my proposed solution to the problem I have described. Common sense as well as my experience and that of many of my friends support it. Why, then, do so few professors give frequent brief exams?

What is the purpose of this question?

9   Some believe that such exams take up too much of the limited class time available to cover the material in the course. Most courses meet 150 minutes a week — three times a week for 50 minutes each time. A 20-minute weekly exam might take 30 minutes to administer, and that is one-fifth of each week's class time. From the student's perspective, however, this time is well spent. Better learning and greater confidence about the course seem a good trade-off for another 30 minutes of lecture. Moreover, time lost to lecturing or discussion could easily be made up in students' learning on their own through careful regular study for the weekly exams. If weekly exams still seem too time-consuming to some professors, their frequency could be reduced to every other week or their length to 5 or 10 minutes. In courses where multiple-choice exams are appropriate, several questions could be designed to take only a few minutes to answer.

10   Moreover, professors object to frequent exams because they take too much time to read and grade. In a 20-minute essay exam, a well-prepared student can easily write two pages. A relatively small class of 30 students might then produce 60 pages, no small amount of material to read each week. A large class of 100 or more students would produce an insurmountable pile of material. There are a number of responses to this objection. Again, professors could give exams every other week or make them very short. Instead of reading them closely, they could skim them quickly to see whether students understand an idea or can apply it to an unfamiliar problem; and instead of numerical or letter grades, they could give a plus, check, or minus. Exams could be collected and responded to only every third or fourth week. Professors who have readers or teaching assistants could rely on them to grade or check exams. And the Scantron machine is always available for instant grading of multiple-choice exams. Finally, frequent exams could be given *in place of* a midterm exam or out-of-class essay assignment.

How does O'Malley argue against possible objections in pars. 9 and 10?

11   Since frequent exams seem to some professors to create too many problems, however, it is reasonable to consider alternative ways to achieve the same goals. One alternative solution is to implement a program that would improve study skills. While such a program might teach students how

How effectively does O'Malley present alternative solutions in pars. 11 and 12?

to study for exams, it cannot prevent procrastination or reduce "large test anxiety" by a substantial amount. One research team studying anxiety and test performance found that study skills training was not effective in reducing anxiety or improving performance (Dendato & Diener, 1986, p. 134). This team, which also reviewed other research that reached the same conclusion, did find that a combination of "cognitive/relaxation therapy" and study skills training was effective. This possible solution seems complicated, however, not to mention time-consuming and expensive. It seems much easier and more effective to change the cause of the bad habit rather than treat the habit itself. That is, it would make more sense to solve the problem at its root: the method of learning and evaluation.

How do the highlighted words and phrases make the argument easy to follow?

12   Still another solution might be to provide frequent study questions for students to answer. These would no doubt be helpful in focusing students' time studying, but students would probably not actually write out the answers unless they were required to. To get students to complete the questions in a timely way, professors would have to collect and check the answers. In that case, however, they might as well devote the time to grading an exam. Even if it asks the same questions, a scheduled exam is preferable to a set of study questions because it takes far less time to write in class, compared to the time students would devote to responding to questions at home. In-class exams also ensure that each student produces his or her own work.

13   Furthermore, professors could help students prepare for midterm and final exams by providing sets of questions from which the exam questions will be selected or announcing possible exam topics at the beginning of the course. This solution would have the advantage of reducing students' anxiety about learning every fact in the textbook, and it would clarify the course goals, but it would not motivate students to study carefully each new unit, concept, or text chapter in the course. I see this as a way of complementing frequent exams, not as substituting for them.

How effective is this conclusion?

14   From the evidence and from my talks with professors and students, I see frequent, brief in-class exams as the only way to improve students' study habits and learning, reduce their anxiety and procrastination, and increase their satisfaction with college. These exams are not a panacea, but only more parking spaces and a winning football team would do as much to improve college

life. Professors can't do much about parking or football, but they can give more frequent exams. Campus administrators should get behind this effort, and professors should get together to consider giving exams more frequently. It would make a difference.

References

Beilock, S. (2010, September 3). Stressing about a high-stakes exam carries consequences beyond the test [Web log post]. Retrieved from http://www.psychologytoday.com/blog/choke/201009/stressing-about-high-stakes-exam-carries-consequences-beyond-the-test

Belluck, P. (2011, January 20). To really learn, quit studying and take a test. *The New York Times*. Retrieved from http://www.nytimes.com

Dendato, K. M., & Diener, D. (1986). Effectiveness of cognitive/relaxation therapy and study skills training in reducing self-reported anxiety and improving the academic performance of test-anxious students. *The Journal of Counseling Psychology, 33*, 131–135.

Frederiksen, N. (1984). The real test bias: Influences of testing on teaching and learning. *American Psychologist, 39*, 193–202.

Karpicke, J. D., & Blunt, J. R. (2011, January 30). Retrieval practice produces more learning than elaborative studying with concept mapping. *Science Online* doi: 10.1126/science.1199327

Light, R. J. (1990). *Explorations with students and faculty about teaching, learning, and student life*. Cambridge, MA: Harvard University Graduate School of Education and Kennedy School of Government.

Rothblum, E. D., Solomon, L., & Murakami, J. (1986). Affective, cognitive, and behavioral differences between high and low procrastinators. *Journal of Counseling Psychology, 33*, 387–394.

ScienceWatch.com (2008, February). Henry L. Roediger and Jeff Karpicke talk with ScienceWatch.com and answer a few questions about this month's fast breaking paper in the field of psychiatry/psychology [Interview]. Retrieved from http://sciencewatch.com/dr/fbp/2008/08febfbp/08febfbpRoedigerETAL

David Bornstein | *Fighting Bullying with Babies*

© JB Reed

DAVID BORNSTEIN has written popular books about solving social problems, including *How to Change the World: Social Entrepreneurs and the Power of New Ideas* (2007) and *Social Entrepreneurship: What Everyone Needs to Know* (2010). The recipient of several awards (for example, from Duke University's Fuqua School of Business), Bornstein co-wrote the PBS documentary *To Our Credit* and founded Dowser.org. The following proposal, "Fighting Bullying with Babies," originally appeared in Bornstein's *New York Times* blog *Fixes* in November 2010. We have converted Bornstein's links to in-text citations and have provided a list of the links at the end of the selection.

As you read, think about Bornstein's goal as described on the Dowser Web site to "present the world through a 'solution frame,' rather than a 'problem frame,'" and consider the following questions:

- What is the tone created by his opening journalistic hook: "Imagine there was a cure for meanness. Well, maybe there is"?

- How does the reference in the next sentence to the Tyler Clementi suicide affect the tone created by the hook? Point to any other passages where the tone seems to change or seems surprising.

- Given his purpose and original *New York Times* blog audience, what do you imagine Bornstein is trying to achieve with tone in this kind of proposal?

1   Imagine there was a cure for meanness. Well, maybe there is. Lately, the issue of bullying has been in the news, sparked by the suicide of Tyler Clementi ("Tyler"), a gay college student who was a victim of cyber-bullying, and by a widely circulated *New York Times* article that focused on "mean girl" bullying in kindergarten (Paul). The federal government has identified bullying as a national problem. In August, it organized the first-ever "Bullying Prevention Summit," and it is now rolling out an anti-bullying campaign aimed at 5- to 8-year-old children (White House). This past month the Department of Education released a guidance letter ("Guidance") urging schools, colleges and universities to take bullying seriously, or face potential legal consequences.

2   The typical institutional response to bullying is to get tough. In the Tyler Clementi case, prosecutors are considering bringing hate-crime charges (Dolnick).[1] But programs like the one I want to discuss today show the potential of augmenting our innate impulses to care for one another instead of just falling back on punishment as a deterrent. And what's the secret formula? A baby.

3   We know that humans are hardwired to be aggressive and selfish. But a growing body of research is demonstrating that there is also a biological basis for human compassion (Angier). Brain scans reveal that when we contemplate violence done to others we activate the same regions in our brains that fire up when mothers gaze at their children, suggesting that caring for

---

[1]Tyler Clementi's roommate, Dharun Ravi, was found guilty in March 2010 of fifteen counts, including invasion of privacy, tampering with evidence, and bias intimidation. [Editor's note]

strangers may be instinctual. When we help others, areas of the brain associated with pleasure also light up. Research by Felix Warneken and Michael Tomasello indicates that toddlers as young as 18 months behave altruistically. (If you want to feel good, watch one of their 15-second video clips [Warneken]. . . .)

4   More important, we are beginning to understand how to nurture this biological potential. It seems that it's not only possible to make people kinder, it's possible to do it systematically at scale—at least with school children. That's what one organization based in Toronto called Roots of Empathy has done. Roots of Empathy was founded in 1996 by Mary Gordon, an educator who had built Canada's largest network of school-based parenting and family-literacy centers after having worked with neglectful and abusive parents (Toronto District School Board). Gordon had found many of them to be lacking in empathy for their children. They hadn't developed the skill because they hadn't experienced or witnessed it sufficiently themselves. She envisioned Roots as a seriously proactive parent education program—one that would begin when the mothers- and fathers-to-be were in kindergarten. Since then, Roots has worked with more than 12,600 classes across Canada, and in recent years, the program has expanded to the Isle of Man, the United Kingdom, New Zealand, and the United States, where it currently operates in Seattle. Researchers have found that the program increases kindness and acceptance of others and decreases negative aggression.

5   Here's how it works: Roots arranges monthly class visits by a mother and her baby (who must be between two and four months old at the beginning of the school year). Each month, for nine months, a trained instructor guides a classroom using a standard curriculum that involves three 40-minute visits—a pre-visit, a baby visit, and a post-visit. The program runs from kindergarten to seventh grade. During the baby visits, the children sit around the baby and mother (sometimes it's a father) on a green blanket (which represents new life and nature) and they try to understand the baby's feelings. The instructor helps by labeling them. "It's a launch pad for them to understand their own feelings and the feelings of others," explains Gordon. "It carries over to the rest of class" (Gordon).

6   I have visited several public schools in low-income neighborhoods in Toronto to observe Roots of Empathy's work. What I find most fascinating is how the baby actually changes the children's behavior. Teachers have confirmed my impressions: tough kids smile, disruptive kids focus, shy kids open up. In a seventh grade class, I found 12-year-olds unabashedly singing nursery rhymes. The baby seems to act like a heart-softening magnet. No one fully understands why. Kimberly Schonert-Reichl, an applied developmental psychologist who is a professor at the University of British Columbia, has evaluated Roots of Empathy in four studies. "Do kids become more empathic and understanding? Do they become less aggressive and kinder to each other? The answer is yes and yes," she explained. "The question is why?" (Schonert-Reichl).

7   Sue C. Carter, a neurobiologist based at the University of Illinois at Chicago, who has conducted pioneering research into the effects of oxytocin, a hormone that has been linked with caring and trusting behavior, suspects that biology is playing a role in the program's impact (Angier). "This may be an oxytocin story," Carter told me. "I believe that being around the baby is somehow putting the children in a biologically different place. We don't know what that place is because we haven't measured it. However, if it works here as it does in other animals, we would guess that exposure to an infant would create a physiological state in which the children would be more social."

Elementary school students are taught empathy with a visit from Baby Leo, five months, through the Roots of Empathy program. Chris So/Toronto Star/Getty Images

8   To parent well, you must try to imagine what your baby is experiencing. So the kids do a lot of "perspective taking." When the baby is too small to raise its own head, for example, the instructor asks the children to lay their heads on the blanket and look around from there. Perspective taking is the cognitive dimension of empathy—and like any skill it takes practice to master. Children learn strategies for comforting a crying baby. They learn that one must never shake a baby. They discover that everyone comes into the world with a different temperament, including themselves and their classmates. They see how hard it can be to be a parent, which helps them empathize with their own mothers and fathers. And they marvel at how capacity develops. Each month, the baby does something that it couldn't do during its last visit: roll over, crawl, sit up, maybe even begin walking. Witnessing the baby's triumphs—even something as small as picking up a rattle for the first time—the children will often cheer.

9   Ervin Staub, professor emeritus of psychology at the University of Massachusetts, has studied altruism in children and found that the best way to create a caring climate is to engage children collectively in an activity that benefits another human being ("Biographical Note"). In Roots, children are enlisted in each class to do something to care for the baby, whether it is to sing a song, speak in a gentle voice, or make a "wishing tree." The results can be dramatic. In a study of first- to third-grade classrooms, Schonert-Reichl focused on the subset of kids who exhibited "proactive aggression"—the deliberate and cold-blooded aggression of bullies who prey on vulnerable kids (Schonert-Reichl et al.). Of those who participated in the Roots program, 88 percent decreased this form of behavior over the school year, while in the control group, only 9 percent did, and many actually increased it. Schonert-Reichl has reproduced these findings with fourth to seventh grade children in a randomized controlled trial. She also found that Roots produced significant drops in "relational aggression"—things like gossiping, excluding others, and backstabbing. Research also found a sharp increase in children's parenting knowledge. "Empathy can't be taught, but it can be caught," Gordon often says—and not just by children. "Programmatically my biggest surprise was that not only did empathy increase in children, but it increased in their teachers," she added. "And that, to me, was glorious, because teachers hold such sway over children."

10   When the program was implemented on a large scale across the province of Manitoba—it's now in 300 classrooms there—it achieved an "effect size" that Rob Santos, the scientific director of

Healthy Child Manitoba, said translates to reducing the proportion of students who get into fights from 15 percent to 8 percent, close to a 50 percent reduction (Healthy Child Manitoba). "For a program that costs only hundreds of dollars per child, the cost-benefit of preventing later problems that cost thousands of dollars per child, is obvious," said Santos. Follow up studies have found that outcomes are maintained or enhanced three years after the program ends. "When you've got emotion and cognition happening at the same time, that's deep learning," explains Gordon. "That's learning that will last."

Links

Angier, Natalie. "The Biology Behind the Milk of Human Kindness." *New York Times*. New York Times, 23 Nov. 2009. Web. 27 Mar. 2012.

Carter, Sue C. Personal interview. N.d.

Dolnick, Sam. "2 Linked to Suicide Case Withdraw from Rutgers." *New York Times*. New York Times, 29 Oct. 2010. Web. 27 Mar. 2012.

Gordon, Mary. Personal interview. N.d.

Healthy Child Manitoba. "Putting Children and Families First." Province of Manitoba, n.d. Web. 27 Mar. 2012.

Paul, Pamela. "The Playground Gets Even Tougher." *New York Times*. New York Times, 8 Oct. 2010. Web. 27 Mar. 2012.

"Roots of Empathy: From Research to Recognition." *Roots of Empathy*. Roots of Empathy, 2012. 27 Mar. 2012.

Schonert-Reichl, Kimberly. Personal interview. N.d.

Schonert-Reichl, Kimberly, et al. "Contextual Considerations in the

Evaluation of a School-Based Social Emotional Competence Program." American Educational Research Association, April 2009. Print.

Staub, Ervin. "Biographical Note." *Ervinstaub.com*. Ervinstaub.com, n.d. Web. 27 Mar. 2012.

Toronto District School Board. "Parenting and Family Literacy Centres." Toronto District School Board, n.d. Web. 27 Mar. 2012.

"Tyler Clementi." Times Topics. *New York Times*. New York Times, 16 Mar. 2012. Web. 27 Mar. 2012.

United States. Dept. of Education. "Guidance Targeting Harassment Outlines Local and Federal Responsibility." *Ed.gov*. Dept. of Education, 26 Oct. 2010. Web. 27 Mar. 2012.

———. Dept. of Health and Human Services. "Stop Bullying Now." *TFK Extra!*. Health Resources and Services Administration, Dept. of Health and Human Services, n.d. Web. 27 Mar. 2012.

———. White House Conference on Bullying Prevention. *White House*. White House, 14 Oct. 2010. Web. 27 Mar. 2012.

Warneken, Felix. "Videoclips." Dept. of Developmental and Comparative Psychology, Max Planck Institute for Evolutionary Anthropology. Max Planck Institute, n.d. Web. 27 Mar. 2012.

Warneken, Felix, and Michael Tomasello. "Altruistic Helping in Human Infants and Young Chimpanzees." *Science* 311.5765 (2006): 1301–3. *Academic Search Complete*. Web. 27 Mar. 2012.

⎡REFLECT⎤ **Make connections: Thinking about perspective taking.**

One of the ways of developing empathy seems to be through "perspective taking," which Bornstein calls "the cognitive dimension of empathy" (par. 8). Think about your own observation and personal experience with perspective taking. Your instructor may ask you to post your thoughts on a class discussion board or to discuss them with other students in class. Use the following suggestions to get started:

- Think of a situation in which you conflicted with someone, such as a sibling, parent, coworker, teacher, or classmate. Reflect on how you felt at the time of the conflict. Then put yourself in the position of the other person and try to imagine how he or she may have felt.

- Consider the insights, if any, you gained from perspective taking in this case. Do you think perspective taking could help while in the middle of a conflict, or do you need distance to empathize with someone else's point of view?

⌈ ANALYZE ⌉ Use the basic features.

A FOCUSED, WELL-DEFINED PROBLEM: ESTABLISHING THE PROBLEM

Every proposal begins with a problem. Student Patrick O'Malley (pp. 197–203) uses his title ("More Testing, More Learning") to hint at both the problem he will identify and the solution he will offer and to capture his readers' attention. He uses a scenario, dramatized by a series of *rhetorical questions,* to frame the problem, and he follows that with citations of research reports that help establish the problem's seriousness. Bornstein's title ("Fighting Bullying with Babies") is designed to surprise readers, and his first two sentences serve as a hook, drawing readers in by his bold claim to find a "cure" for "meanness."

| ANALYZE & WRITE |

Write a few paragraphs analyzing the strategies Bornstein uses to frame the problem of bullying and establish its seriousness and to evaluate how effective these strategies would be for Bornsteln's readers:

1. Skim paragraph 1. In addition to referring to the Tyler Clementi case, with which his original *New York Times* readers would certainly have been familiar, why do you think Bornstein also refers to an article on "mean girl" bullying in kindergarten? What do these two examples have in common?

2. Why do you think Bornstein refers to a White House summit and the Department of Education's "guidance letter"? How do these references help him frame the problem and excite readers' interest in the solution he describes?

3. Bornstein does not directly define *bullying*. Assuming that bullying is a rather wide and varied class of behaviors, how important is it that Bornstein clarify what he means by *bullying*? How does he give readers a sense of what bullying involves?

A WELL-ARGUED SOLUTION: PROVING IT WORKS

Arguing in support of a proposed solution requires evidence that the solution will help solve the problem and that it is feasible (doable and cost-effective). O'Malley cites a number of studies to support his claim that frequent testing reduces anxiety and increases learning.

ANALYZE & WRITE

Write a few paragraphs analyzing and evaluating Bornstein's use of evidence, particularly his use of the Roots of Empathy program, to support his claim:

1 Skim paragraph 5. How does the Roots of Empathy program demonstrate that the proposed solution is feasible and easily implemented? What details about how the program works does Bornstein share with readers?

2 How effectively do you think the information Bornstein provides, as well as the photograph, will convince readers that the Roots of Empathy program will work and that it can be implemented broadly, in a cost-effective way?

AN EFFECTIVE RESPONSE TO OBJECTIONS AND ALTERNATIVE SOLUTIONS: REJECTING THE STANDARD SOLUTION

In addition to arguing for the proposed solution, proposal writers also need to show that their solution is preferable to alternatives their readers might favor. Patrick O'Malley, for example, identifies several alternative solutions his intended audience (instructors) might bring up, including implementing programs to improve students' study skills, giving students study questions, and handing out possible exam topics to help students prepare. He concedes the benefits of some of these solutions, but he also points out their shortcomings, showing how his solution is better.

ANALYZE & WRITE

Write a paragraph analyzing and evaluating how Bornstein anticipates and responds to alternative solutions:

1 Reread the opening paragraphs to identify the actions that have been taken to address the problem of bullying. Consider the words Bornstein uses and the details he provides to describe these programs.

2 Now skim paragraphs 4–10, in which Bornstein describes the Roots of Empathy program. Consider the words he uses and the details he provides about that program. How does he contrast his solution to the alternatives?

3 Given your analysis of Bornstein's choice of words and details, how evenhanded is he in his evaluation of alternative solutions? How persuasive is the solution he offers?

A CLEAR, LOGICAL ORGANIZATION: USING TOPIC SENTENCES

Topic sentences can be especially helpful to readers trying to follow the logic of a proposal. O'Malley, for example, uses topic sentences to introduce the reasons in favor of frequent exams, to identify the reasons opponents offer against frequent exams, and to respond to alternative solutions. He uses transitions such as "The main reason" (par. 4), "Another, closely related argument" (par. 6), and "Moreover" (par. 10), and repeats the key words "frequent exams" and "solution" to guide readers.

ANALYZE & WRITE

Write a couple of paragraphs analyzing and evaluating Bornstein's use of topic sentences to help readers follow his argument:

1 Reread paragraphs 7–9 to see how Bornstein answers the rhetorical question "Why does the solution work?" Look particularly at each of the topic sentences in these paragraphs to see how Bornstein announces the answers.

2 Now review paragraph 3 to see how Bornstein previews two of these answers.

3 Given Bornstein's purpose and audience, how clear and comprehensible is the logic of this proposal argument? If you were to give Bornstein advice on revising this proposal for an audience of college students, what, if anything, would you recommend?

[RESPOND] ## Consider possible topics: Tweaking others' solutions.

The idea behind much of Bornstein's work, as he explains on his Dowser Web site, is to show "Who's solving what and how" with the aim of inspiring creative problem solving in others. Instead of beginning with a problem and then trying to come up with a solution, reflect on solutions with which you are familiar, and then consider how those solutions could be tweaked to help solve another problem. The Roots of Empathy program, for example, might suggest other problems that could be helped by giving people an opportunity to try out a different perspective. Another example featured on the Dowser site that could offer a model to solve problems is Community Spokes, an after-school program that teaches students to fix bicycles in their community. How could this program be adapted to teach other practical, possibly even money-making, skills to children?

Karen Kornbluh | *Win-Win Flexibility*

KAREN KORNBLUH worked in the private sector as an economist and management consultant before becoming deputy chief of staff at the U.S. Treasury Department. She currently serves as the ambassador and U.S. permanent representative to the international Organisation for Economic Co-operation and Development. As founder and director of the Work and Family Program of the New America Foundation—a nonprofit, nonpartisan institute that sponsors research and conferences on public policy issues—Kornbluh led an effort to change the American workplace to accommodate what she calls the "juggler family," in which parents have to juggle their time among caring for their children, their elderly parents, and their work. In 2005, Kornbluh's book *Running Harder to Stay in Place: The Growth of Family Work Hours and Incomes* was published by the New America Foundation, and "Win-Win Flexibility" was published by the Work and Family Program in the same year. Kornbluh's articles have appeared in such distinguished venues as the *New York Times,* the *Washington Post,* and the *Atlantic Monthly.* Kornbluh's proposal in "Win-Win Flexibility" has taken on new meaning in light of contemporary discussions surrounding women's roles in the workplace, popularized by Facebook executive Cheryl Sandberg's "lean in" philosophy and debate surrounding the "opt out" generation of parents who chose to stall or leave careers in order to be stay-at-home parents. As you read, consider who Kornbluh's audience is for this proposal:

- What type of reader do you think made up Kornbluh's (and the New America Foundation's) intended audience?

- Given this audience, why do you think Kornbluh characterizes her proposal as "win-win"?

Introduction

1 Today fully 70 percent of families with children are headed by two working parents or by an unmarried working parent. The "traditional family" of the breadwinner and homemaker has been replaced by the "juggler family," in which no one is home full-time. Two-parent families are working 10 more hours a week than in 1979 (Bernstein and Kornbluh).

2 To be decent parents, caregivers, and members of their communities, workers now need greater flexibility than they once did. Yet good part-time or flex-time jobs remain rare. Whereas companies have embraced flexibility in virtually every other aspect of their businesses (inventory control, production schedules, financing), full-time workers' schedules remain largely inflexible. Employers often demand workers be available around the clock. Moreover, many employees have no right to a minimum number of sick or vacation days; almost two-thirds of all workers—and an even larger percentage of low-income parents—lack the ability to take a day off to care for a family member (Lovell). The Family and Medical Leave Act (FMLA) of 1993 finally guaranteed that workers at large companies could take a leave of absence for the birth or adoption of a baby, or for the illness of a family member. Yet that guaranteed leave is unpaid.

3 Many businesses are finding ways to give their most valued employees flexibility but, all too often, workers who need flexibility find themselves shunted into part-time, temporary, on-call, or contract jobs with reduced wages and career opportunities—and, often, no benefits. A full quarter of American workers are in these jobs. Only 15 percent of women and 12 percent of men in such jobs receive health insurance from their employers (Wenger). A number of European countries provide workers the right to a part-time schedule and all have enacted legislation to implement a European Union directive to prohibit discrimination against part-time workers.

4 In America, employers are required to accommodate the needs of employees with disabilities—even if that means providing a part-time or flexible schedule. Employers may also provide religious accommodations for employees by offering a part-time or flexible schedule. At the same time, employers have no obligation to allow parents or employees caring for sick relatives to work part-time or flexible schedules, even if the cost to the employer would be inconsequential.

5 In the 21st century global economy, America needs a new approach that allows businesses to gain flexibility in staffing without sacrificing their competitiveness and enables workers to gain control over their work-lives without sacrificing their economic security. This win-win flexibility arrangement will not be the same in every company, nor even for each employee working within the same organization. Each case will be different. But flexibility

will not come for all employees without some education, prodding, and leadership. So, employers and employees must be required to come to the table to work out a solution that benefits everyone. American businesses must be educated on strategies for giving employees flexibility without sacrificing productivity or morale. And businesses should be recognized and rewarded when they do so.

6   America is a nation that continually rises to the occasion. At the dawn of a new century, we face many challenges. One of these is helping families to raise our next generation in an increasingly demanding global economy. This is a challenge America must meet with imagination and determination.

Background: The Need for Workplace Flexibility

7   Between 1970 and 2000, the percentage of mothers in the workforce rose from 38 to 67 percent (Smolensky and Gootman). Moreover, the number of hours worked by dual-income families has increased dramatically. Couples with children worked a full 60 hours a week in 1979. By 2000 they were working 70 hours a week (Bernstein and Kornbluh). And more parents than ever are working long hours. In 2000, nearly 1 out of every 8 couples with children was putting in 100 hours a week or more on the job, compared to only 1 out of 12 families in 1970 (Jacobs and Gerson).

8   In addition to working parents, there are over 44.4 million Americans who provide care to another adult, often an older relative. Fifty-nine percent of these caregivers either work or have worked while providing care ("Caregiving").

9   In a 2002 report by the Families and Work Institute, 45 percent of employees reported that work and family responsibilities interfered with each other "a lot" or "some" and 67 percent of employed

parents report that they do not have enough time with their children (Galinsky, Bond, and Hill).

10   Over half of workers today have no control over scheduling alternative start and end times at work (Galinsky, Bond, and Hill). According to a recent study by the Institute for Women's Policy Research, 49 percent of workers—over 59 million Americans—lack basic paid sick days for themselves. And almost two-thirds of all workers—and an even larger percentage of low-income parents—lack the ability to take a day off to care for a family member (Lovell). Thirteen percent of non-poor workers with caregiving responsibilities lack paid vacation leave, while 28 percent of poor caregivers lack any paid vacation time (Heymann). Research has shown that flexible arrangements and benefits tend to be more accessible in larger and more profitable firms, and then to the most valued professional and managerial workers in those firms (Golden). Parents with young children and working welfare recipients—the workers who need access to paid leave the most—are the least likely to have these benefits, according to research from the Urban Institute (Ross Phillips).

11   In the US, only 5 percent of workers have access to a job that provides paid parental leave. The Family and Medical Leave Act grants the right to 12 weeks of unpaid leave for the birth or adoption of a child or for the serious illness of the worker or a worker's family member. But the law does not apply to employees who work in companies with fewer than 50 people, employees who have worked for less than a year at their place of employment, or employees who work fewer than 1,250 hours a year. Consequently, only 45 percent of parents working in the private sector are eligible to take even this unpaid time off (Smolensky and Gootman).

12   Workers often buy flexibility by sacrificing job security, benefits, and pay. Part-time workers are less likely to have employer-provided health insurance or pensions and their hourly wages are lower. One study in 2002 found that 43 percent of employed parents said that using flexibility would jeopardize their advancement (Galinsky, Bond, and Hill).

13   Children, in particular, pay a heavy price for workplace inflexibility (Waters Boots). Almost 60 percent of child care arrangements are of poor or mediocre quality (Smolensky and Gootman). Children in low-income families are even less likely to be in good or excellent care settings. Full-day child care easily costs $4,000 to $10,000 per year—approaching the price of college tuition at a public university. As a result of the unaffordable and low quality nature of child care in this country, a disturbing number of today's children are left home alone: Over 3.3 million children ages 6–12 are home alone after school each day (Vandivere et al.).

14   Many enlightened businesses are showing the way forward to a 21st century flexible workplace. Currently, however, businesses have little incentive to provide families with the flexibility they need. We need to level the playing field and remove the competitive disadvantages for all businesses that do provide workplace flexibility.

15   This should be a popular priority. A recent poll found that 77 percent of likely voters feel that it is difficult for families to earn enough and still have time to be with their families. Eighty-four percent of voters agree that children are being shortchanged when their parents have to work long hours. . . .

Proposal: Win-Win Flexibility

16   A win-win approach in the US to flexibility . . . might function as follows. It would be "soft touch" at first—requiring a process and giving business an out if it would be costly to implement—with a high-profile public education campaign on the importance of workplace flexibility to American business, American families, and American society. A survey at the end of the second year would determine whether a stricter approach is needed.

17   Employees would have the right to make a formal request to their employers for flexibility in the number of hours worked, the times worked, and/or the ability to work from home. Examples of such flexibility would include part-time, annualized hours,[1] compressed hours,[2] flex-time,[3] job-sharing, shift working, staggered hours, and telecommuting.

18   The employee would be required to make a written application providing details on the change in work, the effect on the employer, and solutions to any problems caused to the employer. The employer would be required to meet with the employee and give the employee a decision on the request within two weeks, as well as provide an opportunity for an internal appeal within one month from the initial request.

19   The employee request would be granted unless the employer demonstrated it would require significant difficulty or expense entailing more than ordinary costs, decreased job efficiency, impairment of worker safety, infringement of other employees' rights, or conflict with another law or regulation.

20   The employer would be required to provide an employee working a flexible

---

[1] *Annualized hours* means working different numbers of hours a week but a fixed annual total. [Editor's note]

[2] *Compressed hours* means working more hours a day in exchange for working fewer days a week. [Editor's note]

[3] *Flex-time* means working on an adjustable daily schedule. [Editor's note]

schedule with the same hourly pay and proportionate health, pension, vacation, holiday, and FMLA benefits that the employee received before working flexibly and would be required thereafter to advance the employee at the same rate as full-time employees.

21   *Who would be covered:* Parents (including parents, legal guardians, foster parents) and other caregivers at first. Eventually all workers should be eligible in our flexible, 24×7 economy. During the initial period, it will be necessary to define non-parental "caregivers." One proposal is to define them as immediate relatives or other caregivers of "certified care recipients" (defined as those whom a doctor certifies as having three or more limitations that impede daily functioning—using diagnostic criteria such as Activities of Daily Living [ADL]/Instrumental Activities of Daily Living [IADL]—for at least 180 consecutive days). . . .

22   *Public Education:* Critical to the success of the proposal will be public education along the lines of the education that the government and business schools conducted in the 1980s about the need for American business to adopt higher quality standards to compete against Japanese business. A Malcolm Balridge–like award[4] should be created for companies that make flexibility win-win. A public education campaign conducted by the Department of Labor should encourage small businesses to adopt best practices of win-win flexibility. Tax credits could be used in the first year to reward early adopters.

Works Cited

Bernstein, Jared, and Karen Kornbluh. *Running Faster to Stay in Place: The Growth of Family Work Hours and Incomes*. Washington: New America Foundation, 2005. *New America Foundation*. Web. 22 May 2008.

Galinsky, Ellen, James Bond, and Jeffrey E. Hill. *Workplace Flexibility: What Is It? Who Has It? Who Wants It? Does It Make a Difference?* New York: Families and Work Institute, 2004. Print.

Golden, Lonnie. *The Time Bandit: What U.S. Workers Surrender to Get Greater Flexibility in Work Schedules*. Washington: Economic Policy Institute, 2000. *Economic Policy Institute*. Web. 18 May 2008.

Heymann, Jody. *The Widening Gap: Why America's Working Families Are in Jeopardy—and What Can Be Done About It*. New York: Basic, 2000. Print.

Jacobs, Jerry, and Kathleen Gerson. *The Time Divide: Work, Family and Gender Inequality*. Cambridge: Harvard UP, 2004. Print.

Lovell, Vickey. *No Time to Be Sick: Why Everyone Suffers When Workers Don't Have Paid Sick Leave*. Washington: Institute for Women's Policy Research, 2004. *Institute for Women's Policy Research*. Web. 20 May 2008.

National Alliance for Caregiving and AARP. *Caregiving in the U.S.* Bethesda: NAC, 2004. *National Alliance for Caregiving*. Web. 20 May 2008.

Ross Phillips, Katherin. *Getting Time Off: Access to Leave among Working Parents*. *Assessing the New Federalism* Policy Brief B-57. Washington: Urban Institute, 2004. *Urban Institute*. Web. 21 May 2008.

Smolensky, Eugene, and Jennifer A. Gootman, eds. *Working Families and Growing Kids: Caring for C en and Adolescents*. Washington: The National Academies Press, 2003. Print.

---

4 The Malcolm Balridge National Quality Award is given by the U.S. President to outstanding businesses. [Editor's note]

Vandivere, Sharon, et al. *Unsupervised Time: Family and Child Factors Associated with Self-Care*. Assessing the New Federalism Occasional Paper 71. Washington: Urban Institute, 2003. *Urban Institute*. Web. 21 May 2008.

Waters Boots, Shelley. *The Way We Work: How Children and Their Families Fare*

in a 21st Century Workplace. Washington: New America Foundation, 2004. *New America Foundation*. Web. 22 May 2008.

Wenger, Jeffrey. *Share of Workers in "Nonstandard" Jobs Declines*. Briefing Paper. Washington: Economic Policy Institute, 2003. *Economic Policy Institute*. Web. 18 May 2008.

⎡REFLECT⎤ Make connections: The problem of child care.

Kornbluh asserts in paragraph 13 that it is the children in juggler families who "pay a heavy price." She is particularly critical of child care, which she says is very expensive and low quality. She also cites research indicating that many six- to twelve-year-old children are latchkey kids, "home alone after school each day" (par. 13).

Consider whether your family should be classified as a "juggler" or as a "traditional family" (par. 1). If you are a parent, you might compare the family in which you grew up to the family in which you are a parent and reflect on your personal experience as a child or as a parent. Your instructor may ask you to post your thoughts on a class discussion board or to discuss them with other students during class time. Use the following questions to get started:

- Assess the strengths and weaknesses of your family's arrangements for child care. In your view, how could they be improved? Kornbluh appears to assume that being "home alone" is bad for six- to twelve-year-old children. At what age do you think children can take care of themselves?

- Consider also your family's work situation and whether the kinds of flexibility Kornbluh suggests, such as working part-time, working more hours each day but fewer days per week, being able to adjust your daily schedule, or telecommuting, would be feasible. Which, if any, of these suggestions would help your family and fit your family's workplace conditions?

⎡ANALYZE⎤ Use the basic features.

A FOCUSED, WELL-DEFINED PROBLEM: USING STATISTICS

For problems that are new to readers, writers not only need to explain the problem but also need to convince readers that it exists and is serious enough to justify the actions the writer thinks are necessary to solve it. Kornbluh assumes readers will not be familiar with the problem she is writing about or take it seriously, so she spends the first part of her essay introducing the problem and the second part establishing the problem's existence and seriousness.

Write a couple of paragraphs analyzing and evaluating Kornbluh's use of statistics to present the problem:

1 Reread Kornbluh's opening paragraph. Given that her audience probably combines people in business, labor, and government, what makes the statistics she cites there effective or ineffective?

2 Now reread paragraph 7. Notice that Kornbluh cites statistics from two different time periods in this paragraph. How does this comparison contribute to Kornbluh's presentation of the problem?

3 Finally, skim Kornbluh's proposal to find places where she cites the raw number together with the percentage. Here's one example:

> According to a recent study by the Institute for Women's Policy Research, 49 percent of workers—over 59 million Americans—lack basic paid sick days for themselves. (par. 10)

How, if at all, does giving statistics in both forms help readers? In addition to clarity, for what other reasons might Kornbluh have stated the number in two different ways?

A WELL-ARGUED SOLUTION: GIVING GUIDELINES FOR IMPLEMENTATION

Patrick O'Malley identifies his proposed solution in his title, as does Kornbluh. But whereas O'Malley tries to convince his readers that more frequent exams would indeed help solve the problem he has defined, Kornbluh can safely assume her readers will appreciate that her proposed solution—a flexible work schedule—would help solve the problem. Although she does not have to demonstrate that her proposed solution would solve the problem, Kornbluh does have to convince readers that her proposed solution is feasible—that it could be implemented at little cost and within a reasonable time.

Write a few paragraphs analyzing how Kornbluh argues that her solution is feasible:

1 Reread paragraph 5. Kornbluh states that the "flexibility arrangement will not be the same in every company, nor even for each employee working within the same organization." Given her audience — which includes employers as well as employees — why do you think she includes this statement? How worrisome or reassuring is this statement likely to be?

2 Skim paragraphs 16–22, in which Kornbluh sets out the guidelines for what employees and employers should do to implement her solution. Notice the *would*, *should*, and *could* verb forms she uses, and consider why she uses them.

3 What, if anything, do you think is missing from Kornbluh's description of how to implement her solution? What difficulties would need to be overcome?

AN EFFECTIVE RESPONSE TO OBJECTIONS AND ALTERNATIVE SOLUTIONS: ANTICIPATING ALTERNATIVES

Proposal writers need to anticipate alternative solutions their readers may prefer. O'Malley, for example, brings up several alternatives to improve students' study skills, such as giving students frequent study questions and handing out possible exam topics to help students prepare. He acknowledges the benefits of some of these solutions but also points out their shortcomings, arguing his solution is preferable to others.

ANALYZE & WRITE

Write a few paragraphs analyzing how Kornbluh responds to alternative solutions and an objection to her proposed solution:

1. Reread paragraphs 2–3 and 10–12. Identify the alternative solutions readers could claim are already in place to solve the problem of the "juggler family." How does Kornbluh try to refute these alternative solutions. Is she successful?

2. Reread paragraph 21, in which Kornbluh anticipates an objection. What is the objection, and how does she handle it? How effective is her response in allaying readers' concerns?

3. Now assess the effectiveness of Kornbluh's refutation of the alternative solution and the effectiveness of her response to the objection she anticipates. Has Kornbluh done enough to anticipate and respond to objections and alternative solutions? Why or why not?

A CLEAR, LOGICAL ORGANIZATION: USING HEADINGS

Writers sometimes use headings to make it easy for readers to follow a long, complicated proposal. But what do headings add to a short essay like this one?

ANALYZE & WRITE

Write a couple of paragraphs analyzing and evaluating Kornbluh's use of headings:

1. Highlight each heading.

2. Examine the role each heading plays in relation to the paragraphs that follow it. Look particularly at the relationship between the heading and the topic sentences.

3. Why do you think Kornbluh chose to include these headings? Do they help make the proposal logical and easy to follow? How would omitting the headings affect readers?

⌈RESPOND⌉ ## Consider possible topics: Improving living or working conditions.

If you are interested in the problem Kornbluh describes, you might suggest other ways of helping parents juggle their work and family responsibilities. For example, consider writing a proposal for increasing opportunities for one or more parents to work at home via telecommuting. Alternatively, you might consider a proposal to improve the living or working conditions of a group of people. Focus on a problem a particular category of people face. For example, think of ways to help elderly and infirm people in your community who need transportation, or elementary-school kids who have no after-school programs. Alternatively, devise solutions to problems that affect college students—for example, the creation of job-training or referral programs to help college students find work on or near campus, or recycling and "green" energy solutions that will help students living in dorms limit their impact on the environment.

---

macmillanhighered.com/conciseguide
Does a video report propose a solution as effectively as a print essay?
E-readings > Phoebe Sweet and Zach Wise, *The Problem with Lawns: The Transforming Landscape of Las Vegas*

GUIDE TO WRITING

The Writing Assignment | 218

Writing a Draft: Invention, Research, Planning, and Composing | 219

Evaluating the Draft: Getting a Critical Reading | 229

Improving the Draft: Revising, Formatting, Editing, and Proofreading | 231

The Writing Assignment

Write an essay proposing a solution to a problem. Choose a problem faced by a community or group to which you belong, and address your proposal to one or more members of the group or to outsiders who might help solve the problem.

This Guide to Writing is designed to help you compose your own proposal and apply what you have learned from reading other essays in the same genre. This Starting Points chart will help you find answers to questions you might have about composing a proposal. Use the chart to find the guidance you need, when you need it.

STARTING POINTS: PROPOSING A SOLUTION

A Focused, Well-Defined Problem

How do I come up with a problem to write about?

- Assess the genre's basic features: A focused, well-defined problem. (pp. 193–94)
- Consider possible topics. (pp. 210, 217)
- Choose a problem for which you can propose a solution. (p. 220)
- Test Your Choice (pp. 220–21)

How can I best define the problem for my readers?

- A Focused, Well-Defined Problem: Establishing the Problem (p. 208)
- A Focused, Well-Defined Problem: Using Statistics (pp. 215–16)
- Frame the problem for your readers. (pp. 221–23)
- Use statistics to establish the problem's existence and seriousness. (pp. 223–24)
- Assess how the problem has been framed, and reframe it for your readers. (pp. 224–25)
- A Troubleshooting Guide: A Focused, Well-Defined Problem. (p. 232)

A Well-Argued Solution

How do I come up with a plausible solution?

- Assess the genre's basic features: A well-argued solution. (pp. 195–96)
- A Well-Argued Solution: Proving It Works (pp. 208–209)
- A Well-Argued Solution: Giving Guidelines for Implementation (p. 216)
- Develop a possible solution. (pp. 225–26)
- Research your proposal. (pp. 226–27)

A Well-Argued Solution

How do I construct an argument supporting my solution?

- Assess the genre's basic features: A well-argued solution. (pp. 195–96)
- Explain your solution. (p. 226)
- Research your proposal. (pp. 226–27)
- A Troubleshooting Guide: A Well-Argued Solution (p. 232)

An Effective Response to Objections and Alternative Solutions

How do I respond to possible objections to my solution?

- Assess the genre's basic features: An effective response to objections and alternative solutions (pp. 196–97)
- Develop a response to objections or alternative solutions. (pp. 227–28)

How do I respond to possible alternative solutions?

- Assess the genre's basic features: An effective response to objections and alternative solutions (pp. 196–97)
- An Effective Response to Objections and Alternative Solutions: Rejecting the Standard Solution (p. 209)
- An Effective Response to Objections and Alternative Solutions: Anticipating Alternatives (pp. 216–17)
- Develop a response to objections and alternative solutions. (pp. 227–28).

A Clear, Logical Organization

How can I help my readers follow my argument?

- Assess the genre's basic features: A clear, logical organization. (p. 197)
- A Clear, Logical Organization: Using Topic Sentences (pp. 209–10)
- A Clear, Logical Organization: Using Headings (p. 217)
- Create an outline that will organize your proposal effectively for your readers. (pp. 228–29)
- A Troubleshooting Guide: A Clear, Logical Organization (p. 231)

Writing a Draft: Invention, Research, Planning, and Composing

The activities in this section will help you choose and research a problem as well as develop and organize an argument for your proposed solution. Do the activities in any order that makes sense to you (and your instructor), and return to them as needed as you revise. Your writing in response to many of these activities can be used in a rough draft that you will be able to improve after receiving feedback from your classmates and instructor.

:: Choose a problem for which you can propose a solution.

When choosing a problem, keep in mind that it must be

- important to you and of concern to your readers;
- solvable, at least in part;
- one that you can research sufficiently in the time you have.

Choosing a problem affecting a group to which you belong (for example, as a classmate, teammate, participant in an online game site, or garage band member) or a place at which you have worked (a coffee shop, community pool, or radio station) gives you an advantage: You can write as an expert. You know the history of the problem, you know who to interview, and perhaps you have already thought about possible solutions. Moreover, you know who to address and how to persuade that audience to take action on your proposed solution.

If you already have a problem and possible solution(s) in mind, skip to Test Your Choice below. If you need to find a problem, consider the possible topics following the readings and the suggestions in the following chart. Keeping a chart like this could help you get started exploring creative solutions to real-life problems.

	Problems	**Possible Solutions**
School	Can't get into required courses	Make them large lecture courses.
		Make them online or hybrid courses.
		Give priority to majors.
Community	No safe place for children to play	Use school yards for after-school sports.
		Get high school students or senior citizens to tutor kids.
		Make pocket parks for neighborhood play.
		Offer programs for kids at branch libraries.
Work	Inadequate training for new staff	Make a training video or Web site.
		Assign experienced workers to mentor trainees (for bonus pay).

TEST YOUR CHOICE

After you have made a provisional choice, ask yourself the following questions:

- Do I understand the problem well enough to convince my readers that it really exists and is worth their attention?
- Do I have some ideas about how to solve this problem?
- Do I know enough about the problem, or can I learn what I need to know in the time allotted?

To try out your choice of a problem, get together with two or three other students:

Presenters.   Take turns identifying the problem you're thinking of writing about.

Listeners.   Briefly tell each presenter whether the problem seems important, and why.

As you plan and draft your proposal, you may need to reconsider your choice (for example, if you discover you don't have any good ideas about how to solve the problem) and either refocus it or choose a different problem to write about. If you have serious doubts about your choice, discuss them with your instructor before starting over with a new problem.

⬛ Frame the problem for your readers.

Once you have made a preliminary choice of a problem, consider what you know about it, what research will help you explore what others think about it, and how you can interest your readers in solving it. Then determine how you can frame or reframe it in a way that appeals to readers' values and concerns. Use the questions and sentence strategies that follow as a jumping-off point; you can make them your own as you revise later.

To learn more about conducting surveys and interviews, consult Chapter 16, pp. 414–19. For advice on listing, cubing, and freewriting, see Chapter 8, pp. 282–84, 288, 290–91.

WAYS IN

WHAT IS THE PROBLEM?

What do I already know about the problem?

Brainstorm a list: Spend 10 minutes listing everything you know about the problem. Write quickly, leaving judgment aside for the moment. After the 10 minutes are up, you can review your list and highlight or star the most promising information.

Use cubing: Probe the problem from a variety of perspectives:

- Describe the problem.

- Compare the problem to other, similar problems, or contrast it with other, related problems.

- Connect the problem to other problems in your experience.

- Analyze the problem to identify its parts, its causes, or its effects.

- Apply the problem to a real-life situation.

Freewrite: Write without stopping for 5 or 10 minutes about the problem. Don't stop to reflect or consider; if you hit a roadblock, just keep coming back to the problem. At the end of the specified time, review your writing and highlight or underline promising ideas.

WHY SHOULD READERS CARE?

How can I convince readers the problem is real and deserves attention?

Give an example to make the problem specific:

▶ Recently, _____ has been [in the news/in movies/a political issue] because of [name event].

Example:
> Lately, the issue of bullying has been in the news, sparked by the suicide of Tyler Clementi . . . , a gay college student who was a victim of cyberbullying. (Bornstein, par. 1)

Use a scenario or anecdote to dramatize the problem:

▶ [Describe time and place.] [Describe problem related to time or place.]

Example:
> It's late at night. The final's tomorrow. You got a C on the midterm, so this one will make or break you. (O'Malley, par. 1)

Cite statistics to show the severity of the problem:

▶ It has recently been reported that _____ percent of [name group] are [specify problem].

(continued)

What do others think about the problem? Conduct surveys:

- Talk to a variety of students at your school (your friends and others).
- Discuss the problem with neighbors or survey shoppers at a local mall.
- Discuss the problem with coworkers or people who work at similar jobs.

Conduct interviews:

- Interview faculty experts.
- Discuss the issue with business people in the community.
- Interview local officials (members of the city council, the fire chief, the local labor union representative).

What do most of my readers already think about the problem?

- ▶ Many complain about _____ but do nothing because solving it seems [too hard/too costly].
- ▶ Some think ____ is [someone else's responsibility/not that big of a problem].
- ▶ Others see _____ as a matter of [fairness/human decency].

Who suffers from the problem?

- ▶ Studies have shown that _____ mostly affects [name group(s)].

Example:

> Research has shown that . . . parents with young children and working welfare recipients—the workers who need access to paid leave the most—are the least likely to have these benefits. . . . Children, in particular, pay a heavy price. (Kornbluh, pars. 10, 13)

Example:

> Today fully 70 percent of families with children . . . are working 10 more hours a week than in 1979 (Bernstein and Kornbluh). (Kornbluh, par. 1)

Describe the problem's negative consequences:

- ▶ According to [name expert/study], [state problem] is affecting [name affected group]: [insert quote from expert.]

Example:

> Sian Beilock, a psychology professor at the University of Chicago, points out that "stressing about doing well on an important exam can backfire, leading students to 'choke under pressure' or to score less well than they might otherwise score if the stakes weren't so high." (O'Malley, par. 2)

Why should readers care about solving the problem?

- ▶ We're all in this together. _____ is not a win-lose proposition. If [name group] loses, we all lose.
- ▶ If we don't try to solve _____, no one else will.
- ▶ Doing nothing will only make _____ worse.
- ▶ We have a moral responsibility to do something about _____.

TEST YOUR CHOICE

Ask two or three other students to help you develop your plan to define the problem.

Presenters.   Briefly explain how you are thinking of framing or reframing the problem for your audience. Use the following language as a model for presenting your problem, or use language of your own.

▶ I plan to define the problem [not as _____ but as _____ /in terms of _____] because I think my readers [describe briefly] will share my [concerns, values, or priorities].

Listeners.   Tell the presenter what response this way of framing the problem elicits from you and why. You may also explain how you think other readers might respond. Use the following language as a model for structuring your response, or use your own words.

▶ I'm [also/not] concerned about _____ because [state reasons].

▶ I [agree/disagree] that _____ because [state reasons].

Use statistics to establish the problem's existence and seriousness.

Statistics can be helpful in establishing that a problem exists and is serious. (In fact, using statistics is offered as an option in the preceding Ways In box.) To define her problem, Kornbluh uses statistics in three different forms: percentages, numbers, and proportions.

percentage number proportion	Between 1970 and 2000, the percentage of mothers in the workforce rose from 38 to 67 percent (Smolensky and Gootman). Moreover, the number of hours worked by dual-income families has increased dramatically. Couples with children worked a full 60 hours a week in 1979. By 2000 they were working 70 hours a week (Bernstein and Kornbluh). And more parents than ever are working long hours. In 2000, nearly 1 out of every 8 couples with children was putting in 100 hours a week or more on the job, compared to only 1 out of 12 families in 1970 (Jacobs and Gerson). (par. 7)

Percentages can seem quite impressive, but sometimes without the raw numbers readers may not appreciate just how remarkable the percentages really are. In the following example, readers can see at a glance that the percentage Kornbluh cites is truly significant:

In addition to working parents, there are over 44.4 million Americans who provide care to another adult, often an older relative. Fifty-nine percent of these caregivers either work or have worked while providing care ("Caregiving"). (par. 8)

To establish that there is a widespread perception among working parents that the problem is serious, Kornbluh cites survey results:

In a 2002 report by the Families and Work Institute, 45 percent of employees reported that work and family responsibilities interfered with each other "a lot" or "some" and 67 percent of employed parents report that they do not have enough time with their children (Galinsky, Bond, and Hill). (par. 9)

This example shows that nearly half of all employees have had difficulty juggling work and family responsibilities. The readers Kornbluh is addressing—employers— are likely to find this statistic important because it suggests that their employees are spending time worrying about or attending to family responsibilities instead of focusing on work.

For statistics to be persuasive, they must be from sources that readers consider reliable. Researchers' trustworthiness, in turn, depends on their credentials as experts in the field they are investigating and also on the degree to which they are disinterested, or free from bias. Kornbluh provides a list of works cited that readers can follow up on to check whether the sources are indeed reliable. The fact that some of her sources are books published by major publishers (Harvard University Press and Basic Books, for example) helps establish their credibility. Other sources she cites are research institutes (such as the New America Foundation, Economic Policy Institute, and Families and Work Institute), which readers can easily check out. Another factor that adds to the appearance of reliability is that Kornbluh cites statistics from a range of sources instead of relying on only one or two. Moreover, the statistics are current and clearly relevant to her argument.

To find statistics relating to the problem (or possible solution) you are writing about, explore the state, local, or tribal sections of USA.gov, the U.S. government's official Web portal, or visit the Library of Congress page "State Government Information," www.loc.gov/rr/news/stategov/stategov.html, and follow the links. In particular, visit the U.S. Census Bureau's Web site (www.census.gov), which offers reliable statistics on a wide variety of issues.

To learn more about assessing reliability, consult pp. 421–26 in Chapter 17.

To learn more about finding government documents, see pp. 408–409 in Chapter 16.

Assess how the problem has been framed, and reframe it for your readers.

Once you have a good idea of what you and your readers think about the problem, consider how others have framed the problem and how you might be able to reframe it for your readers.

WAYS IN

HOW HAS THE PROBLEM BEEN FRAMED?	HOW CAN I REFRAME THE PROBLEM?
Sink or Swim Argument	**Teaching Should Not Be Punitive Argument**
Example: Providing tutoring for students who are failing a course is wrong because students should do what they need to do to pass the course or face the consequences. That's the way the system is supposed to work.	**Example:** Providing tutoring for students who are failing a course assumes the purpose of education is learning, not testing for its own sake or punishing those who have not done well.
Don't Reward Failure Argument	**Encourage Success Argument**
Example: Providing tutoring for students who are failing a course is like a welfare	**Example:** Providing tutoring for students who are failing a course encourages students to work hard and value doing well in school.

system that makes underprepared students dependent and second-class citizens.

Reverse Discrimination Argument

Example: Providing tutoring for students who are failing a course is unfair to the other students who don't need assistance.

Win-Lose Argument

Example: Providing tutoring for students who are failing a course ignores the fact that grades should fall on a bell curve—that is, an equal proportion of students should get an *F* as get an *A*.

Level Playing Ground Argument

Example: Providing tutoring for students who are failing a course is a way to make up for inadequacies in previous schooling.

Win-Win Argument

Example: Providing tutoring for students who are failing a course assumes that it would be a good thing if every student earned an *A*. Providing tutoring enhances learning.

Develop a possible solution.

The following activities will help you devise a solution and develop an argument to support it. If you have already found a solution, you may want to skip this activity and go directly to the Explain Your Solution section (p. 226).

WAYS IN

HOW CAN I SOLVE THIS PROBLEM?

One way to generate ideas is to write steadily for at least five minutes, exploring some of the possible ways of solving the problem. Consider using the following approaches as a jumping-off point:

- **Adapt a solution that has been tried or proposed for a similar problem.**

  Example: Bornstein's solution to bullying is to teach children empathy, as the Roots of Empathy program does.

- **Focus on eliminating a cause or minimizing an effect of the problem.**

  Example: O'Malley's solution to stressful high-stakes exams is to eliminate the cause of the stress by inducing instructors to give more frequent low-stakes exams.

- **See the problem as part of a larger system, and explore solutions to the system.**

  Example: Kornbluh's solution is for employers to work with employees to enhance job flexibility.

- **Focus on solving a small part of the problem.**

  Example: Kornbluh could have focused on an aspect of workplace flexibility such as guaranteed paternity leave.

(continued)

- **Look at the problem from different points of view.**

  Example: Consider what students, teachers, parents, or administrators might think could be done to help solve the problem.

- **Think of a specific example of the problem, and consider how you could solve it.**

  Example: O'Malley could have focused on solving the problem of high-stakes exams in his biology course.

For more idea-generating strategies, see Chapter 8.

Explain your solution.

You may not yet know for certain whether you will be able to construct a convincing argument to support your solution, but you should choose a solution that you feel motivated to pursue. Use the questions and sentence strategies that follow to help you put your ideas in writing. You will likely want to revise what you come up with later, but the questions and sentence strategies below may provide a convenient jumping-off point.

WAYS IN

HOW CAN I EXPLAIN HOW MY SOLUTION WOULD HELP SOLVE THE PROBLEM?	HOW CAN I EXPLAIN THAT MY SOLUTION IS FEASIBLE?
It would eliminate a cause of the problem.	**It could be implemented.**
▶ Research shows it would reduce _____.	Describe the major stages or steps necessary to carry out your solution.
It has worked elsewhere.	**We can afford it.**
▶ It works in _____, _____, and _____, as studies evaluating it show.	Explain what it would cost to put the solution into practice.
It would change people's behavior.	**It would not take too much time.**
▶ _____ would [discourage/encourage] people to _____.	Create a rough schedule or timeline to show how long it would take to make the necessary arrangements.

Research your proposal.

You may have already begun researching the problem and familiarizing yourself with alternative solutions that have been offered, or you may have ideas about what you need to research. If you are proposing a solution to a problem about which others have written, use the following research strategies to help you find out what solutions others have proposed or tried. You may also use these strategies to find out how others have defined the problem and demonstrated its seriousness.

   ▪ Enter keywords or phrases related to your solution (or problem) into the search box of an all-purpose database, such as *Academic OneFile* (InfoTrac) or *Academic Search Complete* (EBSCOHost), to find relevant articles in magazines and journals; in the database Lexis/Nexis to find articles in newspapers; or in library catalogs to find books and other resources. (Database names may change, and what is available will differ from school to school. Some libraries may even combine all three into one search link on the library's home page. Ask a librarian if you need help.) Patrick O'Malley could have tried a combination of keywords, such as *learning* and *test anxiety,* or variations on his terms (*frequent testing, improve retention*) to find relevant articles.

   ▪ Bookmark or keep a record of the URLs of promising sites, and download or copy information you could use in your essay. When available, download PDF files rather than HTML files, because these are likely to include visuals, such as graphs and charts. If you copy and paste relevant information into your notes, be careful to distinguish all material from sources from your own ideas.

   ▪ Remember to record source information and to cite and document any sources you use, including visuals and interviews.

For more about searching for information, consult Chapter 16; plagiarism, see Chapter 18; documenting sources, consult Chapter 19 (MLA Style) or Chapter 20 (APA Style).

▪▪ Develop a response to objections and alternative solutions.

The topics you considered when developing an argument for your solution may be the same topics you need to consider when developing a response to likely criticisms of your proposal—answering possible objections to your solution or alternative solutions readers may prefer. The following sentence strategies may help you start drafting an effective response.

⌐ **WAYS IN** →

> **HOW CAN I DRAFT A REFUTATION OR CONCESSION?**
>
> **To draft a refutation, try beginning with sentence strategies like these:**
>
> ▶ Some people think we can't afford to do [name solution], but it would only cost $_____ to put my solution in place compared to $ _____ , the cost of [doing nothing/implementing an alternative solution].
>
> ▶ Although it might take [number of months/years] to implement this solution, it would actually take longer to implement [alternative solution].
>
> ▶ There are critics who think that only a few people would benefit from solving this problem, but _____ would benefit because _____ .

(continued)

▶ Some may suggest that I favor this solution because I would benefit personally; however, the fact is we would all benefit because _____.

▶ Some may claim that this solution has been tried and hasn't worked. But research shows that [explain how proposed solution has worked] *or* my solution differs from past experiments in these important ways: _____, _____, and _____.

To draft a concession, try beginning with sentence strategies like these:

▶ I agree with those who [claim X/object on X grounds]; therefore, instead of _____, I think we should pursue _____.

▶ If _____ seems too [time-consuming/expensive], let's try _____.

▶ Where _____ is a concern, I think [name alternative] should be followed.

▶ Although _____ is the best way to deal with a problem like this, under [describe special circumstances], I agree that _____ should be done.

Create an outline that will organize your proposal effectively for your readers.

Whether you have rough notes or a complete draft, making an outline of what you have written can help you organize your essay effectively for your audience. Compare the possible outlines below to see how you might organize the essay depending on whether your readers agree that a serious problem exists and are open to your solution—or not.

For more on outlining, see pp. 284–87 in Chapter 8.

If you are writing primarily for readers who *acknowledge that the problem exists and are open to your solution*:

  I. Introduce the problem, concluding with a thesis statement asserting your solution.

  II. Demonstrate the problem's seriousness: Frame the problem in a way that prepares readers for the solution.

  III. Describe the proposed solution: Show what could be done to implement it.

  IV. Refute objections.

  V. Conclude: Urge action on your solution.

If you are writing primarily for readers who *do not recognize the problem or are likely to prefer alternative solutions*:

  I. Reframe the problem: Identify common ground, and acknowledge alternative ways readers might see the problem.

  II. Concede strengths, but emphasize the weaknesses of alternative solution(s) that readers might prefer.

  III. Describe the proposed solution: Give reasons and provide evidence to demonstrate that it is preferable to the alternative(s).

  IV. Refute objections.

  V. Conclude: Reiterate shared values.

Whatever organizational strategy you adopt, do not hesitate to change your outline as necessary while drafting and revising. For instance, you might find it more effective to hold back on presenting your solution until you have discussed unacceptable alternatives. The purpose of an outline is to identify the basic components of your proposal and to help you organize it effectively, not to lock you into a particular structure.

Write the opening sentences.

Review your invention writing to see if you have already written something that would work to launch your essay, or try out one or two ways of beginning your essay—possibly from the list that follows:

- A scenario (like O'Malley)
- Statistics (like Kornbluh)
- News events demonstrating the seriousness of the problem (like Bornstein)
- A quotation that highlights support for your solution
- A comparison with other places where the solution has been tried successfully
- A preview of the negative consequences if the problem goes unsolved

Draft your proposal.

By this point, you have done a lot of research and writing to

- focus and define a problem, and develop a solution to it;
- support your solution with reasons and evidence your readers will find persuasive;
- refute or concede objections and alternative solutions;
- organize your ideas to make them clear, logical, and effective for readers.

Now stitch that material together to create a draft. The next two parts of this Guide to Writing will help you evaluate and improve that draft.

Evaluating the Draft: Getting a Critical Reading

Your instructor may arrange a peer review session in class or online, where you can exchange drafts with your classmates and give each other a thoughtful critical reading, pointing out what works well and suggesting ways to improve the draft. A good critical reading does three things:

1. It lets the writer know how well the reader understands the point of the draft.
2. It praises what works best.
3. It indicates where the draft could be improved and makes suggestions on how to improve it.

You can use the Critical Reading Guide on the next page to guide your discussion. Before concluding your peer review, be sure to address any of the writer's concerns that have not been discussed already.

A CRITICAL READING GUIDE

A Focused, Well-Defined Problem

Has the writer framed the problem effectively?

Summarize: Tell the writer what you understand the problem to be.

Praise: Give an example where the problem and its significance come across effectively such as where an example dramatizes the problem or statistics establish its significance.

Critique: Tell the writer where readers might need more information about the problem's causes and consequences, or where more might be done to establish its seriousness.

A Well-Argued Solution

Has the writer argued effectively for the solution?

Summarize: Tell the writer what you understand the proposed solution to be.

Praise: Give an example in the essay where support for the solution is presented especially effectively—for example, note particularly strong reasons, writing strategies that engage readers, or design or visual elements that make the solution clear and accessible.

Critique: Tell the writer where the argument for the solution could be strengthened—for example, where steps for implementation could be laid out more clearly, where the practicality of the solution could be established more convincingly, or where additional support for reasons should be added.

An Effective Response to Objections and Alternative Solutions

Has the writer responded effectively to objections or alternative solutions?

Summarize: Tell the writer what you understand to be the objections or alternative solutions that he or she is responding to.

Praise: Give an example in the essay where the writer effectively concedes or refutes a likely objection to the argument, and where reasons showing the limitations of alternative solutions are most effectively presented.

Critique: Tell the writer where concessions and refutations could be more convincing, where possible objections or reservations should be taken into account or alternative solutions should be discussed, where reasons for not accepting other solutions need to be strengthened, or where common ground should be sought with advocates of other positions.

A Clear, Logical Organization

Is the proposal clearly and logically organized?

Summarize: Underline the sentence(s) in which the writer establishes the problem and proposes a solution. Also identify the places where the writer forecasts the argument, supplies topic sentences, and uses transitions or repeats key words and phrases.

Praise: Give an example of how the essay succeeds in being readable—for example, in its overall organization, its use of forecasting statements or key terms introduced in its thesis and strategically repeated elsewhere, its use of topic sentences or transitions, or an especially effective opening or closing.

Critique: Tell the writer where the readability could be improved. For example, point to places where using key terms would help, where a topic sentence could be made clearer, or where the use of transitions could be improved or added; or indicate whether the beginning or ending could be more effective.

Improving the Draft: Revising, Formatting, Editing, and Proofreading

Start improving your draft by reflecting on what you have written thus far:

- Review the Test Your Choice responses and critical reading comments from your classmates, instructor, or writing center tutor: What are your readers getting at?
- Take another look at the notes from your earlier research and writing activities: What else should you consider?
- Review your draft: What else can you do to make your proposal more effective?

Revise your draft.

If your readers are having difficulty with your draft, or if you think there is room for improvement, try some of the strategies listed in the Troubleshooting Guide that follows. It can help you fine-tune your presentation of the genre's basic features.

A TROUBLESHOOTING GUIDE

A Focused, Well-Defined Problem

My readers aren't convinced that my problem is serious or even exists.

- Change the way you present the problem to address readers' concerns more directly.
- Add information—statistics, examples, description, and so on—that your audience is likely to find persuasive or that they can relate to.
- Consider adding visuals, such as graphs, tables, or charts, if these would help clarify the problem for your audience.

(continued)

A Well-Argued Solution

My readers aren't convinced that my solution is a good one.

- Try to make your solution more convincing by discussing similar solutions used successfully elsewhere or by demonstrating more clearly how it will solve the problem.
- Add evidence (such as facts, statistics, and examples) to support your reasons.
- Review the steps needed to enact your solution; if necessary, lay them out more clearly.

An Effective Response to Objections and Alternative Solutions

My readers have raised objections to my solution.

- Cite research studies, statistics, or examples to refute readers' objections.
- Concede valid points or modify your solution to accommodate the criticism.
- If you can neither refute nor accommodate objections, rethink your solution.

My readers have proposed alternative solutions that I don't discuss.

- If possible, establish common ground with those who propose alternative solutions, but show why their solutions will not work as well as yours.
- If you cannot demonstrate that your solution is preferable, consider arguing that both solutions deserve serious consideration.

A Clear, Logical Organization

My readers are confused by my proposal or find it hard to follow.

- Try outlining your proposal to be sure that the overall organization is strong; if it is not, try moving, adding, or deleting sections to strengthen coherence.
- Consider adding a forecasting statement and using key terms in your thesis and repeating them when you discuss your main points.
- Check to see that you use topic sentences to introduce your main points and that you provide appropriate transitions.
- Consider adding headings to make the structure of your proposal clearer.

Edit and proofread your draft.

Several errors occur often in essays that propose solutions: ambiguous use of *this* and *that,* and sentences that lack an agent. The following guidelines will help you check your essay for these common errors.

Avoiding Ambiguous Use of *This* and *That*

The Problem   Because you must frequently refer to the problem and the solution in a proposal, you will often use pronouns to avoid the monotony or wordiness of repeatedly referring to them by name. Using *this* and *that* vaguely to refer to other words or ideas, however, can confuse readers.

The Correction   Add a specific noun after *this* or *that*. For example, in his essay in this chapter, Patrick O'Malley writes:

> Furthermore, professors could help students prepare for midterm and final exams by providing sets of questions from which the exam questions will be selected. *This solution* would have the advantage of reducing students' anxiety about learning every fact in the textbook. (par. 13)

O'Malley avoids an ambiguous *this* in the second sentence by adding the noun *solution*. (He might just as well have used *preparation* or *action* or *approach*.) Here's another example:

▸ Students would not resist a reasonable fee increase of $40 a year if that~~increase~~ would pay for needed dormitory remodeling.

Revising Sentences That Lack an Agent

The Problem   A writer proposing a solution to a problem usually needs to indicate who should take action to solve it. Those who are in a position to take action are called "agents." Look, for example, at this sentence from Patrick O'Malley's proposal:

> To get students to complete the questions in a timely way, professors would have to collect and check the answers. (par. 12)

In this sentence, *professors* are the agents. They have the authority to assign and collect study questions, and they would need to take this action in order for this solution to be successfully implemented.

Had O'Malley instead written "the answers would have to be collected and checked," the sentence would lack an agent. Failing to name an agent would have made his argument less convincing, because it would have left unclear one of the key parts of any proposal: who is going to take action.

The Correction   When you revise your work, ask yourself *who* or *what* performed the action in any given sentence. If there's no clear answer, rewrite the sentence to give it an agent. Watch in particular for forms of the verb *to be* (the ball *was* dropped, exams should *be* given, etc.), which often signal agentless sentences.

▸ ~~A survey could be planned~~ *Your staff should plan a survey* to find out more about students' problems in scheduling the courses they need.

▸ ~~Extending~~ *The registrar should extend* the deadline to mid-quarter. ~~would make sense.~~

Note: Sometimes, however, agentless sentences are appropriate, as when the agent is clear from the context, unknown, or less important than the person or thing acted upon.

THINKING CRITICALLY

To think critically means to use all of the knowledge you have acquired from the information in this chapter, your own writing, the writing of other students, and class discussions to reflect deeply on your work for this assignment and the genre (or type) of writing you have produced. The benefit of thinking critically is proven and important: Thinking critically about what you have learned will help you remember it longer, ensuring that you will be able to put it to good use well beyond this writing course.

Reflecting on What You Have Learned

In this chapter, you have learned a great deal about this genre from reading several proposals and writing one of your own. To consolidate your learning, reflect not only on what you learned but also on how you learned it.

ANALYZE & WRITE

Write a blog post, a letter to your instructor, or an e-mail message to a student who will take this course next term, using the writing prompt below that seems most productive for you:

- Explain how your purpose and audience influenced *one* of your decisions as a writer, such as how you defined the problem, the strategies you used in presenting your solution, or the ways in which you attempted to counter possible objections.

- Discuss what you learned about yourself as a writer in the process of writing this particular essay. For example, what part of the process did you find most challenging? Did you try anything new, like getting a critical reading of your draft or outlining your draft in order to revise it?

- If you were to give advice to a friend who was about to write an essay proposing a solution to a problem, what would you say?

- Which of the readings in this chapter influenced your essay? Explain the influence, citing specific examples from your essay and the reading.

- If you got good advice from a critical reader, explain exactly how the person helped you—perhaps by questioning the way you addressed your audience or the kinds of evidence you offered in support of your proposed solution.

Reflecting on the Genre

No matter how well researched and well argued, many proposals are simply never carried out. In choosing among competing proposals, decision makers—who usually hold the power of the purse strings and necessarily represent a fairly conservative position—often go for the one that is cheapest, most expedient, and least disruptive. They may also choose small, incremental changes over more fundamental, radical solutions. While sometimes the most pragmatic choice, such immediately feasible solutions may merely patch over a problem, failing to solve it structurally. They may even inadvertently maintain the status quo. Worse, they can cause people to give up all attempts to resolve a problem after superficial treatments fail.

ANALYZE & WRITE

Write a page or two explaining how the genre pushes writers to select problems that are easy to solve or that reinforce the status quo. In your discussion, you might consider one or more of the following:

1. **Consider how proposals, because they invite us to select problems that are solvable, might inadvertently push us to focus on minor problems that are only a small part of a major problem.** Do any of the proposals you have read or written reveal this misdirection? If so, what do you think is the major problem in each case? Is the minor problem worth solving as a first step toward solving the major problem, or is it perhaps an unfortunate diversion?

2. **Reflect on arguments that we should not try to solve fundamental social problems by "throwing money at them."** Do you think this objection is a legitimate criticism of most proposals to solve social problems, or is it a justification for allowing the rich and powerful to maintain the status quo? What else, besides money, is required to solve serious social problems? Where are these other resources to come from?

3. **Write a page or two explaining your ideas about the frustrations of effecting real change.** Connect your ideas to your own essay and to the readings in this chapter.

7

Justifying an Evaluation

Potter collection: Jaap Buitendijk/© 2011 Warner Bros. Ent. Harry Potter publishing rights © J.K.R. Harry Potter characters, names and related indicia are trademarks of © Warner Bros Ent. All rights reserved/Courtesy Everett Collection.

Before you buy a computer, phone, or video game, do you take a look at the reviews? Brief reviews, written by consumers, are easy to find, but some are more helpful than others. The best reviewers know what they're talking about. They don't just say what they like, they justify *why* they like it, giving examples or other evidence. Moreover, their judgment is based not on individual taste alone but on commonly held standards or criteria. For example, no one would consider it appropriate to judge an action film by its poetic dialogue or its subtle characterizations; instead, they would judge it by whether it delivers an exciting roller-coaster ride. The usefulness of an *evaluation*—be it a brief consumer comment or an expert's detailed review—depends on readers sharing or at least respecting the writer's criteria.

IN COLLEGE COURSES

For a film course, a student writes a review evaluating the last two Harry Potter movies in terms of how effectively they adapt J. K. Rowling's much-loved novel *Harry Potter and the Deathly Hallows* (2007). He compares key scenes in the films (like that in Part 2 in which Bellatrix Lestrange and the other Death Eaters attack Hogwarts in the final battle of the Second Wizarding War) with their counterparts in the novel. To support his judgment, he analyzes the sequence of camera shots and angles, which he illustrates with stills from the film and contrasts with quotations from the novel. In refuting critics who think the movies leave out too much detail, he treats his audience—his instructor and classmates—as if they were knowledgeable about the films and novel, and he is careful not to let his review fall into plot summary. He concludes that while some die-hard Harry Potter fans may be reluctant to sacrifice their vision to the director's, the films effectively capture the bleak mood and nerve-racking excitement of the last Harry Potter novel.

IN THE COMMUNITY

A motorcycle enthusiast evaluates the tour he took of the Harley-Davidson factory in York, Pennsylvania, for his blog. In his post, "Hog Heaven," he concedes that some may get restless waiting to get in—he waited over an hour—but he was entertained while he waited by the great old "hogs" from eras past on display. Most of the post focuses on how informative and exciting the factory tour was: his anticipation while donning safety glasses and headset, the buzz he got from being on the factory floor with over a thousand workers, and the thrill of watching a motorcycle roll off the assembly line. He uses photos from his visit to illustrate his post, and he links to Harley-Davidson's handy Ride Planner to help other enthusiasts plan their own trip.

IN THE WORKPLACE

At a conference on innovations in education, an elementary school teacher gives a presentation evaluating the effectiveness of using *Schoolhouse Rock!* videos to teach math to second graders. She tries to maintain objectivity in her voice that matches the objectivity of her evidence: a comparison of her students' test results with those of other students in her district who did not see the videos. She surmises that the *Schoolhouse Rock!* videos are an effective teaching tool because the witty lyrics and catchy tunes make the information memorable and fun, but she concedes that additional research is needed to rule out other factors, such as her own enthusiasm for the videos or the makeup of her class.

In this chapter, we ask you to choose a subject for evaluation that you can examine closely. Analyzing the selections in the Guide to Reading that follows will help you learn how to use appropriate criteria to support your judgment. The Guide to Writing later in the chapter will show you ways to use the basic features of the genre to make your evaluation interesting and persuasive.

PRACTICING THE GENRE

Choosing Appropriate Criteria and Examples

To practice developing an evaluative argument based on appropriate criteria, get together with two or three other students and follow the guidelines below:

Part 1.   Begin by choosing a film everyone in the group has seen fairly recently. It's fine if you differ in your judgment of the film.

Next, discuss how you would classify the film in terms of **genre** (or *type*): comedy, romance, horror, or science fiction, for example. If you think it combines features of different genres, choose the genre you think best fits the film.

Then do the following:

- As a group, agree on one **criterion,** or *standard,* all of you typically use to evaluate a film in this genre. (For example, we usually expect a comedy to be funny.)
- Individually, find an example (such as a scene, a bit of dialogue, or a character) and briefly explain why you think that example supports your judgment that the film either does or does not meet the criterion the group has chosen.

Part 2.   As a group, discuss what you learned from this activity:

- Reflect on the process of classifying a film by genre and choosing a criterion you could all agree was appropriate for evaluating a film of that kind. What disagreements or difficulties did your group have?
- Imagine you had an opportunity to post your film review on the Internet or publish it in the school newspaper. Would the criterion you chose still be appropriate for that audience? Would you have to justify it or choose a different criterion that your audience would be more likely to accept?

Analyzing Evaluations

As you read the selections in this chapter, you will see how different authors justify an evaluation. Analyzing how these writers present their subject, assert and justify their judgment, respond to alternative viewpoints, and organize their writing will help you see how you can use these techniques to make your own evaluations clear and compelling for your readers.

Determine the writer's purpose and audience.

Although writing a review usually helps writers better understand the criteria they use when making evaluations, most writers also hope to influence others. When reading the evaluations that follow, ask yourself questions like these about the writer's purpose and audience:

- What seems to be the writer's main *purpose*—for example, to influence readers' judgments and possibly their actions; to inspire readers to think critically about which criteria are appropriate for judging subjects of this kind; or to get readers to look at the subject in a new way?

- What does the writer assume about the *audience*—for example, that readers will accept the writer's judgment; use the review to make their own independent, informed judgments; already have an independent judgment; or have serious objections to the writer's argument?

Assess the genre's basic features.

> **Basic Features**
> A Well-Presented Subject
> A Well-Supported Judgment
> An Effective Response to Objections and Alternative Judgments
> A Clear, Logical Organization

Use the following to help you analyze and evaluate how reviewers use the genre's basic features. The strategies they typically use to make their evaluations helpful and convincing are illustrated below with examples from the readings in this chapter as well as sentence strategies you can experiment with later as you write your own evaluation.

A WELL-PRESENTED SUBJECT

Read first to identify the subject of the review, which is often named in the title (for example, "The Myth of Multitasking") and described briefly in the opening paragraphs. Look also to see how the writer classifies the subject in terms of its genre. Here's an example from the first reading selection in the chapter, by student William Akana:

subgenres	From start to finish, *Scott Pilgrim vs. the World* delivers intense action in a
genre	hilarious slacker movie that also somehow reimagines romantic comedy. (par. 1)

Even if readers don't recognize the title, Akana makes clear that the film he is reviewing combines elements of three different kinds of movies (or subgenres), so readers can determine whether he is using appropriate criteria, as you will see in the next section.

Knowing the genre is also important because readers need different kinds of information for different genres. For example, most readers of film reviews want to know what the story is about but do not want to know how it turns out. Film reviewers, therefore, try not to give too much plot detail, as you can see in this concise plot summary from Akana's essay:

> Pilgrim's life takes a dramatic turn when he falls in love with Ramona Flowers (Mary Elizabeth Winstead), who is, quite literally, the girl of his dreams. However, he soon discovers that Ramona's former lovers have formed a league of evil exes to destroy him, and he is forced to fight to the death to prove his love. (par. 2)

A WELL-SUPPORTED JUDGMENT

Reviewers assert their judgment of the subject, stating whether it is good or bad, better or worse than other things in the same genre. Typically, writers announce their judgment in a *thesis statement* early in the evaluation. Below are a couple of sentence strategies typically used for thesis statements in evaluations, followed by examples from reviews in this chapter:

▶ Other [genre] have [attempted/succeeded at/failed at] _____ [state goal]; what makes [name of subject] [a success/a failure] is _____ and _____ [state specific characteristics].

EXAMPLE	Genre	But *it's an act of real audacity* when a ranking system tries to be
	Reason	comprehensive and heterogeneous—which is the first thing to
	Subject	keep in mind in any consideration of *U.S. News & World Report's*
	Judgment	annual "Best Colleges" guide. (Gladwell, par. 2)
	(reasons implied)	

▶ [Subject] can be [appreciated/criticized] for _____, _____, and _____ [state/forecast reasons].

EXAMPLE	Genre	Although the film is especially targeted for old-school gamers,
	Subject	anime fans, and comic book fanatics, *Scott Pilgrim vs. the World*
	Judgment	*can be appreciated and enjoyed* by all audiences because of
	Reasons	its inventive special effects, clever dialogue, and artistic
		cinematography and editing. (Akana, par. 2)

When reading an evaluation, look for the thesis and examine it to see whether the writer asserts an *overall judgment* and, if so, what it is. Also note the features of the subject that are being praised or criticized and the *reasons* supporting the judgment. Finally, consider whether the reasons are based on criteria you would expect to be used for evaluating something of this kind. For example, one of William Akana's reasons is that the film uses "special effects" that are "inventive." To support this reason, he devotes two paragraphs to detailing some of the film's special effects. He also gives examples of "video-game-like gimmicks" such as "gamer-tags," describing them and also providing a screen shot to show what they look like (par. 3).

Examples and *visuals* are two common types of evidence reviewers provide. They also may *cite sources*. When reading an evaluation that cites sources, determine whether the writer *quotes, paraphrases,* or *summarizes* the source material. Also notice whether the writer uses a *signal phrase* to identify the source and establish its credibility.

QUOTE

Signal phrase

As the educational researchers Patrick Terenzini and Ernest Pascarella concluded after analyzing twenty-six hundred reports on the effects of college on students:

Quotation
(indented)

> After taking into account the characteristics, abilities, and backgrounds students bring with them to college, we found that . . . (Gladwell, par. 8)

Signal phrase

Quotation
(integrated into
sentence)

As neurologist Jordan Grafman told *Time* magazine: "Kids that are instant messaging while doing homework, playing games online and watching TV, I predict, aren't going to do well in the long run." (Rosen, par. 12)

PARAPHRASE

Signal phrase

Psychologist David Meyer at the University of Michigan believes that rather than a bottleneck in the brain, a process of "adaptive executive control" takes place, which "schedules task processes appropriately to obey instructions about their relative priorities and serial order," as he described to the *New Scientist.* Unlike many other researchers who study multitasking, Meyer is optimistic that, with training, the brain can learn to task-switch more effectively, and there is some evidence that certain simple tasks are amenable to such practice. But his research has also found that multitasking contributes to the release of stress hormones and adrenaline, which can cause long-term health problems if not controlled, and contributes to the loss of short-term memory. (Rosen, par. 8)

For advice on when to indent quotations rather than use quotation marks, see Chapter 18, pp. 434–35

Notice that the writer has quoted specific words and phrases that would be difficult to paraphrase accurately.

SUMMARIZE

Signal phrase

Best-selling business advice author Timothy Ferriss also extols the virtues of "single-tasking" in his book, *The 4-Hour Workweek.* (Rosen, par. 5)

For more on citing sources, see Chapters 18–20.

How writers treat sources depends on the rhetorical situation. Certain formal situations, such as college assignments or scholarly publications, require writers to cite sources in the text and document them in a bibliography (called a list of *works cited* in many humanities disciplines or a list of *references* in the sciences and social sciences), as we can see in Akana's essay. In writing for a general audience—blogs and newspaper articles, for example—readers do not expect references to appear in the article, but they do expect sources to be named and their credentials to be identified in a signal phrase.

Another important strategy reviewers use to support their judgment is *comparison and contrast.* Malcolm Gladwell, for example, sets up his evaluation of the ranking system used by *U.S. News & World Report's* annual "Best Colleges" guide by comparing it to the system used by *Car and Driver* magazine.

Comparison cue

This ranking system looks a great deal like the *Car and Driver* methodology. It is heterogeneous . . . . It is also comprehensive. (Gladwell, (pars. 3, 4)

Christine Rosen also uses comparison and contrast in her description of modern multitasking:

Comparison cue	To readers a century later, that placid portrayal may seem alien—as though
Contrast cue	depicting a bygone world. Instead, today's multitasking adult may find

something more familiar in James's description of the youthful mind. . . . (Rosen, par. 15)

AN EFFECTIVE RESPONSE TO OBJECTIONS AND ALTERNATIVE JUDGMENTS

Reviewers occasionally need to respond to objections to their argument or to alternative judgments readers might prefer. Writers may **concede** (accept) or **refute** (argue against) alternatives, providing a transition or other cues to alert readers:

CONCESSION	"Research shows that the more satisfied students are about their contact with professors," the College Guide's explanation of the category begins, "the more they will learn and the more likely it is they will graduate." That's true. (Gladwell, par. 7)

Often writers use transitions to indicate a concession:

Transition indicating concession	▶ Of course, _____ is an important factor.
	▶ Granted, _____ must be taken into consideration.

REFUTATION	Some reviewers have criticized the film because they think that in the end it fails as a romantic comedy. For example, *Miami Herald* film reviewer Rene Rodriguez argues that the film ultimately fails because of the lack of "chemistry" or "emotional involvement" in the romance between Pilgrim and Ramona. But I agree with *New York Times* reviewer A. O. Scott, who argues that "the movie comes home to the well-known territory of the coming-of-age story, with an account of lessons learned and conflicts resolved." (Akana, par. 9)

The basic structure of a refutation is

Transition indicating opposing or contrasting point	▶ Although _____, I think _____.
	▶ X says _____, but I think _____ because _____.

A CLEAR, LOGICAL ORGANIZATION

Read to see if the reviewer provides cues *to help readers follow the logic of the argument.* Notice, for example, if the reasons are *forecast* in the thesis or elsewhere in the opening and, if so, where they are brought up again later in the essay. Here are examples from William Akana's film review:

Thesis with topics forecast	*Scott Pilgrim vs. the World* can be appreciated and enjoyed by all audiences *because* of its inventive special effects, clever dialogue, and artistic cinematography and editing. (par. 2)
Topic sentences with reasons forecast	*Scott Pilgrim vs. the World* shines bright with superb special effects that serve to reinforce the ideas, themes, and style of the film. (par. 3)
	Another strong point of *Scott Pilgrim vs. the World* is its clever and humorous dialogue. (par. 6)

> The best attribute by far is the film's creative <mark>cinematography and editing.</mark> (par. 7)

Notice that, in addition, Akana provides readers with logical transitions—such as *because* to introduce reasons and *another* to indicate the next reason in a list.

Reviewers may also use *headings* to orient readers, as in these examples from Christine Rosen's evaluation of multitasking:

Key word in heading

Changing Our <mark>Brains</mark>

> To better understand the multitasking phenomenon, neurologists and psychologists have studied the workings of the <mark>brain</mark>. (par. 7)

Paying <mark>Attention</mark>

Key word in topic sentence

> When we talk about multitasking, we are really talking about <mark>attention</mark>: the art of paying <mark>attention</mark>, the ability to shift our <mark>attention</mark>, and, more broadly, to exercise judgment about what objects are worthy of our <mark>attention</mark>. (par. 13)

Finally, where visuals—such as film stills, cartoons, screen shots, and diagrams— are included, determine how they are integrated into the text. Akana, for example, uses the conventional phrase "see fig. 1" in parentheses following his written description and includes a descriptive caption with the visual. Other writers might simply intersperse images following their descriptions to illustrate their points.

See Chapter 10 for more on strategies for cueing readers.

Readings

William Akana | # Scott Pilgrim vs. the World: *A Hell of a Ride*

THIS EVALUATION ESSAY was written by student William Akana for his composition course. The assignment prompt asked students to choose a film and write a review that includes a close analysis of the cinematic techniques used in at least one important scene. Akana's instructor illustrated various cinematic techniques, such as camera angles and movements, and demonstrated how to take screen shots, explaining that students can use visuals for a class project without asking permission, but to publish them they would have to get permission, as we did. As you read, consider these questions as well as those in the margin:

- How well do the screen shots illustrate Akana's analysis and support his evaluation?
- How would you describe Akana's tone in this essay? How is his tone affected by the fact that he uses the first person pronoun "I" to refer to himself only in the opening and closing paragraphs?

Notice that Akana used film stills—screen shots he took from a DVD of the movie— to illustrate his review. Because he used these visuals for a class project and not for public distribution, he did not have to get permission to use them. We did, however.

Basic Features
A Well-Presented Subject
A Well-Supported Judgment
An Effective Response to Objections and Alternative Judgments
A Clear, Logical Organization

How appropriate is this narrative and informality for a film review? For a college paper?

Why do you think Akana gives readers this information?

How well does this thesis statement forecast Akana's argument? Skim the essay, noting where he discusses each of these reasons.

How well do these details and the illustration he chose support Akana's claim that the special effects are "inventive" and "superb"?

1   As I leaned back in the movie theater seat, accompanied by my friends on a typical Saturday night, I knew I was in for something special. I was reassured; not only had my friends and I reached a unanimous vote to watch *Scott Pilgrim vs. the World*, but two of my friends had already seen the film and were eager to see it again. As soon as *Scott Pilgrim vs. the World* began, with its presentation of the classic Universal Studios introduction in old-timer eight-bit music and pixelated format, I knew I was in for one hell of a ride. From start to finish, *Scott Pilgrim vs. the World* delivers intense action in a hilarious slacker movie that also somehow reimagines romantic comedy.

2   *Scott Pilgrim vs. the World*, released in 2010 by Universal Studios, came into production as a comic book adaptation film under the direction of Edgar Wright (best known for the zombie movie masterpiece *Shaun of the Dead*). Scott Pilgrim (Michael Cera) is a twenty-two-year-old Canadian who plays bass for his indie band, Sex Bob-ombs, located in Toronto, Canada. Pilgrim's life takes a dramatic turn when he falls in love with Ramona Flowers (Mary Elizabeth Winstead), who is, quite literally, the girl of his dreams. However, he soon discovers that Ramona's former lovers have formed a league of evil exes to destroy him, and he is forced to fight to the death to prove his love. Although the film is especially targeted for old school gamers, anime fans, and comic book fanatics, *Scott Pilgrim vs. the World* can be appreciated and enjoyed by all audiences because of its inventive special effects, clever dialogue, and artistic cinematography and editing.

3   *Scott Pilgrim vs. the World* shines bright with superb special effects that serve to reinforce the ideas, themes, and style of the film. Special effects are plentiful throughout the entire film, ranging from superimposed annotations echoing classic gaming features to artful backgrounds and action sequences modeled on colorful comic book pages. For example, each of the main characters is described for the first time with "gamertags," short-timed boxes of information that include name, age, and rating (see fig. 1).

4   *Scott Pilgrim vs. the World* contains numerous amounts of other fun video-game-like gimmicks that were made possible through special effects. One humorous scene presents a pee bar that depletes as Pilgrim relieves himself. Another scene presents a bass battle between Pilgrim and one of

Fig. 1. Screen shot showing gamertags
© Universal/Courtesy Everett Collection

the evil exes in the format of PlayStation's popular Guitar Hero (see fig. 2).
It goes without saying that anyone who has ever dabbled in video games
will greatly appreciate the gaming-culture inside jokes. As the reviewer for
the Web site *Cinema Sight* wrote, this film is intended for "the video game
generation" ("Review").

5   Comic book references are also installed using special effects. In
almost every battle between Pilgrim and his enemies, comic-book-like
backgrounds, added through CGI, enhance the eye-popping fight sequences
as characters fly into the air to deliver devastating punches accompanied

Fig. 2. Guitar face-off
© Universal/Courtesy Everett Collection

Fig. 3. Comic-book-style annotations
© Universal/Courtesy Everett Collection

with traditional onomatopoeic "POWs" and "KAPOWs" (see fig. 3). However, comic book annotations are not reserved merely for fight scenes. Annotations range from even the simplest "RIIIINGs" of a telephone to trails of shouting "AAAAHs" of Pilgrim as he is thrown into the air in battle. To make the film even more visually appealing, *Scott Pilgrim vs. the World* portrays flashbacks using white and black comic strips similar to the original Scott Pilgrim comic books. Special effects play a truly vital part in enlivening the style of the film.

6   Another strong point of *Scott Pilgrim vs. the World* is its clever and humorous dialogue. One memorable scene in the film involves Knives Chau (Ellen Wong) and Scott Pilgrim in an awkward situation where Knives states sheepishly: "I've never even kissed a guy." In a supposedly intimate gesture of affection, Pilgrim moves closer only to pause shortly before saying "Hey . . . me neither." Additionally, *Scott Pilgrim vs. the World* is rich in cultural satire that pokes fun at adolescent and young adult behaviors. One scene contains Pilgrim telling Ramona Flowers: "I feel like I'm on drugs when I'm with you, not that I do drugs, unless you do — in which case, I do drugs all the time." Dialogue like this gives the film a raw yet rich sense of humor that is one of the many inventive risks of the film that pay off.

7   The best attribute by far is the film's creative cinematography and editing, which can be illustrated in the ultimate fight scene of the movie.

Pilgrim finally confronts his former band members, who are playing in an underground lair for Ramona's seventh evil ex, Gideon (Jason Schwartzman). As Pilgrim admits his faults and proceeds to apologize to the band for former wrongs, the shot assumes a point of view from Pilgrim's perspective looking up to the band on stage. Shortly before Pilgrim is finished, Gideon, sitting on his throne atop a miniature pyramid, interrupts him. The shot quickly cuts to a close-up of Gideon's eyes, emphasizing his anger at Pilgrim. From this point, soft focusing is utilized to blur the background as a tracking shot follows Pilgrim in a medium close-up as he marches to the base of the pyramid. Then, shot reverse shots are used between high- and low-angled frames to illustrate Pilgrim's challenge to Gideon for a final duel.

8   Gideon, in response to the challenge, asks Pilgrim if he is fighting for Ramona, which leads to a climactic epiphany for Pilgrim as he realizes his true motive, admitting in a tight close-up: "No. I want to fight you for me." As Pilgrim finishes this confession, a deep narrating voice announces that "Scott Pilgrim has earned the power of self-respect," and in turn, he is awarded a magical sword with which he can defeat Gideon. Subsequently, the camera pans from left to right in a subjective shot to illustrate Gideon's goons closing in on Pilgrim. Pilgrim, in a series of fast-paced jump cuts, quickly dispatches the bad guys before charging up the pyramid. After an extended battle, deep focusing is used with a long shot to establish that the hierarchy has changed between hero and villain: Pilgrim is seen standing atop the pyramid, looking down at the kneeling Gideon before Pilgrim kicks him to smithereens.

9   This brilliantly executed scene illustrates the artful cinematography of *Scott Pilgrim vs. the World*. More importantly, it delivers the film's thematic message, which undercuts the cliché "love conquers all" and instead focuses on the fresh concept that, in the grand scheme of things, the only person you are fighting for is yourself. Some reviewers have criticized the film because they think that in the end it fails as a romantic comedy. For example, *Miami Herald* film reviewer Rene Rodriguez argues that the film ultimately fails because of the lack of "chemistry" or "emotional involvement" in the romance between Pilgrim and Ramona. But I agree with *New York Times* reviewer A. O. Scott, who argues that "the movie comes

How do the high-lighted transitions help readers follow Akana's analysis?

For what purposes does Akana use these sources? How effective is his response to an opposing view?

home to the well-known territory of the coming-of-age story, with an account of lessons learned and conflicts resolved." Fighting Ramona's exes forces Pilgrim to wake up out of his slacker stupor. Before he can begin a grown-up relationship with Ramona, he has to come to terms with his own failures, especially in relation to his own exes. The film ends, as director Edgar Wright explained in an interview, on the threshold of a new beginning: "Scott and Ramona might not make it past the end credits, or it might be the start of a beautiful relationship" (Cozzalio).

Fig. 4. Threshold of a new beginning?
© Universal/Courtesy Everett Collection

Works Cited

Cozzalio, Dennis. "Scott Pilgrim's Dreamscape and the Glories of the Wright Stuff II: An interview with director Edgar Wright." *Sergio Leone and the Infield Fly Rule*. SergioLeoneIFR.blogspot.com, 15. Jan. 2011. Web. 30 Mar. 2011.

Rodriguez, Rene. Rev. of *Scott Pilgrim vs. the World*. *Miami Herald*. Miami. com, 11 Aug. 2010. Web. 28 Mar. 2011.

Scott, A. O. "This Girl Has a Lot of Baggage, and He Must Shoulder the Load." *New York Times*. New York Times, 12 Aug. 2010. Web. 29 Mar. 2011.

Rev. of *Scott Pilgrim vs. The World*. *Cinema Sight*. CinemaSight.com, 13 Sept. 2010. Web. 30 Mar. 2011.

Malcolm Gladwell | *What College Rankings Really Tell Us*

Photo by Theo Wargo/WireImage for
Bragman Nyman Cafarelli/Getty Images

MALCOLM GLADWELL is a staff writer for the *New Yorker* magazine and has written a number of best-selling books, including *Outliers: The Story of Success* (2008) and *Blink: The Power of Thinking without Thinking* (2005). He received the American Sociological Association Award for Excellence in the Reporting of Social Issues and was named one of the hundred most influential people by *Time* magazine. As he explains on his Web site (gladwell.com), giving public readings, particularly to academic audiences, has helped him "re-shape and sharpen [his] arguments."

"What College Rankings Really Tell Us" (2011) evaluates the popular *U.S. News* annual "Best Colleges" guide. You may be familiar with this guide and may have even consulted it when selecting a college. Excerpted from a longer *New Yorker* article, Gladwell's evaluation focuses on the *U.S. News* ranking system. As you read Gladwell's review, consider these questions:

- Note the numbered list of "variables" the *U.S. News* uses to rank colleges. For whom do you suppose *U.S. News*'s criteria are important? Why?

- If they are important for you, why? If they are not important for you, why not? What criteria for choosing a college are important for you?

1 *Car and Driver* conducted a comparison test of three sports cars, the Lotus Evora, the Chevrolet Corvette Grand Sport, and the Porsche Cayman S. . . . Yet when you inspect the magazine's tabulations it is hard to figure out why *Car and Driver* was so sure that the Cayman is better than the Corvette and the Evora. The trouble starts with the fact that the ranking methodology *Car and Driver* used was essentially the same one it uses for all the vehicles it tests—from S.U.V.s to economy sedans. It's not set up for sports cars. Exterior styling, for example, counts for four per cent of the total score. Has anyone buying a sports car ever placed so little value on how it looks? Similarly, the categories of "fun to drive" and "chassis"—which cover the subjective experience of driving the car—count for only eighty-five points out of the total of two hundred and thirty-five. That may make sense for S.U.V. buyers. But, for people interested in Porsches and Corvettes and Lotuses, the subjective experience of driving is surely what matters most. In

other words, in trying to come up with a ranking that is heterogeneous—a methodology that is broad enough to cover all vehicles—*Car and Driver* ended up with a system that is absurdly ill-suited to some vehicles. . . .

2 A heterogeneous ranking system works if it focuses just on, say, how much fun a car is to drive, or how good-looking it is, or how beautifully it handles. The magazine's ambition to create a comprehensive ranking system—one that considered cars along twenty-one variables, each weighted according to a secret sauce cooked up by the editors—would also be fine, as long as the cars being compared were truly similar. It's only when one car is thirteen thousand dollars more than another that juggling twenty-one variables starts to break down, because you're faced with the impossible task of deciding how much a difference of that degree ought to matter. A ranking can be heterogeneous, in other words, as long as it doesn't try to be too comprehensive. And it can be comprehensive as long as it doesn't try to measure things that

are heterogeneous. But it's an act of real audacity when a ranking system tries to be comprehensive and heterogeneous—which is the first thing to keep in mind in any consideration of *U.S. News & World Report's* annual "Best Colleges" guide.

3   The *U.S. News* rankings . . . relies on seven weighted variables:

1. Undergraduate academic reputation, 22.5 per cent
2. Graduation and freshman retention rates, 20 per cent
3. Faculty resources, 20 per cent
4. Student selectivity, 15 per cent
5. Financial resources, 10 per cent
6. Graduation rate performance, 7.5 per cent
7. Alumni giving, 5 per cent

From these variables, *U.S. News* generates a score for each institution on a scale of 1 to 100. . . . This ranking system looks a great deal like the *Car and Driver* methodology. It is heterogeneous. It doesn't just compare U.C. Irvine, the University of Washington, the University of Texas–Austin, the University of Wisconsin–Madison, Penn State, and the University of Illinois, Urbana–Champaign—all public institutions of roughly the same size. It aims to compare Penn State—a very large, public, land-grant university with a low tuition and an economically diverse student body, set in a rural valley in central Pennsylvania and famous for its football team—with Yeshiva University, a small, expensive, private Jewish university whose undergraduate program is set on two campuses in Manhattan (one in midtown, for the women, and one far uptown, for the men) and is definitely not famous for its football team.

4   The system is also comprehensive. It doesn't simply compare schools along one dimension—the test scores of incoming freshmen, say, or academic reputation. An algorithm takes a slate of statistics on each college and transforms them into a single score: it tells us that Penn State is a better school than Yeshiva by one point. It is easy to see why the *U.S. News* rankings are so popular. A single score allows us to judge between entities (like Yeshiva and Penn State) that otherwise would be impossible to compare. . . .

5   A comprehensive, heterogeneous ranking system was a stretch for *Car and Driver*—and all it did was rank inanimate objects operated by a single person. The Penn State campus at University Park is a complex institution with dozens of schools and departments, four thousand faculty members, and forty-five thousand students. How on earth does anyone propose to assign a number to something like that?

6   The first difficulty with rankings is that it can be surprisingly hard to measure the variable you want to rank—even in cases where that variable seems perfectly objective. . . . There's no direct way to measure the quality of an institution—how well a college manages to inform, inspire, and challenge its students. So the *U.S. News* algorithm relies instead on proxies for quality—a bit better and the proxies for educational quality turn out to be flimsy at best.

7   Take the category of "faculty resources," which counts for twenty per cent of an institution's score (number 3 on the chart above). "Research shows that the more satisfied students are about their contact with professors," the College Guide's explanation of the category begins, "the more they will learn and the more likely it is they will graduate." That's true. According to educational researchers, arguably the most important variable in a successful college education is a vague but crucial concept called student "engagement"—that is, the extent to which students immerse themselves in the intellectual and social life of their college—and a major component of engagement is the quality of a student's contacts with faculty. . . . So

what proxies does *U.S. News* use to measure this elusive dimension of engagement? The explanation goes on:

> We use six factors from the 2009–10 academic year to assess a school's commitment to instruction. Class size has two components, the proportion of classes with fewer than 20 students (30 percent of the faculty resources score) and the proportion with 50 or more students (10 percent of the score). Faculty salary (35 percent) is the average faculty pay, plus benefits, during the 2008–09 and 2009–10 academic years, adjusted for regional differences in the cost of living. . . . We also weigh the proportion of professors with the highest degree in their fields (15 percent), the student-faculty ratio (5 percent), and the proportion of faculty who are full time (5 percent).

8   This is a puzzling list. Do professors who get paid more money really take their teaching roles more seriously? And why does it matter whether a professor has the highest degree in his or her field? Salaries and degree attainment are known to be predictors of research productivity. But studies show that being oriented toward research has very little to do with being good at teaching. Almost none of the *U.S. News* variables, in fact, seem to be particularly effective proxies for engagement. As the educational researchers Patrick Terenzini and Ernest Pascarella concluded after analyzing twenty-six hundred reports on the effects of college on students:

> After taking into account the characteristics, abilities, and backgrounds students bring with them to college, we found that how much students grow or change has only inconsistent and, perhaps in a practical sense, trivial relationships with such traditional measures of institutional "quality" as educational expenditures per student, student/faculty ratios, faculty salaries,

percentage of faculty with the highest degree in their field, faculty research productivity, size of the library, [or] admissions selectivity. . . .

9   There's something missing from that list of variables, of course: it doesn't include price. That is one of the most distinctive features of the *U.S. News* methodology. Both its college rankings and its law-school rankings reward schools for devoting lots of financial resources to educating their students, but not for being affordable. Why? [Director of Data Research Robert] Morse admitted that there was no formal reason for that position. It was just a feeling. "We're not saying that we're measuring educational outcomes," he explained. "We're not saying we're social scientists, or we're subjecting our rankings to some peer-review process. We're just saying we've made this judgment. We're saying we've interviewed a lot of experts, we've developed these academic indicators, and we think these measures measure quality schools."

10   As answers go, that's up there with the parental "Because I said so." But Morse is simply being honest. If we don't understand what the right proxies for college quality are, let alone how to represent those proxies in a comprehensive, heterogeneous grading system, then our rankings are inherently arbitrary. . . . *U.S. News* thinks that schools that spend a lot of money on their students are nicer than those that don't, and that this niceness ought to be factored into the equation of desirability. Plenty of Americans agree: the campus of Vanderbilt University or Williams College is filled with students whose families are largely indifferent to the price their school charges but keenly interested in the flower beds and the spacious suites and the architecturally distinguished lecture halls those high prices make possible. Of course, given that the rising cost of college has become a significant social problem in the United States

in recent years, you can make a strong case that a school ought to be rewarded for being affordable. . . .

11   The *U.S. News* rankings turn out to be full of these kinds of implicit ideological choices. One common statistic used to evaluate colleges, for example, is called "graduation rate performance," which compares a school's actual graduation rate with its predicted graduation rate given the socioeconomic status and the test scores of its incoming freshman class. It is a measure of the school's efficacy: it quantifies the impact of a school's culture and teachers and institutional support mechanisms. Tulane, given the qualifications of the students that it admits, ought to have a graduation rate of eighty-seven per cent; its actual 2009 graduation rate was seventy-three per cent. That shortfall suggests that something is amiss at Tulane. Another common statistic for measuring college quality is "student selectivity." This reflects variables such as how many of a college's freshmen were in the top ten per cent of their high-school class, how high their S.A.T. scores were, and what percentage of applicants a college admits. Selectivity quantifies how accomplished students are when they first arrive on campus.

12   Each of these statistics matters, but for very different reasons. As a society, we probably care more about efficacy: America's future depends on colleges that make sure the students they admit leave with an education and a degree. If you are a bright high-school senior and you're thinking about your own future, though, you may well care more about selectivity, because that relates to the prestige of your degree. . . .

13   There is no right answer to how much weight a ranking system should give to these two competing values. It's a matter of which educational model you value more—and here, once again, *U.S. News* makes its position clear. It gives twice as much weight to selectivity as it does to efficacy. . . .

14   Rankings are not benign. They enshrine very particular ideologies, and, at a time when American higher education is facing a crisis of accessibility and affordability, we have adopted a defacto standard of college quality that is uninterested in both of those factors. And why? Because a group of magazine analysts in an office building in Washington, D.C., decided twenty years ago to value selectivity over efficacy.

[REFLECT] **Make connections: Ideology underlying judgments.**

Gladwell asserts that "implicit ideological choices" underlie ranking systems (par. 11). The word *ideology* refers to the values and beliefs that influence people's thinking. An important sign of underlying ideology is the fact that the *U.S. News* rankings leave out how much it costs to go to each college. This omission is significant, especially at a time when there is "a crisis of accessibility and affordability" (par. 14).

To think about the role of ideology in your own choice of a college, reflect on your personal experience as well as your observations of others choosing a college. Your instructor may ask you to post your thoughts on a class discussion board or to discuss them with other students in class. Use these questions to get started:

- What colleges did you consider, and what criteria (cost, location, standing in the *U.S. News* college ranking, and so on) did you use?

- Choose one or two of your criteria, and consider what values and beliefs were behind your choice. For example, was it important to you to attend a college with a winning football team, with a particular religious orientation, with opportunities for undergraduates to do scientific research?

■ How would comparing the criteria you used with the criteria your classmates used help you better understand the ideology—values and beliefs—behind your choices?

[ANALYZE] Use the basic features.

A WELL-PRESENTED SUBJECT: INTRODUCING A COMPLICATED SUBJECT

Every year, *U.S. News* publishes a special edition that ranks colleges and universities across the nation. In his essay, Gladwell does not simply evaluate one year's ratings; he evaluates the ranking system itself. But he begins by focusing on the ranking system of another magazine, *Car and Driver*.

| ANALYZE & WRITE |

Write a paragraph or two analyzing and evaluating how Gladwell introduces *U.S. News*'s ranking system:

1. Reread paragraph 1. Why do you think Gladwell begins his evaluation of *U.S. News*'s college ranking system by discussing the system used by another magazine to rank cars? How is Gladwell's evaluation of *Car and Driver*'s ranking system preparing the reader for his evaluation of *U.S. News*'s ranking system?

2. Now reread paragraph 2. What cues does Gladwell provide to help readers follow his transition from the ranking system of *Car and Driver* to that of *U.S. News*?

3. What does Gladwell mean when he describes *U.S. News*'s ranking system as striving to be both comprehensive and heterogeneous?

A WELL-SUPPORTED JUDGMENT: DEFINING CRITERIA

In paragraph 3, Gladwell lists the "seven weighted variables" *U.S. News* uses to represent a school's quality. Then, in paragraph 6, he states his main reason for criticizing any system for ranking colleges: "There's no direct way to measure the quality of an institution. . . . So the *U.S. News* algorithm"—its formula or set of rules—"relies instead on proxies for quality—and the proxies for educational quality turn out to be flimsy at best."

| ANALYZE & WRITE |

Write a few paragraphs analyzing and evaluating how Gladwell supports his claim:

1. Reread paragraphs 7 and 8, in which Gladwell focuses on one criterion — "faculty resources" — from the list of variables *U.S. News* uses to measure a school's quality. Why does *U.S. News* focus on faculty resources, and what do the editors of the magazine use to measure this quality?

2. Now consider Gladwell's claim that faculty resources are an inappropriate criterion for evaluating student engagement. What reasons and evidence does Gladwell supply? Given your own experience as a student, how convincing is this part of his argument?

> **3** What single criterion would you consider most important in evaluating a school's quality? How would you measure that criterion?

AN EFFECTIVE RESPONSE TO OBJECTIONS AND ALTERNATIVE JUDGMENTS: SINGLING OUT A COMMENT FOR RESPONSE

Because it is a negative evaluation, one could say that Gladwell's entire essay is an implied refutation of those who think well of the *U.S. News* college rankings. However, Gladwell also responds specifically to comments made by Robert Morse, the director of data research for *U.S. News & World Report.*

ANALYZE & WRITE

Write a paragraph analyzing Morse's response to Gladwell and Gladwell's response to Morse:

1 Reread paragraph 9. How would you describe Morse's response to Gladwell's criticism: Which of Gladwell's points does Morse concede or refute? Is his response effective?

2 Now reread paragraphs 10–12. How does Gladwell respond to Morse? How does he concede or refute Morse's response? How would you describe the tone, or emotional resonance, of Gladwell's response? Is he fair, mean, sarcastic, something else?

3 Given Gladwell's purpose and audience, how do you imagine readers would react to Morse's response to criticism as well as to Gladwell's handling of Morse's response? How did you respond?

A CLEAR, LOGICAL ORGANIZATION: USING COMPARISON AND CONTRAST

Lengthy evaluations can be difficult to follow, but writers have a number of strategies at their disposal to help guide readers. They may use transitional words and phrases or numbered lists, as Gladwell does. But they may also use more subtle strategies to help create cohesion. Gladwell, for example, uses comparison and contrast and strategic repetition to help readers follow his analysis.

ANALYZE & WRITE

Write a brief analysis of how Gladwell uses these two strategies:

1 Skim paragraphs 1–3, 5, and 10, noting every place that Gladwell mentions *Car and Driver* or compares *Car and Driver*'s ranking system with the ranking system used by *U.S. News*, and highlight every time Gladwell uses the word *heterogeneous* to describe these ranking systems. Consider the comparison Gladwell is making between *Car and Driver*'s and *U.S. News*'s ranking systems. How does this comparison help him structure his article logically?

2 Skim paragraphs 3, 8, and 11–14, underlining the words *selectivity* and *efficacy*. How does Gladwell use the contrast between selectivity and efficacy? How does this contrast help him guide readers and make his point?

3 Finally, evaluate Gladwell's use of these strategies. How effective were they in helping you follow Gladwell's logic? What, if anything, would you suggest Gladwell do to make his analysis easier to follow?

[RESPOND] **Consider possible topics: Evaluating a text.**

List several texts you would consider evaluating, such as an essay from one of the chapters in this book; a children's book that you read when you were young or that you now read to your own children; a magazine for people interested in a particular topic, like computers or cars; or a scholarly article you read for a research paper. If you choose an argument from Chapters 5 to 7, you could evaluate its logic, its use of emotional appeals, or its credibility. You need not limit yourself to texts written on paper. You might also evaluate a Web site or blog, a radio or television program or advertisement, or even a work of art (such as a multimedia selection from this book's online interactive media). Choose one possibility from your list, and then come up with two or three criteria for evaluation.

Christine Rosen | *The Myth of Multitasking*

© Matthew Cavanaugh

CHRISTINE ROSEN has written several books, including *My Fundamentalist Education* (2005) and *The Feminist Dilemma* (2001). She also coedited *Acculturated: 23 Savvy Writers Find Hidden Virtue in Reality TV, Chic Lit, Video Games, and Other Pillars of Pop Culture* (2011). A senior editor of the *New Atlantis: A Journal of Technology and Society,* in which this essay originally appeared, Rosen frequently appears on National Public Radio, CNN, and other news outlets. Her essays have also appeared in such prestigious venues as the *New York Times Magazine, Washington Post, Wall Street Journal,* and *National Review.* As you read, think about your experience, and the experience of Rosen's other readers, with multitasking:

- How frequently do you multitask, and what effect has multitasking had on your productivity?

- How does Rosen try to get readers to consider the idea that there may be a downside to multitasking?

1   In one of the many letters he wrote to his son in the 1740s, Lord Chesterfield offered the following advice: "There is time enough for everything in the course of the day, if you do but one thing at once, but there is not time enough in the year, if you will do two things at a time." To Chesterfield, singular focus was not merely a practical way to structure one's time; it was a mark of intelligence. "This steady and undissipated attention to one object, is a sure mark of a superior genius; as hurry, bustle, and agitation, are the never-failing symptoms of a weak and frivolous mind."

2   In modern times, hurry, bustle, and agitation have become a regular way of life for many people—so much so that we have embraced a word to describe our efforts to respond to the many pressing demands on our time: *multitasking*. Used for decades to describe the parallel processing abilities of computers, multitasking is now shorthand for the human attempt to do simultaneously as many things as possible, as quickly as possible, preferably marshaling the power of as many technologies as possible.

3   In the late 1990s and early 2000s, one sensed a kind of exuberance about the

possibilities of multitasking. Advertisements for new electronic gadgets—particularly the first generation of handheld digital devices—celebrated the notion of using technology to accomplish several things at once. The word *multitasking* began appearing in the "skills" sections of résumés, as office workers restyled themselves as high-tech, high-performing team players. "We have always multitasked—inability to walk and chew gum is a time-honored cause for derision — but never so intensely or self-consciously as now," James Gleick wrote in his 1999 book *Faster*. "We are multitasking connoisseurs—experts in crowding, pressing, packing, and overlapping distinct activities in our all-too-finite moments." An article in the *New York Times Magazine* in 2001 asked, "Who can remember life before multitasking? These days we all do it." The article offered advice on "How to Multitask" with suggestions about giving your brain's "multitasking hot spot" an appropriate workout.

4   But more recently, challenges to the ethos of multitasking have begun to emerge. Numerous studies have shown the sometimes-fatal danger of using cell phones and other electronic devices while driving, for example, and several states have now made that particular form of multitasking illegal. In the business world, where concerns about time-management are perennial, warnings about workplace distractions spawned by a multitasking culture are on the rise. In 2005, the BBC reported on a research study, funded by Hewlett-Packard and conducted by the Institute of Psychiatry at the University of London, that found, "Workers distracted by e-mail and phone calls suffer a fall in IQ more than twice that found in marijuana smokers." The psychologist who led the study called this new "infomania" a serious threat to workplace productivity. One of the *Harvard Business Review*'s "Breakthrough Ideas" for 2007 was Linda Stone's

notion of "continuous partial attention," which might be understood as a subspecies of multitasking: using mobile computing power and the Internet, we are "constantly scanning for opportunities and staying on top of contacts, events, and activities in an effort to miss nothing."

5   Dr. Edward Hallowell, a Massachusetts-based psychiatrist who specializes in the treatment of attention deficit/hyperactivity disorder and has written a book with the self-explanatory title *CrazyBusy*, has been offering therapies to combat extreme multitasking for years; in his book he calls multitasking a "mythical activity in which people believe they can perform two or more tasks simultaneously." In a 2005 article, he described a new condition, "Attention Deficit Trait," which he claims is rampant in the business world. ADT is "purely a response to the hyperkinetic environment in which we live," writes Hallowell, and its hallmark symptoms mimic those of ADD. "Never in history has the human brain been asked to track so many data points," Hallowell argues, and this challenge "can be controlled only by creatively engineering one's environment and one's emotional and physical health." Limiting multitasking is essential. Best-selling business advice author Timothy Ferriss also extols the virtues of "single-tasking" in his book, *The 4-Hour Workweek*.

6   Multitasking might also be taking a toll on the economy. One study by researchers at the University of California at Irvine monitored interruptions among office workers; they found that workers took an average of twenty-five minutes to recover from interruptions such as phone calls or answering e-mail and return to their original task. Discussing multitasking with the *New York Times* in 2007, Jonathan B. Spira, an analyst at the business research firm Basex, estimated that extreme multitasking—information overload—costs the U.S. economy $650 billion a year in lost productivity.

Changing Our Brains

7   To better understand the multitasking phenomenon, neurologists and psychologists
have studied the workings of the brain. In
1999, Jordan Grafman, chief of cognitive
neuroscience at the National Institute of
Neurological Disorders and Stroke (part of
the National Institutes of Health), used
functional magnetic resonance imaging
(fMRI) scans to determine that when
people engage in "task-switching"—that
is, multitasking behavior—the flow of
blood increases to a region of the frontal
cortex called Brodmann area 10. (The flow
of blood to particular regions of the brain
is taken as a proxy indication of activity in
those regions.) "This is presumably the last
part of the brain to evolve, the most mysterious and exciting part," Grafman told
the *New York Times* in 2001—adding, with
a touch of hyperbole, "It's what makes us
most human."

8   It is also what makes multitasking a
poor long-term strategy for learning. Other
studies, such as those performed by psychologist René Marois of Vanderbilt University, have used fMRI to demonstrate the
brain's response to handling multiple tasks.
Marois found evidence of a "response selection bottleneck" that occurs when the brain
is forced to respond to several stimuli at
once. As a result, task-switching leads to
time lost as the brain determines which task
to perform. Psychologist David Meyer at
the University of Michigan believes that
rather than a bottleneck in the brain, a process of "adaptive executive control" takes
place, which "schedules task processes
appropriately to obey instructions about
their relative priorities and serial order," as
he described to the *New Scientist*. Unlike
many other researchers who study multitasking, Meyer is optimistic that, with training, the brain can learn to task-switch more
effectively, and there is some evidence that
certain simple tasks are amenable to such
practice. But his research has also found
that multitasking contributes to the release
of stress hormones and adrenaline, which
can cause long-term health problems if not
controlled, and contributes to the loss of
short-term memory.

9   In one recent study, Russell Poldrack,
a psychology professor at the University of
California, Los Angeles, found that "multitasking adversely affects how you learn.
Even if you learn while multitasking, that
learning is less flexible and more specialized, so you cannot retrieve the information as easily." His research demonstrates
that people use different areas of the brain
for learning and storing new information
when they are distracted: brain scans of
people who are distracted or multitasking
show activity in the striatum, a region of
the brain involved in learning new skills;
brain scans of people who are not distracted show activity in the hippocampus,
a region involved in storing and recalling
information. Discussing his research on
National Public Radio recently, Poldrack
warned, "We have to be aware that there is
a cost to the way that our society is changing, that humans are not built to work this
way. We're really built to focus. And when
we sort of force ourselves to multitask,
we're driving ourselves to perhaps be less
efficient in the long run even though it
sometimes feels like we're being more
efficient."

10   If, as Poldrack concluded, "multitasking changes the way people learn," what
might this mean for today's children and
teens, raised with an excess of new entertainment and educational technology, and
avidly multitasking at a young age?
Poldrack calls this the "million-dollar
question." Media multitasking—that is,
the simultaneous use of several different
media, such as television, the Internet,
video games, text messages, telephones,
and e-mail—is clearly on the rise, as a
2006 report from the Kaiser Family Foundation showed: in 1999, only 16 percent of

the time people spent using any of those media was spent on multiple media at once; by 2005, 26 percent of media time was spent multitasking. "I multitask every single second I am online," confessed one study participant. "At this very moment I am watching TV, checking my e-mail every two minutes, reading a newsgroup about who shot JFK, burning some music to a CD, and writing this message."

11   The Kaiser report noted several factors that increase the likelihood of media multitasking, including "having a computer and being able to see a television from it." Also, "sensation-seeking" personality types are more likely to multitask, as are those living in "a highly TV-oriented household." The picture that emerges of these pubescent multitasking mavens is of a generation of great technical facility and intelligence but of extreme impatience, unsatisfied with slowness and uncomfortable with silence: "I get bored if it's not all going at once, because everything has gaps—waiting for a website to come up, commercials on TV, etc.," one participant said. The report concludes on a very peculiar note, perhaps intended to be optimistic: "In this media-heavy world, it is likely that brains that are more adept at media multitasking will be passed along and these changes will be naturally selected," the report states. "After all, information is power, and if one can process more information all at once, perhaps one can be more powerful." This is techno-social Darwinism, nature red in pixel and claw.

12   Other experts aren't so sure. As neurologist Jordan Grafman told *Time* magazine: "Kids that are instant messaging while doing homework, playing games online and watching TV, I predict, aren't going to do well in the long run." "I think this generation of kids is guinea pigs," educational psychologist Jane Healy told the *San Francisco Chronicle;* she worries that they might become adults who engage in "very quick but very shallow thinking." Or, as the

novelist Walter Kirn suggests in a deft essay in *The Atlantic,* we might be headed for an "Attention-Deficit Recession."

Paying Attention

13   When we talk about multitasking, we are really talking about attention: the art of paying attention, the ability to shift our attention, and, more broadly, to exercise judgment about what objects are worthy of our attention. People who have achieved great things often credit for their success a finely honed skill for paying attention. When asked about his particular genius, Isaac Newton responded that if he had made any discoveries, it was "owing more to patient attention than to any other talent."

14   William James, the great psychologist, wrote at length about the varieties of human attention. In *The Principles of Psychology* (1890), he outlined the differences among "sensorial attention," "intellectual attention," "passive attention," and the like, and noted the "gray chaotic indiscriminateness" of the minds of people who were incapable of paying attention. James compared our stream of thought to a river, and his observations presaged the cognitive "bottlenecks" described later by neurologists: "On the whole easy simple flowing predominates in it, the drift of things is with the pull of gravity, and effortless attention is the rule," he wrote. "But at intervals an obstruction, a set-back, a log-jam occurs, stops the current, creates an eddy, and makes things temporarily move the other way."

15   To James, steady attention was thus the default condition of a mature mind, an ordinary state undone only by perturbation. To readers a century later, that placid portrayal may seem alien—as though depicting a bygone world. Instead, today's multitasking adult may find something more familiar in James's description of the youthful mind: an "extreme mobility of the attention" that "makes the child seem to

belong less to himself than to every object which happens to catch his notice." For some people, James noted, this challenge is never overcome; such people only get their work done "in the interstices of their mind-wandering." Like Chesterfield, James believed that the transition from youthful distraction to mature attention was in large part the result of personal mastery and discipline—and so was illustrative of character. "The faculty of voluntarily bringing back a wandering attention, over and over again," he wrote, "is the very root of judgment, character, and will."

16   Today, our collective will to pay attention seems fairly weak. We require advice books to teach us how to avoid distraction. In the not-too-distant future we may even employ new devices to help us overcome the unintended attention deficits created by today's gadgets. As one *New York Times* article recently suggested, "Further research could help create clever technology, like sensors or smart software that workers could instruct with their preferences and priorities to serve as a high tech 'time nanny' to ease the modern multitasker's plight." Perhaps we will all accept as a matter of course a computer governor—like the devices placed on engines so that people can't drive cars beyond a certain speed. Our technological governors might prompt us with reminders to set mental limits when we try to do too much, too quickly, all at once.

17   Then again, perhaps we will simply adjust and come to accept what James called "acquired inattention." E-mails pouring in, cell phones ringing, televisions blaring, podcasts streaming—all this may become background noise, like the "din of a foundry or factory" that James observed workers could scarcely avoid at first, but which eventually became just another part of their daily routine. For the younger generation of multitaskers, the great electronic din is an expected part of everyday life. And given what neuroscience and anecdotal evidence have shown us, this state of constant intentional self-distraction could well be of profound detriment to individual and cultural well-being. When people do their work only in the "interstices of their mind-wandering," with crumbs of attention rationed out among many competing tasks, their culture may gain in information, but it will surely weaken in wisdom.

⌈ REFLECT ⌉ Make connections: Advantages and disadvantages of multitasking.

Rosen cites studies that show that multitasking can have a number of negative effects—such as increasing stress and making learning less flexible—and that multitaskers have difficulty focusing attention on a single task and tend to be easily distracted, impatient, and bored. Think about whether your experience with multitasking confirms or contradicts these studies. Your instructor may ask you to post your thoughts on a class discussion board or to discuss them with other students in class. Use these questions to get started:

- What do you see as the advantages and disadvantages of multitasking? Have you experienced any of the negative effects Rosen writes about?

- Do you think multitasking is better for certain kinds of tasks than others? If so, what tasks?

- Under what circumstances, if any, do you practice what Timothy Ferriss calls "single-tasking"? Why might certain kinds of tasks or situations be better for single-tasking than for multitasking?

[ANALYZE]   Use the basic features.

A WELL-PRESENTED SUBJECT: USING DEFINITIONS AND EXAMPLES TO REFRAME THE SUBJECT

Because she is writing an evaluation critical of something she knows most of her readers think well of, Rosen needs to reframe her subject. That is, she needs to reintroduce the phenomenon in a way that leads readers to see that multitasking has serious disadvantages.

To do this, she starts the essay by defining the term: She offers synonyms and related words and phrases, gives examples, and contrasts the term with its opposite ("single-tasking"). Let's look at some of the strategies she uses to define what multitasking is and frame the concept for her readers. (Later, we will examine how she defines what it isn't.)

ANALYZE & WRITE

Write a few paragraphs analyzing and evaluating how Rosen reframes her subject:

1 Reread paragraph 1. How does Rosen introduce the concept of multitasking here? Why does she include the quotation from Lord Chesterfield?

2 Now reread paragraph 2. Notice how Rosen begins the paragraph with words from Chesterfield — "hurry, bustle, and agitation." What effect do you think repeating these words would have on the reader? Notice that she constructs her sentence with *multitasking* at the end, introduced by a colon and in italics. Why do you think she positions the word *multitasking* at the end of the sentence in this way? If you did not know what multitasking is, what would you learn about it from this sentence? Consider how Rosen classifies multitasking in the next sentence. How does explaining the history (or *etymology*) of the word *multitasking* help readers understand its meaning and help the writer reframe the concept?

3 A third defining strategy is to give examples of multitasking. Skim paragraphs 3 and 4, noting where Rosen offers examples. How do these examples help readers understand what she means by multitasking?

4 Consider how well Rosen's definition and examples set up readers for her evaluation of the practice in the rest of the essay. How well do her definition and examples fit your own experience and observation of multitasking? (Do not comment now on how she judges multitasking; focus only on how she defines it.)

A WELL-SUPPORTED JUDGMENT: USING AUTHORITIES AND RESEARCH STUDIES

Rosen relies primarily on authorities and research studies to support her argument about the value of multitasking. Because she is not writing for an academic audience, she does not include formal citations. But she does provide the same kinds of information about her sources that formal citations offer—the source author or lead researcher's name, the title of the publication in which the borrowed material appeared, and the year of publication of the source—so that readers can locate and read the source themselves. Notice in the following examples how Rosen presents this information.

Bibliographical information   In one of the many letters he wrote to his son in the 1740s, Lord Chesterfield offered the following advice: "There is time enough for everything." (par. 1)

An article in the New York Times Magazine in 2001 asked, "Who can remember life before multitasking? These days we all do it." (par. 3)

"We have always multitasked . . . but never so intensely or self-consciously as now," James Gleick wrote in his 1999 book *Faster*. "We are multitasking connoisseurs." (par. 3)

Writers often begin with the source's name to provide context and establish credibility. In the third example, Rosen places the source information in the middle of the quotation, possibly because she wants to emphasize the opening phrases of both sentences.

Not all sources are quoted, of course. Writers sometimes summarize the main idea or paraphrase what the source has said:

Summary	One study by researchers at the University of California at Irvine monitored interruptions among office workers; they found that workers took an average of twenty-five minutes to recover from interruptions. (par. 6)
Paraphrase	The psychologist who led the study called this new "infomania" a serious threat to workplace productivity. (par. 4)

Studying how writers use strategies like these can help you as you write your own evaluation.

ANALYZE & WRITE

Write a paragraph analyzing and evaluating how Rosen uses material from other authorities and research studies to support her argument:

1. Skim paragraphs 4–9 to highlight the names of authorities and the research studies Rosen cites.

2. Choose two sources, and determine how Rosen uses them to support her judgment about the value of multitasking. Notice how she integrates them into her text.

3. Why might these sources be convincing (or not) for Rosen's readers? How convincing are they for you?

AN EFFECTIVE RESPONSE TO OBJECTIONS AND ALTERNATIVE JUDGMENTS: USING CONTRAST

Writing about a phenomenon her readers have experienced firsthand, Rosen has to assume that many of them will have a judgment of multitasking that differs from the one she is arguing for. Consequently, Rosen's entire essay can be seen as an attempt to refute an alternative judgment.

Rosen tries to convince readers to see multitasking in a new way by contrasting it with its opposite. In the opening paragraph, she uses a sentence strategy like this to present the contrast:

▶ _____ [the opposite of multitasking] is *not only* _____ [name a good quality]; it is *also* _____ [name another good quality].

EXAMPLE	Opposite of multitasking Good quality 1 Good quality 2	To Chesterfield, singular focus was *not merely* a practical way to structure one's time; it was a mark of intelligence. (par. 1)

| ANALYZE & WRITE | ——————————————————

Write a couple of paragraphs analyzing and evaluating the effectiveness of Rosen's use of contrast to reframe her readers' ideas and attitudes about multitasking:

1. Skim the essay, highlighting with one color (or underlining) the qualities Rosen associates with multitasking, and highlighting with a different color (or circling) the qualities Rosen associates with the opposite of multitasking.

2. Review the words and phrases Rosen uses to describe multitasking and its opposite. What values and ideas does she attach to these two alternatives?

3. Given her purpose and audience, how well do you think this strategy of using contrast is likely to work? What seems to you to be its strengths and weaknesses?

To learn more about patterns of opposition, see pp. 310–11 in Chapter 9.

A CLEAR, LOGICAL ORGANIZATION: CUEING READERS

Rosen's evaluation is complicated. Not only is she juggling multitasking and singular focus, but she is also referring to a range of sources spanning a long period of time. To make clear which phenomenon and which source she is talking about, Rosen uses a variety of explicit cueing devices, including time references, names and titles, transitions, and headings.

| ANALYZE & WRITE | ——————————————————

Write a couple of paragraphs analyzing and evaluating Rosen's use of cues to help readers follow her argument:

1. Skim paragraphs 1–4, highlighting dates and other time references Rosen uses to help readers follow the chronology.

2. Reread paragraphs 7–12, in which Rosen introduces a series of research studies. Highlight the name of the lead researcher (Grafman, for example) or the publication in which the report appeared (the Kaiser Family Foundation) and circle the transitional words and phrases she uses (such as "Other studies") to orient readers.

3. Note the two headings she uses. How do these help readers follow her evaluative argument?

[RESPOND] Consider possible topics: Evaluating technology.

Choose a contemporary phenomenon to evaluate—for example, an Internet site (such as *Wikipedia*), a social networking site (such as *Facebook* or *Twitter*), or a reality television program (such as *The Voice* or *The Bachelorette*). Select a phenomenon about which you already have a strong overall judgment and consider the criteria you would use to persuade others to accept your evaluation. Be sure to consider the evidence you could use to support your judgment.

macmillanhighered.com/conciseguide
Can a crowd-sourced Web site provide an effective evaluation?
E-readings > Yelp, *Kuma's Corner*

The Writing Assignment	263
Writing a Draft: Invention, Research, Planning, and Composing	264
Evaluating the Draft: Getting a Critical Reading	272
Improving the Draft: Revising, Formatting, Editing, and Proofreading	274

The Writing Assignment

Write an essay evaluating a specific subject. Examine your subject closely, and make a judgment about it. Give reasons for your judgment that are based on widely recognized criteria or standards for evaluating a subject like yours. Support your reasons with examples and other details primarily from your subject.

This Guide to Writing is designed to help you compose your own evaluation and apply what you have learned from reading other essays in the same genre. This Starting Points chart will help you find answers to questions you might have about composing an essay evaluating a subject. Use the chart to find the guidance you need, when you need it.

STARTING POINTS: JUSTIFYING AN EVALUATION

A Well-Presented Subject

How do I come up with a subject to write about?

- Consider possible topics. (pp. 255, 262)
- Choose a subject to evaluate. (pp. 264–65)
- Test Your Choice (p. 265)
- Assess your subject and consider how to present it to your readers. (pp. 266–67)

How can I present my subject clearly and convincingly?

- Determine the writer's purpose and audience. (p. 239)
- Assess the genre's basic features: A well-presented subject (pp. 239–40)
- A Well-Presented Subject: Introducing a Complicated Subject (p. 253)
- A Well-Presented Subject: Using Definitions and Examples to Reframe the Subject (p. 260)
- Assess your subject and consider how to present it to your readers. (pp. 266–67)

A Well-Supported Judgment

How do I come up with a thesis statement?

- Assess the genre's basic features: A well-supported judgment (pp. 240–42)
- Formulate a working thesis stating your overall judgment. (p. 267)

(continued)

A Well-Supported Judgment

How do I construct an argument supporting my judgment?

- Assess the genre's basic features: A well-supported judgment (pp. 240–42)
- A Well-Supported Judgment: Defining Criteria (pp. 253–54)
- A Well-Supported Judgment: Using Authorities and Research Studies (pp. 260–61)
- Develop the reasons and evidence supporting your judgment. (pp. 268–69)
- Research your evaluation. (p. 269)

An Effective Response to Objections and Alternative Judgments

How do I respond to possible objections and alternative judgments?

- Assess the genre's basic features: An effective response to objections and alternative judgments (p. 242)
- An Effective Response to Objections and Alternative Judgments: Singling Out a Comment for Response (p. 254)
- An Effective Response to Objections and Alternative Judgments: Using Contrast (pp. 261–62)
- Respond to a likely objection or alternative judgment. (pp. 269–71)

A Clear, Logical Organization

How can I help my readers follow my argument?

- Assess the genre's basic features: A clear, logical organization (pp. 242–43)
- A Clear, Logical Organization: Using Comparison and Contrast (p. 254)
- A Clear, Logical Organization: Cuing Readers (p. 262)
- Organize your draft to appeal to your readers. (pp. 271–72)

Writing a Draft: Invention, Research, Planning, and Composing

The activities in this section will help you choose and research a subject as well as develop and organize an evaluative argument. Do the activities in any order that makes sense to you (and your instructor), and return to them as needed as you revise. Your writing in response to many of these activities can be used in a rough draft that you will be able to improve after receiving feedback from your classmates and instructor.

Choose a subject to evaluate.

When choosing a subject for evaluation, keep in mind that it must be

- one that has strengths or weaknesses you could write about;
- one that you can view and review (for example, a location you can visit; a printed text; or a Web site or digital recording from which you can capture stills or video clips to use as examples in a multimedia presentation);

- one typically evaluated according to criteria or standards of judgment that you understand and share with your readers.

You may already have a subject in mind. If you do, skip to Test Your Choice below. If you do not, the following topics, in addition to those following the readings (pp. 255 and 262), may suggest one you can write about effectively.

Subjects Related to School

- Evaluate some aspect of your high school or college—for example, a particular program or major you are considering; a residence hall, library, or lab; the sports facilities or teams; a campus research institute or center; or campus work-study or student support services.

- Evaluate an article, an essay, a textbook, or another book assigned in a course; a campus newspaper blog, editorial, or opinion piece; or a campus performance, exhibit, or film series.

Subjects Related to Your Community

- Evaluate how well one of the following meets the needs of residents of your town or city: public library, health clinic, neighborhood watch or block parent program, meals-on-wheels program, theater, or symphony.

- Evaluate a law or a proposed law, such as the Dream Act, the Stop Online Piracy Act, the Defense of Marriage Act, the balanced budget amendment, or the equal rights amendment to the Constitution.

Subjects Related to Work

- Evaluate a job you have had or currently have, or evaluate someone else you have observed closely, such as a coworker or supervisor.

- Evaluate a local job-training program, either one in which you have participated or one that will allow you to observe and interview trainees.

| TEST YOUR CHOICE |

After you have made a provisional choice, ask yourself the following questions:

- Do I know enough about the subject, or can I learn enough in the time I have?
- Do I already have a judgment (either tentative or certain) about this subject?
- Do I know what criteria or standards my readers are likely to use for judging something of this kind? Would I use the same criteria?

To try out your choice of a subject and ideas about criteria, get together with two or three other students:

Presenters.   Take turns describing your subject.

Listeners.   Briefly tell the presenter what criteria or standards of judgment you would use to evaluate a subject of this kind.

As you plan and draft your evaluation, you may need to reconsider your choice of subject (for example, if you discover your criteria for evaluating are different from those your readers would use). If you have serious doubts about your choice, discuss them with your instructor before starting over with a new subject.

▪▪ Assess your subject and consider how to present it to your readers.

Once you have made a preliminary choice of a subject, consider how you can frame or reframe it so that readers will be open to your evaluation. To do this, consider first how you regard the subject and what your readers are likely to think. Use the following questions and sentence strategies as a jumping-off point. You can make the sentences you generate your own later, as you revise.

WAYS IN

WHAT DO I THINK?

List those qualities of your subject that you like and dislike, or list its strengths and weaknesses or advantages and disadvantages.

▶ What makes _____ [good/bad] is _____, _____, and _____.

▶ Although _____ is stellar in [these ways], it falls short in [these other ways].

What genre or kind of subject is it?

▶ The _____ is a [name genre or category of subject, such as romantic comedy or horror movie].

▶ It is an innovative [name category in which the subject belongs] that combines elements of _____ and _____.

▶ [Subject] is rather unconventional for a [name category in which your subject belongs].

What criteria or standards of judgment do you usually use to evaluate things of this kind?

▶ I expect _____ to be _____ or _____.

▶ I dislike it when _____ are _____.

How does your subject compare to other examples of the genre?

WHAT DO MY READERS THINK?

Who are your readers, and why will they be reading your review? Is the subject new or familiar to them?

▶ My readers are _____ and are probably reading my review [to learn about the subject or to decide whether to see it, play it, or buy it].

▶ My readers will probably be familiar with the subject [and may have heard or read others' evaluations of it]. They may be curious to know what I think because _____.

How might factors such as the readers' age, gender, cultural background, or work experience affect their judgment of the subject?

▶ [Older/Younger] readers are [less/more] likely to _____.

▶ People who work in _____ or who are familiar with _____ may be [more/less critical, or apply different standards] to a subject like this one.

What criteria or standards of judgment do you expect your readers to use when evaluating subjects of this kind? What other examples of the genre would they be familiar with?

▶ I expect readers to share my criteria.

► Compared to [other subjects], _____ has the [best or worst] _____ [name trait].

► The _____ is like [a comparable subject] in that both [are/do/make] _____, but this subject is [more/less] _____.

► Whereas other [comparable subjects] can be [faulted/praised for] _____, this subject _____.

► If they [like/dislike] [comparable subject], they are sure to [like/dislike] _____.

► Judging [this kind of subject] on the basis of _____ is likely to surprise readers because they probably are more familiar with _____ and _____.

Formulate a working thesis stating your overall judgment.

You may already have a good idea about how you want to assert your thesis: stating whether your subject is good or bad, or better or worse than something else in the same genre or category. Remember that evaluations can be mixed—you can concede shortcomings in a generally favorable review or concede admirable qualities in a mostly negative assessment. If you feel comfortable drafting a working thesis statement now, do so. You may use the following sentence strategies as a jumping-off point—you can always revise them later—or use language of your own. (Alternatively, if you prefer to develop your argument before trying to formulate a thesis, skip this activity now and return to it later.)

As you develop your argument, you may want to rework your thesis to make it more compelling by sharpening the language and perhaps also by forecasting your reasons. You may also need to qualify your judgment with words like *generally, may,* or *in part.*

WAYS IN

HOW CAN I ASSERT A TENTATIVE OVERALL JUDGMENT?

A good strategy is to begin by naming the subject and identifying the kind of subject it is, and then using value terms to state your judgment of the subject's strengths and weaknesses:

► _____ is a brilliant embodiment of [the genre/category], especially notable for its superb _____ and thorough _____.

► Because I admire [another artist's other work], I expected _____ to be _____. But I was [disappointed/surprised] by _____.

► _____ has many good qualities including _____ and _____; however, the pluses do not outweigh its one major drawback, namely that _____.

:: Develop the reasons and evidence supporting your judgment.

The following activities will help you find reasons and evidence to support your evaluation. Begin by writing down what you already know. You can do some focused research later to fill in the details.

For more idea-generating strategies, see Chapter 8.

⌐ WAYS IN ⟶

HOW CAN I COME UP WITH REASONS AND EVIDENCE TO SUPPORT MY JUDGMENT?

List the good and bad qualities of the subject. Begin by reviewing the criteria and the value terms you have already used to describe the good and bad qualities of the subject. These are the potential reasons for your judgment. Try restating them using this basic sentence strategy, which is also illustrated by an example from student William Akana's film review:

▶ _____ is [your overall judgment] *because* _____, _____, and _____.

Example:

> *Scott Pilgrim vs. the World* can be appreciated and enjoyed by all audiences *because* of its inventive special effects, clever dialogue, and artistic cinematography and editing. (par. 2)

Write steadily for at least five minutes, developing your reasons. Ask yourself questions like these:

▶ Why are the characteristics I'm pointing out for praise or criticism so important in judging my subject?

Example:

> Akana singles out special effects, dialogue, cinematography, and editing because of the particular kind of film *Scott Pilgrim vs. the World* is—"a hilarious slacker movie that also somehow reimagines romantic comedy" (par. 1).

▶ How can I prove to readers that the value terms I'm using to evaluate these characteristics are fair and accurate?

Example:

> Akana analyzes the film's special effects and gives readers specific examples, including screen shots, to demonstrate that they are indeed "inventive."

Make notes of the evidence you will use to support your judgment. Evidence you might use to support each reason may include the following:

- Examples
- Quotations from authorities

- Textual evidence (quotations, paraphrases, or summaries)
- Images
- Statistics
- Comparisons or contrasts

You may already have some evidence you could use. If you lack evidence for any of your reasons, make a *Research To Do* note for later.

Research your evaluation.

Consult your *Research To Do* notes to determine what you need to find out. If you are evaluating a subject that others have written about, try searching for articles or books on your topic. Enter keywords or phrases related to the subject, genre, or category into the search box of

- an all-purpose database—such as *Academic OneFile* (InfoTrac) or *Academic Search Complete* (EBSCOHost)—to find relevant articles in magazines and journals;
- the database *Lexis/Nexis* to find newspaper reviews;
- a search engine like *Google* or *Yahoo!* (Akana used *Movie Review Query Engine* [mrqe.com] and *Rotten Tomatoes* to find film reviews of *Scott Pilgrim vs. the World*);
- your library's catalog to locate books on your topic.

Turn to databases and search engines for information on more recent items, like films and popular novels; use books, databases, and search engines to find information on classic topics. (Books are more likely to provide in-depth information, but articles in print or online are more likely to be current.)

Respond to a likely objection or alternative judgment.

Start by identifying an objection or an alternative judgment you expect some readers to raise. To come up with likely objections or alternative judgments, you might try the following:

- *Brainstorm* a list on your own or with fellow students.
- *Freewrite* for ten minutes on this topic.
- Conduct research to learn what others have said about your subject.
- Conduct interviews with experts.
- Distribute a survey to a group of people similar to your intended readers.

Then figure out whether to concede or refute a likely objection or alternative judgment. You may be able simply to acknowledge an objection or alternative judgment. But if the criticism is serious, consider conceding the point and qualifying your judgment. You might also try to refute an objection or alternative judgment by arguing that the standards you are using are appropriate and important. Use the following strategies for generating ideas and sentences as a jumping-off point, and revise them later to make them your own.

For more on idea-generating strategies, see Chapter 8; for more on conducting research, see Chapter 16.

WAYS IN

HOW CAN I RESPOND EFFECTIVELY TO MY READERS?

1. Start by listing objections you expect readers to have as well as their preferred alternative judgments. In the Ways In activity on p. 266, you considered your readers and the criteria they are likely to favor. If their criteria differ from yours, you may need to explain or defend your criteria.

2. Analyze your list of objections and alternative judgments to determine which are likely to be most powerful for your readers.

3. Draft refutations and concession statements:

To Refute

▶ X, reviewer for _____, claims that _____. But I agree with Y, reviewer for _____, who argues that _____.

▶ Some people think _____ is [alternative judgment] because of _____, _____, and _____ [reasons]. Although one can see why they might make this argument, the evidence does not back it up because _____.

▶ Reviewers have remarked that _____ is a pale imitation of [comparable subject]. I disagree. Whereas [comparable subject] is _____, _____ is _____.

▶ This _____ has generated criticism for its supposed _____. But _____ is not _____. Instead, it is _____.

▶ In contrast to popular opinion, a recent study of _____ showed that _____.

To Concede

▶ Indeed, the more hard-core [name enthusiasts] may carp that _____ is not suffi-ciently [shortcomings].

▶ The one justifiable criticism that could be made against _____ is _____.

▶ As some critics have pointed out, _____ follows the tried-and-true formula of _____.

To Concede and Refute

Frequently, writers concede a point only to come back with a refutation. To make the *concession-refutation move*, follow concessions like those above with sentences that begin with a transition like *but, however, yet,* or *nevertheless,* and then explain why you believe that your interpretation or position is more powerful or compelling.

▶ As some critics have pointed out, _____ follows the tried-and-true formula of _____. Still, the [director/writer/artist] is using the formula effectively to _____.

Research Note: You may want to return to this activity after conducting further research. (For example, when he researched published reviews of *Scott Pilgrim*, student William Akana found objections to his argument as well as alternative judgments he could quote and refute.)

For more on the concession-refutation move, see Chapter 5, pp. 150–51 and 179–80.

Organize your draft to appeal to your readers.

Whether you have rough notes or a complete draft, making an *outline* of what you have written can help you organize the essay effectively for your audience. An evaluative essay contains as many as four basic parts:

1. Presentation of the subject
2. Judgment of the subject
3. Presentation of reasons and support
4. Consideration of readers' objections and alternative judgments

These parts can be organized in various ways; two options follow:

If you are writing primarily for readers who disagree with your judgment, you could start by showing them what you think they have overlooked or misjudged about the subject. Then you could anticipate and refute their likely objections before presenting your own reasons.

I. **Presentation of the subject:** Reframe subject in terms that support your judgment

II. **Thesis statement:** State your judgment directly

III. **Refutation of alternative judgments**

IV. **First reason and support with refutation of objection**

V. **Second reason and support (and so on)**

VI. **Conclusion:** Reiterate why your judgment is preferable to the alternatives

If you expect some readers to disagree with your judgment even though they share your standards, you could begin by restating these standards and then demonstrate how the subject fails to meet them. Then you could present your reasons and support before responding to alternative judgments.

I. **Presentation of the issue:** Reassert shared criteria

II. **Thesis statement:** State judgment that subject fails to meet shared criteria

III. **First reason and support showing how subject falls short**

IV. **Second reason and support (and so on)**

V. **Refutation of alternative judgment**

VI. **Conclusion:** Reassert judgment based on shared criteria

There are, of course, many other ways to organize an evaluative essay, but these outlines should help you start planning your draft.

For more on outlining, see pp. 284–87 in Chapter 8.

Never be a slave to an outline: As you draft, you may see ways to improve your original plan, and you should be ready to revise your outline, shift parts around, or drop or add parts as needed. If you use the outlining function of your word processing program, changing your outline will be simple, and you may be able to write the essay simply by expanding that outline.

Write the opening sentences.

You might want to review your invention writing to see if you have already written something that would work to launch your essay. Alternatively, try one or two options from the following list. But do not agonize over the first sentences because you are likely to discover the best way to begin only after you have written a rough draft:

- An anecdote (like Akana)
- A surprising or provocative statement
- A quotation (like Rosen)
- Something comparable that readers are likely to know (like Gladwell)
- Statistics or research study results

Draft your evaluation.

By this point, you have done a lot of writing to

- devise a well-presented subject and make a judgment about it;
- support your judgment with reasons and evidence that your readers will find persuasive;
- refute or concede objections and alternative judgments;
- organize your ideas to make them clear, logical, and effective for readers.

Now stitch that material together to create a draft. The next two parts of this Guide to Writing will help you evaluate and improve that draft.

Evaluating the Draft: Getting a Critical Reading

Your instructor may arrange a peer review session in class or online where you can exchange drafts with your classmates to give each other a thoughtful critical reading, pointing out what works well and suggesting ways to improve the draft. A good critical reading does three things:

1. It lets the writer know how well the reader understands the point of the essay.
2. It praises what works best.
3. It indicates where the draft could be improved and makes suggestions on how to improve it.

One strategy for evaluating a draft is to use the basic features of evaluative essays as a guide.

A CRITICAL READING GUIDE

A Well-Presented Subject

Has the writer presented the subject effectively?

Summarize: Tell the writer what you understand the subject of the evaluation to be, and identify the kind of subject it is.

Praise: Point to a place where the subject is presented effectively — for example, where it is described vividly and accurately, where it is named, or where it is clearly placed in a recognizable genre or category.

Critique: Tell the writer where readers might need more information about the subject, and whether any information about it seems inaccurate or possibly only partly true. Suggest how the writer could clarify the kind of subject it is, either by naming the category or by giving examples of familiar subjects of the same type.

A Well-Supported Judgment

Has the writer supported the judgment effectively?

Summarize: Tell the writer what you understand the overall judgment to be, and list the criteria on which it is based.

Praise: Identify a passage in the essay where support for the judgment is presented effectively — for example, note particularly strong supporting reasons, appeals to criteria readers are likely to share, or especially compelling evidence.

Critique: Let the writer know if you cannot find a thesis statement or think the thesis is vague or overstated. Tell the writer where the evaluation could be improved — for example, suggest another reason that could be added; propose a way to justify one of the criteria on which the evaluation is based; or recommend a source or an example that could be used to bolster support for the judgment.

An Effective Response to Objections and Alternative Judgments

Has the writer responded effectively to objections and alternative judgments?

Summarize: Choose an objection or alternative judgment about the subject, and explain it in your own words.

Praise: Identify a passage in the essay where the writer responds effectively to an objection or alternative judgment. An effective response may include making a concession — for example, agreeing that a subject the writer is primarily criticizing has some good points, or agreeing that the subject has weaknesses as well as strengths.

Critique: Tell the writer where a response is needed or could be made more effective — for example, suggest a likely objection or alternative judgment that should be taken into account, help the writer understand the criteria behind an alternative judgment, or offer an example that could be used to refute an objection.

(continued)

A Clear, Logical Organization

Is the evaluation clearly and logically organized?

Summarize: Briefly describe the strategies used to make the essay clear and easy to follow.

Praise: Give an example of where the essay succeeds in being readable — in its overall organization, in its clear presentation of the thesis, in its effective opening or closing, or by other means.

Critique: Tell the writer where the readability could be improved. Can you, for example, suggest a better beginning or a more effective ending? If the overall organization of the essay needs work, make suggestions for rearranging parts or strengthening connections.

Before concluding your peer review, be sure to address any of the writer's concerns that have not been discussed already.

Improving the Draft: Revising, Formatting, Editing, and Proofreading

Start improving your draft by reflecting on what you have written thus far:

- Review critical reading comments from your classmates, instructor, or writing center tutor: What are your readers getting at?
- Consider whether you can add any of the notes from your earlier writings: What else should you consider?
- Review your draft: What can you do to present your position more compellingly?

Revise your draft.

If your readers are having difficulty with your draft, or if you think there is room for improvement, try some of the strategies listed in the Troubleshooting Guide that follows. It can help you fine-tune your presentation of the genre's basic features:

A TROUBLESHOOTING GUIDE

A Well-Presented Subject

My readers find my subject vague or do not think it has been identified clearly.

- Identify the subject, name the author or director, and give the title.
- Describe the subject — summarize what it is about, cite statistics that establish its importance, or give examples to make it concrete.
- Consider adding visuals — photographs, tables, or charts — to help clarify the subject.

A Well-Presented Subject

My readers aren't sure what kind of subject it is.

- Classify the subject by naming the genre or category it fits into.
- Refer to reviews or reviewers of subjects of this kind.
- Compare your subject to other, better-known subjects of the same kind.

A Well-Supported Judgment

My readers don't find my thesis or overall judgment clear.

- State your thesis early in the essay.
- Clarify the language in your thesis statement to indicate your overall judgment.
- Consider whether your judgment is arguable (not simply a matter of taste). If you cannot provide reasons and support for it, then your judgment probably isn't arguable; ask your instructor about modifying your judgment or writing about a different subject.

My readers aren't convinced that my evaluation is reasonable and/or persuasive.

- Clarify the criteria on which you base your judgment, and justify them by citing authorities or reviews of similar subjects, making comparisons, or explaining why your criteria are appropriate and perhaps preferable to criteria readers may be more familiar with.
- Add support for your reasons by, for example, quoting respected experts or research studies; providing facts or statistics; giving specific examples; or quoting, summarizing, or paraphrasing the subject of your evaluation.

My readers don't understand my evaluation.

- Review the way you present your evaluation to make sure that you have explained it clearly and that you state your supporting reasons clearly.
- Outline your argument to be sure that it is clearly organized; if it is not, try rearranging parts or strengthening connections.
- Make sure that you have cut out any irrelevant content, and revise to strengthen the connections among your ideas.

(continued)

An Effective Response to Objections and Alternative Judgments

My readers raise objections I haven't considered or find fault with my response to alternative judgments.

- If readers raise only a minor concern, you may be able to ignore or dismiss it. (Not every objection requires a response.)
- If readers raise a serious objection, one that undermines your argument, try to refute it by showing that it's not based on widely held or appropriate criteria or that it's based on a misunderstanding of your argument or the subject.
- If readers raise a serious objection that you can't refute, acknowledge it but try to demonstrate that it doesn't invalidate your judgment.

My readers have proposed alternative judgments or have found fault with how I handle alternatives.

- Address the alternative judgments directly by conceding good or bad qualities of the subject that others focus on, but emphasize that you disagree about the overall value of the subject.
- Point out where you and your readers agree on criteria but disagree on how well the subject meets the criteria.
- Where you disagree with readers on criteria, try to justify the standards you are applying by citing authorities or establishing your own authority.

A Clear, Logical Organization

My readers find my essay confusing or hard to follow.

- Outline your essay to review its structure, and move, add, or delete sections as necessary to strengthen coherence.
- Consider adding a forecasting statement early in your essay.
- Repeat your key terms or use synonyms of key terms to keep readers oriented.
- Check to see that you introduce your reasons clearly in topic sentences.
- Check to be sure that you provide appropriate transitions between sentences, paragraphs, and sections of your essay, especially at points where your readers have trouble following your argument.
- Review your opening and closing paragraphs to be sure that your overall judgment is clear and appropriately qualified.

Edit and proofread your draft.

Our research indicates that particular errors occur often in essays that justify an evaluation: incomplete and illogical comparisons, and short, choppy sentences. The following guidelines will help you check your essay for these common errors.

Making Complete, Logical, and Grammatically Correct Comparisons

The Problem   In essays that justify an evaluation, writers often engage in comparison—showing, for example, that one film is stronger than another, a new recording is inferior to an earlier one, or one restaurant is better than another. When comparisons are expressed incompletely, illogically, or incorrectly, however, the point of the comparison can be dulled or lost completely.

The Correction   Reread your comparisons, checking for completeness, logic, and correctness.

A comparison is complete if two terms are introduced, and the relationship between them is clearly expressed:

▶ *Jazz* is as good, if not better than, Morrison's other novels.
    ^*as*

▶ I liked the Lispector story because it's so different‚ *from anything else I've ever read.*
                                                          ^

A comparison is logical if the terms compared are parallel (and therefore comparable):

▶ Will Smith's Muhammad Ali is more serious than any *other* role he's played.
                                                 ^

▶ Ohio State's offense played much better than ~~Michigan.~~ *Michigan's did.*
                                                      ^

Note that *different from* is correct; *different than*, though commonly used, is incorrect:

▶ Carrying herself with a confident and brisk stride, Katherine Parker seems

different ~~than~~ the other women in the office.
          ^ *from*

▶ Films like *Drive*, which glorify violence for its own sake, are different ~~than~~
                                                                        ^ *from*

films like *Apocalypse Now*, which use violence to make a moral point.

Combining Sentences

The Problem   When writers justify an evaluation, they generally present their subject in some detail—defining it, describing it, placing it in some context. Inexperienced writers often present such details one after another, in short, choppy sentences. These sentences can be difficult or irritating to read, and they provide the reader with no help in determining how the different details relate to one another.

The Correction Combine sentences to make your writing more readable and to clarify the relationships among ideas. Two common strategies for sentence combining involve converting full sentences into **appositive phrases** (a noun phrase that renames the noun or pronoun that immediately precedes it) or **verbal phrases** (phrases using words derived from verbs that function as adjectives, adverbs, or nouns). Consider the following example:

▶ In paragraph 5, the details provide a different impression, ~~It is~~ a comic or

  perhaps even pathetic impression, ~~The impression comes~~ *based on* the boy's

  attempts to dress up like a real westerner.

From three separate sentences, this writer smoothly combines details about the "different impression" into a single sentence, using an appositive phrase ("a comic or perhaps even pathetic impression") and a verbal phrase ("based on the boy's attempts to dress up like a real westerner").

Here are two additional examples of the first strategy (conversion into an appositive phrase):

▶ "Something Pacific" was created by Nam June Paik, ~~He is~~ a Korean artist who is considered a founder of video art.

▶ One of Dylan's songs *"Talkin' John Birch Paranoid Blues,"* ridiculed the John Birch Society. ~~This song was called "Talkin' John Birch Paranoid Blues."~~

Finally, here are two additional examples of the second strategy (conversion into a verbal phrase):

▶ Spider-Man's lifesaving webbing sprung from his wristbands, *carrying* ~~They carried~~ Mary Jane Watson and him out of peril.

▶ The coffee bar flanks the bookshelves, *enticing* ~~It entices~~ readers to relax with a book.

THINKING CRITICALLY

To think critically means to use all of the knowledge you have acquired from the information in this chapter, your own writing, the writing of other students, and class discussions to reflect deeply on your work for this assignment and the genre (or type) of writing you have produced. The benefit of thinking critically is proven and important: Thinking critically about what you have learned will help you remember it longer, ensuring that you will be able to put it to good use well beyond this writing course.

Reflecting on What You Have Learned

In this chapter, you have learned a great deal about this genre from reading several essays that justify an evaluation and from writing an evaluation of your own. To consolidate your learning, reflect not only on what you learned but also on how you learned it.

ANALYZE & WRITE

Write a blog post, a letter to your instructor, or an e-mail message to a student who will take this course next term, using the writing prompt that seems most productive for you:

- Explain how your purpose and audience influenced *one* of your decisions as a writer, such as how you presented the subject, the strategies you used in justifying your evaluation, or the ways in which you attempted to counter possible objections.

- Discuss what you learned about yourself as a writer in the process of writing this particular essay. For example, what part of the process did you find most challenging? Did you try anything new, like getting a critical reading of your draft or outlining your draft in order to revise it?

- If you were to give advice to a friend who was about to write an essay justifying an evaluation, what would you say?

- Which of the readings in this chapter influenced your essay? Explain the influence, citing specific examples from your essay and from the reading.

- If you got good advice from a critical reader, explain exactly how the person helped you — perhaps by questioning the way you addressed your audience or the kinds of support you offered for your position.

Reflecting on the Genre

Good evaluative writing provides readers with reasons and support for the writer's judgment. However, the writer's personal experiences, cultural background, and political ideology are also reflected in evaluations. Even the most fair-minded evaluators write from the perspective of their ethnicity, religion, gender, age, social class, sexual orientation, academic discipline, and so on. Writers seldom make their assumptions explicit, however. Consequently, while the reasons presented within an evaluation may make it seem fair and objective, the writer's judgment may result from hidden assumptions that even the writer has not examined critically.

ANALYZE & WRITE

Write a page or two explaining how the genre disguises the writer's assumptions. In your discussion, you might do one or more of the following:

1. **Identify one of the hidden assumptions of a writer in this chapter.** Think of a personal or cultural factor that may have influenced the writer's judgment of the subject. For example, how do you imagine that Akana's gender may have influenced his judgment of the film *Scott Pilgrim vs. the World*?

2. **Reflect on your own experience of writing an evaluation essay.** How do you think factors such as gender, age, social class, ethnicity, religion, geographical region, or political perspective may have influenced your own evaluation? Recall the subjects that you listed as possibilities for your essay and how you chose one to evaluate. Also recall how you arrived at your overall judgment and how you decided which reasons to use and which not to use in your essay.

3. **Write a page or two explaining your ideas about how hidden assumptions play a role in evaluation essays.** Connect your ideas to the readings in this chapter and to your own essay.

© Marek Uliasz/Alamy

PART 2

Strategies for Critical Thinking, Reading, and Writing

8 Strategies for Invention and Inquiry   282

9 Strategies for Reading Critically   294

10 Cueing the Reader   317

11 Analyzing and Synthesizing Arguments   332

12 Analyzing Visuals   352

13 Arguing   366

14 Designing Documents   383

Strategies for Invention and Inquiry

Writers are like scientists: They ask questions, systematically inquiring about how things work, what they are, where they occur, and how more information can be learned about them. Writers are also like artists in that they use what they know and learn to create something new and imaginative.

The invention and inquiry strategies—also known as **heuristics**—described in this chapter are not mysterious or magical. They are available to all writers, and one or more of them may appeal to your common sense and experience. These techniques represent ways creative writers, engineers, scientists, composers—in fact, all of us—solve problems. Once you have mastered these strategies, you can use them to tackle many of the writing situations you will encounter in college, on the job, and in the community.

The strategies for invention and inquiry in this chapter are grouped into two categories:

Mapping: A brief visual representation of your thinking or planning

Writing: The composition of phrases or sentences to discover information and ideas and to make connections among them

These invention and inquiry strategies will help you explore and research a topic fully before you begin drafting, and then help you creatively solve problems as you draft and revise. In this chapter, strategies are arranged alphabetically within each of the two categories.

Mapping

Mapping strategies involve making a visual record of invention and inquiry. In making maps, writers usually use key words and phrases to record material they want to remember, questions they need to answer, and new sources of information they want to check. The maps show the ideas, details, and facts as well as possible ways to connect and focus them. Mapping can be especially useful for working in collaborative writing situations, for preparing oral presentations, and for creating visual aids for written or oral reports. Mapping strategies include *clustering, listing,* and *outlining*.

Create a cluster diagram.

Clustering is a strategy for revealing possible relationships among facts and ideas. Unlike listing (the next mapping strategy), clustering requires a brief period of initial preparation, when you divide your topic into parts or main ideas. Clustering works as follows:

1. In a word or phrase, write your topic in the center of a piece of paper. Circle it.

2. Also in words or phrases, write down the main parts or ideas of your topic. Circle these, and connect them with lines to the topic in the center.

3. Next, write down facts, details, and examples related to these main parts or ideas. Connect them with lines to the relevant main parts or ideas.

Clustering can be useful in the early stages of planning an essay to find subtopics and organize information. You may try out and discard several clusters before finding one that is promising. Many writers also use clustering to plan brief sections of an essay as they are drafting or revising. (A model of clustering is shown in Figure 8.1.)

Make a list.

Listing is a familiar activity. You make shopping lists and lists of errands to do or people to call, but listing can also be a great help in planning an essay. It enables you to recall what you already know about a topic and suggests what else you may need to find out.

A basic activity for all writers, listing is especially useful to those who have little time for planning—for example, reporters facing deadlines and college students taking

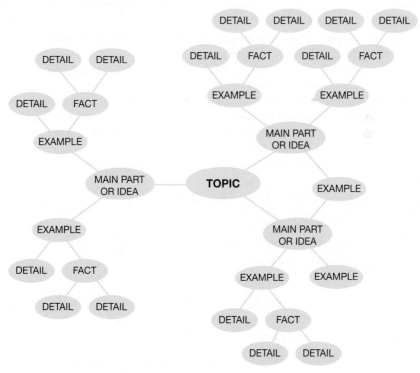

FIGURE 8.1   A Model of Clustering

essay exams. Listing lets you order your ideas quickly. It can also serve as a first step in discovering possible writing topics. Here is how listing works best for invention work:

1. Give your list a title that indicates your main idea or topic.

2. Write as fast as you can, relying on short phrases.

3. Include anything that seems at all useful. Try not to be judgmental at this point.

4. After you have finished or even as you write, reflect on the list, and organize it in the following way:

   - Put an asterisk next to the most promising items.
   - Number key items in order of importance.
   - Put items in related groups.
   - Cross out items that do not seem promising.
   - Add new items.

Create an outline.

Like listing and clustering, **outlining** is both a means of inventing what you want to say in an essay and a way of organizing your ideas and information. As you outline, you nearly always see new possibilities in your subject, discovering new ways of dividing or grouping information and seeing where you need additional information to develop your ideas. Because outlining lets you see at a glance where your essay's strengths and weaknesses lie, outlining can also help you read and revise your essay with a critical eye.

There are two main forms of outlining: informal outlining and formal topic or sentence outlining. Among the several types of informal outlining, *scratch outlines* are perhaps the most adaptable to a variety of situations. Chunking is another useful method. (Clustering also may be considered a type of informal outlining.)

A **scratch outline** is little more than a list of the essay's main points. You have no doubt made scratch outlines many times — to plan essays or essay exams, to revise your own writing, and to analyze a difficult reading passage. Here are sample scratch outlines for two different kinds of essays. The first is an outline of Annie Dillard's essay in Chapter 2 (pp. 18–20), and the second shows one way to organize a position paper (Chapter 5):

Scratch Outline: Essay about a Remembered Event

1. explains what she learned from playing football

2. identifies other sports she learned from boys in the neighborhood

3. sets the scene by describing the time and place of the event

4. describes the boys who were playing with her

5. describes what typically happened: a car would come down the street, they would throw snowballs, and then they would wait for another car

6. describes the iceball-making project she had begun while waiting

7. describes the Buick's approach and how they followed the routine

8. describes the impact of the snowball on the Buick's windshield

9. describes the man's surprising reaction: getting out of the car and running after them

10. narrates the chase and describes the man

11. explains how the kids split up and the man followed her and Mikey

12. narrates the chase and describes how the neighborhood looked as they ran through it

13. continues the narration, describing the way the man threw himself into the chase

14. continues the narration, commenting on her thoughts and feelings

15. narrates the ending or climax of the chase, when the man caught them

16. describes the runners trying to catch their breath

17. describes her own physical state

18. relates the man's words

19. explains her reactions to his words and actions

20. explains her later thoughts and feelings

21. explains her present perspective on this remembered event

Scratch Outline: Essay Arguing a Position

Presentation of the issue

Concession of some aspect of an opposing position

Thesis statement

First reason with support

Second reason with support

(etc.)

Conclusion

Remember that the items in a scratch outline do not necessarily coincide with paragraphs. Sometimes two or more items may be developed in the same paragraph or one item may be covered in two or more paragraphs.

Chunking, a type of scratch outline commonly used by professional writers in business and industry and especially well suited to writing in the electronic age, consists of a set of headings describing the major points to be covered in the final document. What makes chunking distinctive is that the blocks of text—or "chunks"—under each heading are intended to be roughly the same length and scope. These headings can be discussed and passed around among several writers and editors before writing begins, and different chunks may be written by different authors, simply by typing notes into the space under each heading. The list of headings is subject to change during the writing, and new headings may be added or old ones subdivided or discarded as part of the drafting and editing process.

The advantage of chunking in your own writing is that it breaks the large task of drafting into smaller tasks in a simple, evenly balanced way; once the headings are determined, the writing becomes just a matter of filling in the specifics that go in each chunk. Organization tends to improve as you get a sense of the weight of different parts of the document while filling in the blanks. Places where the essay needs more information or there is a problem with pacing tend to stand out because of the chunking structure, and the headings can be either taken out of the finished essay or left in as devices to help guide readers. If they are left in, they should be edited into parallel grammatical form like the items in a formal topic or sentence outline, as discussed below.

Topic outlines and **sentence outlines** are considered more formal than scratch outlines because they follow a conventional format of numbered and lettered headings and subheadings:

I. (Main topic)
   A. (Subtopic of I)
   B.
      1. (Subtopic of I.B)
      2.
         a. (Subtopic of I.B.2)
         b.
            (1) (Subtopic of I.B.2.b)
            (2)
   C.
      1. (Subtopic of I.C)
      2.

The difference between a topic and sentence outline is obvious: Topic outlines simply name the topics and subtopics, whereas sentence outlines use complete or abbreviated sentences. To illustrate, here are two partial formal outlines of an essay arguing a position, Jessica Statsky's "Children Need to Play, Not Compete," from Chapter 5 (pp. 152–57).

Formal Topic Outline

I. Organized sports harmful to children
   A. Harmful physically
      1. Curve ball (Koppett)
      2. Tackle football (Tutko)
   B. Harmful psychologically
      1. Fear of being hurt
         a. Little League Online
         b. Mother
         c. Reporter
      2. Competition
         a. Rablovsky
         b. Studies

Formal Sentence Outline

I. Highly organized competitive sports such as Peewee Football and Little League Baseball can be physically and psychologically harmful to children, as well as counterproductive for developing future players.

A. Physically harmful because sports entice children into physical actions that are bad for growing bodies.
   1. Koppett claims throwing a curve ball may put abnormal strain on developing arm and shoulder muscles.
   2. Tutko argues that tackle football is too traumatic for young kids.
B. Psychologically harmful to children for a number of reasons.
   1. Fear of being hurt detracts from their enjoyment of the sport.
      a. Little League Online ranks fear of injury seventh among the seven top reasons children quit.
      b. One mother says, "kids get so scared. . . . They'll sit on the bench and pretend their leg hurts."
      c. A reporter tells about a child who made himself vomit to get out of playing Peewee Football.
   2. Too much competition poses psychological dangers for children.
      a. Rablovsky reports: "The spirit of play suddenly disappears, and sport becomes joblike."
      b. Studies show that children prefer playing on a losing team to "warming the bench on a winning team."

In contrast to an informal outline in which anything goes, a formal outline must follow many conventions. The roman numerals and capital letters are followed by periods. In both topic and sentence outlines, the first word of each item is capitalized, but items in topic outlines do not end with a period as items in sentence outlines do. Every level of a formal outline except the top level (identified by the roman numeral *I*) must include at least two items. Items at the same level of indentation in a topic outline should be grammatically parallel—all beginning with the same part of speech. For example, *I.A* and *I.B* are parallel when they both begin with an adverb (*Physically harmful* and *Psychologically harmful*) or with an adjective (*Harmful physically* and *Harmful psychologically*); they would not be parallel if one began with an adverb (*Physically harmful*) and the other with an adjective (*Harmful psychologically*).

Writing

Unlike most mapping strategies, **writing strategies** invite you to produce complete sentences. Sentences provide considerable generative power. Because they are complete statements, they take you further than listing or clustering. They enable you to explore ideas and define relationships, bring ideas together or show how they differ, and identify causes and effects. Sentences can also help you develop a logical chain of thought.

Some of these invention and inquiry strategies are systematic, while others are more flexible. Even though they call for complete sentences that are related to one another, they do not require preparation or revision. You can use them to develop oral as well as written presentations.

These writing strategies include *cubing, dialoguing, dramatizing, freewriting, keeping a journal, looping,* and *questioning.*

Use cubing.

Cubing is useful for quickly exploring a writing topic, probing it from six different perspectives. It is known as *cubing* because a cube has six sides. These are the six perspectives in cubing:

> **Describing:** What does your subject look like? What size is it? What is its color? Its shape? Its texture? Name its parts.
>
> **Comparing:** What is your subject similar to? Different from?
>
> **Associating:** What does your subject make you think of? What connections does it have to anything else in your experience?
>
> **Analyzing:** What are the origins of your subject? What are the functions or significance of its parts? How are its parts related?
>
> **Applying:** What can you do with your subject? What uses does it have?
>
> **Arguing:** What arguments can you make for your subject? Against it?

Here are some guidelines to help you use cubing productively.

1. Select a topic, subject, or part of a subject. This can be a person, a scene, an event, an object, a problem, an idea, or an issue. Hold it in focus.

2. Limit your writing to three to five minutes for each perspective. The whole activity should take no more than half an hour.

3. Keep going until you have written about your subject from all six perspectives. Remember that cubing offers the special advantage of enabling you to generate multiple perspectives quickly.

4. As you write from each perspective, begin with what you know about your subject. However, do not limit yourself to your present knowledge. Indicate what else you would like to know about your subject, and suggest where you might find that information.

5. Reread what you have written. Look for bright spots, surprises. Recall the part that was easiest for you to write. Recall the part where you felt a special momentum and pleasure in writing. Look for an angle or an unexpected insight. These special parts may suggest a focus or topic within a larger subject, or they may provide specific details to include in a draft.

Construct a dialogue.

A *dialogue* is a conversation between two or more people. You can use **dialoguing** to search for topics, find a focus, explore ideas, or consider opposing viewpoints. When you write a dialogue as an invention strategy, you need to make up all parts of the conversation (unless, of course, you are writing collaboratively). To construct a dialogue independently or collaboratively, follow these steps:

1. Write a conversation between two speakers. Label the participants *Speaker A* and *Speaker B,* or make up names for them.

2. If you get stuck, you might have one of the speakers ask the other a question.

3. Write brief responses to keep the conversation moving fast. Do not spend much time planning or rehearsing responses. Write what first occurs to you, just as in a real conversation, in which people take quick turns to prevent any awkward silences.

Dialogues can be especially useful in writing based on personal experience and persuasive essays because they help you remember conversations and anticipate objections.

Use the five elements of dramatizing.

Dramatizing is an invention activity developed by the philosopher Kenneth Burke as a way of thinking about how people interact and as a way of analyzing stories and films.

Thinking about human behavior in dramatic terms can be very productive for writers. Drama has action, actors, setting, motives, and methods. Since stars and acting go together, you can use a five-pointed star to remember these five points of dramatizing: Each point on the star provides a different perspective on human behavior (see Figure 8.2).

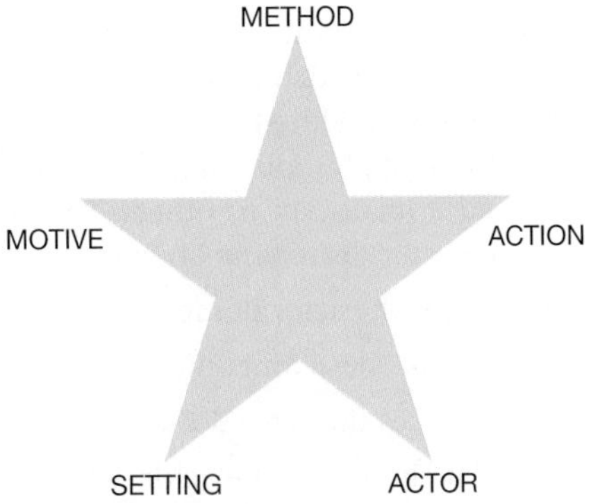

FIGURE 8.2   Dramatizing

Action   An action is anything that happens, has happened, will happen, or could happen. Action includes events that are physical (running a marathon), mental (thinking about a book you have read), and emotional (falling in love).

Actor   The actor is involved in the action—either responsible for it or simply affected by it. (The actor does not have to be a person. It can be a force, something that causes an action. For example, if the action is a rise in the price of gasoline, the actor could be increased demand or short supply.) Dramatizing may also include a number of coactors working together or at odds.

Setting   The setting is the situation or background of the action. We usually think of setting as the place and time of an event, but it may also be the historical background of an event or the childhood of a person.

Motive   The motive is the purpose or reason for an action—the actor's intention. Actions may have multiple, even conflicting, motives.

Method   The method explains how an action occurs, including the techniques an actor uses. It refers to whatever makes things happen.

Each of these points suggests a simple invention question:

Action: What?

Actor: Who?

> *Setting:* When and where?
>
> *Motive:* Why?
>
> *Method:* How?

This list looks like the questions reporters typically ask. But dramatizing goes further: It enables us to consider relations between and among these five elements. We can think about actors' motives, the effect of the setting on the actors, the relations between actors, and so on.

You can use this invention strategy to learn more about yourself or about other significant people in your life. You can use it as well to explore, interpret, or evaluate characters in stories or movies. Moreover, dramatizing is especially useful in understanding the readers you want to inform or convince.

To use dramatizing, imagine the person you want to understand better in a particular situation. Holding this image in mind, write answers to any questions in the following list that apply. You may draw a blank on some questions, have little to say to some, and find a lot to say to others. Be exploratory and playful with the questions. Write responses quickly, relying on words and phrases, even drawings.

- What is the actor doing?
- How did the actor come to be involved in this situation?
- Why does the actor do what he or she does?
- What else might the actor do?
- What is the actor trying to accomplish?
- How do other actors influence — help or hinder — the main actor?
- What do the actor's actions reveal about him or her?
- What does the actor's language reveal about him or her?
- How does the event's setting influence the actor's actions?
- How does the time of the event influence what the actor does?
- Where does the actor come from?
- How is the actor different now from what he or she used to be?
- What might the actor become?
- How is the actor like or unlike the other actors?

Freewrite for a set amount of time.

Freewriting is a technique that requires you to stop judging what you write and simply let your mind wander in order to generate ideas freely and creatively. Freewriting can be useful for generating ideas on a topic you already know. To freewrite, set a certain amount of time, say five or ten minutes, and then simply write, generating as much text as you can in the allotted time. While freewriting, try not to stop; if you cannot think of anything to say, simply write "don't know what to say" over and over until an idea comes to you. If you find it difficult to avoid editing yourself, try turning down the brightness on your monitor until you can no longer see what it says. A variation on freewriting is **focused freewriting.** In focused freewriting, you begin from a specific topic, returning to the beginning topic whenever you find yourself getting off track.

Keep a journal.

Professional writers often use **journals** to keep notes. Starting one is easy. Buy a special notebook, or open a new file on your computer, and start writing. Here are some possibilities:

- Keep a list of new words and concepts you learn in your courses. You could also write about the progress and direction of your learning in particular courses — the experience of being in the course, your feelings about what is happening, and what you are learning.
- Respond to your reading, both assigned and personal. As you read, write about your personal associations, reflections, reactions, and evaluations. Summarize or copy memorable or especially important passages, and comment on them. (Copying and commenting have been practiced by students and writers for centuries in special journals called *commonplace books.*)
- Write to prepare for particular class meetings. Write about the main ideas you have learned from assigned readings and about the relationship of these new ideas to other ideas in the course. After class, write to summarize what you have learned. List questions you have about the ideas or information discussed in class. Journal writing of this kind involves reflecting, evaluating, interpreting, synthesizing, summarizing, and questioning.
- Record observations and overheard conversations.
- Write for ten or fifteen minutes every day about whatever is on your mind. Focus these meditations on your new experiences as you try to understand, interpret, and reflect on them.
- Write sketches of people who catch your attention.
- Organize your time. Write about your goals and priorities, or list specific things to accomplish and what you plan to do.
- Keep a log over several days or weeks about a particular event unfolding in the news—a sensational trial, an environmental disaster, a political campaign, a campus controversy, or the fortunes of a sports team.

You can use a journal in many ways. All of the writing in your journal has value for learning. You may also be able to use parts of your journal for writing in your other courses.

Use looping.

Looping is especially useful for the first stages of exploring a topic. As its name suggests, **looping** involves writing quickly to explore some aspect of a topic and then looping back to your original starting point or to a new starting point to explore another aspect. Beginning with almost any starting point, looping enables you to find a center of interest and eventually a thesis for your essay. The steps are simple:

1. Write down your area of interest. You may know only that you have to write about another person or a movie or a cultural trend that has caught your attention. Or you may want to search for a topic in a broad historical period or for one related to a major political event. Although you may wander from this topic as you write, you will want to keep coming back to it. Your purpose is to find a focus for writing.

2. Write nonstop for ten minutes. Start with the first thing that comes to mind. Write rapidly, without looking back to reread or to correct anything. *Do not stop writing. Keep your pencil moving or keystrokes clacking.* Continuous writing is the key to looping. If you get stuck for a moment, rewrite the last sentence. Follow diversions and digressions, but keep returning to your topic.

3. After ten minutes, pause to reread what you have written. Decide what is most important—a single insight, a pattern of ideas, an emerging theme, a visual detail, anything at all that stands out. Some writers call this a "center of gravity" or a "hot spot." To complete the first loop, restate this center in a single sentence.

4. Beginning with this sentence, write nonstop for another ten minutes.

5. Summarize in one sentence again to complete the second loop.

6. Keep looping until one of your summary sentences produces a focus or thesis. You may need only two or three loops; you may need more.

Ask questions.

Asking questions about a subject is a way to learn about it and decide what to write. When you first encounter a subject, however, your questions may be scattered. Also, you are not likely to think right away of all the important questions you ought to ask. The advantage of having a basic list of questions for invention, like the ones for cubing and for dramatizing discussed earlier in this chapter, is that it provides a systematic approach to exploring a subject.

The questions that follow come from classical rhetoric (what the Greek philosopher Aristotle called *topics*) and a modern approach to invention called *tagmemics*. Based on the work of linguist Kenneth Pike, tagmemics provides questions about different ways we make sense of the world, the ways we sort and classify experience in order to understand it.

Here are the steps in using questions for invention:

1. In a sentence or two, identify your subject. A subject could be any event, person, problem, project, idea, or issue—in other words, anything you might write about.

2. Start by writing a response to the first question in the following list, and move right through the list. Try to answer each question at least briefly with a word or a phrase. Some questions may invite several sentences or even a page or more of writing. You may draw a blank on a few questions. Skip them. Later, when you have more experience with questions for invention, you can start anywhere in the list.

3. Write your responses quickly, without much planning. Follow digressions or associations. Do not screen anything out. Be playful.

What Is Your Subject?

- What is your subject's name? What other names does it have? What names did it have in the past?
- What aspects of the subject do these different names emphasize?
- Imagine a still photograph or a moving picture of your subject. What would it look like?
- What would you put into a time capsule to stand for your subject?
- What are its causes and effects?
- How would it look from different vantage points or perspectives?
- What particular experiences have you had with the subject? What have you learned?

What Parts or Features Does Your Subject Have, and How Are They Related?

- Name the parts or features of your subject.
- Describe each one, using the questions in the preceding subject list.
- How is each part or feature related to the others?

How Is Your Subject Similar to and Different from Other Subjects?

- What is your subject similar to? In what ways?
- What is your subject different from? In what ways?
- What seems to you most unlike your subject? In what ways? Now, just for fun, note how they are alike.

How Much Can Your Subject Change and Still Remain the Same?

- How has your subject changed from what it once was?
- How is it changing now—moment to moment, day to day, year to year?
- How does each change alter your way of thinking about your subject?
- What are some different forms your subject takes?
- What does it become when it is no longer itself?

Where Does Your Subject Fit in the World?

- When and where did your subject originate?
- What would happen if at some future time your subject ceased to exist?
- When and where do you usually experience your subject?
- What is your subject a part of, and what are the other parts?
- What do other people think of your subject?

9

Strategies for Reading Critically

This chapter presents strategies to help you become a thoughtful reader. A thoughtful reader is above all a patient rereader, concerned not only with comprehending and remembering but also with interpreting and evaluating—on the one hand, striving to understand the text on its own terms; on the other hand, taking care to question its ideas.

The reading strategies in this chapter can help you enrich your thinking as a reader and participate in conversations as a writer. These strategies are as follows:

- **Annotating:** Recording your reactions to, interpretations of, and questions about a text as you read it

- **Taking inventory:** Listing and grouping your annotations and other notes to find meaningful patterns

- **Outlining:** Listing the text's main ideas to reveal how it is organized

- **Paraphrasing:** Restating what you have read to clarify or refer to it

- **Summarizing:** Distilling the main ideas or gist of a text

- **Synthesizing:** Integrating into your own writing ideas and information gleaned from different sources

- **Contextualizing:** Placing a text in its historical and cultural context

- **Exploring the significance of figurative language:** Examining how metaphors, similes, and symbols are used in a text to convey meaning and evoke feelings

- **Looking for patterns of opposition:** Inferring the values and assumptions embodied in the language of a text

- **Reflecting on challenges to your beliefs and values:** Examining the bases of your personal responses to a text

- **Evaluating the logic of an argument:** Determining whether an argument is well reasoned and adequately supported

- **Recognizing emotional manipulation:** Identifying texts that unfairly and inappropriately use emotional appeals based on false or exaggerated claims

- **Judging the writer's credibility:** Considering whether writers represent different points of view fairly and know what they are writing about

Although mastering these strategies will not make critical reading easy, it can make your reading much more satisfying and productive and thus help you handle even difficult material with confidence. In addition, these reading strategies will often be useful in your reading outside of school—for instance, these strategies can help you understand, evaluate, and comment on what political figures, advertisers, and competing businesses are saying.

Annotating

Annotations are the marks—underlines, highlights, and comments—you make directly on the page as you read. Annotating can be used to record immediate reactions and questions, outline and summarize main points, and evaluate and relate the reading to other ideas and points of view. Your annotations can take many forms, such as the following:

- Writing comments, questions, or definitions in the margins
- Underlining or circling words, phrases, or sentences
- Connecting ideas with lines or arrows
- Numbering related points
- Bracketing sections of the text
- Noting anything that strikes you as interesting, important, or questionable

Most readers annotate in layers, adding further annotations on second and third readings. Annotations can be light or heavy, depending on your purpose and the difficulty of the material. Your purpose for reading also determines how you use your annotations.

The following selection, excerpted from Martin Luther King Jr.'s "Letter from Birmingham Jail," illustrates some of the ways you can annotate as you read. Add your own annotations, if you like.

Martin Luther King Jr. | *An Annotated Sample from "Letter from Birmingham Jail"*

MARTIN LUTHER KING JR. (1929–1968) first came to national notice in 1955, when he led a successful boycott against the policy of restricting African American passengers to rear seats on city buses in Montgomery, Alabama, where he was minister of a Baptist church. He subsequently formed the Southern Christian Leadership Conference, which brought people of all races from all over the country to the South to fight nonviolently for racial integration. In 1963, King led demonstrations in Birmingham, Alabama, that were met with violence; a bomb was detonated in a black church, killing four young girls. King was arrested for his role in organizing the protests, and while in prison, he wrote his "Letter from Birmingham Jail" to justify his strategy of civil disobedience, which he called "nonviolent direct action."

King begins his letter by discussing his disappointment with the lack of support he has received from white moderates, such as the group of clergy who published criticism of his organization in the local newspaper.

Read the following excerpt, paying attention to the following:

- Try to infer what the clergy's specific criticisms might have been.
- Notice the tone King uses. Would you characterize the writing as apologetic, conciliatory, accusatory, or something else?

I must confess that over the past few years I have been gravely disappointed with the <u>white moderate</u>. I have almost reached the regrettable conclusion that the Negro's [great stumbling block in his stride toward freedom] is not the White Citizen's Counciler or the Ku Klux Klanner, but the white moderate, who is more devoted to "<u>order</u>" than to <u>justice</u>; who prefers a <u>negative peace</u> which is the <u>absence of tension</u> to a <u>positive peace</u> which is the presence of justice; who constantly says: "I agree with you in the <u>goal</u> you seek, but I cannot agree with your <u>methods</u> of direct action"; who (paternalistically) believes he can set the timetable for another man's freedom; who lives by a mythical concept of time and who constantly advises the Negro to wait for a "more convenient season." <u>Shallow understanding from people of good will is more frustrating than absolute misunderstanding from people of ill will.</u> Lukewarm acceptance is much more bewildering than outright rejection. 1

¶1. White moderates block progress.

Contrasts: order vs. justice, negative vs. positive peace, ends vs. means

(treating others like children)

more contrasts

I had hoped that the white moderate would understand that <u>law and order exist for the purpose of establishing justice</u> and that when they fail in this purpose they become the [dangerously structured dams that block the flow of social progress.] I had hoped that the white moderate would understand that the <u>present tension</u> in the South is a <u>necessary phase of the transition</u> from an [obnoxious <u>negative peace</u>,] in which the Negro passively accepted his unjust plight, to a [substantive and <u>positive peace</u>,] in which all men will respect the dignity and worth of human personality. Actually, we who engage in 2

¶2. What the moderates don't understand

metaphor: law and order = dams (faulty?)

repeats contrast (negative/ positive)

nonviolent direct action are not the creators of tension. We merely bring to the surface the hidden tension that is already alive. We bring it out in the open, where it can be seen and dealt with. [Like a boil that can never be cured so long as it is covered up but must be opened with all its ugliness to the natural medicines of air and light, injustice must be exposed, with all the tension its exposure creates, to the light of human conscience and the air of national opinion before it can be cured.]

Tension already exists: We help dispel it. (True?)

simile: hidden tension is "like a boil"

In your statement you assert that our actions, even though peaceful, must be condemned because they precipitate violence. But is this a logical assertion? Isn't this like condemning (a robbed man) because his possession of money precipitated the evil act of robbery? Isn't this like condemning (Socrates) because his unswerving commitment to truth and his philosophical inquiries precipitated the act by the misguided populace in which they made him drink hemlock? Isn't this like condemning (Jesus) because his unique God-consciousness and never-ceasing devotion to God's will precipitated the evil act of crucifixion? We must come to see that, as the federal courts have consistently affirmed, it is wrong to urge an individual to cease his efforts to gain his basic constitutional rights because the question may precipitate violence. [Society must protect the robbed and punish the robber.] 3

¶3. Questions clergymen's logic: condemning his actions = condemning robbery victim, Socrates, Jesus.

repetition ("Isn't this like ...")

(Yes!)

I had also hoped that the white moderate would reject the myth concerning time in relation to the struggle for freedom. I have just received a letter from a white brother in Texas. He writes: "All Christians know that the colored people will receive equal rights eventually, but it is possible that you are in too great a religious hurry. It has taken Christianity almost two thousand years to accomplish what it has. The teachings of Christ take time to come to earth." Such an attitude stems from a tragic misconception of time, from the strangely irrational notion that there is something in the very flow of time 4

example of a white moderate's view

¶4. *Time must be used to do right.*

that will inevitably cure all ills. (Actually, time itself is neutral; it can be used either destructively or constructively.) More and more I feel that the people of ill will have used time much more effectively than have the people of good will. We will have to repent in this generation not merely for the [hateful words and actions of the bad people] but for the [appalling silence of the good people.] Human progress never rolls in on [wheels of inevitability;] it comes through the tireless efforts of men willing to be co-workers with God, and without this hard work, time

Silence/passivity is as bad as hateful words and actions.

metaphor (mechanical?)

(stop developing)

itself becomes an ally of the forces of social (stagnation.) [We must use time creatively, in the knowledge that the time is always ripe to do right.] Now is the time to make real the promise of democracy and transform our pending [national

metaphors (song, natural world)

elegy] into a creative [psalm of brotherhood.] Now is the time to lift our national policy from the [quicksand of racial injustice] to the [solid rock of human dignity.]

You speak of our activity in Birmingham as extreme. 5 At first I was rather disappointed that fellow clergymen would see my nonviolent efforts as those of an extremist. I began thinking about the fact that I stand in the middle of two opposing forces in the Negro community. One is a [force of complacency,] made up in part of Negroes who, as a result of long years of oppression, are so drained of self-respect and a sense of "somebodiness" that they

King accused of being an extremist.

¶5. *Puts self in middle of two extremes: complacency and bitterness.*

have adjusted to segregation; and in part of a few middle-class Negroes, who because of a degree of academic and economic security and because in some ways they profit by segregation, have become insensitive to the problems of the masses. The other [force is one of bitterness and hatred,] and it comes perilously close to advocating violence. It is expressed in the various black nationalist [groups that are springing up] across the nation, the largest and best-known being Elijah Muhammad's Muslim movement. Nourished by the Negro's frustration over the continued existence of racial discrimination, this

Malcolm X?

movement is made up of people who have lost faith in America, who have absolutely repudiated Christianity, and who have concluded that the white man is an incorrigible "devil."

¶6. *Offers better choice: nonviolent protest.*

I have tried to stand between these two forces, saying 6 that we need emulate neither the "do-nothingism" of the complacent nor the hatred and despair of the black nationalist. For there is the more excellent way of love and nonviolent protest. I am grateful to God that, through the influence of the Negro church, the way of nonviolence became an integral part of our struggle.

(How did nonviolence become part of King's movement?)

¶7. *Says movement prevents racial violence. (Threat?)*

If this philosophy had not emerged, by now many 7 streets of the South would, I am convinced, be flowing with blood. And I am further convinced that if our white brothers dismiss as "rabble-rousers" and "outside agitators" those of us who employ nonviolent direct action, and if they refuse to support our nonviolent efforts, millions of Negroes will, out of frustration and despair, seek (solace) and security in black-nationalist ideologies—a development that would inevitably lead to a frightening racial nightmare.

(comfort)

(Oppressed people cannot remain oppressed forever.) 8 The yearning for freedom eventually manifests itself, and that is what has happened to the American Negro. Something within has reminded him of his birthright of freedom, and something without has reminded him that it can be gained. Consciously or unconsciously, he has been caught up by the (Zeitgeist,) and with his black brothers of Africa and his brown and yellow brothers of Asia, South America and the Caribbean, the United States Negro is moving with a sense of great urgency toward the [promised land of racial justice.] If one recognizes this [vital urge that has engulfed the Negro community,] one should readily understand why public demonstrations are taking place. The Negro has many [pent-up resentments] and latent frustrations, and he must release them. So let him

(spirit of the times)

march; let him make prayer pilgrimages to the city hall; let him go on freedom rides—and try to understand why he must do so. If his repressed emotions are not released in nonviolent ways, they will seek expression through violence; this is not a threat but a fact of history. So I have not said to my people: "Get rid of your discontent." Rather, I have tried to say that this normal and healthy discontent can be [channeled into the creative outlet of nonviolent direct action.] And now this approach is being termed extremist.

Not a threat, but a fact — ?

¶18. Discontent is normal, healthy, and historically inevitable, but it must be channeled.

But though I was initially disappointed at being 9 categorized as an extremist, as I continued to think about the matter I gradually gained a measure of satisfaction from the label. Was not Jesus an extremist for love: "Love your enemies, bless them that curse you, do good to them that hate you, and pray for them which despitefully use you, and persecute you." Was not Amos an extremist for justice: "Let justice roll down like waters and righteousness like an ever-flowing stream." Was not Paul an extremist for the Christian gospel: "I bear in my body the marks of the Lord Jesus." Was not Martin Luther an extremist: "Here I stand; I cannot do otherwise, so help me God." And John Bunyan: "I will stay in jail to the end of my days before I make a butchery of my conscience." And Abraham Lincoln: "This nation cannot survive half slave and half free." And Thomas Jefferson: "We hold these truths to be self-evident, that all men are created equal...." So the question is not whether we will be extremists, but what kind of extremists we will be. Will we be extremists for hate or for love? Will we be extremists for the preservation of injustice or for the extension of justice? In that dramatic scene on Calvary's hill three men were crucified. We must never forget that all three were crucified for the same crime — the crime of extremism. Two were extremists for immorality, and thus fell below their environment. The other, Jesus Christ, was an extremist for love, truth

¶19. Redefines "extremism," embraces "extremist" label.

(Hebrew prophet)

(Christian apostle)

(founder of Protestantism)

(English preacher)

Compares self to great "extremists"— including Jesus

Disappointed in the white moderate

and goodness, and thereby rose above his environment. Perhaps the South, the (nation and the world are in dire need of creative extremists.)

I had hoped that the white moderate would see this   10 need. Perhaps I was too optimistic; perhaps I expected too much. I suppose I should have realized that few members of the oppressor race can understand the deep groans and passionate yearnings of the oppressed race, and still fewer have the vision to see that [injustice must be rooted out] by strong, persistent and determined action. I am thankful, however, that some of our white brothers in the South have grasped the meaning of this social revolution and committed themselves to it. They are still all too few in quantity, but they are big in quality. Some—such as Ralph McGill, Lillian Smith, Harry Golden, James McBride Dabbs, Ann Braden and Sarah Patton Boyle—have written about our struggle in eloquent and prophetic terms. Others have marched with us down nameless streets of the South. They have (languished) in filthy, roach-infested jails, suffering the abuse and brutality of policemen who view them as "dirty nigger-lovers." Unlike so many of their moderate brothers and sisters, they have recognized the urgency of the moment and sensed the need for [powerful "action" antidotes] to combat the [disease of segregation.]

¶10. Praises whites who have supported movement.

(Who are they?)

(been left unaided)

Metaphor: segregation is a disease.

ANALYZE & WRITE ──

Annotating

1 Select a reading from chapters 2–7 or from another text, and mark the text using notations like these:

- Circle words to be defined in the margin.
- Underline key words and phrases.
- Bracket important sentences and passages.
- Use lines or arrows to connect ideas or words.

2 Write marginal comments like these:

- Number and summarize each paragraph.
- Define unfamiliar words.
- Note responses and questions.

- Identify interesting writing strategies.
- Point out patterns.
3. Layer additional markings in the text and comments in the margins as you reread for different purposes.

macmillanhighered.com/conciseguide
LearningCurve > Critical Reading

Taking Inventory

Taking inventory helps you analyze your annotations for different purposes. When you take inventory, you make various kinds of lists to explore patterns of meaning you find in the text. For instance, in reading the annotated passage by Martin Luther King Jr., you might have noticed that certain similes and metaphors are used or that many famous people are named. By listing the names (Socrates, Jesus, Luther, Lincoln, and so on) and then grouping them into categories (people who died for their beliefs, leaders, teachers, and religious figures), you could better understand why the writer refers to these particular people. Taking inventory of your annotations can be helpful if you plan to write about a text you are reading.

ANALYZE & WRITE

Taking Inventory

1. Examine the annotations you made in the activity above for patterns or repetitions, such as recurring images, stylistic features, repeated words and phrases, repeated examples or illustrations, and reliance on particular writing strategies.
2. List the items that make up a pattern.
3. Decide what the pattern might reveal about the reading.

Outlining

Outlining is an especially helpful reading strategy for understanding the content and structure of a reading. **Outlining,** which identifies the text's main ideas, may be part of the annotating process, or it may be done separately. Writing an outline in the margins of the text as you read and annotate makes it easier to find information later. Writing an outline on a separate piece of paper gives you more space to work with, and therefore such an outline usually includes more detail.

The key to outlining is distinguishing between the main ideas and the supporting material, such as examples, quotations, comparisons, and reasons. The main ideas form the backbone that holds the various parts of the text together. Outlining the main ideas helps you uncover this structure.

Making an outline, however, is not simple. The reader must exercise judgment in deciding which are the most important ideas. The words used in an outline reflect the reader's interpretation and emphasis. Readers also must decide when to use the writer's words, their own words, or a combination of the two.

You may make either a formal, multileveled outline or an informal scratch outline. A *formal outline* is harder to make and much more time-consuming than a scratch outline. You might choose to make a formal outline of a reading about which you are writing an in-depth analysis or evaluation. For example, here is a formal outline a student wrote for an essay evaluating the logic of the King excerpt.

Formal Outline of "Letter from Birmingham Jail"

I. "[T]he Negro's great stumbling block in his stride toward freedom is . . . the white moderate . . . " (par. 1).

   A. White moderates are more devoted to "order" than to justice; however,

      1. law and order exist only to establish justice (par. 2).

      2. law and order *without* justice actually threaten social order ("dangerously structured dams" metaphor, par. 2).

   B. White moderates prefer "negative peace" (absence of tension) to "positive peace" (justice); however,

      1. tension already exists; it is not created by movement (par. 2).

      2. tension is a necessary phase in progress to a just society (par. 2).

      3. tension must be allowed outlet if society is to be healthy ("boil" simile, par. 2).

   C. White moderates disagree with methods of movement; however,

      1. nonviolent direct action can't be condemned for violent response to it (analogies: robbed man; Socrates; Jesus, par. 3).

      2. federal courts affirm that those who seek constitutional rights can't be held responsible for violent response (par. 3).

   D. White moderates paternalistically counsel patience, saying time will bring change; however,

      1. time is "neutral"—we are obligated to use it *actively* to achieve justice (par. 4).

      2. the time for action is now (par. 4).

II. Contrary to white moderates' claims, the movement is not "extremist" in the usual sense (par. 5 ff.).

   A. It stands between extremes in black community: passivity, seen in the oppressed and the self-interested middle-class; and violent radicalism, seen in Elijah Muhammad's followers (pars. 5–6).

   B. In its advocacy of love and nonviolent protest, the movement has forestalled bloodshed and kept more blacks from joining radicals (pars. 5–7).

   C. The movement helps blacks channel urge for freedom that's part of historical trend and the prevailing *Zeitgeist* (par. 8).

III. The movement can be defined as extremist if the term is redefined: "Creative extremism" is extremism in the service of love, truth, and goodness (examples of Amos, Paul, Luther, Bunyan, Lincoln, Jefferson, Jesus, par. 9).

IV. Some whites—"few in quantity, but . . . big in quality"—have recognized the truth of the arguments above and, unlike the white moderates, have committed themselves to the movement (par. 10).

A *scratch outline* will not record as much information as a formal outline, but it is sufficient for most reading purposes. To make a scratch outline, you first need to locate the topic of each paragraph in the reading. The topic is usually stated in a word or phrase, and it may be repeated or referred to throughout the paragraph. For example, the opening paragraph of the King excerpt (p. 296) makes clear that its topic is the white moderate.

After you have found the topic of the paragraph, figure out what is being said about it. To return to our example: King immediately establishes the white moderate as the topic of the opening paragraph and at the beginning of the second sentence announces the conclusion he has come to—namely, that the white moderate is "the Negro's great stumbling block in his stride toward freedom." The rest of the paragraph specifies the ways the white moderate blocks progress.

The annotations include a summary of each paragraph's topic. Here is a scratch outline that lists the topics:

Scratch Outline of "Letter from Birmingham Jail"

¶1. White moderates block progress

¶2. What the moderates don't understand

¶3. Questions clergymen's logic

¶4. Time must be used to do right

¶5. Puts self in middle of two extremes: complacency and bitterness

¶6. Offers better choice: nonviolent protest

¶7. Says movement prevents racial violence

¶8. Discontent normal, healthy, and historically inevitable, but it must be channeled

¶9. Redefines "extremism," embraces "extremist" label

¶10. Praises whites who have supported movement

ANALYZE & WRITE

Outlining

1   Reread each paragraph of the selection you have been working with in the previous activities in this chapter. Identify the topic and the comments made about the topic. Do not include examples, specific details, quotations, or other explanatory and supporting material.

2   List the author's main ideas in the margin of the text or on a separate piece of paper.

For more on the conventions of formal outlines, see pp. 286–87 in Chapter 8.

Paraphrasing

Paraphrasing is restating a text you have read by using mostly your own words. It can help you clarify the meaning of an obscure or ambiguous passage. It is one of the three ways of integrating other people's ideas and information into your own writing, along with **quoting** (reproducing exactly the language of the source text) and **summarizing** (distilling the main ideas or gist of the source text). You might choose to paraphrase rather than quote when the source's language is not especially arresting or memorable. You might paraphrase short passages but summarize longer ones.

Following are two passages. The first is from paragraph 2 of the excerpt from King's "Letter." The second passage is a paraphrase of the first:

Original

I had hoped that the white moderate would understand that law and order exist for the purpose of establishing justice and that when they fail in this purpose they become the dangerously structured dams that block the flow of social progress. I had hoped that the white moderate would understand that the present tension in the South is a necessary phase of the transition from an obnoxious negative peace, in which the Negro passively accepted his unjust plight, to a substantive and positive peace, in which all men will respect the dignity and worth of human personality.

Paraphrase

King writes that he had hoped for more understanding from white moderates— specifically that they would recognize that law and order are not ends in themselves but means to the greater end of establishing justice. When law and order do not serve this greater end, they stand in the way of progress. King expected the white moderate to recognize that the current tense situation in the South is part of a transition process that is necessary for progress. The current situation is bad because although there is peace, it is an "obnoxious" and "negative" kind of peace based on blacks passively accepting the injustice of the status quo. A better kind of peace — one that is "substantive," real and not imaginary, as well as "positive"— requires that all people, regardless of race, be valued.

When you compare the paraphrase to the original, you can see that the paraphrase contains all the important information and ideas of the original. Notice also that the paraphrase is somewhat longer than the original, refers to the writer by name, and encloses King's original words in quotation marks. The paraphrase tries to be *neutral,* to avoid inserting the reader's opinions or distorting the original writer's ideas.

ANALYZE & WRITE

Paraphrasing

1. Select an important passage from the selection you have been working with. (The passage need be only two or three sentences.) Then reread the passage, looking up unfamiliar words in a college dictionary.

2. Translate the passage into your own words and sentences, putting quotation marks around any words or phrases you quote from the original.

3. Revise to ensure coherence.

Summarizing

Summarizing is important because it helps you understand and remember what is most significant in a reading. Another advantage of summarizing is that it creates a condensed version of the reading's ideas and information, which you can refer to later or insert into your own writing. Along with quoting and paraphrasing, summarizing enables you to integrate other writers' ideas into your own writing.

A **summary** is a relatively brief restatement, primarily in the reader's own words, of the reading's main ideas. Summaries vary in length, depending on the reader's purpose. Some summaries are very brief—a sentence or even a subordinate clause. For example, if you were referring to the excerpt from "Letter from Birmingham Jail" and simply needed to indicate how it relates to your other sources, your summary might look something like this: "There have always been advocates of extremism in politics. Martin Luther King Jr., in 'Letter from Birmingham Jail,' for instance, defends nonviolent civil disobedience as an extreme but necessary means of bringing about racial justice." If, however, you were surveying the important texts of the civil rights movement, you might write a longer, more detailed summary that not only identifies the reading's main ideas but also shows how the ideas relate to one another.

Many writers find it useful to outline the reading as a preliminary to writing a summary. A paragraph-by-paragraph scratch outline (like the one on p. 304) lists the reading's main ideas in the sequence in which they appear in the original. But summarizing requires more than merely stringing together the entries in an outline; it must fill in the logical connections between the author's ideas. Notice also in the following example that the reader repeats selected words and phrases and refers to the author by name, indicating, with verbs like *expresses, acknowledges,* and *explains,* the writer's purpose and strategy at each point in the argument.

Summary

King expresses his disappointment with white moderates who, by opposing his program of nonviolent direct action, have become a barrier to progress toward racial justice. He acknowledges that his program has raised tension in the South, but he explains that tension is necessary to bring about change. Furthermore, he argues that tension already exists, but because it has been unexpressed, it is unhealthy and potentially dangerous.

He defends his actions against the clergy's criticisms, particularly their argument that he is in too much of a hurry. Responding to charges of extremism, King claims that he has actually prevented racial violence by channeling the natural frustrations of oppressed blacks into nonviolent protest. He asserts that extremism is precisely what is needed now—but it must be creative, rather than destructive, extremism. He concludes by again expressing disappointment with white moderates for not joining his effort as some other whites have.

A summary presents only ideas. Although it may use certain key terms from the source, it does not otherwise attempt to reflect the source's language, imagery, or tone; and it avoids even a hint of agreement or disagreement with the ideas it summarizes. Of course, a writer might summarize ideas in a source like "Letter from Birmingham Jail" to show read-ers that he or she has read it carefully and then proceed to use the summary to praise, ques-tion, or challenge King's argument. In doing so, the writer might quote specific language that reveals word choice, imagery, or tone.

ANALYZE & WRITE ───

Summarizing

1. Make a scratch outline of the reading you have been working with, or use the outline you created in the activity on page 304.

2. Write a paragraph or more that presents the author's main ideas largely in your own words. Use the outline as a guide, but reread parts of the original text as necessary.

3. To make the summary coherent, fill in connections between the ideas you present.

Synthesizing

Synthesizing involves presenting ideas and information gleaned from different sources. It can help you see how different sources relate to one another. For example, one reading may provide information that fills out the information in another reading, or a reading could present arguments that challenge arguments in another reading.

When you synthesize material from different sources, you construct a conversation among your sources, a conversation in which you also participate. Synthesizing contrib-utes most when writers use sources, not only to support their ideas but to challenge and extend them as well.

In the following example, the reader uses a variety of sources related to the King pas-sage (pp. 295–301) and brings them together around a central idea. Notice how quota-tion, paraphrase, and summary are all used.

Synthesis

When King defends his campaign of nonviolent direct action against the clergymen's criticism that "our actions, even though peaceful, must be condemned because they precipitate violence" (King excerpt, par. 3), he is using what Vinit Haksar calls Mohandas Gandhi's "safety-valve argument" ("Civil Disobedience and Non-Cooperation" 117). According to Haksar, Gandhi gave a "non-threatening warning of worse things to come" if his demands were not met. King similarly makes clear that advocates of actions more extreme than those he advocates are waiting in the wings: "The other force is one of bitterness and hatred, and it comes perilously close to advocating violence" (King excerpt, par. 5). King identifies this force with Elijah Muhammad, and although he does not name him, King's contemporary readers would have known that he was referring also to his disciple Malcolm X, who, according to Herbert J. Storing, "urged that Negroes take seriously the idea of revolution" ("The Case against Civil Disobedience" 90). In fact, Malcolm X accused King of being a modern-day Uncle Tom, trying "to keep us under control, to keep us passive and peaceful and nonviolent" (*Malcolm X Speaks* 12).

ANALYZE & WRITE

Synthesizing

1 Find and read two or three sources on the topic of the selection you have been working with, annotating the passages that give you ideas about the topic.

2 Look for patterns among your sources, possibly supporting or challenging your ideas or those of other sources.

3 Write a paragraph or more synthesizing your sources, using quotation, paraphrase, and summary to present what they say on the topic.

Contextualizing

All texts reflect historical and cultural assumptions, values, and attitudes that may differ from your own. To read thoughtfully, you need to become aware of these differences. **Contextualizing** is a critical reading strategy that enables you to make inferences about a reading's historical and cultural context and to examine the differences between its context and your own.

The excerpt from King's "Letter from Birmingham Jail" is a good example of a text that benefits from being read contextually. If you knew little about the history of slavery and segregation in the United States, it would be difficult to understand the passion expressed in this passage. To understand the historical and cultural context in which King wrote his "Letter from Birmingham Jail," you could do some library or Internet research. Comparing the situation at the time to situations with which you are familiar would help you understand some of your own attitudes toward King and the civil rights movement.

Here is what one reader wrote to contextualize King's writing:

Notes from a Contextualized Reading

1. I am not old enough to know what it was like in the early 1960s when Dr. King was leading marches and sit-ins, but I have seen television documentaries showing demonstrators being attacked by dogs, doused by fire hoses, beaten and dragged by helmeted police. Such images give me a sense of the violence, fear, and hatred that King was responding to.

   The tension King writes about comes across in his writing. He uses his anger and frustration creatively to inspire his critics. He also threatens them, although he denies it. I saw a film on Malcolm X, so I could see that King was giving white people a choice between his own nonviolent way and Malcolm's more confrontational way.

2. Things have certainly changed since the sixties. Legal segregation has ended, but there are still racists, like the detective in the O. J. Simpson trial. African Americans like Condoleezza Rice and Barack Obama are highly respected and powerful. The civil rights movement is over. So when I'm reading King today, I feel like I'm reading history. But then again, every once in a while there are reports of police brutality because of race (think of Oscar Grant) and of what we now call hate crimes (Trayvon Martin).

Contextualizing

1 Describe the historical and cultural situation as it is represented in the reading you have been working with and in other sources with which you are familiar. Your knowledge may come from other reading, television or film, school, or elsewhere. (If you know nothing about the historical and cultural context, you could do some library or Internet research.)

2 Compare the historical and cultural situation in which the text was written with your own historical and cultural situation. Consider how your understanding and judgment of the reading are affected by your own context.

Exploring the Significance of Figurative Language

Figurative language—*metaphor, simile,* and *symbolism*—enhances literal meaning by implying abstract ideas through vivid images and by evoking feelings and associations.

Metaphor implicitly compares two different things by identifying them with each other. For instance, when King calls the white moderate "the Negro's great stumbling block in his stride toward freedom" (par. 1), he does not mean that the white moderate literally trips the Negro who is attempting to walk toward freedom. The sentence makes sense only if understood figuratively: The white moderate trips up the Negro by frustrating every effort to achieve justice.

Simile, a more explicit form of comparison, uses the word *like* or *as* to signal the relationship of two seemingly unrelated things. King uses simile when he says that injustice is "like a boil that can never be cured so long as it is covered up" (par. 2). This simile makes several points of comparison between injustice and a boil. It suggests that injustice is a disease of society as a boil is a disease of the skin and that injustice, like a boil, must be exposed or it will fester and infect the entire body.

Symbolism compares two things by making one stand for the other. King uses the white moderate as a symbol for supposed liberals and would-be supporters of civil rights who are actually frustrating the cause.

How these figures of speech are used in a text reveals something of the writer's feelings about the subject. Exploring possible meanings in a text's figurative language involves (1) annotating and then listing the metaphors, similes, and symbols you find in a reading; (2) grouping and labeling the figures of speech that appear to express related feelings or attitudes; and (3) writing to explore the meaning of the patterns you have found.

The following example shows the process of exploring figures of speech in the King excerpt.

Listing Figures of Speech

"stumbling block in his stride toward freedom" (par. 1)

"law and order...become the dangerously structured dams" (2)

"the flow of social progress" (2)

"Like a boil that can never be cured" (2)

"the light of human conscience and the air of national opinion" (2)
"the quicksand of racial injustice" (4)

Grouping and Labeling Figures of Speech

Sickness: "like a boil" (2); "the disease of segregation" (10)
Underground: "hidden tension" (2); "injustice must be exposed" (2); "injustice must be rooted out" (10)
Blockage: "dams," "block the flow" (2); "Human progress never rolls in on wheels of inevitability" (4); "pent-up resentments" (8); "repressed emotions" (8)

Writing to Explore Meaning

The patterns labeled Underground and Blockage suggest a feeling of frustration. Inertia is a problem; movement forward toward progress or upward toward the promised land is stalled. The strong need to break through the resistance may represent King's feelings about both his attempt to lead purposeful, effective demonstrations and his effort to write a convincing argument.

The simile of injustice being "like a boil" links the two patterns of underground and sickness, suggesting that something bad, a disease, is inside the people or the society. The cure is to expose or to root out the blocked hatred and injustice as well as to release the tension or emotion that has long been repressed. This implies that repression itself is the evil, not simply what is repressed. Therefore, writing and speaking out through political action may have curative power for individuals and society alike.

ANALYZE & WRITE

Exploring the Significance of Figurative Language

1 Annotate all the figures of speech you find in the reading you have been working with (or another selection) — metaphors, similes, and symbols — and then list them.

2 Group the figures of speech that appear to express related feelings and attitudes, and label each group.

3 Write one or two paragraphs exploring the meaning of these patterns. What do they tell you about the text?

Looking for Patterns of Opposition

All texts carry within themselves voices of opposition. These voices may echo the views and values of readers the writer anticipates or predecessors to whom the writer is responding in some way; they may even reflect the writer's own conflicting values. Careful readers look closely for such a dialogue of opposing voices within the text.

When we think of oppositions, we ordinarily think of polarities: *yes* and *no, up* and *down, black* and *white, new* and *old.* Some oppositions, however, may be more subtle. The excerpt from King's "Letter from Birmingham Jail" is rich in such oppositions: *moderate* versus *extremist, order* versus *justice, direct action* versus *passive acceptance, expression* versus *repression.* These oppositions are not accidental; they form a significant pattern that gives a reader important information about the essay.

A careful reading will show that King always values one of the two terms in an opposition over the other. In the passage, for example, *extremist* is valued over *moderate* (par. 9). This preference for extremism is surprising. The reader should ask why, when white extremists like members of the Ku Klux Klan have committed so many outrages against African Americans, King would prefer extremism. If King is trying to convince his readers to accept his point of view, why would he represent himself as an extremist? Moreover, why would a clergyman advocate extremism instead of moderation?

Studying the **patterns of opposition** in the text enables you to answer these questions. You will see that King sets up this opposition to force his readers to examine their own values and realize that they are in fact misplaced. Instead of working toward justice, he says, those who support law and order maintain the unjust status quo. By getting his readers to think of white moderates as blocking rather than facilitating peaceful change, King brings readers to align themselves with him and perhaps even embrace his strategy of nonviolent resistance.

Looking for patterns of opposition involves annotating words or phrases in the reading that indicate oppositions, listing the opposing terms in pairs, deciding which term in each pair is preferred by the writer, and reflecting on the meaning of the patterns. Here is a partial list of oppositions from the King excerpt, with the preferred terms marked by an asterisk:

Listing Patterns of Opposition

moderate	*extremist
order	*justice
negative peace	*positive peace
absence of justice	*presence of justice
goals	*methods
*direct action	passive acceptance
*exposed tension	hidden tension

ANALYZE & WRITE

Looking for Patterns of Opposition

1. Annotate the selection you have been working with (or another selection) for words or phrases indicating oppositions.

2. List the pairs of oppositions. (You may have to paraphrase or even supply the opposite word or phrase if it is not stated directly in the text.)

3. For each pair of oppositions, put an asterisk next to the term that the writer seems to value or prefer over the other.

4. Study the patterns of opposition. How do they contribute to your understanding of the essay? What do they tell you about what the author wants you to believe?

Reflecting on Challenges to Your Beliefs and Values

To read thoughtfully, you need to scrutinize your own assumptions and attitudes as well as those expressed in the text you are reading. If you are like most readers, however, you will find that your assumptions and attitudes are so ingrained that you are not always fully aware of them. A good strategy for getting at these underlying beliefs and values is to identify and reflect on the ways the text challenges you and how it makes you feel—disturbed, threatened, ashamed, combative, pleased, exuberant, or some other way.

For example, here is what one student wrote about the King passage:

Reflections

In paragraph 1, Dr. King criticizes people who are "more devoted to 'order' than to justice." This criticism upsets me because today I think I would choose order over justice. When I reflect on my feelings and try to figure out where they come from, I realize that what I feel most is fear. I am terrified by the violence in society today. I'm afraid of sociopaths who don't respect the rule of law, much less the value of human life.

I know Dr. King was writing in a time when the law itself was unjust, when order was apparently used to keep people from protesting and changing the law. But things are different now. Today, justice seems to serve criminals more than it serves law-abiding citizens. That's why I'm for order over justice.

ANALYZE & WRITE

Reflecting on Challenges to Your Beliefs and Values

1 Identify challenges by marking the text you have been working with (or another text) where you feel your beliefs and values are being opposed, criticized, or unfairly characterized.

2 Write a few paragraphs reflecting on why you feel challenged. Do not defend your feelings; instead, search your memory to discover where they come from.

Evaluating the Logic of an Argument

An *argument* includes a thesis backed by reasons and support. The **thesis** asserts a position on a controversial issue or a solution to a problem that the writer wants readers to accept. The **reasons** tell readers why they should accept the thesis, and the **support** (such as examples, statistics, authorities, and textual evidence) gives readers grounds for accepting it. For an argument to be considered logically acceptable, it must meet the three conditions of what we call the ABC test:

For more on argument, see Chapter 13.

The ABC Test

A.   The reasons and support must be *appropriate* to the thesis.

B.   The reasons and support must be *believable*.

C.   The reasons and support must be *consistent* with one another as well as *complete*.

Test for appropriateness.

To evaluate the logic of an argument, you first decide whether the argument's reasons and support are appropriate. To test for appropriateness, ask these questions: How does each reason or piece of support relate to the thesis? Is the connection between reasons and support and the thesis clear and compelling?

Readers most often question the appropriateness of reasons and support when the writer argues by analogy or by invoking authority. For example, in paragraph 2, King argues that when law and order fail to establish justice, "they become the dangerously structured dams that block the flow of social progress." The analogy asserts the following logical relationship: Law and order are to progress toward justice what a dam is to water. If you do not accept this analogy, the argument fails the test of appropriateness.

King uses both analogy and authority in paragraph 3: "Isn't this like condemning Socrates because his unswerving commitment to truth and his philosophical inquiries precipitated the act by the misguided populace in which they made him drink hemlock?" Not only must you judge the appropriateness of the analogy comparing the Greeks' condemnation of Socrates to the white moderates' condemnation of King, but you must also judge whether it is appropriate to accept Socrates as an authority. Since Socrates is generally respected for his teachings on justice, his words and actions are likely to be considered appropriate to King's situation in Birmingham.

For more on invoking authorities, see pp. 371–72 in Chapter 13.

Test for believability.

Believability is a measure of your willingness to accept as true the reasons and support the writer gives in defense of a thesis.

To test for believability, ask: On what basis am I being asked to believe this reason or support is true? If it cannot be proved true or false, how much weight does it carry?

In judging facts, examples and anecdotes, statistics, and authorities, consider the following points.

Facts are statements that can be proved objectively to be true. The believability of facts depends on their *accuracy* (they should not distort or misrepresent reality), their *completeness* (they should not omit important details), and the *trustworthiness* of their sources (sources should be qualified and unbiased). King, for instance, asserts as fact that the African American will not wait much longer for racial justice (par. 8). His critics might question the factuality of this assertion by asking: Is it true of all African Americans? How does King know what African Americans will and will not do?

Examples and **anecdotes** are particular instances that may or may not make you believe a general statement. The believability of examples depends on their *representativeness* (whether they are truly typical and thus generalizable) and their *specificity* (whether particular details make them seem true to life). Even if a vivid example or gripping anecdote does not convince readers, it usually strengthens argumentative writing by clarifying the meaning and dramatizing the point. In paragraph 5 of the King excerpt, for example, King supports his generalization that some African American extremists are motivated by bitterness and hatred by citing the specific example of Elijah Muhammad's Black Muslim movement. Conversely, in paragraph 9, he refers to Jesus, Paul, Luther, and others as examples of extremists motivated by love and Christianity. These examples support his assertion that extremism is not in itself wrong and that any judgment of extremism must be based on its motivation and cause.

Statistics are numerical data. The believability of statistics depends on the *comparability* of the data (the price of apples in 1985 cannot be compared with the price of apples in 2012 unless the figures are adjusted to account for inflation), the *precision* of the methods employed to gather and analyze data (representative samples should be used and variables accounted for), and the *trustworthiness* of the sources.

Authorities are people to whom the writer attributes expertise on a given subject. Not only must such authorities be appropriate, as mentioned earlier, but they must be credible as well—that is, the reader must accept them as experts on the topic at hand. King cites authorities repeatedly throughout his essay. He refers to religious leaders (Jesus and Luther) as well as to American political leaders (Lincoln and Jefferson). These figures are likely to have a high degree of credibility among King's readers.

Test for consistency and completeness.

In looking for consistency, you should be concerned that all the parts of the argument work together and that they are sufficient to convince readers to accept the thesis or at least take it seriously. To test for consistency and completeness, ask: Are any of the reasons and support contradictory? Do they provide sufficient grounds for accepting the thesis? Does the writer fail to acknowledge, concede, or refute any opposing arguments or important objections?

A thoughtful reader might regard as contradictory King's characterizing himself first as a moderate and later as an extremist opposed to the forces of violence. (King attempts to reconcile this apparent contradiction by explicitly redefining extremism in par. 9.) Similarly, the fact that King fails to examine and refute every legal recourse available to his cause might allow a critical reader to question the sufficiency of his argument.

For more on responding to opposing views, see pp. 150–51 in Chapter 13.

| ANALYZE & WRITE |

Evaluating the Logic of an Argument

Use the ABC test on the selection you have been working with (or another selection):

- **A** *Test for appropriateness* by checking that the reasons and support are clearly and directly related to the thesis.

- **B** *Test for believability* by deciding whether you can accept the reasons and support as likely to be true.

- **C** *Test for consistency and completeness* by deciding whether the argument has any contradictions and whether any important objections or opposing views have been ignored.

Recognizing Emotional Manipulation

Writers often try to arouse emotions in readers to excite their interest, make them care, or move them to take action. There is nothing wrong with appealing to readers' emotions. What is wrong is manipulating readers with false or exaggerated appeals. Therefore, you should be suspicious of writing that is overly sentimental, that cites alarming statistics and frightening anecdotes, that demonizes others and identifies itself with revered authorities, or that uses potent symbols (for example, the American flag) or emotionally loaded words (such as *racist*).

King, for example, uses the emotionally loaded word *paternalistically* to refer to the white moderate's belief that "he can set the timetable for another man's freedom" (par. 1). In the same paragraph, King uses symbolism to get an emotional reaction from readers when he compares the white moderate to the "Ku Klux Klanner." To get readers to accept his ideas, he also relies on authorities whose names evoke the greatest respect, such as Jesus and Lincoln. But some readers might object that comparing his own crusade to that of Jesus is pretentious and manipulative. A critical reader might also consider King's discussion of African American extremists in paragraph 7 to be a veiled threat designed to frighten readers into agreement.

| ANALYZE & WRITE |

Recognizing Emotional Manipulation

1 Annotate places in the text you have been working with (or another text) where you sense emotional appeals are being used.

2 Assess whether any of the emotional appeals are unfairly manipulative.

Judging the Writer's Credibility

Writers try to persuade readers by presenting an image of themselves in their writing that will gain their readers' confidence. This image must be created indirectly, through the arguments, language, and system of values and beliefs expressed or implied in the writing. Writers establish credibility in their writing in three ways:

- By showing their knowledge of the subject
- By building *common ground* with readers
- By responding fairly to objections and opposing arguments

Test for knowledge.

Writers demonstrate their knowledge through the facts and statistics they marshal, the sources they rely on for information, and the scope and depth of their understanding. You may not be sufficiently expert on the subject yourself to know whether the facts are accurate, the sources are reliable, and the understanding is sufficient. You may need to do some research to see what others say about the subject. You can also check credentials—the writer's educational and professional qualifications, the respectability of the publication in which the selection first appeared, and reviews of the writer's work—to determine whether the writer is a respected authority in the field. For example, King brings with him the authority that comes from being a member of the clergy and a respected leader of the Southern Christian Leadership Conference.

Test for common ground.

One way writers can establish **common ground** with their readers is by basing their reasoning on shared values, beliefs, and attitudes. They use language that includes their readers (*we*) and qualify their assertions to keep them from being too extreme. Above all, they acknowledge differences of opinion. You want to notice such appeals.

King creates common ground with readers by using the inclusive pronoun *we*, suggesting shared concerns between himself and his audience. Notice, however, his use of masculine pronouns and other references ("the Negro . . . he," "our brothers"). Although King addressed his letter to male clergy, he intended it to be published in the local newspaper, where it would be read by an audience of both men and women. By using language that excludes women—a common practice at the time the selection was written—King may have missed the opportunity to build common ground with more than half of his readers.

Test for fairness.

Writers reveal their character by how they handle opposing arguments and objections to their argument. As a critical reader, pay particular attention to how writers treat possible differences of opinion. Be suspicious of those who ignore differences and pretend that everyone agrees with their viewpoints. When objections or opposing views are represented, consider whether they have been distorted in any way; If they are refuted, be sure they are challenged fairly—with sound reasoning and solid support.

One way to gauge the author's credibility is to identify the tone of the argument, for it conveys the writer's attitude toward the subject and toward the reader. Is the text angry? Sarcastic? Evenhanded? Shrill? Condescending? Bullying? Do you feel as if the writer is treating the subject—and you, as a reader—with fairness? King's tone might be characterized in different passages as patient (he doesn't lose his temper), respectful (he refers to white moderates as "people of good will"), or pompous (comparing himself to Jesus and Socrates).

| ANALYZE & WRITE |

Judging the Writer's Credibility

1 Using the selection you have been working with (or another selection), annotate for the writer's knowledge of the subject, how well common ground is established, and whether the writer deals fairly with objections and opposing arguments.

2 Decide what in the essay you find credible and what you question.

10

Cueing the Reader

Readers need guidance. To guide readers through a piece of writing, a writer can provide five basic kinds of **cues,** or signals:

1. Thesis and forecasting statements, to orient readers to ideas and organization
2. Paragraphing, to group related ideas and details
3. Cohesive devices, to connect ideas to one another and bring about clarity
4. Transitions, to signal relationships or shifts in meaning
5. Headings and subheadings, to group related paragraphs and help readers locate specific information quickly

This chapter illustrates how each of these cueing strategies works.

Orienting Statements

To help readers find their way, especially in difficult and lengthy texts, you can provide two kinds of **orienting statements:** a thesis statement, which declares the main point, and a forecasting statement, which previews subordinate points, showing the order in which they will be discussed in the essay.

Use thesis statements to announce the main idea.

To help readers understand what is being said about a subject, writers often provide a thesis statement early in the essay. The **thesis statement,** which can comprise one or more sentences, operates as a cue by letting readers know which is the most important general idea among the writer's many ideas and observations. In "Love: The Right Chemistry" in Chapter 4, Anastasia Toufexis expresses her thesis in the second paragraph:

> O.K., let's cut out all this nonsense about romantic love. Let's bring some scientific precision to the party. Let's put love under a microscope.
>
> When rigorous people with Ph.D.s after their names do that, what they see is not some silly, senseless thing. No, their probe reveals that love rests firmly on the foundations of evolution, biology and chemistry.

Readers naturally look for something that will tell them the point of an essay, a focus for the many diverse details and ideas they encounter as they read. They expect to find some information early on that will give them a context for reading the essay, particularly if they are reading about a new or difficult subject. Therefore, a thesis statement, like Toufexis's, placed at the beginning of an essay enables readers to antici-pate the content of the essay and helps them understand the relationships among its various ideas and details.

Occasionally, however, particularly in fairly short, informal essays and in some auto-biographical and argumentative essays, a writer may save a direct statement of the thesis until the conclusion. In "Why Privacy Matters Even If You Have 'Nothing to Hide,'" for example, from Chapter 5, Daniel J. Solove explicitly states his thesis only in the final paragraph:

> "My life's an open book," people might say. "I've got nothing to hide." But now the government has large dossiers of everyone's activities, interests, reading habits, finances, and health. What if the government leaks the information to the public? What if the government mistakenly determines that based on your pattern of activities, you're likely to engage in a criminal act? What if it denies you the right to fly? What if the govern-ment thinks your financial transactions look odd—even if you've done nothing wrong— and freezes your accounts? What if the government doesn't protect your information with adequate security, and an identity thief obtains it and uses it to defraud you? Even if you have nothing to hide, the government can cause you a lot of harm.

Ending with the thesis brings together the various strands of information or supporting details introduced over the course of the essay and makes clear the essay's main idea.

Some essays, particularly autobiographical essays, offer no direct thesis statement. Although this can make the point of the essay more difficult to determine, it can be appropriate when the essay is more expressive and personal than it is informative. In all cases, careful writers keep readers' needs and expectations in mind when deciding how—and whether—to state the thesis.

EXERCISE 10.1

In the essay by Jessica Statsky in Chapter 5, underline the thesis statement, the last sen-tence in paragraph 1. Notice the key terms: "overzealous parents and coaches," "impose adult standards," "children's sports," "activities . . . neither satisfying nor beneficial." Then skim the essay, stopping to read the sentence at the beginning of each paragraph. Also read the last paragraph.

Consider whether the idea in every paragraph's first sentence is anticipated by the the-sis's key terms. Consider also the connection between the ideas in the last paragraph and the thesis's key terms. What can you conclude about how a thesis might assert the point of an essay, anticipate the ideas that follow, and help readers relate the ideas to one another?

Use forecasting statements to preview topics.

Some thesis statements include a **forecast,** which overviews the way a thesis will be developed, as in the following example:

> In the three years from 1348 through 1350 the pandemic of plague
> known as the Black Death, or, as the Germans called it, the Great Dying,

killed at least a fourth of the population of Europe. It was undoubtedly the worst disaster that has ever befallen mankind. Today we can have no real conception of the terror under which people lived in the shadow of the plague. For more than two centuries plague has not been a serious threat to mankind in the large, although it is still a grisly presence in parts of the Far East and Africa. Scholars continue to study the Great Dying, however, as a historical example of human behavior under the stress of

Thesis forecasts five main categories of effects of the Black Death.

universal catastrophe. In these days when the threat of plague has been replaced by the threat of mass human extermination by even more rapid means, there has been a sharp renewal of interest in the history of the fourteenth-century calamity. With new perspective, students are investigating its manifold effects: demographic, economic, psychological, moral and religious.

—WILLIAM LANGER, "The Black Death"

As a reader would expect, Langer divides his essay into explanations of the research into these five effects, addressing them in the order in which they appear in the forecasting statement.

EXERCISE 10.2

Turn to Patrick O'Malley's essay in Chapter 6, and underline the forecasting statement in paragraph 2. Then skim the essay. Does O'Malley take up every point he mentions in the forecasting statement? Does he stick to the order he promises readers? How well does his forecasting statement help you follow his essay? What suggestions for improvement, if any, would you offer him?

---

 macmillanhighered.com/conciseguide
LearningCurve > Topics and Main Ideas

Paragraphing

Paragraph cues as obvious as indentation keep readers on track. You can also arrange material in a paragraph to help readers see what is significant. For example, you can begin with a topic sentence, show readers the relationship between the previous and present paragraphs with a clear transition, and place the most important information near the end.

Paragraph indents signal related ideas.

One paragraph cue—the indentation that signals the beginning of a new paragraph—is a relatively modern printing convention. Old manuscripts show that paragraph divisions were not always marked. To make reading easier, scribes and printers began to use the symbol ¶ to mark paragraph breaks, and later, indenting became common practice. Indenting has been abandoned by most online and business writers, who now distinguish one paragraph from another by leaving a line of space between paragraphs.

Paragraphing helps readers by signaling when a sequence of related ideas begins and ends. Paragraphing also helps readers judge what is most important in what they are reading. Writers typically emphasize important information by placing it at the two points in the paragraph where readers are most attentive — the beginning and the end.

You can give special emphasis to information by placing it in its own paragraph.

For additional visual cues for readers, see Headings and Subheadings on pp. 329–30.

EXERCISE 10.3

Turn again to Patrick O'Malley's essay in Chapter 6, and read paragraphs 4–7 with the following questions in mind: Does all the material in each paragraph seem to be related? Do you feel a sense of closure at the end of each paragraph? Does the last sentence offer the most important or significant or weighty information in the paragraph?

Topic sentences announce the paragraph's focus.

A **topic sentence** lets readers know the focus of a paragraph in simple and direct terms. It is a cueing strategy for the paragraph, much as a thesis or forecasting statement is for the whole essay. Because paragraphing usually signals a shift in focus, readers expect some kind of reorientation in the opening sentence. They need to know whether the new paragraph will introduce another aspect of the topic or develop one already introduced.

Announcing the Topic   Some topic sentences simply announce the topic. Here are some examples taken from Barry Lopez's book *Arctic Dreams:*

> A polar bear walks in a way all its own.

> What is so consistently striking about the way Eskimos used parts of an animal is the breadth of their understanding about what would work.

> The Mediterranean view of the Arctic, down to the time of the Elizabethan mariners, was shaped by two somewhat contradictory thoughts.

The following paragraph shows how one of Lopez's topic sentences (highlighted) is developed:

> What is so consistently striking about the way Eskimos used parts of an animal is the breadth of their understanding about what would work. Knowing that muskox horn is more flexible than caribou antler, they preferred it for making the side prongs of a fish spear. For a waterproof bag in which to carry sinews for clothing repair, they chose salmon skin. They selected the strong, translucent intestine of a bearded seal to make a window for a snowhouse — it would fold up for easy traveling and it would not frost over in cold weather. To make small snares for sea ducks, they needed a springy material that would not rot in salt water — baleen fibers. The down feather of a common eider, tethered at the end of a stick in the snow at an angle, would reveal the exhalation of a quietly surfacing seal. Polar bear bone was used anywhere a stout, sharp point was required, because it is the hardest bone.
>
> —Barry Lopez, *Arctic Dreams*

EXERCISE 10.4

Turn to Jessica Statsky's essay in Chapter 5. Underline the topic sentence (the first sentence) in paragraphs 3 and 5. Consider how these sentences help you anticipate the paragraph's topic and method of development.

---

 macmillanhighered.com/conciseguide
LearnngCurve > Topic Sentences and Supporting Details

Making a Transition   Not all topic sentences simply point to what will follow. Some refer to earlier sentences that work both as topic sentences, stating the paragraph's main point, and as *transitions,* linking that paragraph to the previous one. Here are a few topic sentences from "Quilts and Women's Culture," by Elaine Hedges, with transitions highlighted:

> Transitions tie each topic sentence to a previous statement.

> Within its broad traditionalism and anonymity, however, variations and distinctions developed.

> Regionally, too, distinctions were introduced into quilt making through the interesting process of renaming.

> Finally, out of such regional and other variations come individual, signed achievements.

> Quilts, then, were an outlet for creative energy, a source and emblem of sisterhood and solidarity, and a graphic response to historical and political change.

Sometimes the first sentence of a paragraph serves as a transition, and a subsequent sentence states the topic, as in the following example:

> What a convenience, what a relief it will be, they say, never to worry about how to dress for a job interview, a romantic tryst, or a funeral!

> Transition sentences

> Convenient, perhaps, but not exactly a relief. Such a utopia would give most of us the same kind of chill we feel when a stadium full of Communist-bloc athletes in identical sports outfits, shouting slogans in unison, appears on TV. Most people do not want to be told what to wear any more than they want to be told what to say. In Belfast recently four hundred Irish Republican prisoners "refused to wear any clothes at all, draping themselves day and night in blankets," rather than put on prison uniforms. Even the offer of civilian-style dress did not satisfy them; they insisted on wearing their own clothes brought from home, or nothing. Fashion is free speech, and one of the privileges, if not always one of the pleasures, of a free world.

> —ALISON LURIE, *The Language of Clothes*

Occasionally, whole paragraphs serve as transitions, linking one sequence of paragraphs with those that follow, as in the following:

> Transition paragraph summarizes contrasts and sets up an analysis of the similarities.

> Yet it was not all contrast, after all. Different as they were —in background, in personality, in underlying aspiration—these two great soldiers had much in common. Under everything else, they

were marvelous fighters. Furthermore, their fighting qualities were really very much alike.

—Bruce Catton, "Grant and Lee: A Study in Contrasts"

EXERCISE 10.5

Turn to Jessica Statsky's essay in Chapter 5 and read paragraphs 3–7. As you read, underline the part of the first sentence in paragraphs 4, 5, and 7 that refers to the previous paragraph, creating a transition from one to the next. Notice the different ways Statsky creates these transitions. Consider whether they are all equally effective.

Positioning the Topic Sentence Although topic sentences may occur anywhere in a paragraph, stating the topic in the first sentence has the advantage of giving readers a sense of how the paragraph is likely to be developed. The beginning of the paragraph is therefore the most common position.

A topic sentence that does not open a paragraph is most likely to appear at the end. When a topic sentence concludes a paragraph, it usually summarizes or generalizes preceding information:

> Even black Americans sometimes need to be reminded about the deceptiveness of television. Blacks retain their fascination with black characters on TV: Many of us buy *Jet* magazine primarily to read its weekly television feature, which lists every black character (major or minor) to be seen on the screen that week. Yet our fixation with the presence of black characters on TV has blinded us to an important fact that *Cosby,* which began in 1984, and its offshoots over the years demonstrate convincingly: There is very little connection between the social status of black Americans and the fabricated images of black people that Americans consume each day. The representation of blacks on TV is a very poor index to our social advancement or political progress.
>
> —Henry Louis Gates Jr., "TV's Black World Turns—but Stays Unreal"

Topic is not stated until the last sentence.

When a topic sentence is used in a narrative, it often appears as the last sentence as a way to evaluate or reflect on events:

> A cold sun was sliding down a gray fall sky. Some older boys had been playing tackle football in the field we took charge of every weekend. In a few years, they'd be called to Southeast Asia, some of them. Their locations would be tracked with pushpins in red, white, and blue on maps on nearly every kitchen wall. But that afternoon, they were quick as young deer. They leapt and dodged, dove from each other and collided in midair. Bulletlike passes flew to connect them. Or the ball spiraled in a high arc across the frosty sky one to another. In short, they were mindlessly agile in a way that captured as audience every little kid within running distance of the yellow goalposts.
>
> —Mary Karr, *Cherry*

Topic sentence reflects on narrated events described earlier in paragraph.

It is possible for a single topic sentence to introduce two or more paragraphs. Subsequent paragraphs in such a sequence have no separate topic sentences of their own:

Topic sentence states topic of this paragraph and next.	Anthropologists Daniel Maltz and Ruth Borker point out that boys and girls socialize differently. Little girls tend to play in small groups or, even more common, in pairs. Their social life usually centers around a best friend, and friendships are made, maintained, and broken by talk—especially "secrets." If a little girl tells her friend's secret to another little girl, she may find herself with a new best friend. The secrets themselves may or may not be important, but the fact of telling them is all-important. It's hard for newcomers to get into these tight groups, but anyone who is admitted is treated as an equal. Girls like to play cooperatively; if they can't cooperate, the group breaks up.

Little boys tend to play in larger groups, often outdoors, and they spend more time doing things than talking. It's easy for boys to get into the group, but not everyone is accepted as an equal. Once in the group, boys must jockey for their status in it. One of the most important ways they do this is through talk: verbal display such as telling stories and jokes, challenging and sidetracking the verbal displays of other boys, and withstanding other boys' challenges in order to maintain their own story — and status. Their talk is often competitive talk about who is best at what.

—Deborah Tannen, *That's Not What I Meant!*

EXERCISE 10.6

Consider the variety and effectiveness of the topic sentences in your most recent essay. Begin by underlining the topic sentence in each paragraph after the first one. The topic sentence may not be the first sentence in a paragraph, though it will often be.

Then double-underline the part of the topic sentence that provides an explicit transition from one paragraph to the next. You may find a transition that is separate from the topic sentence. You may not always find a topic sentence.

Reflect on your topic sentences, and evaluate how well they serve to orient your readers to the sequence of topics or ideas in your essay.

Cohesive Devices

Cohesive devices guide readers, helping them follow your train of thought by connecting key words and phrases throughout a passage. Among such devices are pronoun reference, word repetition, synonyms, sentence structure repetition, and collocation.

Pronouns connect phrases or sentences.

One common cohesive device is *pronoun reference*. As noun substitutes, pronouns refer to nouns that either precede or follow them and thus serve to connect phrases or sentences. The nouns that come before pronouns are called **antecedents**.

In New York from dawn to dusk to dawn, day after day, you can hear the steady rumble of tires against the concrete span of the George Washington Bridge. The bridge is never completely still. It trembles with traffic. It moves in the wind. Its great veins of steel swell when hot and contract when cold; its span often is ten feet closer to the Hudson River in summer than in winter.

Pronouns form a chain of connection with antecedent.

—GAY TALESE, "New York"

This example has only one pronoun-antecedent chain, and the antecedent comes first, so all the pronouns refer back to it. When there are multiple pronoun-antecedent chains with references forward as well as back, writers have to make sure that readers will not mistake one pronoun's antecedent for another's.

Word repetition aids cohesion.

To avoid confusion, writers often use *word repetition*. The device of repeating words and phrases is especially helpful if a pronoun might confuse readers:

Repeated words

Some odd optical property of our highly polarized and unequal society makes the poor almost invisible to their economic superiors. The poor can see the affluent easily enough—on television, for example, or on the covers of magazines. But the affluent rarely see the poor or, if they do catch sight of them in some public space, rarely know what they're seeing, since—thanks to consignment stores and, yes, Wal-Mart—the poor are usually able to disguise themselves as members of the more comfortable classes.

—BARBARA EHRENREICH, *Nickel and Dimed*

In the next example, several overlapping chains of word repetition prevent confusion and help the reader follow the ideas:

Repeated words with some variation of form

Natural selection is the central concept of Darwinian theory—the fittest survive and spread their favored traits through populations. Natural selection is defined by Spencer's phrase "survival of the fittest," but what does this famous bit of jargon really mean? Who are the fittest? And how is "fitness" defined? We often read that fitness involves no more than "differential reproductive success"—the production of more surviving offspring than other competing members of the population. Whoa! cries Bethell, as many others have before him. This formulation defines fitness in terms of survival only. The crucial phrase of natural selection means no more than "the survival of those who survive"—a vacuous tautology. (A tautology is a phrase—like "my father is a man"—containing no information in the predicate ["a man"] not inherent in the subject ["my father"]. Tautologies are fine as definitions, but not as testable scientific statements—there can be nothing to test in a statement true by definition.)

— STEPHEN JAY GOULD, *Ever Since Darwin*

Synonyms connect ideas.

In addition to word repetition, you can use **synonyms,** words with identical or very similar meanings, to connect important ideas. In the following example, the author develops a careful chain of synonyms and word repetitions:

Synonym sequences:
region, particular
landscape

local residents, native

stories, narratives

are remembered,
does not become lost

intricate, . . . view,
complex . . . "reality"

Over time, small bits of knowledge about a region accumulate among local residents in the form of stories. These are remembered in the community; even what is unusual does not become lost and therefore irrelevant. These narratives comprise for a native an intricate, long-term view of a particular landscape. . . . Outside the region this complex but easily shared "reality" is hard to get across without reducing it to generalities, to misleading or imprecise abstraction.

—Barry Lopez, *Arctic Dreams*

The result is a coherent paragraph that constantly reinforces the author's point.

Sentence structure repetition emphasizes connections.

Writers occasionally use *sentence structure repetition* to emphasize the connections among their ideas, as in this example:

Repeats the if/then
sentence structure

But the life forms are as much part of the structure of the Earth as any inanimate portion is. It is all an inseparable part of a whole. If any animal is isolated totally from other forms of life, then death by starvation will surely follow. If isolated from water, death by dehydration will follow even faster. If isolated from air, whether free or dissolved in water, death by asphyxiation will follow still faster. If isolated from the Sun, animals will survive for a time, but plants would die, and if all plants died, all animals would starve.

— Isaac Asimov, "The Case against Man"

Collocation creates networks of meaning.

Collocation—the positioning of words together in expected ways around a particular topic—occurs quite naturally to writers and usually forms recognizable networks of meaning for readers. For example, in a paragraph on a high school graduation, a reader might expect to encounter such words as *valedictorian, diploma, commencement, honors, cap* and *gown,* and *senior class.* The paragraph that follows uses five collocation chains:

housewife, cooking, neighbor, home

clocks, calculated, progression, precise

obstinacy, vagaries, problem

sun, clear days, cloudy ones, sundial, cast its light, angle, seasons, sun, weather

cooking, fire, matches, hot coals smoldering, ashes, go out, bed-warming pan

The seventeenth-century housewife not only had to make do without thermometers, she also had to make do without clocks, which were scarce and dear throughout the sixteen hundreds. She calculated cooking times by the progression of the sun; her cooking must have been more precise on clear days than on cloudy ones. Marks were sometimes painted on the floor, providing her with a rough sundial, but she still had to make allowance for the obstinacy of the sun in refusing to cast its light at the same angle as the seasons changed; but she was used to allowing for the vagaries of sun and weather. She also had a problem starting her fire in the morning; there were no matches. If she had allowed the hot coals smoldering under the ashes to go out, she had to borrow some from a neighbor, carrying them home with care, perhaps in a bed-warming pan.

—Waverly Root and Richard de Rouchement, *Eating in America*

EXERCISE 10.7

Now that you know more about pronoun reference, word repetition, synonyms, sentence structure repetition, and collocation, turn to Brian Cable's essay in Chapter 3 and identify the cohesive devices you find in paragraphs 1–5. Underline each cohesive device you can find; there will be many. You might also want to connect with lines the various pronoun, related-word, and synonym chains you find. You could also try listing the separate collocation chains. Consider how these cohesive devices help you read and make sense of the passage.

EXERCISE 10.8

Choose one of your recent essays, and select any three contiguous paragraphs. Underline every cohesive device you can find; there will be many. Try to connect with lines the various pronoun, related-word, and synonym chains you find. Also try listing the separate collocation chains.

You will be surprised and pleased at how extensively you rely on cohesive ties. Indeed, you could not produce readable text without cohesive ties. Consider these questions relevant to your development as a writer: Are all of your pronoun references clear? Are you straining for synonyms when repeated words would do? Do you ever repeat sentence structures to emphasize connections? Do you trust yourself to put collocation to work?

Transitions

A **transition** serves as a bridge to connect one paragraph, sentence, clause, or word with another. It also identifies the kind of connection by indicating to readers how the item preceding the transition relates to the one that follows it. Transitions help readers anticipate how the next paragraph or sentence will affect the meaning of what they have just read. There are three basic groups of transitions, based on the relationships they indicate: logical, temporal, and spatial.

Transitions emphasize logical relationships.

Transitions help readers follow the *logical relationships* within an argument. How such transitions work is illustrated in this tightly and passionately reasoned paragraph by James Baldwin:

Transitions
reinforce the logic
of the argument.

> The black man insists, by whatever means he finds at his disposal, that the white man cease to regard him as an exotic rarity and recognize him as a human being. This is a very charged and difficult moment, for there is a great deal of will power involved in the white man's naïveté. Most people are not naturally malicious, and the white man prefers to keep the black man at a certain human remove because it is easier for him thus to preserve his simplicity and to avoid being called to account for crimes committed by his forefathers, or his neighbors. He is inescapably aware, nevertheless, that he is in a better position in the world than black men are, nor can he quite put to death the suspicion that he is hated by black men therefore. He does not wish to be hated, neither does he wish to change places, and at this point in his uneasiness he can scarcely avoid having recourse to those legends which white men have created about black men, the most unusual effect of which is that the white man finds himself enmeshed, so to speak, in his own language which describes hell, as well as the attributes which lead one to hell, as being black as night.
>
> —James Baldwin, "Stranger in the Village"

Transitions Showing Logical Relationships

- *To introduce another item in a series:* first . . . , second; in the second place; for one thing . . . , for another; next; then; furthermore; moreover; in addition; finally; last; also; similarly; besides; and; as well as

- *To introduce an illustration or other specification:* in particular; specifically; for instance; for example; that is; namely

- *To introduce a result or a cause:* consequently; as a result; hence; accordingly; thus; so; therefore; then; because; since; for

- *To introduce a restatement:* that is; in other words; in simpler terms; to put it differently

- *To introduce a conclusion or summary:* in conclusion; finally; all in all; evidently; clearly; actually; to sum up; altogether; of course

- *To introduce an opposing point:* but; however; yet; nevertheless; on the contrary; on the other hand; in contrast; still; neither; nor

- *To introduce a concession to an opposing view:* certainly; naturally; of course; it is true; to be sure; granted

- *To resume the original line of reasoning after a concession:* nonetheless; all the same; even though; still; nevertheless

Transitions can indicate a sequence in time.

In addition to showing logical connections, transitions may indicate **temporal relationships**—a sequence or progression in time—as this example illustrates:

Transitions to relationships of time

That night, we drank tea and then vodka with lemon peel steeped in it. The four of us talked in Russian and English about mutual friends and American railroads and the Rolling Stones. Seryozha loves the Stones, and his face grew wistful as we spoke about their recent album, *Some Girls*. He played a tape of "Let It Bleed" over and over, until we could translate some difficult phrases for him; after that, he came out with the phrases at intervals during the evening, in a pretty decent imitation of Jagger's Cockney snarl. He was an adroit and oddly formal host, inconspicuously filling our teacups and politely urging us to eat bread and cheese and chocolate. While he talked to us, he teased Anya, calling her "Piglet," and she shook back her bangs and glowered at him. It was clear that theirs was a fiery relationship. After a while, we talked about ourselves. Anya told us about painting and printmaking and about how hard it was to buy supplies in Moscow. There had been something angry in her dark face since the beginning of the evening; I thought at first that it meant she didn't like Americans; but now I realized that it was a constant, barely suppressed rage at her own situation.

— ANDREA LEE, *Russian Journal*

Transitions Showing Temporal Relationships

- **To indicate frequency:** frequently; hourly; often; occasionally; now and then; day after day; every so often; again and again
- **To indicate duration:** during; briefly; for a long time; minute by minute; while
- **To indicate a particular time:** now; then; at that time; in those days; last Sunday; next Christmas; in 2003; at the beginning of August; at six o'clock; first thing in the morning; two months ago; when
- **To indicate the beginning:** at first; in the beginning; since; before then
- **To indicate the middle:** in the meantime; meanwhile; as it was happening; at that moment; at the same time; simultaneously; next; then
- **To indicate the end and beyond:** eventually; finally; at last; in the end; subsequently; later; afterward

Transitions can indicate relationships in space.

Transitions showing **spatial relationships** orient readers to the objects in a scene, as illustrated in these paragraphs:

Transitions to show relationships in space

On Georgia 155, I crossed Troublesome Creek, then went through groves of pecan trees aligned one with the next like fenceposts. The pastures grew a green almost blue, and syrupy water the color of a dusty sunset filled the ponds. Around the farmhouses, from wires strung high above the ground, swayed gourds hollowed out for purple martins.

The land rose again on the other side of the Chattahoochee River, and Highway 34 went to the ridgetops where long views over the hills opened in all directions. Here was the tail of the Appalachian backbone, its gradual descent to the Gulf. Near the Alabama stateline stood a couple of LAST CHANCE! bars.

— WILLIAM LEAST HEAT MOON, *Blue Highways*

Transitions Showing Spatial Relationships

- *To indicate closeness:* close to; near; next to; alongside; adjacent to; facing
- *To indicate distance:* in the distance; far; beyond; away; there
- *To indicate direction:* up/down; sideways; along; across; to the right/left; in front of/behind; above/below; inside/outside; toward/away from

---

EXERCISE 10.9

Turn to William Akana's essay in Chapter 7. Relying on the lists of transitions just given, underline the transitions in paragraphs 4–6. Consider how the transitions connect the ideas from sentence to sentence. Suggest any further transitions that could be added to make the relationships even clearer.

EXERCISE 10.10

Select a recent essay of your own. Choose at least three paragraphs, and underline the logical, temporal, and spatial transitions. Depending on the kind of writing you were doing, you may find few, if any, transitions in one category or another. For example, an essay speculating about causes may not include any spatial transitions; writing about a remembered event might not contain transitions showing logical relationships.

Consider how your transitions relate the ideas from sentence to sentence. Compare your transitions with those in the lists in this text. Do you find that you are making full use of the repertoire? Do you find gaps between any of your sentences that a well-chosen transition would close?

Headings and Subheadings

Headings and **subheadings** — brief phrases set off from the text in various ways — can provide visible cues to readers about the content and organization of a text. Headings can be distinguished from the text in numerous ways, including the selective use of capital letters, bold or italic type, or different sizes of type. To be most helpful to readers, headings should be phrased similarly and follow a predictable system.

Headings indicate sections and levels.

In this chapter, the headings in the section Paragraphing, beginning on p. 319, provide a good example of a system of headings that can readily be outlined:

Paragraphing

Paragraph indents signal related ideas

Topic sentences announce the paragraph's focus

Announcing the Topic

Making a Transition

Positioning the Topic Sentence

Notice that in this example, the heading system has three levels. The first-level heading sits on its own line and is set in a large, red font; this heading stands out most visibly among the others. (It is one of five such headings in this chapter.) The second-level heading also sits on its own line but is set in a smaller font (and uses black type). The first of these second-level headings has no subheadings beneath it, while the second has three. These third-level headings, in black, do not sit on their own lines but run into the paragraph they introduce, as you can see if you turn back to pp. 320–22.

All of these headings follow a parallel grammatical structure: short nouns at the first level; complete sentences at the second level; and "-ing" noun phrases at the third level.

To learn more about distinguishing headings from surrounding text and about setting up systems of headings, see p. 387 in Chapter 14.

Headings are not common in all genres.

Headings may not be necessary in short essays: thesis statements, forecasting statements, well-positioned topic sentences, and transition sentences may be all the cues the reader needs. Headings are rare in some genres, such as essays about remembered events (Chapter 2) and essays profiling people and places (Chapter 3). Headings appear more frequently in such genres as concept explanations, position papers, public policy proposals, and evaluations (Chapters 4–7).

At least two headings are needed at each level.

Before dividing their essays into sections with headings and subheadings, writers need to make sure their discussion is detailed enough to support at least two headings at each level. The frequency and placement of headings depend entirely on the content and how it is divided and organized. Keep in mind that headings do not reduce the need for other cues to keep readers on track.

EXERCISE 10.11

Turn either to Karen Kornbluh's "Win-Win Flexibility" in Chapter 6 or to Christine Rosen's "The Myth of Multitasking" in Chapter 7, and survey that essay's system of headings. If you have not read the essay, read or skim it now. Consider how the headings help readers anticipate what is coming and how the argument is organized. Decide whether the headings substitute for or complement other cues for keeping readers on track. Consider whether the headings are grammatically parallel.

EXERCISE 10.12

Select one of your essays that might benefit from headings. Develop a system of headings, and insert them where appropriate. Be prepared to justify your headings in light of the discussion about headings in this section.

11

Analyzing and Synthesizing Arguments

Analyzing and synthesizing are complementary strategies: Whereas analyzing involves taking something apart, synthesizing involves bringing different things together. Anytime you use multiple sources, you need to begin by analyzing each source so that you can then synthesize the various sources' ideas, information, and arguments.

While any text — or anything, for that matter — can be analyzed, the skills involved are particularly critical in the realm of argument. For this reason, this chapter provides a set of strategies for analyzing and synthesizing arguments.

Analysis and synthesis do not have to be exhaustive. In fact, cataloging everything indiscriminately as if every detail were equally important is counterproductive. To be effective, analysis and synthesis must be selective and focus on what is significant in a text or group of texts.

Because arguments serve to express writers' views and aim to convince readers of the validity of those views, their most significant features are the ways in which they convey the writers' thoughts and attempt to influence readers. An **analysis** of an individual argument essay, then, examines how the writer's presentation of particular reasons or kinds of evidence reflects his or her views and how this presentation would likely appeal to the intended readers. If you examine multiple essays arguing about a controversial issue, their significant features for the purpose of a **synthesis** are the points of agreement and disagreement in the arguments.

Analyzing Arguments

To analyze an argument, you need to read it closely and critically, asking questions about how it is put together and what its underlying assumptions are. (Note that you will almost certainly need to read the text several times to get all you can out of it.) The Criteria for Analyzing Arguments chart on p. 333 will help you do a probing critical analysis of any argument.

Applying the criteria for analyzing arguments.

The Criteria for Analyzing Arguments include two categories: basic features and motivating factors. The basic features include the issue, the position, the argument, and the counterargument. The motivating factors include values, ideology, concerns, and priorities.

CRITERIA FOR ANALYZING ARGUMENTS

Features of the Argument

- **Issue.** What issue does the writer address? How does the writer define or frame the issue?

- **Position.** What is the writer's position on the issue (thesis statement)?

- **Argument.** What are the main reasons and kinds of evidence (facts, statistics, examples, authorities, etc.) the writer uses to support his or her position?

- **Counterargument.** What opposing arguments does the writer anticipate? Does the writer **concede** (agree with) or **refute** (disagree with) these arguments? How does the writer attempt to refute opposing arguments?

Motivating Factors

Factors such as the following may be stated explicitly or implied. If you find any other factor that you consider important but that is not on the list, give it a name and include it in your annotations.

- **Values—Moral, Ethical, or Religious Principles** (for example, justice, equality, the public good, "do unto others," social responsibility, stewardship of the natural environment)

- **Ideology and Ideals** (for example, democratic ideals — everyone is created equal and has the right to life, liberty, and the pursuit of happiness; capitalist ideals; socialist ideals; feminist ideals)

- **Needs and Interests** (for example, food, shelter, work, respect, privacy, choice)

- **Fears and Concerns** (for example, regarding safety, socioeconomic status, power, consequences of actions taken or not taken)

- **Priorities and Agendas** about what is most important or urgent (for example, whether law and order is more important than securing justice and equality, whether the right to life trumps all other concerns, whether combating global warming ought to be a principal concern of government)

- **Binary Thinking** (the assumption that things are "either/or" — for example, that only one of two outcomes is possible, that there can only be winners or losers in a situation, that only two positions are possible, that the world is divided into "us" against "them")

Analyzing motivating factors is important because it helps you better understand the argument's basic features. You accomplish this analysis by considering the writer's reasons for choosing particular way(s) of framing the issue, establishing a position, constructing the argument, and anticipating and responding to counterarguments. For example, an analysis of the motivating factors behind the writer's way of framing the issue can lead to a deeper understanding of the argument in its rhetorical context.

Let's take as an example the issue of whether the government should be allowed to torture suspected terrorists. Those in favor of torture often frame this issue in either/or terms: Either we use torture, or terrorists will destroy us. These proponents usually illustrate this way of framing by invoking the so-called "ticking time-bomb" scenario, which assumes that there is limited time to avert a disaster and that the government can only do so by forcing a wrongdoer to disclose the plans for it. Framing the issue in this way involves certain underlying assumptions: namely, that no action other than torture will elicit the needed information, and that the information gained through torture is reliable. It also implies a set of specific underlying values, including the following two judgments: that the terrorist's life and/or well-being is less important than the lives of those potentially harmed in a disaster, and that the torturer has the moral right to make this distinction. Throughout the rest of this chapter, we will show you how one student built an analysis and synthesis of this argument by applying the Criteria for Analyzing Arguments.

Annotating a text and creating a chart.

Annotating a given text and creating a chart like the one on p. 335 will make it easy for you to locate the argument's key features.

1. Begin by carefully reading and annotating the text, marking key passages, and adding questions, comments, and notes to the margins where you identify basic features and motivating factors.

2. Record the argument's basic features in a chart like the one on p. 335. Add paragraph numbers to the chart directing yourself to the places where the feature is evident. Add brief notes to the chart, or jot down key phrases to jog your memory.

3. Chart the argument's motivating factors, adding paragraph numbers and notes (if appropriate and helpful).

4. Chart any additional significant factors you might find, naming them appropriately.

Remember you may not find *every* basic feature or motivating factor in each essay.

macmillanhighered.com/conciseguide
Tutorials > Critical Reading > Active Reading Strategies

Coming up with a focus for your analysis.

Simply re-presenting the notes you have recorded in your chart would constitute a summary of the argument, not an analysis. To write an effective analysis of an argument, you need to explain the significance of what you have found.

To do so, reread the notes you recorded on your chart, and try to identify something — either a basic feature or a motivating factor, or some combination — that strikes you as interesting, unusual, perplexing, or otherwise worth examining further. Try to express this insight in the form of an assertion about the text that will help your reader see it as you do. This insight will provide the focus for your analysis. You may use the sentence strategies following as a jumping-off point—you can always revise them later—or you can use language of your own from the start.

Annotations Chart: Analyzing [title of text]

Features of the Text	Issue	
	Position (Thesis)	
	Argument (Main supporting reasons and evidence)	
	Counterargument (Refutation, concession)	
Motivating Factors	Values (Moral, ethical, religious)	
	Ideology and Ideals (Cultural, legal, political)	
	Needs and Interests	
	Fears and Concerns	
	Priorities and Agendas	
	Binary Thinking?	
Other Factors		

Sentence Strategies for Analysis

Write a paragraph presenting each important point of disagreement or agreement:

To summarize or paraphrase the disagreement or potential agreement

▶ [Author X] takes the position that _____ because _____. [In contrast/Similarly], [author Y] thinks _____ because _____.

To choose quotations from each writer to analyze and compare their perspectives

▶ [Author X] claims: [quotation].

▶ X's use of [quoted word or phrase] shows that _____ [name motivating factor] is central to [her/his] way of thinking about the issue.

▶ [Author Y's] argument that [quotation], [however/also], shows that [she/he] values _____ more highly than _____.

To explain what you think are the different or similar motivating factors influencing the writers' perspectives, and why you think so

▶ Whereas [author X's] argument is based on _____ [name motivating factor], [author Y's] is primarily concerned with [name motivating factor].

▶ Like [author X], [author Y] is primarily concerned about _____ [motivating factor].

A Sample Analysis

In this section, you will see how student Melissa Mae used the Criteria for Analyzing Arguments to plan and write an analysis of "A Case for Torture," an essay that originally appeared in 2005 in the *Age*, a newspaper published in Melbourne, Australia. "A Case for Torture" was co-written by Mirko Bagaric, Dean and Head of the Deakin Law School in Melbourne, Australia, and Julie Clarke, Associate Head of Teaching and Learning in the same program. Bagaric and Clarke also coauthored a book, *Torture: When the Unthinkable Is Morally Permissible* (2006).

Mirko Bagaric and Julie Clarke │ *A Case for Torture*

1 Recent events stemming from the "war on terrorism" have highlighted the prevalence of torture. This is despite the fact that torture is almost universally deplored.

The formal prohibition against torture is absolute — there are no exceptions to it.

2 The belief that torture is always wrong is, however, misguided and symptomatic of

the alarmist and reflexive responses typically emanating from social commentators. It is this type of absolutist and short-sighted rhetoric that lies at the core of many distorted moral judgements that we as a community continue to make, resulting in an enormous amount of injustice and suffering in our society and far beyond our borders.

3   Torture is permissible where the evidence suggests that this is the only means, due to the immediacy of the situation, to save the life of an innocent person. The reason that torture in such a case is defensible and necessary is because the justification manifests from the closest thing we have to an inviolable right: the right to self-defence, which of course extends to the defence of another. Given the choice between inflicting a relatively small level of harm on a wrongdoer and saving an innocent person, it is verging on moral indecency to prefer the interests of the wrongdoer.

4   The analogy with self-defence is sharpened by considering the hostage-taking scenario, where a wrongdoer takes a hostage and points a gun to the hostage's head, threatening to kill the hostage unless a certain (unreasonable) demand is met. In such a case it is not only permissible, but desirable for police to shoot (and kill) the wrongdoer if they get a "clear shot." This is especially true if it's known that the wrongdoer has a history of serious violence, and hence is more likely to carry out the threat.

5   There is no logical or moral difference between this scenario and one where there is overwhelming evidence that a wrongdoer has kidnapped an innocent person and informs police that the victim will be killed by a co-offender if certain demands are not met.

6   In the hostage scenario, it is universally accepted that it is permissible to violate the right to life of the aggressor to save an innocent person. How can it be wrong to violate an even less important right (the right to physical integrity) by torturing the aggressor in order to save a life in the second scenario?

7   There are three main [objections] to even the above limited approval of torture. The first is the slippery slope argument: if you start allowing torture in a limited context, the situations in which it will be used will increase.

8   This argument is not sound in the context of torture. First, the floodgates are already open — torture is used widely, despite the absolute legal prohibition against it. Amnesty International has recently reported that it had received, during 2003, reports of torture and ill-treatment from 132 countries, including the United States, Japan and France. It is, in fact, arguable that it is the existence of an unrealistic absolute ban that has driven torture beneath the radar of accountability, and that legalisation in very rare circumstances would in fact reduce instances of it.

9   The second main argument is that torture will dehumanise society. This is no more true in relation to torture than it is with self-defence, and in fact the contrary is true. A society that elects to favour the interests of wrongdoers over those of the innocent, when a choice must be made between the two, is in need of serious ethical rewiring.

10   A third [objection] is that we can never be totally sure that torturing a person will in fact result in us saving an innocent life. This, however, is the same situation as in all cases of self-defence. To revisit the hostage example, the hostage-taker's gun might in fact be empty, yet it is still permissible to shoot. As with any decision, we must decide on the best evidence at the time.

11   Torture in order to save an innocent person is the only situation where it is clearly justifiable. This means that the recent high-profile incidents of torture, apparently undertaken as punitive measures or in a bid to acquire information where there was no evidence of an immediate risk to the life of an innocent person, were reprehensible.

12   Will a real-life situation actually occur where the only option is between torturing

a wrongdoer or saving an innocent person? Perhaps not. However, a minor alteration to the Douglas Wood situation illustrates that the issue is far from moot. If Western forces in Iraq arrested one of Mr. Wood's captors, it would be a perverse ethic that required us to respect the physical integrity of the captor, and not torture him to ascertain Mr. Wood's whereabouts, in preference to taking all possible steps to save Mr. Wood.*

13   Even if a real-life situation where torture is justifiable does not eventuate, the above argument in favour of torture in limited circumstances needs to be made because it will encourage the community to think more carefully about moral judgements we collectively hold that are the cause of an enormous amount of suffering in the world.

14   First, no right or interest is absolute. Secondly, rights must always yield to consequences, which are the ultimate criteria upon which the soundness of a decision is gauged. Lost lives hurt a lot more than bent principles.

15   Thirdly, we must take responsibility not only for the things that we do, but also for the things that we can — but fail to — prevent. The retort that we are not responsible for the lives lost through a decision not to torture a wrongdoer because we did not create the situation is code for moral indifference.

16   Equally vacuous is the claim that we in the affluent West have no responsibility for more than 13,000 people dying daily due to starvation. Hopefully, the debate on torture will prompt us to correct some of these fundamental failings.

---

*Douglas Wood was taken hostage in Iraq in 2005. — Ed.

Melissa Mae's annotations.

Mae used the Criteria for Analyzing Arguments to guide her close reading of Bagaric and Clarke's argument. When she first read the essay, she used a highlighter to mark important passages, and she made a few annotations about the argument's basic features. When she began to record her observations in a chart, she realized that her annotations were too scanty to help her (or her reader) understand the essay deeply. She therefore returned to the essay and reread it, this time using the Criteria more systematically.

When she was done, Mae was surprised by how much she had written in the margins. She found herself not only marking where each of the basic features appears in the text, but also going deeper in her analysis by identifying the moral values and ideological principles that energize the argument. Mae also added several questions to her annotations that reflect her uncertainty about the argument's validity.

Below is an excerpt from Mae's annotations. Following this excerpt is the annotation chart she completed for the entire essay.

Thesis: Torture justified, even required to save innocent victim	Torture is permissible where the evidence suggests 3 that this is the only means, due to the immediacy of the situation, to save the life of an innocent person. The reason that torture in such a case is defensible and necessary is because the justification manifests from the
Ideology (legal rights) True?	closest thing we have to an inviolable right: the right to

self-defence, which of course extends to the defence of another. Given the choice between inflicting a relatively small level of harm on a wrongdoer and saving an innocent person, it is verging on moral indecency to prefer the interests of the wrongdoer.

Saving victim outweighs harming wrongdoer

The analogy with self-defence is sharpened by con- 4 sidering the hostage-taking scenario, where a wrongdoer takes a hostage and points a gun to the hostage's head, threatening to kill the hostage unless a certain (unreasonable) demand is met. In such a case it is not only permissible, but desirable for police to shoot (and kill) the wrongdoer if they get a "clear shot." This is especially true if it's known that the wrongdoer has a history of serious violence, and hence is more likely to carry out the threat.

Does self-defense analogy hold up?

There is no logical or moral difference between this 5 scenario and one where there is overwhelming evidence that a wrongdoer has kidnapped an innocent person and informs police that the victim will be killed by a co-offender if certain demands are not met.

Closer to terrorist situation?

In the hostage scenario, it is universally accepted that 6 it is permissible to violate the right to life of the aggressor to save an innocent person. How can it be wrong to violate an even less important right (the right to physical integrity) by torturing the aggressor in order to save a life in the second scenario?

True?

Logic: If killing to save life OK, then torturing to save life also OK.

Melissa Mae's analysis

In reviewing her annotations of "A Case for Torture," Mae decided that Bagaric and Clarke's essay fell short in three areas: its assumptions about moral "truths," its use of a faulty analogy, and its confusion of moral and legal imperatives. Mae decided that her challenge to the argument's validity on these three grounds was strong enough to provide the focus of her analysis, which she envisioned as inviting further discussion on the issue of government-sponsored torture.

Melissa Mae's Annotation Chart: Analyzing "A Case for Torture"

Features of the Text	*Issue*	war on terrorism (par. 1)
	Position **(Thesis)**	"Torture permissible . . . only means . . . to save the life of an innocent person." (3)
	Argument **(Main supporting reasons and evidence)**	torture sometimes OK: analogy: self-defense (3) analogy: hostage-talking scenario ⟶ b/c If it's right to kill to save innocent life, then it's right to torture (4–6) b/c it's necessary in real life — Wood example (12) b/c "no right or interest is absolute" (14)
	Counterargument **(Refutation, concession)**	refutes "absolute" prohibition against torture argument (1–2) refutes slippery slope, dehumanizes society, & info untrustworthy arguments (7–10) concedes cases torture is wrong ⟶ therefore qualifies thesis: not when punitive, only in immediate risk (9–11)
Motivating Factors	*Values* **(Moral, ethical, religious)**	save innocent life (2–3) need "to think more carefully about moral judgments" (13–16)
	Ideology and Ideals **(Cultural, legal, political)**	right to self-defense (3) "universally accepted . . . to violate the right to life of the aggressor to save an innocent person" (6) "Lost lives hurt a lot more than bent principles." (14)
	Fears and Concerns	post–9/11 fear of terrorism (1)
	Priorities and Agendas	save innocent life (3)
	Binary Thinking?	"only option is between torturing a wrongdoer or saving an innocent person? Perhaps not. However . . ." (12)

"A Case for Torture": A Questionable Argument

Melissa Mae

1   In 2004, when the abuse of detainees at Abu Ghraib was revealed, many Americans became concerned that the United States was using torture as part of its interrogation of war-on-terror detainees. Although the government denied a torture program existed, we now know that the Bush administration did order what it called "enhanced interrogation techniques" such as waterboarding and sleep deprivation, which clearly fell under the common understanding of torture.

2   The central question of whether torture should be used has been the subject of much heated debate. In a 2005 article, "A Case for Torture," Mirko Bagaric and Julie Clarke, law faculty at Australia's Deakin University, argue that torture is justifiable, morally as well as legally. In fact, they claim that torture is not only "defensible" but "necessary" under certain circumstances (par. 3). The authors raise some interesting points, but their argument has several fundamental problems: They present debatable moral claims as obvious truths, they make use of a faulty analogy, and they do not consider the crucial distinction between what is morally justified and what is legally prudent.

3   In their opening paragraphs, Bagaric and Clarke make clear that they are arguing against the position that torture is always wrong and should never be used. They call this view "absolutist" and therefore "misguided" (par. 2). Although they claim that torture is "almost universally deplored" (par. 1), they assert that there are times when it would be morally indecent *not* to use torture (par. 3).

4   These are assertions that appeal to the pragmatic inclinations of many people but do little to advance a moral argument. Bagaric and Clarke conclude the essay by asserting that "no right or interest is absolute" and that consequences "are the ultimate criteria upon which the soundness of a decision is gauged" (par. 14). This is an assumption, however, not an argument. There are plenty of thinkers who argue that consequences are *not* the ultimate criteria for making moral decisions. Simply asserting the opposite is not an adequate substitute for a real argument.

5   One of the authors' major claims is that using torture in order to extract information needed to avert an imminent tragedy is analogous to self-defense, which they say is "an inviolable right . . . , which of course extends to the defence of another" (par. 3). They refine this analogy by claiming that the so-called "ticking time-bomb" scenario parallels a scenario in which a wrongdoer kidnaps someone (pars. 4–6). Since we would allow a police officer to shoot the kidnapper, they reason, and since killing is obviously worse than torture, then torture should be allowed in "ticking time-bomb" situations.

6   Even granting Bagaric and Clarke some questionable assumptions — specifically, that killing is always worse than torture, and that it is indeed morally acceptable for the police to shoot someone holding a gun to a hostage's head — their analogy does not work. Asserting that self-defense "of course" extends to "defense of another" is just that — an assertion, not an argument. Similarly, claiming that torturing someone for information is equivalent to the defense of an innocent "other" is a muddier proposition than the authors seem to acknowledge. In the hostage-taking case, killing the wrongdoer with a clean shot stops him from killing the hostage. In the ticking time-bomb case, torture only yields the *possibility* that the wrongdoer will divulge accurate information that *might* enable the police to disarm the bomb.

7   Further, the authors are unable to produce a single real-life example of the ticking time-bomb situation. While the image of police sharp-shooters poised to take a "clear shot" of the hostage-taker/terrorist is vivid and familiar from television news as well as from innumerable crime programs and films, it poorly represents the situations in which war-on-terror detainees have actually been tortured.

8   The authors seem to acknowledge the importance of this point by asking, "Will a real-life situation actually occur where the only option is between torturing a wrongdoer or saving an innocent person? Perhaps not." (par. 12). They seem to suggest that such cases *do* exist, however, by immediately afterwards bringing up the case of Douglas Wood, who was taken hostage in Iraq and held for six weeks until he was rescued by U.S. and Iraqi soldiers. In doing so, Bagaric and Clarke attempt at the same time to put a face to the hostage scenario and thereby tap into readers' emotions.

9   However, a news report about the rescue of Wood published in the *Age*, where Bagaric and Clarke's essay was also published, says that the soldiers "effectively 'stumbled across Wood' during a 'routine' raid on a suspected insurgent weapons cache" ("Firefight"). Wood's rescuers appear to have acted on information they got from ordinary informants rather than through torture. This explains the need for the "minor alteration" (par. 12) that Bagaric and Clarke suggest would be necessary for the case to fulfill the requirements of their scenario. People caught up in the drama of the situation may overlook the detail that Bagaric and Clarke call "minor." But the authors' failure to provide this or indeed any real-world situation to bolster their analogy and the hypothetical scenario they propose is an important, indeed a crucial, detail that undercuts their argument.

10   The authors argue (though, as we have seen, with questionable effectiveness) that there are some extreme instances in which torture is moral, and they want to move from this conclusion to the conclusion that the law should be amended to allow for torture in these situations. There are, however, many situations in which what is moral to do and what is legal to do part ways. For instance, most people would accept that it is morally acceptable to break the law and run a red light to take a critically ill child to the hospital. It does not follow from this, however, that a variety of exceptions for obeying traffic signals should be incorporated into the law. Accordingly, then, Bagaric and Clarke need to do more than show that torture is morally acceptable in some instances — they need to show that these instances are significant enough to justify changes in legislation. The authors fail to offer any convincing evidence that such legal change is necessary.

Works Cited

Bagaric, Mirko, and Julie Clarke. "A Case for Torture." *theage.com.au*. The Age, 17 May 2005. Web. 1 May 2009.

"Firefight as Wood Rescued." *theage.com.au*. The Age, 16 June 2005. Web. 2 May 2009.

From Analysis to Synthesis

Synthesizing involves presenting ideas and information gleaned from different sources, and it suggests the ways in which those sources relate to one another. For example, one source may provide information that expands on the information in another source, or it may present arguments that challenge arguments in another reading. When you synthesize material from different sources, you construct a conversation among your sources, a conversation in which you also participate.

Synthesis is a critical step in the process of writing on any topic in which you use multiple sources. In order to create an effective synthesis, you need first to read the sources to see what you want to focus on. This kind of reading will be faster and at least initially more superficial than the kind of close analysis that is required to write an essay analyzing just one or two sources, as illustrated above in Mae's analysis essay, "'A Case for Torture': A Questionable Argument." For an essay based on a multisource synthesis, you read to identify the important arguments offered by the sources, and you search for quotes to illustrate these arguments.

Before you can do any of this, of course, you have to find credible sources that speak in interesting ways to the topic on which you are writing. For helpful information on finding and evaluating sources, see Chapters 16 and 17.

A Sample Synthesis
Melissa Mae's process

After analyzing "A Case for Torture" (see pp. 335–38), Melissa Mae continued to work on the issue of government-sponsored torture. In looking through additional sources that treated the issue, Mae realized that what interested her most was the ways in which various sources addressed the ticking time-bomb scenario, so she decided to focus her synthesis on this scenario.

Mae annotated the sources, highlighting passages where they discuss the scenario. She also tried to identify the topic or argument of each highlighted passage. As she worked with the sources, Mae began to identify several arguments that she thought she might be able to use in her essay. She created a Synthesis Chart by collecting quotes and evidence from the sources and by organizing them under headings that each quote or piece of evidence supported. She found that a number of the sources discussed several of the arguments, so there were numerous good quotes to choose from. For other arguments, she could only use one or two possible quotes. (A small portion of her chart appears on the next page.)

After Mae had charted her sources, she reread the chart, thinking about which arguments she should include and what order would make the most sense. Her solution to this challenge, and her way of illuminating the various arguments for her readers, appear in the sample synthesis essay after the chart, on pp. 346–51.

Melissa Mae's Synthesis Chart

Argument	*Supporting Quotes/Evidence*
The ticking time-bomb (TTB) scenario's frequent discussion may have increased support for torture.	Bellamy describes TTB's ubiquity in discussion and fictional portrayals (141) 1.7 million search results for TTB on Google On *24*: "Each season of *24*, which has been airing . . . But on our show it happens every week" (Mayer) — use whole thing? Television Council Chart "tolerance for torture" (Ip, 40) Henry Shue: "moral reasons for not saying it . . ." (47) — quote all? Žižek quote: "And, in a way, essays like Alter's . . ." (from *London Review of Books*)
The TTB scenario supports the government's practice of torture.	Mayerfeld quote starting "the main justification for . . ." (110) quote from the Bybee memo in Ip (44)
The TTB scenario shows that absolute prohibition on torture is unsustainable.	Bagaric and Clarke use in "A Case for Torture" from Bagaric and Clarke: "Torture is permissible where . . ." Brecher's take on Dershowitz Scarry quote on Dershowitz: ""Alan Dershowitz has asked . . ." (285) Marc Thiessen quote: "The fact is, in real life . . ." (192) Jeff McMahan: "If nothing else, this example exposes . . ." (114)

The Centrality of the Ticking Time-bomb Scenario
in Arguments Justifying Torture

Melissa Mae

1 In the post-9/11 world, the ticking time-bomb scenario has played a central role in arguments justifying the use of torture. As Alex J. Bellamy, professor of peace and conflict studies at the University of Queensland, has pointed out, the scenario is ubiquitous (141). A Google search of "ticking bomb scenario" and "ticking time-bomb scenario" calls up more than 1.7 million results. The scenario dominates discussion of torture in much mass-media reporting, commentary, and debate. It is also an important focus of the numerous scholarly books and articles published about torture in the last decade.

2 But possibly the most persuasive evocation of the scenario was in the television program *24*, which aired on the Fox network from 2001 to 2010. Here's how the program was described in a 2007 *New Yorker* article by investigative reporter Jane Mayer, author of *The Dark Side: The Inside Story of How the War on Terror Turned into a War on American Ideals* (2008), a study of the legal and political debate over torture inside President George W. Bush's administration:

> Each season of *24*, which has been airing on Fox since 2001, depicts a single, panic-laced day in which Jack Bauer . . . must unravel and undermine a conspiracy that imperils the nation. Terrorists are poised to set off nuclear bombs or bioweapons, or in some other way annihilate entire cities. . . . Frequently, the dilemma is stark: a resistant suspect can either be accorded due process — allowing a terrorist plot to proceed — or be tortured in pursuit of a lead. Bauer invariably chooses coercion. With unnerving efficiency, suspects are beaten, suffocated, electrocuted, drugged, assaulted with knives, or more exotically abused; almost without fail, these suspects divulge critical secrets.
>
> The show's appeal, however, lies less in its violence than in its giddily literal rendering of a classic thriller trope: the "ticking time bomb" plot. . . . Bob Cochran, who created the show with Surnow, admitted, "Most terrorism experts will tell you that the 'ticking time

bomb' situation never occurs in real life, or very rarely. But on our
show it happens every week." (Mayer)

As the Parents Television Council has demonstrated (see Fig. 1), scenes of
torture dominated television in the period following 9/11 and may have
intensified the persuasive power of the ticking time-bomb scenario. In
fact, John Ip argues that the rise in the public's "tolerance for torture" can
be attributed mainly to the ticking bomb scenario (40). In order to take
a responsible position on the critical issue of government-supported
torture, it is necessary to understand the power — and the real-world
applicability — of this well-known scenario.

3   Not only is the ticking bomb scenario ubiquitous, but according to
Jamie Mayerfeld the scenario is "the main justification for the use of
torture by the U.S. government in the 'War on Terror'" (110). The scenario
was often part of official statements, most notably the Bybee memos
justifying harsh interrogation methods:

> [A] detainee may possess information that could enable the
> United States to prevent attacks that potentially could equal or

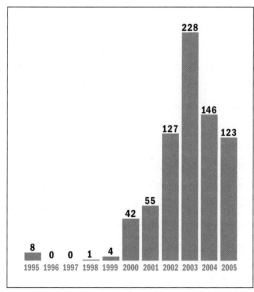

Fig. 1. Graph courtesy Human Rights First.
Source: Parents Television Council.

surpass the September 11 attacks in their magnitude. Clearly, any harm that might occur during an interrogation would pale to insignificance compared to the harm avoided by preventing such an attack, which could take hundreds or thousands of lives. (qtd in Ip 44)

4   It is relatively easy to find examples of the scenario used by proponents of government-sponsored torture: The article "A Case for Torture" by legal scholars Mirko Bagaric and Julie Clarke is one of many that uses the scenario to argue for the limited use of the otherwise "universally deplored" practice of torture. Bob Brecher, like many other commentators, is especially concerned that the influential Harvard Law professor Alan Dershowitz bases his argument that torture is justified on the scenario. A number of essays have been published refuting Dershowitz's argument — for example, Brecher's chapter titled "The Fantasy of the Ticking Bomb Scenario" in his book *Torture and the Ticking Bomb* and Elaine Scarry's "Five Errors in the Reasoning of Alan Dershowitz." Scarry writes: "Alan Dershowitz has asked us to put aside our commitment to an unwavering prohibition on torture, to enter into an open debate with him, and to step into that debate by passing through the threshold of the ticking bomb case, a case whose framing assumptions are erroneous" (285).

5   The scenario is used by virtually everyone, however — critics as well as proponents of torture. In a review of a collection of scholarly essays on torture published by Oxford University Press, Corey Robin wrote: "Neo-cons in the White House are not the only ones in thrall to romantic notions of danger and catastrophe. Academics are, too. Every scholarly discussion of torture . . . begins with the ticking time-bomb scenario" (qtd. in Brecher 16-17). What Bob Brecher finds "remarkable . . . is that so many *opponents* of interrogational torture appear not to have given much more thought to the 'facts' of the ticking bomb scenario examples than its supporters" (18).

6   The primary argument against the ticking bomb scenario is that it is unrealistic, a "fantasy," as Brecher says. Jamie Mayerfeld asserts that "in the long history of counter-terrorist campaigns there has not been one verified report of a genuine ticking bomb torture scenario. There

has not been a verified incident that even comes close to the ticking bomb torture scenario" (111). Former Bush administration officials such as Vice President Dick Cheney and CIA Director George Tenet and supporters like columnist Charles Krauthammer disagree, claiming that "enhanced interrogation techniques" used on Khalid Sheik Mohammed and Abu Zubaydah produced information that forestalled terrorist attacks.

7   However, an August 2009 *Newsweek* article referring to recently released CIA documents makes the point that the documents are vague as to "whether, under the stress and pain of intense interrogation, detainees gave false information that their questioners wanted to hear" and "whether the same information could have been obtained through nonviolent interrogation tactics." Moreover, the article calls into question the claims of immediacy and imminent threat on which justifications of torture are based:

> A former intelligence officer . . . noted that in selling the notion of "enhanced" interrogation techniques to congressional leaders, the Bush administration regularly argued that the main purpose of the techniques was to extract information that could be used to foil imminent terror plots. But the inspector general said his investigation failed to "uncover any evidence that these plots were imminent." (Hosenball)

If torture is used even when there is no ticking bomb — and no credible evidence to suggest there is one — then shouldn't the argument based on the scenario be called into question?

8   David Luban makes the point that if there is no imminent threat — what in the law is referred to as necessity — then torture is revealed to be merely "a fishing expedition" and should not be justifiable under "[t]he limitation to emergency exceptions, implicit in the ticking-bomb story" (1441). Everyone agrees that the scenario dramatizes the necessity of acting quickly and aggressively to prevent disaster. It has been used to open the door for torture under extraordinary circumstances. But if torture is used when we are in a continual state of war but there is no immediate threat, then torture becomes normalized. As Luban argues, "any responsible discussion of torture must address the practice of

torture, not the ticking-bomb hypothetical. . . . But somehow, we always manage to forget this and circle back to the ticking bomb. Its rhetorical power has made it indispensable" (1445).

9   The ticking time-bomb scenario as a justification for torture is a rhetorical ploy — Luban calls it "an intellectual fraud" (1452). The scenario provides a powerful visual image that manipulates our emotions, so vulnerable after the appalling visual images of 9/11. It makes us believe that we are reasonable people, following the law and not acting out of a desire for vengeance. As Luban points out, the ticking bomb scenario converts the torturer from a "cruel" sadist into a "conscientious public servant" like Jack Bauer, the hero of *24* (1436, 1441). In order to take an informed position on issues, like government-sponsored torture, that are literally matters of life and death, we need to be particularly careful in challenging received wisdom and, in this case, in responding viscerally to powerful rhetorical moves.

Works Cited

Bagaric, Mirko, and Julie Clarke. "A Case for Torture." *theage.com.au*. The Age, 17 May 2005. Web. 1 May 2011.

Bellamy, Alex J. "No Pain, No Gain? Torture and Ethics in the War on Terror." *International Affairs* 82.1 (2006): 121-48. Print.

Brecher, Bob. *Torture and the Ticking Bomb*. New York: Wiley, 2007. Print.

Dershowitz, Alan. *Why Terrorism Works*. New York: Yale UP, 2002. Print.

Hosenball, Mark. "Did Waterboarding Actually Work?" *Newsweek*. Newsweek, 24 Aug. 2009. Web. 21 Apr. 2011.

Ip, John. "Two Narratives of Torture." *Northwestern Journal of International Human Rights* 7.1 (2009): 35-77. Print.

Krauthammer, Charles. "The Torture Debate, Continued." *Washington Post*. Washington Post, 15 May 2009. Web. 11 June 2011.

Luban, David. "Liberalism and the Unpleasant Question of Torture." *Virginia Law Review* 91.6 (2005): 1425-61. Web. 20 Apr. 2011.

Mayer, Jane. "Whatever It Takes." *New Yorker*. Condé Nast Digital, 19 Feb. 2007. Web. 20 Apr. 2011.

Mayerfeld, Jamie. "In Defense of the Absolute Prohibition of Torture."
Public Affairs Quarterly 22.2 (2008): 109-28. Print.

Scarry, Elaine. "Five Errors in the Reasoning of Alan Dershowitz." *Torture: A Collection*. Ed. Sanford Levinson. New York: Oxford UP, 2004. Print.

12

Analyzing Visuals

We live in a highly visual world. Every day we are deluged with a seemingly endless stream of images from television, magazines, billboards, books, Web pages, newspapers, flyers, storefront signs, and more, all of them competing for our attention, and all of them loaded with information and ideas. Forms of communication that traditionally used only the written word (letters, books, term papers) or the spoken word (telephone conversations, lectures) are today increasingly enhanced with visual components (PowerPoint slides, smartphone graphics, video, photos, illustrations, graphs, and the like) for greater impact. And most of us would agree that visuals do, indeed, have an impact: A picture, as the saying goes, is worth a thousand words.

In part because of their potentially powerful effect on us, visuals and visual texts* should be approached the way we approach written texts: analytically and critically. Whether their purpose is to sell us an idea or a car, to spur us to action or inspire us to dream, visuals invite analysis both of their key components and their *rhetorical context*. As

FIGURE 12.1 Times Square at Dusk
© Amanda Hall/Robert Harding/Newscom

---

* In this chapter, we use the word *image* to refer primarily to photographs. We use the word *visual* as a broader designation for visual elements of texts (including images, but also such components as diagrams, charts, and graphs), and *visual text* for documents such as ads, brochures, and the like, in which visuals are strongly featured, but which consist of more than a single image.

we "read" a visual, therefore, we should ask ourselves a series of questions: Who created it? Where was it published? What *audience* is it addressing? What is it trying to get this audience to think and feel about the subject? How does it attempt to achieve this *purpose*?

Let's look, for example, at the visual text in Figure 12.2 a public service announcement (PSA) from the World Wildlife Fund (WWF).

The central image in this PSA is a smiling fisherman holding up a fish. Most of us will immediately recognize his posture and facial expression as those of a man excited about and proud of an impressive catch; the photo's wooden frame makes the image seem like a real photo from a fishing trip, as opposed to an ad agency's creation (which

FIGURE 12.2 "Fishing," from the WWF's "Beautiful Day U.S." Series
Courtesy WWF

would be easier to ignore). After noting these things, however, we are immediately struck by what is wrong with the picture: the fish is tiny — a far cry from the sort of catch any normal fisherman would be satisfied with — the lake in the background is almost entirely dried up, and the fisherman is covered in bloody sores from severe sun damage.

So what do we make of the disruption of the convention (the vacation photo) on which the PSA image is based? In trying to decide, most of us will look next to the text below the image: "Ignoring global warming won't make it go away." The disjunction between the fisherman's pleased expression and the barren lake and measly catch — not to mention his grotesquely sunburned skin — turns out to be the point of the PSA: Like the fisherman in the picture, the PSA implies, we are all blithely ignoring the impending disaster that global warming represents. The reputable, nonprofit WWF's logo and URL, which constitute its "signature," are meant to be an assurance that this threat is real, and not just an idea a profit-seeking ad agency dreamed up to manipulate us.

Not everyone will be convinced by this PSA to support the work of the WWF, and some viewers may feel manipulated by the visual image. They may disagree that the problem is as dire as the depiction implicitly claims it is. They may feel that our resources and energy would be better directed toward other problems facing the world. Nevertheless, most people would agree that with a single cleverly constructed image, a single line of text, and a logo, the PSA delivers its message clearly and forcefully.

CRITERIA FOR ANALYZING VISUALS

KEY COMPONENTS

Composition

- Of what elements is the visual composed?
- What is the focal point—that is, the place your eyes are drawn to?
- From what perspective do you view the focal point? Are you looking straight ahead at it, down at it, or up at it? If the visual is a photograph, what angle was the image shot from— straight ahead, looking down or up?
- What colors are used? Are there obvious special effects employed? Is there a frame, or are there any additional graphical elements? If so, what do these elements contribute to your "reading" of the visual?

People/Other Main Figures

- If people are depicted, how would you describe their age, gender, sub-culture, ethnicity, profession, level of attractiveness, and socioeconomic class? How do these factors relate to other elements of the image?
- Who is looking at whom? Do the people represented seem conscious of the viewer's gaze?
- What do the facial expressions and body language tell you about power relationships (equal, subordinate, in charge) and attitudes (self-confident, vulnerable, anxious, subservient, angry, aggressive, sad)?

Scene

- If a recognizable scene is depicted, what is its setting? What is in the background and the foreground?
- What has happened just before the image was "shot"? What will happen in the next scene?
- What, if anything, is happening just outside of the visual frame?

Words

- If text is combined with the visual, what role does the text play? Is it a slogan? A famous quote? Lyrics from a well-known song?
- If the text help you interpret the visual's overall meaning, what interpretive clues does it provide?
- What is the tone of the text? Humorous? Elegiac? Ironic?

Tone

- What tone, or mood, does the visual convey? Is it lighthearted, somber,

Criteria for Analyzing Visuals

The primary purpose of this chapter is to help you analyze visuals and write about them. In your college courses, some of you will be asked to write entire papers in which you analyze one or more visuals (a painting or a photo, for example). Some of you will write papers in which you include analysis of one or more visual texts within the context of a larger written essay (say, by analyzing the brochures and ads authorized by a political candidate, in an argument about her campaign).

---

frightening, shocking, joyful? What elements in the visual (color, composition, words, people, setting) convey this tone?

CONTEXT(S)

Rhetorical Context

- **What is the visual's main purpose?** Are we being asked to buy a product? Form an opinion or judgment about something? Support a political party's candidate? Take some other kind of action?

- **Who is its target audience?** Children? Men? Women? Some sub- or super-set of these groups (e.g., African American men, "tweens," seniors)?

- **Who is the author? Who sponsored its publication?** What background/ associations do the author and the sponsoring publication have? What other works have they produced?

- **Where was it published, and in what form?** Online? On television? In print? In a commercial publication (a sales brochure, billboard, ad) or an informational one (newspaper, magazine)?

- **If the visual is embedded within a document that is primarily written text, how do the written text and** the visual relate to each other? Do they convey the same message, or are they at odds in any way? What does the image contribute to the written text? Is it essential or just eye candy?

- **Social Context. What is the immediate social and cultural context within which the visual is operating?** If we are being asked to support a certain candidate, for example, how does the visual reinforce or counter what we already know about this candidate? What other social/ cultural knowledge does the visual assume its audience already has?

- **Historical Context. What historical knowledge does it assume the audience already possesses?** Does the visual refer to other historical images, figures, events, or stories that the audience would recognize? How do these historical references relate to the visual's audience and purpose?

- **Intertextuality. How does the visual connect, relate to, or contrast with any other significant texts, visual or otherwise, that you are aware of?** How do such considerations inform your ideas about this particular visual?

Of course, learning to analyze visuals effectively can also help you gain a more complete understanding of any document that *uses* visuals but that is not entirely or predominantly composed of them. Why did the author of a remembered event essay, for example, choose a particular photo of a person mentioned in the text—does it reinforce the written description, add to it, or contradict it in some way? If there is a caption under the photo, how does it affect the way we read it? In a concept explanation, why are illustrations of one process included but not those of another? How well do the charts and graphs work with the text to help us understand the author's explanation? Understanding what visuals can do for a text can also help you effectively integrate images, charts, graphs, and other visuals into your own essays, whatever your topic.

FIGURE 12.3 *American Gothic, Washington D.C.,*Gordon Parks (1942)
Photograph by Gordon Parks. Copyright © The Gordon Parks Foundation. Courtesy The Gordon Parks Foundation.

The chart on pages 354–55 outlines key criteria for analyzing visuals and provides questions for you to ask about documents that include them.

A Sample Analysis

In a composition class, students were asked to do a short written analysis of a photograph. In looking for ideas, Paul Taylor came across the Library of Congress's *Documenting America,* an exhibit of photographs taken 1935–45. Gordon Parks's photographs struck Paul as particularly interesting, especially those of Ella Watson, a poorly paid office cleaner employed by the federal government. (See Figure 12.3.)

After studying the photos, Paul read about Parks's first session with Watson:

> My first photograph of [Watson] was unsubtle. I overdid it and posed her, Grant Wood style, before the American flag, a broom in one hand, a mop in the other, staring straight into the camera.[1]

Paul didn't understand Parks's reference to Grant Wood in his description of the photo, so he did an Internet search and discovered that Parks was referring to a classic painting by

---

[1]Gordon Parks, *A Choice of Weapons* (New York: Harper & Row, 1966), 230–31.

Wood called *American Gothic*. Reading further about the connection, he discovered that Parks's photo of Watson is itself commonly titled *American Gothic* and discussed as a parody of Grant Wood's painting.

After learning about the connection with *American Gothic,* Paul read more about the context of Parks's photos:

> Gordon Parks was born in Kansas in 1912. . . . During the Depression a variety of jobs . . . took him to various parts of the northern United States. He took up photography during his travels. . . . In 1942, an opportunity to work for the Farm Security Administration brought the photographer to the nation's capital; Parks later recalled that "discrimination and bigotry were worse there than any place I had yet seen."[2]

Intrigued by what he had learned so far, Paul decided to delve into Parks's later career. A 2006 obituary of Parks in the *New York Times* reproduced his 1952 photo *Emerging Man* (Figure 12.4), which Paul decided to analyze for his assignment. First he did additional research on the photo. Then he made notes on his responses to the photo using the criteria for analysis provided on pp. 354–55.

FIGURE 12.4 *Emerging Man, Harlem, New York* **Gordon Parks (1952)**

Photograph by Gordon Parks. Copyright © The Gordon Parks Foundation. Courtesy The Gordon Parks Foundation.

---

[2] Martin H. Bush, "A Conversation with Gordon Parks," in *The Photographs of Gordon Parks* (Wichita, KS: Wichita State University, 1983), 36.

PAUL TAYLOR'S ANALYSIS OF *EMERGING MAN*

KEY COMPONENTS OF THE VISUAL

Composition

- **Of what elements is the visual composed?** It's a black-and-white photo showing the top three-quarters of a man's face and his hands (mostly fingers). He appears to be emerging out of the ground--out of a sewer? There's what looks like asphalt in the foreground, and buildings (out of focus) in the far background.

- **What is the focal point—that is, the place your eyes are drawn to?** The focal point is the face of the man staring directly into the camera's lens. There's a shaft of light angled (slightly from the right?) onto the lower-middle part of his face. His eyes appear to glisten slightly. The rest of his face, his hands, and the foreground are in shadow.

- **From what perspective do you view the focal point?** We appear to be looking at him at eye level--weird, since eye level for him is just a few inches from the ground. Was the photographer lying down? The shot is also a close-up--a foot or two from the man's face. Why so close?

- **What colors are used? Are there obvious special effects employed? Is there a frame, or are there any additional graphical elements?** There's no visible frame or any graphic elements. The image is in stark black and white, and there's a "graininess" to it: we can see the texture of the man's skin and the asphalt on the street.

People/Other Main Figures

- **If people are depicted, how would you describe their age, gender, subculture, ethnicity, profession, level of attractiveness, and socioeconomic class?** The man is African American and probably middle-aged (or at least not obviously very young or very old). We can't see his clothing or any other marker of class, profession, etc. The fact that he seems to be emerging from a sewer implies that he's not hugely rich or prominent, of course--a "man of the people"?

- **Who is looking at whom? Do the people represented seem conscious of the viewer's gaze?** The man seems to be looking directly into the camera and at the viewer (who's in the position of the photographer). I guess, yes, he seems to look straight at the viewer--perhaps in a challenging or questioning way.

- **What do the facial expressions and body language tell you about power relationships (equal, subordinate, in charge) and attitudes (self-confident, vulnerable, anxious, subservient, angry, aggressive, sad)?** We can only see his face from the nose up, and his fingertips. It looks like one eyebrow is slightly raised, which might mean he's questioning or skeptical. The expression in his eyes is definitely serious. The position of his fingers implies that he's clutching the rim of the manhole--that, and the title, indicate that he's pulling himself up out of the hole. But since we see only the fingers, not the whole hand, does his hold seem tenuous--he's "holding on by his fingertips"? Not sure.

Scene

- **If a recognizable scene is depicted, what is its setting? What is in the background and the foreground?** It looks like an urban setting (asphalt, manhole cover, buildings, and lights in the blurry distant background). Descriptions of the photo note that Parks shot the image in Harlem. Hazy buildings and objects are in the distance. Only the man's face and fingertips are in focus. The sky behind him is light gray, though--is it dawn?

- **What has happened just before the image was "shot"? What will happen in the next scene?** He appears to be coming up and out of the hole in the ground (the sewer).

- **What, if anything, is happening just outside of the visual frame?** It's not clear. There's no activity in the background at all. It's deserted, except for him.

Words

- **If text is combined with the visual, what role does the text play?** There's no text on or near the image. There is the title, though--*Emerging Man*.

- **Does the text help you interpret the visual's overall meaning?** The title is a literal description, but it might also refer to the civil rights movement--the gradual racial and economic integration--of African Americans into American society.

- **What is the tone of the text?** Hard to say. I guess, assuming wordplay is involved, it's sort of witty (merging traffic?).

Tone

- **What tone, or mood, does the visual convey? What elements in the visual (color, composition, words, people, setting) convey this tone?** The tone is serious, even perhaps a bit spooky. The use of black and white and heavy shadows lends a somewhat ominous feel, though the ray of light on the man's face, the lightness of the sky, and the lights in the background counterbalance this to an extent. The man's expression is somber, though not obviously angry or grief-stricken.

CONTEXT(S)

Rhetorical Context

- **What is the visual's main purpose?** Given Parks's interest in politics and social justice, it seems fair to assume that the image of the man emerging from underground--from the darkness into the light?--is a reference to social progress (civil rights movement) and suggests rebirth of a sort. The use of black and white, while certainly not unusual in photographs of the era, emphasizes the division between black and white that is in part the photo's subject.

- **Who is its target audience?** Because it appeared first in Life, the target audience was mainstream--a broad cross-section of the magazine-reading U.S. population at mid-twentieth century.

- **Who is the author? Who sponsored its publication?** During this era, Gordon Parks was best known as a photographer whose works documented and commented on social conditions. The fact that this photo was originally published in *Life* (a mainstream periodical read by white Americans throughout the country) is probably significant.

- **If the visual is embedded within a document that is primarily written text, how do the written text and the visual relate to each other?** The photo accompanied an article about Ellison's *Invisible Man*, a novel about a man who goes underground to escape racism and conflicts within the early civil rights movement. Now the man is reentering mainstream society?

- **Social Context. What is the immediate social and cultural context within which the visual is operating?** The civil rights movement was gaining ground in post–World War II society.

- **Historical Context. What historical knowledge does it assume the audience already possesses?** For a viewer in 1952, the image would call to mind the current and past situation of African Americans. Uncertainty about what the future would hold (Would the emergence be successful? What kind of man would eventually emerge?) would be a big part of the viewer's response. Viewers today obviously feel less suspense about what would happen in the immediate (post-1952) future. The "vintage" feel of the photo's style and even the man's hair, along with the use of black and white, probably have a "distancing" effect on the viewer today. At the same time, the subject continues to be relevant--most viewers will likely think about the progress we've made in race relations and where we're currently headed.

- **Intertextuality. How does the visual connect, relate to, or contrast with any other significant texts, visual or otherwise, that you are aware of?** Invisible Man, which I've already discussed, was a best-seller and won the National Book Award in 1953.

After writing and reviewing these notes and doing some further research to fill in gaps in his knowledge about Parks, Ellison, and the civil rights movement, Paul drafted his analysis. He submitted this draft to his peer group for comments, and then revised. His final draft follows.

Taylor 1

Paul Taylor

Professor Stevens

Writing Seminar I

4 October 2012

The Rising

Gordon Parks's 1952 photograph *Emerging Man* (Fig. 1) is as historically significant a reflection of the civil rights movement as are the speeches of Martin Luther King and Malcolm X, the music of Mahalia Jackson, and the books of Ralph Ellison and James Baldwin. Through striking use of black and white—a reflection of the racial divisions plaguing American cities and towns throughout much of the nineteenth and twentieth centuries—and a symbolically potent central subject—an African American man we see literally "emerging" from a city manhole—Parks's photo evokes the centuries of racial and economic marginalization of African Americans, at the same time as it projects a spirit of determination and optimism regarding the civil rights movement's eventual success.

In choosing the starkest of urban settings and giving the image a gritty feel, Parks alerts the viewer to the gravity

Fig. 1. Gordon Parks, *Emerging Man, Harlem, New York* (1952)

Taylor 2

Fig. 2. *American Gothic, Washington D.C.,* Gordon Parks (1942)

of his subject and gives it a sense of immediacy. As with the documentary photographs Parks took of office cleaner Ella Watson for the Farm Security Administration in the 1940s— see Fig. 2 for one example—the carefully chosen setting and the spareness of the treatment ensure the viewer's focus on the social statement the artist is making (*Documenting*). Whereas the photos of Ella Watson document a particular woman and the actual conditions of her life and work, however, *Emerging Man* strips away any particulars, including any name for the man, with the result that the photo enters the symbolic or even mythic realm.

The composition of *Emerging Man* makes it impossible for us to focus on anything other than the unnamed subject rising from the manhole—we are, for instance, unable to consider what the weather might be, though we might surmise from the relatively light tone of the sky and the emptiness of the street that it is dawn. Similarly, we are not given any specifics of the setting, which is simply urban and, apart from the central figure, unpopulated. Reducing the elements to their outlines in this way keeps the viewer focused on the grand central theme of the piece: the role of race in mid-twentieth-century America and the future of race relations.

The fact that the man is looking directly at the camera, in a way that's challenging but not hostile, speaks to the racial optimism of the period among many African Americans and whites alike. President Truman's creation of the President's Committee on Civil Rights in 1946 and his 1948 Executive Order for the integration of all armed services were significant steps toward the emergence of the full-blown civil rights movement, providing hope that African Americans would be able, for perhaps the first time in American history, to look directly into the eyes of their white counterparts and fearlessly emphasize their shared humanity (Leuchtenburg). The "emerging man" seems to be daring us to try to stop his rise from the manhole, his hands gripping its sides, his eyes focused intently on the viewer.

According to several sources, Parks planned and executed the photograph as a photographic counterpart to Ralph Ellison's 1952 *Invisible Man,* a breakthrough novel about race and society that was both a best-seller and a critical success. *Invisible Man* is narrated in the first person by an unnamed African American man who traces his experiences from boyhood. The climax of the novel shows the narrator hunted by policemen controlling a Harlem race riot; escaping down a manhole, the narrator is trapped at first but eventually decides to live permanently underground, hidden from society ("Ralph Ellison"). The correspondences between the photo and the book are apparent. In fact, according to the catalog accompanying an exhibit of Parks's photos selected by the photographer himself before his death in 2006, Ellison actually collaborated on the staging of the photo (*Bare Witness*).

More than just a photographic counterpart, however, it seems that Parks's *Emerging Man* can be read as a sequel to

Taylor 4

Invisible Man, with the emphasis radically shifted from resig-
nation to optimism. The man who had decided to live underground now decides to emerge, and does so with determination.
In this compelling photograph, Parks—himself an "emerging
man," considering he was the first African American photographer to be hired full-time by the widely respected mainstream
Life magazine—created a photograph that celebrated the
changing racial landscape in American society.

Works Cited

Bare Witness: Photographs by Gordon Parks. Catalog. Milan:
 Skira; Stanford, CA: Iris & B. Gerald Cantor Center for
 Visual Arts at Stanford University, 2006. Traditional Fine
 Arts Organization. *Resource Library*. Web. 29 Sept. 2012.

Documenting America: Photographers on Assignment. 15 Dec. 1998.
 *America from the Great Depression to World War II: Black-and-
 White Photographs from the FSA-OWI, 1935-1945*. Prints and
 Photographs Div., Lib. of Cong. Web. 27 Sept. 2012.

Leuchtenburg, William E. "The Conversion of Harry Truman."
 American Heritage 42.7 (1991): 55-68. *America: History
 & Life*. Web. 29 Sept. 2012.

Parks, Gordon. *Ella Watson*. Aug. 1942. *America from the
 Great Depression to World War II: Black-and-White
 Photographs from the FSA-OWI, 1935-1945*. Prints and
 Photographs Div., Lib. of Cong. Web. 27 Sept. 2012.

———. *Emerging Man*. 1952. *PhotoMuse*. George Eastman
 House and ICP, n.d. Web. 26 Sept. 2012.

"Ralph Ellison: *Invisible Man*." *Literature and Its Times: Profiles
 of 300 Notable Literary Works and the Historical Events
 That Influenced Them*. Ed. Joyce Moss and George Wilson.
 Vol. 4. Gale Research, 1997. *Literature Resource Center*.
 Web. 30 Sept. 2012.

Dorothea Lange's *First-Graders at the Weill Public School* shows children of Japanese descent reciting the Pledge of Allegiance in San Francisco, California, in 1942. Following the steps below, write an essay suggesting what the image means.

First-Graders at the Weill Public School, **Dorothea Lange (1942)**
Library of Congress, Prints & Photographs Division, LC-USZ62-42810

1. Do some research on Lange's work. (Like Paul Taylor, you might start at the Library of Congress's online exhibit *Documenting America,* which features Lange, along with Gordon Parks and other photographers.)

2. Analyze the image using the criteria for analysis presented on pp. 354–55.

3. From this preliminary analysis, develop a tentative thesis that says what the image means and how it communicates that meaning.

4. With this thesis in mind, plan your essay, using your analysis of the image to illustrate your thesis. Be aware that as you draft your essay, your thesis will develop and may even change substantially.

Analyze one of the ads that follow by using the criteria for visual analysis on pp. 354–55. Be sure to consider the role that writing plays in the ad's overall meaning. Write an essay with a thesis that discusses the ad's central meaning and significance.

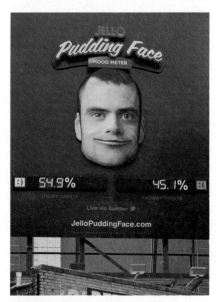

Magazine Ad for Jell-O (2012)
© Andrew Burton/Getty Images

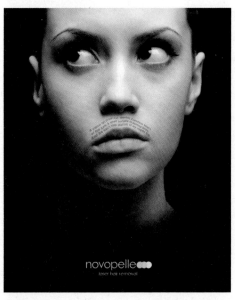

Magazine Ad for Novopelle Laser Hair Removal (2008)
(Text reads: "A closet full of low-cut blouses. Countless hours at the gym. A small fortune in pushup bras. And he can't stop staring at my upper lip.")
Courtesy of Novopelle. Carlos Cortinas, Art Director; Glen Day, Writer

Find an ad or public service announcement that you find compelling in its use of visuals. Analyze the ad by using the criteria for visual analysis on pp. 354–55. Be sure to consider the role that writing plays in the ad's overall meaning. Write an essay with a thesis that discusses the ad's central meaning and significance.

13

Arguing

This chapter presents the basic strategies for making *arguments* in writing. In it, we focus on asserting a thesis, backing it up with reasons and support, and anticipating readers' questions and objections. It concludes with some sentence strategies you might use when composing an argument.

Asserting a Thesis

Central to any argument is the **thesis**. In a sentence or two, a thesis asserts or states the main point of any argument you want to make. It can be assertive only if you make it clear and direct. The thesis statement usually appears at the beginning of an argument essay.

There are three kinds of argument essays in Part One of this book. Each of these essays requires a special kind of assertion and reasoning:

- **Assertion of opinion:** What is your position on a controversial issue? (Chapter 5, "Arguing a Position")

  When overzealous parents and coaches impose adult standards on children's sports, the result can be activities that are neither satisfying nor beneficial to children.
  — JESSICA STATSKY, "Children Need to Play, Not Compete"

- **Assertion of policy:** What is your understanding of a problem, and what do you think should be done to solve it? (Chapter 6, "Proposing a Solution")

  Although this last-minute anxiety about midterm and final exams is only too familiar to most college students, many professors may not realize how such major, infrequent, high-stakes exams work against the best interests of students both psychologically and cognitively. . . . If professors gave brief exams at frequent intervals, students would be spurred to learn more and worry less.
  — PATRICK O'MALLEY, "More Testing, More Learning"

- **Assertion of evaluation:** What is your judgment of a subject? (Chapter 7, "Justifying an Evaluation")

  Although the film is especially targeted for old school gamers, anime fans, and comic book fanatics, *Scott Pilgrim vs. the World* can be appreciated and enjoyed by all audiences because of its inventive special effects, clever dialogue, and artistic cinematography and editing.
  —WILLIAM AKANA, "*Scott Pilgrim vs. the World:* A Hell of a Ride"

Chapters 5–7 contain essays that argue for each of these kinds of assertions, along with guidelines for constructing an argument to support such an assertion.

366

As these different thesis statements indicate, the kind of thesis you assert depends on the occasion for which you are writing and the question you are trying to answer for your readers. Whatever the writing situation, to be effective, every thesis must satisfy the same three standards: It must be *arguable, clear,* and *appropriately qualified.*

Make arguable assertions.

Reasoned argument is called for when informed people disagree over an issue or remain divided over how best to solve a problem, as is so often the case in social and political life. Hence, the thesis statements in reasoned arguments make **arguable assertions**— possibilities or probabilities, not certainties.

Therefore, a statement of fact could not be an arguable thesis statement because facts are easy to verify—whether by checking an authoritative reference book, asking an authority, or observing the fact with your own eyes. For example, these statements assert facts:

Jem has a Ph.D. in history.

I am less than five feet tall.

Eucalyptus trees were originally imported into California from Australia.

Each of these assertions can be easily verified. To find out Jem's academic degree, you can ask him, among other things. To determine a person's height, you can use a tape measure. To discover where California got its eucalyptus trees, you can search the library or Internet. There is no point in arguing such statements (though you might question the authority of a particular source or the accuracy of someone's measurement). If a writer asserts something as fact and attempts to support the assertion with *authorities* or *statistics,* the resulting essay is not an argument but a *report.*

Like facts, expressions of personal feelings are not arguable assertions. Whereas facts are unarguable because they can be definitively proved true or false, feelings are unarguable because they are purely subjective.

You can declare, for example, that you detest eight o'clock classes, but you cannot offer an argument to support this assertion. All you can do is explain why you feel as you do. If, however, you were to restate the assertion as "Eight o'clock classes are counterproductive," you could then construct an argument that does not depend solely on your subjective feelings, memories, or preferences. Your argument could be based on *reasons* and *support* that apply to others as well as to yourself. For example, you might argue that students' ability to learn is at an especially low ebb immediately after breakfast and provide scientific support for this assertion — in addition, perhaps, to personal experience and reports of interviews with your friends.

Use clear and precise wording.

The way a thesis is worded is as important as its arguability. The wording of a thesis, especially its key terms, must be *clear* and *precise.*

Consider the following assertion: "Democracy is a way of life." The meaning of this claim is uncertain, partly because the word *democracy* is abstract and partly because the phrase *way of life* is inexact. Abstract ideas like democracy, freedom, and patriotism are by their very nature hard to grasp, and they become even less clear with overuse. Too often, such words take on *connotations* that may obscure the meaning you want to emphasize. *Way of life* is fuzzy: What does it mean? Does it refer to daily life, to a general philosophy or attitude toward life, or to something else?

Thus, a thesis is vague if its meaning is unclear; it is ambiguous if it has more than one possible meaning. For example, the statement "My English instructor is mad" can be understood in two ways: The teacher is either angry or insane. Obviously, these are two very different assertions. You would not want readers to think you mean one when you actually mean the other.

Whenever you write argument, you should pay special attention to the way you phrase your thesis and take care to avoid vague and ambiguous language.

Qualify the thesis appropriately.

In addition to being arguable and clear, an argument thesis must make **appropriate qualifications** that suit your writing situation. If you are confident that your case is so strong that readers will accept your argument without question, state your thesis emphatically and unconditionally. If, however, you expect readers to challenge your assumptions or conclusions, you must qualify your statement. Qualifying a thesis makes it more likely that readers will take it seriously. Expressions like *probably, very likely, apparently,* and *it seems* all serve to qualify a thesis.

EXERCISE 13.1

Write an assertion of opinion that states your position on one of the following controversial issues:

- Should English be the official language of the United States and the only language used in local, state, and federal governments' oral and written communications?
- Should teenagers be required to get their parents' permission to obtain birth control information and contraceptives?
- Should high schools or colleges require students to perform community service as a condition for graduation?
- Should marriage between same-sex couples be legal?

Constructing a persuasive argument on any of these issues would obviously require careful deliberation and research. For this exercise, however, all you need to do is construct an arguable, clear, and appropriately qualified thesis.

EXERCISE 13.2

Find the thesis in one of the argument essays in Chapters 5–7. Then decide whether the thesis meets the three requirements: that it be arguable, clear, and appropriately qualified.

EXERCISE 13.3

If you have written or are currently working on one of the argument assignments in Chapters 5–7, consider whether your essay thesis is arguable, clear, and appropriately qualified. If you believe it does not meet these requirements, revise it accordingly.

Giving Reasons and Support

Whether you are arguing a position, proposing a solution, justifying an evaluation, or speculating about causes, you need to give reasons and support for your thesis.

Think of **reasons** as the main points supporting your thesis. Often they answer the question, Why do you think so? For example, if you assert among friends that you value a certain movie highly, one of your friends might ask, "Why do you like it so much?" And you might answer, "*Because* it has challenging ideas, unusual camera work, and memorable acting." Similarly, you might oppose restrictions on students' use of offensive language at your college *because* such restrictions would make students reluctant to enter into frank debates, *because* offensive speech is hard to define, and *because* restrictions violate the free-speech clause of the First Amendment. These *because* phrases are your reasons. You may have one or many reasons, depending on your subject and your writing situation.

For your argument to succeed with your readers, you must not only give reasons but also support your reasons. The main kinds of **support** writers use are examples, statistics, authorities, anecdotes, and textual evidence. Following is a discussion and illustration of each kind of support, along with standards for judging its reliability.

Use representative examples for support.

Examples may be used as support in all types of arguments. For examples to be believable and convincing, they must be representative (typical of all the relevant examples you might have chosen), consistent with the experience of your readers (familiar to them and not extreme), and adequate in number (numerous enough to be convincing and yet not likely to overwhelm readers).

The following illustration comes from a book on illiteracy in America by Jonathan Kozol, a prominent educator and writer:

> Kozol presents several examples to support his argument that the human costs of illiteracy are high.

Illiterates cannot read the menu in a restaurant.

They cannot read the cost of items on the menu in the window of the restaurant before they enter.

Illiterates cannot read the letters that their children bring home from their teachers. They cannot study school department circulars that tell them of the courses that their children must be taking if they hope to pass the SAT exams. They cannot help with homework. They cannot write a letter to the teacher. They are afraid to visit in the classroom. They do not want to humiliate their child or themselves.

Illiterates cannot read instructions on a bottle of prescription medicine. They cannot find out when a medicine is past the year of safe consumption; nor can they read of allergenic risks, warnings to diabetics, or the potential sedative effect of certain kinds of nonprescription pills. They cannot observe preventive health care admonitions. They cannot read about "the seven warning signs of cancer" or the indications of blood-sugar fluctuations or the risks of eating certain foods that aggravate the likelihood of cardiac arrest.

— Jonathan Kozol, *Illiterate America*

Kozol collected these examples in his many interviews with people who could neither read nor write. Though all of his readers are literate and have presumably never experienced the frustrations of adult illiterates, Kozol assumes they will accept that the experiences are a familiar part of illiterates' lives. Most readers will believe the experiences to be neither atypical nor extreme.

| EXERCISE 13.4 |

Identify the examples in paragraphs 9 and 11 in Jessica Statsky's essay "Children Need to Play, Not Compete" and paragraphs 16–18 in Amitai Etzioni's essay "Working at McDonald's" (both in Chapter 5). If you have not read the essays, pause to skim them so that you can evaluate these examples within the context of the entire essay. How well do the examples meet the standards of representativeness, consistency with experience of readers, and adequacy in number? You will not have all the information you need to evaluate the examples — you rarely do unless you are an expert on the subject — but make a judgment based on the information available to you in the headnotes and the essays.

Use up-to-date, relevant, and accurate statistics.

In many kinds of arguments about economic, educational, or social issues, statistics may be essential. When you use statistics in your own arguments, you will want to ensure that they are up-to-date, relevant, and accurate. In addition, take care to select statistics from reliable sources and to cite them from the sources in which they originally appeared if at all possible. For example, you would want to get medical statistics directly from a reputable and authoritative professional periodical like the *New England Journal of Medicine* rather than secondhand from a supermarket tabloid or an unaffiliated Web site, neither of which can be relied on for accuracy. If you are uncertain about the most authoritative sources, ask a reference librarian or a professor who knows your topic.

The following selection, written by a Harvard University professor, comes from an argument speculating about the decline of civic life in the United States. Civic life includes all of the clubs, organizations, and communal activities in which people choose to participate:

Putnam uses statistics to support his opinion that since the early 1960s, Americans have devoted less and less time to civic life because they are watching more and more television.

The culprit is television.

First, the timing fits. The long civic generation was the last cohort of Americans to grow up without television, for television flashed into American society like lightning in the 1950s. In 1950 barely 10 percent of American homes had television sets, but by 1959, 90 percent did. . . . The reverberations from this lightning bolt continued for decades, as viewing hours grew by 17–20 percent during the 1960s and by an additional 7–8 percent during the 1970s. In the early years, TV watching was concentrated among the less educated sectors of the population, but during the 1970s the viewing time of the more educated sectors of the population began to converge upward. Television viewing increases with age, particularly upon retirement, but each generation since the introduction of television has begun its life cycle at a higher starting point. By 1995 viewing per TV household was more than 50 percent higher than it had been in the 1950s.

Most studies estimate that the average American now watches roughly four hours per day (excluding periods in which television is merely playing in the background). Even a more conservative estimate of three hours means that television absorbs 40 percent of the average American's free time, an increase of about one-third since 1965. Moreover, multiple sets have proliferated: By the late 1980s three-quarters of all U.S. homes had more than one set, and these numbers too are rising steadily, allowing ever more private viewing. . . . This massive change in the way Americans spend their days and nights occurred precisely during the years of generational civic disengagement.

— Robert D. Putnam, "The Strange Disappearance of Civic America"

These statistics come primarily from the U.S. Bureau of the Census, a nationwide count of the number of Americans and a survey, in part, of their buying habits, levels of education, and leisure activities. The Census reports are widely considered to be accurate and trustworthy. They qualify as original sources of statistics.

Chapter 16, pp. 408–409, provides help finding statistical data in the library.

| EXERCISE 13.5 |

In Chapter 5, underline the statistics in paragraphs 5 and 6 of Jessica Statsky's essay. If you have not read the essay, pause to skim it so that you can evaluate the writer's use of statistics within the context of the whole essay. How well do the statistics meet the standards of up-to-dateness, relevance, accuracy, and reliance on the original source? Does the writer indicate where the statistics come from? What do the statistics contribute to the argument?

Cite reputable authorities on relevant topics.

To support an argument, writers often cite experts on the subject. *Quoting, paraphrasing,* or even just referring to a respected **authority** can add to a writer's *credibility.* Authorities must be selected as carefully as are facts and statistics, however. One qualification for authorities is suggested by the way we refer to them: They must be authoritative—that is, trustworthy and reputable. They must also be specially qualified to contribute to the subject you are writing about. For example, a well-known expert on the American presidency might be a perfect choice to support an argument about the achievements of a past president but a poor choice to support an argument on whether adolescents who commit serious crimes should be tried as adults. Finally, qualified authorities must have training at respected institutions or have unique real-world experiences, and they must have a record of research and publications recognized by other authorities.

The following example comes from a *New York Times* article about some parents' and experts' heightened concern over boys' behavior. The author believes that the concern is exaggerated and potentially dangerous. In the full argument, she is particularly concerned about the number of boys who are being given Ritalin, a popular drug for treating attention-deficit hyperactivity disorder (ADHD):

> Today, the world is no longer safe for boys. A boy being a shade too boyish risks finding himself under the scrutiny of parents, teachers, guidance counselors, child therapists—all of them on watch for the early glimmerings of a medical syndrome, a bona fide behavioral disorder. Does the boy disregard authority, make snide comments in class, push other kids around and play hooky? Maybe he has a conduct disorder. Is he fidgety, impulsive, disruptive, easily bored? Perhaps he is suffering from attention-deficit hyperactivity disorder, or ADHD, the disease of the hour and the most frequently diagnosed behavioral disorder of childhood. Does he prefer computer games and goofing off to homework? He might have dyslexia or another learning disorder.
>
> "There is now an attempt to pathologize what was once considered the normal range of behavior of boys," said Melvin Konner of the departments of anthropology and psychiatry at Emory University in Atlanta. "Today, Tom Sawyer and Huckleberry Finn surely would have been diagnosed with both conduct disorder and ADHD." And both, perhaps, would have been put on Ritalin, the drug of choice for treating attention-deficit disorder.
>
> — NATALIE ANGIER, "Intolerance of Boyish Behavior"

Angier establishes Melvin Konner's professional qualifications by naming the university where he teaches and his areas of study.

In this example, Angier relies on **informal citation** within her essay to introduce Melvin Konner, the authority she quotes, along with a reference to his professional qualifications. Such informal citation is common in newspapers, magazines, and some books intended for general audiences. In other books and in academic contexts, writers use **formal citation,** providing a list of works cited at the end of the essay.

For examples of two formal citation styles often used in college essays, see Chapters 19 and 20.

EXERCISE 13.6

Analyze how authorities are used in paragraphs 4 and 6 of Patrick O'Malley's essay "More Testing, More Learning" in Chapter 6 (pp. 198–203). Begin by underlining the authorities' contributions to these paragraphs, whether through quotation, summary, or paraphrase. On the basis of the evidence you have available, decide to what extent each source is authoritative on the subject: qualified to contribute to the subject, trained appropriately, and recognized widely. How does O'Malley establish each authority's credentials? Then decide what each authority contributes to the argument as a whole. (If you have not read the essay, take time to read or skim it.)

Use vivid, relevant anecdotes.

Anecdotes are brief stories about events or experiences. If they are relevant to the argument, well told, and true to life, they can provide convincing support. To be relevant, an anecdote must strike readers as more than an entertaining diversion; it must seem to make an irreplaceable contribution to an argument. A well-told story is easy to follow, and the people and scenes are described memorably, even vividly. A true-to-life anecdote seems believable, even if the experience is foreign to readers' experiences.

The following anecdote appeared in an argument taking a position on gun control. The writer, an essayist, poet, and environmentalist who is also a rancher in South Dakota, always carries a pistol and believes that other people should have the right to do so:

> To support her argument, Hasselstrom tells an engaging anecdote and, in the last paragraph, explains its relevance.

One day, while driving to the highway mailbox, I saw a vehicle parked about halfway to the house. Several men were standing in the ditch, relieving themselves. I have no objection to emergency urination; we always need moisture. But I noticed they'd also dumped several dozen beer cans, which can blow into pastures and slash a cow's legs or stomach.

As I drove slowly closer, the men zipped their trousers ostentatiously while walking toward me, and one of them demanded what the hell I wanted.

"This is private land. I'd like you to pick up the beer cans."

"What beer cans?" said the belligerent one, putting both hands on the car door and leaning in my window. His face was inches from mine, and the beer fumes were strong. The others laughed. One tried the passenger door, locked; another put his foot on the hood and rocked the car. They circled, lightly thumping the roof, discussing my good fortune in meeting them and the benefits they were likely to bestow upon me. I felt small and trapped; they knew it.

"The ones you just threw out," I said politely.

"I don't see no beer cans. Why don't you get out here and show them to me, honey?" said the belligerent one, reaching for the handle inside my door.

"Right over there," I said, still being polite, "—there and over there." I pointed with the pistol, which had been under my thigh. Within one minute the cans and the men were back in the car and headed down the road.

I believe this incident illustrates several important principles. The men were trespassing and knew it; their judgment may have been impaired by alcohol. Their response to the polite request of a woman alone was to use their size and numbers to inspire fear. The pistol was a response in the same language. Politeness didn't work; I couldn't intimidate them. Out of the car, I'd have been more vulnerable. The pistol just changed the balance of power.

— LINDA M. HASSELSTROM, "Why One Peaceful Woman Carries a Pistol"

Most readers would readily agree that this anecdote is well told: It has many concrete, memorable details; there is action, suspense, climax, resolution, and even dialogue. It is about a believable, possible experience. Finally, the anecdote is clearly relevant to the author's argument about gun control.

See Chapter 2, "Remembering an Event," for more information about narrating anecdotes.

EXERCISE 13.7

Evaluate the way an anecdote is used in paragraph 16 of Amitai Etzioni's essay "Working at McDonald's" in Chapter 5 (pp. 158–60). Consider whether the story is well told and true to life. Decide whether it seems to be relevant to the whole argument. Does the writer make the relevance clear? Does the anecdote support Etzioni's argument?

Use relevant textual evidence.

When you argue claims of value (Chapter 7), **textual evidence** will be very important. In your college courses, if you are asked to evaluate a controversial article, you must quote, paraphrase, or *summarize* passages so that readers can understand why you think the author's argument is or is not credible. If you are analyzing a novel, you must include numerous excerpts to show just how you arrived at your conclusion.

For textual evidence to be considered effective support for an argument, it must be carefully selected to be relevant. You must help readers see the connection between each piece of evidence and the reason it supports. Textual evidence must also be highly selective—that is, chosen from among all the available evidence to provide the support needed without overwhelming the reader or weakening the argument with marginally relevant evidence. Textual evidence usually has more impact if it is balanced between quotation and paraphrase, and quotations must be smoothly *integrated* into the sentences of the argument.

The following example comes from a student essay in which the writer argues that the main character (referred to as "the boy") in the short story "Araby" by James Joyce is so self-absorbed that he learns nothing about himself or other people:

Crane cites textual evidence from "Araby" to convince readers to take her argument seriously.	The story opens and closes with images of blindness — a framing device that shows the boy does not change but ends up with the same lack of understanding that he began with. The street is "blind" with an "uninhabited house . . . at the blind end" (par. 1). As he spies on Mangan's sister, from his own house, the boy intentionally limits what he is able to see by lowering the "blind" until it is only an inch from the window sash (par. 4). At the bazaar in the closing scene, the "light was out," and the upper part of the hall was "completely dark" (par. 36). The boy is left "gazing up into the darkness," seeing nothing but an inner torment that burns his eyes (par. 37).

The boy's blindness appears to be caused by his obsession with Mangan's sister. When he tries to read at night, for example, the girl's "image [comes] between [him] and the page," in effect blinding him (par. 12). In fact, he seems blind to everything except this "image" of the "brown-clad figure cast by [his] imagination" (par. 16). The girl's "brown-clad figure" is also associated with the houses on "blind" North Richmond Street, with their "brown imperturbable faces" (par. 1). The houses stare back at the boy, unaffected by his presence and gaze.

— Sally Crane, "Gazing into the Darkness"

Notice how the writer quotes selected words and phrases about blindness to support her reasoning that the boy learns nothing because he is blinded. There are twelve smoothly integrated quotations in these two paragraphs, along with a number of paraphrases, all of them relevant. The writer does not assume that the evidence speaks for itself; she comments and interprets throughout.

For more information on paraphrasing, see pp. 304–305 in Chapter 9 and pp. 435–37 in Chapter 18.

EXERCISE 13.8

Analyze the use of evidence in paragraphs 2–5 of Melissa Mae's essay "'A Case for Torture': A Questionable Argument" in Chapter 11 (pp. 335–38). If you have not read this essay, read it now. Identify the quotes and paraphrases Mae uses, and then try to identify the phrases or sentences that comment on or explain this evidence. Consider whether Mae's evidence in these two paragraphs seems relevant to her thesis and reasons, appropriately selective, well balanced between quotes and paraphrases, integrated smoothly into the sentences she creates, and explained helpfully.

Responding to Objections and Alternatives

Asserting a thesis and backing it with reasons and support are essential to a successful argument. Thoughtful writers go further, however, by anticipating and responding to their readers' objections or their alternative position or solutions to a problem.

To respond to objections and alternatives, writers rely on three basic strategies: acknowledging, conceding, and refuting. Writers show they are aware of readers' objections and questions (*acknowledge*), modify their position to accept readers' concerns they think are legitimate (*concede*), or explicitly argue that readers' objections may be invalid or that their concerns may be irrelevant (*refute*). Writers may use one or more of these three strategies in the same essay. Readers find arguments more convincing when writers have anticipated their concerns in these ways.

Acknowledge readers' concerns.

When you **acknowledge** readers' questions or objections, you show that you are aware of their point of view and take it seriously even if you do not agree with it, as in the following example:

> Marin acknowledges three doubts his readers may have regarding his argument that some of America's homeless have chosen that way of life.

The homeless, it seems, can be roughly divided into two groups: those who have had marginality and homelessness forced upon them and want nothing more than to escape them, and a smaller number who have at least in part chosen marginality, and now accept, or, in a few cases, embrace it.

I understand how dangerous it can be to introduce the idea of choice into a discussion of homelessness. It can all too easily be used for all the wrong reasons by all the wrong people to justify indifference or brutality toward the homeless, or to argue that they are getting only what they deserve.

And I understand, too, how complicated the notion can become: Many of the veterans on the street, or battered women, or abused and runaway children, have chosen this life only as the lesser of evils, and because, in this society, there is often no place else to go.

And finally, I understand how much that happens on the street can combine to create an apparent acceptance of homelessness that is nothing more than the absolute absence of hope.

Nonetheless we must learn to accept that there may indeed be people on the street who have seen so much of our world, or have seen it so clearly, that to live in it becomes impossible.

— Peter Marin, "Go Ask Alice"

You might think that acknowledging readers' objections in this way—addressing readers directly, listing their possible objections, and discussing each one—would weaken your argument. It might even seem reckless to suggest objections that not all readers would think of. On the contrary, however, most readers respond positively to this strategy because it makes you seem thoughtful and reasonable. By researching your subject and your readers, you will be able to use this strategy confidently in your own argumentative essays. And you will learn to look for it in arguments you read and use it to make judgments about the writer's credibility.

| EXERCISE 13.9 |

Patrick O'Malley acknowledges readers' concerns in paragraphs 6 and 10 of his essay in Chapter 6 (pp. 198–203). How, specifically, does O'Malley attempt to acknowledge his readers' concerns? What do you find most and least successful in his acknowledgment? How does the acknowledgment affect your judgment of the writer's credibility?

Concede readers' concerns.

To argue effectively, you must often take special care to acknowledge readers' objections; questions; and alternative positions, causes, or solutions. Occasionally, however, you may have to go even further. Instead of merely acknowledging your readers' concerns, you may decide to accept some of them and incorporate them into your own argument. This strategy, called **concession,** can be very disarming to readers, for it recognizes that opposing views have merit. The following example comes from an essay enthusiastically endorsing e-mail:

After supporting his own reasons for embracing e-mail, Kinsley accommodates readers' likely reservations by conceding that e-mail poses certain problems.

To be sure, egalitarianism has its limits. The ease and economy of sending email, especially to multiple recipients, makes us all vulnerable to any bore, loony, or commercial or political salesman who can get our email address. It's still a lot less intrusive than the telephone, since you can read and answer or ignore email at your own convenience. But as normal people's email starts mounting into the hundreds daily, . . . filtering mechanisms and conventions of etiquette that are still in their primitive stage will be desperately needed.

Another supposed disadvantage of email is that it discourages face-to-face communication. At Microsoft, where people routinely send email back and forth all day to the person in the next office, this is certainly true. Some people believe this tendency has more to do with the underdeveloped social skills of computer geeks than with Microsoft's role in developing the technology email relies on. I wouldn't presume to comment on that. Whether you think email replacing live conversation is a good or bad thing depends, I guess, on how much of a misanthrope you are. I like it.

— Michael Kinsley, "Email Culture"

Notice that Kinsley's accommodation or concession is not grudging. He readily concedes that e-mail brings users a lot of unwanted messages and may discourage conversation in the workplace.

| EXERCISE 13.10 |

How does Jessica Statsky respond to readers' objections and alternatives in paragraphs 6 and 10 of her essay in Chapter 5 (pp. 152–57) arguing against the competitive culture of children's sports? What seems successful or unsuccessful in her argument? How do her efforts to make concessions affect her argument and her credibility?

Refute readers' objections.

Your readers' possible objections and views cannot always be conceded. Sometimes they must be refuted. When you **refute readers' objections,** you assert that they are wrong and argue against them. Refutation does not have to be delivered arrogantly or dismissively, however. Because differences are inevitable, reasoned argument provides a peaceful and constructive way for informed, well-intentioned people who disagree strongly to air their differences.

In the following example, social sciences professor Todd Gitlin refutes one argument for giving college students the opportunity to purchase lecture notes prepared by someone else:

Gitlin first concedes a possible objection, and then even partially agrees with this view. In the second paragraph, however, he begins to refute the objection.

Now, it may well be argued that universities are already shortchanging their students by stuffing them into huge lecture halls where, unlike at rock concerts or basketball games, the lecturer can't even be seen on a giant screen in real time. If they're already shortchanged with impersonal instruction, what's the harm in offering canned lecture notes?

The amphitheater lecture is indeed, for all but the most engaging professors, a lesser form of instruction, and scarcely to be idealized. Still, Education by Download misses one of the keys to learning. Education is a meeting of minds, a process through which the student educes, draws from within, a response to what the teacher teaches.

The very act of taking notes—not reading someone else's notes, no matter how stellar—is a way of engaging the material, wrestling

> with it, struggling to comprehend or take issue, but in any case entering into the work. The point is to decide, while you are listening, what matters in the presentation. And while I don't believe that most of life consists of showing up, education does begin with that—with immersing yourself in the activity at hand, listening, thinking, judging, offering active responses. A download is a poor substitute.
> — Todd Gitlin, "Disappearing Ink"

As this selection illustrates, writers cannot simply dismiss readers' possible concerns with a wave of their hand. Gitlin states a potential objection fully and fairly but then goes on to refute it by claiming that students need to take their own lecture notes to engage and comprehend the material that is being presented to them.

Effective refutation requires a restrained tone and careful argument. Although you may not accept this particular refutation, you can agree that it is well reasoned and supported. You need not feel attacked personally because the writer disagrees with you.

EXERCISE 13.11

Evaluate Daniel J. Solove's acknowledgment of the opposing argument in paragraph 4 of "Why Privacy Matters Even If You Have 'Nothing to Hide'" and his refutation in the paragraphs that follow (Chapter 5, pp. 163–67). How does Solove signal or announce the points of his refutation? How does he support the refutation? What is the tone of the refutation, and how effective do you think the tone would be in convincing readers to take the writer's argument seriously?

Recognizing Logical Fallacies

Fallacies are errors or flaws in reasoning. Although essentially unsound, fallacious arguments seem superficially plausible and often have great persuasive power. Fallacies are not necessarily deliberate efforts to deceive readers. Writers may introduce a fallacy accidentally by not examining their own reasons or underlying assumptions, by failing to establish solid support, or by using unclear or ambiguous words. Here is a summary of the most common logical fallacies (listed alphabetically):

- **Begging the question:** Arguing that a claim is true by repeating the claim in different words (also called *circular reasoning*)
- **Confusing chronology with causality:** Assuming that because one thing preceded another, the former caused the latter (also called *post hoc, ergo propter hoc*—Latin for "after this, therefore because of this")
- **Either-or reasoning:** Assuming that there are only two sides to a question and representing yours as the only correct one
- **Equivocating:** Misleading or hedging with ambiguous word choices
- **Failing to accept the burden of proof:** Asserting a claim without presenting a reasoned argument to support it

- *False analogy:* Assuming that because one thing resembles another, conclusions drawn from one also apply to the other
- *Hasty generalization:* Offering only weak or limited evidence to support a conclusion
- *Overreliance on authority:* Assuming that something is true simply because an expert says so and ignoring evidence to the contrary
- *Oversimplifying:* Giving easy answers to complicated questions, often by appealing to emotions rather than logic
- *Personal attack:* Demeaning the proponents of a claim instead of refuting their argument (also called *ad hominem*—Latin for "against the man"—*attack*)
- *Red herring:* Attempting to misdirect the discussion by raising an essentially unrelated point
- *Slanting:* Selecting or emphasizing the evidence that supports your claim and suppressing or playing down other evidence
- *Slippery slope:* Pretending that one thing inevitably leads to another
- *Sob story:* Manipulating readers' emotions to lead them to draw unjustified conclusions
- *Straw man:* Directing the argument against a claim that nobody actually makes or that everyone agrees is very weak

Sentence Strategies for Argument

Writers in college courses, in the community, and in the workplace argue to persuade others, so you are likely to write sentences that assert and support a position or that respond to alternative positions and concede or refute objections. Sentence strategies like these may provide a jumping-off point for articulating your thoughts. Of course, you will probably want to rework the sentences they inspire.

To Assert a Position

▶ When [issue/event] happens, most people think _____, but I think _____ because _____.

▶ [People] focus on [X], which is characterized by _____, and they don't even notice [Y], which is characterized by _____.

▶ Although many people take _____ for granted, [list individuals/groups] oppose it on the grounds that _____.

▶ Whereas supporters of _____ have argued that _____, opponents such as [list individuals/groups] contend that _____.

▶ Though others may view it as a matter of _____, for me, the issue hinges on _____.

▶ According to _____, what's at stake in this issue is _____. For me, however, what is most important is _____.

▶ On this issue, X and Y say _____. Although I understand and to some degree sympathize with their point of view, this is ultimately a question of _____. What's at stake is not _____ but _____. Therefore, we must _____.

▶ This issue is dividing our community. Some people argue _____. Others contend _____. And still others believe _____. It is in all of our interests to _____, however, because _____.

▶ Conventional wisdom is that _____. But I take a different view: _____.

▶ [Subject] has many good qualities, including _____ and _____; however, the pluses do not outweigh its one major drawback, namely that _____.

▶ [Subject] is a brilliant embodiment of [genre or category], especially notable for its superb _____ and thorough _____.

▶ Because I admire [another artist's other work], I expected [subject] to be _____. But I was [disappointed/surprised] by _____ because _____.

▶ Many complain about _____ but do nothing because solving it seems [too hard/too costly].

To Support a Position

▶ What makes _____ [problematic/praiseworthy] is _____.

▶ Because _____, I [support/oppose] _____.

▶ Studies such as _____ have shown that [problem] mostly affects _____ [name group(s)].

▶ Studies by X, Y, and Z show that [solution] has worked in _____, _____, and _____.

▶ The reasons for _____ may surprise you, such as _____, _____, and _____.

▶ The cause(s) of [subject] may be [surprising/alarming/disturbing/amazing], but they are clear: _____ [state cause(s) and provide evidence].

▶ [Cause] plays a [surprising/alarming/disturbing/amazing] role in [our lives/our families/ our communities/our workplaces]: It [does/is/provides] _____ [describe role].

▶ For many years, [name group] has believed that _____. Now there is research supporting this claim, but not for the reasons you may think. It's not _____ that has been causing this phenomenon but _____.

▶ Researchers studying _____ have shown a causal connection between _____ [my causes] and _____ [my subject]. They claim _____ [quote/paraphrase/summarize information from source] (cite source).

▶ A large number of people have been polled on this question, and it appears that _____ was an important factor in their decision to _____.

▶ Reliable research by _____ shows _____.

To Refute an Opposing Position

▶ One problem with [opposing view] is that _____.

▶ Some claim [opposing view], but in reality _____.

▶ My opponents cite research to support their argument, but the credibility of that research is questionable because _____.

▶ This argument seems plausible because it is consistent with our preconceptions. Nevertheless, evidence shows _____.

▶ Activists insist _____. Still, in spite of their good intentions, _____ would [take away a basic right/make things even worse].

▶ X and Y think this issue is about _____. But what is really at stake here is _____.

▶ Proponents object to my argument on the grounds that _____. However, they are confusing results with causes. What I am arguing is _____.

▶ Polls show that most people favor _____, but an opinion's popularity does not make it true or right.

▶ Though most would agree that _____ is true, it does not necessarily follow that _____.

▶ One common complaint is _____. In recent years, however, _____.

▶ Some people think we can't afford to do _____ [name solution], but it would only cost $_____ [insert dollar amount] to put my solution in place compared to $_____, the cost of [doing nothing/implementing an alternative solution].

▶ Although it might take _____ [months/years] to implement this solution, it would actually take longer to implement [alternative solution].

▶ Some may suggest that I favor this solution because I would benefit personally; however, the fact is we would all benefit because _____.

▶ Some may claim that this solution has been tried and hasn't worked. But research shows that _____ [explain how my solution differs from past experiments in several important ways]: _____, _____, and _____ (list differences).

▶ X, reviewer for _____, claims that _____. But I agree with Y, reviewer for _____, who argues that _____.

▶ Some people think [subject] is [alternative judgment] because of _____, _____, and _____ [reasons]. Although it is easy to see why they might make this argument, the evidence does not back it up: _____ [explanation].

▶ Reviewers have remarked that [subject] is a pale imitation of [comparable subject]. I disagree. Whereas [comparable subject] is _____, [subject] is _____.

▶ This [subject] has generated criticism for its supposed _____. But [subject] is not _____. Instead, it is _____.

▶ A recent study of [subject] showed that _____.

To Concede an Objection

► I agree that _____ .

► _____ is certainly an important factor.

► To be sure, _____ is true.

► Granted, _____ must be taken into consideration.

► Some people argue that _____ . I understand this reservation, and therefore, I think we should _____ .

► A common concern about this issue is _____ . That's why my argument focuses on [this other aspect] of the issue.

► I agree with those who [claim X/object on X grounds]; therefore, instead of [option A], I think we should pursue [option B].

► If _____ seems too [time-consuming/expensive], let's try _____ .

► Where _____ is a concern, I think [name alternative] should be followed.

► Although _____ is the best way to deal with a problem like this, under [describe special circumstances], I agree that _____ should be done.

► Indeed, the more hard-core [name enthusiasts] may complain that [subject] is not sufficiently _____ [shortcomings].

► The one justifiable criticism that could be made against [subject] is _____ .

► As some critics have pointed out, [subject] does follow the tried-and-true formula of _____ .

To Concede and Refute an Objection

► _____ may be true for X but not for Y.

► Although _____ , I think _____ .

► X and Y insist that _____ . Nevertheless, in spite of their good intentions, _____ .

► I agree that _____ is important, but so is _____ .

► I agree that _____ is important, but my opponents need to consider _____ .

► On the one hand, I accept X's argument that _____ , but on the other hand, I still think _____ is ultimately more important because _____ .

► As some critics have pointed out, [subject] does follow the tried-and-true formula of _____ . Still, the [director/writer/artist] is using the formula effectively to _____ .

► Those who disagree about _____ often see it as a choice between _____ and _____ . But both are important. We don't have to choose between them because _____ .

14

Designing Documents

The way a document is designed—the arrangement of text, visuals, and white space on a page—has a major impact on the readability of a document and may influence the reader's attitude toward it. This chapter introduces basic components of document design, offers guidelines for designing effective documents, and discusses some common formats for documents you may be asked to create in your college courses or in the workplace. You may also want to look at the student essays in Chapters 2–7 to analyze how they formatted and integrated visuals into their college writing projects. In addition, Chapters 19 and 20 includes a research project annotated to point out the formatting requirements in MLA and APA style.

The Impact of Document Design

When we read a well-designed document, part of the meaning we take away from it is attributable to design. When we read a poorly designed document, however, it may be difficult to discern its meaning at all. We can probably all agree that effectively written documents are easy to navigate, and their meanings are accessible to the intended audience. Good design should accordingly make readability easier and make the intended meaning clearer and more vivid.

The ways in which design affects the way we read documents can be illustrated fairly simply. Consider the following familiar phrase, rendered in four different ways:

The words in each rendering are the same, but the different uses of fonts, colors, and white space encourage us to read them very differently. The first message is vaguely unsettling (is that a ransom note? a message from a stalker?); the second seems conventionally sweet; the third carries no emotional or context clues, but the spacing makes it irritatingly difficult to read; and the fourth offers no tone or context clues at all (though this in itself might strike us as odd, given the meaning of the words). Thus, design does far more than add visual interest: It actually directs how we read and, to a certain extent, determines the meaning we derive from texts.

The freedom you have in terms of using design elements and visuals in your college writing projects will vary quite a bit, depending on your instructors' preferences and the nature of the projects. As you write, however, you should always remain aware of the impact document design can have on your reader. And any time you read a document—whether it is a textbook, a blog, or even an ad on the bus—you should stop to think about how that document was designed and how that design affects your reading of it.

Considering Context, Audience, and Purpose

Context, audience, and *purpose* are the key components to consider in designing any document. For instance, if you are writing an essay for a college course, you can expect that your instructor and your classmates will read it carefully. Your design decisions should therefore make sustained reading as easy as possible; fonts that are too small to read easily or print that is too light to see clearly will make the reader's job unnecessarily difficult. Additionally, instructors usually ask students to submit hard-copy work that is double-spaced text with one-inch margins to give the reviewers room to write comments on the page.*

In most college courses, guidelines on design have traditionally followed a "less is more" rule—written assignments were generally expected to be printed on white, 8.5- by 11-inch paper, and the use of colors, extravagant fonts, sheerly decorative visuals, and the like, was in most cases discouraged. However, in many college classrooms, what constitutes an acceptable course "paper" or project is in transition; many instructors now allow or in some cases require the creation of multimodal projects — Web sites, video, PowerPoint presentations, playlists, and the like—in place of traditional papers.

Developments like these, driven largely by advances in technology, have obviously required some adjustments to traditional notions of acceptable design for college writing. "Less is more" still applies, however, in principle. Good design gives priority to clarity:

---

* It is important to note that MLA, APA, and other style systems have specific rules regarding such things as spacing, margins, and heading formats. Be sure to ask your instructor whether you will be expected to adhere closely to these rules; if so, your choices regarding document design will be limited. For more on MLA and APA style, see pp. 438–75.

Whatever the project, you should use design not for its own sake but to make your points as clearly, effectively, and efficiently as possible.

Of course, the same principle of clarity applies to most *non*academic documents you will write. In writing for nonacademic audiences, however, you cannot necessarily expect all readers to read your writing closely. Some readers may skim through your blog entries looking for interesting points; others might scan a report or memo for information important specifically to them. Design elements such as *headings, bullets,* and *chunking* will help these readers find the information of most interest to them.

Frequently, too, your document design decisions will be predetermined by the kind of document you are preparing. Business letters and memos, for example, traditionally follow specific formats. Because your readers will bring certain expectations to these kinds of documents, altering an established format can cause confusion and should therefore be avoided.

To analyze the context in which a document is read or used, ask yourself the following questions:

- **Where will my document be read?** Will the document be read on paper in a well-lighted, quiet room, or in another context — perhaps on a laptop in a noisy, dimly lit coffee shop?

- **Do my readers have specific expectations for this kind of document?** Am I writing a memo, letter, or report that requires certain design conventions? Does my instructor expect me to follow MLA style, APA style, or another system?

- **How will the information be used?** Are my readers reading to learn or to be entertained? Do I expect them to skim the document or to read it carefully?

Elements of Document Design

Readable *fonts;* informative *headings; bulleted or numbered lists;* and appropriate use of *color, white space,* and *visuals* like photographs, charts, and diagrams all help readers learn from your document.

Choose readable fonts.

Typography is a design term for the letters and symbols that make up the print on a page or a screen. You are already using important aspects of typography when you use capital letters, italics, boldface, or different sizes of type to signal a new sentence, identify the title of a book, or distinguish a heading from body text.

Word processing programs enable you to use dozens of different **fonts,** or typefaces; bold and italic versions of these fonts; and a range of font sizes. Fortunately, you can rely on some simple design principles to make good typographic choices for your documents.

Perhaps the most important advice for working with typography is to choose fonts that are easy to read. Some fonts are meant for decorative or otherwise very minimal use, and are hard to read in extended passages. Font style, font size, and combinations of style and size are features that can add to or detract from readability.

Considering Font Style   For most academic and business writing, you will probably want to choose a traditional font that is easy to read, such as Arial or Times New Roman. This book is set in Stone Serif. Sentences and paragraphs printed in fonts that imitate *calligraphy* (typically called script fonts) or those that mimic **Handwriting** are not only difficult to read but also too informal in appearance for most academic and business purposes.

Some Fonts Appropriate for Academic and Business Writing

Arial

Georgia

Tahoma

Times New Roman

Verdana

Considering Font Size   To ensure that your documents can be read easily, you also need to choose an appropriate font size (traditionally measured in units called **points**). For most types of academic writing, a 12-point font is standard for the main (body) text. For Web pages, however, you should consider using a slightly larger font to compensate for the difficulty of reading from a computer monitor. For computer-projected displays, you should use an even larger font size (such as 32-point, and typically no smaller than 18-point) to ensure that the text can be read from a distance.

Combining Font Styles and Sizes   Although computers now make hundreds of font styles and sizes available to writers, you should avoid confusing readers with too many different fonts in one document. Limit the fonts in a document to one or two that complement each other well. A common practice, for instance, is to choose one font for all titles and headings (such as Arial, 14-point, boldface) and another for the body text (such as Times New Roman, 12-point), as shown in the example here.

This Is an Example Heading

This is body text. This is body text.
This is body text. This is body text.
This is body text. This is body text.

This Is an Example Heading

This is body text. This is body text.
This is body text. This is body text.
This is body text. This is body text.

Use headings to organize your writing.

Titles and headings are often distinguished from body text by boldface, italics, or font size. Headings are helpful in calling attention to certain parts or sections of a piece of writing and in offering readers visual cues to its overall organization. Always check with your instructor about the conventions for using (or not using) these elements in the particular discipline you are studying.

Distinguishing between Headings and Subheadings   Typically, headings for major sections (level-one headings) must have more visual impact than those subdividing these sections (level-two headings), which should be more prominent than headings within the subdivisions (level-three headings). The typography should reflect this hierarchy of headings. Here is one possible system for distinguishing among three levels of headings:

LEVEL-ONE HEADING
Level-Two Heading
Level-Three Heading

Notice that the level-one and level-two headings are given the greatest prominence by the use of boldface and that they are distinguished from one another by the use of all capital letters for the major heading versus capital and lowercase letters for the subheading. The third-level heading, italicized but not boldfaced, is less prominent than the other two headings but can still be readily distinguished from body text. Whatever system you use to distinguish headings and subheadings, be sure to apply it consistently throughout your document.

Positioning Headings Consistently   In addition to keeping track of the font size and style of headings, you need to position headings in the same way throughout a piece of writing. You will want to consider the spacing above and below headings and determine whether the headings should be aligned with the left margin, indented a fixed amount of space, or centered. In this book, headings like the one that begins this paragraph—**Positioning Headings Consistently**—are aligned with the left margin and followed by a fixed amount of space.

Using Type Size to Differentiate Headings from Text   In documents that do not need to observe MLA or APA style, which have specific rules about formatting, you may wish to use font size to help make headings visually distinct from the body of the text. If you do so, avoid making the headings too large. To accompany 12-point body text, for instance, a 14-point heading will do. The default settings for heading and body text styles on most word processing and desktop publishing programs are effective, and you may want to use them to autoformat your heading and text styles.

For more on selecting appropriate headings and subheadings, see Chapter 10, pp. 329–30.

Use lists to highlight steps or key points.

Lists are often an effective way to present information in a logical and visually coherent way. Use a **numbered list** (1, 2, 3) to present the steps in a process or to list items that readers will need to refer to easily (for instance, see the numbered steps under the heading "Edit and proofread your draft" on pp. 45–46). Use a **bulleted list** (marking each new item with a "bullet"—a dash, circle, or box) to highlight key points when the order of the items is not significant (for instance, see the bulleted lists under the heading "Choose a concept to write about" on p. 127). Written instructions, such as recipes, are typically formatted using numbered lists, whereas a list of supplies, for example, is more often presented in the form of a bulleted list.

Use colors with care.

Color printers, photocopiers, and online technology facilitate the use of color, but color does not necessarily make text easier to read. In most academic print documents, the only color you should use is black. Though color is typically used more freely in academic writing produced in other media (for example, Web pages or slideshow presentations), it should still be used in moderation and always with the aim of increasing your readers' understanding of what you have to say. Always consider, too, whether your readers might be color-blind and whether they will have access to a full-color version of the document.

Although the slideshow design in Figure 14.1 is visually interesting and the heading is readable, the bulleted text is very hard to read because there is too little contrast between the text color and the background color.

In Figure 14.2, it is clear that the person who created the pie chart carefully chose the colors to represent the different data. What the person did not consider, however, is how the colors would look when printed out on a black-and-white printer. It is nearly impossible to associate the labels with the slices of the pie and thus to read the chart. If your work is likely to be photocopied, consider using patterns to distinguish pie slices or lines and bars in graphs.

FIGURE 14.1   Document with Too Little Color Contrast

**Number and Distribution of Fatal
Occupational Injuries by Age among
Young Workers, 1992–2002 (N = 644)**

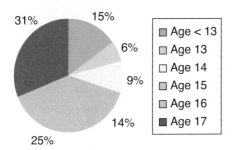

**Number and Distribution of Fatal
Occupational Injuries by Age among
Young Workers, 1992–2002 (N = 644)**

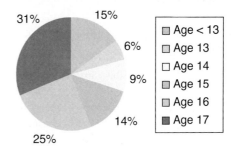

FIGURE 14.2 A Pie Chart That Requires a Color Printer to Be Understandable
Source: National Institute for Occupational Safety and Health, "Data on Young Worker Injuries and Illnesses in Worker Health" (2004).

Also consider the meanings associated with different colors. For example, in the United States and other Western cultures, white is typically associated with goodness and purity; in China, however, white represents grief and mourning. Although your use of color in an essay, a Web page, or a slideshow presentation might not carry such deep meaning, bear in mind that most people have emotional or psychological responses to colors and color combinations.

Use white space to make text readable.

Another basic element of document design, **white space,** is the open, or blank, space surrounding the text. White space is usually used between a heading and the paragraph that follows the heading. You also use white space when you set the margins on the page, and even when you double-space between lines of text and indent paragraphs. In all of these cases, the space makes your document easier to read. When used generously, white space facilitates reading by keeping the pages of a document uncluttered and by helping the eye find and follow the text.

Chunking   Chunking, the breaking up of text into smaller units, also facilitates reading. **Paragraphing** is a form of chunking that divides text into units of closely related information. In most academic essays and reports, text is double-spaced, and paragraphs are distinguished by indenting the first line one-half inch.

In single-spaced text or text that will be read on-screen, you may want to make reading easier by adding extra space between paragraphs rather than indenting the first lines of paragraphs. This format, referred to as **block style,** is often used in memos, letters, and electronic documents. When creating electronic documents, especially Web pages, you might consider chunking your material into separate "pages" or screens, with links connecting the chunks.

Margins   Adequate margins are an important component of readability. If the margins are too small, your page will seem cluttered. For academic essays, use one-inch margins on all sides unless your instructor (or the style manual you are following) advises differently.

Adding Visuals

Tables, graphs, charts, diagrams, photographs, maps, and screen shots add visual interest and are often more effective in conveying information than prose alone. Be certain, however, that each visual has a valid role to play in your work; if the visual is merely a decoration, leave it out or replace it with a visual that is more appropriate.

You can create visuals on a computer, using the drawing tools of a word processing program, the charting tools of a spreadsheet program, or software specifically designed for creating visuals. You can also download visuals from the Internet or photocopy or scan visuals from print materials. If your essay is going to be posted on the Web on a site that is not password-protected and a visual you want to use is from a source that is copyrighted, you should request written permission from the copyright holder (such as the photographer, publisher, or site sponsor). For any visual that you borrow from or create based on data from a source, be sure to cite the source in the caption, your bibliography, or both, according to the guidelines of the documentation system you are using.

Choose and design visuals with their final use in mind.

Select the types of visuals that will best suit your purpose (see Figure 14.3, pp. 391–93).

macmillanhighered.com/conciseguide
Turorials > Digital Writing > Presentations
        > Photo Editing Basics with GIMP

Number, title, and label visuals.

Number your visuals in sequential order, and give each one a title. Refer to tables as *Table 1, Table 2,* and so on, and to other types of visuals as *Figure 1, Figure 2,* and so on. (In a long work with chapters or sections, also include the chapter or section number [*Figure 14.1*], as is done here.) In MLA style, use the abbreviation *fig.*

Make sure each visual has a title that reflects its subject (for example, income levels) and its purpose (to compare changes in those income levels over time): *Figure 1. Percentage of U.S. Households in Three Income Ranges, 2000–2012.* MLA style requires that the title be placed above a table and below a figure.

To help readers understand a visual, clearly label all of its parts. For instance, give each of a table's columns a heading, and label each section of a pie chart with the percentage and the item it represents. You may place the label on the chart itself if it is readable, or in a legend next to the chart.

Some visuals may require a caption to provide a fuller description or explanation than the title alone can. (See Figure 14.2, for example.)

<table>
<tr><th>Use a/an . . .</th><th>to . . .</th><th></th></tr>
<tr><td>table</td><td>display detailed numerical or textual data</td><td>
<table>
<tr><th colspan="5">TABLE 21.1 Population Change for the Ten Largest U.S. Cities, 1990 to 2000</th></tr>
<tr><th></th><th colspan="2">Population</th><th colspan="2">Change, 1990 to 2000</th></tr>
<tr><th>City and State</th><th>April 1, 2000</th><th>April 1, 1990</th><th>Number</th><th>Percentage</th></tr>
<tr><td>New York, NY</td><td>8,008,278</td><td>7,322,564</td><td>685,714</td><td>9.4</td></tr>
<tr><td>Los Angeles, CA</td><td>3,694,820</td><td>3,485,398</td><td>209,422</td><td>6.0</td></tr>
<tr><td>Chicago, IL</td><td>2,896,016</td><td>2,783,726</td><td>112,290</td><td>4.0</td></tr>
<tr><td>Houston, TX</td><td>1,953,631</td><td>1,630,553</td><td>323,078</td><td>19.8</td></tr>
<tr><td>Philadelphia, PA</td><td>1,517,550</td><td>1,585,577</td><td>68,027</td><td>4.3</td></tr>
<tr><td>Phoenix, AZ</td><td>1,321,045</td><td>983,403</td><td>337,642</td><td>34.3</td></tr>
<tr><td>San Diego, CA</td><td>1,223,400</td><td>1,110,549</td><td>112,851</td><td>10.2</td></tr>
<tr><td>Dallas, TX</td><td>1,188,580</td><td>1,006,877</td><td>181,703</td><td>18.0</td></tr>
<tr><td>San Antonio, TX</td><td>1,144,646</td><td>935,933</td><td>208,713</td><td>22.3</td></tr>
<tr><td>Detroit, MI</td><td>951,270</td><td>1,027,974</td><td>76,704</td><td>7.5</td></tr>
</table>
</td></tr>
<tr><td>bar graph</td><td>compare one or more variables</td><td>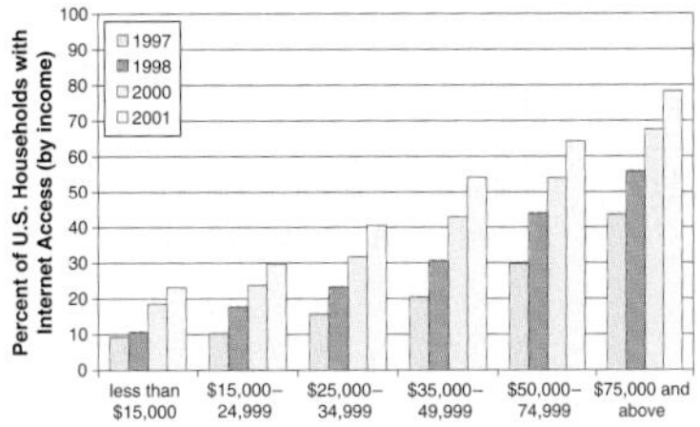
Percent of U.S. Households with Internet Access (by income)
1997
1998
2000
2001
less than $15,000
$15,000–24,999
$25,000–34,999
$35,000–49,999
$50,000–74,999
$75,000 and above</td></tr>
<tr><td>line graph</td><td>compare one or more variables, usually over time</td><td>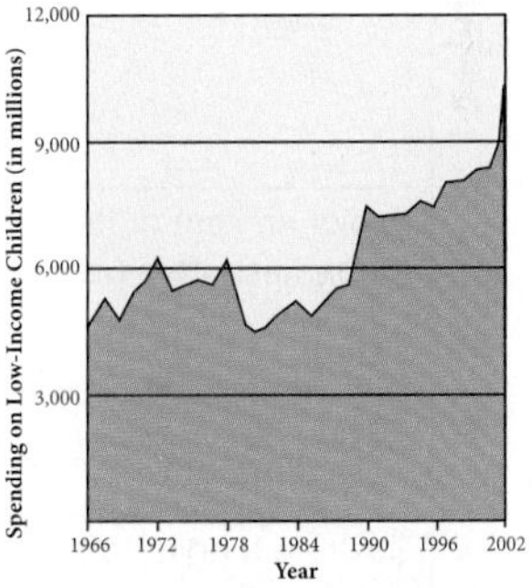
Spending on Low-Income Children (in millions)
12,000
9,000
6,000
3,000
1966 1972 1978 1984 1990 1996 2002
Year</td></tr>
<tr><td>pie chart</td><td>show the parts that make up a whole (usually adding up to 100%)</td><td>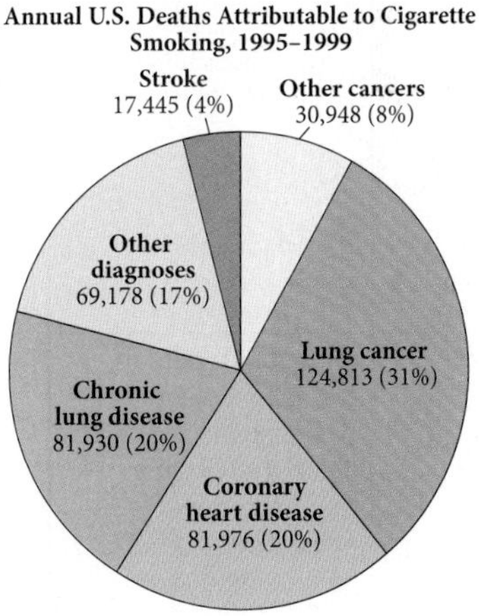
Annual U.S. Deaths Attributable to Cigarette Smoking, 1995–1999
Stroke 17,445 (4%)
Other cancers 30,948 (8%)
Other diagnoses 69,178 (17%)
Lung cancer 124,813 (31%)
Chronic lung disease 81,930 (20%)
Coronary heart disease 81,976 (20%)</td></tr>
</table>

FIGURE 14.3 When to Use a Visual ***(continued)***

Use a/an . . .	to . . .	
flowchart	show a process broken down into steps or stages	**Should You Change Your Oil?** Has the car been driven 3,000 miles since last changed? **If YES** Change the oil. **If NO** Has it been three months since last changed? **If YES** Change the oil. **If NO** No need to change the oil.
organization chart	map lines of authority within an organization	**Newsroom Staff** Managing Editor News Editor City Editor Sports Editor Copy Editors Photographers Reporters Sports Reporters
diagram	depict an item or its properties, often using symbols	cerebral hemisphere pituitary gland cerebellum brainstem spinal cord
drawing or cartoon	illustrate a point, often with humor	BUT I'M **HONORING** YOU, DUDE! GO SAVAGES KILL 'EM INDI **LALO ALCARAZ** ©2002† DISTRIBUTED BY UNIVERSAL PRESS SYNDICATE LALO ALCARAZ © 2002. Dist. by UNIVERSAL UCLICK. Reprinted with permission. All rights reserved.
photograph	represent a person, place, or object discussed in the text (Note that photos that have been altered should be so identified.)	© JH Pete Carmichael/Getty Images

map	show geographical areas, lay out spatial relationships, or make a historical or political point	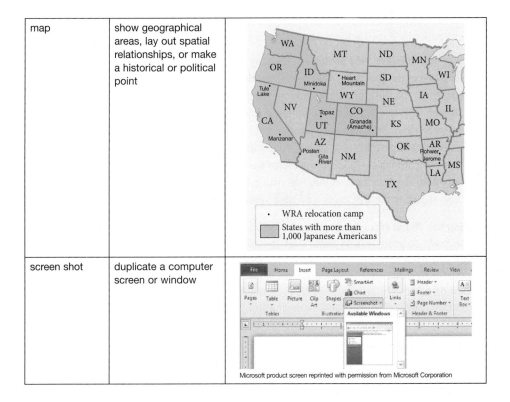
screen shot	duplicate a computer screen or window	

Cite visual sources.

Finally, if you borrow a visual from another source or create a visual from borrowed information, you must cite the source, following the guidelines for the documentation style you are using. In addition, be sure to document the source in your list of works cited or references at the end of your document.

Integrate the visual into the text.

Visuals should facilitate, not disrupt, the reading of the body text. To achieve this goal, you need to first introduce and discuss the visual in your text and then insert the visual in an appropriate location.

Introducing the Visual Ideally, you should introduce each visual by referring to it in your text immediately *before* the visual appears. An effective textual reference answers the following questions:

- What is the number of the visual?
- Where is it located?
- What kind of information does it contain?
- What important point does it make or support?

Here is an example of a paragraph that effectively refers to a visual; it is taken from the student paper by Paul Taylor that appears in Chapter 12 (pp. 360–63):

> Gordon Parks's 1952 photograph *Emerging Man* (Fig. 1) is as historically significant a reflection of the civil rights movement as are the speeches of Martin Luther King and Malcolm X, the music of Mahalia Jackson, and the books of Ralph Ellison and James Baldwin. Through striking use of black and white—a reflection of the racial divisions plaguing American cities and towns throughout much of the nineteenth and twentieth centuries—and a symbolically potent central subject—an African American man we see literally "emerging" from a city manhole—Parks's photo evokes the centuries of racial and economic marginalization of African Americans, at the same time as it projects a spirit of determination and optimism regarding the civil rights movement's eventual success.

Placing the Visual in an Appropriate Location   MLA style requires that you place a visual in the body of your text as soon after the discussion as possible, particularly when the reader will need to consult the visual. See, for example, Paul Taylor's paper in Chapter 12 (pp. 360–63). (Note that he discusses the figures in the text and places them as close after he first mentions them as he can. He also includes them in his list of works cited (p. 363), with a descriptive title and source information.)

Use common sense when creating visuals on a computer.

If you use a computer program to create visuals, keep this advice in mind:

- *Make the decisions that your computer cannot make for you.* A computer can automatically turn spreadsheet data into a pie chart or bar graph, but only you can decide which visual—or what use of color, if any—is most appropriate for your purpose.

- *Avoid "chart junk."* Many computer programs provide an array of special effects that can be used to alter visuals, including three-dimensional renderings, textured backgrounds, and shadowed text. Such special effects often detract from the intended message of the visual by calling attention to themselves instead. Use them sparingly, and only when they emphasize key information.

- *Use clip art sparingly, if at all.* Clip art consists of icons, symbols, and other simple, typically abstract, copyright-free drawings. Because clip art simplifies ideas, it is of limited use in conveying the complex information contained in most academic writing.

15 Planning a Research Project   396

16 Finding Sources and Conducting Field Research   404

17 Evaluating Sources   420

18 Using Sources to Support Your Ideas   427

19 Citing and Documenting Sources in MLA Style   438

20 Citing and Documenting Sources in APA Style   466

PART 3

Strategies for Research

15

Planning a Research Project

To research a topic effectively at the college level requires a plan. A clear sense of your rhetorical situation, as well as the practical needs of your research task (such as the due date and the level of detail required), will help you create one. Figure 15.1 lists common elements that you will need to consider as you plan your research project, and also as you continue to find and evaluate sources and draft your project.

Define your research task and set a schedule.

Analyze your rhetorical situation.

- Determine your purpose.
- Analyze your audience to understand the interest and background your readers bring to the project, and analyze your attitude to determine how you want your readers to think of you.
- Determine the genre, or type, of research project you are creating, such as a proposal or laboratory report, and the expectations for research, writing, and design associated with this genre.

Understand the assignment.

- Check your syllabus or consult your instructor about the number and types of resources required, the length of the project, and so forth.
- Determine the final due date, and assign interim due dates to keep your project on track.

Establish a research log.

- Create a list of keywords.
- Create a working bibliography, and annotate entries.
- Take notes on your sources.

Choose a topic, get an overview, and narrow your topic.

Choose a topic that is appropriate to the assignment and of interest to you and your readers.

- Consult with your instructor.
- Review textbooks and other course materials.
- Explore newspapers, magazines, and Internet sites.

Get an overview, and narrow your topic (if necessary).

- Consult subject guides or a librarian to determine the availability of sources on your topic.
- Get necessary background by consulting encyclopedias and other general reference sources.
- Start a working bibliography (list of sources) to keep track of the sources you are beginning to explore.
- Draft questions to guide your research.

FIGURE 15.1 Overview of a Research Project

Search for in-depth information on your topic.

Conduct a search for sources, using carefully selected search terms.

- Check the library's resources (such as the catalog, databases, or home page) for books, articles, and multimedia.
- Check Internet sites for relevant Web sites, blogs, groups.

- Keep a list of search terms in a research log, and annotate your working bibliography to keep track of sources.
- Add relevant sources to your working bibliography, and annotate entries to record the sources' main points and how you would use the source.
- Refine your research questions, and draft a thesis.

Refine your search.

Ask yourself questions like these:

- Is this what I expected to find?
- Am I finding enough?
- Am I finding too much?
- Do I need to modify my keywords?

- Do I need to recheck background sources?
- Do I need to revise my research questions?
- Do I need to modify my thesis statement?

Continue searching for relevant and reliable sources in response to your answers.

Evaluate your sources.

Determine the relevance of potential sources.

- Does the source explain terms or concepts or provide background?
- Does the source provide evidence to support your claims?
- Does the source offer alternative viewpoints or lend authority?

Determine the reliability of potential sources.

- Who wrote it?
- When was it published?
- Who published it?
- Is the source scholarly or popular (or something else)?
- Is the source printed or online?
- What does the source say?

Continue to evaluate and refine your search strategy based on your research results.

Use your research to support your ideas.

Use evidence from sources to support your ideas.

- Synthesize ideas from multiple sources.
- Support your ideas with summaries, paraphrases, and quotations as appropriate.

Avoid plagiarism.

- Paraphrase carefully to avoid plagiarism.
- Carefully integrate source material into your text.
- Cite sources using an appropriate citation style.

Analyzing Your Rhetorical Situation and Setting a Schedule

Making your research project manageable begins with defining the scope and goals of your research project. Begin by analyzing your *rhetorical situation:*

- What is your *purpose*? Is it to explain a concept, report on or argue for a position, or analyze the causes of an event or a behavior?

- Who is your *audience* and what will their interests, attitudes, and expectations for the project be? How many and what kinds of resources does your audience expect you to consult? (For college research projects, your audience will likely be your instructor.)

- What *genre* is the research project, and how will that affect the kinds of sources you use? An observational report in the social sciences may demand mainly *primary research,* whereas an argument essay for a history course may require a variety of *secondary* and primary sources.

Also be sure you consider the following practical issues before you begin your research project:

- How long should the research project be?

- When is it due?

- Are any interim assignments required (such as an outline or an annotated bibliography)?

If you're not sure of the answers to these questions, ask your instructor to clarify the assignment or define any confusing terms so that you can work most efficiently.

Finally, set a schedule. Be sure to take into consideration the projects you have due for other classes as well as other responsibilities (to work or family, for example) or activities. A sample schedule is shown in Figure 15.2.

To learn more about primary and secondary research, see Chapter 16.

Sunday	Monday	Tuesday	Wednesday	Thursday	Friday	Saturday
	1 Analyze writing situation & choose topic	**2**	**3** Check resources available and get an overview	**4**	**5** Draft research questions & narrow topic further (?)	**6**
7	**8** Set up a working bibliog.	**9** List search terms and start searching for sources	**10** Topic and working bib with 3 sources due!	**11** Evaluate the sources I've found so far	**12**	**13** Draft a thesis statement
14 Write a first draft	**15** Peer review—in class	**16** More research? Revise research questions and search terms?	**17** Don't forget to evaluate new sources!	**18** Start revising!	**19**	**20**
21	**22** Draft the works-cited list	**23**	**24** Revise the 2nd draft	**25**	**26**	**27**
28 Edit, spell-check, and proofread	**29** Final project due in class today!	**30**	**31**			

FIGURE 15.2   Sample Schedule for a 3- to 5-Page Research Project

Some library Web sites may offer an online scheduler to help you with this process. Look for a link on your library's Web site, or try out an assignment calculator, such as the one found at the University of Minnesota library's Web site, www.lib.umn.edu /help/calculator/.

Choosing a Topic and Getting an Overview

Often students will be assigned a topic for a research project. If you are free to choose your own topic, consult course materials, such as textbooks and handouts, to get ideas, and consult your instructor to make sure your topic is appropriate. Sometimes conducting an Internet search may give you an idea for a topic.

Once you've chosen an appropriate topic, an overview can help you determine the kinds of issues you should consider.

General Encyclopedias

General encyclopedias, such as *Britannica Online* and the *Columbia Encyclopedia,* provide basic information about many topics. Your library will likely have one or more general encyclopedias, available either on the shelf or through the library's digital portal. Often, encyclopedias are part of an online reference package. *Wikipedia,* too, offers a wealth of information, and it is often the first stop for students who are accustomed to consulting the Internet first for information. Be aware, though, that *Wikipedia* is user generated rather than traditionally published, and for this reason, the quality of information found there can be inconsistent. Many instructors do not consider *Wikipedia* a reliable source, so you should ask your teacher for advice on consulting it at this stage. Whichever general encyclopedia you consult, bear in mind that general encyclopedias should be used only for an overview of a topic; the information is not sufficiently in-depth to be an appropriate resource for college research.

Specialized Encyclopedias and Other Overview Resources

Specialized, or **subject-specific, encyclopedias** cover topics in more depth than general encyclopedias do. Here are some examples:

> *Encyclopedia of Computer Science and Technology*
>
> *Encyclopedia of Addictions*
>
> *Encyclopedia of Global Warming and Climate Change*
>
> *Encyclopedia of Human Rights*
>
> *The Encyclopedia of Punk*
>
> *Grove Dictionary of Art* or *Grove Art Online*

In addition to providing an overview of a topic, specialized encyclopedias often include an explanation of issues related to the topic, definitions of specialized terminology, and selective bibliographies of additional sources. As starting points, specialized encyclopedias have two distinct advantages:

1. They provide a comprehensive introduction to your topic, including the key terms you will need to find relevant material in catalogs and databases.

2. They present subtopics, enabling you to see many possibilities for focusing your research.

Frequently, libraries prepare **guides to a subject**—lists of reliable sources on popular topics. A guide can offer very useful suggested resources for research, so check your library to find out if such a guide is available. You may also find resources that provide good overviews of topics, such as *CQ Researcher*. A reference librarian can help point you in the right direction.

Narrowing Your Topic and Drafting Research Questions

After you have gotten a sense of the kinds of sources available on your topic, you may be ready to narrow it. Focus on a topic that you can explore thoroughly in the number of pages assigned and the length of time available. Finding your own take on a subject can help you narrow it as well. The invention strategies in Chapter 8 can help you focus in on one aspect of your topic.

You may also want to write questions about your topic and then focus in on one or two that can be answered through research. These will become the research questions that will guide your search for information. You may need to add or revise these questions as you conduct your search. The answers you devise can form the basis for your thesis statement.

Establishing a Research Log

One of the best ways to keep track of your research is to keep all your notes in one place, in a **research log.** Your log may be digital (a folder on your computer with files for notes, lists of keywords, and your working bibliography) or analog (a notebook with pockets for copies of sources).

Listing Keywords

Finding useful sources depends on determining the right **keywords**—words or phrases that describe your topic—to use while searching catalogs, databases, and the Internet. Start your list of keywords by noting the main words from your research question or thesis statement. Look for useful terms in your search results, and use these to expand your list. Then add synonyms (or words with a similar meaning) to expand your list.

For example, student Cristina Dinh might have started with a term like *home schooling*. She might have added *home education* or *home study*. After reading an article in an encyclopedia about her subject, she might have added *student-paced education* or *autonomous learning* to expand her scope.

To see Dinh's completed research essay, go to pp. 457–65.

Creating a Working Bibliography

A **working bibliography** is an ongoing record of the sources you discover as you research your subject. In your final project, you will probably not end up citing all the sources you list in your working bibliography, but recording the information you will need to cite a source—*as you identify it*—will save you time later. (Just be sure to double-check that your entries are accurate!)

Your working bibliography should include the following for each source:

- **Author(s) name(s)**

- **Title and subtitle**

- **Publication information:** A book's edition number (for example, *revised edition, 3rd ed.*), the name and location of the book's publisher, and the page numbers of the section you consulted; a periodical's name, volume and issue number or date, and the article's page numbers

- **Access information:** The call number of a book; the name of the database through which you accessed the source; the URL of the article (if available without a subscription), the URL of the source's home page, or the **DOI** (digital object identifier—a permanent identifying code that won't change over time or from database to database); the date you last accessed the source (for a Web page or Web site)

- **Medium of publication:** *Print* for printed books and articles, *Web* for online books and articles accessed through a database or found online, *DVD* for a film you watched at home, *MP3* for a music file, and so on

You can store your working bibliography in a computer file, in specialized bibliography software, or even on note cards. Each method has its advantages:

- A **computer file** allows you to move citations into order and incorporate the bibliography into your research project easily using standard software (such as Word or Excel).

- **Specialized bibliography software** (such as RefWorks or Zotero) designed for creating bibliographies helps you create the citation in the specific citation style (such as MLA or APA) required by your discipline. These software programs are not perfect, however; you still need to double-check your citations against the models in the style manual you are using or in Chapter 19 or 20 of this text.

- **Index cards** (one card per source) are easy to arrange and rearrange and allow you to include notes on the cards themselves.

- **A notebook** allows you to keep everything—working bibliography, annotations, notes, copies of chapters or articles—all in one place.

Chapters 19 and 20 present two common documentation styles—one created by the Modern Language Association (MLA) and widely used in the humanities, and the other advocated by the American Psychological Association (APA) and used in the social sciences. Other disciplines have their own preferred styles of documentation. Confirm with your instructor which documentation style is required for your assignment so that you can follow that style for all the sources you put into your working bibliography.

Annotating Your Working Bibliography

An **annotated bibliography** provides an overview of sources that you have considered for your research project. Instructors sometimes ask students to create an annotated bibliography as a separate assignment to demonstrate that each student has done some preparatory research and has considered the usefulness of the sources he or she has found. But researchers frequently create annotated bibliographies for their own use, to keep a record of sources and their thoughts about them, especially when their research occurs over a lengthy period of time. Researchers sometimes also publish annotated bibliographies to provide others with a useful tool for beginning a research project of their own.

What an annotated bibliography includes depends on the researcher's writing situation. If the annotated bibliography is intended for publication, the emphasis is on the source's main claims and major supporting evidence. If the annotated bibliography is for the researcher's use (or if it is for a class assignment), the annotation may also include information about how the source could be used in the research project.

Most annotated bibliographies created for publication or a class assignment also include an introduction that explains the subject, purpose, and scope of the annotated references and may describe how and why the author selected those sources. For instance, an annotated bibliography featuring works about computer animation might have the following introduction:

> Early animations of virtual people in computer games tended to be oblivious to their surroundings, reacting only when hit by moving objects, and then in ways that were not always appropriate—that is, a small object might generate a large effect. In the past few years, however, computer animators have turned their attention to designing virtual people who react appropriately to events around them. The sources below represent the last two years' worth of publications on the subject from the *IEEE Xplore* database.

To annotate your working bibliography, answer these three questions about each source:

- What kind of source is this?
- What does the source say?
- How can I use the source?

Here are two example annotations:

MLA Style	APA Style
Drennan, Tammy. "Freedom of Education in Hard Times." *Alliance for the Separation of School and State*. Schoolandstate.org, 26 Mar. 2010. Web. 9 May 2012.	Castelvecchi, D. (2008, August 30). Carbon tubes leave nano behind. *Science News, 174*(5), 9-9. Retrieved from http://www.sciencenews.org
This Web page discusses the benefits of brainstorming ideas and tapping the community as options for overcoming economic hardships faced by home-schoolers. I have concerns about the reliability of this source, since it does not identify its members or funding sources. (It seems to be a one-woman show, with all the documents on the site written by Tammy Drennan.) But it's interesting because it is written by a home schooling parent herself. I might be able to use this as evidence of the limitations of home schooling—a lack of resources such as lab equipment and subject-matter experts.	This news article, which describes a new, flexible lightweight material 30 times stronger than Kevlar and possibly useful for better bulletproof vests, provides evidence of yet another upcoming technology that might be useful to law enforcement. I can focus on the ways in which lighter, stronger bulletproof materials might change SWAT tactics—for instance, enabling officers to carry more gear, protect police vehicles, or blend into crowds better.

Taking Notes on Your Sources

The summaries that you include in a working bibliography or that you make on a printed or digital copy of a source are useful reminders, but you should also make notes that analyze the text, that synthesize what you are learning with ideas you have gleaned elsewhere or with your own ideas, and that evaluate the quality of the source.

You will mine your notes for language to use in your draft, so be careful to

- summarize accurately, using your own words and sentence structures;
- paraphrase without borrowing the language or sentence structure of the source;
- quote accurately and place all language from the source in quotation marks.

You can take notes on a photocopy of a printed text or use comments or highlighting to annotate a digital text. Whenever possible, download, print, photocopy, or scan useful sources, so that you can read and make notes at your leisure and so that you can double-check your summaries, paraphrases, and quotations of sources against the original. These strategies, along with those discussed in Chapter 18, "Using Sources to Support Your Ideas," will keep you from plagiarizing inadvertently.

For more on synthesizing, see pp. 307–308 and 344–51; for more on annotation, see pp. 295–302 and 333–43.

16

Finding Sources and Conducting Field Research

Students today are surrounded by a wealth of information—in print, online, even face to face! This wealth can make finding the information you need to support your ideas exciting, but it also means you will have to develop a research strategy and sift through possible sources carefully. What you are writing about and who will read your writing project will help you decide whether journal articles about your topic written by experts in the field will be most appropriate or whether you should rely on articles from newspapers and magazines you access online, or even whether blog posts or tweets from politicians and other public figures, information about legislation, a historic document, or a video will best help you support your claims. Does your writing project require you to depend mainly on **secondary sources**—works that analyze and summarize a subject—or develop **primary sources,** such as interviews with experts, surveys, or observational studies you conduct yourself? Whatever sources you decide will best help you support your claims, this chapter will help you find or develop the resources you need.

To learn how to devise a research strategy, see Chapter 15; to learn how to evaluate sources, see Chapter 17.

Searching Library Catalogs and Databases

For most college research projects, finding appropriate sources starts with your library's home page, where you can

- use your library's catalog to find books, reference sources (such as encyclopedias and dictionaries), reports, documents, multimedia resources (such as films and audio recordings), and much more;
- use your library's databases to find articles in newspapers, magazines, and scholarly journals.

Your library's home page is also the place to find information about the brick-and-mortar library—its floor plan, its hours of operation, and the journals it has available in print. You might even be able to find research guides, find links to what you need in other libraries, or get online help from a librarian.

Use appropriate search terms.

Just as with a search engine like *Google,* you can search a library catalog or database by typing your search terms—an author's name, the title of a work, a subject term or keyword, even a call number—into the search box. To search successfully, put yourself in the position of the people writing about your topic to figure out what words they might have used. If your topic is "ecology," for example, you may find information under the keywords *ecosystem, environment, pollution,* and *endangered species,* as well as a number of other related keywords, depending on the focus of the research.

Narrow (or expand) your results.

When conducting a search, you may get too few hits and have to broaden your topic. To broaden your search, try the following:

Replace a specific term with a more general term	Replace *sister* or *brother* with *sibling*
Substitute a synonym for one of your keywords	Replace *home study* with *home schooling* or *student-paced education*
Combine terms with *or* **to get results with either or both terms**	Search *home study or home schooling* to get results that include *home study* and results that include *home schooling*
Add a wildcard character, usually an asterisk (*) or question mark (?) (Check the search tips to find out which wildcard character is in use.)	Search *home school** or *home school?* to retrieve results for *home school, home schooling,* and *home-schooler*

Most often, you'll get too many hits and need to narrow your search. To narrow a search, try the following:

Add a specific term	Search not just *home schooling* but *home schooling statistics*
Combine search terms into phrases or word strings	Search *Home schooling in California*

In many cases, using phrases or word strings will limit your results to items that include *all* the words you have specified. In a few cases, you may need to insert quotation marks around the terms or insert the word *and* between them to create a search phrase or word string. Check the search tips for the database, catalog, or search engine you are using.

Find books (and other sources) through your library's catalog.

Books housed in academic library collections offer two distinct advantages to the student researcher:

1. They provide in-depth coverage of topics.
2. They are more likely to be published by reputable presses that strive for standards of accuracy and reliability.

FIGURE 16.1   A Book's Catalog Record

An item's record provides a lot more information than just the author, title, and call number **(A, C)**. You can also find the subject terms by which it was cataloged **(B)** and perhaps also the item's status—checked out or available—and its location **(C)**. Some libraries may allow you to place a hold on a book **(D)** or find similar items **(E)**. Some libraries, such as the one whose catalog is depicted here, even allow you to capture the book's record with your smartphone **(F)** or have the information texted or e-mailed to you **(G)**. Many libraries also give you the option to chat directly with a librarian through your computer **(H)**.

Used by permission of the UCR Libraries, University of California, Riverside

To find books (as well as reference works and multimedia resources) on your topic, turn to your library's catalog (see Figure 16.1). You can generally search the online catalog by author's name, title, keyword, or subject heading, and narrow your search by using the catalog's advanced search options.

Though you can search by keywords, most college library catalog sources use special *subject headings* devised by the Library of Congress (the national library of the United States). Finding and using the subject headings most relevant to your search will make your research more productive. You can locate the subject headings your library uses by pulling up the record of a relevant book you have already found and looking for the list of words under the heading "Subject" or "Subject headings" (Figure 16.1). Including these terms in your search may help you find additional relevant resources. Ask a librarian for help if you cannot identify the headings.

Some library catalogs allow you to search by call number, which makes it easy to find other items on the same or a similar topic. (You might think of a call-number search as the electronic equivalent of looking at books shelved nearby.) For example, typing LC40 (the first part of the call number from the library record shown in Figure 16.1) into the search box calls up the records of other items on the subject of home schooling:

Title	Call number
Well-Trained Mind: A Guide to Classical Education at Home	**LC40**.B39 2004
Love in a Time of Homeschooling: A Mother and Daughter's Uncommon Year	**LC40**.B76 2010
Homeschool: An American History	**LC40**.G34 2008
Family Matters: Why Homeschooling Makes Sense	**LC40**.G88 1992
Home Schooling: Parents as Educators	**LC40**.H65 1995
How Children Learn at Home	**LC40**.T48 2007

If your search for books in your college library turns up little that is useful to you, do not give up. Consider using *WorldCat* (www.worldcat.org), which includes records for many libraries in the United States and worldwide. You may be able to request an item from another library via your library's interlibrary loan service. Inquire at your library for services available to you that can connect you to resources in other libraries.

Though library catalogs are the place to go to find books, you can also use your library's catalog to find

- ■ *Audio:* recordings of music, speeches, plays, and readings
- ■ *Video:* films and documentaries in a variety of formats
- ■ *Art:* drawings, paintings, photographs, and engravings; some libraries may also own collections of artwork

Many libraries also house **archives and special collections** comprising manuscripts, rare books, and specialized materials or resources of local or worldwide interest. Whereas some libraries may list these items in their online catalog, others may provide links to these special collections in a different location on their Web sites; still others may provide access only through a catalog in the archives or special-collections room. Ask a librarian whether such materials may be useful to you.

Find articles in periodicals using your library's databases.

Much of the information you will use to write your research project will come from articles in **periodicals,** publications such as newspapers, magazines, or scholarly journals that are published at regular intervals. To locate relevant articles on your topic, start your search with one of your library's databases. Why not just start with a *Google* search? There are two very good reasons:

1. *Google* will pull up articles from any publication it indexes, from freely available personal Web sites to scholarly journals. Results rise to the top of the list based on a number of factors but not necessarily the reliability of the source. A *Google* search will turn up helpful sources, but you will need to spend a good deal of time sifting

through the numerous hits you get to find sources that are both relevant and reliable. (*Google Scholar* may help you locate more reliable sources than those you might find through a typical *Google* search.)

2. Sources you find through *Google* may ask you to pay for access to articles, or they may require a subscription. Your library already subscribes to these sources on your behalf. Also, adding databases to your search strategy will round out and diversify your search, and provide you with access to resources not available through a search engine such as *Google*.

Most college libraries subscribe at least to **general databases** and **subject-specific databases** as well as databases that index newspapers. General databases (such as *Academic OneFile, Academic Search Premier* or *Elite* or *Complete,* and *ProQuest Central*) index articles from both scholarly journals and popular magazines.[1] Subject-specific databases (such as *ERIC—Education Resources Information Center, MLA International Bibliography, PsycINFO,* and *General Science Full Text*) index articles only in their discipline. Newspaper databases (such as *Alt-Press Watch, LexisNexis Academic, National Newspaper Index,* and *ProQuest Newspapers*) index newspaper articles. For college-level research projects, you may use all three types of databases to find appropriate articles. (Note that many libraries also offer ways to search multiple databases at once.) For the research project on home schooling that appears in Chapter 19, "Citing and Documenting Sources in MLA Style," Cristina Dinh might have consulted both a general database and a subject-specific database like *ERIC.*

If your database search returns too many unhelpful results, use the search strategies discussed at the beginning of this chapter (p. 404) or use the database's advanced search options to refine your search. Many databases allow users to restrict results to articles published in academic journals, for example, or to articles that were published only after a certain date (see Figure 16.2). Use the Help option or ask a librarian for assistance.

Increasingly, databases provide access to full-text articles, either in HTML or PDF format. When you have the option, choose the PDF format, as this will provide you with photographs, graphs, and charts in context, and you will be able to include the page numbers in your citation. If you find a citation to an article that is not accessible through a database, however, do not ignore it. Check with a librarian to find out how you can get a copy of the article.

Find government documents and statistical information.

Federal, state, and local governments make many of their documents available directly through the Web. For example, you can access statistical data about the United States through the U.S. Census Bureau's Web site (www.census.gov), and you can learn a great deal about other countries through the Web sites of the U.S. State Department (travel.state.gov) and the CIA (www.cia.gov/library/publications/the-world-factbook).

The Library of Congress provides a useful portal for finding government documents (federal, state, local, and international) through its Web site (www.loc.gov), and the U.S.

---

[1] The names of these databases change over time and vary from library to library, so ask your instructor or a reference librarian if you need help identifying a general database.

FIGURE 16.2 Database Search Results

Database search results may allow you to access an article directly or provide the information you need to locate (and cite) it, including the title, the author(s), and the article's publication information. Click on the title to retrieve an article's full record **(B)**. Click a magnifying glass to view the abstract (summary) of an article **(C)**. Check to see whether the article is available in PDF format **(D)**, or both HTML and PDF formats **(E)**. The database may also provide options for narrowing a search by publication date, source type, and so on; in this example from the database titled *Academic Search Complete* **(A)**, these options are available in the left column **(F)**.

Courtesy of EBSCO Publishing

Government Printing Office provides free electronic access to documents produced by the federal government through its FDsys Web page (www.gpo.gov/fdsys).

Some libraries have collections of government publications and provide access to government documents through databases or catalogs. Your library may also offer statistical resources and data sets. See if your library has a guide to these resources, or ask a librarian for advice. You can also find government documents online using an advanced *Google* search (www.google.com/advanced_search) and specifying *.gov* as the type of site or domain you want to search (see Figure 16.3).

To learn more about the domains of Web sites, see Chapter 17, p. 424.

Find Web sites and interactive sources.

By now, you are likely quite familiar with searching the Web. This section introduces you to some tools and strategies to use it more efficiently. But first, a few cautions:

- *Your research project will be only as credible as the sources you use.* Because search engines index Web sources without evaluating them, not all the results a search engine like *Google* generates will be reliable and relevant to your purposes.

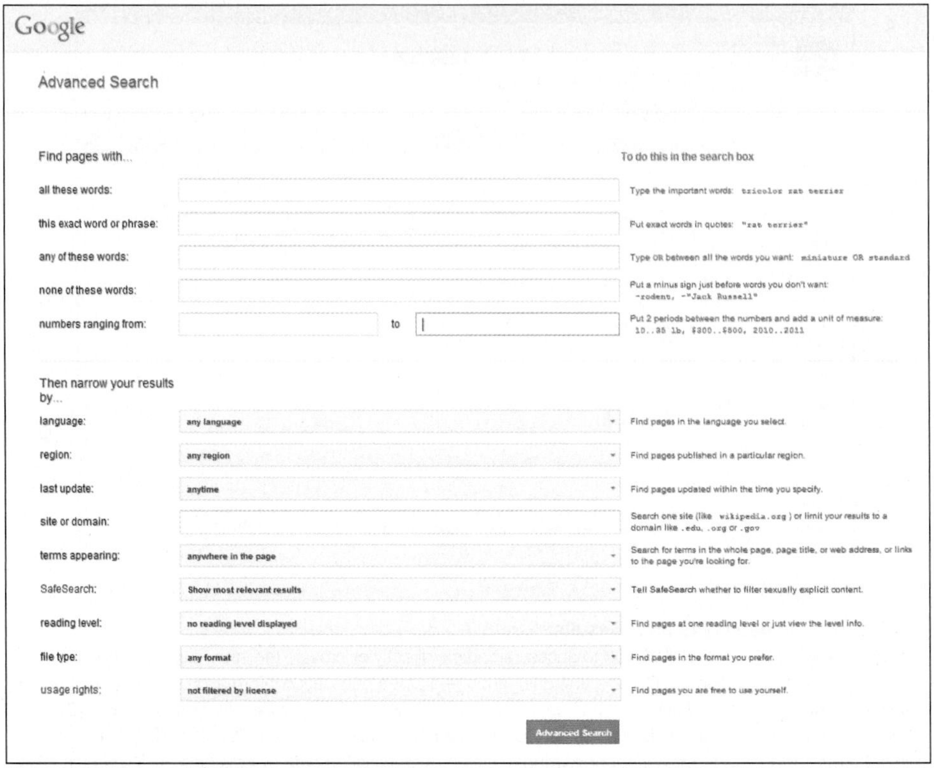

FIGURE 16.3   An Advanced *Google* Search
Use *Google's* advanced search (www.google.com/advanced_search) to locate information within specific sites or domains (such as *.edu* or *.gov*) or to narrow results to sites that include or exclude specific words, appear only in English or another language, and so on. Courtesy of Google

- **Web sources may not be stable.** A Web site that existed last week may no longer be available today, or its content may have changed. Be sure to record the information you need to cite a source when you first find it.

- **Web sources must be documented.** No matter what your source—a library book, a scholarly article, or a Web site or Web page—you will need to cite and document your source in your list of works cited or references. If you are publishing your report online, check also to determine whether you will need permission to reproduce an image or any other elements.

For guidelines on how to cite Web sources, see pp. 454–56 (MLA style); or pp. 473–74 (APA style); for more on evaluating sources, especially Web sources, see Chapter 17.

Google Scholar and *Google Book Search*

Although you may use search engines like *Google* with great rapidity and out of habit, as a college researcher you are likely to find it worthwhile to familiarize yourself with other parts of the *Google* search site. Of particular interest to the academic writer are *Google*

Scholar and *Google Book Search*. *Google Scholar* retrieves articles from a number of scholarly databases and a wide range of general-interest and scholarly books. *Google Book Search* searches both popular and scholarly books. Both *Google Scholar* and *Google Book Search* offer overviews and, in some cases, the full text of a source.

Note: Whatever search engine you use, always click on the link called *Help, Hints,* or *Tips* on the search tool's home page to find out more about the commands and advanced-search techniques it offers. Most search engines allow searches using the techniques discussed on p. 405. Many also provide advanced searching options that allow you to limit results to those created between specific dates, in specific languages, and so on.

Other Useful Search Options

No matter how precisely you search the Web with a standard search engine, you may not hit on the best available resources. Starting your search from a subject guide, such as those provided by the *Internet Public Library* (www.ipl.org/div/subject), *Infomine* (infomine.ucr.edu), or the librarians at your school, can direct you to relevant and reliable sources of online information.

Interactive Sources

Interactive sources, including blogs, wikis, RSS feeds, social networking sites (like *Facebook and Twitter*), and discussion lists, can also be useful sources of information, especially if your research project focuses on a current event or late-breaking news.

- **Blogs** are Web sites that are updated regularly, often many times a day. They are usually organized chronologically, with the newest posts at the top, and may contain links or news stories, but generally focus on the opinions of the blog host and visitors. Blogs by experts in the field are likely to be more informative than blogs by amateurs or fans.

- **Wikis**—of which *Wikipedia* is the best known example—offer content contributed and modified collaboratively by a community of users. Wikis can be very useful for gleaning background information, but because (in most cases) anyone can write or revise wiki entries, many instructors will not accept them as reliable sources for college-level research projects. Use wikis cautiously.

- **RSS (Really Simple Syndication) feeds** aggregate frequently updated sites, such as news sites and blogs, into links in a single Web page or e-mail. Most search engines provide this service, as do sites such as *FeedDemon* (www.feeddemon.com) and apps such as *Feedly* (www.feedly.com). RSS feeds can be useful if you are researching news stories or political campaigns.

- **Social networking sites,** like *Facebook* and *Twitter,* allow users to create groups or pages on topics of interest or to follow the thoughts and activities of newsmakers.

- **Discussion lists** are electronic mailing lists that allow members to post comments and get feedback from others interested in the same topic. The most reliable discussion lists are moderated and attract experts on the topic. Many online communities provide some kind of indexing or search mechanism so that you can look for "threads" (conversations) related to your topic.

Although you need to evaluate the information you find in all sources carefully, you must be especially careful with information from social networking sites and discussion lists. However, such sources can provide up-to-the-minute information. Also be aware that whereas most online communities welcome guests and newcomers, others may perceive your questions as intrusive or naive. It may be useful to "lurk" (that is, just to read posts) before making a contribution.

Conducting Field Research

In universities, government agencies, and the business world, field research can be as important as library research. In some majors, like education or sociology, as well as in service-learning courses, primary research projects are common. Even in the writing projects covered in Chapters 2–7, observations, interviews, and surveys may be useful or even necessary. As you consider how you might use field research in your writing projects, ask your instructor whether your institution requires you to obtain approval, and check Chapters 19 and 20 for information about citing interviews you conduct yourself.

Conduct observational studies.

Observational studies, such as profiling a place (see Chapter 3) for a writing course or studying how children play for a psychology or sociology course, are common in college. To conduct an observational study effectively, follow these guidelines.

Planning an Observational Study

To ensure that your observational visits are productive, plan them carefully:

- **Arrange access if necessary.** Visits to a private location (such as a day-care center or school) require special permission, so be sure to arrange your visit in advance. When making your request, state your intentions and goals for your study directly and fully. You may be surprised at how receptive people can be to a college student on assignment. But have a fallback plan in case your request is refused or the business or institution places constraints on you that hamper your research.

- **Develop a hypothesis.** In advance, write down a tentative assumption about what you expect to learn from your study—your **hypothesis.** This will guide your observations and notes, and you can adjust your expectations in response to what you observe if necessary. Consider, too, how your presence will affect those whom you are observing, so you can minimize your impact or take the effect of your presence into consideration.

- **Consider how best to conduct the observation.** Decide where to place yourself to make your observations most effective. Should you move around to observe from multiple vantage points, or will a single perspective be more productive?

Making Observations

Strategies for conducting your observation include the following:

- **Description:** *Describe* in detail the setting and the people you are observing. Note the physical arrangement and functions of the space, and the number, activities, and appearance of the people. Record as many details as possible, draw diagrams or sketches if helpful, and take photographs or videos if allowed (and if those you are observing do not object).

- **Narration:** *Narrate* the activities going on around you. Try initially to be an innocent observer: Pretend that you have never seen anything like this activity or place before, and explain what you are seeing step by step, even if what you are writing seems obvious. Include interactions among people, and capture snippets of conversations (in quotation marks) if possible.

- **Analysis and classification:** Break the scene down into its component parts, identify common threads, and organize the details into categories.

Take careful notes during your visit if you can do so unobtrusively, or immediately afterward if you can't. You can use a notebook and pencil, a laptop or tablet, or even a smartphone to record your notes. Choose whatever is least disruptive to those around you. You may need to use abbreviations and symbols to capture your observations on-site, but be sure to convert such shorthand into words and phrases as soon as possible after the visit so that you don't forget its significance.

Writing Your Observational Study

Immediately after your visit, fill in any gaps in your notes, and review your notes to look for meaningful patterns. You might find *mapping strategies,* such as *clustering* or *outlining,* useful for discovering patterns in your notes. Take some time to reflect on what you saw. Asking yourself questions like these might help:

- How did what I observed fit my own or my readers' likely preconceptions of the place or activity? Did my observations upset any of my preconceptions? What, if anything, seemed contradictory or out of place?

- What interested me most about the activity or place? What are my readers likely to find interesting about it?

- What did I learn?

Your purpose in writing about your visit is to share your insights into the meaning and significance of your observations. Assume that your readers have never been to the place, and provide enough detail for it to come alive for them. Decide on the perspective you want to convey, and choose the details necessary to convey your insights.

For more about mapping, clustering, or outlining strategies, see Chapter 8.

PRACTICING THE GENRE

Collaborating on an Observational Study

Arrange to meet with a small group (three or four students) for an observational visit somewhere on campus, such as the student center, gym, or cafeteria. Have each group member focus on a specific task, such as recording what people are wearing, doing, or saying, or capturing what the place looks, sounds, and smells like. After twenty to thirty minutes, report to one another on your observations. Discuss any difficulties that arise.

Conduct interviews.

A successful interview involves careful planning before the interview, but it also requires keen listening skills and the ability to ask appropriate follow-up questions while conducting the interview. Courtesy and consideration for your subject are crucial at all stages of the process.

Planning the Interview

Planning an interview involves the following:

- **Choosing an interview subject.** For a profile of an individual, your interview will be with one person; for a profile of an organization, you might interview several people, all with different roles or points of view. Prepare a list of interview candidates, as busy people might turn you down.

- **Arranging the interview.** Give your prospective subject a brief description of your project, and show some sincere enthusiasm for your project. Keep in mind that the person you want to interview will be donating valuable time to you, so call ahead to arrange the interview, allow your subject to specify the amount of time she or he can spare, and come prepared.

Preparing for the Interview

In preparation for the interview, consider your objectives;

- Do you want details or a general orientation (the "big picture") from this interview?
- Do you want this interview to lead you to interviews with other key people?
- Do you want mainly facts or opinions?
- Do you need to clarify something you have observed or read? If so, what?

Making an observational visit and doing some background reading beforehand can be helpful. Find out as much as you can about the organization or company (size, location, purpose, etc.), as well as the key people.

Good questions are key to a successful interview. You will likely want to ask a few **closed questions** (questions that request specific information) and a number of **open questions** (questions that give the respondent range and flexibility and encourage him or her to share anecdotes, personal revelations, and expressions of attitudes):

Open Questions	Closed Questions
What do you think about _____ ?	How do you do _____ ?
Describe your reaction when _____ happened.	What does _____ mean?
Tell me about a time you were _____ .	How was _____ developed?

The best questions encourage the subject to talk freely but stick to the point. You may need to ask a follow-up question to refocus the discussion or to clarify a point, so be prepared. If you are unsure about a subject's answer, follow up by rephrasing the subject's answer, prefacing it by saying something like "Let me see if I have this right" or "Am I correct in saying that you feel _____ ?" Avoid *forced-choice questions* ("Which do you think is the better approach: _____ or _____ ?") and *leading questions* ("How well do you think _____ is doing?").

During the Interview

Another key to good interviewing is flexibility. Ask the questions you have prepared, but also be ready to shift gears to take full advantage of what your subject can offer.

- **Take notes.** Take notes during the interview, even if you are recording your discussion. You might find it useful to divide several pages of a notebook into two columns or to set up a word processing file in two columns. Use the left-hand column to note details about the scene and your subject or about your impressions overall; in the right-hand column, write several questions and record answers to your questions. Remember that how something is said is as important as what is said. Look for material that will give texture to your writing—gesture, verbal inflection, facial expression, body language, physical appearance, dress, hair, or anything that makes the person an individual.

- **Listen carefully.** Avoid interrupting your subject or talking about yourself; rather, listen carefully and guide the discussion by asking follow-up questions and probing politely for more information.

- **Be considerate.** Do not stay longer than the time you were allotted unless your subject agrees to continue the discussion, and show your appreciation for the time you have been given by thanking your subject and offering her or him a copy of your finished project.

Following the Interview

After the interview, do the following:

- **Reflect on the interview.** As soon as you finish the interview, find a quiet place to reflect on it and to review and amplify your notes. Asking yourself questions like these might help: What did I learn? What seemed contradictory or surprising about the interview? How did what was said fit my own or my readers' likely expectations about the person, activity, or place? How can I summarize my impressions?

  Also make a list of any questions that arise. You may want to follow up with your subject for more information, but limit yourself to one e-mail or phone call to avoid becoming a bother.

- **Thank your subject.** Send your interview subject a thank-you note within twenty-four hours of the interview. Try to reference something specific from the interview, something you thought was surprising or thought provoking. And send your subject a copy of your finished project with a note of appreciation.

Interviewing a Classmate

In pairs, practice the genre by interviewing a classmate:

- First, spend five to ten minutes writing questions and thinking about what you'd like to learn. Then, during a ten-minute interview, ask the questions you have prepared, but also ask one or more follow-up questions in response to something your classmate has told you.

- Following the interview, spend a few minutes thinking about what you learned about your classmate and about conducting an interview. What might you do differently when conducting a formal interview?

Conduct surveys.

Surveys let you gauge the opinions and knowledge of large numbers of people. You might conduct a survey to gauge opinion in a political science course or to assess familiarity with a television show for a media studies course. You might also conduct a survey to assess the seriousness of a problem for a service-learning class or in response to an assignment to propose a solution to a problem (Chapter 6). This section briefly outlines procedures you can follow to carry out an informal survey, and it highlights areas where caution is needed. Colleges and universities have restrictions about the use and distribution of questionnaires, so check your institution's policy or obtain permission before beginning the survey.

Designing Your Survey

Use the following tips to design an effective survey:

- **Conduct background research.** You may need to conduct background research on your topic. For example, to create a survey on scheduling appointments at the student health center, you may first need to contact the health center to determine its scheduling practices, and you may want to interview health center personnel.

- **Focus your study.** Before starting out, decide what you expect to learn (your *hypothesis*). Make sure your focus is limited—focus on one or two important issues—so you can craft a brief questionnaire that respondents can complete quickly and easily and so that you can organize and report on your results more easily.

- **Write questions.** Plan to use a number of *closed questions* (questions that request specific information), such as *two-way questions, multiple-choice questions, ranking scale questions,* and *checklist questions* (see Figure 16.4). You will also likely want to include a few *open questions* (questions that give respondents the opportunity to write their answers in their own words). Closed questions are easier to tally, but open questions are likely to provide you with deeper insight and a fuller sense of respondents' opinions. Whatever questions you develop, be sure that you provide all the answer options your respondents are likely to want, and make sure your questions are clear and unambiguous.

- **Identify the population you are trying to reach.** Even for an informal study, you should try to get a reasonably representative group. For example, to study

This is a survey about scheduling appointments at the student health center. Your participation will help determine how long students have to wait to use the clinic's services and how these services might be more conveniently scheduled. The survey should take only 3 to 4 minutes to complete. All responses are confidential.

Two-way question — 1. Have you ever made an appointment at the clinic?
❏ Yes ❏ No

Filter — If you answered "No" to question 1, skip to question 5.

Multiple-choice questions —
2. How frequently have you had to wait more than 10 minutes at the clinic for a scheduled appointment?
❏ Always ❏ Usually ❏ Occasionally ❏ Never

3. Have you ever had to wait more than 30 minutes at the clinic for a scheduled appointment?
❏ Yes ❏ No ❏ Uncertain

4. Based on your experience with the clinic, how would you rate its system for scheduling appointments?

❏ 1 (poor) ❏ 2 (adequate) ❏ 3 (good) ❏ 4 (excellent)

5. Given your present work and class schedule, which times during the day (Monday through Friday) would be the most and least convenient for you to schedule appointments at the clinic? (Rank your choices from 1 for most convenient time to 4 for least convenient time.)

Ranking questions —

	1 (most convenient)	2 (more convenient)	3 (less convenient)	4 (least convenient)
morning (7 a.m.–noon)	❏	❏	❏	❏
afternoon (noon–5 p.m.)	❏	❏	❏	❏
dinnertime (5–7 p.m.)	❏	❏	❏	❏
evening (7–10 p.m.)	❏	❏	❏	❏

6. If you have had an appointment at the student health center within the last six months, please evaluate your experience.

7. If you have had an appointment at the student health center within the last six months, please indicate what you believe would most improve scheduling of appointments at the clinic.

Open questions —

8. If you have *never* had an appointment at the student health center, please indicate why you have not made use of this service.

Thank you for your participation.

FIGURE 16.4   Sample Questionnaire: Scheduling at the Student Health Center

satisfaction with appointment scheduling at the student health center, you would need to include a representative sample of all the students at the school—not only those who have visited the health center. Determine the demographic makeup of your school, and arrange to reach out to a representative sample.

- **Design the questionnaire.** Begin your questionnaire with a brief, clear introduction stating the purpose of your survey and explaining how you intend to use the results. Give advice on answering the questions, estimate the amount of time needed to complete the questionnaire, and—unless you are administering the survey in person—indicate the date by which completed surveys must be returned. Organize your questions from least to most complicated or in any order that seems logical, and format your questionnaire so that it is easy to read and complete.

- **Test the questionnaire.** Ask at least three readers to complete your questionnaire before you distribute it. Time them as they respond, or ask them to keep track of how long they take to complete it. Discuss with them any confusion or problems they experience. Review their responses with them to be certain that each question is eliciting the information you want it to elicit. From what you learn, revise your questions and adjust the format of the questionnaire.

Administering the Survey

The more respondents you have, the better, but constraints of time and expense will almost certainly limit the number. As few as twenty-five could be adequate for an informal study, but to get twenty-five responses, you may need to solicit fifty or more participants.

You can conduct the survey in person or over the telephone; use an online service such as *SurveyMonkey* (surveymonkey.com); e-mail the questionnaires; or conduct the survey using a social media site such as *Facebook*. You may also distribute surveys to groups of people in class or around campus and wait to collect their responses.

Each method has its advantages and disadvantages. For example, face-to-face surveys allow you to get more in-depth responses, but participants may be unwilling to answer personal questions face to face. Though fewer than half the surveys you solicit using survey software are likely to be completed (your invitations may wind up in a spam folder), online software will tabulate responses automatically.

Writing the Report

When writing your report, include a summary of the results, as well as an interpretation of what the results mean.

- **Summarize the results.** Once you have the completed questionnaires, tally the results from the closed questions. (If you conducted the survey online, this will have already been done for you.) You can give the results from the closed questions as percentages, either within the text of your report or in one or more tables or graphs. Next, read all respondents' answers to each open question to determine the variety of responses they gave. Summarize the responses by classifying the answers. You might classify them as positive, negative, or neutral or by grouping them into more specific categories. Finally, identify quotations that express a range of responses succinctly and engagingly to use in your report.

- **Interpret the results.** Once you have tallied the responses and read answers to open questions, think about what the results mean. Does the information you gathered support your hypothesis? If so, how? If the results do not support your hypothesis, where did you go wrong? Was there a problem with the way you worded your questions or with the sample of the population you contacted? Or was your hypothesis in need of adjustment?

- **Write the report.** Reports in the social sciences use a standard format, with headings introducing the following categories of information:
  - **Abstract:** A brief summary of the report, usually including one sentence summarizing each section
  - **Introduction:** Includes context for the study (other similar studies, if any, and their results), the question or questions the researcher wanted to answer and why this question (or these questions) are important, and the limits of what the researcher expected the survey to reveal
  - **Methods:** Includes the questionnaire, identifies the number and type of participants, and describes the methods used for administering the questionnaire and recording data
  - **Results:** Includes the data from the survey, with limited commentary or interpretation
  - **Discussion:** Includes the researcher's interpretation of results, an explanation of how the data support the hypothesis (or not), and the conclusions the researcher has drawn from the research

macmillanhighered.com/conciseguide
Tutorials>Digital Writing>Online Research Tools

17

Evaluating Sources

As soon as you start your search for sources, you should begin evaluating what you find not only to decide whether they are *relevant* to your research project but also to determine how *credible* or *reliable* they are.

Choosing Relevant Sources

Sources are **relevant** when they help you achieve your aims with your readers. Relevant sources may

- explain terms or concepts;
- provide background information;
- provide evidence in support of your claims;
- provide alternative viewpoints or interpretations;
- lend authority to your point of view.

A search for sources may reveal many seemingly relevant books and articles—more than any researcher could ever actually consult. A search on the term *home schooling* in one database, for example, got 1,172 hits. Obviously, a glance at all the hits to determine which are most relevant would take far too much time. To speed up the process, resources such as library catalogs, databases, and search engines provide tools to narrow the results. For example, in one popular all-purpose database, you can limit results by publication date, language, and publication or source type, among other options. (Check the Help screen to learn how to use these tools.) In this database, limiting the *home schooling* results to articles published in scholarly journals in English over the last ten years reduced the number of hits to fifty-six, a far more reasonable number to review. (Remember that if you have too few results or your results are not targeted correctly, you can expand your search by removing limits selectively.)

Once you've reduced your search results to a manageable number, click on the remaining titles to look closely at each record. The analysis of an article's detailed record in Figure 17.1 shows what to look for.

After you have identified a reasonable number of relevant sources, examine the sources themselves:

- Read the preface, introduction, or conclusion of books, or the first or last few paragraphs of articles, to determine which aspect of the topic is addressed or which approach to the topic is taken. To obtain a clear picture of a topic, researchers need to consider sources that address different aspects of the topic or take different approaches.

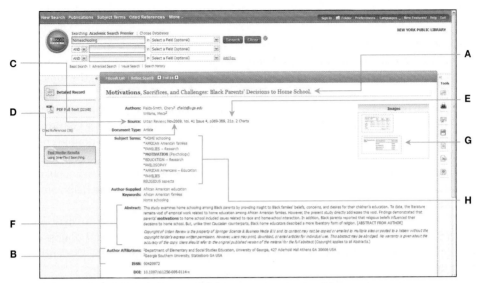

FIGURE 17.1   Analyzing the Detailed Record of an Article from a Periodicals Database
Analyze the detailed record of an article to determine whether the article itself is worth reading by asking yourself the following questions: Does the **title (A)** suggest that the article addresses your topic? Are the **authors (B)** experts in the field and do they have relevant background? Was the article **published (C)** in a periodical that is likely to be reliable, was it published at a recent **date (D)**, and is it **lengthy (E)** enough to indicate that the topic is treated in depth? Does the **abstract (or summary) (F)** suggest that the article addresses your topic? If so, what angle does it take? Are there any **illustrations (G)** that may illuminate concepts? Check the **subject terms (H)**, too: Are any of your keywords listed? Should any of these terms be added to your keywords list?
Courtesy of EBSCO Publishing

- Look at the headings or references in articles, or the table of contents and index in books, to see how much of the content relates specifically to your topic.
- Consider the way the source is written: Sources written for general readers may be accessible but may not analyze the subject in depth. Extremely specialized works may be too technical. Poorly written sources may be unreliable. (See Choosing Reliable Sources below, for more on scholarly versus popular sources and for a discussion of why researchers should avoid sources that are poorly written or riddled with errors.)

If close scrutiny leaves you with too few sources—or too many sources from too few perspectives—conduct a search using additional or alternative keywords, or explore links to related articles, look at the references in a particularly useful article, or look for other sources by an author whose work you find useful.

Choosing Reliable Sources

Choosing relevant sources is crucial to assembling a useful working bibliography. Determining which of those relevant sources are also likely to be *reliable* is even more important. To determine reliability, ask yourself the questions that follow.

Who wrote it?

Consider, first, whether the author is an *expert* in the field. The fact that someone has a PhD in astrophysics is no indication that he or she will be an expert in military history, for example, so make sure that the area of expertise is directly relevant to the topic.

To determine the author's area of expertise, look for the author's professional affiliation (where he or she works or teaches). This may be indicated at the bottom of the first page of an article or in an "About the Author" section in a book or on a Web site. Frequently, Googling the author will also reveal the author's affiliation, but double-check to make sure the affiliation is current and that you have located the right person. You may also consult a biographical reference source available through your library. Looking to see what other works the author has published, and with whom, can also help you ascertain his or her areas of expertise.

Contributors to blogs, wikis, and online discussion forums may or may not be experts in the field. Determine whether the site screens contributors, and double-check any information taken from sites for which you cannot determine the credentials of contributors.

Also consider the author's *perspective*. Most writing is not neutral or objective and does not claim to be. Knowledge of the author's perspective enables you to assess *bias* and determine whether the author's perspective affects the presentation of his or her argument. To determine the author's perspective, look for the main point and ask yourself question like these:

- What evidence does the author provide to support this point? Is it from authoritative sources? Is it persuasive?
- Does the author make concessions to or refute opposing arguments?
- Does the author avoid fallacies, confrontational phrasing, and loaded words?

For more details on these argumentative strategies, see Chapter 13.

When was it published?

In general, especially when you are writing about science or technology, current events, or emerging trends, you should consult the most up-to-date sources available on your subject. The date of publication for articles you locate should be indicated in your search results. For a print book, look for the copyright date on the copyright page (usually on the back of the title page); for an e-book, look for the copyright date at the beginning or end of the electronic file. If your source is a Web site, consider when it, and the content within it, was last updated (often indicated at the bottom of the Web page or home page).

You may also need older, "classic" sources that establish the principles, theories, and data on which later work is based and may provide a useful perspective for evaluating other works. To determine which sources are classics, note the ones that are cited most often in encyclopedia articles, lists of works cited or references, and recent works on the subject. You may also want to consult your instructor or a librarian to help you determine which works are classics in your field.

Is the source scholarly, popular, or for a trade group?

Scholarly sources (whether books or articles) are written by and for experts in a field of study, frequently professors or academic researchers. They can be challenging to read and understand because they use the language of the field and terminology that may be unfamiliar to those outside the discipline, but they are considered reliable because the contents are written by specialists and peer-reviewed (reviewed by specialists) before publication. Scholarly sources also tend to delve deeply into a subject, often a narrowly defined subject. Scholarly sources may be published by a university press, a scholarly organization, or a commercial publisher (such as Kluwer Academic or Wiley-Blackwell). Though scholarly sources may provide an overview of the subject, they generally focus on a specific issue or argument and generally contain a great deal of original research.

In contrast, **popular sources** are written to entertain and educate the general public. For the most part, they are written by journalists who have conducted research and interviewed experts. They may include original research, especially on current events or emerging trends. Mainly, though, they report on and summarize original research and are written for interested, nonspecialist readers.

Of course, popular sources range widely along the reliability spectrum. Highly respected newspapers and magazines, such as the *New York Times,* the *Guardian,* the *Economist,* and *Harper's Magazine,* publish original research on news and culture. These newspapers and magazines check facts carefully and are often considered appropriate sources for research projects in entry-level courses (although you should check with your instructor to find out her or his expectations). Magazines that focus on celebrity gossip, such as *People* and *Us Weekly,* are unlikely to be considered appropriate sources for a college-level research project. Table 17.1 summarizes some of the important differences between scholarly journals and popular magazines.

Trade publications—periodicals that report on news and technical advances in a specific industry—are written for those employed in the industry and include such titles as *World Cement* and *American Machinist.* Some trade publications may be appropriate for college research projects, especially in the sciences, but keep in mind that these publications are intended for a specialist audience and may focus on marketing products to professionals in the field.

Who published it?

Determining who published or sponsored a source you are considering can help you gauge its reliability and ascertain the publication's slant (or point of view). Look to see whether the source was published by a commercial publisher (such as St. Martin's Press or Random House); a university press (such as the University of Nebraska Press); a corporation, an organization, or an interest group (such as the RAND Corporation, the World Wildlife Fund, or the National Restaurant Association); a government agency (such as the Internal Revenue Service or the U.S. Census Bureau); or the author on his or her own. Determining the publisher or sponsor is particularly important for material published on the Web.

TABLE 17.1 Scholarly Journals versus Popular Magazines

Scholarly Journals	*Popular Magazines*
Journals are usually published 4 to 6 times per year.	Magazines are usually published weekly or monthly.
Articles are usually written by scholars (with *Ph.D.* or academic affiliations after their names).	Authors of articles are journalists but may quote experts.
Many articles have more than one author.	Most articles have a single author.
In print journals, the title page often appears on the cover, and the covers frequently lack artwork.	Photographs, usually in color, appear on the covers of most print magazines.
Articles may include charts, tables, figures, and quotations from other scholarly sources.	Articles frequently include color pictures and sidebars.
An abstract (summary) of the article may appear on the first page.	A headline or engaging description may precede the article.
Most articles are fairly long—5 to 20 pages.	Most articles are fairly short—1 to 5 pages.
Articles cite sources and provide a bibliography (works-cited or reference list).	Articles rarely include a list of works cited or references but may mention or quote experts.

All photos: Bill Aron/PhotoEdit

If your source is a Web page, look at the URL (uniform resource locator) to find its top-level domain, which is indicated by a suffix. Some of the most useful ones are listed here:

.gov   U.S. federal government and some state or local
       government institutions

.org   nonprofit organizations

.edu   educational institutions

.com   businesses and commercial enterprises

.net   usually businesses or organizations associated with networks

.mil   the U.S. military

For the most part, *.gov* and *.edu* are the most likely to offer reliable sources of information for a college research project. However, sources with any of these domains may vary in reliability. For example, a file with a *.com* suffix may offer a highly reliable history of a corporation and be an appropriate source for someone writing a history of corporate America, whereas a file with an *.edu* suffix may have been posted by a student or by a faculty member outside his or her area of expertise. It is essential to look at Web sites carefully. Determine who sponsors the site: Is it a business, a professional group, a private organization, an educational institution, a government agency, or an individual? Look for a link, usually at the top or the bottom of the home page, called something like "Who We Are" or "About Us." If you cannot determine who sponsors a site, carefully double-check any information you find there.

Consider, too, checking how often the Web site has been linked to and the types of links provided by the Web site. That a site has been linked to repeatedly does not guarantee reliability, but the information may be helpful in conjunction with other recommendations in this chapter. To determine the number of times a Web page has been linked to, type *link:* plus the URL into a *Google* search box. To check the links provided, click on them and apply the criteria in this chapter.

If the source was published by a commercial publisher, check out the publisher's Web site, and ask yourself questions like these:

- Does the publisher offer works from a single perspective or from multiple perspectives?

- Do the works it publishes cover a wide variety of topics or focus on a particular array?

- Does the publisher's Web site host links to a particular type of site?

Consider the Web sites shown in Figure 17.2. The screenshot on the left is from the Web site of the *Nation*; the screenshot on the right is from the online version of the *National Review*. Compare the titles of the articles, and look at the photographs and advertisements. Do you notice any particular slant to the coverage?

The Web sites of book publishers may offer a link to a catalog. If so, look at the works it lists. Does the publisher seem to publish works on a particular topic or from a particular point of view? Does the publisher generally offer popular, academic, or professional works?

If your source is a periodical (a magazine, newspaper, newsletter, or scholarly journal), consider whether it focuses on a particular topic or offers a single point of view. In addition to looking at the article you are considering, visit the publisher's Web site, which may help you determine this.

FIGURE 17.2   Assessing a Publisher's Perspective
Consulting a publisher's Web site can help you determine the publisher's slant or point of view. A careful look at the Web sites of the *Nation* and the *National Review* indicates that one takes a liberal perspective on politics, while the other takes a conservative one. After looking carefully at the Web sites, can you determine which is which? (left) Reprinted with permission from the February 6, 2012 issue of *The Nation*. Portions of each week's *Nation* magazine can be accessed at http://www.thenation.com; (right) Courtesy of National Review

How is the source written?

Most works that are published professionally (including popular newspapers and magazines, as well as scholarly journals and trade magazines) will have been edited carefully. These sources will generally avoid errors of grammar, punctuation, and spelling. Web sites sponsored by professional organizations, too, will generally avoid these kinds of errors. Personal Web sites, however, are unlikely to have been professionally edited and fact-checked. If a Web site is riddled with errors, be very careful to double-check any information you take from that site.

What does the source say?

Finally, and perhaps most importantly, consider the source itself. Answering the following questions can help you determine whether the source is worth consideration:

- What is the intended audience of the source? Does the source address an audience of experts, or is it intended for a general audience?
- What is the purpose of the source? Does it review a number of different positions, or does it argue for a position of its own? If it makes its own argument, analyze the argument closely.
- What is the tone of the source? Is the tone reasonable? Does the source respond to alternative viewpoints, and are those responses logical and reasonable?
- What evidence is offered to support the argument? Is the evidence relevant and reliable? What kinds of citations or links does the source supply?

To learn more about analyzing an argument, see Chapter 13.

18

Using Sources to Support Your Ideas

Writing a college research project requires you to

- analyze sources to understand the arguments those sources are making, the information they are using to support their claims, and the ways those arguments and the supporting evidence they use relate to your topic;
- synthesize information from sources to support, extend, and challenge your own ideas;
- integrate information from sources with your own ideas to contribute something new to the "conversation" on your topic.

Synthesizing Sources

Synthesizing means making connections among ideas from texts and from the writer's own experience. Once you have analyzed a number of sources on your topic, consider questions like the following to help you synthesize ideas and information:

- Do any of the sources you read use similar approaches or come to similar conclusions? What common themes do they explore? Do any of them use the same evidence (facts, statistics, research studies, examples) to support their claims?
- What differentiates their various positions? Where do the writers disagree, and why? Does one writer seem to be responding to or challenging one or more of the others?
- Do you agree with some sources and disagree with others? What makes one source more convincing than the others? Do any of the sources you have read offer support for your claims? Do any of them challenge your conclusions? If so, can you *refute* the challenge or do you need to *concede* a point?

Sentence strategies like the following can help you clarify where you differ from or agree with the sources you have read:

- ▶ A study by X supports my position by demonstrating that _____.

- ▶ X and Y think this issue is about _____. But what is really at stake here is _____.

- ▶ X claims that _____. But I agree with Y, who argues that _____.

- ▶ On this issue, X and Y say _____. Although I understand and to some degree sympathize with their point of view, I agree with Z that this is ultimately a question of _____.

The paragraph from Patrick O'Malley's paper on pp. 429–30 shows how ideas and information from sources can be synthesized to support the writer's claim.

Acknowledging Sources and Avoiding Plagiarism

In your college writing, you will be expected to use and acknowledge **secondary sources**— books, articles, published or recorded interviews, Web sites, computer bulletin boards, lectures, and other print and nonprint materials—in addition to your own ideas, insights, and field research. The following information will help you decide what does and does not need to be acknowledged and will enable you to avoid *plagiarizing* from sources inadvertently.

What does and does not need to be acknowledged?

For the most part, any ideas, information, or language you borrow from a source—whether the source is in print or online—must be acknowledged by including an in-text citation and an entry in your list of works cited (MLA style) or references (APA style). The only types of information that do not require acknowledgment are common knowledge (for example, John F. Kennedy was assassinated in Dallas), facts widely available in many sources (U.S. presidents used to be inaugurated on March 4 rather than January 20), well-known quotations ("To be or not to be /That is the question"), and material you created or gathered yourself, such as photographs that you took or data from surveys that you conducted.

You need to acknowledge the source of any visual (photograph, table, chart, graph, diagram, drawing, map, screenshot) that you did not create yourself as well as the source of any information that you used to create your own visual. (You should also request permission from the source of a visual if your essay is going to be posted online without password protection.) When in doubt, acknowledge the source.

The documentation guidelines in the next two chapters present two styles for citing sources: MLA and APA. Whichever style you use, the most important thing is that your readers be able to tell where words or ideas that are not your own begin and end: Take and transcribe notes carefully, place parenthetical source citations correctly, and separate your words from those of the source with **signal phrases** such as "According to Smith," and "As Olmos asserts." (When you cite a source for the first time in a signal phrase, use the author's full name; after that, use just the last name.)

Avoid plagiarism by acknowledging sources and quoting, paraphrasing, and summarizing carefully.

When you use material from another source, you need to acknowledge the source, usually by citing the author and page or publication date in your text and including a list of works cited or references at the end of your essay. Failure to acknowledge sources—even by accident— constitutes plagiarism, a serious transgression. By citing sources correctly, you give appropriate credit to the originator of the words and ideas you are using, offer your readers the information they need to consult those sources directly, and build your own credibility.

Writers—students and professionals alike—occasionally fail to acknowledge sources properly. Students sometimes mistakenly assume that plagiarizing occurs only when another writer's exact words are used without acknowledgment. In fact, plagiarism can also apply to paraphrases as well as to such diverse forms of expression as musical compositions, visual images, ideas, and statistics. Therefore, keep in mind that you must indicate the source of any borrowed information, idea, language, or visual or audio material you use in your essay, whether you have *paraphrased, summarized,* or *quoted* directly from the source or have reproduced it or referred to it in some other way.

Remember especially the need to document electronic sources fully and accurately. Perhaps because it is so easy to access and distribute text and visuals online and to copy material from one electronic document and paste it into another, some students do not realize, or may forget, that information, ideas, and images from electronic sources require acknowledgment in even more detail than those from print sources. At the same time, the improper (unacknowledged) use of online sources is often very easy for readers to detect.

Some people plagiarize simply because they do not know the conventions for using and acknowledging sources. Others plagiarize because they keep sloppy notes and thus fail to distinguish between their own and their sources' ideas. If you keep a working bibliography and careful notes, you will not make this serious mistake. If you are unfamiliar with the conventions for documentation, this and the next two chapters will clarify how you can incorporate sources into your writing and properly acknowledge your use of those sources.

Another reason some people plagiarize is that they feel intimidated by the writing task or the deadline. If you experience this anxiety about your work, speak to your instructor. Do not run the risk of failing a course or being expelled from your college because of plagiarism.

If you are confused about what is and what is not plagiarism, be sure to ask your instructor.

Using Information from Sources to Support Your Claims

When writing a research project, remember that the goal is to use the ideas and information you find in sources *to support your own ideas*. Make sure that each of your supporting paragraphs does three things:

1. States a claim that supports your thesis
2. Provides evidence that supports your claim
3. Explains to readers how the evidence supports your claim

Consider this paragraph from Patrick O'Malley's proposal in Chapter 6, "More Testing, More Learning" (pp. 198–203):

States claim	The main reason professors should give frequent exams is that when they do
Explains how evidence supports claim	and when they provide feedback to students on how well they are doing, students learn more in the course and perform better on major exams, projects, and papers. It makes sense that in a challenging course containing a great deal

Provides evidence

of material, students will learn more of it and put it to better use if they have to apply or "practice" it frequently on exams, which also helps them find out how much they are learning and what they need to go over again. A 2006 study reported in *Psychological Science* journal concluded that "taking repeated tests on material leads to better long-term retention than repeated studying," according to the study's coauthors, Henry L. Roediger and Jeffrey Karpicke (ScienceWatch.com, 2008). When asked what the impact of this breakthrough research would be, they responded: "We hope that this research may be picked up in educational circles as a way to improve educational practices, both for students in the classroom and as a study strategy outside of class." The new field of mind, brain, and education research advocates the use of "retrieval testing." For example, research by Karpicke and Blunt (2011) published in *Science* found that testing was more effective than other, more traditional methods of studying both for comprehension and for analysis.

O'Malley connects this body paragraph to his thesis by beginning with the transition *The main reason* and by repeating the phrase *perform better* from his forecasting statement. He synthesizes information from a variety of sources. For example, he uses quotations from some sources and a summary of another to provide evidence. And he doesn't merely stitch quotations and summary together; rather, he explains how the evidence supports his claim by stating that it "makes sense" that students "apply or 'practice'" what they learn on frequent exams.

For more on synthesis, see pp. 307–308, Chapter 9.

Decide whether to quote, paraphrase, or summarize.

As illustrated in O'Malley's paragraph, above, writers integrate supporting evidence by quoting, paraphrasing, or summarizing information or ideas from sources. This section provides guidelines for deciding when to use each of these three methods and how to quote, paraphrase, and summarize effectively. Note that all examples in this section follow MLA style for in-text citations, which is explained in detail in Chapter 19.

As a rule, quote only in these situations:

- When the wording of the source is particularly memorable or vivid or expresses a point so well that you cannot improve it
- When the words of reliable and respected authorities would lend support to your position
- When you wish to cite an author whose opinions challenge or vary greatly from those of other experts
- When you are going to discuss the source's choice of words

Paraphrase passages whose details you wish to use but whose language is not particularly striking. Summarize any long passages whose main points you wish to record as support for a point you are making.

Copy quotations exactly, or use italics, ellipses, and brackets to indicate changes.

Quotations should duplicate the source exactly, even if they contain spelling errors. Add the notation *sic* (Latin for "thus") in brackets immediately after any such error to indicate that it is not your error but your source's. As long as you signal them appropriately, you may make changes to

- emphasize particular words;
- omit irrelevant information;
- insert information necessary for clarity;
- make the quotation conform grammatically to your sentence.

Using Italics for Emphasis   You may italicize any words in the quotation that you want to emphasize; add a semicolon and the words *emphasis added* (in regular type, not italicized or underlined) to the parenthetical citation:

> In her 2001 exposé of the struggles of the working class, Ehrenreich writes, "The wages Winn-Dixie is offering—*$6 and a couple of dimes to start with*—are not enough, I decide, to compensate for this indignity" (14; emphasis added).

Using Ellipsis Marks for Omissions   You may decide to omit words from a quotation because they are not relevant to the point you are making. When you omit words from within a quotation, use **ellipses**—three spaced periods (. . .) — in place of the missing words. When the omission occurs within a sentence, include a space before the first ellipsis mark and after the last mark:

> Hermione Roddice is described in Lawrence's *Women in Love* as a "woman of the new school, full of intellectuality and . . . nerve-worn with consciousness" (17).

When the omission falls at the end of a sentence, place a period *directly after* the final word of the sentence, followed by a space and three spaced ellipsis marks:

> But Grimaldi's commentary contends that for Aristotle rhetoric, like dialectic, had "no limited and unique subject matter upon which it must be exercised. . . . Instead, rhetoric as an art transcends all specific disciplines and may be brought into play in them" (6).

A period plus ellipses can indicate the omission not just of the rest of a sentence but also of whole sentences, paragraphs, or even pages.

When a parenthetical reference follows the ellipses at the end of a sentence, place the three spaced periods after the quotation, and place the sentence period after the final parenthesis:

> But Grimaldi's commentary contends that for Aristotle rhetoric, like dialectic, had "no limited and unique subject matter upon which it must be exercised. . . . Instead, rhetoric as an art transcends all specific disciplines . . ." (6).

When you quote only single words or phrases, you do not need to use ellipses because it will be obvious that you have left out some of the original:

More specifically, Wharton's imagery of suffusing brightness transforms Undine before her glass into "some fabled creature whose home was in a beam of light" (21).

For the same reason, you need not use ellipses if you omit the beginning of a quoted sentence unless the rest of the sentence begins with a capitalized word and still appears to be a complete sentence.

Using Brackets for Insertions or Changes   Use brackets around an insertion or a change needed to make a quotation conform grammatically to your sentence, such as a change in the form of a verb or pronoun or in the capitalization of the first word of the quotation. In this example from an essay on James Joyce's short story "Araby," the writer adapts Joyce's phrases "we played till our bodies glowed" and "shook music from the buckled harness" to fit the grammar of her sentences:

In the dark, cold streets during the "short days of winter," the boys must generate their own heat by "play[ing] till [their] bodies glowed." Music is "[shaken] from the buckled harness" as if it were unnatural, and the singers in the market chant nasally of "the troubles in our native land" (30).

You may also use brackets to add or substitute explanatory material in a quotation:

Guterson notes that among Native Americans in Florida, "education was in the home; learning by doing was reinforced by the myths and legends which repeated the basic value system of their [the Seminoles'] way of life" (159).

Some changes that make a quotation conform grammatically to another sentence may be made without any signal to readers:

- A period at the end of a quotation may be changed to a comma if you are using the quotation within your own sentence.
- Double quotation marks enclosing a quotation may be changed to single quotation marks when the quotation is enclosed within a longer quotation.

Adjusting the Punctuation within Quotations   Although punctuation within a quotation should reproduce the original, some adaptations may be necessary. Use single quotation marks for quotations within the quotation:

Original from David Guterson's **_Family Matters_ (pp. 16–17)**	**Quoted Version**
E. D. Hirsch also recognizes the connection between family and learning, suggesting in his discussion of family background and academic achievement "that the significant part of our children's education has been going on outside rather than inside the schools."	Guterson claims that E. D. Hirsch "also recognizes the connection between family and learning, suggesting in his discussion of family background and academic achievement 'that the significant part of our children's education has been going on outside rather than inside the schools' " (16-17).

If the quotation ends with a question mark or an exclamation point, retain the original punctuation:

"Did you think I loved you?" Edith later asks Dombey (566).

If a quotation ending with a question mark or an exclamation point concludes your sentence, retain the question mark or exclamation point, and put the parenthetical reference and sentence period outside the quotation marks:

Edith later asks Dombey, "Did you think I loved you?" (566).

Avoiding Grammatical Tangles   When you incorporate quotations into your writing, and especially when you omit words from quotations, you run the risk of creating ungrammatical sentences. Avoid these three common errors:

- Verb incompatibility
- Ungrammatical omissions
- Sentence fragments

Verb incompatibility occurs when the verb form in the introductory statement is grammatically incompatible with the verb form in the quotation. When your quotation has a verb form that does not fit in with your text, it is usually possible to use just part of the quotation, thus avoiding verb incompatibility:

▶ The narrator suggests his bitter disappointment when "*he describes seeing himself "*~~I saw myself~~ as a creature

driven and derided by vanity" (35).

As this sentence illustrates, use the present tense when you refer to events in a literary work.

Ungrammatical omissions may occur when you delete text from a quotation. To avoid this problem, try adapting the quotation (with brackets) so that its parts fit together grammatically, or use only one part of the quotation:

▶ From the moment of the boy's arrival in Araby, the bazaar is presented as a commercial

enterprise: "I could not find any sixpenny entrance and . . . *hand[ed]* ~~handing~~ a shilling to a

weary-looking man" (34).

▶ From the moment of the boy's arrival in Araby, the bazaar is presented as a

commercial enterprise: *He "* "I could not find any sixpenny entrance ~~and~~ *"*

so had to pay a shilling to get in
~~. . . handing a shilling to a weary-looking man~~" (34).

Sentence fragments sometimes result when writers forget to include a verb in the sentence introducing a quotation, especially when the quotation itself is a complete sentence. Make sure you introduce a quotation with a complete sentence:

leads

▶ The girl's interest in the bazaar ~~leading~~ the narrator to make what amounts to a sacred

oath: "If I go . . . I will bring you something" (32).

Use in-text or block quotations.

Depending on its length, you may incorporate a quotation into your text by enclosing it in quotation marks or by setting it off from your text in a block without quotation marks. In either case, be sure to integrate the quotation into your essay using the strategies described here:

In-Text Quotations Incorporate brief quotations (no more than four typed lines of prose or three lines of poetry) into your text. You may place a quotation virtually anywhere in your sentence:

At the Beginning

"To live a life is not to cross a field," Sutherland, quoting Pasternak, writes at the beginning of her narrative (11).

In the Middle

Woolf begins and ends by speaking of the need of the woman writer to have "money and a room of her own" (4)—an idea that certainly spoke to Plath's condition.

At the End

In *The Second Sex*, Simone de Beauvoir describes such an experience as one in which the girl "becomes an object, and she sees herself as object" (378).

Divided by Your Own Words

"Science usually prefers the literal to the nonliteral term," Kinneavy writes, "—that is, figures of speech are often out of place in science" (177).

When you quote poetry within your text, use a slash (/) with spaces before and after to signal the end of each line of verse:

Alluding to St. Augustine's distinction between the City of God and the Earthly City, Lowell writes that "much against my will / I left the City of God where it belongs" (4-5).

Block Quotations In MLA style, use the block form for prose quotations of five or more typed lines and for poetry quotations of four or more lines. Indent the quotation an inch from the left margin, as shown in the following example:

In "A Literary Legacy from Dunbar to Baraka," Margaret Walker says of Paul Lawrence Dunbar's dialect poems:

> He realized that the white world in the United States tolerated his literary genius only because of his "jingles in a broken tongue," and they found the old "darky" tales and speech amusing and within the vein of folklore

> into which they wished to classify all Negro life. This troubled Dunbar
> because he realized that white America was denigrating him as a writer
> and as a man. (70)

In APA style, use block form for quotations of forty words or more. Indent the block quotation half an inch.

In a block quotation, double-space between lines just as you do in your text. *Do not* enclose the passage within quotation marks. Use a colon to introduce a block quotation unless the context calls for another punctuation mark or none at all. When quoting a single paragraph or part of one in MLA style, do not indent the first line of the quotation more than the rest. In quoting two or more paragraphs, indent the first line of each paragraph an extra quarter inch. If you are using APA style, indent the first line of subsequent paragraphs in the block quotation an additional half inch from the indention of the block quotation.

Note that in MLA style the parenthetical page reference follows the period in block quotations.

Use punctuation to integrate quotations into your writing.

Statements that introduce in-text quotations take a range of punctuation marks and lead-in words. Here are some examples of ways writers typically introduce quotations:

Introducing a Quotation Using a Colon   A colon usually follows an independent clause placed before the quotation:

> As George Williams notes, protection of white privilege is critical to patterns of discrim-
> ination: "Whenever a number of persons within a society have enjoyed for a consider-
> able period of time certain opportunities for getting wealth, for exercising power and
> authority, and for successfully claiming prestige and social deference, there is a strong
> tendency for these people to feel that these benefits are theirs 'by right' " (727).

Introducing a Quotation Using a Comma   A comma usually follows an introduction that incorporates the quotation in its sentence structure:

> Similarly, Duncan Turner asserts, "As matters now stand, it is unwise to talk about communi-
> cation without some understanding of Burke" (259).

Introducing a Quotation Using *That*   No punctuation is generally needed with *that*, and no capital letter is used to begin the quotation:

> Noting this failure, Alice Miller asserts that "the reason for her despair was not her suffering
> but the impossibility of communicating her suffering to another person" (255).

Paraphrase sources carefully.

In a **paraphrase,** the writer restates in his or her own words all the relevant information from a passage, without any additional comments or any suggestion of agreement or disagreement with the source's ideas. A paraphrase is useful for recording details of the passage when the order of the details is important but the source's wording is not. Because all the details of the passage are included, a paraphrase is often about the same length as the original passage. It is better to paraphrase than to quote ordinary material in which the author's way of expressing things is not worth special attention.

Here is a passage from a book on home schooling and an example of an acceptable paraphrase of it:

Original Source	Acceptable Paraphrase
Bruner and the discovery theorists have also illuminated conditions that apparently pave the way for learning. It is significant that these conditions are unique to each learner, so unique, in fact, that in many cases classrooms can't provide them. Bruner also contends that the more one discovers information in a great variety of circumstances, the more likely one is to develop the inner categories required to organize that information. Yet life at school, which is for the most part generic and predictable, daily keeps many children from the great variety of circumstances they need to learn well.	According to Guterson, the "discovery theorists," particularly Bruner, have found that there seem to be certain conditions that help learning to take place. Because individuals require different conditions, many children are not able to learn in the classroom. According to Bruner, when people can explore information in many different situations, they learn to classify and order what they discover. The general routine of the school day, however, does not provide children with the diverse activities and situations that would allow them to learn these skills (172).

—David Guterson, *Family Matters: Why Homeschooling Makes Sense*, p. 172

The highlighting shows that some words in the paraphrase were taken from the source. Indeed, it would be nearly impossible for paraphrasers to avoid using any key terms from the source, and it would be counterproductive to try to do so, because the original and the paraphrase necessarily share the same information and concepts. Notice, though, that of the total of eighty-five words in the paraphrase, the paraphraser uses only a name (*Bruner*) and a few other key nouns and verbs for which it would be awkward to substitute other words or phrases. If the paraphraser had wanted to use other, more distinctive language from the source—for example, the description of life at school as "generic and predictable"—these adjectives would need to be enclosed in quotation marks. In fact, the paraphraser puts quotation marks around only one of the terms from the source: "discovery theorists"—a technical term likely to be unfamiliar to readers.

Paraphrasers must, however, avoid borrowing too many words and repeating the sentence structures from a source. Here is an unacceptable paraphrase of the first sentence in the Guterson passage:

Unacceptable Paraphrase: Too Many Borrowed Words and Phrases

Repeated sentence
structure

Repeated words

Apparently, some conditions, which have been illuminated by Bruner and other discovery theorists, pave the way for people to learn.

Here, the paraphrase borrows almost all of its key language from the source sentence, including the entire phrase *pave the way for*. Even if you cite the source, this heavy borrowing would be considered plagiarism.

Here is another unacceptable paraphrase of the same sentence:

Unacceptable Paraphrase: Sentence Structure Repeated Too Closely

Repeated words
Synonyms
Repeated sentence
structure

Bruner and other *researchers* have also *identified circumstances* that *seem to ease the path* to learning.

If you compare the source's first sentence and this paraphrase of it, you will see that the paraphraser has borrowed the phrases and clauses of the source and arranged them in an almost identical sequence, simply substituting synonyms for most of the key terms. This paraphrase would also be considered plagiarism.

Summaries should present the source's main ideas in a balanced and readable way.

Unlike a paraphrase, a **summary** presents only the main ideas of a source, leaving out examples and details.

Here is one student's summary of five pages from Guterson's book *Family Matters*. You can see at a glance how drastically summaries can condense information, in this case from five pages to five sentences. Depending on the summarizer's purpose, the five pages could be summarized in one sentence, the five sentences here, or two or three dozen sentences.

> In looking at different theories of learning that discuss individual-based programs (such as home schooling) versus the public school system, Guterson describes the disagreements among "cognitivist" theorists. One group, the "discovery theorists," believes that individual children learn by creating their own ways of sorting the information they take in from their experiences. Schools should help students develop better ways of organizing new material, not just present them with material that is already categorized, as traditional schools do. "Assimilationist theorists," by contrast, believe that children learn by linking what they don't know to information they already know. These theorists claim that traditional schools help students learn when they present information in ways that allow children to fit the new material into categories they have already developed (171–75).

Summaries like this one are more than a dry list of main ideas from a source. They are instead a coherent, readable new text composed of the source's main ideas. Summaries provide balanced coverage of a source, following the same sequence of ideas and avoiding any hint of agreement or disagreement with them.

19

Citing and Documenting Sources in MLA Style

When using the MLA system of documentation, include both an in-text citation and a list of works cited. **In-text citations** tell your readers where the ideas or words you have borrowed come from, and the entries in the **works-cited list** allow readers to locate your sources so that they can read more about your topic.

In most cases, include the author's last name and the page number on which the borrowed material appears in the text of your research project. You can incorporate this information in two ways, often used together:

SIGNAL PHRASE   By naming the author in the text of your research project with a signal phrase (*Simon described*) and including the page reference (in parentheses) at the end of the borrowed passage:

author's last name   *appropriate verb*

Simon, a well-known figure in New York literary society, described the impression Dr. James made on her as a child in the Bronx: He was a "not-too-skeletal Ichabod Crane" (68).

page number

PARENTHETICAL CITATION   By including the author's name and the page number together in parentheses at the end of the borrowed passage:

author's last name + page number

Dr. James is described as a "not-too-skeletal Ichabod Crane" (Simon 68).

WORKS-CITED ENTRY   Simon, Kate. "Birthing." *Bronx Primitive: Portraits in a Childhood.* New York: Viking, 1982. 68–77. Print.

In most cases, you will want to use a *signal phrase* because doing so lets you put your source in context. The signal-phrase-plus-page-reference combination also allows you to make crystal clear where the source information begins and ends. Use a parenthetical citation alone when you have already identified the author or when citing the source of an uncontroversial fact.

The in-text citation (with or without a signal phrase) should include only as much information as is needed to lead readers to the source in your list of works cited and allow them to find the passage you are citing in that source. In most cases, that means the author's last name and the page number on which the borrowed material appears. In some cases, you may need to include other information in your in-text citation (such as a brief version of the title if the author is unknown or if you cite more than one work by this author). In a few cases, you may not be able to include a page reference, as, for example, when you cite a Web site that does not include page numbers. In such cases, you may include other identifying information, such as a paragraph number or section heading.

The most common types of in-text citations follow. For other, less common citation types, consult the *MLA Handbook for Writers of Research Papers,* Seventh Edition. Most libraries will own a copy. If the handbook does not provide a model citation, use the information here to create a citation that will lead your readers to the source.

macmillanhighered.com/conciseguide
Tutorials > Documentation and Working with Sources > How to Cite an Article in MLA Style
> How to Cite a Book in MLA Style
> How to Cite a Database in MLA Style
> How to Cite a Web Site in MLA Style

Citing Sources in the Text

Directory to In-Text-Citation Models

One author   439
More than one author   440
Unknown author   440
Two or more works by the same author   440
Two or more authors with the same last name   440
Corporation, organization, or government agency as author   440
Literary work (novel, play, poem)   441

Work in an anthology   441
Religious work   441
Indirect citation (quotation from a secondary source)   442
Entire work   442
Work without page numbers or a one-page work (with/without other section numbers)   442
Two or more works cited in the same parentheses   442

One author   When citing most works with a single author, include the author's name (usually the last name is enough) and the page number on which the cited material appears.

author's last name + appropriate verb   *page number*

SIGNAL PHRASE   Simon describes Dr. James as a "not-too-skeletal Ichabod Crane" (68).

author's last name + page number

PARENTHETICAL CITATION   Dr. James is described as a "not-too-skeletal Ichabod Crane" (Simon 68).

author's name

BLOCK QUOTATION   In Kate Simon's story "Birthing," the description of Dr. James captures both his physical appearance and his role in the community:

> He looked so much like a story character—the gentled Scrooge of a St. Nicholas Magazine Christmas issue, a not-too-skeletal Ichabod Crane. . . . Dr. James was, even when I knew him as a child, quite an old man, retired from a prestigious and lucrative

> practice in Boston. . . . His was a prosperous intellectual family, the famous New England Jameses that produced William and Henry, but to the older Bronx doctors, *the* James was the magnificent old driven scarecrow. (68)
> page number

(A works-cited entry for "Birthing" appears on page 438.)

More than one author   To cite a source by two or three authors, include all the authors' last names. To cite a source with four or more authors, model your in-text citation on the entry in your works-cited list: Use either all the authors' names or just the first author's name followed by *et al.* ("and others" in Latin, not italicized).

SIGNAL PHRASE	Dyal, Corning, and Willows (1975) identify several types of students, including the "Authority-Rebel" (4).
PARENTHETICAL CITATION	The Authority-Rebel "tends to see himself as superior to other students in the class" (Dyal, Corning, and Willows 4).
	The drug AZT has been shown to reduce the risk of transmission from HIV-positive mothers to their infants by as much as two-thirds (Van de Perre et al. 4-5).

Unknown author   If the author's name is unknown, use a shortened version of the title, beginning with the word by which the title is alphabetized in the works-cited list.

> An international pollution treaty still to be ratified would prohibit ships from dumping plastic at sea ("Plastic Is Found" 68).

The full title of the work is "Plastic Is Found in the Sargasso Sea; Pieces of Apparent Refuse Cover Wide Atlantic Region."

Two or more works by the same author   If you cite more than one work by the same author, include a shortened version of the title.

> When old paint becomes transparent, it sometimes shows the artist's original plans: "a tree will show through a woman's dress" (Hellman, *Pentimento* 1).

Two or more authors with the same last name   When citing works by authors with the same last name, include each author's first initial in the citation. If the first initials are also the same, spell out the authors' first names.

> Chaplin's *Modern Times* provides a good example of montage used to make an editorial statement (E. Roberts 246).

Corporation, organization, or government agency as author   In a signal phrase, use the full name of the corporation, organization, or government agency. In a parenthetical citation, use the full name if it is brief or a shortened version if it is long.

SIGNAL PHRASE   According to the Washington State Board for Community and Technical Colleges, a tuition increase . . . from Initiative 601 (4).

PARENTHETICAL CITATION   A tuition increase has been proposed for community and technical colleges to offset budget deficits from Initiative 601 (Washington State Board 4).

Literary work (novel, play, poem)   Provide information that will help readers find the passage you are citing no matter what edition of the novel, play, or poem they are using. For a novel or other prose work, provide the part or chapter number as well as the page numbers from the edition you used.

NOVEL OR OTHER PROSE WORK   In *Hard Times,* Tom reveals his utter narcissism by blaming Louisa for his own failure: " 'You have regularly given me up. You never cared for me'" (Dickens 262; bk. 3, ch. 9).

For a play in verse, use act, scene, and line numbers instead of page numbers.

PLAY (IN VERSE)   At the beginning, Regan's fawning rhetoric hides her true attitude toward Lear: "I profess / myself an enemy to all other joys . . . / And find that I am alone felicitate / In your dear highness' love" (*King Lear* 1.1.74–75, 77–78).

For a poem, indicate the line numbers and stanzas or sections (if they are numbered) instead of page numbers.

POEM   In "Song of Myself," Whitman finds poetic details in busy urban settings, as when he describes "the blab of the pave, tires of carts . . . the driver with his interrogating thumb" (8.153–54).

If the source gives only line numbers, use the term *lines* in your first citation and use only the numbers in subsequent citations.

In "Before you thought of spring," Dickinson at first identifies the spirit of spring with a bird, possibly a robin—"A fellow in the skies / Inspiriting habiliments / Of indigo and brown" (lines 4, 7–8)—but by the end of the poem, she has linked it with poetry and perhaps even the poet herself, as the bird, like Dickinson, "shouts for joy to nobody / But his seraphic self!" (15–16)

Work in an anthology   Use the name of the author of the work, not the editor of the anthology, in your in-text citation.

SIGNAL PHRASE   In "Six Days: Some Rememberings," Grace Paley recalls that when she was in jail for protesting the Vietnam War, her pen and paper were taken away and she felt "a terrible pain in the area of my heart—a nausea" (191).

PARENTHETICAL CITATION   Writers may have a visceral reaction—"a nausea" (Paley 191)—to being deprived of access to writing implements.

Religious work   In your first citation, include the element that begins your entry in the works-cited list, such as the edition name of the religious work you are citing, and include the book or section name (using standard abbreviations in parenthetical citations) and any chapter or verse numbers.

> She ignored the admonition "Pride goes before destruction, and a haughty spirit before a fall" (*New Oxford Annotated Bible,* Prov. 16.18).

Indirect citation (quotation from a secondary source)   If possible, locate the original source and cite that. If not possible, name the original source but also include the secondary source in which you found the material you are citing, plus the abbreviation *qtd. in.* Include the secondary source in your list of works cited.

> E. M. Forster says, "the collapse of all civilization, so realistic for us, sounded in Matthew Arnold's ears like a distant and harmonious cataract" (qtd. in Trilling 11).

Entire work   Include the reference in the text without any page numbers or parentheses.

> In *The Structure of Scientific Revolutions,* Thomas Kuhn discusses how scientists change their thinking.

Work without page numbers or a one-page work (with/without other section numbers) If a work (such as a Web page) has no page numbers or is only one page long, omit the page number. If it uses screen numbers or paragraph numbers, insert a comma after the author's name, an identifying term (such as *screen*) or abbreviation (*par.* or *pars.*), and the number.

WITHOUT PAGE OR OTHER NUMBERS	The average speed on Montana's interstate highways, for example, has risen by only 2 miles per hour since the repeal of the federal speed limit, with most drivers topping out at 75 (Schmid).
WITH OTHER SECTION NUMBERS	Whitman considered African American speech "a source of a native grand opera" (Ellison, par. 13).

Two or more works cited in the same parentheses   If you cite two or more sources for a piece of information, include them in the same parentheses, separated by semicolons.

> A few studies have considered differences between oral and written discourse production (Scardamalia, Bereiter, and Goelman; Gould).

If the parenthetical citation is likely to prove disruptive for your reader, cite multiple sources in a footnote or an end note.

Creating a List of Works Cited

Directory to Works-Cited-List Models

Author Listings
One author   444
Two or three authors   444
Four or more authors   444

Unknown author   444
Corporation, organization, or government agency as author   445
Two or more works by the same author   445

Books (Print, Electronic, Database)
Basic format   445
Anthology or edited collection   445
Work in an anthology or edited
   collection   445
Introduction, preface, foreword, or
   afterword   446
Translation   446
Graphic narrative   446
Religious work   446
Later edition of a book   446
Republished book   446
Title within a title   446
Book in a series   446
Dictionary entry or article in another
   reference book   447
Government document   447
Pamphlet or brochure   447
Doctoral dissertation   448

Articles (Print, Online, Database)
From a scholarly journal   448
From a newspaper   449
From a magazine   449
Editorial or letter to the editor   449
Review   449

**Multimedia Sources (Live, Print,
Electronic, Database)**
Lecture or public address   451
Letter   451
Map or chart   451
Cartoon or comic strip   451
Advertisement   451
Work of art   452
Performance   452
Television or radio program   452
Podcast   452
Film   453
Online video   453
Music recording   453
Interview   453

Other Electronic Sources
Web page or other document on a
   Web site   454
Entire Web site   454
Online scholarly project   454
Book or a short work in an online
   scholarly project   454
Blog   454
Wiki article   456
E-mail message   456

In your MLA-style research paper, every source you cite must have a corresponding entry in the list of works cited, and every entry in your list of works cited must correspond to at least one citation in your research project.

Follow these rules when formatting your list of works cited in MLA style:

- Double-space the whole works-cited list.

- Alphabetize entries by the first word in the citation (usually the first author's last name, or the title if the author is unknown, ignoring *A, An,* or *The*).

- Use a "hanging indent" for all entries: Do not indent the first line, but indent second and subsequent lines of the entry by half an inch (or five spaces).

- Shorten publishers' names: Abbreviate compound or hyphenated names to the first name only (*Bedford/St. Martin's* becomes *Bedford,* for example); omit words like *Company* or *Books;* and for university presses, shorten the words *University* and *Press* to *U* and *P.*

Nowadays, many print sources are also available in an electronic format, either online or through a database your school's library subscribes to. For most online versions of a source, follow the form of the corresponding print version. For example, if you are citing an article from an online periodical, put the article title in quotation marks and italicize the name of the periodical. If the source has also been published in print (as with most e-books and many magazines and newspapers that appear online), include the print publication information if it is available. Also include information specific to the version of the source you used.

For sources accessed through a database, include the following:

- Title of the database (in italics)
- Medium of publication (*Web*)
- Date you last accessed the source

For other online sources, include the following:

- Title of the Web site (in italics)
- Version or edition used (if any)
- Publisher or sponsor of the site; if not available, use *N.p.*
- Date of publication or last update; if not available, use *n.d.*
- Medium of publication (*Web*)
- Date you last accessed the source

Content on the Web frequently changes or disappears, and because the same information that traditionally published books and periodicals provide is not always included for Web sources, giving your reader a complete citation is not always possible. Always keep your goal in mind: to provide enough information so that your reader can track down the source. If you cannot find all of the information listed here, include what you can.

Author Listings

One author   List the author last name first (followed by a comma), and insert a period at the end of the name.

Isaacson, Walter.

Two or three authors   List the first author last name first (followed by a comma). List the other authors in the usual first-name/last-name order. Insert the word *and* before the last author's name, and follow it with a period.

Saba, Laura, and Julie Gattis.

Wilmut, Ian, Keith Campbell, and Colin Tudge.

Four or more authors   List the first author last name first (followed by a comma). Then either list all the authors' names (in the usual first-name/last-name order, with a comma between authors, the word *and* before the last name, and a period after it) *or* insert *et al.* (which means *and others* in Latin) in regular type (not italics). Whichever you decide to do, be sure to use the same format in your in-text citation.

Hunt, Lynn, Thomas R. Martin, Barbara H. Rosenwein, R. Po-chia Hsia, and Bonnie G. Smith.

Hunt, Lynn, et al.

Unknown author   Begin the entry with the title.

Primary Colors: A Novel of Politics.

"Out of Sight."

Corporation, organization, or government agency as author   Use the name of the corporation, organization, or government agency as the author.

RAND Corporation.

United States. National Commission on Terrorist Attacks.

Two or more works by the same author   Replace the author's name in subsequent entries with three hyphens, and alphabetize the works by the first important word in the title:

Eugenides, Jeffrey. *The Marriage Plot*.

---. "Walkabout."

Books (Print, Electronic, Database)

Basic format (print, e-book, database)

Anthology or edited collection   If you are referring to the anthology as a whole, put the editor's name first.

Masri, Heather, ed. *Science Fiction: Stories and Contexts*. Boston: Bedford, 2009. Print.

Work in an anthology or edited collection   If you're referring to a selection in an anthology, begin the entry with the name of the selection's author.

Hopkinson, Nalo. "Something to Hitch Meat To." *Science Fiction: Stories and Contexts*. Ed.
    Heather Masri. Boston: Bedford, 2009. 838–50. Print.

If you cite more than one selection from an anthology or collection, you may create an entry for the collection as a whole (see the model above) and then cross-reference individual selections to that entry.

Introduction, preface, foreword, or afterword

> Murfin, Ross C. Introduction. *Heart of Darkness*. By Joseph Conrad. 3rd ed. Boston: Bedford,
> 2011. 3–16. Print.

Translation

> Tolstoy, Leo. *War and Peace*. Trans. Richard Pevear and Larissa Volokhonsky. New York:
> Vintage, 2009. Print.

Graphic narrative   If the graphic narrative was a collaboration between a writer and an illustrator, begin your entry with the name of the person on whose work your research project focuses. If the author also created the illustrations, then follow the basic model for a book with one author (p. 444).

> Pekar, Harvey, and Joyce Brabner. *Our Cancer Year*. Illus. Frank Stack. New York: Four Walls
> Eight Windows, 1994. Print.

Religious work   Include an entry in the list of works cited only if you cite a specific edition of a sacred text.

> *The Qu'ran: English Translation and Parallel Arabic Text*. Trans. M. A. S. Abdel Haleem.
> New York: Oxford UP, 2010. Print.

Later edition of a book   Include the edition name (such as *Revised*) or number following the title.

> Rottenberg, Annette T , and Donna Haisty Winchell. *The Structure of Argument*. 6th ed.
> Boston: Bedford, 2009. Print.

Republished book   Provide the original year of publication after the title of the book, followed by publication information for the edition you are using.

> *Original publication date*
> Alcott, Louisa May. *An Old-Fashioned Girl*. |1870.| New York: Puffin, 1995. Print.
> *Republication information*

Title within a title   When a title that is normally italicized appears within a book title, do not italicize it. If the title within the title would normally be enclosed in quotation marks, include the quotation marks and also set the title in italics.

> Hertenstein, Mike. *The Double Vision of* Star Trek: *Half-Humans, Evil Twins, and Science Fiction*.
> Chicago: Cornerstone, 1998. Print.

> Miller, Edwin Haviland. *Walt Whitman's "Song of Myself": A Mosaic of Interpretation*. Iowa
> City: U of Iowa P, 1989. Print.

Book in a series   Include the series title and number (if any) after the medium of publication. If the word *Series* is part of the name, include the abbreviation *Ser.* before the series number. (This information will appear on the title page or on the page facing the title page.) Abbreviate any commonly abbreviated words in the series title.

Zigova, Tanya, et al. *Neural Stem Cells: Methods and Protocols.* Totowa: Humana, 2002. Print. Methods in Molecular Biology 198.

Dictionary entry or article in another reference book (print, online, database)   If no author is listed, begin with the entry's title. (But check for initials following the entry or article and a list of authors in the front of the book.) If the reference work is familiar, omit the publication information.

PRINT   "Homeopathy." *Webster's New World College Dictionary.* 4th ed. 1999. Print.

PRINT   Trenear-Harvey, Glenmore S. "Farm Hall." *Historical Dictionary of Atomic Espionage.*
Lanham: Scarecrow, 2011. Print.

ONLINE   "Homeopathy." *Merriam-Webster.com.* Merriam-Webster, Inc., 2013. Web.
29 Nov. 2013.

Web site (italics) *Pub./Sponsor* *Medium* *Access date*

DATABASE   Powell, Jason L. "Power Elite." *Blackwell Encyclopedia of Sociology.* Ed. George
Ritzer. Wiley-Blackwell, 2007. *Blackwell Reference Online.* Web. 29 Nov. 2013.

Database (italics) *Medium* *Access date*

Government document (print, online)   If no author is named, begin with the government and agency that issued the document. If the author is named, include that information either before or after the document's title (introduced with the word *By*). In the United States, the publication information for most print government documents is *Washington: GPO.* (*GPO* stands for *Government Printing Office.*) But most government documents are now published online.

PRINT   United States. Dept. of Health and Human Services. *Trends in Underage
Drinking in the United States, 1991-2007.* By Gabriella Newes-Adeyi et al.
Washington: GPO, 2009. Print.

Issuing government *Issuing department* *Authors*

ONLINE   United States. Centers for Disease Control. "Youth Risk Behavior Surveillance—
United States, 2011." *Morbidity and Mortality Weekly Report.*
Centers for Disease Control. Dept. of Health and Human Services,
8 June 2012. Web. 30 Nov. 2013.

Issuing agency *Web site (italics)* *Pub./Sponsor* *Publication date* *Medium* *Access date*

Pamphlet or brochure

U.S. Foundation for Boating Safety and Clean Water. *Hypothermia and Cold Water Survival.* Alexandria: U.S. Foundation for Boating, 2001. Print.

Doctoral dissertation (published, unpublished)   Cite a published dissertation as you would a book, but add pertinent dissertation information before the publication data. Enclose the title of an unpublished dissertation in quotation marks.

Title in italics

PUBLISHED   Jones, Anna Maria. *Problem Novels/Perverse Readers: Late-Victorian Fiction and the Perilous Pleasures of Identification.* Diss. U of Notre Dame, 2001. Ann Arbor: UMI, 2001. Print.

Dissertation information

Title in quotation marks

UNPUBLISHED   Bullock, Barbara. "Basic Needs Fulfillment among Less Developed Countries: Social Progress over Two Decades of Growth." Diss. Vanderbilt U, 1986. Print.

Dissertation information

Articles (Print, Online, Database)

Articles appear in periodicals—works that are issued at regular intervals—such as scholarly journals, newspapers, and magazines. Most periodicals today are available both in print and in electronic form (online or through an electronic database); some are available only in electronic format. If you are using the online version of an article, use the models provided here. If no model matches your source exactly, choose the closest print match, and add the site publisher or sponsor, the medium, and the date you last accessed the site, along with any other information your reader will need to track down the source.

From a scholarly journal (print, online, database)   Scholarly journals are typically identified using their volume and issue numbers, separated by a period. If a journal does not use volume numbers, provide the issue number only.

Author, last name first   *Title of article (in quotation marks)*

PRINT   Haas, Heather A. "The Wisdom of Wizards—and Muggles and Squibs: Proverb Use in the World of Harry Potter." *Journal of American Folklore* 124.492 (2011): 29–54. Print.

Year   Pages   Medium   *Title of journal (in italics)   Volume   Issue*

ONLINE   Markel, J. D. "Religious Allegory and Cultural Discomfort in Mike Leigh's *Happy-Go-Lucky*: And Why *Larry Crowne* Is One of the Best Films of 2011." *Bright Lights* 74 (2011): n. pag. Web. 14 Sept. 2013.

Issue number only   No page numbers   Medium   Access date

DATABASE   Haas, Heather A. "The Wisdom of Wizards—and Muggles and Squibs: Proverb Use in the World of *Harry Potter*." *Journal of American Folklore* 124.492 (2011): 29–54. *Academic Search Complete.* Web. 29 Nov. 2011.

Database (italics)   Medium   Access date

Article from a Scholarly Journal

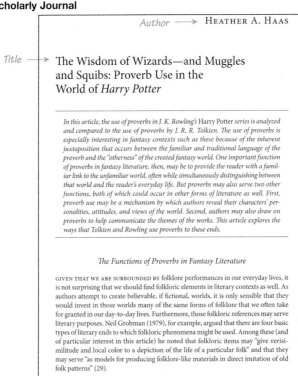

Author → HEATHER A. HAAS

Title → The Wisdom of Wizards—and Muggles and Squibs: Proverb Use in the World of *Harry Potter*

In this article, the use of proverbs in J. K. Rowling's Harry Potter series is analyzed and compared to the use of proverbs by J. R. R. Tolkien. The use of proverbs is especially interesting in fantasy contexts such as these because of the inherent juxtaposition that occurs between the familiar and traditional language of the proverb and the "otherness" of the created fantasy world. One important function of proverbs in fantasy literature, then, may be to provide the reader with a familiar link to the unfamiliar world, often while simultaneously distinguishing between that world and the reader's everyday life. But proverbs may also serve two other functions, both of which could occur in other forms of literature as well. First, proverb use may be a mechanism by which authors reveal their characters' personalities, attitudes, and views of the world. Second, authors may also draw on proverbs to help communicate the themes of the works. This article explores the ways that Tolkien and Rowling use proverbs to these ends.

The Functions of Proverbs in Fantasy Literature

GIVEN THAT WE ARE SURROUNDED BY folklore performances in our everyday lives, it is not surprising that we should find folkloric elements in literary contexts as well. As authors attempt to create believable, if fictional, worlds, it is only sensible that they would invest in those worlds many of the same forms of folklore that we often take for granted in our day-to-day lives. Furthermore, those folkloric references may serve literary purposes. Neil Grobman (1979), for example, argued that there are four basic types of literary ends to which folkloric phenomena might be used. Among these (and of particular interest in this article) he noted that folkloric items may "give verisimilitude and local color to a depiction of the life of a particular folk" and that they may serve "as models for producing folklore-like materials in direct imitation of old folk patterns" (29).

HEATHER A. HAAS is Associate Professor of Psychology, LaGrange College, LaGrange, Georgia

Journal — *Journal of American Folklore* 124(492):29–54
Copyright © 2011 by the Board of Trustees of the University of Illinois

Year —

Database **Database Results List**

Author → ... *Article title* ... *Publication information: journal, year, volume, issue, page numbers*

FIGURE 19.1 Documentation Map for a Journal Article Look for the title of the journal on the first page of the article (shown here). The information you will need to cite an article accessed through a database will appear in the list of results, the detailed record of the article, and the PDF (or HTML) version of the article itself. For an article published in an electronic journal, look for the information you need to create the works-cited entry on the journal's home page or on the page on which the article appears.

Online journals may not include page numbers; if paragraph or other section numbers are provided, use them instead. Otherwise, insert *n. pag.* (for *no page numbers*). If the article is not on a continuous sequence of pages, give the first page number followed by a plus sign. (Figure 19.1 on page 449 shows where to find the source information.)

From a newspaper (print, online, database)   Newspapers are identified by date, not volume and issue numbers, with the names of months longer than four letters abbreviated. If the article is from a special edition of the newspaper (*early ed., natl ed.*), include the edition name after the date. If articles are not on a continuous series of pages, give only the first page number followed by a plus sign. For unpaginated articles accessed through a database, use *n. pag.*

PRINT   Stoll, John D., et al. "U.S. Squeezes Auto Creditors." *Wall Street Journal*
          10 Apr. 2009: A1+. Print.
                                Noncontinuous pages

                                                      Web site (italics)   Pub./Sponsor
ONLINE   Angier, Natalie, "The Changing American Family." *New York Times.* New York Times,
          26 Nov. 2013. Web. 26 Nov. 2013.
          Publication date   Medium   Access date

DATABASE   Lopez, Steve. "Put Occupy L.A. on the Bus." *Los Angeles Times* 30 Nov. 2011,
            Home ed.; n. pag. *LexisNexis Academic.* Web. 30 Nov. 2011.
            Edition name   No page   Database (italics)
                            numbers

From a magazine (print, online, database)   Magazines (like newspapers) are identified by date, with the names of months longer than four letters abbreviated. For magazines published weekly or biweekly, include the day, month, and year; for magazines published monthly or bimonthly, include the month and year. If the article is unsigned, alphabetize by the first important word in the title (ignoring *A, An,* and *The*).

                                                      Publication date (monthly)
PRINT   Branch, Taylor. "The Shame of College Sports." *Atlantic* Oct. 2011: 80–110. Print.
                                                          Publication date
                                Web site (italic)   Site sponsor   (weekly)
ONLINE   Harrell, Eben. "A Flicker of Consciousness." *Time.* Time, Inc. 28 Nov. 2011.
          Web. 26 Nov. 2013.
          Medium   Access date

DATABASE   Harrell, Eben. "A Flicker of Consciousness." *Time* 28 Nov. 2011: 42–47.
            Academic Search Premier. Web. 26 Nov. 2013.
            Database (italics)   Medium   Access date

Editorial or letter to the editor

"Stay Classy." Editorial. *New Republic* 1 Dec. 2011: 1. Print.

Wegeiser, Art. "How Does He Know?" Letter. *Pittsburgh Post-Gazette* 30 Nov. 2011: B6. Print.

Review   If the review does not include an author's name, start the entry with the title of the review. If the review is untitled, begin with *Rev. of* and alphabetize under the title of the work being reviewed. For a review in an online newspaper or magazine, add the site sponsor and access date and change the medium to *Web*. For a review accessed through a database, add the database title (in italics) and access date and change the medium to *Web*.

> Cassidy, John. "Master of Disaster." Rev. of *Globalization and Its Discontents,* by Joseph
> Stiglitz. *New Yorker* 12 July 2002: 82–86. Print.

Multimedia Sources (Live, Print, Electronic, Database)

Lecture or public address

Title of lecture   *Conference title*

> Birnbaum, Jack. "The Domestication of Computers." Conf. of the Usability Professionals
> Association. Hyatt Grand Cypress Resort, Orlando. 10 July 2002. Lecture.
>
> *Location*   *Date of lecture*   *Medium*

Letter   If the letter has been published, treat it like a work in an anthology (p. 445), but add the recipient, the date, and any identifying number after the author's name. If the letter is unpublished, change the medium to *MS* ("manuscript") if written by hand or *TS* ("typescript") if typed.

Sender   *Recipient*   *Date*   *Medium*

> DuHamel, Grace. Letter to the author. 22 Mar. 2008. TS.

Map or chart (print, online)

PRINT   *Map of Afghanistan and Surrounding Territory*. Map. Burlington: GiziMap, 2001. Print.

ONLINE   "North America, 1797." Map. *Perry-Castañeda Library Map Collection*. U of Texas,
              21 June 2011. Web. 1 Dec. 2011.

Cartoon or comic strip (print, online)   Provide the title (if given) in quotation marks directly following the artist's name.

PRINT   Cheney, Tom. Cartoon. *New Yorker* 10 Oct. 2005: 55. Print.

ONLINE   Hunt, Tarol. "Goblins." Comic strip. *Goblinscomic.com*. Tarol Hunt, 29 Sept. 2011.
              Web. 30 Nov. 2013.

Advertisement (print, broadcast, online)

PRINT   Hospital for Special Surgery. Advertisement. *New York Times* 13 Apr. 2009:
              A7. Print.

BROADCAST   Norweigian Cruise Line. Advertisement. *WNET.org*. PBS, 29 Apr. 2012.
              Television.

ONLINE   Samsung Galaxy Note. Advertisement. *Slate*. Slate Group, 26 Nov. 2013. Web.
              26 Nov. 2013.

Work of art (museum, print, Web site)   Include the year the work was created, the medium (*Oil on canvas*), and the museum or collection and its location. If the work was accessed online, include the Web site name and your date of access and change the medium to *Web*.

MUSEUM   Palmer Payne, Elsie. *Sheep Dipping Time*. c. 1930s. Oil on canvas.
          Nevada Museum of Art, Reno.

PRINT   Chihuly, Dale. *Carmine and White Flower Set*. 1987. Glass. Tacoma Art Museum,
        Tacoma. New York: Abrams, 2011. 109. Print.

WEB SITE   Sekaer, Peter. *A Sign Business Shop*, New York. 1935. International Center
           of Photography, New York. *International Center of Photography*.
           Web. 27 Nov. 2013.

Performance

The Agony and the Ecstasy of Steve Jobs. Writ. and perf. Mike Daisey. Dir. Jean-Michele
   Gregory. Public Theater, New York. 25 Nov. 2011. Performance.

Television or radio program   Include the network, local station, and broadcast date. Treat a show you streamed as you would a Web page, but include information about key contributors (host or performers, for example) as you would for a broadcast television or radio program. If you downloaded the program as a podcast, include the information as for a broadcast program, but change the medium to match the type of file you accessed (*MP3, JPEG file*).

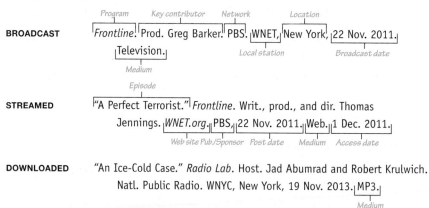

BROADCAST   *Frontline*. Prod. Greg Barker. PBS. WNET, New York, 22 Nov. 2011.
            Television.

STREAMED   "A Perfect Terrorist." *Frontline*. Writ., prod., and dir. Thomas
           Jennings. *WNET.org*. PBS, 22 Nov. 2011. Web. 1 Dec. 2011.

DOWNLOADED   "An Ice-Cold Case." *Radio Lab*. Host. Jad Abumrad and Robert Krulwich.
             Natl. Public Radio. WNYC, New York, 19 Nov. 2013. MP3.

Podcast (streamed, downloaded)   Treat a podcast you listened to or watched online as you would an online television or radio program (see "A Perfect Terrorist" entry above).

Treat a podcast you downloaded as you would a television or radio program you downloaded (see "An Ice-Cold Case" entry above).

Film (theater, DVD, streamed)

THEATER *Space Station*. Prod. and dir. Toni Myers. Narr. Tom Cruise. IMAX, 2002. Film.

DVD *Casablanca*. Dir. Michael Curtiz. Perf. Humphrey Bogart, Ingrid Bergman, and Paul Henreid. 1942. Warner Home Video, 2003. DVD.

STREAMED *The Social Network*. Dir. David Fincher. Writ. Aaron Sorkin. Perf. Jesse Eisenberg, Justin Timberlake, and Andrew Garfield. Columbia Pictures, 2010. iTunes. Web. 21 Mar. 2013.

Online video

Film School. "Sunny Day." *YouTube*. YouTube, 12 June 2010. Web. 8 Aug. 2013.

Music recording

Beethoven, Ludwig van. *Violin Concerto in D Major, Op. 61*. U.S.S.R. State Orchestra. Cond. Alexander Gauk. Perf. David Oistrakh. Allegro, 1980. CD.

Maroon 5. "Moves Like Jagger." *Hands All Over*. A&M/Octone Records, 2011. MP3.

Interview (print, broadcast, personal) If a personal interview takes place through e-mail, change "Personal interview" to "E-mail interview."

PRINT Ashrawi, Hanan. "Tanks vs. Olive Branches." Interview by Rose Marie Berger. *Sojourners* Feb. 2005: 22–26. Print.

BROADCAST Zimmer, Carl. "Manipulating Science Reporting." Interview by Brooke Gladstone. *On the Media*. Natl. Public Radio. WNYC, New York, 28 Sept. 2013. Web. 26 Nov. 2013.

PERSONAL Ellis, Trey. Personal interview. 3 Sept. 2008.

Other Electronic Sources

Online sources have proliferated in the last ten years. With that proliferation has come access to more information than ever before. But not all of that information is of equal value. Before including a source found on *Google* in your research project, be sure that it is appropriate for a college-level writing project, and evaluate its reliability carefully.

If you are using the online version of a source for which there is no model shown here, choose the model that best matches your source, change the medium as appropriate, add the date you last accessed the source, and add any other information that readers will need to find the source themselves.

For help evaluating online sources, see Chapter 17.

Web page or other document on a Web site

Author/editor, last name first   *Document title (in quotation marks)*

McGann, Jerome J., ed. "Introduction to the Final Installment of the Rossetti Archive."

Title of site (italicized)

The Complete Writings and Pictures of Dante Gabriel Rossetti: A Hypermedia Archive.

Pub./Sponsor

Institute for Advanced Technology in the Humanities, U of Virginia,

Publication date/last update   Access date

2008. Web. 16 Oct. 2012.

Figure 19.2 (p. 455) shows where to find the source information you will need to create a works-cited entry for the Web page cited here.

Entire Web site   If the author's name is not given, begin the citation with the title. For an untitled personal site, put a description such as *Home page* where the Web site's title would normally appear (but with no quotation marks or italics). If no site sponsor or publisher is named, insert *N.p.* (for *No publisher*).

> Chesson, Frederick W. Home page. N.p., 1 Apr. 2003. Web. 26 Apr. 2008.

> *The Complete Writings and Pictures of Dante Gabriel Rossetti: A Hypermedia Archive*. Ed.
> Jerome J. McGann. Institute for Advanced Technology in the Humanities, U of Virginia,
> 2008. Web. 16 Oct. 2012.

> Gardner, James Alan. *A Seminar on Writing Prose*. N.p., 2001. Web. 1 Dec. 2012.

Online scholarly project   Treat an online scholarly project as you would a Web site, but include the name of the editor, if given.

> *The Darwin Correspondence Project*. Ed. Janet Browne. American Council of Learned Societies
> and U Cambridge, 2013. Web. 19 Nov. 2013.

Book or a short work in an online scholarly project   Treat a book or a short work in an online scholarly project as you would a Web page or another document on a Web site, but set the title in italics if the work is a book and in quotation marks if it is an article, essay, poem, or other short work, and include the print publication information (if any) following the title.

Original publication information

> Corelli, Marie. *The Treasure of Heaven*. London: Constable, 1906. *Victorian Women Writer's
> Project*. Ed. Percy Willett. Indiana U, 10 July 1999. Web. 10 Sept. 2008.

Blog (entire blog, blog post)   If the author of the blog post uses a pseudonym, begin with the pseudonym and put the blogger's real name in brackets. Cite an entire blog as you would an entire Web site (see above).

❷ Publication Date

❹ Title of Site

❶ Author (s)

❸ Document Title

FIGURE 19.2   Documentation Map for a Web Page

Look for the author or editor and title of the Web page on the Web page itself. The title of the Web site may appear on the Web page, on the site's home page, or both. The sponsor may be listed at the bottom of the Web page, on the home page, or somewhere else. (Look for a page entitled "About Us," "Who We Are," or "Contact Us.") If no publication or copyright date or "last update" appears on the Web page, the home page, or elsewhere on the site, insert *n.d.* in its place.

Blog title   *Pub./Sponsor*

Talking Points Memo. Ed. Josh Marshall. TPM Media, 26 Nov. 2013. Web. 26 Nov. 2013.

Pseudonym   *Real name*

Negative Camber [Todd McCandless]. *Formula1blog.* F1b., 2013. Web. 1 Dec. 2013.

Post author   *Post title*

Marshall, Josh. "Beneath the Headlines on Healthcare.gov." *Talking Points Memo.* TPM Media,
17 Nov. 2013. Web. 26 Nov. 2013.

Wiki article   Since wikis are written and edited collectively, start your entry with the title of the article you are citing. But check with your instructor before using information from a wiki in your research project; because content is written and edited collectively, it is difficult to assess its reliability and impossible to determine the expertise of the contributors.

"John Lydon." *Wikipedia.* Wikipedia Foundation, 22 Nov. 2013. Web. 25 Nov. 2013.

E-mail message

Sender   *Subject line*   *Recipient*   *Date sent*

Olson, Kate. "Update on State Legislative Grants." Message to the author. 5 Nov. 2008.
E-mail.

Medium

Student Research Project in MLA Style

On the following pages is a student research paper speculating about the causes of a trend—the increase in home schooling. The author, Cristina Dinh, cites statistics, quotes authorities, and paraphrases and summarizes background information and support for her argument. She uses the MLA documentation style.

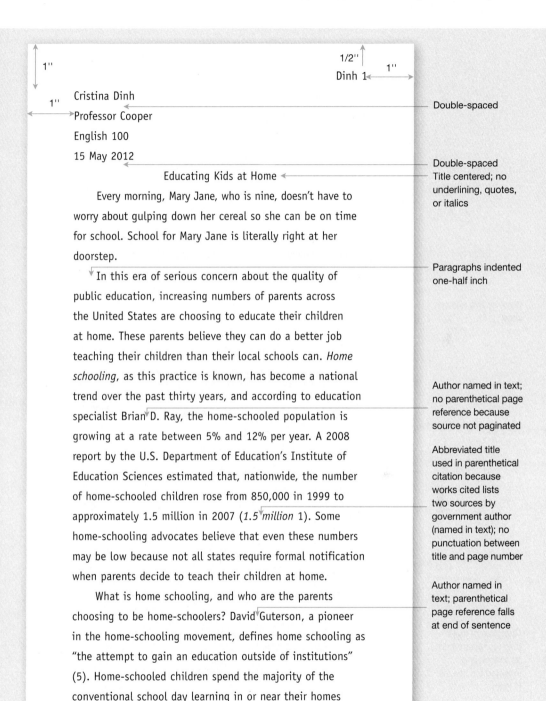

1"

1/2"

Dinh 1

1"

1"

Cristina Dinh

Professor Cooper

English 100

15 May 2012

Educating Kids at Home

    Every morning, Mary Jane, who is nine, doesn't have to worry about gulping down her cereal so she can be on time for school. School for Mary Jane is literally right at her doorstep.

    In this era of serious concern about the quality of public education, increasing numbers of parents across the United States are choosing to educate their children at home. These parents believe they can do a better job teaching their children than their local schools can. *Home schooling*, as this practice is known, has become a national trend over the past thirty years, and according to education specialist Brian D. Ray, the home-schooled population is growing at a rate between 5% and 12% per year. A 2008 report by the U.S. Department of Education's Institute of Education Sciences estimated that, nationwide, the number of home-schooled children rose from 850,000 in 1999 to approximately 1.5 million in 2007 (*1.5 million* 1). Some home-schooling advocates believe that even these numbers may be low because not all states require formal notification when parents decide to teach their children at home.

    What is home schooling, and who are the parents choosing to be home-schoolers? David Guterson, a pioneer in the home-schooling movement, defines home schooling as "the attempt to gain an education outside of institutions" (5). Home-schooled children spend the majority of the conventional school day learning in or near their homes

1"

Double-spaced

Double-spaced
Title centered; no underlining, quotes, or italics

Paragraphs indented one-half inch

Author named in text; no parenthetical page reference because source not paginated

Abbreviated title used in parenthetical citation because works cited lists two sources by government author (named in text); no punctuation between title and page number

Author named in text; parenthetical page reference falls at end of sentence

Dinh 2

rather than in traditional schools; parents or guardians are the prime educators. Former teacher and home-schooler Rebecca Rupp notes that home-schooling parents vary considerably in what they teach and how they teach, ranging from those who follow a highly traditional curriculum within a structure that parallels the typical classroom to those who essentially allow their children to pursue whatever interests them at their own pace (3). Home-schoolers commonly combine formal instruction with life skills instruction, learning fractions, for example, in terms of monetary units or cooking measurements (Saba and Gattis 89). According to the U.S. Department of Education's 2008 report, while home-schoolers are also a diverse group politically and philosophically—libertarians, conservatives, Christian fundamentalists—most say they home school for one of three reasons: they are concerned about the quality of academic instruction, the general school environment, or the lack of religious or moral instruction (*1.5 million* 2).

> The first group generally believes that children need individual attention and the opportunity to learn at their own pace to learn well. This group says that one teacher in a classroom of twenty to thirty children (the size of typical public-school classes) cannot give this kind of attention. These parents believe they can give their children greater enrichment and more specialized instruction than public schools can provide. At home, parents can work one-on-one with each child and be flexible about time, allowing their children to pursue their interests at earlier ages. Many of these parents, like home-schooler Peter Bergson, believe that home schooling provides more of an opportunity to continue the natural learning process that's in evidence in all children. [In school,] you

Work by two authors cited

Quotation of more than four lines typed as a block and indented ten spaces (1 inch)

Brackets indicate alteration of quotation

Dinh 3

change the learning process from self-directed to
other-directed, from the child asking questions to
the teacher asking questions. You shut down areas
of potential interest. (qtd. in Kohn 22)

Parenthetical citation
of secondary source
falls after period
when quotation
indented as a block

This trend can be traced back to the 1960s, when many
people began criticizing traditional schools. Various types of
"alternative schools" were created, and some parents began
teaching their children at home (Friedlander 150). Parents
like this mention several reasons for their disappointment
with public schools and for their decision to home school.
A lack of funding, for example, leaves children without new
textbooks. In a 2002 survey, 31% of teachers said that their
students are using textbooks that are more than ten years
old, and 29% said that they do not have enough textbooks
for all of their students (National Education Association).

Corporate author's
name cited

Many schools also cannot afford to buy laboratory equipment
and other teaching materials. At my own high school, the
chemistry teacher told me that most of the lab equipment
we used came from a research firm he worked for. In a 2006
Gallup poll, lack of proper financial support ranked first on
the list of the problems in public schools (Rose and Gallup).

Parents also cite overcrowding as a reason for taking
their kids out of school. The more students in a classroom,
the less learning that goes on, as Cafi Cohen discovered
before choosing to home school; after spending several
days observing what went on in her child's classroom,
she found that administrative duties, including disciplining,
took up to 80% of a teacher's time, with only 20% of the
day devoted to learning (6). Moreover, faced with a large
group of children, a teacher ends up gearing lessons to the
students in the middle level, so children at both ends miss

Dinh 4

out. Gifted children and those with learning disabilities particularly suffer in this situation. At home, parents of these children say they can tailor the material and the pace for each child. Studies show that home-schooling methods seem to work well in preparing children academically. Lawrence Rudner, director of the ERIC Clearinghouse on Assessment and Evaluation at the University of Maryland and a researcher on home schooling, found that testing of home-schooled students showed them to be between one and three years ahead of public school students their age (xi). Home-schooled children have also made particularly strong showings in academic competitions; since the late 1990s, 10% of National Spelling Bee participants have been home schooled, as have two National Spelling Bee and two National Geographic Bee winners (Lyman). More and more selective colleges are admitting, and even recruiting, home-schooled applicants (Basham, Merrifield, and Hepburn 15).

Parents in the second group—those concerned with the general school environment—claim that their children are more well-rounded than those in school. Because they don't have to sit in classrooms all day, home-schooled kids can pursue their own projects, often combining crafts or technical skills with academic subjects. Home-schoolers participate in outside activities, such as 4-H competitions, field trips with peers in home-school support groups, science fairs, musical and dramatic productions, church activities, and Boy Scouts or Girl Scouts (Saba and Gattis 59–62). In fact, they may even be able to participate to some extent in actual school activities. A 1999 survey conducted by the U.S. Department of Education's Institute of Education Sciences found that 28% of public schools allowed home-schooled students to participate in extracurricular activities alongside enrolled students, and

20% allowed home-schooled students to attend some classes
(*Homeschooling* 12).

Many home-schooling parents believe that these
activities provide the social opportunities kids need without
exposing their children to the peer pressure they would have
to deal with as regular school students. For example, many
kids think that drinking and using drugs are cool. When I
was in high school, my friends would tell me a few drinks
wouldn't hurt or affect driving. If I had listened to them,
I wouldn't be alive today. Four of my friends were killed
under the influence of alcohol. Between 1992 and 2008, the
number of high school seniors surveyed who had used any
illicit drug in the last year climbed from 27.1% to 36.6%
(Johnston et al. 59). ⟵ ————————————————— Work by four or more
                                                       authors cited

Another reason many parents decide to home school their
kids is that they are concerned for their children's safety. Samuel
L. Blumenfeld notes that "physical risk" is an important reason
many parents remove their children from public schools as "[m]
ore and more children are assaulted, robbed, and murdered in
school" and a "culture of violence, abetted by rap music, drug
trafficking, . . . and racial tension, has engulfed teenagers"
(4). Beginning in the mid-1990s, a string of school
shootings—including the 1999 massacres in Littleton,
Colorado, and Conyers, Georgia, and the 2001 massacre in
Santee, California—has led to increasing fears that young
people are simply not safe at school.

While all of the reasons mentioned so far are important,
perhaps the single most significant cause of the growing home-
schooling trend is Christian fundamentalist dissatisfaction with
"godless" public schools. Sociologist Mitchell L. Stevens, author
of one of the first comprehensive studies of home schooling,
cites a mailing sent out by Basic Christian Education, a

Dinh 6

company that markets home-schooling materials, titled "What Really Happens in Public Schools." This publication sums up the fears of fundamentalist home-schoolers about public schools: that they encourage high levels of teenage sexual activity and pregnancies "out of wedlock"; expose children to "violence, crime, lack of discipline, and, of course, drugs of every kind"; present positive portrayals of communism and socialism and negative portrayals of capitalism; and undermine children's Christian beliefs by promoting "New Age philosophies, Yoga, Transcendental Meditation, witchcraft demonstrations, and Eastern religions" (51).

As early as 1988, Luanne Shackelford and Susan White, two Christian home-schooling mothers, were claiming that because schools expose children to "[p]eer pressure, perverts, secular textbooks, values clarification, TV, pornography, rock music, bad movies . . . [h]ome schooling seems to be the best plan to achieve our goal [to raise good Christians]" (160). As another mother more recently put it:

> I don't like the way schools are going. . . . What's wrong with Christianity all of a sudden? You know? This country was founded on Christian, on religious principles. [People] came over here for religious freedom, and now all of a sudden all religious references seem to be stricken out of the public school, and I don't like that at all. (qtd. in Stevens 67)

Although many nonfundamentalist home-schoolers make some of these same criticisms, those who cite the lack of "Christian values" in public schools have particular concerns of their own. For example, home-schooling leader Raymond Moore talks of parents who are "'sick and tired of the teaching of evolution in the schools as a cut-and-dried fact,' along

Brackets used to indicate changes in capitalization and addition to quotation for clarification

Ellipsis marks used to indicate words left out of quotations

Quotation cited in a secondary source

Single quotation marks indicate a quotation within a quotation

Dinh 7

with other evidence of so-called secular humanism" (Kohn 21), such as textbooks that contain material contradicting Christian beliefs. Moreover, parents worry that schools undermine their children's moral values. In particular, some Christian fundamentalist parents object to sex education in schools, saying that it encourages children to become sexually active early, challenging values taught at home. They see the family as the core and believe that the best place to instill family values is within the family. These Christian home-schooling parents want to provide their children not only with academic knowledge but also with a moral grounding consistent with their religious beliefs.

Still other home-schooling parents object to a perceived government-mandated value system that they believe attempts to override the values, not necessarily religious in nature, of individual families. For these parents, home schooling is a way of resisting what they see as unwarranted intrusion by the federal government into personal concerns (*Alliance*).

Armed with their convictions, parents such as those who belong to the Christian Home School Legal Defense Association have fought in court and lobbied for legislation that allows them the option of home schooling. In the 1970s, most states had compulsory attendance laws that made it difficult, if not illegal, to keep school-age children home from school. Today, home schooling is permitted in every state, with strict regulation required by only a few (Home School). As a result, Mary Jane is one of hundreds of thousands of American children who can start their school day without leaving the house.

Citation placed close to quotation, before comma but after quotation marks

Internet source cited by shortened form of title; author's name and page numbers unavailable

Shortened form of corporate author's name cited

Works-cited entries begin on a new page; entries are in alphabetical order.

Title centered

Double-spaced

Entries begin flush with left margin; subsequent lines indent half an inch.

Periods separate author, title, publication information, medium, and date of access.

1/2"

1"

Dinh 8

1"

Works Cited

Alliance for the Separation of School and State. Home page. Alliance for the Separation of School and State, 26 Feb. 2009. Web. 10 Apr. 2012.

Basham, Patrick, John Merrifield, and Claudia R. Hepburn. *Home Schooling: From the Extreme to the Mainstream.* 2nd ed. Vancouver: Fraser Institute, 2007. Studies in Education Policy. *Fraser Institute.* Web. 13 Apr. 2012.

Blumenfeld, Samuel L. *Homeschooling: A Parent's Guide to Teaching Children.* Bridgewater: Replica, 1999. Print.

Cohen, Cafi. *And What about College? How Home-Schooling Leads to Admissions to the Best Colleges and Universities.* Cambridge: Holt, 1997. Print.

Friedlander, Tom. "A Decade of Home Schooling." *The Home School Reader.* Ed. Mark Hegener and Helen Hegener. Tonasket: Home Education, 1988. 147–56. Print.

Guterson, David. *Family Matters: Why Homeschooling Makes Sense.* San Diego: Harcourt, 1992. Print.

Home School Legal Defense Association. "State Action Map." HSLDA, 2009. Web. 5 Apr. 2012.

Johnston, Lloyd D., et al. *Monitoring the Future: National Results on Adolescent Drug Use, Overview of Key Findings, 2008.* Bethesda: National Institute on Drug Abuse, 2009. Web. 20 Apr. 2012.

Kohn, Alfie. "Home Schooling." *Atlantic Monthly* Apr. 1988: 20–25. Print.

Lyman, Isabel. "Generation Two." *American Enterprise* Oct./ Nov. 2002: 48–49. *InfoTrac OneFile.* Web. 10 May 2012.

National Education Association. *2002 Instructional Materials Survey.* Sept. 2002. Association of American Publishers, 2002. Web. 21 Apr. 2012.

Dinh 9

Ray, Brian D. "Research Facts on Home Schooling." *National
    Home Education Research Institute*. NHERI, 2008. Web.
    10 Apr. 2012.

Rose, Lowell C., and Alec M. Gallup. "The 38th Annual PDK/
    Gallup Poll of the Public's Attitudes toward the Public
    Schools." *Phi Delta Kappan* 88.1 (2006): n. pag. *Phi
    Delta Kappa International*. Web. 1 May 2009.

Rudner, Lawrence. Foreword. *The McGraw-Hill Home-Schooling
    Companion*. By Laura Saba and Julie Gattis. New York:
    McGraw, 2002. Print.

Rupp, Rebecca. *The Complete Home Learning Source Book*.
    New York: Three Rivers, 1998. Print.

Saba, Laura, and Julie Gattis. *The McGraw-Hill Home-
    Schooling Companion*. New York: McGraw, 2002. Print.

Shackelford, Luanne, and Susan White. *A Survivor's Guide to
    Home Schooling*. Westchester: Crossway, 1988. Print.

Stevens, Mitchell L. *Kingdom of Children: Culture and
    Controversy in the Homeschooling Movement*. Princeton:
    Princeton UP, 2001. Print.

United States. Dept. of Education. Institute of Education
    Sciences. *Homeschooling in the United States: 1999*.
    Washington: GPO, 2001. *National Center for Education
    Statistics*. Web. 23 Apr. 2009.

---. *1.5 Million Homeschooled Students in the United States
    in 2007*. Washington: GPO, 2008. *National Center for
    Education Statistics*. Web. 23 Apr. 2009.

Source with no pagination marked *n. pag.*

Untitled section labeled

For multiple sources by the same author, replace author's name with three hyphens followed by a period. (The name of this government source has three separate components.)

20

Citing and Documenting Sources in APA Style

When using the APA system of documentation, include both an in-text citation and a list of references at the end of the research project. **In-text citations** tell your readers where the ideas or words you have borrowed come from, and the entries in the **list of references** allow readers to locate your sources so that they can read more about your topic.

The most common types of in-text citations follow. For other, less common citation types, consult the *Publication Manual of the American Psychological Association,* Sixth Edition. Most libraries will own a copy.

 macmillanhighered.com/conciseguide
Tutorials > Documentation and Working with Sources > How to Cite a Database in APA Style
> How to Cite a Web Site in APA Style

Citing Sources in the Text

Directory to In-Text-Citation Models

One author   467
More than one author   467
Unknown author   467
Two or more works by the same author in the same year   467
Two or more authors with the same last name   468
Corporation, organization, or government agency as author   468
Indirect citation (quotation from a secondary source)   468
Two or more works cited in the same parentheses   468

When citing ideas, information, or words borrowed from a source, include the author's last name and the date of publication in the text of your research project. In most cases, you will want to use a *signal phrase* to introduce the works you are citing, since doing so gives you the opportunity to put the work and its author in context. A signal phrase includes the author's last name, the date of publication, and a verb that describes the author's attitude or stance:

Smith (2011) complains that . . .

Jones (2012) defends her position by . . .

Use a parenthetical citation—*(Jones, 2012)*—when you have already introduced the author or the work or when citing the source of an uncontroversial fact. When quoting from a source, also include the page number: *Smith (2011) complains that he "never gets a break" (p. 123).* When you are paraphrasing or summarizing, you may omit the page reference, although including it is not wrong.

One author

SIGNAL PHRASE Upton Sinclair (2005), a crusading journalist, wrote that workers sometimes "fell into the vats; and when they were fished out, there was never enough of them left to be worth exhibiting" (p. 134).

PARENTHETICAL CITATION *The Jungle*, a naturalistic novel inspired by the French writer Zola, described in lurid detail the working conditions of the time, including what became of unlucky workers who fell into the vats while making sausage (Sinclair, 2005).

author's last name + date

REFERENCE-LIST ENTRY Sinclair, U. (2005). *The jungle*. New York, NY: Oxford University Press. (Original work published 1906)

More than one author   In a signal phrase, use the word *and* between the authors' names; in a parenthetical citation, use an ampersand (&). When citing a work by three to five authors, list all the authors in your first reference; in subsequent references, just list the first and use *et al.* (Latin for *and others*).

SIGNAL PHRASE As Jamison and Tyree (2001) have found, racial bias does not diminish merely through exposure to individuals of other races.

PARENTHETICAL CITATION Racial bias does not diminish through exposure (Jamison & Tyree, 2001).

FIRST CITATION Rosenzweig, Breedlove, and Watson (2005) wrote that biological psychology is an interdisciplinary field that includes scientists from "quite different backgrounds" (p. 3).

LATER CITATIONS Biological psychology is "the field that relates behavior to bodily processes, especially the workings of the brain" (Rosenzweig et al., 2005, p. 3).

For works with six or more authors, cite only the first and use *et al.*

Unknown author   To cite a work when the author is unknown, the APA suggests using a shortened version of the title.

An international pollution treaty still to be ratified would prohibit all plastic garbage from being dumped at sea ("Plastic Is Found," 1972).

The full title of the article is "Plastic Is Found in the Sargasso Sea; Pieces of Apparent Refuse Cover Wide Atlantic Region."

Two or more works by the same author in the same year   When your list of references includes two works by the same author, the year of publication is usually enough to distinguish them. Occasionally, though, you may have two works by the same author in the same year. If this happens, alphabetize the works by title in your list of references, and add a lowercase letter after the date (2005a, 2005b).

Middle-class unemployed workers are better off than their lower-class counterparts, because "the white collar unemployed are likely to have some assets to invest in their job search" (Ehrenreich, 2005b, p. 16).

Two or more authors with the same last name   Include the author's initials.

F. Johnson (2010) conducted an intriguing study on teen smoking.

Corporation, organization, or government agency as author   Spell out the name of the organization the first time you use it, but abbreviate it in subsequent citations.

(National Institutes of Health, 2012)

(NIH, 2012)

Indirect citation (quotation from a secondary source)   To quote material taken not from the original source but from a secondary source that quotes the original, give the secondary source in the reference list, and in your essay acknowledge the original source and cite the secondary source.

E. M. Forster said "the collapse of all civilization, so realistic for us, sounded in Matthew Arnold's ears like a distant and harmonious cataract" (as cited in Trilling, 1955, p. 11).

Two or more works cited in the same parentheses   List sources in alphabetical order separated by semicolons.

(Johnson, 2010; NIH, 2012)

Creating a List of References

Directory to Reference-List Models

Author Listings
One author   469
More than one author   469
Unknown author   470
Corporation, organization, or government agency as author   470
Two or more works by the same author   470

Books (Print, Electronic)
Basic format for a book   470
Author and editor   471
Edited collection   471
Work in an anthology or edited collection   471
Translation   471

Dictionary entry or article in another reference book   471
Introduction, preface, foreword, or afterword   471
Later edition of a book   471
Government document   471
Unpublished doctoral dissertation   471

Articles (Print, Electronic)
From a scholarly journal   472
From a newspaper   472
From a magazine   472
Editorial or letter to the editor   472
Review   473

Multimedia Sources (Print, Electronic)

Television program   473
Film, video, or DVD   473
Sound recording   473
Interview   473

Other Electronic Sources

Web site   473
Web page or document on a Web site   474
Blog post   474
Wiki entry   474
E-mail message   474

Author Listings

When the list of references includes several works by the same author, the APA provides the following rules for arranging these entries in the list:

- Same-name single-author entries precede multiple-author entries:

Zettelmeyer, F. (2000).

Zettelmeyer, F., Morton, F. S., & Silva-Risso, J. (2006).

- Entries with the same first author and a different second author are alphabetized under the first author according to the second author's last name:

Dhar, R., & Nowlis, S. M. (2004).

Dhar, R., & Simonson, I. (2003).

- Entries by the same authors are arranged by year of publication, in chronological order:

Golder, P. N., & Tellis, G. J. (2003).

Golder, P. N., & Tellis, G. J. (2004).

- Entries by the same authors with the same publication year should be arranged alphabetically by title (according to the first word after *A, An,* or *The*), and lower-case letters (*a, b, c,* and so on) should be appended to the year in parentheses:

Aaron, P. (1990a). Basic . . .

Aaron, P. (1990b). Elements . . .

One author

Ehrenreich, B. (2001). *Nickel and dimed: On (not) getting by in America*. New York, NY: Metropolitan.

More than one author

Saba, L., & Gattis, J. (2002). *The McGraw-Hill homeschooling companion*. New York, NY: McGraw-Hill.

Hunt, L., Po-Chia Hsia, R., Martin, T. R., Rosenwein, B. H., Rosenwein, H., & Smith, B. G. (2001). *The making of the West: Peoples and cultures*. Boston, MA: Bedford.

If there are more than seven authors, list only the first six, insert an ellipsis (. . .), and add the last author's name.

Unknown author   Begin the entry with the title.

> Communities blowing whistle on street basketball. (2003). *USA Today*, p. 20A.

If an author is designated as "Anonymous," include the word *Anonymous* in place of the author, and alphabetize it as "Anonymous" in the reference list.

> Anonymous. (2006). *Primary colors*. New York, NY: Random House.

Corporation, organization, or government agency as author

> American Medical Association. (2004). *Family medical guide*. Hoboken, NJ: Wiley.

Two or more works by the same author

When you cite two or more works by the same author, arrange them in chronological (time) order.

> Pinker, S. (2005). So how does the mind work? *Mind and Language, 20*(1): 1–24. doi:10.1111
>   /j.0268-1064.2005.00274.x

> Pinker, S. (2011). *The better angels of our nature: Why violence has declined*. New York, NY:
>   Viking.

When you cite two works by the same author in the same year, alphabetize entries by title and then add a lowercase letter following each year.

> Pinker, S. (2005a). *Hotheads*. New York, NY: Pocket Penguins.

> Pinker, S. (2005b). So how does the mind work? *Mind and Language, 20*(1), 1–24. doi:
>   10.1111/j.0268-1064.2005.00274.x

Books (Print, Electronic)

When citing a book, capitalize only the first word of the title and subtitle and any proper nouns (*Dallas, Darwin*). Book titles are italicized.

Basic format for a book

          Author   *Year*   *Title: Subtitle*

PRINT   Pinker, S. (2011). *The better angels of our nature: Why violence has declined.*
           New York, NY: Viking.
           City, State (abbr)   *Publisher*

E-BOOK   Pinker, S. (2011). *The better angels of our nature: Why violence has declined.*
           New York, NY: Viking. [Nook Book Edition].
                      E-publication information

DATABASE   Darwin, C. (2001). *The origin of species.* Retrieved from http://bartleby.com
           (Original work published 1909–14)   *Database Information*

If an e-book has been assigned a **digital object identifier** (or DOI)—a combination of numbers and letters assigned by the publisher to identify the work—add that information at the end of the citation.

Author and editor

Arnold, M. (1994). *Culture and anarchy* (S. Lipman, Ed.). New Haven, CT: Yale University Press. (Original work published 1869)

Edited collection

Waldman, D., & Walker, J. (Eds.). (1999). *Feminism and documentary*. Minneapolis, MN: University of Minnesota Press.

Work in an anthology or edited collection

Fairbairn-Dunlop, P. (1993). Women and agriculture in western Samoa. In J. H. Momsen & V. Kinnaird (Eds.), *Different places, different voices* (pp. 211–226). London, England: Routledge.

Translation

Tolstoy, L. (2002). *War and peace* (C. Garnett, Trans.). New York, NY: Modern Library. (Original work published 1869)

Dictionary entry or article in another reference book

Rowland, R. P. (2001). Myasthenia gravis. In *Encyclopedia Americana* (Vol. 19, p. 683). Danbury, CT: Grolier.

Introduction, preface, foreword, or afterword

Graff, G., & Phelan, J. Preface (2004). In M. Twain, *Adventures of Huckleberry Finn* (pp. iii–vii). Boston, MA: Bedford.

Later edition of a book

Axelrod, R., & Cooper, C. (2013). *The St. Martin's guide to writing* (10th ed.). Boston, MA: Bedford.

Government document

U.S. Department of Health and Human Services. (2009). *Trends in underage drinking in the United States, 1991–2007*. Washington, DC: Government Printing Office.

Note: when the author and publisher are the same, use the word *Author* (not italicized) as the name of the publisher.

Unpublished doctoral dissertation

Bullock, B. (1986). *Basic needs fulfillment among less developed countries: Social progress over two decades of growth* (Unpublished doctoral dissertation). Vanderbilt University, Nashville, TN.

Articles (Print, Electronic)

For articles, capitalize only the first word of the title, proper nouns (*Barclay, Berlin*), and the first word following a colon (if any). Omit quotation marks around the titles of articles, but capitalize all the important words of journal, newspaper, and magazine titles, and set them in italics. If you are accessing an article through a database, follow the model for a comparable source.

From a scholarly journal

PRINT   Tran, D. (2002). Personal income by state, second quarter 2002. *Current Business, 82*(11), 55–73.

Include the digital object identifier (or DOI) when available. When a DOI has not been assigned, include the journal's URL with the words *Retrieved from* (not italicized).

ELECTRONIC   Tharp, R. G. (1989). Psychocultural variables and constants: Effects on teaching and learning in schools. *American Psychologist, 44*(2), 349–359. doi:10.1037/0003-066X.44.2.349

From a newspaper

PRINT   Peterson, A. (2003, May 20). Finding a cure for old age. *The Wall Street Journal*, pp. D1, D5.

ELECTRONIC   Barboza, D., & LaFraniere, S. (2012, May 17). 'Princelings' in China use family ties to gain riches. *The New York Times*. Retrieved from www.nytimes.com

From a magazine   If a magazine is published weekly or biweekly (every other week), include the full date following the author's name. If it is published monthly or bimonthly, include just the year and month (or months).

PRINT   Gross, M. J. (2003, April 29). Family life during war time. *The Advocate*, 42–48.

Shelby, A. (2005, September/October). Good going: Alaska's glacier crossroads. *Sierra, 90*, 23.

ELECTRONIC   Marche, S. (2012, May). Is Facebook making us lonely? *The Atlantic*. Retrieved from http://theatlantic.com

Editorial or letter to the editor

Kosinski, T. (2012, May 15). Who cares what she thinks? [Letter to the editor]. *The Chicago Sun-Times*. Retrieved from www.suntimes.com/opinions/letters/12522890-474 /who-cares-what-she-thinks.html

Review

"Review of" + item type + title of item reviewed

Cassidy, J. (2002, July 12). Master of disaster [Review of the book *Globalization and its discontents*]. *The New Yorker,* 82–86.

If the review is untitled, use the bracketed information as the title, retaining the brackets.

Multimedia Sources (Print or Electronic)

Television program

Label

Charlsen, C. (Writer and producer). (2003, July 14). Murder of the century [Television series episode]. In M. Samels (Executive producer), *American Experience*. Boston, MA: WGBH.

Film, video, or DVD

Label

Nolan, C. (Writer and director). (2010). *Inception* [Motion picture]. Los Angeles, CA: Warner Bros.

Sound recording

PODCAST   Dubner, S. (2012, May 17). Retirement kills [Audio podcast]. *Freakonomics Radio*. Retrieved from www.freakonomics.com

Label

RECORDING   Maroon 5. (2010). Moves like Jagger. On *Hands all over* [CD]. New York, NY: A&M/Octone Records.

Interview   Do not list personal interviews in your reference list. Instead, cite the interviewee in your text (last name and initials), and in parentheses give the notation *personal communication* (in regular type, not italicized) followed by a comma and the date of the interview. For published interviews, use the appropriate format for an article.

Other Electronic Sources

A rule of thumb for citing electronic sources not covered in one of the preceding sections is to include enough information to allow readers to access and retrieve the source. For most online sources, provide as much of the following as you can:

- Name of author
- Date of publication or most recent update (in parentheses; if unavailable, use the abbreviation *n.d.*)
- Title of document (such as a Web page)
- Title of Web site
- Any special retrieval information, such as a URL; include the date you last accessed the source only when the content is likely to change or be updated (as on a wiki, for example)

Web site   The APA does not require an entry in the list of references for entire Web sites. Instead, give the name of the site in your text with its Web address in parentheses.

Web page or document on a Web site

American Cancer Society. (2011, Oct. 10). *Child and teen tobacco use.* Retrieved from http://www.cancer.org/Cancer/CancerCauses/TobaccoCancer/ChildandTeenTobaccoUse/child-and-teen-tobacco-use-what-to-do

Heins, M. (2003, January 24). The strange case of Sarah Jones. *The Free Expression Policy Project.* Retrieved from http://www.fepproject.org/commentaries/sarahjones.html

Blog post

Label

Mestel, R. (2012, May 17). Fructose makes rats dumber. [Web log post]. Retrieved from http://www.latimes.com/health/boostershots/la-fructose-makes-rats-stupid-brain-20120517,0,2305241.story?track=rss

Wiki entry   Start with the article title and include the post date (or *n.d.,* if there is no date), since wikis may be updated frequently, as well as the retrieval date.

Sleep. (2011, November 26). Retrieved May 21, 2011, from Wiki of Science: http://wikiofscience.wikidot.com/science:sleep

E-mail message   Personal correspondence, including e-mail, should not be included in your reference list. Instead, cite the person's name in your text, and in parentheses give the notation *personal communication* (in regular type, not italicized) and the date.

A Sample Reference List

To see the complete text of Patrick O'Malley's research project in APA style, see Chapter 6, pp. 198–203.

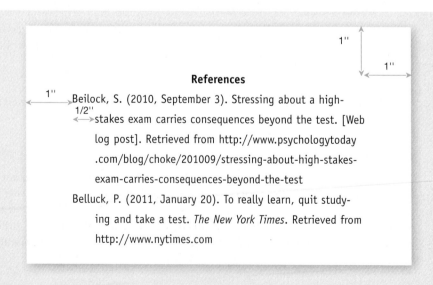

References

1″

Beilock, S. (2010, September 3). Stressing about a high-
1/2″
stakes exam carries consequences beyond the test. [Web

log post]. Retrieved from http://www.psychologytoday

.com/blog/choke/201009/stressing-about-high-stakes-

exam-carries-consequences-beyond-the-test

Belluck, P. (2011, January 20). To really learn, quit study-

ing and take a test. *The New York Times.* Retrieved from

http://www.nytimes.com

Dendato, K. M., & Diener, D. (1986). Effectiveness of cognitive/relaxation therapy and study skills training in reducing self-reported anxiety and improving the academic performance of test-anxious students. *The Journal of Counseling Psychology, 33,* 131–135.

Frederiksen, N. (1984). The real test bias: Influences of testing on teaching and learning. *American Psychologist, 39,* 193–202.

Karpicke, J. D., & Blunt, J. R. (2011, January 30). Retrieval practice produces more learning than elaborative studying with concept mapping. *Science Online.* doi: 10.1126/science.1199327

Light, R. J. (1990). *Explorations with students and faculty about teaching, learning, and student life.* Cambridge, MA: Harvard University Graduate School of Education and Kennedy School of Government.

Rothblum, E. D., Solomon, L., & Murakami, J. (1986). Affective, cognitive, and behavioral differences between high and low procrastinators. *Journal of Counseling Psychology, 33,* 387–394.

ScienceWatch.com (2008, February). Henry L. Roediger and Jeff Karpicke talk with ScienceWatch.com and answer a few questions about this month's fast breaking paper in the field of psychiatry/psychology [Interview]. Retrieved from http://sciencewatch.com/dr/fbp/2008/08febfbp/08febfbpRoedigerETAL

Acknowledgments

Text Credits

David Bornstein. "Fighting Bullying with Babies" from *The New York Times,* Nov. 8, 2010. Copyright © 2010 by The New York Times. All rights reserved. Used by permission and protected by the Copyright Laws of the United States. The printing, copying, redistribution, or retransmission of this Content without express written permission is prohibited.

Susan Cain. "Shyness: Evolutionary Tactic?" from *The New York Times,* June 26, 2011. Copyright © 2011 by The New York Times Company. All rights reserved. Used by permission and protected by the Copyright Laws of the United States. The printing, copying, redistribution, or retransmission of this Content without express written permission is prohibited.

Amanda Coyne. "The Long Good-Bye: Mother's Day in Federal Prison" is reproduced from the May issue of *Harper's* magazine by special permission. Copyright © 1997 by Harper's Magazine. All rights reserved.

Jenee Desmond-Harris. "Tupac and My Non-Thug Life" from *The Root,* Sept. 13, 2011. Copyright © 2011 by The Slate Group. All Rights Reserved. Used by permission and protected by the Copyright Laws of the United States. The printing, copying, redistribution, or retransmission of this Content without express written permission is prohibited.

Annie Dillard. From AN AMERICAN CHILDHOOD, copyright © 1987 by Annie Dillard. Reprinted by permission of HarperCollins Publishers and Russell & Volkening as agents for the author.

Amitai Etzioni. "Working at McDonald's." Copyright © 1986 by Amitai Etzioni. Reproduced with the permission of the author.

Malcolm Gladwell. "The Order of Things: What College Rankings Really Tell Us," first published in *The New Yorker,* Feb. 14, 2011. Reprinted by permission of the author.

Martin Luther King, Jr. From "Letter from Birmingham Jail," copyright © 1963 by Dr. Martin Luther King, Jr., copyright renewed 1991 by Coretta Scott King. Reprinted by arrangement with The Heirs to the Estate of Martin Luther King, Jr., c/o Writers House as agent for the proprietor, New York, NY.

Karen Kornbluh. "Win-Win Flexibility." Originally published in the *Atlantic* (January/February 2003). Copyright © 2003 by Karen Kornbluh. Reprinted with the permission of the author.

Christine Rosen. "The Myth of Multitasking" from *The New Atlantis,* Number 20, Spring 2008. Copyright © 2008 by The New Atlantis. Reprinted by permission of the publisher.

Daniel Solove. "Why Privacy Matters Even If You Have 'Nothing to Hide'" excerpt as published in *The Chronicle of Higher Education,* May 15, 2011, adapted from NOTHING TO HIDE: THE FALSE TRADEOFF BETWEEN PRIVACY AND SECURITY. Copyright © 2011 by Daniel J. Solove. Reprinted by permission of the publisher, Yale University Press.

Gabriel Thompson. "The Last Word: A Gringo In the Lettuce Fields," published in *The Week,* 2010, adapted from WORKING IN THE SHADOWS: A YEAR OF DOING THE JOBS (MOST) AMERICANS WON'T DO. Copyright © 2010 by Gabriel Thompson. Reprinted by permission of Nation Books, a member of the Perseus Books Group.

Anastasia Toufexis. "Love: The Right Chemistry" from TIME, June 24, 2001, first published February 15, 1993. Reported by Hannah Bloch and Sally B. Donnelly. Copyright © by Time Inc. Reprinted by permission. TIME is a registered trademark of Time Inc. All rights reserved.

Index

Entries followed by an [e] may be found in the LaunchPad Solo. For more information visit **macmillanhighered.com/conciseguide.**

ABC test, for logic of argument, 312–14
abstract ideas, connotations of, 367–68
Academic OneFile, 177, 227, 269, 408
Academic Search Complete, 177, 227, 269, 408, 409
Academic Search Premier, 408
accuracy, of facts, 313
action, in writing
　in drama, 289
　dramatic arc structure, 12, 33–34
　prepositional phrases, 20–21
　in remembered event essays, 12, 22, 34
　time transitions and, 35, 47
actor, in drama, 289, 290
ad hominem (personal) attack, 151, 379
adjective clauses, commas with, 141
adjective order, multilingual writers and, 95
adverbs, conjunctive, 186–87
advertisements, 365
　MLA style documentation, 447
afterword of book
　APA style documentation, 471
　MLA style documentation, 446
agentless sentences, revising, 233
Akana, William, "Scott Pilgrim vs. the World: A Hell of a Ride," 239–40, 242–48, 268, 366
although, 150, 196
Alt-Press Watch, 408
"American Childhood, An" (Dillard), 17–21, 22

analogy, 342
　appropriateness of, 313
　false, 151, 379
analyzing
　argument. *See* arguments and arguing, analyzing
　in cubing, 288
　of observation study, 413
　of visuals. *See* visuals, analyzing
anecdotes
　believability, test for, 313–14
　illustrating concepts with, 135
　in profiles, 65, 81
　relevant, to support argument, 372–74
　and scenarios, in framing problem, 193, 221
Angier, Natalie, "Intolerance of Boyish Behavior," 371–72
annotated bibliography, 402–3
annotations and annotating, 294, 333
　Annotations Chart, 336, 340
　examples
　　"A Case for Torture" (Bagaric and Clarke), 338–39
　　"Letter from Birmingham Jail" (King), 295–301
antecedents, pronouns and, 323–24
anthology, work in
　APA style documentation, 471
　MLA style documentation, 441
APA style, 403
　block quotations in, 435, 468
　in-text citations, 466–68
　　book by one author, 467

　corporate, organization, or government author, 468
　more than one author, 467
　secondary source, quotation from, 468
　several by same author/same year, 467–68
　two or more authors with same last name, 468
　two or more works in same parentheses, 468
　unknown author, 467
reference list (print, electronic), 468–75
　anthology or edited collection, 471
　articles, 471–73
　author listings, 469–70
　blogs, 474
　corporate, organization, or government author, 470
　dictionary entry, 471
　doctoral dissertation, unpublished, 471
　editorial, 472
　e-mail message, 474
　film or video recording, 473
　government documents, 471
　interview, 473
　introduction, preface, foreword, or afterword, 471
　later edition of book, 471
　letter to editor, 470
　magazine articles, 470
　more than one author, 469
　multimedia sources, 473
　newspaper articles, 470
　one author, 469
　reference book article, 471

APA style (*continued*)
review, 473
sample, 474–75
scholarly journal article, 470
sound recordings, 473
television programs, 473
translations, 471
two or more works by same author, 470
unknown author, 470
Web site, 473–74
wiki entry, 474
applying, in cubing, 288
appositives
defined, 133
to integrate sources, 133–34
phrases, in combining sentences, 278
appropriateness, test for, 313, 314
appropriate qualifications, 368
archives, in libraries, 407
Arctic Dreams **(Lopez)**, 320, 325
argument essays
evaluations. *See* evaluations
proposing solutions. *See* proposals for solutions
stating position. *See* position arguments
arguments and arguing, 366–82
analyzing, 332–44
annotations, 333, 336, 338–39, 340
applying criteria for, 332–33, 334–35
example, "A Case for Torture" (Bagaric and Clarke), 335–43
focus for analysis, 333–34
motivating factors in, 334–35, 336, 340
sentence strategies for, 334–35
concessions, 376–77, 382
cubing, 288
evaluating logic of, 312–14
logical fallacies, 378–79
readers' objections and concerns, responding to, 375–78
reasons and support, giving, 369–75
representative examples, 369–70

reputable authorities, citing, 371–72
textual evidence, relevant, 374–75
up-to-date, relevant statistics, 370–71
vivid, relevant anecdotes, 372–74
refutation, 377–78, 381, 382
sentence strategies for, 379–82
synthesizing, 332
sample synthesis, 344–51
thesis, asserting, 318, 366–68
articles, in periodicals, 407–8
APA style documentation, 472–73
MLA style documentation, 448–52
art works
library collections, 407
MLA documentation style, 452
as, in time transitions, 35
Asimov, Isaac, "The Case against Man," 325
assertion, of thesis, 318, 366–68
arguable, 366–67
clear and precise wording, 367–68
"Attachment: Someone to Watch over You" (Lyu), 104–10
audience. *See also* readers
document design and, 384–85
for evaluations, 239
for explanations of concepts, 101
for position arguments, 147
for proposals for solutions, 193
for remembered event essays, 11, 29, 39
visual analysis and, 355, 359
writer's purpose, in profile, 53
audio recordings, 407
of interviews, 81, 415
authority, 3–4
appropriateness of, 313, 314
citing reputable, 371–72
credibility of, 314
in evaluations, 260
overreliance on, 379
in position arguments, 161
in proposals for solutions, 194
statistics and, 314
authors

citing. *See* APA style; MLA style
expertise of, 371, 422
names of, for bibliography, 401
perspective of, 422
autobiography, 318
present perspective in, 13, 22
and remembered events. *See* remembered event essays
showing and telling in, 21–22
significance, creating, 13, 21–22, 27, 30, 39–40, 42
thoughts and feelings, remembered in, 13

Bagaric, Mirko, "A Case for Torture," 335–43, 348
Baldwin, James, "Stranger in the Village," 327
bar graph, as visual, 391
begging the question, 378
beliefs and values, challenges to, 294, 312
example, "Letter from Birmingham Jail" (King), 312
believability, 369
test for, 313–14
bias, of author, 422
bibliography, 104, 135, 241. *See also* Works Cited
access information in, 401
annotated, 402–3
working bibliography, 401–3, 429
binary thinking, 335
"Black Death, The" (Langer), 318–19
block quotations
APA style, 435, 468
MLA style, 434–35, 439–40
block style document design, 389
blogs (Web logs), 411
APA style documentation, 474
MLA style documentation, 454
Blue Highways, **(Least Heat Moon),** 328–29
bookmarking, Web site, 128, 177, 227
books
documentation style. *See* APA style; MLA style
library, finding, 405–7

Bornstein, David, "Fighting Bullying with Babies," 195, 204–10, 225
brackets, in quotations, for insertions or changes, 432
brainstorming, 221, 269
Brandt, Jean, "Calling Home," 13–17
Britannica Online, 399
brochure, MLA style documentation, 447
bulleted lists, 388
burden of proof, failing to accept, 378
but, 150, 196–97

Cable, Brian, "The Last Stop," 55–60
Cain, Susan, "Shyness: Evolutionary Tactic?," 117–24
calendar and clock time. *See also* time management
in profiles, 72–73, 78–79
in remembered event essays, 35, 54
"Calling Home" (Brandt), 13–17
call number, in library search, 406–7
capitalization, in outlines, 287
caption, for visuals, 243, 390
cartoons
MLA style documentation, 451
as visual, 392
"Case against Man, The" (Asimov), 325
"Case for Torture, A" (Bagaric and Clarke), 335–43
annotations, 336, 338–39, 340
student analysis (Melissa Mae), 339–43, 375
catalogs, online library, 404–7
archives and special collections, 407
search guidelines, 404–7
subject headings, 406
Catton, Bruce, "Grant and Lee: A Study in Contrasts," 321–22
causality, confusing chronology with, 378
cause and effect, 169–70
as explanatory strategy, 103, 132

in profiles, 55
in proposals for solutions, 195, 197
charts, 391–92, 394
MLA style documentation, 451
pie charts, 388–89, 391
Cherry (Karr), 322
"Children Need to Play, Not Compete" (Statsky), 148, 150, 152–57, 177–78, 366
topic outline, 286–87
chronology
calendar and clock time, 35, 54, 72–73
confusing causality with, 378
chunking
and outlining, 285–86
of text, design element, 389
citations. *See also* Works Cited
in evaluations, 260–61
informal *versus* formal, 372
in-text, 135, 178
in parentheses, 135
of visual sources, 390, 393
claims, 2
supported by sources, 429–30
clarity, in design, 384–85
Clarke, Julia, "A Case for Torture," 335–43, 348
classification
as explanatory strategy, 103, 132
of observation study, 413
climax, in dramatic arc, 12, 34
clip art, 394
clock time. *See* calendar and clock time
closed questions, in interviews, 414–15
clustering, 282–83
cohesive devices, 323–26
collocation, 325–26
pronouns, 323–24
sentence structure repetition, 325
synonyms, 325
word repetition, 324, 325
Coleman, Molly, "Missing the Fun" 🅴
collaborative activities
evaluations, 238, 272
explanations of concepts, 100, 130

in observation study, 413–14
position arguments, 146
profiles, 52, 78
proposals for solutions, 192, 219, 220
remembered event essays, 10, 34
college and school courses
document design for, 384
evaluations, 236, 265
explanations of concepts, 98, 127
position arguments, 144, 173
profiles, 50
proposals for solutions, 190, 220
remembered event essays, 8
collocation, networks of meaning and, 325–26
colon, introducing quotation with, 435
colors, in document design, 388–89
comic strip, MLA style documentation, 451
commas
adjective clauses, setting off, 141
appositives, setting off, 134
introducing quotation with, 435
with quotation marks, 94
used before coordinating conjunctions, 186
comma splice, correcting, 186–87
multilingual writers and, 187
common ground, 180
test for, 316
common knowledge, 428
community and writing
in evaluations, 237, 265
explanations of concepts, 99, 127
position arguments, 145, 173
profiles, 51
proposals for solutions, 191, 220
remembered event essays, 9
comparison, 288
in evaluations, 241–42, 277
in explanations of concepts, 103, 122–23, 132
metaphor, 38, 296, 298, 301, 309

comparison (*continued*)
in profiles, 53, 58, 81
in proposals for solutions, 1
95
simile, 38, 297, 309, 310
symbolism, 309
completeness, test for, 313,
314
composition, in visual analysis,
354, 358
compound sentences, 186
computer file, for working
bibliography, 401
computers. *See also* Internet
research
creating visuals on, 394
concepts, explaining. *See*
explanations of concepts
concession (accepts objections),
376–77
concession-refutation move,
150–51, 180, 181, 196, 382
counterargument, 334, 340
in evaluations, 242, 270–71
in position arguments,
150–51, 179, 180, 181
in proposals for solutions,
196, 197, 228
sentence strategies for, 382
conclusion
in profiles, 55
in proposals for solutions, 197
thus used to indicate, 186
conjunctions, coordinating,
186, 187
conjunctive adverbs
comma splices with, 186–87
multilingual writers and, 187
semicolons to join clauses
with, 187
connecting to issues
in evaluations, 252–53, 259
in explanations of concepts,
121
in position arguments, 160,
167–68
in profiles, 65, 71–72
in proposals for solutions,
207–8, 215
in remembered event essays,
20, 25–26
connectives. *See* transitions
(words or phrases)
consistency, testing for, 314

context, 308–9
in analysis of visuals, 352–53,
355, 359
in document design, 384–85
social and historical, 308, 355,
359
contextualizing
example, "Letter from
Birmingham Jail" (King),
308–9
as reading strategy, 294, 308
contradiction, in profiles, 55
contrast
in evaluations, 241–42, 261–62
example, "Letter from
Birmingham Jail" (King), 296
in explanations of concepts,
103, 122–23, 132
juxtaposition and, 67
reframing argument through,
168
conversation, 288–89. *See also*
dialogue
coordinating conjunctions,
commas before, 186, 187
copyright date, 422
copyright permissions, for
visuals, 390
corporate author
APA style, 468
MLA style, 440–41
counterargument, 334, 340. *See*
also concession; refutation
Coyne, Amanda, "The Long
Good-Bye: Mother's Day
in Federal Prison," 61–67
Crane, Sally, "Gazing into the
Darkness," 374
credibility of writer
assessing, as reading strategy,
294, 315–16
authority and, 314, 371
example, "Letter from
Birmingham Jail" (King),
316
sources to reinforce, 177–78,
194, 224, 240, 261, 409
Critical Reading Guide, A
evaluations, 272–74
explanations of concepts,
136–37
position arguments, 182–83
profiles, 88–90
proposals for solutions, 229–31

remembered event essays,
41–43
critical thinking
about evaluations, 279–80
about explanations of concepts, 142–43
about personal experience, 6
about position arguments,
188–89
about profiles, 96–97
about proposals for solutions,
234–35
about remembered event
essays, 48–49
cubing
as invention and inquiry
strategy, 288
in proposals for solutions, 221
cueing strategies, 317–31
cohesive devices, 323–26
collocation, 325–26
in explanations of concepts,
115
headings and subheadings,
329–31
in logical organization, 162,
170, 197
orienting statements, 317–19
paragraphing, 319–23
repetition, 324, 325
in reviews and evaluations,
242–43, 262
topic sentences, 320–23
transitions (words or phrases),
115, 321, 326–29
cultural context, 308–9

"Daily Grind, The" (Roy) e
dashes, appositives set off with,
134
databases, for research
in explaining concept, 128
keywords in, 227, 405, 406
library catalogs and, 404–7
general *versus* subject-
specific databases, 408
periodicals, articles in, 407–8
search results, 409
for reviews and evaluations,
269
definition
appositives used in, 134
as explanatory strategy, 102,
132

mixed constructions and, 141
  in reframing subject, 260
description
  in cubing, 288
  naming, 21, 37, 53
  of observation study, 413
  people and places, 12–13, 21,
    26, 30, 36–38, 42
  remembered event essays,
    12–13, 21, 26–27, 30,
    36–39, 42
descriptive verbs, in signal
  phase, 134
design elements (document),
  383–90
  chunking texts, 389–90
  clarity in, 384–85
  color choices in, 388–89
  context, audience, and
    purpose in, 384–85
  font style and size, 385–86
  impact of, 383–84
  lists, numbered and bulleted,
    387–88
  margins, 390
  surveys, 416–18
  visuals. *See* visuals
  white space, 389
**Desmond-Harris, Jenée "Tupac
  and My Non-Thug Life,"**
  23–28, 35
detailing
  in profiles, 53
  in remembered event essays, 21
diagrams, use of, 392
dialogue, in remembered event
  essays
  quotation in, 12, 26, 35–36,
    46–47
  speaker tags in, 12, 26, 33, 36,
    46
  summarizing in, 26, 36
dialoguing, as invention
  strategy, 288–89
digital object identifier (DOI),
  401, 470
**Dillard, Anne, "American
  Childhood, An,"** 17–21, 22
"Disappearing Ink" (Gitlin),
  377–78
discussion lists, online, 411–12
doctoral dissertation
  APA documentation style
    for, 471

MLA documentation style
  for, 448
documentation, of sources, 428.
  See also APA style; MLA
  style
  Web sources, 410
document design. *See* design
  elements (document)
Documenting America, visual
  analysis of, 356–63
dominant impression
  in profiles, 58, 87
  in remembered event essays,
    13, 40
drafting, 5. See also drafting
  under specific types of essays
  evaluations, 264–72
  explanations of concepts,
    127–36
  position arguments, 172–82
  profiles, 76–88
  proposals for solutions,
    219–29
  remembered event essays,
    30–41
  research questions, 400
dramatic arc, elements of, 12,
  33–34
dramatizing, as writing strategy,
  33, 289–90
  motive and, 289, 290
drawings, 392
DVD, APA style documentation,
  473

***Eating in America* (Root and
  Rouchement),** 326
EBSCOHost, 177, 227, 269, 408
edited works
  APA style documentation, 471
  MLA style documentation,
    445
editing and proofreading
  evaluation, 277–78
  explanations of concepts,
    140–41
  position arguments, 185–87
  profiles, 93–95
  proposals for solutions,
    231–33
  remembered event essays,
    45–47
  on Web sites, 426
edition of book

APA style documentation, 471
  MLA style documentation,
    446
editorials
  APA documentation style, 472
  MLA documentation style,
    449–50
effects. *See* cause and effect
Ehrenreich, Barbara, *Nickel
  and Dimed,* 324
either-or reasoning, 378
Ella Watson (photograph),
  356, 361
ellipsis marks, for omissions,
  431–32
e-mail
  APA documentation style for,
    474
  example of concession, 376–77
  MLA documentation style for,
    459
"Email Culture" (Kinsley),
  376–77
Emerging Man (photograph),
  357–63, 394
emotional manipulation, 294
  example, "Letter from
    Birmingham Jail" (King),
    315
emotions
  personal feelings, expression
    of, 367
  in remembered event essays,
    22, 27, 40
empathy, 206, 225
  perspective taking and, 207–8
encyclopedias
  general, 399
  as overview resources,
    399–400
  specialized, 399–400
*ERIC (Educational Resource
  Information Center),* 408
ethics, in research, 77
ethos
  defined, 177
  in positions argument,
    149–50, 151
**Etzioni, Amitai, "Working at
  McDonald's,"** 149, 151,
  157–62, 181
evaluations
  assertion of, 366
  drafting, 264–72

evaluations (*continued*)
  alternative judgments,
    responding to, 242, 269–70
  audience and purpose, as-
    sessing, 239
  concession-refutation
    move, 242, 270
  ideas into words, Ways In,
    266–70
  judgment, stating, 267
  organization, logical,
    242–43
  outline, 271–72
  reasons and evidence,
    presenting, 268–69
  subject, choosing, 264–65
  testing topic with others, 265
  transitions (words or
    phrases) in, 242
evaluating draft, Critical
  Reading Guide, 272–74
genre
  basic features of, 239–43,
    253–54, 260–62
  practicing with group, 238
  reflecting on, 279–80
Guide to Reading, 239–62
  making connections,
    252–53, 259
  "Myth of Multitasking,
    The" (Rosen), 255–62
  "*Scott Pilgrim vs. the World*:
    A Hell of a Ride"
    (Akana), 239, 243–48
  topics for essays, consider-
    ing, 255, 262
  "What College Rankings
    Really Tell Us"
    (Gladwell), 249–54
Guide to Writing, 263–64
learning, reflecting on, 279
research sources, types of,
  260, 269, 271
revising draft, 274–78
  combining sentences,
    277–78
  comparisons, checking
    logic of, 277
  editing and proofreading,
    277–78
  Troubleshooting Guide,
    274–76
Thinking Critically about,
  279–80

writing situations
  in college courses, 236, 265
  in community, 237, 265
  in workplace, 237, 265
writing strategies
  alternative judgments,
    responding to, 254, 261–
    62, 264, 269–70, 273, 276
  comparison and contrast,
    241–42, 277
  complicated subject, pre-
    senting, 253
  concessions, making, 242,
    270
  criteria, defining, 253–54
  forecasting statement, 242
  headings, 243
  judgment, well-supported,
    240–42, 253, 263–64,
    273, 275
  organization, logical,
    242–43, 254, 262, 264,
    274, 276
  quotations, paraphrasing,
    summarizing, 240–41,
    261
  reader objections, response
    to, 264, 273, 276
  reframing, 260
  sources, citing, 240
  thesis statement, 240, 244,
    267
  transitions (words or
    phrases), 242, 243
  visuals in, 240, 243, 245,
    246, 248
  well-presented subject,
    239–40, 263, 273, 274–75
***Ever Since Darwin* (Gould)**,
  324
evidence, supporting. *See*
  supporting evidence
examples
  appositives and, 134
  believability of, 313–14
  in evaluation, 238, 240, 260
  as explanatory strategy, 103,
    132
  listing negative consequences,
    194, 221, 222
  representativeness of, 313,
    369–70
exclamation points, with
  quotation marks, 94, 433

expert credentials, appositives
  and, 133–34
expertise, author, 371, 422.
    See also authority; authors
explanations of concepts,
  98–143
  drafting, 127–36
    appositives, use of, 133–34
    concept, identifying, 127
    descriptive verbs, used in
      signal phrases, 134–35
    explanatory strategies, con-
      sidering, 131–32
    ideas into words, Ways In,
      128–32
    information from sources,
      introducing, 134–35
    opening sentences, 135
    summaries, paraphrases,
      quotations, 133
    testing topic with others,
      130
    thesis statement, working,
      130–31
  evaluating draft, with Critical
    Reading, 136–37
  genre
    features of, 101–4, 115,
      121–24
    practicing with groups, 100
    reflecting on, 142–43
  Guide to Reading
    "Attachment: Someone to
      Watch over You" (Lyu)
      104–10
    audience and purpose, 101
    connections, making, 121
    "Love: The Right
      Chemistry" (Toufexis),
      111–17
    "Shyness: Evolutionary
      Tactic?" (Cain), 117–24
    topics for essays, consider-
      ing, 116–17, 124
  Guide to Writing, 125–41
  learning, reflecting on, 142
  research
    in-depth, 130
    initial, types of, 128
  revising draft, 137–41
    adjective clauses, commas
      with, 141
    editing and proofreading,
      140–41

mixed constructions, avoiding, 141
Troubleshooting Guide, 138–40
Thinking Critically about, 142–43
visuals and illustrations in, 103, 106, 113, 116, 133
writing situation for
college courses, 98, 127
community, 99, 127
workplace, 99, 127
writing strategies
causes and effects, 103
classification, 103
comparing and contrasting, 103, 122–23
definitions, 102, 132
examples, 103, 132
explanations, focused, 101–2, 105, 121–22, 125, 136, 138
explanatory strategies, types of, 102–3, 105, 116, 122–23, 126, 137, 139–40
organization, logical, 102, 105, 115, 122, 126, 136, 138–39
sources, integration of, 103–4, 105, 116, 123–24, 126, 137, 140
thesis statements, 102, 130–31
exposition
in dramatic arc, 12, 34
in remembered event essays, 12, 34
eyewitness, writer as. *See* spectator

facts, believability of, 313
fairness, test for, 316
fallacies, in logic, 151, 378–79
falling action, in dramatic arc, 12, 34
false analogy, 151, 379
familiar expressions, errors in, 45–46
"Fatty's Custom Tattooz and Body Piercing" (O'Leary)
ⓔ
FeedDemon, 411
field research, conducting, 412–19

interviews, 414–16
observation studies, 412–14
"Fighting Bullying with Babies" (Bornstein), 195, 204–10
figurative language, 294, 309–10. *See also* figures of speech
figures, numbering, 106, 243, 390
figures of speech
metaphors, 38, 296, 298, 301, 309
similes, 38, 297, 309, 310
symbolism, 309
First-Graders at the Weill Public School (photograph), 364
first person, pros/cons of, in profiles, 84–85
"Fishing" (photograph), 353
flowchart, use of, 392
focus
for analysis, 333–34
in explanations of concepts, 101–2, 105, 121–22, 125, 136, 138
in position arguments, 147–49, 160–61
in proposals for solutions, 193–94, 218
topic sentence, 320–23
focused freewriting, 291
fonts, readability of, 385–86
forecasting statement
cueing reader with, 115
in positions essay, 149, 151
previewing topics with, 317, 318–19
in thesis, 242
foreword of book
APA style documentation, 471
MLA style documentation, 446
framing. *See also* reframing issue
in position arguments, 148–49, 171, 174–75
in proposals for solutions, 193, 221–25, 230
rhetorical questions, 208
freewriting, 269
focused, 291
in framing problem, 221
invention and inquiry strategy, 290–91

Gale Virtual Reference Library, 128
Gates, Henry Louis, Jr.,"TV's Black World Turns—but Stays Unreal," 322
"Gazing into the Darkness" (Crane), 374
generalization, hasty, 379
General Science Full Text, 408
genres
defined, 2
evaluations, 239–43, 253–54, 260–62
explanations of concepts, 101–4, 115, 121–24
headings and, 330
position arguments, 147–51, 160–62, 168–70
profiles, 53–55, 96–97
proposals for solutions, 193–97, 208–10, 215–17
remembered event essays, 11–13, 48–49
Gitlin, Todd, "Disappearing Ink," 377–78
Gladwell, Malcolm, "What College Rankings Really Tell Us," 241, 249–54
"Go Ask Alice" (Marin), 375–76
Google Book Search, 410–11
Google Scholar, 408, 410–11
Google search, 269, 407–8, 409–11
checking links in, 425
Gould, Stephen Jay, *Ever Since Darwin,* 324
government information
APA style documentation, 468
.gov Web sites, 177, 408–9, 424
Library of Congress and, 177, 408
MLA style documentation, 440–41, 447
"Grant and Lee: A Study in Contrasts" (Catton), 321–22
graphic narrative, MLA style documentation, 446
graphs, use of, 391
"Gringo in the Lettuce Fields, A" (Thompson), 68–74

Hasselstrom, Linda M., "Why One Peaceful Woman Carries a Pistol," 373
hasty generalization, 379
headings and subheadings
  cueing reader with, 329–31
  distinguishing between, 387
  document design and, 386–87
  font style and size for, 386, 387
  organization with, 217, 243, 387
  in outlines, 286
  positioning of, 387
Hedges, Elaine, "Quilts and Women's Culture," 321
heuristics, 282
historical context, 308
  of visuals, 355, 359
however, 150, 186, 187, 196
hypothesis, for observation study, 412

ideology and ideals, 335
Illiterate America **(Kozol),** 369–70
illustrations. *See* photographs; visuals
inciting incident, in remembered event, 12, 34
indentation
  hanging indent, in MLA format, 443
  paragraphs and, 319
independent clauses, linking of
  with conjunctive adverbs, 186–87
  with coordinating conjunctions, 186
indirect quotation
  APA style documentation, 468
  MLA style documentation, 442
Infomine, 411
InfoTrac, 177, 227, 269, 408
inquiry strategies. *See* invention and inquiry, strategies for
interactive sources, for research, 411–12
Internet Public Library, 411
Internet research (Web sites), 408–12
  acknowledgement of, 429
  bookmarking, 128, 177, 227

credentials of contributors, 422
documentation and, 410
government information, 177, 408–9, 424
interactive sources, 411–12
publisher or sponsor, determining, 423, 424–25, 426
quotations from, 178
reliability of, 424, 425
in remembered event essays, 31
screen shots, 393, 425
Internet (Web page). *See also* Internet research
  APA style documentation, 473–74
  blogs, 411, 454, 474
  e-mail, 376–77, 459, 474
  MLA style documentation, 454–56
  wikis, 411, 456, 474
intertextuality, visuals and, 355, 359
interviews
  APA documentation style, 473
  conducting, 414–16
    follow-up on, 415
    preparation for, 414–15
    questions for, 414–15
  with experts, 269
  MLA documentation style, 453
  notetaking in, 52, 81, 415
  for profiles, 52, 79–82
  in proposals for solutions, 222
"Intolerance of Boyish Behavior" (Angier), 371–72
introduction of book
  APA style documentation, 471
  MLA style documentation, 446
invention and inquiry, strategies for, 282–93. *See also* outlining
  chunking, 285–86
  clustering, 282–83
  listing, 283–84
  mapping, 282–87
  writing strategies, 282, 287–93
    dialoguing, 288–89
    dramatizing, 289–90
    freewriting, 221, 269, 290–91
    journal keeping, 291

looping, 291–92
questioning, 292–93
inventory, taking, 294, 302
issue, argument and, 334. *See also* position arguments
italics, used for emphasis, 431
"'It's Only Another Beer' Black and Tan, The" (U.S. Department of Transportation/Ad Council) 🄴
"It's Time to Ban Head First Tackles and Blocks" (Niechayev) 🄴

journals, 291
Joyce, James, "Araby," 374
judgment, in evaluations, 240–42, 253, 267, 269, 273. *See also* evaluations

Karr, Mary, *Cherry,* 322
key words
  appositives to define, 134
  in database search, 227, 405, 406
  listing, in research log, 400–401
  in mapping, 282
  in thesis, 367
  in topic sentence, 243
King, Martin Luther, Jr., "Letter from Birmingham Jail," 295–301, 303–4, 306–16
Kinsley, Michael, "Email Culture," 376–77
knowledge of writer, testing, 315–16
Kornbluh, Karen, "Win-Win Flexibility," 194, 210–17, 222, 223–24, 225
Kozol, Jonathan, *Illiterate America,* 369–70
Kramer, Sarah Kate, "Niche Market: Fountain Pen Hospital" 🄴
"Kuma's Corner" (Yelp) 🄴

Lange, Dorothea, 364
Langer, William, "The Black Death," 318–19
Language of Clothes, The **(Lurie),** 321

"Last Stop, The" (Cable), 55–60

learning to write, 1, 3

St. Martin's Guide and, 4–6

Least Heat Moon, William, *Blue Highways*, 328–29

lectures, MLA style documentation, 451

Lee, Andrea, *Russian Journal*, 328

Lemus, Brittany, "*Requiem for a Dream*: Fantasy versus Reality" [e]

"less is more" principle, in design, 384

"Letter from Birmingham Jail" (King), 295–301, 303–4, 306–16

letters, MLA style documentation, 451

letters to the editor
APA style documentation, 472
MLA style documentation, 449–50

Lewis, Shannon, "We Were Here" [e]

LexisNexis, 177, 227, 269

LexisNexis Academic, 408

Library of Congress
as research source, 177, 406, 408
subject headings, 406
Web site, 408

library research, 404–12
archives and special collections, 407
books, finding, 405–7
call numbers, 406–7
catalogs and databases, 227, 269, 404–12
general *versus* subject-specific databases in, 408
government information in, 409
interactive sources, 411–12
narrowing or expanding results, 405
online catalogs, 404–7
periodicals, articles in, 407–8
search terms, choosing, 404–5
statistical information in, 408–9
subject guides in, 400
Web sites, 409–11

line graphs, uses of, 391

listing, 283–84
of key points, 387–88

literacy narrative, 1, 6

literary works, MLA style documentation, 441

logic, of argument, 294, 297
ABC test for, 312–14

logical fallacies, recognizing, 151, 378–79

logical transitions, 327
in position arguments, 151
in profiles, 55

logos, in position arguments, 149–50, 151

"Long Good-Bye, The: Mother's Day in Federal Prison" (Coyne), 61–67

looping, exploring topic with, 291–92

Lopez, Barry, *Arctic Dreams*, 320, 325

"Love: The Right Chemistry" (Toufexis), 111–17, 317–18

Lurie, Alison, *The Language of Clothes*, 321

Lyu, Patricia, "Attachment: Someone to Watch over You," 104–10

magazine articles
APA documentation style, 470
MLA documentation style, 449

magazines
advertising in, 365
popular *versus* scholarly, 423, 424

"Mapping Memory" (National Geographic) [e]

mapping strategies, 282–87.
See also outlining
clustering, 282–83
listing, 283–84, 387–88

maps
MLA style documentation, 451
uses as visual, 393

margins, readability and, 390

Marin, Peter, "Go Ask Alice," 375–76

meaning, writing to explore, 310

memorabilia, in remembered event essays, 37

metaphor
description and, 38
examples, "Letter from Birmingham Jail" (King), 296, 298, 301, 309

method, in drama, 289–90

"Missing the Fun" (Coleman) [e]

mixed constructions, avoiding, 141

MLA International Bibliography, 408

MLA style
articles (print, online, database), 448–51
block quotations in, 434–35, 439–40
in-text citations, 403, 438–42
corporate, organization, or government author, 440–41
entire work, 442
literary work (novel, play, poem), 441
quotation from secondary source, 442
religious work, 441–42
two or more authors with same last name, 440
two or more works by same author, 440
two or more works in same parentheses, 442
work in anthology, 441
work with more than one author, 440
work with one author, 439–40
work without page numbers, 442
work with unknown author, 440

research paper, example of, 456–65

works cited list (print, electronic, database), 438, 442–56
advertisements, 451
anthology, or edited collection, 445
article from reference book, 447
art works, 452
author listings, 444–45

MLA style (*continued*)
blogs, 454
book in series, 446–47
corporate, organization, or agency as author, 445
dictionary entry, 447
doctoral dissertation, 448
editorials, 449–50
e-mail message, 456
films, 453
government document, 447
graphic narrative, 446
hanging indent, 443
introduction, preface, foreword, or afterword, 446
later edition of book, 446
lecture or public address, 451
letters, 451
letters to editor, 449–50
magazine article, 449
maps or charts, 451
multimedia sources, 451–53
musical recordings, 453
newspaper article, 448–49
online scholarly project, 454
pamphlet or brochure, 447
performances, 452
podcast, 452–53
publisher names, shortened, 443
radio programs, 452
religious work, 446
republished book, 446
review, 451
scholarly journal, article from, 448–49, 450
television programs, 452
title within title, 446
translation, 446
video, online, 453
Web site, 444, 454, 455
wiki article, 456
"More Testing, More Learning" (O'Malley), 193, 196, 197–203, 216, 233, 366, 429–30
motivating factors, in argument, 333, 334–35
in annotations chart, 336, 340
motive, in drama, 289, 290
Movie Review Query Engine, 269
multilingual writers, troubleshots for

adjective order, 95
past participles, 47
past perfect tense, 47
subtle differences in meaning, 187
verb tenses, 47
multimedia, to enhance explanations, 133
multimedia sources
APA documentation style, 473
MLA style documentation, 451–53
multimodal projects, 384
music recording, MLA documentation style, 453
"Myth of Multitasking, The" (Rosen), 241–42, 255–62

naming
in profiles, 53
in remembered event essays, 21, 37
narration
dialogue strategy in, 26
in observation study, 413
in profiles, 54, 73
in remembered event essays, 33, 54
topic sentence in, 322
narrative literacy, 1, 6
National Geographic, "Mapping Memory" e
National Newspaper Index, 408
negative effects, of problem, 194, 221, 222
nevertheless, 150, 187, 196
newspaper articles
APA documentation style, 470
databases for, 408
MLA documentation style, 449
"New York" (Talese), 324
"Niche Market: Fountain Pen Hospital" (Kramer) e
Nickel and Dimed (Ehrenreich), 324
Niechayev, Michael, "It's Time to Ban Head First Tackles and Blocks" e
notebook, for working bibliography, 401
note taking
in interviews, 52, 81, 415
in observations, 81, 413
sources and, 403

novels, MLA style documentation, 441
numbered list, 387–88
numerical data, 223, 314. *See also* statistics

observation
conducting, 412–14
preparing, 79–80, 412
for profiles, 79–82
writing up, 82, 413
O'Leary, Briana, "Fatty's Custom Tattooz and Body Piercing" e
O'Malley, Patrick, "More Testing, More Learning," 193, 196–203, 209, 216, 222, 225, 233, 366, 372, 376, 429–30
online sources, documenting, 429. *See also* Internet research (Web sites)
opening sentences. *See also* topic sentences
evaluations, 272
explanations of concepts, 135
position arguments, 181–82
proposals for solutions, 229
remembered event essays, 41
opinion, assertion of, 366
opposing positions
exploring. *See* position arguments
patterns of opposition, 294, 310–11
responding to. *See* concessions; refutations
organization. *See also* outlining
as author, in MLA style, 440–41
dramatic arc, 12, 33–34
evaluations, 242–43, 254, 262, 264, 274
explanations of concepts, 102, 105, 115, 122, 126, 136, 138–39
position arguments, 151, 162, 172, 183, 185
profiles, 54–55, 72
proposals for solutions, 197, 209–10, 217, 219, 231
organization chart, 392
orienting statements, 317–19. *See also* thesis and thesis statement

outlining, 284–87
  in arguing positions, 180–81,
    285, 286–87
  chunking and, 285–86
  in evaluations, 271–72
  example, "Letter from
    Birmingham Jail" (King),
    303–4
  in explanations of concepts,
    131
  formal *versus* informal, 284,
    287
  in profiles, 83–84
  in proposals for solutions,
    228–29
  as reading strategy, 294,
    302–4, 306
  in remembered event essays,
    284–85
  scratch outline, 131, 284–85,
    304, 306
  sentence outline, 286–87
  topic outline, 286, 287
oversimplifying, 151, 379

pamphlet, MLA style documen-
    tation, 447
paragraphing, 318–23
  chunking and, 389
  quotation and, 36
  related ideas and, 319–20
  topic sentences and, 320–23
paraphrasing, 430, 435–37
  in arguing positions, 169,
    177–78
  disagreement, 334
  in evaluations, 240, 241, 261
  example, "Letter from
    Birmingham Jail" (King), 305
  in explanations of concepts,
    103, 133, 140
  plagiarism, avoiding, 428–29,
    437
  in profiles, 54, 72
  as reading strategy, 294,
    304–5
  in remembered event essays,
    12, 26, 35, 36
  signal phrases to introduce,
    134
  writer's credibility and, 371
parentheses
  in-text citations in, 135, 466,
    467

MLA citation style, 438, 439,
    440, 441
Parks, Gordon, *Emerging Man,*
    356–63, 394
participant-observer, writer as,
    55, 66–67
  pros and cons of, 84–85
participial phrases, integrating,
    94–95
past perfect tense, multilingual
    writers and, 47
past tense, remembered events
    and, 35
pathos, in position arguments,
    149–50, 151
patterns of opposition, 294
  example, "Letter from
    Birmingham Jail" (King),
    310–11
PDF file format, 227, 408, 409
peer critique, 5
peer-reviewed research, 161
people
  in analysis of visuals, 354, 358
  appositives used with, 134
  description of, 12–13, 21, 26,
    30, 36–38, 42, 413
  profiling. *See* profiles
percentages, in statistics, 223
periodicals, articles in
  APA style documentation,
    472–73
  in library database, 407–8
  MLA style documentation,
    448–52
personal *(ad hominem)* attack,
    151, 379
perspective on subject, 422
  in profiles, 55, 60, 67, 71–72,
    73, 76, 81, 85–87, 90, 93
photographs, 352, 392
  analysis of, 357–63, 394
  in explanations of concepts, 108
  film stills, in movie review,
    243, 245, 246, 248
  memorabilia and, 37
  in proposals for solutions, 206
  in remembered event essays,
    24, 26–27
pie charts, 388–89, 391
plagiarism, avoiding, 428–29,
    437
plays, MLA style documenta-
    tion, 441

podcasts
  APA style documentation, 473
  MLA style documentation,
    452–53
poetry
  MLA style documentation, 441
  quoting within text, 434
policy, assertion of, 366
popular sources, 423, 424
position arguments, 144–89, 334
  drafting, 172–82
    framing issue, 148–49, 171,
      175
    ideas into words, Ways In,
      174–77
    opening sentences, 181–82
    organization, logical, 151,
      162, 172, 183, 185
    outline, 180–81, 285, 286–87
    purpose and audience,
      clarifying, 147
    quotations, paraphrasing,
      summarizing, 169,
      177–78
    reasons, developing,
      176–77
    refutation-concession move,
      150–51, 179, 180, 181
    response to opposing views,
      172, 183, 185
    statistics, use of, 161
    supporting evidence, 162,
      171–72
    thesis statement, working,
      149, 151, 176, 181
    topic (issue), choosing,
      172–73
  evaluating draft, Critical
    Reading Guide, 182–83
  genre
    features of, 147–51, 160–62,
      168–70
    practicing with group, 146
    reflecting on, 188–89
  Guide to Reading, 147–70
    audience and writer's
      purpose, 147
    "Children Need to Play,
      Not Compete" (Statsky),
      152–57, 160, 287
    connections, making, 160,
      167–68
    logical fallacies, checking
      for, 151

position arguments (*continued*)
topics for essays, considering, 162–63, 170
"Why Privacy Matters Even If You Have Nothing to Hide" (Solove), 163–70
"Working at McDonald's" (Etzioni), 157–62
Guide to Writing, 171–87
learning, reflecting on, 188
research
sources, types of, 177
statistics, sources of, 161
revising draft, 184–87
conjunctive adverbs, avoiding comma splices with, 186–87
coordinating conjunctions, commas before, 186
editing and proofreading, 185–87
tone, editing for, 185
Troubleshooting Guide, 184–85
sentence strategies for, 379–82
Thinking Critically about, 188–89
writing situation for
in college courses, 144, 173
in community, 145, 173
in workplace, 145, 173
writing strategies
cause and effect in, 169–70
concession-refutation move, 150–51, 179, 180
focused, well-presented issue, 147–49, 160–61
forecasting statement, 149
framing issue, 148–49, 171, 174–75
hypothetical quotations, 169
logical transitions in, 151
organization, logical, 162, 170, 172
reader's objections, anticipating, 162, 178–80
statistics in, 161
supporting evidence, 149
thesis statements, 149, 151, 176, 181
writer's position, support for, 161, 169

preface of book
APA style documentation, 471
MLA style documentation, 446
prepositional phrases, 54
present perspective, autobiographical significance and, 13, 22
present tense, 35
"Problem with Lawns, The: The Transforming Landscape of Las Vegas," (Sweet and Wise) e
process analysis, in proposing solutions, 195
process narratives, 81
profiles
drafting, 76–88
dominant impression, clarifying, 58, 87
information to include, 87
main point, considering, 87
opening sentence, 88
organization, logical, 72–73, 92
outline, 83–84
perspective on subject, 55, 60, 67, 71–72, 73, 76, 81, 85–87, 90, 93
purpose for writing, refining, 86
quotations, integrating into essay, 62, 82–83
subject to profile, choosing, 77–78
testing topic with others, 77–78
writer's role, 76, 84–85, 89, 93
evaluating draft, Critical Reading guide, 88–90
field research, 54, 78–83
artifacts, photographs, or videos, 81
ethics in, 77
interview notes, 81
interviews, 52, 79–82
interview write-up, 82–83
observations, 79–82
schedule, 78–79
genre
basic features, 53–55
practicing with group, 52
reflecting on, 96–97

Guide to Reading
audience and purpose, 53
connections, making, 65, 71–72
features of genre, 53–55, 65, 72
"A Gringo in the Lettuce Fields" (Thompson), 68–74
"Last Stop, The" (Cable), 55–60
"Long Good-Bye, The: Mother's Day in Federal Prison" (Coyne), 61–67
perspective on subject, 55, 60, 67, 71–72, 73, 76
topics for, considering, 67, 74
writer's role in, 55, 57, 66, 73
Guide to Writing, 75–90
revising draft, 90–95
for adjective order, 95
editing and proofreading, 93–95
participial phrases, integrating, 94–95
quotations, punctuation in, 93–94
Troubleshooting Guide, 91–93
Thinking Critically about, 96–97
writing situation for
in college courses, 50
in community, 51
in workplace, 51
writing strategies
anecdotes, use of, 65
contrast and juxtaposition, 67
descriptions, 57
dominant impression, creating, 58, 87
interview write-up, 82–83
logical transitions, 55, 58
organization, logical, 54–55, 66, 72–73, 76, 89, 92
outlining, 83–84
quoting, paraphrasing, summarizing, 54, 72
subject, detailed information about, 53–54, 72, 75, 89, 91
pronoun reference, as cohesive device, 323–24

proofreading. *See* editing and proofreading
proposals for solutions
    drafting, 219–29
        alternative solutions, offering, 196, 227–28
        authority or expert information in, 194
        developing possible solution, 225–26
        explaining solutions, 226
        framing problem, 193–94, 198, 221–25, 230
        ideas into words, Ways In, 221–23, 224–28
        opening sentences, 229
        outline, 228–29
        purpose and audience, determining, 193
        reframing issue, 224–25
        refutation/concession, 196, 197, 227–28
        testing topic with others, 220, 223
        topics, considering, 210, 217
    evaluating draft, Critical Reading Guide, 229–31
    genre
        basic features, 193–97, 208–10, 215–17
        practicing with group, 192
        reflecting on, 234–35
    Guide to Reading, 193–217
        connections, making, 207–8, 215
        "Fighting Bullying with Babies" (Bornstein), 195, 204–10
        "More Testing, More Learning" (O'Malley), 193, 196, 197–203
        purpose and audience, 193
        "Win-Win Flexibility" (Kornbluh), 210–17
    Guide to Writing, 218–19
    research, 226–27
        databases for, 227
        Internet search, 227
        sources, types of, 194
    revising draft, 231–33
        agentless sentences, revising, 233
        editing and proofreading, 232–33

this, that, avoiding ambiguous use of, 232
Troubleshooting Guide, 232–33
Thinking Critically about, 234–35
writing situation
    in college courses, 190, 220
    in community, 191, 220
    in workplace, 191, 220
writing strategies
    alternative solutions, offering, 201–2, 209, 216–17, 219, 230
    anecdotes and examples, 221, 222
    authority or expert information in, 194
    comparing, 195
    focused, well-defined problem, 193–94, 218
    framing issue, 148–49, 171, 174–75
    organization, logical, 197, 209–10, 217, 219, 231
    reader's objections, response to, 209, 216–17, 219, 227, 230
    reframing problem, 224–25
    refutation or concession, 196, 227–28
    rhetorical questions, 208
    statistics, using, 194, 196, 215–16, 221, 223–24
    supporting evidence, 195, 429–30
    thesis statement, 197
    topic sentences, 197–98, 209–10
    transitions (words or phrases) in, 196, 197, 209
    well-argued solution, 195–96, 208–9, 216, 218–19, 230
ProQuest Central, 408
ProQuest Newspapers, 408
PsycINFO, 408
public address, MLA style documentation, 451
publication information, 422–26
    for bibliography, 401
    up-to-date, 422
    Web sites, 424–25

public service announcement (PSA), 353–54
punctuation and punctuation marks
    colon, 435
    commas, 134, 141, 186, 187, 435
    question marks, 94, 433
    quotation marks, 33, 36, 46, 94, 178, 432, 433
    semicolon, 187
purpose for writing
    in concept explanations, 101
    in document design, 384–85
    in evaluations, 239
    in position arguments, 147
    in proposals for solutions, 193
    in remembered event essays, 11, 39
Putnam, Robert D., "The Strange Disappearance of Civic America," 370–71

qualification
    of authority, 371
    of thesis, 368
question marks, 94, 433
questionnaire, in survey, 417–18
questions, asking
    in interviews, 414–15
    as invention and inquiry strategy, 292–93
    rhetorical, 102, 131, 208
    in surveys, 416, 417
"Quilts and Women's Culture" (Hedges), 321
quotation marks, 33, 36, 178
    commas with, 46, 94
    exclamation points with, 94, 433
    question marks with, 94, 433
    single, 432
quotations
    APA style documentation, 435, 468
    block (in-text), 434–35, 439–40
    brackets used in, 431
    in dialogue, 12, 26, 35–36, 46–47
    ellipses used in to mark omissions in, 431–32
    in evaluations, 240–41, 261
    in explanations of concepts, 103, 133, 140

quotations (*continued*)
    grammatical tangles in,
        avoiding, 433–34
    hypothetical, 169
    integrating
        into argument, 62, 374–75
        block quotations, 434–35
        in position arguments, 169,
            177–78
        in profiles, 54, 72, 82–83,
            93–94
        with punctuation, 432, 435
    from interviews, 81, 82–83
    introducing
        with colons, 435
        with commas, 435
        with signal phrases, 134, 169
        with *that*, 435
    italics used for emphasis in,
        431
    MLA style documentation,
        439–40, 442
    plagiarism, avoiding, 428–29
    quotation marks with. *See*
        quotation marks
    as reading strategy, 305
    in remembered event essays,
        12, 26, 35–36, 46–47
    speaker tags for, 82–83, 94
    supporting evidence, 430–35
    writer's credibility and, 371

readers. *See also* audience
    concept explanations and,
        131
    cueing. *See* cueing strategies
    document design and, 384, 385
    objections, responding to,
        375–78
        conceding. *See* concession
        evaluations, 264, 270, 273,
            276
        position arguments, 178–80
        proposals for solutions,
            209, 216–17, 219, 227,
            230
        refutation. *See* refutation
    thesis statement and, 317
    reading, critical. *See* Critical
        Reading Guide
    reading strategies
        annotating, 295–302
        beliefs and values, challenges
            to, 312

contextualizing, 308–9
emotional manipulation,
    recognizing, 315
figurative language, exploring,
    309–10
inventory, taking, 302
"Letter from Birmingham Jail"
    (King), 295–301, 303–4,
    306–16
logic of argument, evaluating,
    312–14
outlining, 302–4, 306
paraphrasing, 304–5
patterns of opposition, find-
    ing, 310–11
summarizing, 305, 306–7
synthesizing, 307–8
writer's credibility, judging,
    315–16
the reason is because, avoiding,
    141
reasons (supporting thesis),
    369–75
    See also supporting evidence
    ABC test and, 312–14
    in position arguments,
        149–50
    in proposals for solutions, 195
red herring, 379
reference book article
    APA style documentation,
        471
    MLA style documentation,
        447
references, list of, 104, 135, 203,
    241, 467
    See also APA style
reflecting
    on challenges to beliefs and
        values, 294, 312
    on interviews, 82, 415
    on observations, 82
reframing issue. *See also* framing
    in evaluations, 260
    in proposals for solutions,
        224–25
    through contrast, 168
refutation (argues against)
    in argument, 377–78, 381–82
    concession-refutation move,
        150–51, 180, 181, 196, 270,
        382
    counterargument and, 334,
        340

in evaluation, 242, 270–71
in positions argument, 150–
    51, 179, 180, 181
in proposals for solutions,
    196, 197, 227–28
sentence strategies for, 381,
    382
religious works, MLA style docu-
    mentation, 441–42
remembered event essays, 8–49
    drafting, 30–41
    autobiographical signifi-
        cance, 13, 21–22, 27, 30
    choosing event, 31–32
    conflict, exploring, 39–40
    descriptive details,
        incorporating, 38–39
    dialogue, 284–85
    dominant impression,
        conveying, 13, 40
    dramatic arc, 12, 33–34
    emotions, exploring, 22, 27
    main point, considering, 39
    memorabilia/photos,
        exploring, 37
    opening sentence, 41
    outline, 32, 284–85
    present perspective,
        exploring, 40
    shaping story, Ways In,
        32–33
    testing story with others,
        34
    time sequence and verb
        tenses, 35, 47
    topics (events) choosing,
        22, 28
    evaluating draft, Critical
        Reading Guide, 41–43
    genre
        basic features, 11–13
        practicing with group, 10
        reflecting on, 48–49
    Guide to Reading, 11–28
        "American Childhood, An"
            (Dillard), 17–20
        audience and purpose, 39
        "Calling Home" (Brandt),
            13–17
        connections, making, 20,
            25–26
        features of genre, 11–13
        purpose for writing, 11, 39
        topics, considering, 22

"Tupac and My Non-Thug Life" (Desmond-Harris), 23–28
Guide to Writing, 29–47
  revising draft, 43–47
    for dialogue issues, 46–47
    editing and proofreading, 45–47
    for right words/expressions, 45–46
    Troubleshooting Guide, 43–45
    for verb tense, 47
  Thinking Critically about, 48–49
  writing situation for
    in college courses, 8
    in community, 9
    in workplace, 9
  writing strategies
    action sequences, 20–21, 38
    autobiographical significance, conveying, 39–40
    descriptions, 12–13, 21, 26–27, 30, 36–38, 42
    dialogue, 12, 35–36, 46–47
    dominant impression, conveying, 13, 40
    dramatic arc, 12, 33–34
    present perspective, 13, 22
    showing and telling, 21
    stream of consciousness, 22
    thoughts and feelings, presenting, 13
    well-told story, elements of, 11–12, 29, 32–33, 42
  repetition, as aid to cohesion, 324, 325
"Requiem for a Dream: Fantasy versus Reality" (Lemus) e
research. See also Internet research
  for concept explanations, 128, 130
  in evaluations, 260, 269, 271
  field research, conducting, 412–19
    interviews, conducting, 414–16
    surveys, 416–19
  peer-reviewed, 161
  in positions argument, 177

in profile writing, 52, 54, 77, 78–83
in proposals for solutions, 194, 226–27
surveys, 196, 222, 223, 269
research papers, planning, 396–403
  documentation styles for. See APA style; MLA style
  keywords, listing, 400–401
  overview resources, 399–400
  research log, 396, 400–401
  rhetorical situation, analyzing, 396, 397–98
  schedule for, 398–99
  topic, choosing, 399
  working bibliography for, 402–3
research questions, drafting, 400
resolution, in dramatic arc, 12, 34
reviews
  APA documentation style, 473
  essays as. See evaluations
  MLA documentation style, 451
revising. See also specific types of essays
  agentless sentences, 233
  evaluations, 274–78
  explanations of concepts, 137–41
  position arguments, 184–87
  profiles, 90–95
  proposals for solutions, 231–33
  remembered event essays, 43–47
rhetorical context, of visuals, 352–53, 355, 359
rhetorical questions
  in explanations of concept, 102, 131
  in framing problem, 208
rhetorical situation, 2
  analyzing, 396, 397–98
  in evaluations, 241
  in explanations of concepts, 115
  success in, 3
rising action, in dramatic arc, 12, 34
Roman numerals, in outlines, 228, 287

Root, Waverly, *Eating in America*, 326
Rosen, Christine, "The Myth of Multitasking," 241–42, 255–62
Rotten Tomatoes, 269
Rouchement, Richard de, *Eating in America*, 326
Roy, Kelsey C., "Daily Grind, The" e
RSS (Really Simple Syndication) feeds, 411
Russian Journal (Lee), 328

scenarios, in framing problem, 193, 221
scene, in visual analysis, 354, 358
schedule, for research, 398–99
scholarly sources, 423, 424
  MLA documentation style, 448–49, 450
"*Scott Pilgrim vs. the World*: A Hell of a Ride" (Akana), 239–40, 242–48, 268, 366
scratch outlines, 131. See also outlining
  versus formal outline, 304, 306
  for remembered event, 284–85
screen shots, 243, 393, 425
script fonts, 386
search terms, appropriate, 404–5
self-discovery, 3
  in remembered events essays, 48–49
semicolon, before conjunctive adverb, 187
sentence combining, 277–78
sentence fragments, in quotations, 433–34
sentence outlines, 286–87
sentence strategies
  agentless, revising, 233
  for analysis, 334–35
  for argument, 379–82
sentence structure, repetition of, 325
setting, in drama, 289, 290
showing, in remembered event essays, 21, 22
"Shyness: Evolutionary Tactic?" (Cain), 117–24

signal phrase, 177
  author named with, in cita-
    tion, 438, 439, 440, 441,
    467
  descriptive verbs in, 134–35
  in evaluations, 240–41
  in integrating sources, 103,
    428
  introducing quotation with,
    134, 169
significance, creating, 11, 13,
  21–22, 27
simile
  description and, 38
  example of, "Letter from
    Birmingham Jail" (King),
    297, 309, 310
slanting, 151, 379
slippery slope, 379
sob story, 379
social context, of visuals, 355,
  359
social networking Web sites, 411
**Solove, Daniel J., "Why
  Privacy Matters Even If
  You Have 'Nothing to
  Hide,'"** 147–48, 163–70,
  181, 318, 378
solutions, proposals for. *See*
  proposals for solutions
sound recording, APA documentation style for, 473
sources, 420–37
  citing of, for visuals, 390, 393
  credibility of, 224
  evaluation of, 420–26
    choosing relevant sources,
      420–21
    choosing reliable sources,
      421–26
    popular *versus* scholarly,
      423, 424
  ideas supported by, 427–37
    acknowledging, 428
    plagiarism, avoiding, 428–29
    supporting claims, 429–30
    synthesizing sources,
      427–28
  integration of, in explaining
    concepts, 103–4, 105, 116,
    123–24, 140
  in proposals for solutions, 194
  reinforcing credibility with,
    177–78

secondary *versus* primary, 404
signal phrases to introduce,
  103, 134–35, 428
taking notes on, 403
trustworthiness of, 313, 314
spatial relationships, transitions
  of, 55, 328–29
speaker tags
  in dialogue, 12, 26, 33, 36, 46
  in direct quotations, 82–83, 94
special collections, in libraries,
  407
specialized encyclopedias,
  399–400
spectator
  pros and cons of role, 84–85
  writer as, 55, 66–67
speculation, in profiles, 55
statistics
  believability of, 314
  government documents and,
    408–9
  in position arguments, 161
  in proposals for solutions,
    194, 196, 215–16, 221,
    223–24
  up-to-date, relevant, and
    accurate, 370–71
**Statsky, Jessica, "Children
  Need to Play, Not
  Compete,"** 148, 150,
  152–57, 160, 177–78, 181,
  286–87, 318, 366, 377
storytelling, 10
  remembered events. *See* re-
    membered event essays
**"Strange Disappearance of
  Civic America, The"
  (Putnam),** 370–71
**"Stranger in the Village"
  (Baldwin),** 327
straw man fallacy, 179, 379
stream of consciousness, 22
subheadings. *See* headings and
  subheadings
subject, in profiles. *See also*
  profiles
  detailed information about,
    53–54, 72, 75, 89, 91
  perspective on (*See* perspective
    on subject)
subject guides, in libraries, 400
subject headings, in library
  catalogs, 406

subject-specific encyclopedias,
  399–400
summaries and summarizing
  in arguing positions, 169,
    177–78
  defined, 294
  disagreement in, 334
  in evaluations, 240, 241, 261,
    374
  example, "Letter from
    Birmingham Jail" (King),
    306–7
  in explanations of concepts,
    104, 133, 140
  main ideas and, 430, 437
  paraphrasing and, 305
  plagiarism, avoiding, 428–29
  in profiles, 54, 72
  in remembered event essays,
    12, 26, 35, 36
  signal phrases to introduce, 134
  survey results, 418
supporting evidence
  anecdotes as, 372–74
  authority or expert informa-
    tion, 371–72
  in evaluations, 268–69
  examples as, 369–70
  in positions argument, 149,
    176–77
  in proposals for solutions,
    195, 429–30
  statistics as, 370–71
  textual evidence as, 374–75
  for thesis statement, 312,
    369–75
surveys
  administering, 418
  designing, 416–18
  in field research, 269, 416–19
  in proposals for solutions,
    196, 222, 223
  questions for, 416, 417
  reporting results, 418–19
**Sweet, Phoebe, and Zach Wise,
  "The Problem with
  Lawns: The Transforming
  Landscape of Las Vegas"**
  e
symbolism
  defined, 309
  example, "Letter from
    Birmingham Jail" (King),
    309

synonyms, ideas connected with, 325
synthesizing, 294, 307–8
  arguments, 332, 344–51
  example, "Letter from Birmingham Jail" (King), 307
  sources, 427–28
  synthesis chart, 345

table, as visual, 391
Talese, Gay, "New York," 324
Tannen, Deborah, *That's Not What I Meant,* 323
Taylor, Paul (student), 356–63, 394
television programs
  APA style documentation, 473
  MLA style documentation, 452
telling, in remembered event essays, 21–22
temporal transitions, 328. *See also* time entries
  past perfect tense, 47
tenses. *See* verb tenses
testing
  appropriateness, believability, completeness, 312–14
  for common ground, 316
  topics for essays
    evaluations, 265
    explanations of concepts, 130
    profiles, 77–78
    proposals for solutions, 220, 223
    remembered event essays, 34
  for writer's knowledge, 315–16
textual evidence, supporting position with, 374–75. *See also* supporting evidence
that, 233
  adjective clause with, 141
  ambiguous use of, avoiding, 233
  introducing quotation with, 435
***That's Not What I Meant* (Tannen),** 323
thesis and thesis statement
  ABC test and, 312–14
  asserting, 366–68
    appropriate qualification of, 368
    arguable assertions, 366–67

wording, clear and precise, 367–68
evaluations, 240, 244, 267
explanations of concepts, 115, 130–31
forecast included in, 318–19
main idea, announcing, 317–18
position arguments, 149, 151, 176, 181
proposals for solutions, 195
reasons and support for, 312, 369–75
  anecdotes, 372–74
  authority or expert information, 371–72
  examples, 369–70
  statistics, 370–71
  textual evidence, 374–75
research questions and, 400
thinking, writing and, 2–3. *See also* critical thinking
this, avoiding ambiguous use of, 232
Thompson, Gabriel, "A Gringo in the Lettuce Fields," 68–74
time management
  backward planning in, 78–79
  scheduling research, 398–99
time markers and verb tenses
  in profiles, 54, 72–73
  in remembered event essays, 35, 47
  calendar and clock time, 35, 54, 72–73, 78–79
time sequence, transitions and, 328
"Times Square at Dusk" (photograph), 352
title and subtitle, in bibliography, 401
tone
  in position argument, 185
  in proposals for solutions, 197
  in visual analysis, 354–55, 359
topic outlines, 286, 287. *See also* outlining
topics, for essays
  evaluations, 255, 262
  explanations of concepts, 116–17, 124
  position arguments, 162–63, 170

profiles, 67, 74
proposals for solutions, 210, 217
remembered event essays, 22, 28
research strategies and, 399
topic sentences
  announcing topic with, 320–21
  in evaluations, 243
  making transitions with, 151, 197, 209, 321–22
  paragraph's focus in, 320–23
  positioning of, 322–23
  in proposals for solutions, 197–98, 209–10
Toufexis, Anastasia, "Love: The Right Chemistry," 111–17, 317–18
trade publications, 423, 424
transitions (words or phrases), 3
  contrast, in proposals, 196, 197, 209
  cueing reader with, 115, 321, 326–29
  in evaluations, 242, 243
  logical, 327
    in position arguments, 151
    in profiles, 55
    in paragraphs, 321–22
  spatial relationships, indicating, 55, 328–29
  temporal relationships, indicating, 328
  in topic sentences, 151, 197, 209, 321–22
translations
  APA style documentation, 471
  MLA style documentation, 446
Troubleshooting Guide, A
  evaluations, 274–76
  explanations of concepts, 138–40
  position arguments, 184–85
  profiles, 91–93
  proposals for solutions, 232–33
  remembered event essays, 43–45
trustworthiness, of sources, 313, 314
"Tupac and My Non-Thug Life" (Desmond-Harris), 23–28, 35
"TV's Black World Turns—but Stays Unreal" (Gates), 322
typography, in document design, 385–86

underlining, in annotation, 295
URL (uniform resource locator),
    177, 227, 424, 425
**U.S. Department of
    Transportation/Ad
    Council, "'It's Only
    Another Beer' Black and
    Tan, The"** e
U.S. government printing office,
    408–9

values, as motivating factor,
    334–35, 340
values and beliefs, challenges to,
    294, 312
verbal phrases, in sentence-
    combining, 278
verbs, descriptive, in signal
    phrases, 134
verb tenses
    in profiles, 54
    in remembered event essays,
        35, 47
video recordings, 407
    APA style documentation, 473
    MLA style documentation, 453
visuals
    analyzing, 352–65
        criteria for, 354–56
        rhetorical context of,
            352–53, 355, 359
        sample analysis,
            Documenting America,
            356–63
        social context of, 355, 359
    captions for, 243, 390
    citing sources for, 390, 393
    computer tools for, 394
    in document design, 390–94
    in evaluations, 243, 245, 246,
        248
    in explanations of concepts,
        103, 106, 113, 116, 133,
        139
    graphs, 391
    integrating into text, 243,
        393–94
    maps and mapping, 282–87,
        393
    number, title, and label for,
        390
    in PDF files, 227
    photographs. *See* photographs

in proposals for solutions, 197
screen shots, 393, 425
vivid description and, 24,
    26–27

"We Were Here" (Lewis) e
Web of Science, 128
Web sites
    APA style documentation,
        473–74
    MLA style documentation,
        444, 454, 455
Web sites, in research, 409–12.
    See also Internet research
    (Web sites)
**"What College Rankings
    Really Tell Us"
    (Gladwell),** 241, 249–54
which, with adjective clause, 141
white space, in document
    design, 389
who, with adjective clause, 141
**"Why One Peaceful Woman
    Carries a Pistol"
    (Hasselstrom),** 373
**"Why Privacy Matters Even If
    You Have 'Nothing to
    Hide'" (Solove),** 147–48,
    163–70, 318
Wikipedia, 399, 411
wikis
    APA style documentation, 474
    MLA style documentation, 456
    as research source, 411
**"Win-Win Flexibility"
    (Kornbluh),** 194, 210–17,
    223–24
**"Working at McDonald's"
    (Etzioni),** 151, 157–62
working bibliography, 401–3,
    429
    annotating, 402–3
working thesis. *See also* thesis
    and thesis statement
    evaluations, 267
    explanations of concepts,
        130–31
    position arguments, 176
workplace, writing in
    evaluations, 237, 265
    explanations of concepts, 99,
        127
    position arguments, 145, 173

profiles, 51
proposals for solutions, 191,
    220
remembered event essays, 9
Works Cited. *See also* MLA style
    in arguing positions, 156–57,
        167
    in evaluations, 241, 248
    in explanations of concepts,
        104, 110, 135
    in proposals for solutions,
        214–15, 224
    in student analysis and
        synthesis, 343, 350–51
    student research paper,
        464–65
    student visual analysis, 363
World Cat, 407
World Wildlife Fund, 353–54
writer
    credibility of. *See* credibility,
        of writer
    as participant observer, 55,
        66–67, 84–85
    purpose for. *See* purpose, and
        writing
    as spectator, 55, 66–67,
        84–85
writing
    importance of, 1–4
    interviews, 82
    observation study, 82, 413
    strategies for (*See* writing
        strategies)
    survey report, 418–19
    thinking and, 2–3
writing strategies
    arguments and arguing,
        366–82
    cueing strategies, 317–31
    invention and inquiry,
        282–93
        cubing, 221, 288
        dialoguing, 288–89
        dramatizing, 289–90
        freewriting, 221, 269,
            290–91
        journal keeping, 291
        looping, 291–92
        questioning, 292–93

Yahoo! search, 269
Yelp, "Kuma's Corner" e

Edit and Proofread Your Draft

Chapter 2

Using the Right Word or Expression   45
Incorporating Dialogue   46
Using the Past Perfect   47

Chapter 3

Checking the Punctuation of Quotations   93
Integrating Participial Phrases   94
A Common Problem for Multilingual Writers: Determining Adjective Order   95

Chapter 4

Avoiding Mixed Constructions   141
Using Punctuation with Adjective Clauses   141

Chapter 5

Editing for Tone   185
Using Commas before Coordinating Conjunctions   186
Avoiding Comma Splices When Using Conjunctive Adverbs to Link Independent Clauses   186
A Common Problem for Multilingual Writers: Detecting Subtle Differences in Meaning   187

Chapter 6

Avoiding Ambiguous Use of *This* and *That*   232
Revising Sentences That Lack an Agent   233

Chapter 7

Making Complete, Logical, and Grammatically Correct Comparisons   277
Combining Sentences   277

LaunchPad Solo

Missing something? Instructors may assign the online materials that accompany this text. For access to them, visit **macmillanhighered.com/conciseguide**.

Inside LaunchPad Solo for *The Concise St. Martin's Guide to Writing*

 E-readings

Chapter 2: Remembering an Event
Shannon Lewis, *We Were Here* [STUDENT ESSAY]
Kelsey Cartwright Roy, *The Daily Grind* [COMIC]

Chapter 3: Writing Profiles
Briana O'Leary, *Fatty's Custom Tattooz and Body Piercing* [STUDENT ESSAY]
Sarah Kate Kramer / WNYC, *Niche Market: Fountain Pen Hospital* [ARTICLE AND SLIDESHOW]

Chapter 4: Explaining a Concept
Ammar Rana: *Jihad: The Struggle in the Way of God* [STUDENT ESSAY]
National Geographic Online, *Mapping Memory* [INTERACTIVE GRAPHIC]

Chapter 5: Arguing a Position
Michael Niechayev, *It's Time to Ban Head First Tackles and Blocks* [STUDENT ESSAY]

Ad Council/U.S. Department of Transportation, *The "It's Only Another Beer" Black and Tan* [ADVERTISEMENT]

Chapter 6: Proposing a Solution
Molly Coleman, *Missing the Fun* [STUDENT ESSAY]
Phoebe Sweet and Zach Wise, *The Problem with Lawns: The Transforming Landscape of Las Vegas* [VIDEO]

Chapter 7: Justifying an Evaluation
Brittany Lemus, Requiem for a Dream: *Fantasy versus Reality* [STUDENT ESSAY]
Yelp, *Kuma's Korner* [WEB PAGE]

 Tutorials

Critical Reading
Active Reading Strategies
Reading Visuals: Purpose
Reading Visuals: Audience

Documentation and Working with Sources
Do I Need to Cite That?
How to Cite an Article in MLA Style

How to Cite a Book in MLA Style
How to Cite a Database in MLA Style
How to Cite a Database in APA Style
How to Cite a Web Site in MLA Style
How to Cite a Web Site in APA Style

Digital Writing
Photo Editing Basics with GIMP
Audio Editing with Audacity
Presentations
Word Processing
Online Research Tools
Job Search/Personal Branding

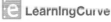 **LearningCurve**
Critical Reading
Topic Sentences and Supporting Details
Topics and Main Ideas
Working with Sources (MLA)
Working with Sources (APA)
Commas
Fragments
Run-ons and Comma Splices
Active and Passive voice
Appropriate Language
Subject-Verb Agreement

Missing something? To access the online material that accompanies this text, visit **macmillanhighered.com/conciseguide**. Students who do not buy a new book can purchase access at this site.